Principles of Political [Economy]

Abridged with Critical, Bibliographical, and Explanatory Notes, and a Sketch of the History of Political Economy

John Stuart Mill, (Editor: J. Laurence Laughlin)

Alpha Editions

This edition published in 2024

ISBN 9789362516534

Design and Setting By
Alpha Editions
www.alphaedis.com
Email - info@alphaedis.com

As per information held with us this book is in Public Domain.
This book is a reproduction of an important historical work.
Alpha Editions uses the best technology to reproduce historical work
in the same manner it was first published to preserve its original nature.
Any marks or number seen are left intentionally to preserve.

Contents

Preface.	- 1 -
Book I. Production.	- 29 -
Chapter I. Of The Requisites Of Production.	- 30 -
Chapter II. Of Unproductive Labor.	- 36 -
Chapter III. Of Capital.	- 40 -
Chapter IV. Fundamental Propositions Respecting Capital.	- 48 -
Chapter V. On Circulating And Fixed Capital.	- 68 -
Chapter VI. Of Causes Affecting The Efficiency Of Production.	- 74 -
Chapter VII. Of The Law Of The Increase Of Labor.	- 85 -
Chapter VIII. Of The Law Of The Increase Of Capital.	- 93 -
Chapter IX. Of The Law Of The Increase Of Production From Land.	- 101 -
Chapter X. Consequences Of The Foregoing Laws.	- 118 -
Book II. Distribution.	- 127 -
Chapter I. Of Property.	- 128 -
Chapter II. Of Wages.	- 144 -
Chapter III. Of Remedies For Low Wages.	- 161 -
Chapter IV. Of The Differences Of Wages In Different Employments.	- 172 -
Chapter VI. Of Rent.	- 198 -
Book III. Exchange.	- 211 -
Chapter I. Of Value.	- 212 -
Chapter II. Ultimate Analysis Of Cost Of Production.	- 228 -
Chapter III. Of Rent, In Its Relation To Value.	- 242 -
Chapter IV. Of Money.	- 250 -

Chapter V. Of The Value Of Money, As Dependent On
Demand And Supply. - 258 -

Chapter VI. Of The Value Of Money, As Dependent On
Cost Of Production. - 265 -

Chapter VII. Of A Double Standard And Subsidiary Coins. - 275 -

Chapter VIII. Of Credit, As A Substitute For Money. - 290 -

Chapter IX. Influence Of Credit On Prices. - 299 -

Chapter X. Of An Inconvertible Paper Currency. - 307 -

Chapter XI. Of Excess Of Supply. - 327 -

Chapter XII. Of Some Peculiar Cases Of Value. - 332 -

Chapter XIII. Of International Trade. - 337 -

Chapter XIV. Of International Values. - 350 -

Chapter XV. Of Money Considered As An Imported Commodity. - 362 -

Chapter XVI. Of The Foreign Exchanges. - 367 -

Chapter XVII. Of The Distribution Of The Precious Metals
Through The Commercial World. - 375 -

Chapter XVIII. Influence Of The Currency On
The Exchanges And On Foreign Trade. - 384 -

Chapter XIX. Of The Rate Of Interest. - 392 -

Chapter XX. Of The Competition Of Different
Countries In The Same Market. - 401 -

Chapter XXI. Of Distribution, As Affected By Exchange. - 415 -

Book IV. Influence Of The Progress Of Society
On Production And Distribution. - 421 -

Chapter I. Influence Of The Progress Of Industry
And Population On Values And Prices. - 422 -

Chapter II. Influence Of The Progress Of Industry
And Population On Rents, Profits, And Wages. - 436 -

Chapter III. Of The Tendency Of Profits To A Minimum. - 444 -

Chapter IV. Consequences Of The Tendency Of Profits To A Minimum, And The Stationary State.	- 456 -
Chapter V. On The Possible Futurity Of The Laboring-Classes.	- 462 -
Book V. On The Influence Of Government.	- 481 -
Chapter I. On The General Principles Of Taxation.	- 482 -
Chapter II. Of Direct Taxes.	- 492 -
Chapter III. Of Taxes On Commodities, Or Indirect Taxes.	- 501 -
Chapter IV. Comparison Between Direct And Indirect Taxation.	- 517 -
Chapter V. Of A National Debt.	- 531 -
Chapter VI. Of An Interference Of Government Grounded On Erroneous Theories.	- 538 -
Appendix I. Bibliographies.	- 563 -
A Brief Bibliography Of The Tariffs Of The United States.	- 564 -
A Brief Bibliography Of Bimetallism.	- 567 -
A Brief Bibliography Of American Shipping.	- 570 -
Appendix II. Examination Questions.	- 572 -
Footnotes	- 598 -

Preface.

An experience of five years with Mr. Mill's treatise in the class-room not only convinced me of the great usefulness of what still remains one of the most lucid and systematic books yet published which cover the whole range of the study, but I have also been convinced of the need of such additions as should give the results of later thinking, without militating against the general tenor of Mr. Mill's system; of such illustrations as should fit it better for American students, by turning their attention to the application of principles in the facts around us; of a bibliography which should make it easier to get at the writers of other schools who offer opposing views on controverted questions; and of some attempts to lighten those parts of his work in which Mr. Mill frightened away the reader by an appearance of too great abstractness, and to render them, if possible, more easy of comprehension to the student who first approaches Political Economy through this author. Believing, also, that the omission of much that should properly be classed under the head of Sociology, or Social Philosophy, would narrow the field to Political Economy alone, and aid, perhaps, in clearer ideas, I was led to reduce the two volumes into one, with, of course, the additional hope that the smaller book would tempt some readers who might hesitate to attack his larger work. In consonance with the above plan, I have abridged Mr. Mill's treatise, yet have always retained his own words; although it should be said that they are not always his consecutive words. Everything in the larger type on the page is taken literally from Mr. Mill, and, whenever it has been necessary to use a word to complete the sense, it has been always inserted in square brackets. All additional matter introduced by me has been printed in a smaller but distinctive type. The reader can see at a glance which part of the page is Mr. Mill's and which my own.

It has seemed necessary to make the most additions to the original treatise under the subjects of the Wages Question; of Wages of Superintendence; of Socialism; of Cost of Production; of Bimetallism; of the Paper Money experiments in this country; of International Values; of the Future of the Laboring-Classes (in which the chapter was entirely rewritten); and of Protection. The treatment of Land Tenures has not been entirely omitted, but it does not appear as a separate subject, because it has at present less value as an elementary study for American students. The chapters on Land Tenures, the English currency discussion, and much of Book V, on the Influence of Government, have been simply omitted. In one case I have changed the order of the chapters, by inserting Chap. XV of Book III, treating of a standard of value, under the chapter treating of money and its functions. In other respects, the same order has been followed as in the original work.

Wherever it has seemed possible, American illustrations have been inserted instead of English or Continental ones.

To interest the reader in home problems, twenty-four charts have been scattered throughout the volume, which bear upon our own conditions, with the expectation, also, that the different methods of graphic representation here presented would lead students to apply them to other questions. They are mainly such as I have employed in my class-room. The use and preparation of such charts ought to be encouraged. The earlier pages of the volume have been given up to a "Sketch of the History of Political Economy," which aims to give the story of how we have arrived at our present knowledge of economic laws. The student who has completed Mill will then have a very considerable bibliography of the various schools and writers from which to select further reading, and to select this reading so that it may not fall wholly within the range of one class of writers. But, for the time that Mill is being first studied, I have added a list of the most important books for consultation. I have also collected, in Appendix I, some brief bibliographies on the Tariff, on Bimetallism, and on American Shipping, which may be of use to those who may not have the means of inquiring for authorities, and in Appendix II a number of questions and problems for the teacher's use.

In some cases I have omitted Mr. Mill's statement entirely, and put in its stead a simpler form of the same exposition which I believed would be more easily grasped by a student. Of such cases, the argument to show that Demand for Commodities is not Demand for Labor, the Doctrine of International Values, and the Effect of the Progress of Society on wages, profits, and rent, are examples. Whether I have succeeded or not, must be left for the experience of the teacher to determine. Many small figures and diagrams have been used throughout the text, in order to suggest the concrete means of getting a clear grasp of a principle.

In conclusion, I wish to acknowledge my indebtedness to several friends for assistance in the preparation of this volume, among whom are Professor Charles F. Dunbar, Dr. F. W. Taussig, Dr. A. B. Hart, and Mr. Edward Atkinson.

J. LAURENCE LAUGHLIN.
HARVARD UNIVERSITY, CAMBRIDGE, MASSACHUSETTS,
September, 1884.

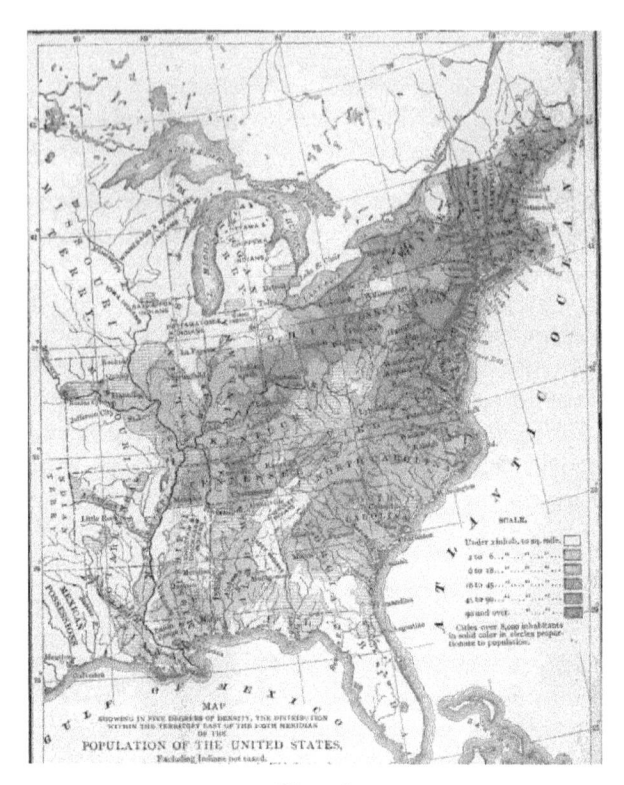

Chart I

Chart II

Introductory.
A Sketch Of The History Of Political Economy.

GENERAL BIBLIOGRAPHY.—There is no satisfactory general history of political economy in English. Blanqui's "Histoire de l'économie politique en Europe" (Paris, 1837) is disproportioned and superficial, and he labors under the disadvantage of not understanding the English school of economists. He studies to give the history of economic facts, rather than of economic laws. The book has been translated into English (New York, 1880).

Villeneuve-Bargemont, in his "Histoire de l'économie politique" (Paris, 1841), aims to oppose a "Christian political economy" to the "English" political economy, and indulges in religious discussions.

Travers Twiss, "View of the Progress of Political Economy in Europe since the Sixteenth Century" (London, 1847), marked an advance by treating the subject in the last four centuries, and by separating the history of principles from the history of facts. It is brief, and only a sketch. Julius Kautz has published in German the best existing history, "Die geschichtliche Entwickelung der National-Oekonomie und ihrer Literatur" (Vienna, 1860). (See Cossa, "Guide to the Study of Political Economy," page 80.) Cossa in his book has furnished a vast amount of information about writers, classified by epochs and countries, and a valuable discussion of the divisions of political economy by various writers, and its relation to other sciences. It is a very desirable little hand-book. McCulloch, in his "Introduction to the Wealth of Nations," gives a brief sketch of the growth of economic doctrine. The editor begs to acknowledge his great indebtedness for information to his colleague, Professor Charles F. Dunbar, of Harvard University.

Systematic study for an understanding of the laws of political economy is to be found no farther back than the sixteenth century. The history of political economy is not the history of economic institutions, any more than the history of mathematics is the history of every object possessing length, breadth, and thickness. Economic history is the story of the gradual evolution in the thought of men of an understanding of the laws which to-day constitute the science we are studying. It is essentially modern.[1]

Aristotle[2] and Xenophon had some comprehension of the theory of money, and Plato[3] had defined its functions with some accuracy. The economic laws of the Romans were all summed up in the idea of enriching the metropolis at the expense of the dependencies. During the middle ages no systematic study was undertaken, and the nature of economic laws was not even suspected.

It is worth notice that the first glimmerings of political economy came to be seen through the discussions on money, and the extraordinary movements of gold and silver. About the time of Charles V, the young study was born, accompanied by the revival of learning, the Reformation, the discovery of America, and the great fall in the value of gold and silver. Modern society was just beginning, and had already brought manufactures into existence— woolens in England, silks in France, Genoa, and Florence; Venice had become the great commercial city of the world; the Hanseatic League was carrying goods from the Mediterranean to the Baltic; and the Jews of Lombardy had by that time brought into use the bill of exchange. While the supply of the precious metals had been tolerably constant hitherto, the steady increase of business brought about a fall of prices. From the middle of the fourteenth to the end of the fifteenth century the purchasing power of money increased in the ratio of four to ten. Then into this situation came the great influx of gold and silver from the New World. Prices rose unequally; the trading and manufacturing classes were flourishing, while others were depressed. In the sixteenth century the price of wheat tripled, but wages only doubled; the laboring-classes of England deteriorated, while others were enriched, producing profound social changes and the well-known flood of pauperism, together with the rise of the mercantile classes. Then new channels of trade were opened to the East and West. Of course, men saw but dimly the operation of these economic causes; although the books now began to hint at the right understanding of the movements and the true laws of money.

Even before this time, however, Nicole Orêsme, Bishop of Lisieux (died 1382), had written intelligently on money;[4] but, about 1526, the astronomer Copernicus gave a very good exposition of some of the functions of money. But he, as well as Latimer,[5] while noticing the economic changes, gave no correct explanation. The Seigneur de Malestroit, a councilor of the

King of France, however, by his errors drew out Jean Bodin[6] to say that the rise of prices was due to the abundance of money brought from America. But he was in advance of his time, as well as William Stafford,[7] the author of the first English treatise on money, which showed a perfect insight into the subject. Stafford distinctly grasped the idea that the high prices brought no loss to merchants, great gain to those who held long leases, and loss to those who did not buy and sell; that, in reality, commodities were exchanged when money was passed from hand to hand.

Such was the situation[8] which prefaced the first general system destined to be based on supposed economic considerations, wrongly understood, to be sure, but vigorously carried out. I refer to the well-known mercantile system which over-spread Europe.[9] Spain, as the first receiver of American gold and silver, attributed to it abnormal power, and by heavy duties and prohibitions tried to keep the precious metals to herself. This led to a general belief in the tenets of the mercantile system, and its adoption by all Europe. 1. It was maintained that, where gold and silver abounded, there would be found no lack of the necessaries of life; 2. Therefore governments should do all in their power to secure an abundance of money. Noting that commerce and political power seemed to be in the hands of the states having the greatest quantity of money, men wished mainly to create such a relation of exports and imports of goods as would bring about an importation of money. The natural sequence of this was, the policy of creating a favorable "balance of trade" by increasing exports and diminishing imports, thus implying that the gain in international trade was not a mutual one. The error consisted in supposing that a nation could sell without buying, and in overlooking the instrumental character of money. The errors even went so far as to create prohibitory legislation, in the hope of shutting out imported goods and keeping the precious metals at home. The system spread over Europe, so that France (1544) and England (1552) forbade the export of specie. But, with the more peaceful conditions at the end of the sixteenth century, the expansion of commerce, the value of money became steadier, and prices advanced more slowly.

Italian writers were among the first to discuss the laws of money intelligently,[10] but a number of acute Englishmen enriched the literature of the subject,[11] and it may be said that any modern study of political economy received its first definite impulse from England and France.

The prohibition of the export of coin was embarrassing to the East India Company and to merchants; and Mun tried to show that freedom of exportation would increase the amount of gold and silver in a country, since the profits in foreign trade would bring back more than went out. It probably was not clear to them, however, that the export of bullion to the East was advantageous, because the commodities brought back in return were more valuable in England than the precious metals. The purpose of the mercantilists was to increase the amount of gold and silver in the country. Mun, with some penetration, had even pointed out that too much money was an evil; but in 1663 the English Parliament removed the restriction on the exportation of coin. The balance-of-trade heresy, that exports should always exceed imports (as if merchants would send out goods which, when paid for in commodities, should be returned in a form of less value than those sent out!), was the outcome of the mercantile system, and it has continued in the minds of many men to this day. The policy which aimed at securing a favorable balance of trade, and the plan of protecting home industries, had the same origin. If all consumable goods were produced at home, and none imported, that would increase exports, and bring more gold and silver into the country. As all the countries of Europe had adopted the mercantile theory after 1664, retaliatory and prohibitory tariffs were set up against each other by England, France, Holland, and Germany. Then, because it was seen that large sums were paid for carrying goods, in order that no coin should be required to pay foreigners in any branch of industry, navigation laws were enacted, which required goods to be imported only in ships belonging to the importing nation. These remnants of the mercantile system continue to this day in the shipping laws of this and other countries.[12]

A natural consequence of the navigation acts, and of the mercantile system, was the so-called colonial policy, by which the colonies were excluded from all trade except with the mother-country. A plantation like New England, which produced commodities in competition with England, was looked upon with disfavor for her enterprise; and all this because of the fallacy, at the foundation of the mercantile system, that the gain in international trade is not mutual, but that what one country gains another must lose.[13]

An exposition of mercantilism would not be complete without a statement of the form it assumed in France under the guidance of Colbert,[14] the great minister of Louis XIV, from 1661 to 1683. In order to create a favorable balance of trade, he devoted himself to fostering home productions, by attempts to abolish vexatious tolls and customs within the country, and by an extraordinary system of supervision in manufacturing establishments (which has been the stimulus to paternal government from which France has never since been able to free herself). Processes were borrowed from England, Germany, and Sweden, and new establishments for making tapestries and silk goods sprang up; even the sizes of fabrics were regulated by Colbert, and looms unsuitable for these sizes destroyed. In 1671 wool-dyers were given a code of detailed instructions as to the processes and materials that might be used. Long after, French industry felt the difficulty of struggling with stereotyped processes. His system, however, naturally resulted in a series of tariff measures (in 1664 and 1667). Moderate duties on the exportation of raw materials were first laid on, followed by heavy customs imposed on the importation of foreign goods. The shipment of coin was forbidden; but Colbert's criterion of prosperity was the favorable balance of trade. French agriculture was overlooked. The tariff of 1667 was based on the theory that foreigners must of necessity buy French wines, lace, and wheat; that the French could sell, but not buy; but the act of 1667 cut off the demand for French goods, and Portuguese wines came into the market. England and Holland retaliated and shut off the foreign markets from France. The wine and wheat growers of the latter country were ruined, and the rural population came to the verge of starvation. Colbert's last years were full of misfortune and disappointment; and a new illustration was given of the fallacy that the gain from international trade was not mutual.

From this time, economic principles began to be better apprehended. It is to be noted that the first just observations arose from discussions upon money, and thence upon international trade. So far England has furnished the most acute writers: now France became the scene of a new movement. Marshal Vauban,[15] the great soldier, and Boisguillebert[16] both began to emphasize the truth that wealth really consists, not in money alone, but in an abundance of commodities; that countries which have plenty of gold and silver are not wealthier than others, and that money is only a medium of exchange. It was not, however, until 1750 that evidences of any real advance began to appear; for Law's famous scheme (1716-1720) only served as a drag upon the growth of economic truth. But in the middle of the eighteenth century an intellectual revival set in: the "Encyclopædia" was published, Montesquieu wrote his "l'Ésprit des Lois," Rousseau was beginning to write, and Voltaire was at the height of his power. In this movement political economy had an important share, and there resulted the first school of Economists, termed the Physiocrats.

The founder and leader of this new body of economic thinkers was François Quesnay,[17] a physician and favorite at the court of Louis XV. Passing by his ethical basis of a natural order of society, and natural rights of man, his main doctrine, in brief, was that the cultivation of the soil was the only source of wealth; that labor in other industries was sterile; and that freedom of trade was a necessary condition of healthy distribution. While known as the "Economists," they were also called the "Physiocrats,"[18] or the "Agricultural School." Quesnay and his followers distinguished between the creation of wealth (which could only come from the soil) and the union of these materials, once created, by labor in other occupations. In the latter case the laborer did not, in their theory, produce wealth. A natural consequence of this view appeared in a rule of taxation, by which all the burdens of state expenditure were laid upon the landed proprietors alone, since they alone received a surplus of wealth (the famous *net produit*) above their sustenance and expenses of production. This position, of course, did not recognize the old mercantile theory that foreign commerce enriched a nation solely by increasing the quantity of money. To a physiocrat the wealth of a community was increased not by money, but by an abundant produce from its own soil. In fact, Quesnay argued that the right of property included the right to dispose of it freely at home or abroad, unrestricted by the state. This doctrine was formulated in the familiar expression, "*Laissez faire, laissez passer.*"[19] Condorcet and Condillac favored the new ideas. The "Economists" became the fashion in France; and even included in their number Joseph II of Austria, the Kings of Spain, Poland, Sweden, Naples, Catharine of Russia, and the Margrave of Baden.[20] Agriculture, therefore, received a great stimulus.

Quesnay had many vigorous supporters, of whom the most conspicuous was the Marquis de Mirabeau[21] (father of him of the Revolution), and the culmination of their popularity was reached about 1764. A feeling that the true increase of wealth was not in a mere increase of money, but in the products of the soil, led them naturally into a reaction against mercantilism, but also made them dogmatic and overbearing in their one-sided system, which did not recognize that labor in all industries created wealth. As the mercantile system found a great minister in Colbert to carry those opinions into effect on a national scale, so the Physiocrats found in Turgot[22] a minister, under Louis XVI, who gave them a national field in which to try the doctrines of the new school. Benevolently devoted to bettering the condition of the people while Intendant of Limoges (1751), he was made comptroller-general of the finances by Louis XVI in 1774. Turgot had the ability to separate political economy from politics, law, and ethics. His system of freeing industry from governmental interference resulted in abolishing many abuses, securing a freer movement of grain, and in lightening the taxation. But the rigidity of national prejudices was too strong to allow him success. He had little tact, and raised many difficulties in his way. The proposal to abolish the *corvées* (compulsory repair of roads by the peasants), and substitute a tax on land, brought his king into a costly struggle (1776), and attempts to undermine Turgot's power were successful. With his downfall ended the influence of the Economists. The last of them was Dupont de Nemours,[23] who saw a temporary popularity of the Physiocrats in the early years of the French Revolution, when the Constituent Assembly threw the burden of taxes on land. But the fire blazed up fitfully for a moment, only to die away entirely.

All this, however, was the slow preparation for a newer and greater movement in political economy than had yet been known, and which laid the foundation of the modern study as it exists to-day. The previous discussions on money and the prominence given to agriculture and economic considerations by the Economists made possible the great achievements of Adam Smith and the English school. A reaction in England against the mercantile system produced a complete revolution in political economy. Vigorous protests against mercantilism had appeared long before,[24] and the true functions of money had come to be rightly understood.[25] More than that, many of the most important doctrines had been either discussed, or been given to the public in print. It is at least certain that hints of much that made so astonishing an effect in Adam Smith's "Wealth of Nations" (1776) had been given to the world before the latter was written. To what sources, among the minor writers, he was most indebted, it is hard to say. Two, at least, deserve considerable attention, David Hume and Richard Cantillon. The former published his "Economic Essays" in 1752, which contained what even now would be considered enlightened views on money, interest, balance of trade, commerce, and taxation; and a personal friendship existed between Hume and Adam Smith dating back as far as 1748, when the latter was lecturing in Edinburgh on rhetoric. The extent of Cantillon's acquirements and Adam Smith's possible indebtedness to him have been but lately recognized. In a recent study[26] on Cantillon, the late Professor Jevons has pointed out that the former anticipated many of the doctrines later ascribed to Adam Smith, Malthus, and Ricardo. Certain it is that the author of the "Wealth of Nations" took the truth wherever he found it, received substantial suggestions from various sources, but, after having devoted himself in a peculiarly successful way to collecting facts, he wrought out of all he had gathered the first rounded system of political economy the world had yet known; which pointed out that labor was at the basis of production, not merely in agriculture, as the French school would have it, but in all industries; and which battered down all the defenses of the mediæval mercantile system. In a marked degree Adam Smith[27] combined a logical precision and a power of generalizing results out of confused data with a practical and intuitive regard for facts which are absolutely necessary for great achievements in the science of political economy. At Glasgow (1751-1764) Adam Smith gave lectures on natural theology, ethical philosophy, jurisprudence, and political economy, believing that these subjects were complementary to each other.

A connected and comprehensive grasp of principles was the great achievement of Adam Smith;[28] for, although the "Wealth of Nations" was naturally not without faults, it has been the basis of all subsequent discussion and advance in political economy. In Books I and II his own system is elucidated, while Book IV contains his discussion of the Agricultural School and the attacks on the mercantile system. Seeing distinctly that labor was the basis of all production (not merely in agriculture), he shows (Books I and II) that the wealth of a country depends on the skill with which its labor is applied, and upon the proportion of productive to unproductive laborers. The gains from division of labor are explained, and money appears as a necessary instrument after society has reached such a division. He is then led to discuss prices (market price) and value; and, since from the price a distribution takes place among the factors of production, he is brought to wages, profit, and rent. The functions of capital are explained in general; the separation of fixed from circulating capital is made; and he discusses the influence of capital on the distribution of productive and unproductive labor; the accumulation of capital, money, paper money, and interest. He, therefore, gets a connected set of ideas on production, distribution, and exchange. On questions of production not much advance has been made since his day; and his rules of taxation are now classic. He attacked vigorously the balance-of-trade theory, and the unnatural diversion of industry in England by prohibitions, bounties, and the arbitrary colonial system. In brief, he held that a plan for the regulation of industry by the Government was indefensible, and that to direct private persons how to employ their capital was either hurtful or useless. He taught that a country will be more prosperous if its neighbors are prosperous, and that nations have no interest in injuring each other. It was, however, but human that his work should have been somewhat defective.[29] A new period in the history of political economy, however, begins with Adam Smith. As Roscher says, he stands in the center of economic history.

New writers now appear who add gradually stone after stone to the good foundation already laid, and raise the edifice to fairer proportions. The first considerable addition comes from a contribution by a country clergyman, Thomas Robert Malthus,[30] in his "Essay on the Principles of Population" (1798). Against the view of Pitt that "the man who had a large family was a benefactor to his country," Malthus argued conclusively that "a perfectly happy and virtuous community, by physical law, is constrained to increase very rapidly.... By nature human food increases in a slow arithmetical ratio; man himself increases in a quick geometrical ratio, unless want and vice stop him." In his second edition (1803), besides the positive check of vice and want, he gave more importance to the negative check of "self-restraint, moral and prudential." The whole theory was crudely stated at first; and it raised the cry that such a doctrine was inconsistent with the belief in a benevolent Creator. In its essence, the law of population is simply that a tendency and ability exist in mankind to increase its numbers faster than subsistence, and that this result actually will happen unless checks retard it, or new means of getting subsistence arise. If an undue increase of population led to vice and misery, in Malthus's theory, he certainly is not to be charged with unchristian feelings if he urged a self-restraint by which that evil result should be avoided. Malthus's doctrines excited great discussion: Godwin says that by 1820 thirty or forty answers to the essay had been written; and they have continued to appear. The chief contributions have been by A. H. Everett, "New Ideas on Population" (1823), who believed that an increase of numbers increased productive power; by M. T. Sadler, "Law of Population" (1830), who taught that human fertility varied inversely with numbers, falling off with density of population; by Sir Archibald Alison, "Principles of Population" (1840), who reasoned inductively that the material improvement of the human race is a proof that man can produce more than he consumes, or that in the progress of society preventive checks necessarily arise; by W. R. Greg, "Enigmas of Life" (1873); and by Herbert Spencer, "Westminster Review" (April, 1852), and "Principles of Biology," (part vi, ch. xii and xiii), who worked out a physiological check, in that with a mental development out of lower stages there comes an increased demand upon the nervous energy which causes a diminution of fertility. Since Darwin's studies it has been very generally admitted that it is the innate *tendency* of all organic life to increase until numbers press upon the limit of food-production; not that population has always done so in every country.[31] Malthus's teachings resulted in the modern poor-house system, beginning with 1834 in England, and they corrected some of the abuses of indiscriminate charity.

While Adam Smith had formulated very correctly the laws of production, in his way Malthus was adding to the means by which a better knowledge of the principles of distribution was to be obtained; and the next advance, owing to the sharp discussions of the time on the corn laws, was, by a natural progress, to the law of diminishing returns and rent. An independent discovery of the law of rent is to be assigned to no less than four persons,[32] but for the full perception of its truth and its connection with other principles of political economy the credit has been rightly given to David Ricardo,[33] next to Adam Smith without question the greatest economist of the English school. Curiously enough, although Adam Smith was immersed in abstract speculations, his "homely sagacity" led him to the most practical results; but while Ricardo was an experienced and successful man of business, he it was, above all others, who established the abstract political economy, in the sense of a body of scientific laws to which concrete phenomena, in spite of temporary inconsistencies, must in the end conform. His work, therefore, supplemented that of Adam Smith; and there are very few doctrines fully worked out to-day of which hints have not been found in Ricardo's wonderfully compact statements. With no graces of exposition, his writings seem dry, but are notwithstanding mines of valuable suggestions.

In the field of distribution and exchange Ricardo made great additions. Malthus and West had shown that rent was not an element in cost of production; but both Malthus and Ricardo seemed to have been familiar with the doctrine of rent long before the former published his book. Ricardo, however, saw into its connection with other parts of a system of distribution.[34] The Malthusian doctrine of a pressure of population on subsistence naturally forced a recognition of the law of diminishing returns from land;[35] then as soon as different qualities of land were simultaneously cultivated, the best necessarily gave larger returns than the poorest; and the idea that the payment of rent was made for a superior instrument, and in proportion to its superiority over the poorest instrument which society found necessary to use, resulted in the law of rent. Ricardo, moreover, carried out this principle as it affected wages, profits, values, and the fall of profits; but did not give sufficient importance to the operation of forces in the form of improvements acting in opposition to the tendency toward lessened returns. The theory of rent still holds its place, although it has met with no little opposition.[36] A doctrine, quite as important in its effects on free exchange, was clearly established by Ricardo, under the name of the doctrine of "Comparative Cost," which is the reason for the existence of any and all international trade.

The work of Adam Smith was soon known to other countries, apart from translations. A most lucid and attractive exposition was given to the French by J. B. Say, "Traité d'économie politique" (1803), followed, after lecturing in Paris from 1815-1830, by a more complete treatise,[37] "Cours complète d'économie politique" (1828). While not contributing much that was new, Say did a great service by popularizing previous results in a happy and lively style, combined with good arrangement, and many illustrations. The theory that general demand and supply are identical is his most important contribution to the study. Although he translated Ricardo's book, he did not grasp the fact that rent did not enter into price. Say's work was later supplemented by an Italian, Pellegrino Rossi,[38] who, in his "Cours d'économie politique" (1843-1851), naturalized the doctrines of Malthus and Ricardo on French soil. His work is of solid value, and he and Say have given rise to an active school of political economy in France. In Switzerland, Sismondi expounded Adam Smith's results in his "De la richesse commerciale" (1803), but was soon led into a new position, explained in his "Nouveaux principes d'économie politique" (1819). This has made him the earliest and most distinguished of the humanitarian economists. Seeing the sufferings caused by readjustments of industries after the peace, and the warehouses filled with unsold goods, he thought the excess of production over the power of consumption was permanent, and attacked division of labor, labor-saving machinery, and competition. Discoveries which would supersede labor he feared would continue, and the abolition of patents, together with the limitation of population,[39] was urged. These arguments furnished excellent weapons to the socialistic agitators. Heinrich Storch[40] aimed to spread the views of Adam Smith[41] in Russia, by his "Cours d'économie politique" (1815). Without further developing the theory of political economy, he produced a book of exceptional merit by pointing out the application of the principles to Russia, particularly in regard to the effect of a progress of wealth on agriculture and manufactures; to the natural steps by which a new country changes from agriculture to a manufacturing *régime*; and to finance and currency, with an account of Russian depreciated paper since Catharine II.

For the next advance, we must again look to England. Passing by McCulloch[42] and Senior, a gifted writer, the legitimate successor of Ricardo is John Stuart Mill.[43] His father, James Mill,[44] introduced him into a circle of able men, of which Bentham was the ablest, although his father undoubtedly exercised the chief influence over his training. While yet but twenty-three, in his first book, "Essays on some Unsettled Questions of Political Economy" (1829-1830), he gained a high position as an economist. In one form or another, all his additions to the study are to be found here in a matured condition. The views on productive and unproductive consumption, profits, economic methods, and especially his very clever investigation on international values, were there presented. His "Logic" (1843) contains (Book VI) a careful statement of the relation of political economy to other sciences, and of the proper economic method to be adopted in investigations. Through his "Principles of Political Economy" (1848) he has exercised a remarkable influence upon men in all lands; not so much because of great originality, since, in truth, he only put Ricardo's principles in better and more attractive form, but chiefly by a method of systematic treatment more lucid and practical than had been hitherto reached, by improving vastly beyond the dry treatises of his predecessors (including Ricardo, who was concise and dull), by infusing a human element into his aims, and by illustrations and practical applications. Even yet, however, some parts of his book show the tendency to too great a fondness for abstract statement, induced probably by a dislike to slighting his reasons (due to his early training), and by the limits of his book, which obliged him to omit many possible illustrations. With a deep sympathy for the laboring-classes, he was tempted into the field of sociology in this book, although he saw distinctly that political economy was but one of the sciences, a knowledge of which was necessary to a legislator in reaching a decision upon social questions. Mill shows an advance beyond Ricardo in this treatise, by giving the study a more practical direction. Although it is usual to credit Mill with originating the laws of international values, yet they are but a development of Ricardo's doctrine of international trade, and Mill's discussions of the progress of society toward the stationary state were also hinted at, although obscurely, by Ricardo. In the volumes of Mr. Mill the subject is developed as symmetrically as a proof in geometry. While he held strongly to free trade,[45] he gave little space to the subject in his book. All in all, his book yet remains the best systematic treatise in the English language, although much has been done since his day.[46]

He who has improved upon previous conceptions, and been the only one to make any very important advance in the science since Mill's day, is J. E. Cairnes,[47] in his "Leading Principles of Political Economy newly expounded" (1874). Scarcely any previous writer has equaled him in logical clearness, originality, insight into economic phenomena, and lucidity of style. He subjected value, supply and demand, cost of production, and international trade, to a rigid investigation, which has given us actual additions to our knowledge of the study. The wages-fund theory was re-examined, and was stated in a new form, although Mr. Mill had given it up. Cairnes undoubtedly has given it its best statement. His argument on free trade (Part III, chapter iv) is the ablest and strongest to be found in modern writers. This volume is, however, not a systematic treatise on all the principles of political economy; but no student can properly pass by these great additions for the right understanding of the science. His "Logical Method of Political Economy" (1875) is a clear and able statement of the process to be adopted in an economic investigation, and is a book of exceptional merit and usefulness, especially in view of the rising differences in the minds of economists as to method.

A group of English writers of ability in this period have written in such a way as to win for them mention in connection with Cairnes and Mill. Professor W. Stanley Jevons[48] put himself in opposition to the methods of the men just mentioned, and applied the mathematical process to political economy, but without reaching new results. His most serviceable work has been in the study of money, which appears in an excellent form, "The Money and Mechanism of Exchange" (1875), and in an investigation which showed a fall of the value of gold since the discoveries of 1849. In this latter he has furnished a model for any subsequent investigator. Like Professor Jevons, T. E. Cliffe Leslie[49] opposed the older English school (the so-called "orthodox"), but in the different way of urging with great ability the use of the historical method, of which more will be said in speaking of later German writers.[50] He also distinguished himself by a study of land tenures, in his "Land Systems and Industrial Economy of Ireland, England, and Continental Countries" (1870), which was a brilliant exposition of the advantages of small holdings.

By far the ablest of the group, both by reason of his natural gifts and his training as a banker and financial editor, was Walter Bagehot.[51] In his "Economic Studies" (1880) he has discussed with a remarkable economic insight the postulates of political economy, and the position of Adam Smith, Ricardo, and Malthus; in his "Lombard Street" (fourth edition, 1873), the money market is pictured with a vivid distinctness which implies the possession of rare qualities for financial writing; indeed, it is in this practical way also, as editor of the London "Economist,"[52] that he made his great reputation.

Of living English economists, Professor Henry Fawcett,[53] in his "Manual of Political Economy" (1865; sixth edition, 1883), is a close follower of Mill, giving special care to co-operation, silver, nationalization of land, and trades-unions. He is an exponent of the strict wages-fund theory, and a vigorous free-trader. Professor J. E. Thorold Rogers, of Oxford, also holds aloof from the methods of the old school. His greatest contribution has been a "History of Agriculture and Prices in England," from 1255 to 1793, in four volumes[54] (1866-1882).

Of all the writers[55] since Cairnes, it may be said that, while adding to the data with which political economy has to do, and putting principles to the test of facts, they have made no actual addition to the existing body of principles; although questions of distribution and taxation are certainly not yet fully settled, as is seen by the wide differences of opinion expressed on subjects falling within these heads by writers of to-day.

It now remains to complete this sketch of the growth of political economy by a brief account of the writers on the Continent and in the United States, beginning with France. About the time of the founding of the London "Economist" (1844) and "The Statistical Journal" (1839) in England, there was established in Paris the "Journal des Économistes" (1842), which contains many valuable papers. On the whole, the most popular writer since J. B. Say has been Bastiat,[56] who aspired to be the French Cobden. He especially urged a new[57] view of value, which he defined as the relation established by an exchange of services; that nature's products are gratuitous, so that man can not exact anything except for a given service. Chiefly as a foe of protection, which he regarded as qualified socialism, he has won a reputation for popular and clever writing; and he was led to believe in a general harmony of interests between industrial classes; but in general he can not be said to have much influenced the course of French thought. On value, rent, and population, he is undoubtedly unsound. A writer of far greater depth than Bastiat, with uncommon industry and wide knowledge, was Michel Chevalier,[58] easily the first among modern French economists. He has led in the discussion upon the fall of gold, protection, banking, and particularly upon money; an ardent free-trader, he had influence enough to induce France to enter into the commercial treaty of 1860 with England. One of the ablest writers on special topics is Levasseur,[59] who has given us a history of the working-classes before and since the Revolution, and the best existing monograph on John Law. The most industrious and reliable of the recent writers is the well-known statistician, Maurice Block,[60] while less profound economists were J. A. Blanqui[61] and Wolowski.[62] The latter devoted himself enthusiastically to banks of issue, and bimetallism. A small group gave themselves up chiefly to studies on agriculture and land-tenures—H. Passy,[63] Laveleye, and Lavergne.[64] The latter is by far the most important, as shown by his "L'économie rurale de la France depuis 1789" (1857), which gives a means of comparing recent French agriculture with that before the Revolution, as described in Arthur Young's "Travels in France" (1789). The best systematic treatise in French is the "Précis de la science économique" (1862), by Antoine-Élise Cherbuliez,[65] a Genevan. The French were the first to produce an alphabetical encyclopædia of economics, by Coquelin and Guillaumin, entitled the "Dictionnaire de l'économie politique" (1851-1853, third edition, 1864). Courcelle-Seneuil,[66] by his "Traité théorique et pratique d'économie politique" (second edition, 1867); and Baudrillart, by a good compendium. Joseph Garnier, Dunoyer,[67] Paul Leroy-Beaulieu,[68] Reybaud,[69] De Parieu,[70] Léon Say,[71] Boiteau, and others, have done excellent work in France, and Walras[72] in Switzerland.

As Cobden had an influence on Bastiat, so both had an influence in Germany in creating what has been styled by opponents the "Manchester school," led by Prince-Smith (died 1874). They have worked to secure complete liberty of commerce and industry, and include in their numbers many men of ability and learning. Yearly congresses have been organized for the purpose of disseminating liberal ideas, and an excellent review, the "Vierteljahrschrift für Volkswirthschaft, Politik, und Kulturgeschichte,"[73] has been established. They have devoted themselves successfully to reforms of labor-laws, interest, workingmen's dwellings, the money system, and banking, and strive for the abolition of protective duties. Schulze-Delitzsch has acquired a deserved reputation for the creation of people's banks, and other forms of co-operation. The translator of Mill into German, Adolph Soetbeer,[74] is the most eminent living authority on the production of the precious metals, and a vigorous monometallist. The school is represented in the "Handwörterbuch der Volkswirthschaftslehre" (1865) of Reutzsch. The other writers of this group are Von Böhmert,[75] Faucher, Braun, Wolff, Michaelis, Emminghaus,[76] Wirth,[77] Hertzka, and Von Holtzendorf. The best known of the German protectionists is Friedrich List, the author of "Das nationale System der politischen Oekonomie" (1841), whose doctrines are very similar to those of H. C. Carey in this country.[78] An able writer on administrative functions and finance[79] is Lorenz Stein, of Vienna.

But German economists are of interest, inasmuch as they have established a new school who urge the use of the historical method in political economy, and it is about the question of method that much of the interest of to-day centers. In 1814 Savigny introduced this method into jurisprudence, and about 1850 it was applied to political economy. The new school claim that the English "orthodox" writers begin by an *a priori* process, and by deductions reach conclusions which are possibly true of imaginary cases, but are not true of man as he really acts. They therefore assert that economic laws can only be truly discovered by induction, or a study of phenomena first, as the means of reaching a generalization. To them Bagehot[80] answers that scientific bookkeeping, or collections of facts, in themselves give no results ending in scientific laws; for instance, since the facts of banking change and vary every day, no one can by induction alone reach any laws of banking; or, for example, the study of a panic from the concrete phenomena would be like trying to explain the bursting of a boiler without a theory of steam. More lately,[81] since it seems that the new school claim that induction does not preclude deduction, and as the old school never intended to disconnect themselves from "comparing conclusions with external facts," there is not such a cause of difference as has previously appeared. Doubtless the insistence upon the merits of induction will be fruitful of good to "orthodox" writers, in the more general resort to the collection of statistics and means of verification. It is suggestive also that the leaders of the new school in Germany and England have reached no different results by their new method, and in the main agree with the laws evolved by the old English school. The economist does not pretend that his assumptions are descriptions of economic conditions existing at a given time; he simply considers them as forces (often acting many on one point or occasion) to be inquired into separately, inasmuch as concrete phenomena are the resultants of several forces, not to be known until we know the separate operation of each of the conjoined forces.

The most prominent of the new school is Wilhelm Roscher,[82] of Leipsic, who wrote a systematic treatise, "System der Volkswirthschaft" (1854, sixteenth edition, 1883), in the first division of which the notes contain a marvelous collection of facts and authorities. He agrees in results with Adam Smith, Ricardo, Malthus, and Mill, but does not seem to have known much of Cairnes. This book, however, is only a first of four treatises eventually intended to include the political economy of (2) agriculture, (3) industry and commerce, and (4) the state and commune. The ablest contemporary of Roscher, who was probably the first to urge the historical method, is Karl Knies,[83] in "Die politische Oekonomie vom Standpunkte der geschichtlichen Methode" (1853, second edition, 1881-1883). The third of the group who founded the historical school is Bruno Hildebrand,[84] of

Jena, author of "Die Nationalökonomie der Gegenwart und Zukunft" (1848).

The German mind has always been familiar with the interference of the state, and a class of writers has arisen, not only advocating the inductive method, but strongly imbued with a belief in a close connection of the state with industry; and, inasmuch as the essence of modern socialism is a resort to state-help, this body of men, with Wagner at their head, has received the name of "Socialists[85] of the Chair," and now wield a wide influence in Germany. Of these writers,[86] Wagner, Engel, Schmoller, Von Scheel, Brentano, Held, Schönberg, and Schäffle are the most prominent.

The historical school has received the adhesion of Émile de Laveleye,[87] in Belgium, and other economists in England and the United States. While Cliffe Leslie has been the most vigorous opponent of the methods of the old school, there have been many others of less distinction. Indeed, the period, the close of which is marked by J. R. McCulloch's book, was one in which the old school had seemingly come to an end of its progress, from too close an adhesion to deductions from assumed premises. Mill's great merit was that he began the movement to better adapt political economy to society as it actually existed; and the historical school will probably give a most desirable impetus to the same results, even though its exaggerated claims as to the true method[88] can not possibly be admitted.

Italian writers have not received hitherto the attention they deserve. After 1830, besides Rossi, who went to France, there was Romagnosi, who dealt more with the relations of economics to other studies; Cattanes, who turned to rural questions and free trade (combating the German, List); Scialoja, at the University of Turin; and Francesco Ferrara, also at Turin from 1849 to 1858. The latter was a follower of Bastiat and Carey, as regards value and rent, and at the same time was a radical believer in *laissez-faire*. Since the union of Italy there has been a new interest in economic study, as with us after our war. The most eminent living Italian economist is said to be Angelo Messedaglia, holding a chair at Padua since 1858. He has excelled in statistical and financial subjects, and is now engaged on a treatise on money, "Moneta," of which one part has been issued (1882). Marco Minghetti and Fedele Lampertico stand above others, the former for a study of the connection of political economy with morals, and for his public career as a statesman; the latter for his studies on paper money and other subjects. Carlo Ferrais presented a good monograph on "Money and the Forced Currency" (1879); and Boccardo issued a library of selected works of the best economists, and a large Dictionary of Political Economy, "Dizionario universale di Economia Politica e di Commercio" (2 vols., second edition, 1875). Luigi Luzzati is a vigorous advocate of co-operation; and Elia Lattes has made a serious study of the early Venetian banks.

Political economy has gained little from American writers. Of our statesmen none have made any additions to the science, and only Hamilton and Gallatin can properly be called economists. Hamilton, in his famous "Report on Manufactures" (1791), shared in some of the erroneous conceptions of his day; but this paper, together with his reports on a national bank and the public credit, are evidences of a real economic power. Gallatin's "Memorial in Favor of Tariff Reform" (1832) is as able as Hamilton's report on manufactures, and a strong argument against protection. Both men made a reputation as practical financiers.

"With few exceptions, the works produced in the United States have been prepared as text-books[89] by authors engaged in college instruction, and therefore chiefly interested in bringing principles previously worked out by others within the easy comprehension of undergraduate students."[20] Of these exceptions, Alexander H. Everett's "New Ideas on Population"[21] (1822), forms a valuable part in the discussion which followed the appearance of Malthus's "Essay." The writer, however, who has drawn most attention, at home and abroad, for a vigorous attack on the doctrines of Ricardo is Henry Charles Carey.[22] Beginning with "The Rate of Wages" (1835), he developed a new theory of value (see "Principles of Political Economy," 1837-1840), "which he defined as a measure of the resistance to be overcome in obtaining things required for use, or the measure of the power of nature over man. In simpler terms, value is measured by the cost of reproduction. The value of every article thus declines as the arts advance, while the general command of commodities constantly increases. This causes a constant fall in the value of accumulated capital as compared with the results of present labor, from which is inferred a tendency toward harmony rather than divergence of interests between capitalist and laborer." This theory of value[23] he applied to land, and even to man, in his desire to give it universality. He next claimed to have discovered a law of increasing production from land in his "Past, Present, and Future" (1848), which was diametrically opposed to Ricardo's law of diminishing returns. His proof was an historical one, that in fact the poorer, not the richer lands, were first taken into cultivation. This, however, did not explain the fact that different grades of land are simultaneously under cultivation, on which Ricardo's doctrine of rent is based. The constantly increasing production of land naturally led Carey to believe in the indefinite increase of population. He, however, was logically brought to accept the supposed law of an ultimate limit to numbers suggested by Herbert Spencer, based on a diminution of human fertility. He tried to identify physical and social laws, and fused his political economy in a system of "Social Science" (1853), and his "Unity of Law" (1872). From about 1845 he became a protectionist, and his writings were vigorously controversial. In his doctrines on money he is distinctly a mercantilist;[24] but, by his earnest attacks on all that has been gained in the science up to his day, he has done a great service in stimulating inquiry and causing a better statement of results. While undoubtedly the best known of American writers, yet, because of a prolix style and an illogical habit of mind, he has had no extended influence on his countrymen.[25]

The effect of the civil war is now beginning to show itself in an unmistakable drift toward the investigation of economic questions, and there is a distinctly energetic tone which may bring new contributions from American writers. General Francis A. Walker,[26] in his study on "The Wages Question" (1876), has combated the wages-fund theory, and proposed in its place a doctrine that wages are paid out of the product, and not out of accumulated capital. Professor W. G. Sumner[27] is a vigorous writer in the school of Mill and Cairnes, and has done good work in the cause of sound money doctrines. Both General Walker and Professor Sumner hold to the method of economic investigation as expounded by Mr. Cairnes; although several younger economists show the influence of the German school. Professor A. L. Perry,[28] of Williams College, adopted Bastiat's theory of value. He also accepts the wages-fund theory, rejects the law of Malthus, and, although believing in the law of diminishing returns from land, regards rent as the reward for a service rendered. Another writer, Henry George,[29] has gained an abnormal prominence by a plausible book, "Progress and Poverty" (1880), which rejects the doctrine of Malthus, and argues that the increase of production of any kind augments the demand for land, and so raises its value. His conclusions lead him to advocate the nationalization of land. Although in opposition to almost all that political economy has yet produced, his writing has drawn to him very unusual notice. The increasing interest in social questions, and the general lack of economic training, which prevents a right estimate of his reasoning by people in general, sufficiently account for the wide attention he has received.

Of late, however, new activity has been shown in the establishment of better facilities for the study of political economy in the principal seats of learning—Harvard, Yale, Cornell, Columbia, Michigan, and Pennsylvania: and a "Cyclopædia of Political Science" (1881-1884, three volumes) has been published by J. J. Lalor, after the example of the French dictionaries.

Books For Consultation (From English, French, And German Authors).

GENERAL TREATISES FORMING A PARALLEL COURSE OF READING WITH MILL.

Professor Fawcett's "Manual of Political Economy" (London, sixth edition, 1883) is a brief statement of Mill's book, with additional matter on the precious metals, slavery, trades-unions, co-operation, local taxation, etc.

Antoine-Élise Cherbuliez's "Précis de la science économique" (Paris, 1862, 2 vols.) follows the same arrangement as Mill, and is considered the best treatise on economic science in the French language. He is methodical, profound, and clear, and separates pure from applied political economy.

Other excellent books in French are: Courcelle-Seneuil's "Traité théorique et pratique d'économie politique" (1858), (Paris, second edition, 1867, 2 vols.), and a compendium by Henri Baudrillart, "Manuel d'économie politique" (third edition, 1872).

Roscher's "Principles of Political Economy" is a good example of the German historical method; its notes are crowded with facts; but the English translation (New York, 1878) is badly done. There is an excellent translation of it into French by Wolowski.

A desirable elementary work, "The Economics of Industry" (London, 1879), was prepared by Mr. and Mrs. Marshall.

Professor Jevons wrote a "Primer of Political Economy" (1878), which is a simple, bird's-eye view of the subject in a very narrow compass.

IMPORTANT GENERAL WORKS.

Adam Smith's "Wealth of Nations" (1776). The edition of McCulloch is perhaps more serviceable than that of J. E. T. Rogers.

Ricardo's "Principles of Political Economy and Taxation" (1817).

J. S. Mill's "Principles of Political Economy" (2 vols., 1848—sixth edition, 1865).

Schönberg's "Handbuch der politischen Oekonomie" (1882). This is a large co-operative treatise by twenty-one writers from the historical school.

Cairnes's "Leading Principles of Political Economy" (1874); "Logical Method" (1875), lectures first delivered in Dublin in 1857.

Carey's "Social Science" (1877). This has been abridged in one volume by Kate McKean.

F. A. Walker's "Political Economy" (1883). This author differs from other economists, particularly on wages and questions of distribution.

H. George's "Progress and Poverty" (1879). In connection with this, read F. A. Walker's "Land and Rent" (1884).

Treatises on Special Subjects.

W. T. Thornton's "On Labor" (1869).

McLeod's "Theory and Practice of Banking" (second edition, 1875-1876).

M. Block's "Traité théorique et pratique de statistique" (1878).

Goschen's "Theory of Foreign Exchanges" (eighth edition, 1875).

J. Caird's "Landed Interest" (fourth edition, 1880), treating of English land and the food-supply.

W. G. Sumner's "History of American Currency" (1874).

John Jay Knox's "United States Notes" (1884).

Jevons's "Money and the Mechanism of Exchange" (1875).

Tooke and Newmarch's "History of Prices" (1837-1856), in six volumes.

Leroy-Beaulieu's "Traité de la science des finances" (1883). This is an extended work, in two volumes, on taxation and finance; "Essai sur la répartition des richesses" (second edition, 1883).

F. A. Walker's "The Wages Question" (1876); "Money" (1878).

L. Reybaud's "Études sur les réformateurs contemporains, ou socialistes modernes" (seventh edition, 1864).

Dictionaries.

McCulloch's "Commercial Dictionary" (new and enlarged edition, 1882).

Lalor's "Cyclopædia of Political Science" (1881-84) is devoted to articles on political science, political economy, and American history.

Coquelin and Guillaumin's "Dictionnaire de l'économie politique" (1851-1853, third edition, 1864), in two large volumes.

Reports and Statistics.

The "Compendiums of the Census" for 1840, 1850, 1860, and 1870, are desirable. The volumes of the tenth census (1880) are of great value for all questions; as is also F. A. Walker's "Statistical Atlas" (1874).

The United States Bureau of Statistics issues quarterly statements; and annually a report on "Commerce and Navigation," and another on the "Internal Commerce of the United States."

The "Statistical Abstract" is an annual publication, by the same department, compact and useful. It dates only from 1878.

The Director of the Mint issues an annual report dealing with the precious metals and the circulation. Its tables are important.

The Comptroller of the Currency (especially during the administration of J. J. Knox) has given important annual reports upon the banking systems of the United States.

The reports of the Secretary of the Treasury deal with the general finances of the United States. These, with the two last mentioned, are bound together in the volume of "Finance Reports," but often shorn of their tables.

There are valuable special reports to Congress of commissioners on the tariff, shipping, and other subjects, published by the Government.

The report on the "International Monetary Conference of 1878" contains a vast quantity of material on monetary questions.

The British parliamentary documents contain several annual "Statistical Abstracts" of the greatest value, of which the one relating to other European states is peculiarly convenient and useful. These can always be purchased at given prices.

A. R. Spofford's "American Almanac" is an annual of great usefulness.

Preliminary Remarks.

Writers on Political Economy profess to teach, or to investigate, the nature of Wealth, and the laws of its production and distribution; including, directly or remotely, the operation of all the causes by which the condition of mankind, or of any society of human beings, in respect to this universal object of human desire, is made prosperous or the reverse.

> It will be noticed that political economy does not include ethics, legislation, or the science of government. The results of political economy are offered to the statesman, who reaches a conclusion after weighing them in connection with moral and political considerations. Political Economy is distinct from Sociology; although it is common to include in the former everything which concerns social life. Some writers distinguish between the pure, or abstract science, and the applied art, and we can speak of a science of political economy only in the sense of a body of abstract laws or formulas. This, however, does not make political economy less practical than physics, for, after a principle is ascertained, its operation is to be observed in the same way that we study the force of gravitation in a falling stone, even when retarded by opposing forces. An economic force, or tendency, can be likewise distinctly observed, although other influences, working at the same time, prevent the expected effect from following its cause. It is, in short, the aim of political economy to investigate the laws which govern the phenomena of material wealth. (Cf. Cossa, "Guide," chap. iii.)

While the [Mercantile] system prevailed, it was assumed, either expressly or tacitly, in the whole policy of nations, that wealth consisted solely of money; or of the precious metals, which, when not already in the state of money, are capable of being directly converted into it. According to the doctrines then prevalent, whatever tended to heap up money or bullion in a country added to its wealth.

> More correctly the Mercantilists (in the sixteenth and seventeenth centuries) held that where money was most plentiful, there would be found the greatest abundance of the necessaries of life.[100]

Whatever sent the precious metals out of a country impoverished it. If a country possessed no gold or silver mines, the only industry by which it could be enriched was foreign trade, being the only one which could bring in money. Any branch of trade which was supposed to send out more money than it brought in, however ample and valuable might be the returns in another shape, was looked upon as a losing trade. Exportation of goods was favored and encouraged (even by means extremely onerous to the real resources of the country), because, the exported goods being stipulated to be paid for in money, it was hoped that the returns would actually be made in gold and silver. Importation of anything, other than the precious metals, was regarded as a loss to the nation of the whole price of the things imported; unless they were brought in to be re-exported at a profit, or unless, being the materials or instruments of some industry practiced in the country itself, they gave the power of producing exportable articles at smaller cost, and thereby effecting a larger exportation. The commerce of the world was looked upon as a struggle among nations, which could draw to itself the largest share of the gold and silver in existence; and in this competition no nation could gain anything, except by making others lose as much, or, at the least, preventing them from gaining it.

The Mercantile Theory could not fail to be seen in its true character when men began, even in an imperfect manner, to explore into the foundations of things. Money, as money, satisfies no want; its worth to any one consists in its being a convenient shape in which to receive his incomings of all sorts, which incomings he afterwards, at the times which suit him best, converts into the forms in which they can be useful to him. The difference between a country with money, and a country altogether without it, would be only one of convenience; a saving of time and trouble, like grinding by water instead of by hand, or (to use Adam Smith's illustration) like the benefit derived from roads; and to mistake money for wealth is the same sort of error as to mistake the highway, which may be the easiest way of getting to your house or lands, for the house and lands themselves.

Money, being the instrument of an important public and private purpose, is rightly regarded as wealth; but everything else which serves any human purpose, and which nature does not afford gratuitously, is wealth also. To be wealthy is to have a large stock of useful articles, or the means of purchasing them. Everything forms, therefore, a part of wealth, which has a power of purchasing; for which anything useful or agreeable would be given in exchange. Things for which nothing could be obtained in exchange, however useful or necessary they may be, are not wealth in the sense in which the term is used in Political Economy. Air, for example, though the most absolute of necessaries, bears no price in the market, because it can be obtained gratuitously; to accumulate a stock of it would yield no profit or advantage to any one; and the laws of its production and distribution are the subject of a very different study from Political Economy. It is possible to imagine circumstances in which air would be a part of wealth. If it became customary to sojourn long in places where the air does not naturally penetrate, as in diving-bells sunk in the sea, a supply of air artificially furnished would, like water conveyed into houses, bear a price: and, if from any revolution in nature the atmosphere became too scanty for the consumption, or could be monopolized, air might acquire a very high marketable value. In such a case, the possession of it, beyond his own wants, would be, to its owner, wealth; and the general wealth of mankind might at first sight appear to be increased, by what would be so great a calamity to them. The error would lie in not considering that, however rich the possessor of air might become at the expense of the rest of the community, all persons else would be poorer by all that they were compelled to pay for what they had before obtained without payment.

Wealth, then, may be defined, all useful or agreeable things which possess exchangeable value; or, in other words, all useful or agreeable things except those which can be obtained, in the quantity desired, without labor or sacrifice.

> This is the usual definition of wealth. Henry George (see "Progress and Poverty," pp. 34-37) regards wealth as consisting "of natural products that have been secured, moved, combined, separated, or in other ways *modified by human exertion*, so as to fit them for the gratification of human desires.... Nothing which Nature supplies to man without his labor is wealth.... All things which have an exchange value are, therefore, not wealth. Only such things can be wealth the production of which increases and the destruction of which decreases the aggregate of wealth.... Increase in land values does not represent increase in the common wealth, for what land-owners gain by higher prices the

tenants or purchasers who must pay them will lose." Jevons ("Primer," p. 13) defines wealth very properly as what is transferable, limited in supply, and useful. F. A. Walker defines wealth as comprising "all articles of value and nothing else" ("Political Economy," p. 5). Levasseur's definition ("Précis," p. 15) is, "all material objects possessing utility" (i.e., the power to satisfy a want). (Cf. various definitions in Roscher's "Political Economy," section 9, note 3.) Perry ("Political Economy," p. 99) rejects the term *wealth* as a clog to progress in the science, and adopts *property* in its stead, defining it as that "which can be bought or sold." Cherbuliez ("Précis," p. 70) defines wealth as the material product of nature appropriated by labor for the wants of man. Carey ("Social Science," i, 186) asserts that wealth consists in the power to command Nature's services, including in wealth such intangible things as mental qualities.

Book I. Production.

Chapter I. Of The Requisites Of Production.

§ 1. The Requisites of Production are Two: Labor, and Appropriate Natural Objects.

> There is a third requisite of production, capital (see page 58). Since the limitation to only two requisites applies solely to a primitive condition of existence, so soon as the element of *time* enters into production, then a store of capital becomes necessary; that is, so soon as production requires such a term that during the operation the laborer can not at the same time provide himself with subsistence, then capital is a requisite of production. This takes place also under any general division of labor in a community. When one man is making a pin-head, he must be supplied with food by some person until the pins are finished and exchanged.

Labor is either bodily or mental; or, to express the distinction more comprehensively, either muscular or nervous; and it is necessary to include in the idea, not solely the exertion itself, but all feelings of a disagreeable kind, all bodily inconvenience or mental annoyance, connected with the employment of one's thoughts, or muscles, or both, in a particular occupation.

> The word "sacrifice" conveys a just idea of what the laborer undergoes, and it corresponds to the abstinence of the capitalist.

Of the other requisite—appropriate natural objects—it is to be remarked that some objects exist or grow up spontaneously, of a kind suited to the supply of human wants. There are caves and hollow trees capable of affording shelter; fruits, roots, wild honey, and other natural products, on which human life can be supported; but even here a considerable quantity of labor is generally required, not for the purpose of creating, but of finding and appropriating them.

Of natural powers, some are unlimited, others limited in quantity. By an unlimited quantity is of course not meant literally, but practically unlimited: a quantity beyond the use which can in any, or at least in present circumstances, be made of it. Land is, in some newly settled countries, practically unlimited in quantity: there is more than can be used by the existing population of the country, or by any accession likely to be made to it for generations to come. But, even there, land favorably situated with regard to markets, or means of carriage, is generally limited in quantity: there is not so much of it as persons would gladly occupy and cultivate, or otherwise turn to use. In all old countries, land capable of cultivation, land at least of any tolerable fertility, must be ranked among agents limited in quantity. Coal, metallic ores, and other useful substances found in the earth, are still more limited than land.

For the present I shall only remark that, so long as the quantity of a natural agent is practically unlimited, it can not, unless susceptible of artificial monopoly, bear any value in the market, since no one will give anything for what can be obtained gratis. But as soon as a limitation becomes practically operative—as soon as there is not so much of the thing to be had as would be appropriated and used if it could be obtained for asking—the ownership or use of the natural agent acquires an exchangeable value.

> Rich lands in our Western Territories a few years ago could be had practically for the asking; but now, since railways and an increase of population have brought them nearer to the markets, they have acquired a distinct exchange value. The value of a commodity (it may be anticipated) is the quantity of other things for which it can be exchanged.

When more water-power is wanted in a particular district than there are falls of water to supply it, persons will give an equivalent for the use of a fall of water. When there is more land wanted for cultivation than a place possesses, or than it possesses of a certain quality and certain advantages of situation, land of that quality and situation may be sold for a price, or let for an annual rent.

§ 2. The Second Requisite of Production, Labor.

It is now our purpose to describe the second requisite of production, labor, and point out that it can be either direct or indirect. This division and subdivision can be seen from the classification given below. Under the head of indirect labor are to be arranged all the many employments subsidiary to the production of any one article, and which, as they furnish but a small part of labor for the one article (e.g., bread), are subsidiary to the production of a vast number of other articles; and hence we see the interdependence of one employment on another, which comes out so conspicuously at the time of a commercial depression.

"We think it little to sit down to a table covered with articles from all quarters of the globe and from the remotest isles of the sea—with tea from China, coffee from Brazil, spices from the East, and sugar from the West Indies; knives from Sheffield, made with iron from Sweden and ivory from Africa; with silver from Mexico and cotton from South Carolina; all being lighted with oil brought from New Zealand or the Arctic Circle. Still less do we think of the great number of persons whose united agency is required to bring any one of these finished products to our homes—of the merchants, insurers, sailors, ship-builders, cordage and sail makers, astronomical-instrument makers, men of science, and others, before a pound of tea can appear in our market."[101]

The labor[102] which terminates in the production of an article fitted for some human use is either employed directly about the thing, or in previous operations destined to facilitate, perhaps essential to the possibility of, the subsequent ones. In making bread, for example, the labor employed about the thing itself is that of the baker; but the labor of the miller, though employed directly in the production not of bread but of flour, is equally part of the aggregate sum of labor by which the bread is produced; as is also the labor of the sower, and of the reaper. Some may think that all these persons ought to be considered as employing their labor directly about the thing; the corn, the flour, and the bread being one substance in three different states. Without disputing about this question of mere language, there is still the plowman, who prepared the ground for the seed, and whose labor never came in contact with the substance in any of its states; and the plow-maker, whose share in the result was still more remote. We must add yet another kind of labor; that of transporting the produce from the place of its production to the place of its destined use: the labor of carrying the corn to market, and from market to the miller's, the flour from the miller's to the baker's, and the bread from the baker's to the place of its final consumption.

> Besides the two classes of indirect laborers here mentioned, those engaged in producing materials and those in transportation, there are several others who are paid fractions out of the bread. Subsidiary to the direct labor of the bread-maker is the labor of all those who make the instruments employed in the process (as, e.g., the oven). Materials are completely changed in character by one use, as when the coal is burned, or the flour baked into bread; while an instrument, like an oven, is capable of remaining intact throughout many operations. The producer of materials and the transporter are paid by the bread-maker in the price of his coal and flour when left at his door, so that the price of the loaf is influenced by these payments. Those persons, moreover, who, like the police and officers of our government, act to protect property and life, are also to be classed as laborers indirectly aiding in the production of the given article, bread (and by his taxes the bread-maker helps pay the wages of these officials). Shading off into a more distant, although essential, connection is another class—that of those laborers who train human beings in the branches of knowledge necessary to the attainment of proper skill in managing the processes and instruments of an industry. The acquisition of the rudiments of education, and, in many cases, the most profound knowledge of chemistry, physics and recondite studies, are essential to production; and teachers are indirect laborers in producing almost every article in the market. In this country, especially, are inventors a class of indirect laborers essential to all ultimate production as it now goes on. The improvements in the instruments of production are the results of an inventive ability which has made American machinery known all over the world. They, too, as well as the teacher, are paid (a small fraction, of course) out of the

> ultimate result, by an indirect path, and materially change the ease or difficulty, cheapness or dearness, of production in nearly every branch of industry. In the particular illustration given they have improved the ovens, ranges, and stoves, so that the same or better articles are produced at a less cost than formerly. All these indirect laborers receive, in the way of remuneration, a fraction, some more, some less (the farther they are removed from the direct process), of the value of the final result.

§ 3. Of Capital as a Requisite of Production.

> But another set of laborers are to be placed in distinct contrast with these, so far as the grounds on which they receive their remuneration is concerned. These are the men engaged previously in providing the subsistence, and articles by which the former classes of labor can carry on their operations.

The previous employment of labor is an indispensable condition to every productive operation, on any other than the very smallest scale. Except the labor of the hunter and fisher, there is scarcely any kind of labor to which the returns are immediate. Productive operations require to be continued a certain time before their fruits are obtained. Unless the laborer, before commencing his work, possesses a store of food, or can obtain access to the stores of some one else, in sufficient quantity to maintain him until the production is completed, he can undertake no labor but such as can be carried on at odd intervals, concurrently with the pursuit of his subsistence.

> The possession of capital is thus a third requisite of production, together with land and labor, as noted above. Henry George ("Progress and Poverty," chap. iv) holds an opposite opinion: "The subsistence of the laborers who built the Pyramids was drawn, not from a previously hoarded stock" (does he not forget the story of Joseph's store of corn?), "but from the constantly recurring crops of the Nile Valley."

He can not obtain food itself in any abundance; for every mode of so obtaining it requires that there be already food in store. Agriculture only brings forth food after the lapse of months; and, though the labors of the agriculturist are not necessarily continuous during the whole period, they must occupy a considerable part of it. Not only is agriculture impossible without food produced in advance, but there must be a very great quantity in advance to enable any considerable community to support itself wholly by agriculture. A country like England or the United States is only able to carry on the agriculture of the present year because that of past years has provided, in those countries or somewhere else, sufficient food to support their agricultural population until the next harvest. They are only enabled to produce so many other things besides food, because the food which was in store at the close of the last harvest suffices to maintain not only the agricultural laborers, but a large industrious population besides.

The claim to remuneration founded on the possession of food, available for the maintenance of laborers, is of another kind; remuneration for abstinence, not for labor. If a person has a store of food, he has it in his power to consume it himself in idleness, or in feeding others to attend on him, or to fight for him, or to sing or dance for him. If, instead of these things, he gives it to productive laborers to support them during their work, he can, and naturally will, claim a remuneration from the produce. He will not be content with simple repayment; if he receives merely that, he is only in the same situation as at first, and has derived no advantage from delaying to apply his savings to his own benefit or pleasure. He will look for some equivalent for this forbearance:[103] he will expect his advance of food to come back to him with an increase, called, in the language of business, a profit; and the hope of this profit will generally have been a part of the inducement which made him accumulate a stock, by economizing in his own consumption; or, at any rate, which made him forego the application of it, when accumulated, to his personal ease or satisfaction.

Chapter II. Of Unproductive Labor.

§ 1. Definition of Productive and Unproductive Labor.

Labor is indispensable to production, but has not always production for its effect. There is much labor, and of a high order of usefulness, of which production is not the object. Labor has accordingly been distinguished into Productive and Unproductive. Productive labor means labor productive of wealth. We are recalled, therefore, to the question touched upon in our [Preliminary Remarks], what Wealth is.

By Unproductive Labor, on the contrary, will be understood labor which does not terminate in the creation of material wealth. And all labor, according to our present definition, must be classed as unproductive, which terminates in a permanent benefit, however important, provided that an increase of material products forms no part of that benefit. The labor of saving a friend's life is not productive, unless the friend is a productive laborer, and produces more than he consumes.

> The principle on which the distinction is made is perfectly clear, but in many cases persons may be misled chiefly in regard to matters of fact. A clergyman may at first sight be classed as an unproductive laborer; but, until we know the facts, we can not apply the principle of our definition. Unless we know that no clergyman, by inculcating rules of morality and self-control, ever caused an idler or wrong-doer to become a steady laborer, we can not say that a clergyman is a laborer unproductive of material wealth. Likewise the army, or the officers of our government at Washington, may or may not have aided in producing material wealth according as they do or do not, in fact, accomplish the protective purposes for which they exist. So with teachers. There is, however, no disparagement implied in the word unproductive; it is merely an economic question, and has to do only with forces affecting the production of wealth.

Unproductive may be as useful as productive labor; it may be more useful, even in point of permanent advantage; or its use may consist only in pleasurable sensation, which when gone leaves no trace; or it may not afford even this, but may be absolute waste. In any case, society or mankind grow no richer by it, but poorer. All material products consumed by any one while he produces nothing are so much subtracted, for the time, from the material products which society would otherwise have possessed.

To be wasted, however, is a liability not confined to unproductive labor. Productive labor may equally be waste, if more of it is expended than really conduces to production. If defect of skill in laborers, or of judgment in those who direct them, causes a misapplication of productive industry, labor is wasted. Productive labor may render a nation poorer, if the wealth it produces, that is, the increase it makes in the stock of useful or agreeable things, be of a kind not immediately wanted: as when a commodity is unsalable, because produced in a quantity beyond the present demand; or when speculators build docks and warehouses before there is any trade.

§ 2. Productive and Unproductive Consumption.

The distinction of Productive and Unproductive is applicable to Consumption as well as to Labor. All the members of the community are not laborers, but all are consumers, and consume either unproductively or productively. Whoever contributes nothing directly or indirectly to production is an unproductive consumer. The only productive consumers are productive laborers; the labor of direction being of course included, as well as that of execution. But the consumption even of productive laborers is not all of it Productive Consumption. There is unproductive consumption by productive consumers. What they consume in keeping up or improving their health, strength, and capacities of work, or in rearing other productive laborers to succeed them, is Productive Consumption. But consumption on pleasures or luxuries, whether by the idle or by the industrious, since production is neither its object nor is in any way advanced by it, must be reckoned Unproductive: with a reservation, perhaps, of a certain quantum of enjoyment which may be classed among necessaries, since anything short of it would not be consistent with the greatest efficiency of labor. That alone is productive consumption which goes to maintain and increase the productive powers of the community; either those residing in its soil, in its materials, in the number and efficiency of its instruments of production, or in its people.

I grant that no labor really tends to the enrichment of society, which is employed in producing things for the use of unproductive consumers. The tailor who makes a coat for a man who produces nothing is a productive laborer; but in a few weeks or months the coat is worn out, while the wearer has not produced anything to replace it, and the community is then no richer by the labor of the tailor than if the same sum had been paid for a stall at the opera. Nevertheless, society has been richer by the labor while the coat lasted. These things also [such as lace and pine-apples] are wealth until they have been consumed.

§ 3. Distinction Between Labor for the Supply of Productive Consumption and Labor for the Supply of Unproductive Consumption.

We see, however, by this, that there is a distinction more important to the wealth of a community than even that between productive and unproductive labor; the distinction, namely, between labor for the supply of productive, and for the supply of unproductive, consumption; between labor employed in keeping up or in adding to the productive resources of the country, and that which is employed otherwise. Of the produce of the country, a part only is destined to be consumed productively; the remainder supplies the unproductive consumption of producers, and the entire consumption of the unproductive class. Suppose that the proportion of the annual produce applied to the first purpose amounts to half; then one half the productive laborers of the country are all that are employed in the operations on which the permanent wealth of the country depends. The other half are occupied from year to year and from generation to generation in producing things which are consumed and disappear without return; and whatever this half consume is as completely lost, as to any permanent effect on the national resources, as if it were consumed unproductively. Suppose that this second half of the laboring population ceased to work, and that the government maintained them in idleness for a whole year: the first half would suffice to produce, as they had done before, their own necessaries and the necessaries of the second half, and to keep the stock of materials and implements undiminished: the unproductive classes, indeed, would be either starved or obliged to produce their own subsistence, and the whole community would be reduced during a year to bare necessaries; but the sources of production would be unimpaired, and the next year there would not necessarily be a smaller produce than if no such interval of inactivity had occurred; while if the case had been reversed, if the first half of the laborers had suspended their accustomed occupations, and the second half had continued theirs, the country at the end of the twelvemonth would have been entirely impoverished. It would be a great error to regret the large proportion of the annual produce, which in an opulent country goes to supply unproductive consumption. That so great a surplus should be available for such purposes, and that it should be applied to them, can only be a subject of congratulation.

This principle may be seen by the following classification:

(A) Idlers; or unproductive laborers—e.g., actors.
(B) Productive laborers—e.g., farmers.
   (C) Producing wealth for productive consumption, one half the annual produce.
   (D) Producing wealth for unproductive consumption (A), one half the annual produce.

Group D are productive laborers, and their *own necessaries* are productively consumed, but they are supplied by C, who keep themselves and D in existence. So long as C work, both C and D can go on producing. If D stopped working, they could be still subsisted as before by C; but A would be forced to produce for themselves. But, if C stopped working, D and C would be left without the necessaries of life, and would be obliged to cease their usual work. In this way it may be seen how much more important to the increase of material wealth C are than D, who labor "for the supply of unproductive consumption." Of course, group D are desirable on other than economic grounds, because their labor represents what can be enjoyed beyond the necessities of life.

Chapter III. Of Capital.

§ 1. Capital is Wealth Appropriated to Reproductive Employment.

It has been seen in the preceding chapters that besides the primary and universal requisites of production, labor and natural agents, there is another requisite without which no productive operations beyond the rude and scanty beginnings of primitive industry are possible—namely, a stock, previously accumulated, of the products of former labor. This accumulated stock of the produce of labor is termed Capital. What capital does for production is, to afford the shelter, protection, tools, and materials which the work requires, and to feed and otherwise maintain the laborers during the process. These are the services which present labor requires from past, and from the produce of past, labor. Whatever things are destined for this use—destined to supply productive labor with these various prerequisites—are Capital.

> Professor Fawcett, "Manual" (chap. ii), says: "Since the laborer must be fed by previously accumulated food, ... some of the results of past labor are required to be set aside to sustain the laborer while producing. The third requisite of production, therefore, is a fund reserved from consumption, and devoted to sustain those engaged in future production.... Capital is not confined to the food which feeds the laborers, but includes machinery, buildings, and, in fact, every product due to man's labor which can be applied to assist his industry" (chap. iv). General Walker ("Political Economy," pages 68-70) defines capital as that portion of wealth (excluding unimproved land and natural agents) which is employed in the production of new forms of wealth. Henry George ("Progress and Poverty," page 41) returns to Adam Smith's definition: "That part of a man's stock which he expects to yield him a revenue is called his capital." Cherbuliez ("Précis," page 70) points out the increasing interdependence of industrial operations as society increases in wealth, and that there

> is not a single industry which does not demand the use of products obtained by previous labor. "These auxiliary products accumulated with a view to the production to which they are subservient" form what is called capital. Carey ("Social Science," iii, page 48) regards as capital all things which in any way form the machinery by which society obtains wealth. Roscher's definition is, "Every product laid by for purposes of further production." ("Political Economy," section 42.) By some, labor is regarded as capital.[104]

A manufacturer, for example, has one part of his capital in the form of buildings, fitted and destined for carrying on this branch of manufacture. Another part he has in the form of machinery. A third consists, if he be a spinner, of raw cotton, flax, or wool; if a weaver, of flaxen, woolen, silk, or cotton thread; and the like, according to the nature of the manufacture. Food and clothing for his operatives it is not the custom of the present age that he should directly provide; and few capitalists, except the producers of food or clothing, have any portion worth mentioning of their capital in that shape. Instead of this, each capitalist has money, which he pays to his work-people, and so enables them to supply themselves. What, then, is his capital? Precisely that part of his possessions, whatever it be, which he designs to employ in carrying on fresh production. It is of no consequence that a part, or even the whole of it, is in a form in which it can not directly supply the wants of laborers.

> Care should be taken to distinguish between wealth, capital, and money. Capital may be succinctly defined as *saved wealth devoted to reproduction*, and the relations of the three terms mentioned may be illustrated by the following figure: The area of the circle, A, represents the wealth of a country; the area of the inscribed circle, B, the quantity out of the whole wealth which is saved and devoted to reproduction and called capital. But money is only one part of capital, as shown by the area of circle C. Wherefore, it can be plainly seen that not all capital, B, is money; that not all wealth, A, is capital, although all capital is necessarily wealth as included within it. It is not always understood that money is merely a convenient article by which other forms of wealth are exchanged against each other, and that a man may have capital without ever having any actual

money in his possession. In times of commercial depression, that which is capital to-day may not to-morrow satisfy any desires (i.e., not be in demand), and so for the time it may, so to speak, drop entirely out of our circles above. For the moment, not having an exchange value, it can not be wealth, and so can the less be capital.

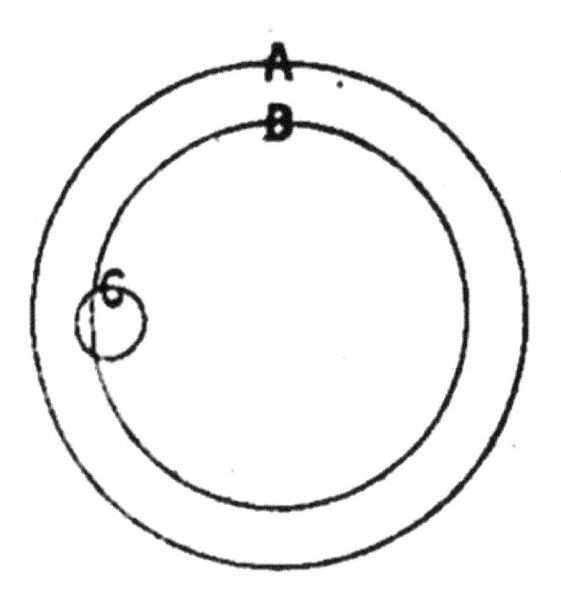

Suppose, for instance, that the capitalist is a hardware manufacturer, and that his stock in trade, over and above his machinery, consists at present wholly in iron goods. Iron goods can not feed laborers. Nevertheless, by a mere change of the destination of the iron goods, he can cause laborers to be fed. Suppose that [the capitalist changed into wages what he had before spent] in buying plate and jewels; and, in order to render the effect perceptible, let us suppose that the change takes place on a considerable scale, and that a large sum is diverted from buying plate and jewels to employing productive laborers, whom we shall suppose to have been previously, like the Irish peasantry, only half employed and half fed. The laborers, on receiving their increased wages, will not lay them out in plate and jewels, but in food. There is not, however, additional food in the country; nor any unproductive laborers or animals, as in the former case, whose food is set free for productive purposes. Food will therefore be imported if possible; if not possible, the laborers will remain for a season on their short allowance: but the consequence of this change in the demand for commodities, occasioned by the change in the expenditure of capitalists from unproductive to productive, is that next year more food will be produced, and less plate and jewelry. So that again, without having had anything to do with the food of the laborers directly, the conversion by individuals of a portion of their property, no matter of what sort, from an unproductive destination to a productive, has had the effect of causing more food to be appropriated to the consumption of productive laborers. The distinction, then, between Capital and Not-capital, does not lie in the kind of commodities, but in the mind of the capitalist—in his will to employ them for one purpose rather than another; and all property, however ill adapted in itself for the use of laborers, is a part of capital, so soon as it, or the value to be received from it, is set apart for productive reinvestment.

§ 2. More Capital Devoted to Production than Actually Employed in it.

As whatever of the produce of the country is devoted to production is capital, so, conversely, the whole of the capital of the country is devoted to production. This second proposition, however, must be taken with some limitations and explanations. (1) A fund may be seeking for productive employment, and find none adapted to the inclinations of its possessor: it then is capital still, but unemployed capital. (2) Or the stock may consist of unsold goods, not susceptible of direct application to productive uses, and not, at the moment, marketable: these, until sold, are in the condition of unemployed capital.

> This is not an important distinction. The goods are doubtless marketable at some price, if offered low enough. If no one wants them, then, by definition, they are not wealth so long as that condition exists.

(3) [Or] suppose that the Government lays a tax on the production in one of its earlier stages, as, for instance, by taxing the material. The manufacturer has to advance the tax, before commencing the manufacture, and is therefore under a necessity of having a larger accumulated fund than

is required for, or is actually employed in, the production which he carries on. He must have a larger capital to maintain the same quantity of productive labor; or (what is equivalent) with a given capital he maintains less labor. (4) For another example: a farmer may enter on his farm at such a time of the year that he may be required to pay one, two, or even three quarters' rent before obtaining any return from the produce. This, therefore, must be paid out of his capital.

(5) Finally, that large portion of the productive capital of a country which is employed in paying the wages and salaries of laborers, evidently is not, all of it, strictly and indispensably necessary for production. As much of it as exceeds the actual necessaries of life and health (an excess which in the case of skilled laborers is usually considerable) is not expended in supporting labor, but in remunerating it, and the laborers could wait for this part of their remuneration until the production is completed.

> The previous accumulation of commodities requisite for production must inevitably be large enough to cover necessaries, but need not be more, if the laborer is willing to wait for the additional amount of his wages (the amount of his unproductive consumption) until the completion of the industrial operation. In fact, however, the accumulation must be sufficient to pay the laborer all his wages from week to week, by force of custom (wherever there is any considerable division of labor), and also sufficient to purchase tools and materials. The various elements of capital are materials, instruments, and subsistence, giving "instruments" its wide signification which includes money (the tool of exchange), and other necessary appliances of each special kind of production.

In truth, it is only after an abundant capital had already been accumulated that the practice of paying in advance any remuneration of labor beyond a bare subsistence could possibly have arisen: since whatever is so paid is not really applied to production, but to the unproductive consumption of productive laborers, indicating a fund for production sufficiently ample to admit of habitually diverting a part of it to a mere convenience.

It will be observed that I have assumed that the laborers are always subsisted from capital:[105] and this is obviously the fact, though the capital need not necessarily be furnished by a person called a capitalist.

The peasant does not subsist this year on the produce of this year's harvest, but on that of the last. The artisan is not living on the proceeds of the work he has in hand, but on those of work previously executed and disposed of. Each is supported by a small capital of his own, which he periodically replaces from the produce of his labor. The large capitalist is, in like manner, maintained from funds provided in advance.

§ 3. Examination of Cases Illustrative of the Idea of Capital.

That which is virtually capital to the individual is or is not capital to the nation, according as the fund which by the supposition he has not dissipated has or has not been dissipated by somebody else.

> Let the reader consider, in the four following suppositions, whether or not the given capital has wholly dropped out of the circle in the diagram, page 67. In (3) and (4) the wealth is entirely dissipated; as it can not longer be in circle A, it can not, of course, be in circle B.

(1.) For example, let property of the value of ten thousand pounds, belonging to A, be lent to B, a farmer or manufacturer, and employed profitably in B's occupation. It is as much capital as if it belonged to B. A is really a farmer or manufacturer, not personally, but in respect of his property. Capital worth ten thousand pounds is employed in production— in maintaining laborers and providing tools and materials—which capital belongs to A, while B takes the trouble of employing it, and receives for his remuneration the difference between the profit which it yields and the interest he pays to A. This is the simplest case.

(2.) Suppose next that A's ten thousand pounds, instead of being lent to B, are lent on mortgage to C, a landed proprietor, by whom they are employed in improving the productive powers of his estate, by fencing, draining, road-making, or permanent manures. This is productive employment. The ten thousand pounds are sunk, but not dissipated. They yield a permanent return; the land now affords an increase of produce, sufficient in a few years, if the outlay has been judicious, to replace the amount, and in time to multiply it manifold. Here, then, is a value of ten thousand pounds, employed in increasing the produce of the country. This constitutes a capital, for which C, if he lets his land, receives the returns in the nominal form of increased rent; and the mortgage entitles A to receive from these returns, in the shape of interest, such annual sum as has been agreed on.

(3.) Suppose, however, that C, the borrowing landlord, is a spendthrift, who burdens his land not to increase his fortune but to squander it, expending the amount in equipages and entertainments. In a year or two it is dissipated, and without return. A is as rich as before; he has no longer his ten thousand pounds, but he has a lien on the land, which he could still sell for that amount. C, however, is ten thousand pounds poorer than formerly; and nobody is richer. It may be said that those are richer who have made profit out of the money while it was being spent. No doubt if C lost it by gaming, or was cheated of it by his servants, that is a mere transfer, not a destruction, and those who have gained the amount may employ it productively. But if C has received the fair value for his expenditure in articles of subsistence or luxury, which he has consumed on himself, or by means of his servants or guests, these articles have ceased to exist, and nothing has been produced to replace them: while if the same sum had been employed in farming or manufacturing, the consumption which would have taken place would have been more than balanced at the end of the year by new products, created by the labor of those who would in that case have been the consumers. By C's prodigality, that which would have been consumed with a return is consumed without return. C's tradesmen may have made a profit during the process; but, if the capital had been expended productively, an equivalent profit would have been made by builders, fencers, tool-makers, and the tradespeople who supply the consumption of the laboring-classes; while, at the expiration of the time (to say nothing of an increase), C would have had the ten thousand pounds or its value replaced to him, which now he has not. There is, therefore, on the general result, a difference, to the disadvantage of the community, of at least ten thousand pounds, being the amount of C's unproductive expenditure. To A, the difference is not material, since his income is secured to him, and while the security is good, and the market rate of interest the same, he can always sell the mortgage at its original value. To A, therefore, the lien of ten thousand pounds on C's estate is virtually a capital of that amount; but is it so in reference to the community? It is not. A had a capital of ten thousand pounds, but this has been extinguished—dissipated and destroyed by C's prodigality. A now receives his income, not from the produce of his capital, but from some other source of income belonging to C, probably from the rent of his land, that is, from payments made to him by farmers out of the produce of *their* capital.

(4.) Let us now vary the hypothesis still further, and suppose that the money is borrowed, not by a landlord, but by the state. A lends his capital to Government to carry on a war: he buys from the state what are called government securities; that is, obligations on the Government to pay a certain annual income. If the Government employed the money in making a railroad, this might be a productive employment, and A's property would still be used as capital; but since it is employed in war, that is, in the pay of officers and soldiers who produce nothing, and in destroying a quantity of gunpowder and bullets without return, the Government is in the situation of C, the spendthrift landlord, and A's ten thousand pounds are so much national capital which once existed, but exists no longer—virtually thrown into the sea, as wealth or production is concerned; though for other reasons the employment of it may have been justifiable. A's subsequent income is derived, not from the produce of his own capital, but from taxes drawn from the produce of the remaining capital of the community; to whom his capital is not yielding any return, to indemnify them for the payment; it is all lost and gone, and what he now possesses is a claim on the returns to other people's capital and industry.

The breach in the capital of the country was made when the Government spent A's money: whereby a value of ten thousand pounds was withdrawn or withheld from productive employment, placed in the fund for unproductive consumption, and destroyed without equivalent.

> The United States had borrowed in the late civil war, by August 31, 1865, $2,845,907,626; and, to June 30, 1881, the Government had paid in interest on its bonds, "from taxes drawn from the produce of the remaining capital," $1,270,596,784, as an income to bondholders. From this can be seen the enormous waste of wealth to the United States during the war, and consequently the less existing capital to-day in this country; since, under the same inducements to save, the smaller the outside circle (wealth), the less the inside circle (capital) must be.

Chapter IV. Fundamental Propositions Respecting Capital.

§ 1. Industry is Limited by Capital.

The first of these propositions is, that industry is limited by capital. To employ labor in a manufacture is to invest capital in the manufacture. This implies that industry can not be employed to any greater extent than there is capital to invest. The proposition, indeed, must be assented to as soon as it is distinctly apprehended. The expression "applying capital" is of course metaphorical: what is really applied is labor; capital being an indispensable condition. The food of laborers and the materials of production have no productive power; but labor can not exert its productive power unless provided with them. There can be no more industry than is supplied with materials to work up and food to eat. Self-evident as the thing is, it is often forgotten that the people of a country are maintained and have their wants supplied, not by the produce of present labor, but of past.

> Therefore, as capital increases, more labor can be employed. When the Pittsburg rioters, in 1877, destroyed property, or the product of past labor, they did not realize then that that property might, but now could never again, be employed for productive purposes, and thereby support laborers.

They consume what has been produced, not what is about to be produced. Now, of what has been produced, a part only is allotted to the support of productive labor; and there will not and can not be more of that labor than the portion so allotted (which is the capital of the country) can feed, and provide with the materials and instruments of production.

Because industry is limited by capital, we are not, however, to infer that it always reaches that limit. There may not be as many laborers obtainable as the capital would maintain and employ. This has been known to occur in new colonies, where capital has sometimes perished uselessly for want of labor.

> In the farming districts of our Middle and Western States, in harvest-time, crops have been often of late years ruined because farm-hands could not be obtained. In earlier days, President John Adams was unable to hire a man in Washington to cut wood in the surrounding forests with which to warm the White House.

The unproductive consumption of productive laborers, the whole of which is now supplied by capital, might cease, or be postponed, until the produce came in; and additional productive laborers might be maintained with the amount.

[Governments] can create capital. They may lay on taxes, and employ the amount productively. They may do what is nearly equivalent: they may lay taxes on income or expenditure, and apply the proceeds toward paying off the public debts. The fund-holder, when paid off, would still desire to draw an income from his property, most of which, therefore, would find its way into productive employment, while a great part of it would have been drawn from the fund for unproductive expenditure, since people do not wholly pay their taxes from what they would have saved, but partly, if not chiefly, from what they would have spent.

§ 2. Increase of Capital gives Increased Employment to Labor, Without Assignable Bounds.

While, on the one hand, industry is limited by capital, so, on the other, every increase of capital gives, or is capable of giving, additional employment to industry; and this without assignable limit. I do not mean to deny that the capital, or part of it, may be so employed as not to support laborers, being fixed in machinery, buildings, improvement of land, and the like. In any large increase of capital a considerable portion will generally be thus employed, and will only co-operate with laborers, not maintain them.

> It will be remembered, however, that subsistence is but one part or element of capital; that instruments and materials form a large part of capital. But still the question of mere maintenance is rightfully discussed, because it is asserted to-day that, while the rich are

> growing richer, the poor lack even the food to keep them alive; and throughout this discussion Mr. Mill has in view the fact that laborers may exist in the community either "half fed or unemployed."

What I do intend to assert is, that the portion which is destined to their maintenance may (supposing no alteration in anything else) be indefinitely increased, without creating an impossibility of finding the employment: in other words, that if there are human beings capable of work, and food to feed them, they may always be employed in producing something. It is very much opposed to common doctrines.[106] There is not an opinion more general among mankind than this, that the unproductive expenditure of the rich is necessary to the employment of the poor.

> It is to be noticed that, in fact, after the arts have so far advanced in a community that mankind can obtain by their exertion more than the amount of the mere necessaries of life sufficient on the average for the subsistence of all, any further production rendered possible to the human race by new discoveries and processes is naturally unproductively consumed, and that consequently a demand for labor for unproductive consumption is essential for the employment of all existing laborers. This, however, can be done, because enough capital has been brought into existence to create the demand for the labor. Yet it is clear that it is not *expenditure*, but capital, by which employment is given to the poor.

Suppose that every capitalist came to be of opinion that, not being more meritorious than a well-conducted laborer, he ought not to fare better; and accordingly laid by, from conscientious motives, the surplus of his profits; unproductive expenditure is now reduced to its lowest limit: and it is asked, How is the increased capital to find employment? Who is to buy the goods which it will produce? There are no longer customers even for those which were produced before. The goods, therefore (it is said), will remain unsold; they will perish in the warehouses, until capital is brought down to what it was originally, or rather to as much less as the demand of the customers has lessened. But this is seeing only one half of the matter. In the case supposed, there would no longer be any demand for luxuries on the part of capitalists and land-owners. But, when these classes turn their income into capital, they do not thereby annihilate their power of consumption; they do but transfer it from themselves to the laborers to whom they give employment. Now, there are two possible suppositions in regard to the laborers: either there is, or there is not, an increase of their numbers proportional to the increase of capital. (1.) If there is, the case offers no difficulty. The production of necessaries for the new population takes the place of the production of luxuries for a portion of the old, and supplies exactly the amount of employment which has been lost. (2.) But suppose that there is no increase of population. The whole of what was previously expended in luxuries, by capitalists and landlords, is distributed among the existing laborers, in the form of additional wages. We will assume them to be already sufficiently supplied with necessaries.

What follows? That the laborers become consumers of luxuries; and the capital previously employed in the production of luxuries is still able to employ itself in the same manner; the difference being, that the luxuries are shared among the community generally, instead of being confined to a few, supposing that the power of their labor were physically sufficient to produce all this amount of indulgences for their whole number. Thus the limit of wealth is never deficiency of consumers, but of producers and productive power. Every addition to capital gives to labor either additional employment or additional remuneration.

> That laborers should get more (*a*) by capitalists abstaining from unproductive expenditure than (*b*) by expenditure in articles unproductively consumed is a question difficult for many to comprehend, and needs all the elucidation possible. To start with, no one ever knew of a community all of whose wants were satisfied: in fact, civilization is constantly leading us into new fields of enjoyment, and results in a constant differentiation of new desires. To satisfy these wants is the spring to nearly all production and industry. There can, therefore, be no stop to production arising from lack of desire for commodities. "The limit of wealth is never deficiency of consumers," but of productive power.
>
> Now, in supposition (2) of the text, remember that the laborers are supposed not to be employed up to their full productive power. If all capitalists abstain from unproductive consumption, and devote that amount of wealth to production, then, since there can be no

production without labor, the same number of laborers have offered to them in the aggregate a larger sum of articles for their exertions, which is equivalent to saying they receive additional wages.

But some persons want to see the process in the concrete, and the same principle may be illustrated by a practical case. It is supposed that all laborers have the necessaries of life only, but none of the comforts, decencies, and luxuries. Let A be a farmer in New York, who can also weave carpets, and B a lumberman in Maine. A begins to want a better house, and B wishes a carpet, both having food, clothing, and shelter. One of the capitalists abstaining from unproductive consumption, as above, is X, who, knowing the two desires of A and B, presents himself as a middle-man (i.e., he gives a market for both men, as is found in every center of trade, as well as in a country store), furnishing A the tools, materials, etc., and giving him the promise of lumber if he will create the carpet, and promising B the carpet if he will likewise produce the additional lumber. To be more matter of fact, X buys the carpet of A, and sells it to B for the lumber. Thus two new articles have been created, and for their exertions A has received additional wages (either in the form of lumber, or of the money paid him for the carpet), and B has received additional wages (either in the form of a carpet, or the money paid him by X for the lumber). If A and B are regarded as typifying all the laborers, and X all the above capitalists, in the multiplicity of actual exchanges, it will be seen that A and B are creating new articles to satisfy their own demand, instead of meeting the demands of X. If their primary wants are already supplied, then they take their additional wages in the form of comforts and decencies. When Class X forego their consumption, but add that amount to capital, they do not give up their title to that capital, but they transfer the use of it, or their consuming power, to others for the time being. This question will be more fully discussed in § 6.

§ 3. Capital is the result of Saving, and all Capital is Consumed.

A second fundamental theorem respecting capital relates to the source from which it is derived. It is the result of saving.

If all persons were to expend in personal indulgences all that they produce, and all the income that they receive from what is produced by others, capital could not increase. Some saving, therefore, there must have been, even in the simplest of all states of economical relations; people must have produced more than they used, or used less than they produced. Still more must they do so before they can employ other laborers, or increase their production beyond what can be accomplished by the work of their own hands. If it were said, for instance, that the only way to accelerate the increase of capital is by increase of saving, the idea would probably be suggested of greater abstinence and increased privation. But it is obvious that whatever increases the productive power of labor, creates an additional fund to make savings from, and enables capital to be enlarged, not only without additional privation, but concurrently with an increase of personal consumption. Nevertheless, there is here an increase of saving, in the scientific sense. Though there is more consumed, there is also more spared. There is a greater excess of production over consumption. To consume less than is produced is saving; and that is the process by which capital is increased; not necessarily by consuming less, absolutely.

> The economic idea of saving involves, of course, the intention of using the wealth in reproduction. Saving, without this meaning, results only in hoarding of wealth, and while hoarded this amount is not capital. To explain the process by which capital comes into existence, Bastiat has given the well-known illustration of the plane in his "Sophisms of Protection."[107]

A fundamental theorem respecting capital, closely connected with the one last discussed, is, that although saved, and the result of saving, it is nevertheless consumed. The word saving does not imply that what is saved is not consumed, nor even necessarily that its consumption is deferred; but only that, if consumed immediately, it is not consumed by the person who saves it. If merely laid by for future use, it is said to be hoarded; and, while hoarded, is not consumed at all. But, if employed as capital, it is all consumed, though not by the capitalist. Part is exchanged for tools or machinery, which are worn out by use; part for seed or materials, which are destroyed as such by being sown or wrought up, and destroyed altogether by the consumption of the ultimate product. The remainder is paid in wages to productive laborers, who consume it for their daily wants; or if they in their turn save any part, this also is not, generally speaking, hoarded, but (through savings-banks, benefit clubs, or some other channel) re-employed as capital, and consumed. To the vulgar, it is not at all apparent that what is saved is consumed. To them, every one who saves appears in the light of a person who hoards. The person who expends his fortune in unproductive consumption is looked upon as diffusing benefits all around, and is an object of so much favor, that some portion of the same popularity attaches even to him who spends what does not belong to him; who not only destroys his own capital, if he ever had any, but, under pretense of borrowing, and on promise of repayment, possesses himself of capital belonging to others, and destroys that likewise.

This popular error comes from attending to a small portion only of the consequences that flow from the saving or the spending; all the effects of either, which are out of sight, being out of mind. There is, in the one case, a wearing out of tools, a destruction of material, and a quantity of food and clothing supplied to laborers, which they destroy by use; in the other case, there is a consumption, that is to say, a destruction, of wines, equipages, and furniture. Thus far, the consequence to the national wealth has been much the same; an equivalent quantity of it has been destroyed in both cases. But in the spending, this first stage is also the final stage; that particular amount of the produce of labor has disappeared, and there is nothing left; while, on the contrary, the saving person, during the whole time that the destruction was going on, has had laborers at work repairing it; who are ultimately found to have replaced, with an increase, the equivalent of what has been consumed.

Almost all expenditure being carried on by means of money, the money comes to be looked upon as the main feature in the transaction; and since that does not perish, but only changes hands, people overlook the destruction which takes place in the case of unproductive expenditure. The money being merely transferred, they think the wealth also has only been handed over from the spendthrift to other people. But this is simply confounding money with wealth. The wealth which has been destroyed was not the money, but the wines, equipages, and furniture which the money purchased; and, these having been destroyed without return, society collectively is poorer by the amount. In proportion as any class is improvident or luxurious, the industry of the country takes the direction of producing luxuries for their use; while not only the employment for productive laborers is diminished, but the subsistence and instruments which are the means of such employment do actually exist in smaller quantity.

§ 4. Capital is kept up by Perpetual Reproduction, as shown by the Recovery of Countries from Devastation.

To return to our fundamental theorem. Everything which is produced is consumed—both what is saved and what is said to be spent—and the former quite as rapidly as the latter. All the ordinary forms of language tend to disguise this. When people talk of the ancient wealth of a country, of riches inherited from ancestors, and similar expressions, the idea suggested is, that the riches so transmitted were produced long ago, at the time when they are said to have been first acquired, and that no portion of the capital of the country was produced this year, except as much as may have been this year added to the total amount. The fact is far otherwise. The greater part, in value, of the wealth now existing [in the United States] has been produced by human hands within the last twelve months.

> "In the State of Massachusetts it is estimated that the capital, on the average, belonging to each individual does not exceed $600, and that the average annual product *per capita* is about $200; so that the total capital is the product of only two or three years' labor."[108]

The land subsists, and the land is almost the only thing that subsists. Everything which is produced perishes, and most things very quickly. Most kinds of capital are not fitted by their nature to be long preserved. Westminster Abbey has lasted many centuries, with occasional repairs; some Grecian sculptures have existed above two thousand years; the Pyramids perhaps double or treble that time. But these were objects devoted to unproductive use. Capital is kept in existence from age to age not by preservation, but by perpetual reproduction; every part of it is used and destroyed, generally very soon after it is produced, but those who consume it are employed meanwhile in producing more. The growth of capital is similar to the growth of population. Every individual who is born, dies, but in each year the number born exceeds the number who die; the population, therefore, always increases, though not one person of those composing it was alive until a very recent date.

This perpetual consumption and reproduction of capital afford the explanation of what has so often excited wonder, the great rapidity with which countries recover from a state of devastation. The possibility of a rapid repair of their disasters mainly depends on whether the country has been depopulated. If its effective population have not been extirpated at the time, and are not starved afterward, then, with the same skill and knowledge which they had before, with their land and its permanent improvements undestroyed, and the more durable buildings probably unimpaired, or only partially injured, they have nearly all the requisites for their former amount of production. If there is as much of food left to them, or of valuables to buy food, as enables them by any amount of privation to remain alive and in working condition, they will, in a short time, have raised as great a produce, and acquired collectively as great wealth and as great a capital, as before, by the mere continuance of that ordinary amount of exertion which they are accustomed to employ in their occupations. Nor does this evince any strength in the principle of saving, in the popular sense of the term, since what takes place is not intentional abstinence, but involuntary privation.

> The world has at any given period the power, under existing conditions of production and skill, to create a certain amount of wealth, as represented by the inner rectangle, W. Each increased power of production arising from conquests over Nature's forces, as the use of steam and labor-saving machinery, permits the total wealth to be enlarged, as, in the figure, to rectangle W'. For the production of wealth are required labor, capital, and land; therefore, if the labor and land are not destroyed by war, there need not necessarily be in existence all the previous capital. If there are the necessaries for all, and only sufficient tools to accomplish the work, they will, in a few years, again recreate all the wealth that formerly existed, regain the same position as before, and go on slowly increasing the total wealth just as fast as improvements in the arts of production render it possible.

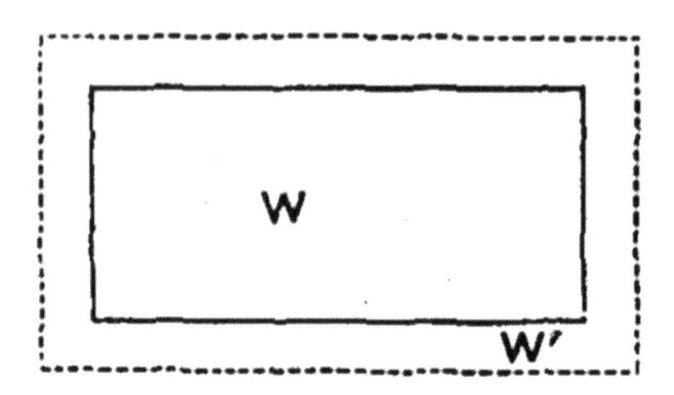

§ 5. Effects of Defraying Government Expenditure by Loans.

[An application of this truth has been made to the question of raising government supplies for war purposes.] Loans, being drawn from capital (in lieu of taxes, which would generally have been paid from income, and made up in part or altogether by increased economy), must, according to the principles we have laid down, tend to impoverish the country: yet the years in which expenditure of this sort has been on the greatest scale have often been years of great apparent prosperity: the wealth and resources of the country, instead of diminishing, have given every sign of rapid increase during the process, and of greatly expanded dimensions after its close.

> During our civil war, at the same time that wealth was being destroyed on an enormous scale, there was a very general feeling that trade was good, and large fortunes were made. At the close of the war a period of speculation and overtrading continued until it was brought to a disastrous close by the panic of 1873. Much of this speculation, however, was due to an inflated paper currency.

We will suppose the most unfavorable case possible: that the whole amount borrowed and destroyed by the Government was abstracted by the lender from a productive employment in which it had actually been invested. The capital, therefore, of the country, is this year diminished by so much. But, unless the amount abstracted is something enormous, there is no reason in the nature of the case why next year the national capital should not be as great as ever. The loan can not have been taken from that portion of the capital of the country which consists of tools, machinery, and buildings. It must have been wholly drawn from the portion employed in paying laborers: and the laborers will suffer accordingly. But if none of them are starved, if their wages can bear such an amount of reduction, or if charity interposes between them and absolute destitution, there is no reason that their labor should produce less in the next year than in the year before. If they produce as much as usual, having been paid less by so many millions sterling, these millions are gained by their employers. The breach made in the capital of the country is thus instantly repaired, but repaired by the privations and often the real misery of the laboring-class.

> As Mr. Mill points out, during the Napoleonic wars, in France the withdrawal of laborers from industry into the army was so large that it caused a rise of wages, and a fall in the profits of capital; while in England, inasmuch as capital, rather than men, was sent to the Continent in the war, the very reverse took place: the diversion of "hundreds of millions of capital from productive employment" caused a fall of wages, and the prosperity of the capitalist class, while the permanent productive resources did not fall off.

This leads to the vexed question to which Dr. Chalmers has very particularly adverted: whether the funds required by a government for extraordinary unproductive expenditure are best raised by loans, the interest only being provided by taxes, or whether taxes should be at once laid on to the whole amount; which is called, in the financial vocabulary, raising the whole of the supplies within the year. Dr. Chalmers is strongly for the latter method. He says the common notion is that, in calling for the whole amount in one year, you require what is either impossible, or very inconvenient; that the people can not, without great hardship, pay the whole at once out of their yearly income; and that it is much better to require of them a small payment every year in the shape of interest, than so great a sacrifice once for all. To which his answer is, that the sacrifice is made equally in either case. Whatever is spent can not but be drawn from yearly income. The whole and every part of the wealth produced in the country forms, or helps to form, the yearly income of somebody. The privation which it is supposed must result from taking the amount in the shape of taxes is not avoided by taking it in a loan. The suffering is not averted, but only thrown upon the laboring-classes, the least able, and who least ought, to bear it: while all the inconveniences, physical, moral, and political, produced by maintaining taxes for the perpetual payment of the interest, are incurred in pure loss. Whenever capital is withdrawn from production, or from the fund destined for production, to be lent to the state and expended unproductively, that whole sum is withheld from the laboring-classes: the loan, therefore, is in truth paid off the same year; the whole of the sacrifice necessary for paying it off is actually made: only it is paid to the wrong persons, and therefore does not extinguish the claim; and paid by the very worst of taxes, a tax exclusively on the laboring-class. And, after having, in this most painful and unjust of ways, gone through the whole effort necessary for extinguishing the debt, the country remains charged with it, and with the payment of its interest in perpetuity.

> The United States, for example, borrows capital from A, with which it buys stores from B. If the loan all comes from within the country, A's capital is *borrowed*, when the United States should have taken that amount outright by taxation. When the money is borrowed of A, the laborers undergo the sacrifice, the title to the whole sum remains in A's hands, and the claim against the Government by A still exists; while, if the amount were taken by taxation, the title to the sum raised is in the state, and it is paid to the right person.
>
> The experience of the United States during the civil war is an illustration of this principle. It is asserted that, as a matter of fact, the total expenses of the war were defrayed by the Northern States, during the four years of its continuance, out of surplus earnings; and yet at the close of the conflict a debt of $2,800,000,000 was saddled on the country.
>
> The United States borrowed $2,400,000,000
> Revenue during that time   1,700,000,000
> Total cost of the war $4,100,000,000
>
> In reality we borrowed only about $1,500,000,000 instead of $2,400,000,000, since (1) the Government issued paper which depreciated, and yet received it at

par in subscriptions for loans. Moreover, the total cost would have been much reduced had we issued no paper and (2) thereby not increased the prices of goods to the state, and (3) if no interest account had been created by borrowing. But could the country have raised the whole sum each year by taxation? In the first fiscal year after the war the United States paid in war taxes $650,000,000. At the beginning of the struggle, to June 30, 1862, the expenditure was $515,000,000, and by June 30, 1863, it had amounted to $1,098,000,000; so that $600,000,000 of taxes a year would have paid the war expenses, and left us free of debt at the close.

A confirmatory experience is that of England during the Continental wars, 1793-1817:

Total war expenditures	£1,060,000,000
Interest charge on the existing debt	235,000,000
Total amount required	£1,295,000,000
Revenue for that period	1,145,000,000
Deficit	£150,000,000

To provide for this deficit, the Government actually increased its debt by £600,000,000. A slight additional exertion would have provided £150,000,000 more of revenue, and saved £450,000,000 to the taxpayers.[109]

The practical state of the case, however, seldom exactly corresponds with this supposition. The loans of the less wealthy countries are made chiefly with foreign capital, which would not, perhaps, have been brought in to be invested on any less security than that of the Government: while those of rich and prosperous countries are generally made, not with funds withdrawn from productive employment, but with the new accumulations constantly making from income, and often with a part of them which, if not so taken, would have migrated to colonies, or sought other investments abroad.

§ 6. Demand for Commodities is not Demand for Labor.

Mr. Mill's statement of the theorem respecting capital, discussed in the argument that "demand for commodities is not demand for labor," needs some simplification. For this purpose represent by the letters of the alphabet, A, B, C, ... X, Y, Z, the different kinds of commodities produced in the world which are exchanged against each other in the process of reaching the consumers. This exchange of commodities for each other, it need hardly be said, does not increase the number or quantity of commodities already in existence; since their production, as we have seen, requires labor and capital in connection with natural agents. Mere exchange does not alter the quantity of commodities produced.

To produce a plow, for example, the maker must have capital (in the form of subsistence, tools, and materials) of which some one has foregone the use by a process of saving in order that something else, in this case a plow, may be produced. This saving must be accomplished first to an amount sufficient to keep production going on from day to day. This capital is all consumed, but in a longer or shorter term (depending on the particular industrial operation) it is reproduced in new forms adapted to the existing wants of man. Moreover, without any new exertion of abstinence, this amount of capital may be again consumed and reproduced, and so go on forever, after once being saved (if never destroyed in the mean while, thereby passing out of the category not only of capital, but also of wealth). The total capital of the country, then, is not the sum of one year's capital added to that of another; but that of last year reproduced in a new form this year, plus a fractional increase arising from new savings. But, once saved, capital can go on constantly aiding in production forever. This plow when made is exchanged (if a plow is wanted, and the production is properly adjusted to meet desires) for such other products, food, means for repairing tools, etc., as give back to the plow-maker all the commodities consumed in its manufacture (with an increase, called profit).

Returning to our illustration of the alphabet, it is evident that a certain amount of capital united with labor (constituting what may be called a productive engine) lies behind the production of A (such as the plow, for example), and to which its existence is due. The same is true of Z. Suppose that 5,000 of Z is produced, of which 4,000 is enough to reimburse the capital used up by labor in the operation, and that the owner of commodity Z spends the remaining 1,000 Z in exchange for 1,000 of commodity A. It is evident (no money being used as yet) that this exchange of goods is regulated entirely by the desires of the two parties to the transaction. No more goods are created simply by the exchange; the simple process of exchange does not keep the laborers engaged on A occupied. And yet the owner of Z had a demand for commodity A; his demand was worthless, except through the fact of his production, which gave him actual wealth, or purchasing power, in the form of Z. His demand for commodity A was not the thing which employed the laborers engaged in producing A, although the demand (if known beforehand) would cause them to produce A rather than some other article—that is, the demand of one quantity of wealth for a certain thing determines the *direction* taken by the owner of capital A. But, since the exchange is merely the form in which the demand manifests itself, it is clear that the demand does not add to production, and so of itself does not employ labor. Of course, if there were no desires, there would be no demand, and so no production and employment of labor. But we may conclude by formulating the proposition, that wealth (Z) offered for commodities (A) necessitates the use of other wealth (than Z) as capital to support the operation by which those commodities (A) are produced. It makes no difference to the existing employment of labor what want is supplied by the producers of A, whether it is velvet (intended for unproductive consumption) or plows (intended for productive consumption). Even if Z is no longer offered in exchange for A, and if then A is no longer to be made, the laborers formerly occupied in producing A—if warning is given of the coming change; if not, loss results—having the plant, can produce something else wanted by the owner of Z.

Now into a community, as here pictured, all laborers supposed to be occupied, and all capital employed in producing A, B, C, ... X, Y, Z, imagine the coming of a shipwrecked crew. Instead of exchanging Z for A, as before, the owner of Z may offer his wealth to the crew to dance for him. The essential question is, Is more employment offered to labor by this action than the former exchange for A? That is, it is a question merely of distribution of wealth among the members of a community. The labor engaged on A is not thrown out of employment (if they have warning). There is no more wealth in existence, but it is differently distributed than before: the crew, instead of the former owner, now have 1,000 of Z. So far as the question of employment is concerned, it makes no difference on what terms the crew got it: they might have been hired to stand in a row and admire the owner of Z when he goes out. But yet it may naturally be assumed that the crew were employed productively. In this case, after they have consumed the wealth Z, they have brought into existence articles in the place of those they consumed. But, although this last operation is economically more desirable for the future growth of wealth, yet no more laborers for the time were employed than if the crew had merely danced. The advantages or disadvantages of productive consumption are not to be discussed here. It is intended, however, to establish the proposition that *wealth paid out in wages, or advanced to producers, itself supports labor*; that wealth offered directly to laborers in this way employs more labor than when merely offered in exchange for other goods, or, in other words, by a demand for commodities; that an increased demand for commodities does not involve an increased demand for labor, since this can only be created by capital. The essential difference is, that the owner of Z in one case, by exchanging goods for A, did not forego his consuming power; in the other case, by giving Z to the unemployed crew, he actually went through the process of saving by foregoing his personal consumption, and handing it over to the crew. If the crew use it unproductively, it is in the end the same as if the owner of Z had done it; but meanwhile the additional laborers were employed. If the crew be employed productively, then the saving once made will go on forever, as explained above, and the world will be the richer by the wealth this additional capital can create.

It may now be objected that, if A is no longer in demand, the laborers in that industry will be thrown out of employment. Out of that employment certainly, but not out of every other. One thousand of Z was able to purchase certain results of labor and capital in industry A, when in the hands of its former owner; and now when in the hands of the crew it will control, as purchasing power, equivalent results of labor and capital. The crew may not want the same articles as the former owner of Z, but they will want the equivalents of 1,000 of Z in something, and that something will be produced now instead of A. The whole process may be represented by this diagram.

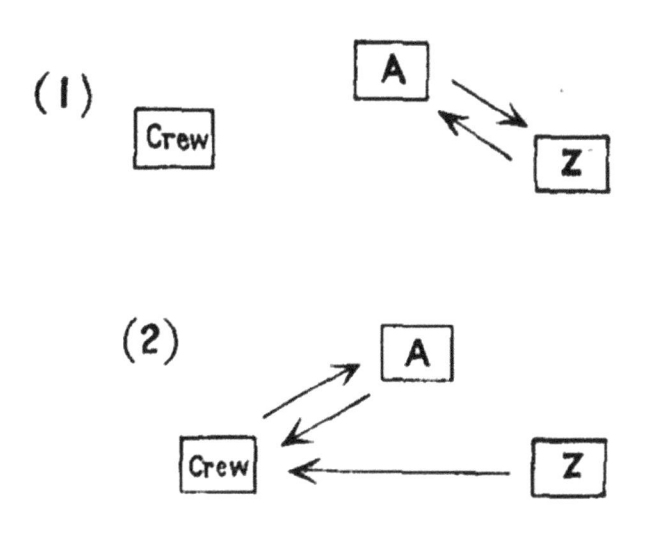

(1) Crew   A ⇄ Z

(2) Crew ⇄ A ← Z

1. Z is exchanged against A, and the crew remain unemployed.

2. Here the crew possess Z, and they themselves exchange Z for whatever A may produce in satisfaction of their wants, and the crew are then employed.

It is possible that the intervention of money blinds some minds to a proper understanding of the operations described above. The supposition, as given, applies to a condition of barter, but is equally true if money is used.[110] Imagine a display of all the industries of the world, A, B, C, ... X, Y, Z, presented within sight on one large field, and at the central spot the producer of gold and silver. When Z is produced, it is taken to the gold-counter, and exchanged for money; when A is produced, the same is done. Then the former money is given for A, and the latter for Z, so that in truth A is exchanged against Z through the medium of money, just as before money was considered. Now, it may be said by an objector, "If A is not wanted, after it is produced, and can not be sold, because the demand from Z has been withdrawn, then the capital used for A will not be returned, and the laborers in A will be thrown out of employment." The answer is, of course, that the state of things here contemplated is a permanent and normal one wherein production is correctly adapted to human desires. If A is found not to be wanted, after the production of it, an industrial blunder has been committed, and wealth is wasted just as when burned up. It is ill-assorted production. The trouble is not in a lack of demand for what A may produce (of something else), but with the producers of A in not making that for which there were desires, from ignorance or lack of early information of the disposition of wealth Z. In practice, however, it will be found that most goods are made upon "orders," and, except under peculiar circumstances, not actually produced unless a market is foreseen. Indeed, as every man knows, the most important function of a successful business man is the adaptation of production to the market, that is, to the desires of consumers.

One other form of this question needs brief mention. It is truly remarked that a large portion of industrial activity is engaged to-day, not in supplying productive consumption, such as food, shelter, and clothing, but in supplying the comforts and luxuries of low and high alike, or unproductive consumption; now, if there were not a demand for luxuries and comforts, many vast industries would cease to exist, and labor would be thrown out of employment. Is not a demand for such commodities, then, a cause of the present employment of labor? No, it is not. Luxuries and comforts are of course the objects of human wants; but a desire alone, without purchasing power, can not either buy or produce these commodities. To obtain a piano, one must produce goods, and this implies the possession of capital, by which to bring into existence goods, or purchasing power, to be offered for a piano. Nor is this sufficient. Even after a man, A, for example, offers purchasing power, he will not get a piano unless there exists an accumulation of unemployed capital, together with labor ready to manufacture the instrument. If capital were all previously occupied, no piano could be made, although A stood offering an equivalent in valuable goods. It may be said that A himself has the means. He has the *wealth*, and if he is willing to forego the use of this wealth, or, in other words, save it by devoting it to reproduction in the piano industry—that is, create the capital necessary for the purpose—then the piano can be made. But this shows again that, not a mere desire, but the existence of capital, is necessary to the production, and so to the employment of labor. An increased demand for commodities, therefore, does not give additional employment to labor, unless there be capital to support the labor.

Some important corollaries result from this proposition: (*a.*) When a country by legislation creates a home demand for commodities, that does not of itself give additional employment to labor. If the goods had before been purchased abroad, under free discretion, then if produced at home they must require more capital and labor, or they would not have been brought from foreign countries. If produced at home, it would require, to purchase them, more of what was formerly sent abroad; or some must do without. The legislation can not, *ipso facto*, create capital, and only by an increase of capital can more employment result. It is possible, however, that legislation might cause a more effective use of existing capital; but that must be a question of fact, to be settled by circumstances in each particular case. It is not a thing to be governed by principles.

(*b.*) It follows from the above proposition also that taxes levied on the rich, and paid by a saving from their consumption of luxuries, do not fall on the poor because of a lessened demand for commodities; since, as we have seen, that demand does not create or diminish the demand for labor. But, if the taxes levied on the rich are paid by savings from what the rich would have expended in wages, then if the Government spends the amount of revenue thus taken in the direct purchase of labor, as of soldiers and sailors, the tax does not fall on the laboring-class taken as a whole. When the Government takes that wealth which was formerly capital, burns it up, or dissipates it in war, it ceases to exist any longer as a means of again producing wealth, or of employing labor.

Chapter V. On Circulating And Fixed Capital.

§ 1. Fixed and Circulating Capital.

Of the capital engaged in the production of any commodity, there is a part which, after being once used, exists no longer as capital; is no longer capable of rendering service to production, or at least not the same service, nor to the same sort of production. Such, for example, is the portion of capital which consists of materials. The tallow and alkali of which soap is made, once used in the manufacture, are destroyed as alkali and tallow. In the same division must be placed the portion of capital which is paid as the wages, or consumed as the subsistence, of laborers. That part of the capital of a cotton-spinner which he pays away to his work-people, once so paid, exists no longer as his capital, or as a cotton-spinner's capital. Capital which in this manner fulfills the whole of its office in the production in which it is engaged, by a single use, is called Circulating Capital. The term, which is not very appropriate, is derived from the circumstance that this portion of capital requires to be constantly renewed by the sale of the finished product, and when renewed is perpetually parted with in buying materials and paying wages; so that it does its work, not by being kept, but by changing hands.

Another large portion of capital, however, consists in instruments of production, of a more or less permanent character; which produce their effect not by being parted with, but by being kept; and the efficacy of which is not exhausted by a single use. To this class belong buildings, machinery, and all or most things known by the name of implements or tools. The durability of some of these is considerable, and their function as productive instruments is prolonged through many repetitions of the productive operation. In this class must likewise be included capital sunk (as the expression is) in permanent improvements of land. So also the capital expended once for all, in the commencement of an undertaking, to prepare the way for subsequent operations: the expense of opening a mine, for example; of cutting canals, of making roads or docks. Other examples might be added, but these are sufficient. Capital which exists in any of these durable shapes, and the return to which is spread over a period of corresponding duration, is called Fixed Capital.

Of fixed capital, some kinds require to be occasionally or periodically renewed. Such are all implements and buildings: they require, at intervals, partial renewal by means of repairs, and are at last entirely worn out. In other cases the capital does not, unless as a consequence of some unusual accident, require entire renewal. A dock or a canal, once made, does not require, like a machine, to be made again, unless purposely destroyed. The most permanent of all kinds of fixed capital is that employed in giving increased productiveness to a natural agent, such as land.

To return to the theoretical distinction between fixed and circulating capital. Since all wealth which is destined to be employed for reproduction comes within the designation of capital, there are parts of capital which do not agree with the definition of either species of it; for instance, the stock of finished goods which a manufacturer or dealer at any time possesses unsold in his warehouses. But this, though capital as to its destination, is not yet capital in actual exercise; it is not engaged in production, but has first to be sold or exchanged, that is, converted into an equivalent value of some other commodities, and therefore is not yet either fixed or circulating capital, but will become either one or the other, or be eventually divided between them.

§ 2. Increase of Fixed Capital, when, at the Expense of Circulating, might be Detrimental to the Laborers.

There is a great difference between the effects of circulating and those of fixed capital, on the amount of the gross produce of the country. Circulating capital being destroyed as such, the result of a single use must be a reproduction equal to the whole amount of the circulating capital used, and a profit besides. This, however, is by no means necessary in the case of fixed capital. Since machinery, for example, is not wholly consumed by one use, it is not necessary that it should be wholly replaced from the product of that use. The machine answers the purpose of its owner if it brings in, during each interval of time, enough to cover the expense of repairs, and the deterioration in value which the machine has sustained during the same time, with a surplus sufficient to yield the ordinary profit on the entire value of the machine.

From this it follows that all increase of fixed capital, when taking place at the expense of circulating, must be, at least temporarily, prejudicial to the interests of the laborers. This is true, not of machinery alone, but of all improvements by which capital is sunk; that is, rendered permanently incapable of being applied to the maintenance and remuneration of labor.

> It is highly probable that in the twenty-five years preceding the panic of 1873, owing to the progress of invention, those industries in the United States employing much machinery were unduly stimulated in comparison with other industries, and that the readjustment was a slow and painful process. After the collapse vast numbers left the manufacturing to enter the extractive industries.

The argument relied on by most of those who contend that machinery can never be injurious to the laboring-class is, that by cheapening production it creates such an increased demand for the commodity as enables, ere long, a greater number of persons than ever to find employment in producing it. The argument does not seem to me to have the weight commonly ascribed to it. The fact, though too broadly stated, is, no doubt, often true. The copyists who were thrown out of employment by the invention of printing were doubtless soon outnumbered by the compositors and pressmen who took their place; and the number of laboring persons now employed in the cotton manufacture is many times greater than were so occupied previously to the inventions of Hargreaves and Arkwright, which shows that, besides the enormous fixed capital now embarked in the manufacture, it also employs a far larger circulating capital than at any former time. But if this capital was drawn from other employments, if the funds which took the place of the capital sunk in costly machinery were supplied not by any additional saving consequent on the improvements, but by drafts on the general capital of the community, what better are the laboring-classes for the mere transfer?

> There is a machine used for sizing the cotton yarn to prepare it for weaving, by which it is dried over a steam cylinder, the wages for attendance on which were only two dollars per day, as compared with an expenditure for labor of fourteen dollars per day to accomplish the same ends before the machine was invented.

All attempts to make out that the laboring-classes as a collective body *can not* suffer temporarily by the introduction of machinery, or by the sinking of capital in permanent improvements, are, I conceive, necessarily fallacious.[111] That they would suffer in the particular department of industry to which the change applies is generally admitted, and obvious to common sense; but it is often said that, though employment is withdrawn from labor in one department, an exactly equivalent employment is opened for it in others, because what the consumers save in the increased cheapness of one particular article enables them to augment their consumption of others, thereby increasing the demand for other kinds of labor. This is plausible, but, as was shown in the last chapter, involves a fallacy; demand for commodities being a totally different thing from demand for labor. It is true, the consumers have now additional means of buying other things; but this will not create the other things, unless there is capital to produce them, and the improvement has not set at liberty any capital, even if it has not absorbed some from other employments.

> If the improvement has lowered the cost of production, it has often required less capital (as well as less labor) to produce the same quantity of goods; or, what is the same thing, an increased product with the same capital.

§ 3. —This seldom, if ever, occurs.

Nevertheless, I do not believe that, as things are actually transacted, improvements in production are often, if ever, injurious, even temporarily, to the laboring-classes in the aggregate. They would be so if they took place suddenly to a great amount, because much of the capital sunk must necessarily in that case be provided from funds already employed as circulating capital. But improvements are always introduced very gradually, and are seldom or never made by withdrawing circulating capital from actual production, but are made by the employment of the annual increase. I doubt if there would be found a single example of a great increase of fixed capital, at a time and place where circulating capital was not rapidly increasing likewise.

> In the United States, while the cost per yard of the manufactured goods has decreased, and so made accessible to poorer classes than before, the capital engaged in manufactures has increased so as to allow a vastly greater number of persons to be employed, as will be seen by the following comparison of 1860 with 1880 taken from the last census returns. (Compendium, 1880, pp. 928, 930.)

	Number of establishments.	Capital (Thousands).	Average number of hands employed.	Total amount paid in wages during the year.
1860	140,433	$1,009,855	1,311,246	$378,878,966
1880	253,852	2,790,272	2,732,595	947,953,795

> "A hundred years ago, one person in every family of five or six must have been absolutely needed to spin and weave by hand the fabrics required for the scanty clothing of the people; now one person in two hundred or two hundred and fifty only need work in the factory to produce the cotton and woolen fabrics of the most amply clothed nation of the world."[112]

To these considerations must be added, that, even if improvements did for a time decrease the aggregate produce and the circulating capital of the community, they would not the less tend in the long run to augment both. This tendency of improvements in production to cause increased accumulation, and thereby ultimately to increase the gross produce, even if temporarily diminishing it, will assume a still more decided character if it should appear that there are assignable limits both to the accumulation of capital and to the increase of production from the land, which limits once attained, all further increase of produce must stop; but that improvements in production, whatever may be their other effects, tend to throw one or both of these limits farther off. Now, these are truths which will appear in the clearest light in a subsequent stage of our investigation. It will be seen that the quantity of capital which will, or even which can, be accumulated in any country, and the amount of gross produce which will, or even which can, be raised, bear a proportion to the state of the arts of production there existing; and that every improvement, even if for the time it diminish the circulating capital and the gross produce, ultimately makes room for a larger amount of both than could possibly have existed otherwise. It is this which is the conclusive answer to the objections against machinery; and the proof thence arising of the ultimate benefit to laborers of mechanical inventions, even in the existing state of society, will hereafter be seen to be conclusive.[113]

Chapter VI. Of Causes Affecting The Efficiency Of Production.

§ 1. General Causes of Superior Productiveness.

The most evident cause of superior productiveness is what are called natural advantages. These are various. Fertility of soil is one of the principal. The influence of climate [is another advantage, and] consists in lessening the physical requirements of the producers.

> In spinning very fine cotton thread, England's natural climate gives in some parts of the country such advantages in proper moisture and electric conditions that the operation can be carried on out-of-doors; while in the United States it is generally necessary to create an artificial atmosphere. In ordinary spinning in our country more is accomplished when the wind is in one quarter than in another. The dry northwest wind in New England reduces the amount of product, while the dry northeast wind in England has a similar effect, and it is said has practically driven the cotton-spinners from Manchester to Oldham, where the climate is more equably moist. The full reasons for these facts are not yet ascertained.
>
> Experts in the woolen industry, also, explain that the quality and fiber of wool depend upon the soil and climate where the sheep are pastured. When Ohio sheep are transferred to Texas, in a few years their wool loses the distinctive quality it formerly possessed, and takes on a new character belonging to the breeds of Texas. The wool produced by one set of climatic conditions is quite different from that of another set, and is used by the manufacturers for different purposes.

In hot regions, mankind can exist in comfort with less perfect housing, less clothing; fuel, that absolute necessary of life in cold climates, they can almost dispense with, except for industrial uses. They also require less aliment. Among natural advantages, besides soil and climate, must be mentioned abundance of mineral productions, in convenient situations, and capable of being worked with moderate labor. Such are the coal-fields of Great Britain, which do so much to compensate its inhabitants for the disadvantages of climate; and the scarcely inferior resource possessed by this country and the United States, in a copious supply of an easily reduced iron-ore, at no great depth below the earth's surface, and in close proximity to coal-deposits available for working it. But perhaps a greater advantage than all these is a maritime situation, especially when accompanied with good natural harbors; and, next to it, great navigable rivers. These advantages consist indeed wholly in saving of cost of carriage. But few, who have not considered the subject, have any adequate notion how great an extent of economical advantage this comprises.

As the second of the [general] causes of superior productiveness, we may rank the greater energy of labor. By this is not to be understood occasional, but regular and habitual energy. The third element which determines the productiveness of the labor of a community is the skill and knowledge therein existing, whether it be the skill and knowledge of the laborers themselves or of those who direct their labor. That the productiveness of the labor of a people is limited by their knowledge of the arts of life is self-evident, and that any progress in those arts, any improved application of the objects or powers of nature to industrial uses, enables the same quantity and intensity of labor to raise a greater produce. One principal department of these improvements consists in the invention and use of tools and machinery.[114]

The deficiency of practical good sense, which renders the majority of the laboring-class such bad calculators—which makes, for instance, their domestic economy so improvident, lax, and irregular—must disqualify them for any but a low grade of intelligent labor, and render their industry far less productive than with equal energy it otherwise might be. The moral qualities of the laborers are fully as important to the efficiency and worth of their labor as the intellectual. Independently of the effects of intemperance upon their bodily and mental faculties, and of flighty, unsteady habits upon the energy and continuity of their work (points so easily understood as not to require being insisted upon), it is well worthy of meditation how much of the aggregate effect of their labor depends on their trustworthiness.

Among the secondary causes which determine the productiveness of productive agents, the most important is Security. By security I mean the completeness of the protection which society affords to its members.

§ 2. Combination and Division of Labor Increase Productiveness.

In the enumeration of the circumstances which promote the productiveness of labor, we have left one untouched, which is co-operation, or the combined action of numbers. Of this great aid to production, a single department, known by the name of Division of Labor, has engaged a large share of the attention of political economists; most deservedly, indeed, but to the exclusion of other cases and exemplifications of the same comprehensive law. In the lifting of heavy weights, for example, in the felling of trees, in the sawing of timber, in the gathering of much hay or corn during a short period of fine weather, in draining a large extent of land during the short season when such a work may be properly conducted, in the pulling of ropes on board ship, in the rowing of large boats, in some mining operations, in the erection of a scaffolding for building, and in the breaking of stones for the repair of a road, so that the whole of the road shall always be kept in good order: in all these simple operations, and thousands more, it is absolutely necessary that many persons should work together, at the same time, in the same place, and in the same way. [But] in the present state of society, the breeding and feeding of sheep is the occupation of one set of people; dressing the wool to prepare it for the spinner is that of another; spinning it into thread, of a third; weaving the thread into broadcloth, of a fourth; dyeing the cloth, of a fifth; making it into a coat, of a sixth; without counting the multitude of carriers, merchants, factors, and retailers put in requisition at the successive stages of this progress.

Without some separation of employments, very few things would be produced at all. Suppose a set of persons, or a number of families, all employed precisely in the same manner; each family settled on a piece of its own land, on which it grows by its labor the food required for its own sustenance, and, as there are no persons to buy any surplus produce where all are producers, each family has to produce within itself whatever other articles it consumes. In such circumstances, if the soil was tolerably fertile, and population did not tread too closely on the heels of subsistence, there would be, no doubt, some kind of domestic manufactures; clothing for the family might, perhaps, be spun and woven within it, by the labor, probably, of the women (a first step in the separation of employments); and a dwelling of some sort would be erected and kept in repair by their united labor. But beyond simple food (precarious, too, from the variations of the seasons), coarse clothing, and very imperfect lodging, it would be scarcely possible that the family should produce anything more.

Suppose that a company of artificers, provided with tools, and with food sufficient to maintain them for a year, arrive in the country and establish themselves in the midst of the population. These new settlers occupy themselves in producing articles of use or ornament adapted to the taste of a simple people; and before their food is exhausted they have produced these in considerable quantity, and are ready to exchange them for more food. The economical position of the landed population is now most materially altered. They have an opportunity given them of acquiring comforts and luxuries. Things which, while they depended solely upon their own labor, they never could have obtained, because they could not have produced, are now accessible to them if they can succeed in producing an additional quantity of food and necessaries. They are thus incited to increase the productiveness of their industry. The new settlers constitute what is called a *market* for surplus agricultural produce; and their arrival has enriched the settlement, not only by the manufactured articles which they produce, but by the food which would not have been produced unless they had been there to consume it.

There is no inconsistency between this doctrine and the proposition we before maintained,[115] that a market for commodities does not constitute employment for labor. The labor of the agriculturists was already provided with employment; they are not indebted to the demand of the new-comers for being able to maintain themselves. What that demand does for them is to call their labor into increased vigor and efficiency; to stimulate them, by new motives, to new exertions.

From these considerations it appears that a country will seldom have a productive agriculture unless it has a large town population, or, the only available substitute, a large export trade in agricultural produce to supply a population elsewhere. I use the phrase "town population" for shortness, to imply a population non-agricultural.

It is found that the productive power of labor is increased by carrying the separation further and further; by breaking down more and more every process of industry into parts, so that each laborer shall confine himself to an ever smaller number of simple operations. And thus, in time, arise those remarkable cases of what is called the division of labor, with which all readers on subjects of this nature are familiar. Adam Smith's illustration from pin-making, though so well known, is so much to the point that I will venture once more to transcribe it: "The business of making a pin is divided into about eighteen distinct operations. One man draws out the wire, another straights it, a third cuts it, a fourth points it, a fifth grinds it at the top for receiving the head; to make the head requires two or three distinct operations; to put it on, is a peculiar business; to whiten the pins is another; it is even a trade by itself to put them into the paper.... I have seen a small manufactory where ten men only were employed, and where some of them, consequently, performed two or three distinct operations. But though they were very poor, and therefore but indifferently accommodated with the necessary machinery, they could, when they exerted themselves, make among them about twelve pounds of pins in a day. There are in a pound upward of four thousand pins of a middling size. Those ten persons, therefore, could make among them upward of forty-eight thousand pins in a day. Each person, therefore, making a tenth part of forty-eight thousand pins, might be considered as making four thousand eight hundred pins in a day. But if they had all wrought separately and independently, and without any of them having been educated to this peculiar business, they certainly could not each of them have made twenty, perhaps not one pin in a day."

§ 3. Advantages of Division of Labor.

The causes of the increased efficiency given to labor by the division of employments are some of them too familiar to require specification; but it is worth while to attempt a complete enumeration of them. By Adam Smith they are reduced to three: "First, the increase of dexterity in every particular workman; secondly, the saving of the time which is commonly lost in passing from one species of work to another; and, lastly, the invention of a great number of machines which facilitate and abridge labor, and enable one man to do the work of many."

(1.) Of these, the increase of dexterity of the individual workman is the most obvious and universal. It does not follow that because a thing has been done oftener it will be done better. That depends on the intelligence of the workman, and on the degree in which his mind works along with his hands. But it will be done more easily. This is as true of mental operations as of bodily. Even a child, after much practice, sums up a column of figures with a rapidity which resembles intuition. The act of speaking any language, of reading fluently, of playing music at sight, are cases as remarkable as they are familiar. Among bodily acts, dancing, gymnastic exercises, ease and brilliancy of execution on a musical instrument, are examples of the rapidity and facility acquired by repetition. In simpler manual operations the effect is, of course, still sooner produced.

(2.) The second advantage enumerated by Adam Smith as arising from the division of labor is one on which I can not help thinking that more stress is laid by him and others than it deserves. To do full justice to his opinion, I will quote his own exposition of it: "It is impossible to pass very quickly from one kind of work to another, that is carried on in a different place, and with quite different tools. A country weaver, who cultivates a small farm, must lose a good deal of time in passing from his loom to the field, and from the field to his loom. When the two trades can be carried on in the same workhouse, the loss of time is no doubt much less. It is even in this case, however, very considerable. A man commonly saunters a little in turning his hand from one sort of employment to another." I am very far from implying that these considerations are of no weight; but I think there are counter-considerations which are overlooked. If one kind of muscular or mental labor is different from another, for that very reason it is to some extent a rest from that other; and if the greatest vigor is not at once obtained in the second occupation, neither could the first have been indefinitely prolonged without some relaxation of energy. It is a matter of common experience that a change of occupation will often afford relief where complete repose would otherwise be necessary, and that a person can work many more hours without fatigue at a succession of occupations, than if confined during the whole time to one.[116] Different occupations employ different muscles, or different energies of the mind, some of which rest and are refreshed while others work. Bodily labor itself rests from mental, and conversely. The variety itself has an invigorating effect on what, for want of a more philosophical appellation, we must term the animal spirits—so important to the efficiency of all work not mechanical, and not unimportant even to that.

(3.) The third advantage attributed by Adam Smith to the division of labor is, to a certain extent, real. Inventions tending to save labor in a particular operation are more likely to occur to any one in proportion as his thoughts are intensely directed to that occupation, and continually employed upon it.

> This also can not be wholly true. "The founder of the cotton manufacture was a barber. The inventor of the power-loom was a clergyman. A farmer devised the application of the screw-propeller. A fancy-goods shopkeeper is one of the most enterprising experimentalists in agriculture. The most remarkable architectural design of our day has been furnished by a gardener. The first person who supplied London with water was a goldsmith. The first extensive maker of English roads was a blind man, bred to no trade. The father of English inland navigation was a duke, and his engineer was a millwright. The first great builder of iron bridges was a stone-mason, and the greatest railway engineer commenced his life as a colliery engineer."[117]

(4.) The greatest advantage (next to the dexterity of the workmen) derived from the minute division of labor which takes place in modern manufacturing industry, is one not mentioned by Adam Smith, but to which attention has been drawn by Mr. Babbage: the more economical distribution of labor by classing the work-people according to their capacity. Different parts of the same series of operations require unequal degrees of skill and bodily strength; and those who have skill enough for the most difficult, or strength enough for the hardest parts of the labor, are made much more useful by being employed solely in them; the operations which everybody is capable of being left to those who are fit for no others.

The division of labor, as all writers on the subject have remarked, is limited by the extent of the market. If, by the separation of pin-making into ten distinct employments, forty-eight thousand pins can be made in a day, this separation will only be advisable if the number of accessible consumers is such as to require, every day, something like forty-eight thousand pins. If there is only a demand for twenty-four thousand, the division of labor can only be advantageously carried to the extent which will every day produce that smaller number. The increase of the general riches of the world, when accompanied with freedom of commercial intercourse, improvements in navigation, and inland communication by roads, canals, or railways, tends to give increased productiveness to the labor of every nation in particular, by enabling each locality to supply with its special products so much larger a market that a great extension of the division of labor in their production is an ordinary consequence. The division of labor is also limited, in many cases, by the nature of the employment. Agriculture, for example, is not susceptible of so great a division of occupations as many branches of manufactures, because its different operations can not possibly be simultaneous.

> (5.) "In the examples given above the advantage obtained was derived from the mere fact of the separation of employments, altogether independently of the mode in which the separated employments were distributed among the *persons* carrying them on, as well as of the *places* in which they were conducted. But a further gain arises when the employments are of a kind which, in order to their effective performance, call for special capacities in the workman, or special natural resources in the scene of operation. There would be a manifest waste of special power in compelling to a mere mechanical or routine pursuit a man who is fitted to excel in a professional career; and similarly, if a

branch of industry were established on some site which offered greater facilities to an industry of another sort, a waste, analogous in character, would be incurred. In a word, while a great number of the occupations in which men engage are such as, with proper preparation for them, might equally well be carried on by any of those engaged in them, or in any of the localities in which they are respectively established, there are others which demand for their effective performance special personal qualifications and special local conditions; and the general effectiveness of productive industry will, other things being equal, be proportioned to the completeness with which the adaptation is accomplished between occupation on the one hand and individuals and localities on the other."[118]

§ 4. Production on a Large and Production on a Small Scale.

Whenever it is essential to the greatest efficiency of labor that many laborers should combine, the scale of the enterprise must be such as to bring many laborers together, and the capital must be large enough to maintain them. Still more needful is this when the nature of the employment allows, and the extent of the possible market encourages, a considerable division of labor. The larger the enterprise the further the division of labor may be carried. This is one of the principal causes of large manufactories. Every increase of business would enable the whole to be carried on with a proportionally smaller amount of labor.

As a general rule, the expenses of a business do not increase by any means proportionally to the quantity of business. Let us take as an example a set of operations which we are accustomed to see carried on by one great establishment, that of the Post-Office. Suppose that the business, let us say only of the letter-post, instead of being centralized in a single concern, were divided among five or six competing companies. Each of these would be obliged to maintain almost as large an establishment as is now sufficient for the whole. Since each must arrange for receiving and delivering letters in all parts of the town, each must send letter-carriers into every street, and almost every alley, and this, too, as many times in the day as is now done by the Post-Office, if the service is to be as well performed. Each must have an office for receiving letters in every neighborhood, with all subsidiary arrangements for collecting the letters from the different offices and redistributing them. To this must be added the much greater number of superior officers who would be required to check and control the subordinates, implying not only a greater cost in salaries for such responsible officers, but the necessity, perhaps, of being satisfied in many instances with an inferior standard of qualification, and so failing in the object.

Whether or not the advantages obtained by operating on a large scale preponderate in any particular case over the more watchful attention and greater regard to minor gains and losses usually found in small establishments, can be ascertained, in a state of free competition, by an unfailing test. Wherever there are large and small establishments in the same business, that one of the two which in existing circumstances carries on the production at greatest advantage will be able to undersell the other. The power of permanently underselling can only, generally speaking, be derived from increased effectiveness of labor; and this, when obtained by a more extended division of employment, or by a classification tending to a better economy of skill, always implies a greater produce from the same labor, and not merely the same produce from less labor; it increases not the surplus only, but the gross produce of industry. If an increased quantity of the particular article is not required, and part of the laborers in consequence lose their employment, the capital which maintained and employed them is also set at liberty, and the general produce of the country is increased by some other application of their labor.

A considerable part of the saving of labor effected by substituting the large system of production for the small, is the saving in the labor of the capitalists themselves. If a hundred producers with small capitals carry on separately the same business, the superintendence of each concern will probably require the whole attention of the person conducting it, sufficiently, at least, to hinder his time or thoughts from being disposable for anything else; while a single manufacturer possessing a capital equal to the sum of theirs, with ten or a dozen clerks, could conduct the whole of their amount of business, and have leisure, too, for other occupations.

Production on a large scale is greatly promoted by the practice of forming a large capital by the combination of many small contributions; or, in other words, by the formation of stock companies. The advantages of the principle are important, [since] (1) many undertakings require an amount of capital beyond the means of the richest individual or private partnership. [Of course] the Government can alone be looked to for any of those works for which a great combination of means is requisite, because it can obtain those means by compulsory taxation, and is already accustomed to the conduct of large operations. For reasons, however, which are tolerably well known, government agency for the conduct of industrial operations is generally one of the least eligible of resources when any other is available. Of [the advantages referred to above] one of the most important is (2) that which relates to the intellectual and active qualifications of the directing head. The stimulus of individual interest is some security for exertion, but exertion is of little avail if the intelligence exerted is of an inferior order, which it must necessarily be in the majority of concerns carried on by the persons chiefly interested in them. Where the concern is large, and can afford a remuneration sufficient to attract a class of candidates superior to the common average, it is possible to select for the general management, and for all the skilled employments of a subordinate kind, persons of a degree of acquirement and cultivated intelligence which more than compensates for their inferior interest in the result. It must be further remarked that it is not a necessary consequence of joint-stock management that the persons employed, whether in superior or in subordinate offices, should be paid wholly by fixed salaries. In the case of the managers of joint-stock companies, and of the superintending and controlling officers in many private establishments, it is a common enough practice to connect their pecuniary interest with the interest of their employers, by giving them part of their remuneration in the form of a percentage on the profits.

The possibility of substituting the large system of production for the small depends, of course, in the first place, on the extent of the market. The large system can only be advantageous when a large amount of business is to be done: it implies, therefore, either a populous and flourishing community, or a great opening for exportation.

In the countries in which there are the largest markets, the widest diffusion of commercial confidence and enterprise, the greatest annual increase of capital, and the greatest number of large capitals owned by individuals, there is a tendency to substitute more and more, in one branch of industry after another, large establishments for small ones. These are almost always able to undersell the smaller tradesmen, partly, it is understood, by means of division of labor, and the economy occasioned by limiting the employment of skilled agency to cases where skill is required; and partly, no doubt, by the saving of labor arising from the great scale of the transactions; as it costs no more time, and not much more exertion of mind, to make a large purchase, for example, than a small one, and very much less than to make a number of small ones. With a view merely to production, and to the greatest efficiency of labor, this change is wholly beneficial.

A single large company very often, instead of being a monopoly, is generally better than two large companies; for there is little likelihood of competition and lower prices when the competitors are so few as to be able to agree not to compete. As Mr. Mill says in regard to parallel railroads: "No one can desire to see the enormous waste of capital and land (not to speak of increased nuisance) involved in the construction of a second railway to connect the same places already united by an existing one; while the two would not do the work better than it could be done by one, and after a short time would probably be amalgamated." The actual tendency of charges to diminish on the railways, before the matter of parallel railways was suggested is clearly seen by reference to Chart V (p. 137).

Chapter VII. Of The Law Of The Increase Of Labor.

§ 1. The Law of the Increase of Production Depends on those of Three Elements—Labor. Capital, and Land.

Production is not a fixed but an increasing thing. When not kept back by bad institutions, or a low state of the arts of life, the produce of industry has usually tended to increase; stimulated not only by the desire of the producers to augment their means of consumption, but by the increasing number of the consumers.

We have seen that the essential requisites of production are three—labor, capital, and natural agents; the term capital including all external and physical requisites which are products of labor, the term natural agents all those which are not. The increase of production, therefore, depends on the properties of these elements. It is a result of the increase either of the elements themselves, or of their productiveness. We proceed to consider the three elements successively, with reference to this effect; or, in other words, the law of the increase of production, viewed in respect of its dependence, first on Labor, secondly on Capital, and lastly on Land.

§ 2. The Law of Population.

The increase of labor is the increase of mankind; of population. The power of multiplication inherent in all organic life may be regarded as infinite. There are many species of vegetables of which a single plant will produce in one year the germs of a thousand; if only two come to maturity, in fourteen years the two will have multiplied to sixteen thousand and more. It is but a moderate case of fecundity in animals to be capable of quadrupling their numbers in a single year; if they only do as much in half a century, ten thousand will have swelled within two centuries to upward to two millions and a half. The capacity of increase is necessarily in a geometrical progression: the numerical ratio alone is different.

To this property of organized beings, the human species forms no exception. Its power of increase is indefinite, and the actual multiplication would be extraordinarily rapid, if the power were exercised to the utmost. It never is exercised to the utmost, and yet, in the most favorable circumstances known to exist, which are those of a fertile region colonized from an industrious and civilized community, population has continued, for several generations, independently of fresh immigration, to double itself in not much more than twenty years.

Years.	Population.	Food.
25	11 mills	x
25	22 mills	$2x$
25	44 mills	$3x$
25	88 mills	$4x$
25	176 mills	$5x$

By this table it will be seen that if population can double itself in twenty-five years, and if food can only be increased by as much as x (the subsistence of eleven millions) by additional application of another equal quantity of labor on the same land in each period, then at the end of one hundred years there would be the disproportion of one hundred and seventy-six millions of people, with subsistence for only fifty-five millions. Of course, this is prevented either by checking population to the amount of the subsistence; by sending off the surplus population; or by bringing in food from new lands.

In the United States to 1860 population has doubled itself about every twenty years, while in France there is practically no increase of population. It is stated that the white population of the United States between 1790 and 1840 increased 400.4 per cent, deducting immigration. The extraordinary advance of population with us, where subsistence is easily attainable, is to be seen in the chart on the next page (No. III), which shows the striking rapidity of increase in the United

States when compared with the older countries of Europe. The steady demand for land can be seen by the gradual westward movement of the center of population, as seen in chart No. IV (p. 116), and by the rapid settlement of the distant parts of our country, as shown by the two charts (frontispieces), which represent to the eye by heavier colors the areas of the more densely settled districts in 1830 and in 1880.

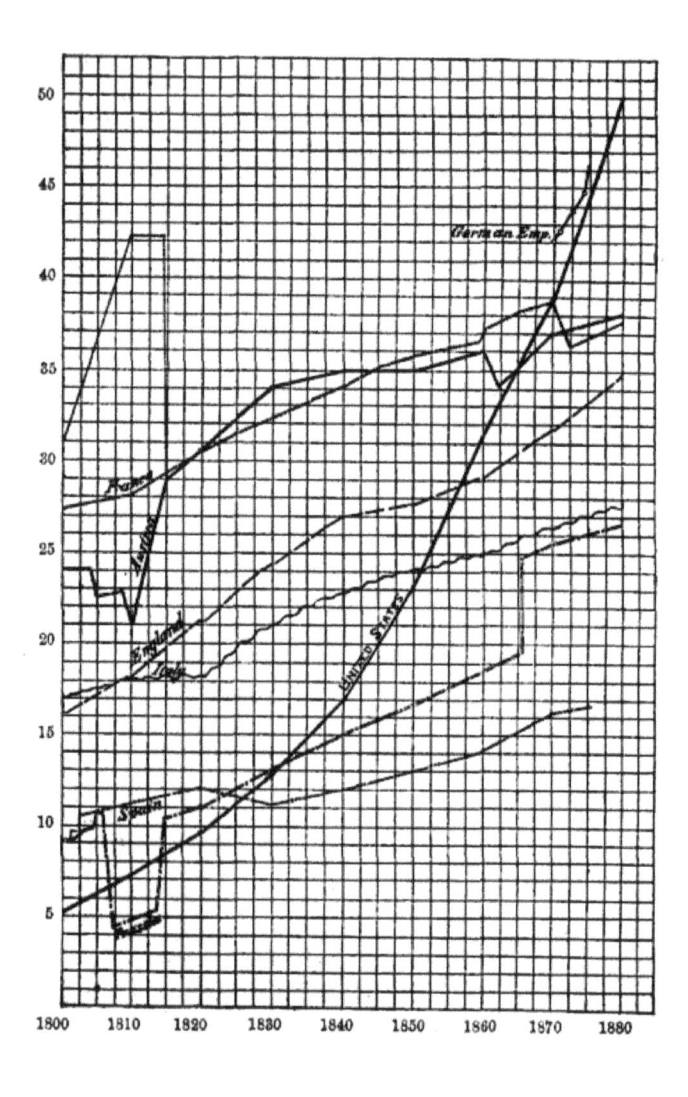

Chart III: Population of European Countries, XIXth Century.

§ 3. By what Checks the Increase of Population is Practically Limited.

The obstacle to a just understanding of the subject arises from too confused a notion of the causes which, at most times and places, keep the actual increase of mankind so far behind the capacity.

The conduct of human creatures is more or less influenced by foresight of consequences, and by some impulses superior to mere animal instincts; and they do not, therefore, propagate like swine, but are capable, though in very unequal degrees, of being withheld by prudence, or by the social affections, from giving existence to beings born only to misery and premature death.

> Malthus found an explanation of the anomaly that in the Swiss villages, with the longest average duration of life, there were the fewest births, by noting that no one married until a cow-herd's cottage became vacant, and precisely because the tenants lived so long were the new-comers long kept out of a place.

In proportion as mankind rise above the condition of the beast, population is restrained by the fear of want, rather than by want itself. Even where there is no question of starvation, many are similarly acted upon by the apprehension of losing what have come to be regarded as the decencies of their situation in life. Among the middle classes, in many individual instances, there is an additional restraint exercised from the desire of doing more than maintaining their circumstances—of improving them; but such a desire is rarely found, or rarely has that effect, in the laboring-classes. If they can bring up a family as they were themselves brought up, even the prudent among them are usually satisfied. Too often they do not think even of that, but rely on fortune, or on the resources to be found in legal or voluntary charity.

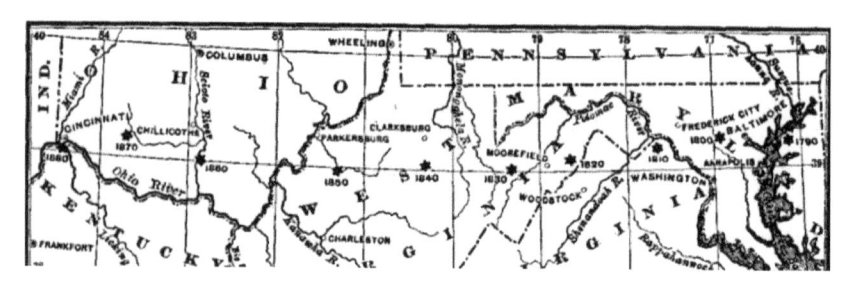

Chart IV: Westward Movement of Center of Population.

This, in effect, is the well-known Malthusian doctrine. The thorough reader will also consult the original "Essay" of Malthus. Mr. Bowen[119] and other writers oppose it, saying it has "no relation to the times in which we live, or to any which are near at hand." He thinks the productive power of the whole world prevents the necessity of considering the pressure of population upon subsistence as an actuality now or in the future. This, however, does not deny the existence of Malthus's principles, but opposes them only on the methods of their action. Mr. Rickards[120] holds that man's food—as, e.g., wheat—has the power to increase geometrically faster than man; but he omits to consider that for the growth of this food land is demanded; that land is not capable of such geometrical increase; and that without it the food can not be grown. Of course, any extension of the land area, as happened when England abolished the corn laws and drew her food from our prairies, removes the previous pressure of population on subsistence. No believer in the Malthusian doctrine is so absurd as to hold that the growth of population actually exceeds subsistence, but that there is a "constant *tendency* in all animated life to increase beyond the nourishment prepared for it," no one can possibly doubt. This is not inconsistent with the fact that subsistence has at any time increased faster than population. It is as if a block of wood on the floor were acted on by two opposing forces, one tending to move it forward, one backward: if it moves backward, that does not prove the absence of any force working to move it forward, but only that the other force is the stronger of the two, and that the final motion is the resultant of the two forces. It is only near-sighted generalization to say that since the block moves forward, there is therefore no opposing force to its advance.[121] Mr. Doubleday maintains that, as people become better fed, they become unprolific. Mr. Mill's answer, referring to the large families of the English peerage, is unfortunate.[122] In Sweden the increase of the peasantry is six times that of the middle classes, and fourteen times that of the nobility. The diminishing fertility of New England families gives a truer explanation, when it is seen that with the progress in material wealth later marriages are the rule. When New-Englanders emigrate to the Western States, where labor is in demand and where it is less burdensome to have large families, there is no question as to their fertility.[123]

(1.) In a very backward state of society, like that of Europe in the middle ages, and many parts of Asia at present, population is kept down by actual starvation. The starvation does not take place in ordinary years, but in seasons of scarcity, which in those states of society are much more frequent and more extreme than Europe is now accustomed to. (2.) In a more improved state, few, even among the poorest of the people, are limited to actual necessaries, and to a bare sufficiency of those: and the increase is kept within bounds, not by excess of deaths, but by limitation of births.[124] The limitation is brought about in various ways. In some countries, it is the result of prudent or conscientious self-restraint. There is a condition to which the laboring-people are habituated; they perceive that, by having too numerous families, they must sink below that condition, or fail to transmit it to their children; and this they do not choose to submit to.

There are other cases in which the prudence and forethought, which perhaps might not be exercised by the people themselves, are exercised by the state for their benefit; marriage not being permitted until the contracting parties can show that they have the prospect of a comfortable support. There are places, again, in which the restraining cause seems to be not so much individual prudence, as some general and perhaps even accidental habit of the country. In the rural districts of England, during the last century, the growth of population was very effectually repressed by the difficulty of obtaining a cottage to live in. It was the custom for unmarried laborers to lodge and board with their employers; it was the custom for married laborers to have a cottage: and the rule of the English poor-laws, by which a parish was charged with the support of its unemployed poor, rendered land-owners averse to promote marriage. About the end of the century, the great demand for men in war and manufactures made it be thought a patriotic thing to encourage population: and about the same time the growing inclination of farmers to live like rich people, favored as it was by a long period of high prices, made them desirous of keeping inferiors at a greater distance, and, pecuniary motives arising from abuses of the poor-laws being superadded, they gradually drove their laborers into cottages, which the landowners now no longer refused permission to build.

It is but rarely that improvements in the condition of the laboring-classes do anything more than give a temporary margin, speedily filled up by an increase of their numbers. Unless, either by their general improvement in intellectual and moral culture, or at least by raising their habitual standard of comfortable living, they can be taught to make a better use of favorable circumstances, nothing permanent can be done for them; the most promising schemes end only in having a more numerous but not a happier people. There is no doubt that [the standard] is gradually, though slowly, rising in the more advanced countries of Western Europe.[125] Subsistence and employment in England have never increased more rapidly than in the last forty years, but every census since 1821 showed a smaller proportional increase of population than that of the period preceding; and the produce of French agriculture and industry is increasing in a progressive ratio, while the population exhibits, in every quinquennial census, a smaller proportion of births to the population.

> This brings forward the near connection between land-tenures and population. France is pre-eminently a country of small holdings, and it is undoubtedly true that the system has checked the thoughtless increase of numbers. On his few hectares, the French peasant sees in the size of his farm and the amount of its produce the limit of subsistence for himself and his family; as in no other way does he see beforehand the results of any lack of food from his lack of prudence.[126] From 1790 to 1815 the average yearly increase of population was 120,000; from 1815 to 1846, the golden age of French agriculture, 200,000; from 1846 to 1856, when agriculture was not prosperous, 60,000; from 1856 to 1880 the increase has been not more than 36,000 yearly. In France the question shapes itself to the peasant proprietor, How many can be subsisted by the amount of produce, not on an unlimited area of land in

other parts of the world, but on this particular property of a small size? While in England there are ten births to six deaths, in France there are about ten births to every nine deaths.[127] In no country has the doctrine of Malthus been more attacked than in France, and yet in no other country has there been a more marked obedience to its principles in actual practice. Since the French are practically not at all an emigrating people, population has strictly adapted itself to subsistence. For the relative increase of population in France and the United States, see also the movement of lines indicating the increase of population in chart No. III (p. 114).

Chapter VIII. Of The Law Of The Increase Of Capital.

§ 1. Means for Saving in the Surplus above Necessaries.

The requisites of production being labor, capital, and land, it has been seen from the preceding chapter that the impediments to the increase of production do not arise from the first of these elements. But production has other requisites, and, of these, the one which we shall next consider is Capital. There can not be more people in any country, or in the world, than can be supported from the produce of past labor until that of present labor comes in [although it is not to be supposed that capital consists wholly of food]. We have next, therefore, to inquire into the conditions of the increase of capital: the causes by which the rapidity of its increase is determined, and the necessary limitations of that increase.

Since all capital is the product of saving, that is, of abstinence from present consumption for the sake of a future good, the increase of capital must depend upon two things—the amount of the fund from which saving can be made, and the strength of the dispositions which prompt to it.

(1.) The fund from which saving can be made is the surplus of the produce of labor, after supplying the necessaries of life to all concerned in the production (including those employed in replacing the materials, and keeping the fixed capital in repair). More than this surplus can not be saved under any circumstances. As much as this, though it never is saved, always might be. This surplus is the fund from which the enjoyments, as distinguished from the necessaries of the producers, are provided; it is the fund from which all are subsisted who are not themselves engaged in production, and from which all additions are made to capital. The capital of the employer forms the revenue of the laborers, and, if this exceeds the necessaries of life, it gives them a surplus which they may either expend in enjoyments or save.

> It is evident that the whole unproductive consumption of the laborer can be saved. When it is considered how enormous a sum is spent by the working-classes in drink alone (and also in the great reserves of the Trades-Unions collected for purposes of strikes), it is indisputable that the laborers have the margin from

which savings can be made, and by which they themselves may become capitalists. The great accumulations in the savings-banks by small depositors in the United States also show somewhat how much is actually saved. In 1882-1883 there were 2,876,438 persons who had deposited in the savings-banks of the United States $1,024,856,787, with an average to each depositor of $356.29. The unproductive consumption, however, of all classes—not merely that of the working-men—is the possible fund which may be saved. That being the amount which *can* be saved, how much *will* be saved depends on the strength of the desire to save.

The greater the produce of labor after supporting the laborers, the more there is which *can* be saved. The same thing also partly contributes to determine how much *will* be saved. A part of the motive to saving consists in the prospect of deriving an income from savings; in the fact that capital, employed in production, is capable of not only reproducing itself but yielding an increase. The greater the profit that can be made from capital, the stronger is the motive to its accumulation.

§ 2. Motive for Saving in the Surplus above Necessaries.

But the disposition to save does not wholly depend on the external inducement to it; on the amount of profit to be made from savings. With the same pecuniary inducement, the inclination is very different, in different persons, and in different communities.

(2.) All accumulation involves the sacrifice of a present, for the sake of a future good.

This is the fundamental motive underlying the effective desire of accumulation, and is far more important than any other. It is, in short, the test of civilization. In order to induce the laboring-classes to improve their condition and save capital, it is absolutely necessary to excite in them (by education or religion) a belief in a future gain greater than the present sacrifice. It is, to be sure, the whole problem of creating character, and belongs to sociology and ethics rather than to political economy.

In weighing the future against the present, the uncertainty of all things future is a leading element; and that uncertainty is of very different degrees. "All circumstances," therefore, "increasing the probability of the provision we make for futurity being enjoyed by ourselves or others, tend" justly and reasonably "to give strength to the effective desire of accumulation. Thus a healthy climate or occupation, by increasing the probability of life, has a tendency to add to this desire. When engaged in safe occupations and living in healthy countries, men are much more apt to be frugal, than in unhealthy or hazardous occupations and in climates pernicious to human life. Sailors and soldiers are prodigals. In the West Indies, New Orleans, the East Indies, the expenditure of the inhabitants is profuse. The same people, coming to reside in the healthy parts of Europe, and not getting into the vortex of extravagant fashion, live economically. War and pestilence have always waste and luxury among the other evils that follow in their train. For similar reasons, whatever gives security to the affairs of the community is favorable to the strength of this principle. In this respect the general prevalence of law and order and the prospect of the continuance of peace and tranquillity have considerable influence."[128]

> It is asserted that the prevalence of homicide in certain parts of the United States has had a vital influence in retarding the material growth of those sections. The Southern States have received but a very small fraction (from ten to thirteen per cent) of foreign immigration. "A country where law and order prevail to perfection may find its material prosperity checked by a deadly and fatal climate; or, on the other hand, a people may destroy all the advantages accruing from matchless natural resources and climate by persistent disregard of life and property. A rather startling confirmation of this economic truth is afforded by the fact that homicide has been as destructive of life in the South as yellow fever. Although there have been forty thousand deaths from yellow fever since the war, the deaths from homicide, for the same period, have been even greater."[129] The influence of the old slave *régime*, and its still existing influences, in checking foreign immigration into the South can be seen by the colored chart, No. VIII, showing the relative density of

foreign-born inhabitants in the several parts of the United States. The deeper color shows the greater foreign-born population.

The more perfect the security, the greater will be the effective strength of the desire of accumulation. Where property is less safe, or the vicissitudes ruinous to fortunes are more frequent and severe, fewer persons will save at all, and, of those who do, many will require the inducement of a higher rate of profit on capital to make them prefer a doubtful future to the temptation of present enjoyment.

In the circumstances, for example, of a hunting tribe, "man may be said to be necessarily improvident, and regardless of futurity, because, in this state, the future presents nothing which can be with certainty either foreseen or governed.... Besides a want of the motives exciting to provide for the needs of futurity through means of the abilities of the present, there is a want of the habits of perception and action, leading to a constant connection in the mind of those distant points, and of the series of events serving to unite them. Even, therefore, if motives be awakened capable of producing the exertion necessary to effect this connection, there remains the task of training the mind to think and act so as to establish it."

§ 3. Examples of Deficiency in the Strength of this Desire.

For instance: "Upon the banks of the St. Lawrence there are several little Indian villages. The cleared land is rarely, I may almost say never, cultivated, nor are any inroads made in the forest for such a purpose. The soil is, nevertheless, fertile, and, were it not, manure lies in heaps by their houses. Were every family to inclose half an acre of ground, till it, and plant it in potatoes and maize, it would yield a sufficiency to support them one half the year. They suffer, too, every now and then, extreme want, insomuch that, joined to occasional intemperance, it is rapidly reducing their numbers. This, to us, so strange apathy proceeds not, in any great degree, from repugnance to labor; on the contrary, they apply very diligently to it when its reward is immediate. It is evidently not the necessary labor that is the obstacle to more extended culture, but the distant return from that labor. I am assured, indeed, that among some of the more remote tribes, the labor thus expended much exceeds that given by the whites. On the Indian, succeeding years are too distant to make sufficient impression; though, to obtain what labor may bring about in the course of a few months, he toils even more assiduously than the white man."

This view of things is confirmed by the experience of the Jesuits, in their interesting efforts to civilize the Indians of Paraguay. The real difficulty was the improvidence of the people; their inability to think for the future; and the necessity accordingly of the most unremitting and minute superintendence on the part of their instructors. "Thus at first, if these gave up to them the care of the oxen with which they plowed, their indolent thoughtlessness would probably leave them at evening still yoked to the implement. Worse than this, instances occurred where they cut them up for supper, thinking, when reprehended, that they sufficiently excused themselves by saying they were hungry."

As an example intermediate, in the strength of the effective desire of accumulation, between the state of things thus depicted and that of modern Europe, the case of the Chinese deserves attention. "Durability is one of the chief qualities, marking a high degree of the effective desire of accumulation. The testimony of travelers ascribes to the instruments formed by the Chinese a very inferior durability to similar instruments constructed by Europeans. The houses, we are told, unless of the higher ranks, are in general of unburnt bricks, of clay, or of hurdles plastered with earth; the roofs, of reeds fastened to laths. A greater degree of strength in the effective desire of accumulation would cause them to be constructed of materials requiring a greater present expenditure, but being far more durable. From the same cause, much land, that in other countries would be cultivated, lies waste. All travelers take notice of large tracts of lands, chiefly swamps, which continue in a state of nature. To bring a swamp into tillage is generally a process to complete which requires several years. It must be previously drained, the surface long exposed to the sun, and many operations performed, before it can be made capable of bearing a crop. Though yielding, probably, a very considerable return for the labor bestowed on it, that return is not made until a long time has elapsed. The cultivation of such land implies a greater strength of the effective desire of accumulation than exists in the empire. The amount of self-denial would seem to be small. It is their great deficiency in forethought and frugality in this respect which is the cause of the scarcities and famines that frequently occur."

That it is defect of providence, not defect of industry, that limits production among the Chinese, is still more obvious than in the case of the semi-agriculturized Indians. "Where the returns are quick, where the instruments formed require but little time to bring the events for which they were formed to an issue," it is well known that "the great progress which has been made in the knowledge of the arts suited to the nature of the country and the wants of its inhabitants" makes industry energetic and effective. "What marks the readiness with which labor is forced to form the most difficult materials into instruments, where these instruments soon bring to an issue the events for which they are formed, is the frequent occurrence, on many of their lakes and rivers, of structures resembling the floating gardens of the Peruvians, rafts covered with vegetable soil and cultivated. Labor in this way draws from the materials on which it acts very speedy returns. Nothing can exceed the luxuriance of vegetation when the quickening powers of a genial sun are ministered to by a rich soil and abundant moisture. It is otherwise, as we have seen, in cases where the return, though copious, is distant. European travelers are surprised at meeting these little floating farms by the side of swamps which only require draining to render them tillable."

When a country has carried production as far as in the existing state of knowledge it can be carried with an amount of return corresponding to the average strength of the effective desire of accumulation in that country, it has reached what is called the stationary state; the state in which no further addition will be made to capital, unless there takes place either some improvement in the arts of production, or an increase in the strength of the desire to accumulate. In the stationary state, though capital does not on the whole increase, some persons grow richer and others poorer. Those whose degree of providence is below the usual standard become impoverished, their capital perishes, and makes room for the savings of those whose effective desire of accumulation exceeds the average. These become the natural purchasers of the lands, manufactories, and other instruments of production owned by their less provident countrymen.

In China, if that country has really attained, as it is supposed to have done, the stationary state, accumulation has stopped when the returns to capital are still as high as is indicated by a rate of interest legally twelve per cent, and practically varying (it is said) between eighteen and thirty-six. It is to be presumed, therefore, that no greater amount of capital than the country already possesses can find employment at this high rate of profit, and that any lower rate does not hold out to a Chinese sufficient temptation to induce him to abstain from present enjoyment. What a contrast with Holland, where, during the most flourishing period of its history, the government was able habitually to borrow at two per cent, and private individuals, on good security, at three!

§ 4. Examples of Excess of this Desire.

In [the United States and] the more prosperous countries of Europe, there are to be found abundance of prodigals: still, in a very numerous portion of the community, the professional, manufacturing, and trading classes, being those who, generally speaking, unite more of the means with more of the motives for saving than any other class, the spirit of accumulation is so strong that the signs of rapidly increasing wealth meet every eye: and the great amount of capital seeking investment excites astonishment, whenever peculiar circumstances turning much of it into some one channel, such as railway construction or foreign speculative adventure, bring the largeness of the total amount into evidence.

There are many circumstances which, in England, give a peculiar force to the accumulating propensity. The long exemption of the country from the ravages of war and the far earlier period than elsewhere at which property was secure from military violence or arbitrary spoliation have produced a long-standing and hereditary confidence in the safety of funds when trusted out of the owner's hands, which in most other countries is of much more recent origin, and less firmly established.

> The growth of deposit-banking in Great Britain, therefore, advances with enormous strides, while in Continental countries it makes very little headway. The disturbed condition of the country in France, owing to wars, leads the thrifty to hoard instead of depositing their savings. But in the United States the same growth is seen as among the English. The net deposits of the national banks of the United States in 1871 were $636,000,000, but in 1883 they had increased more than 83 per cent to $1,168,000,000. Deposit accounts are the rule even with small tradesmen; and the savings-banks of Massachusetts alone show deposits in 1882-1883 of $241,311,362, and those of New York of $412,147,213. The United States also escapes from the heavy taxation which in Europe is imposed to maintain an extravagant army and navy chest. The effect of institutions, moreover, in stimulating the growth of material prosperity is far more true of the United States than of England, for the barriers raised against the movement from lower to higher social classes in the latter country are non-existent here, and consequently there is more stimulus toward acquiring the means of bettering a man's social condition.

The geographical causes which have made industry rather than war the natural source of power and importance to Great Britain [and the United

States] have turned an unusual proportion of the most enterprising and energetic characters into the direction of manufactures and commerce; into supplying their wants and gratifying their ambition by producing and saving, rather than by appropriating what has been produced and saved. Much also depended on the better political institutions of this country, which, by the scope they have allowed to individual freedom of action, have encouraged personal activity and self-reliance, while, by the liberty they confer of association and combination, they facilitate industrial enterprise on a large scale. The same institutions, in another of their aspects, give a most direct and potent stimulus to the desire of acquiring wealth. The earlier decline of feudalism [in England] having removed or much weakened invidious distinctions between the originally trading classes and those who had been accustomed to despise them, and a polity having grown up which made wealth the real source of political influence, its acquisition was invested with a factitious value independent of its intrinsic utility. And, inasmuch as to be rich without industry has always hitherto constituted a step in the social scale above those who are rich by means of industry, it becomes the object of ambition to save not merely as much as will afford a large income while in business, but enough to retire from business and live in affluence on realized gains.

In [the United States,] England, and Holland, then, for a long time past, and now in most other countries in Europe, the second requisite of increased production, increase of capital, shows no tendency to become deficient. So far as that element is concerned, production is susceptible of an increase without any assignable bounds. The limitation to production, not consisting in any necessary limit to the increase of the other two elements, labor and capital, must turn upon the properties of the only element which is inherently, and in itself, limited in quantity. It must depend on the properties of land.

Chapter IX. Of The Law Of The Increase Of Production From Land.

§ 1. The Law of Production from the Soil, a Law of Diminishing Return in Proportion to the Increased Application of Labor and Capital.

Land differs from the other elements of production, labor, and capital, in not being susceptible of indefinite increase. Its extent is limited, and the extent of the more productive kinds of it more limited still. It is also evident that the quantity of produce capable of being raised on any given piece of land is not indefinite. This limited quantity of land and limited productiveness of it are the real limits to the increase of production.

The limitation to production from the properties of the soil is not like the obstacle opposed by a wall, which stands immovable in one particular spot, and offers no hindrance to motion short of stopping it entirely. We may rather compare it to a highly elastic and extensible band, which is hardly ever so violently stretched that it could not possibly be stretched any more, yet the pressure of which is felt long before the final limit is reached, and felt more severely the nearer that limit is approached.

After a certain, and not very advanced, stage in the progress of agriculture—as soon, in fact, as mankind have applied themselves to cultivation with any energy, and have brought to it any tolerable tools—from that time it is the law of production from the land, that in any given state of agricultural skill and knowledge, by increasing the labor, the produce is not increased in an equal degree; doubling the labor does not double the produce; or, to express the same thing in other words, every increase of produce is obtained by a more than proportional increase in the application of labor to the land. This general law of agricultural industry is the most important proposition in political economy. Were the law different, nearly all the phenomena of the production and distribution of wealth would be other than they are.

> It is not generally considered that in the United States, where in many sparsely settled parts of the country new land is constantly being brought into cultivation, an additional population under existing conditions of

- 101 -

> agricultural skill can be maintained with constantly increasing returns up to a certain point before the law of diminishing returns begins to operate. Where more laborers are necessary, and more capital wanted, to co-operate in a new country before all the land can give its maximum product, in such a stage of cultivation it can not be said that the law of diminishing returns has yet practically set in.

When, for the purpose of raising an increase of produce, recourse is had to inferior land, it is evident that, so far, the produce does not increase in the same proportion with the labor. The very meaning of inferior land is land which with equal labor returns a smaller amount of produce. Land may be inferior either in fertility or in situation. The one requires a greater proportional amount of labor for growing the produce, the other for carrying it to market. If the land A yields a thousand quarters of wheat to a given outlay in wages, manure, etc., and, in order to raise another thousand, recourse must be had to the land B, which is either less fertile or more distant from the market, the two thousand quarters will cost more than twice as much labor as the original thousand, and the produce of agriculture will be increased in a less ratio than the labor employed in procuring it.

Instead of cultivating the land B, it would be possible, by higher cultivation, to make the land A produce more. It might be plowed or harrowed twice instead of once, or three times instead of twice; it might be dug instead of being plowed; after plowing, it might be gone over with a hoe instead of a harrow, and the soil more completely pulverized; it might be oftener or more thoroughly weeded; the implements used might be of higher finish, or more elaborate construction; a greater quantity or more expensive kinds of manure might be applied, or, when applied, they might be more carefully mixed and incorporated with the soil.

> The example of market-gardens in the vicinity of great cities and towns shows how the intensive culture permits an increase of labor and capital with larger returns. These lands, by their situation, are superior lands for this particular purpose, although they might be inferior lands as regards absolute productiveness when compared with the rich wheat-lands of Dakota. New England and New Jersey farms, generally speaking, no longer attempt the culture of grains, but

(when driven out of that culture by the great railway lines which have opened up the West) they have arranged themselves in a scale of adaptability for stock, grass, fruit, dairy, or vegetable farming; and have thereby given greater profits to their owners than the same land did under the old *régime*. Even on lands where any grain can still be grown, corn, buckwheat, barley, oats, and rye, cover the cultivated areas instead of wheat.

Inferior lands, or lands at a greater distance from the market, of course yield an inferior return, and an increasing demand can not be supplied from them unless at an augmentation of cost, and therefore of price. If the additional demand could continue to be supplied from the superior lands, by applying additional labor and capital, at no greater proportional cost than that at which they yield the quantity first demanded of them, the owners or farmers of those lands could undersell all others, and engross the whole market. Lands of a lower degree of fertility or in a more remote situation might indeed be cultivated by their proprietors, for the sake of subsistence or independence; but it never could be the interest of any one to farm them for profit. That a profit can be made from them, sufficient to attract capital to such an investment, is a proof that cultivation on the more eligible lands has reached a point beyond which any greater application of labor and capital would yield, at the best, no greater return than can be obtained at the same expense from less fertile or less favorably situated lands.

"It is long," says a late traveler in the United States,[130] "before an English eye becomes reconciled to the lightness of the crops and the careless farming (as we should call it) which is apparent. One forgets that, where land is so plentiful and labor so dear as it is here, a totally different principle must be pursued from that which prevails in populous countries, and that the consequence will of course be a want of tidiness, as it were, and finish, about everything which requires labor." Of the two causes mentioned, the plentifulness of land seems to me the true explanation, rather than the dearness of labor; for, however dear labor may be, when food is wanted, labor will always be applied to producing it in preference to anything else. But this labor is more effective for its end by being applied to fresh soil than if it were employed in bringing the soil already occupied into higher cultivation.

> The Western movement of what might be called the "wheat-center" is quite perceptible. Until recently Minnesota has been a great wheat-producing State, and vast tracts of land were there planted with that grain when the soil was first broken. The profits on the first few crops have been enormous, but it is now said to be more desirable for wheat-growers to move onward to newer lands, and to sell the land to cultivators of a different class (of fruit and varied products), who produce for a denser population. So that (in 1884) Dakota, instead of Minnesota, has become the district of the greatest wheat production.[131]

Only when no soils remain to be broken up, but such as either from distance or inferior quality require a considerable rise of price to render their cultivation profitable, can it become advantageous to apply the high farming of Europe to any American lands; except, perhaps, in the immediate vicinity of towns, where saving in cost of carriage may compensate for great inferiority in the return from the soil itself.

The principle which has now been stated must be received, no doubt, with certain explanations and limitations. Even after the land is so highly cultivated that the mere application of additional labor, or of an additional amount of ordinary dressing, would yield no return proportioned to the expense, it may still happen that the application of a much greater additional labor and capital to improving the soil itself, by draining or permanent manures, would be as liberally remunerated by the produce as any portion of the labor and capital already employed. It would sometimes be much more amply remunerated. This could not be, if capital always sought and found the most advantageous employment.

§ 2. Antagonist Principle to the Law of Diminishing Return; the Progress of Improvements in Production.

That the produce of land increases, *cæteris paribus*, in a diminishing ratio to the increase in the labor employed, is, as we have said (allowing for occasional and temporary exceptions), the universal law of agricultural industry. This principle, however, has been denied. So much so, indeed, that (it is affirmed) the worst land now in cultivation produces as much food per acre, and even as much to a given amount of labor, as our ancestors contrived to extract from the richest soils in England.

> The law of diminishing returns is the physical fact upon which the economic doctrine of rent is based, and requires careful attention. Carey asserts, instead, that there is a law of increasing productiveness, since, as men grow in numbers and intelligence, there arises an ability to get more from the soil.[132] Some objectors even deny that different grades of land are cultivated, and that there is no need of taking inferior soils into cultivation. If this were true, why would not one half an acre of land be as good as a whole State? Johnston[133] says: "In a country and among poor settlers ... poor land is a relative term. Land is called poor which is not suitable to a poor man, which on mere clearing and burning will not yield good first crops. Thus that which is poor land for a poor man may prove rich land to a rich man."[134] Moreover, as is constantly the case in our country, it often happens that a railway may bring new lands into competition with old lands in a given market; of which the most conspicuous example is the competition of Western grain-fields with the Eastern farms. In these older districts, before the competition came, there was a given series of grades in the cultivated land; after the railway was built there was a disarrangement of the old series, some going out of cultivation, some remaining, and some of the new lands entering the list. The result is a new series of grades better suited to satisfy the wants of men.

This, however, does not prove that the law of which we have been speaking does not exist, but only that there is some antagonizing principle at work, capable for a time of making head against the law. Such an agency there is, in habitual antagonism to the law of diminishing return from land; and to the consideration of this we shall now proceed. It is no other than the progress of civilization. The most obvious [part of it] is the progress of agricultural knowledge, skill, and invention. Improved processes of agriculture are of two kinds: (1) some enable the land to yield a greater absolute produce, without an equivalent increase of labor; (2) others have not the power of increasing the produce, but have that of diminishing the labor and expense by which it is obtained. (1.) Among the first are to be reckoned the disuse of fallows, by means of the rotation of crops; and the introduction of new articles of cultivation capable of entering advantageously into the rotation. The change made in agriculture toward the close of the last century, by the introduction of turnip-husbandry, is spoken of as amounting to a revolution. Next in order comes the introduction of new articles of food, containing a greater amount of sustenance, like the potato, or more productive species or varieties of the same plant, such as the Swedish turnip. In the same class of improvements must be placed a better knowledge of the properties of manures, and of the most effectual modes of applying them; the introduction of new and more powerful fertilizing agents, such as guano, and the conversion to the same purpose of substances previously wasted; inventions like subsoil-plowing or tile-draining, by which the produce of some kinds of lands is so greatly multiplied; improvements in the breed or feeding of laboring cattle; augmented stock, of the animals which consume and convert into human food what would otherwise be wasted; and the like. (2.) The other sort of improvements, those which diminish labor, but without increasing the capacity of the land to produce, are such as the improved construction of tools; the introduction of new instruments which spare manual labor, as the winnowing and thrashing machines. These improvements do not add to the productiveness of the land, but they are equally calculated with the former to counteract the tendency in the cost of production of agricultural produce, to rise with the progress of population and demand.

§ 3. —In Railways.

Analogous in effect to this second class of agricultural improvements are improved means of communication. Good roads are equivalent to good tools. It is of no consequence whether the economy of labor takes place in extracting the produce from the soil, or in conveying it to the place where it is to be consumed.

> The functions performed by railways in the system of production is highly important. They are among the most influential causes affecting the cost of producing commodities, particularly those which satisfy the primary wants of man, of which food is the chief. The amount of tonnage carried is enormous; and the cost of this service to the producers and consumers of the United States is a question of very great magnitude.

The serious reduction in the cost of transportation on the railways will be a surprise to all who have not followed the matter very closely; the more so, that it has been brought about by natural causes, and independent of legislation. Corn, meat, and dairy products form, it is said, at least 50 per cent, and coal and timber about 30 per cent, of the tonnage moved on all the railways of the United States. If a lowered cost of transportation has come about, it has then cost less to move the main articles of immediate necessity. Had the charge in 1880 remained as high even as it was from 1866 to 1869, the number of tons carried in 1880 would have cost the United States from $500,000,000 to $800,000,000 more than the charge actually made, owing to the reductions by the railways. It seems, however, that this process of reduction culminated about 1879. In order to show the facts of this process, note the changes in the following chart, No. V. The railways of the State of New York are taken, but the same is also true of those of Ohio:

Chart V.

Cost of 20 Barrels of Flour, 10 Beef, 10 Pork, 100 Bushels Wheat, 100 Corn, 100 Oats, 100 Pounds Butter, 100 Lard, and 100 Fleece Wool, in New York City, at the Average of each Year, Compiled by Months, in Gold; Compared Graphically with the Decrease in the Charge per Ton per Mile, on all the Railroads of the State of New York, during the Same Period.

Year.	Price in gold of staple farm products. (Dollars)	Charge for carrying one ton one mile. (Cents)	Decrease in the railroad expenses per ton. (Cents)	Decrease in the profits of the railroads for carrying one ton. (Cents)

1870 776.02	1.7016	1.1471	.5545
1871 735.33	1.7005	1.1450	.5555
1872 675.92	1.6645	1.1490	.5155
1873 662.50	1.6000	1.0864	.5136
1874 748.54	1.4480	.9730	.4750
1875 696.40	1.3039	.9587	.3452
1876 651.74	1.1604	.8561	.3043
1877 751.95	1.0590	.7740	.2850
1878 569.81	.9994	.6900	.3094
1879 568.34	.8082	.5847	.2295
1880 631.32	.9220	.6030	.3190
1881 703.10	.8390	.5880	.2510
1882 776.12	.8170	.6010	.2160
1883 662.11	.8990	.6490	.2500

In 1855 the charge per ton per mile was 3.27 cents, as compared with 0.89 in 1883.

Tons moved 1 m. in 1883 by railroads of N.Y.	9,286,216,628
At rate of 1855, would cost	$303,659,283
Actual cost in 1883	83,464,919
Saving to the State	$220,194,364

The explanation of this reduced cost is given by Mr. Edward Atkinson[135] as (1) the competition of waterways, (2) the competition of one railway with another, and (3) the competition of other countries, which forces our railways to try to lay our staple products down in foreign markets at a price which will warrant continued shipment. Besides these reasons, much ought also (4) to be assigned to the progress of inventions and the reduced cost of steel and all appliances necessary to the railways.

The large importance of the railways shows itself in an influence on general business prosperity, and as a place for large investments of a rapidly growing capital. The building of railways, however, has been going on, at some times with greater speed than at others. Instead of 33,908 miles of railways at the close of our war, we have now (1884) over 120,000 miles. How the additional mileage has been built year by year, with two distinct eras of increased building—one from 1869 to 1873, and another from 1879 to 1884—may be seen by the shorter lines of the subjoined chart, No. VI.

That speculation has been excited at different times by the opening up of our Western country, there can be no doubt. And if a comparison be made with Chart No. XVII (Book IV, Chap. III), which gives the total grain-crops of the United States, it will be seen that since 1879, although our population has increased from 12-½ per cent to 14 per cent, our grain-crops only 5 per cent, yet our railway mileage has increased 40 per cent.

The extent to which the United States has carried railway-building, as compared with European countries, although we have a very much greater area, is distinctly shown by Chart No. VII. This application of one form of improvement to oppose the law of diminishing returns in the United States has produced extraordinary results, especially when we consider that we are probably not yet using all our best lands, or, in other words, that we have not yet felt the law of diminishing returns in some large districts.

Chart VI.

Miles of Railroad in Operation on the 1st January in each Year, and the Miles added in the Year Ensuing.

Year.	Miles of Railroad.	Miles added.
1865	33,908	1,177
1866	35,085	1,716
1867	36,801	2,449
1868	39,250	2,979
1869	42,229	4,615
1870	46,844	6,070
1871	52,914	7,379
1872	60,293	5,878
1873	66,171	4,107
1874	70,278	2,105
1875	72,383	1,713
1876	74,096	2,712
1877	76,808	2,281
1878	79,089	2,687
1879	81,776	4,721
1880	86,497	7,048
1881	93,545	9,789
1882	103,334	11,591
1883	114,925	6,618

Railways and canals are virtually a diminution of the cost of production of all things sent to market by them; and literally so of all those the appliances and aids for producing which they serve to transmit. By their means land can be cultivated, which would not otherwise have remunerated the cultivators without a rise of price. Improvements in navigation have, with respect to food or materials brought from beyond sea, a corresponding effect.

§ 4. —In Manufactures.

From similar considerations, it appears that many purely mechanical improvements, which have, apparently, at least, no peculiar connection with agriculture, nevertheless enable a given amount of food to be obtained with a smaller expenditure of labor. A great improvement in the process of smelting iron would tend to cheapen agricultural implements, diminish the cost of railroads, of wagons and carts, ships, and perhaps buildings, and many other things to which iron is not at present applied, because it is too costly; and would thence diminish the cost of production of food. The same effect would follow from an improvement in those processes of what may be termed manufacture, to which the material of food is subjected after it is separated from the ground. The first application of wind or water power to grind corn tended to cheapen bread as much as a very important discovery in agriculture would have done; and any great improvement in the construction of corn-mills would have, in proportion, a similar influence.

Those manufacturing improvements which can not be made instrumental to facilitate, in any of its stages, the actual production of food, and therefore do not help to counteract or retard the diminution of the proportional return to labor from the soil, have, however, another effect, which is practically equivalent. What they do not prevent, they yet, in some degree, compensate for.[136]

Chart VII.

Ratio of Miles of Railroad to the Areas of States and Countries—United States and Europe. The relative proportion is 1 Mile Railroad to 4 Square Miles of Area.

No.	Name.	Rank in Size.	Relative.
1	Massachusetts	67	98
2	Belgium	62	96
3	England and Wales	29	88
4	New Jersey	62	81
5	Connecticut	68	80
6	Rhode Island	71	65
7	Ohio	44	60
8	Illinois	32	59
9	Pennsylvania	40	55

10	Delaware	69	53
11	Indiana	50	52
12	New Hampshire	65	45
13	Switzerland	59	44
14	New York	39	41
15	Iowa	33	39
16	German Empire	4	38
17	Scotland	52	37
18	Maryland	63	36
19	Vermont	64	35
20	Ireland	51	29
21	Michigan	31	28
22	France	5	27
23	Denmark	60	26
24	Netherlands	57	25
25	Missouri	26	24
26	Wisconsin	34	23
27	Austrian Empire	3	21
28	Virginia	45	19
29	Italy	13	18
30	Georgia	30	17
31	Kansas	22	16
32	Kentucky	46	15
33	South Carolina	49	14
34	Tennessee	42	14
35	Minnesota	21	13
36	Alabama	36	13
37	West Virginia	55	12
38	Roumania	41	12

39	North Carolina	37	12
40	Maine	48	12
41	Nebraska	23	10
42	Mississippi	38	9
43	Spain	6	9
44	Portugal	47	9
45	Sweden	7	9
46	Arkansas	35	8
47	Louisiana	43	8
48	Colorado	16	8
49	California	8	7
50	Turkey	27	7
51	Texas	2	7
52	Utah	20	6
53	Florida	28	6
54	Dakota	7	6
55	Russia in Europe	1	5
56	Nevada	15	5
57	Norway	11	5
58	Oregon	18	4
59	Bulgaria	54	4
60	New Mexico	12	3
61	Wyoming	17	2
62	Indian Territory	25	2
63	Washington	24	1
64	Arizona	14	1
65	Idaho	19	1
66	Greece	58	0
67	Montana	10	0

68	Bosnia and Herzegovina	53	0
69	Servia	56	0
70	Eastern Roumelia	61	0
71	Montenegro	70	0
72	Andorra	72	0

(The United States have substantially one mile of railway to each 540 inhabitants. Europe has one mile to each 3,000 inhabitants, if Russia be included; about one mile to each 2,540, exclusive of Russia.)

The materials of manufactures being all drawn from the land, and many of them from agriculture, which supplies in particular the entire material of clothing, the general law of production from the land, the law of diminishing return, must in the last resort be applicable to manufacturing as well as to agricultural history. As population increases, and the power of the land to yield increased produce is strained harder and harder, any additional supply of material, as well as of food, must be obtained by a more than proportionally increasing expenditure of labor. But the cost of the material forming generally a very small portion of the entire cost of the manufacture, the agricultural labor concerned in the production of manufactured goods is but a small fraction of the whole labor worked up in the commodity.

Mr. Babbage[137] gives an interesting illustration of this principle. Bar-iron of the value of £1 became worth, when manufactured into—

	£
Slit-iron, for nails	1.10
Natural steel	1.42
Horseshoes	2.55
Gun-barrels, ordinary	9.10
Wood-saws	14.28
Scissors, best	446.94

Penknife-blades	657.14
Sword-handles, polished steel	972.82

It can not, however, be said of such manufactures as coarse cotton cloth, wherein the increased cost of raw cotton causes an immediate effect upon the price of the cloth, that the cost of the materials forms but a small portion of the cost of the manufacture.[138]

All the labor [not engaged in preparing materials] tends constantly and strongly toward diminution, as the amount of production increases. Manufactures are vastly more susceptible than agriculture of mechanical improvements and contrivances for saving labor. In manufactures, accordingly, the causes tending to increase the productiveness of industry preponderate greatly over the one cause which tends to diminish it; and the increase of production, called forth by the progress of society, takes place, not at an increasing, but at a continually diminishing proportional cost. This fact has manifested itself in the progressive fall of the prices and values of almost every kind of manufactured goods during two centuries past; a fall accelerated by the mechanical inventions of the last seventy or eighty years, and susceptible of being prolonged and extended beyond any limit which it would be safe to specify. The benefit might even extend to the poorest class. The increased cheapness of clothing and lodging might make up to them for the augmented cost of their food.

There is, thus, no possible improvement in the arts of production which does not in one or another mode exercise an antagonistic influence to the law of diminishing return to agricultural labor. Nor is it only industrial improvements which have this effect. Improvements in government, and almost every kind of moral and social advancement, operate in the same manner. We may say the same of improvements in education. The intelligence of the workman is a most important element in the productiveness of labor. The carefulness, economy, and general trustworthiness of laborers are as important as their intelligence. Friendly relations and a community of interest and feeling between laborers and employers are eminently so. In the rich and idle classes, increased mental energy, more solid instruction, and stronger feelings of conscience, public spirit, or philanthropy, would qualify them to originate and promote the most valuable improvements, both in the economical resources of their country and in its institutions and customs.

§ 5. Law Holds True of Mining.

We must observe that what we have said of agriculture is true, with little variation, of the other occupations which it represents; of all the arts which extract materials from the globe. Mining industry, for example, usually yields an increase of produce at a more than proportional increase of expense.

It does worse, for even its customary annual produce requires to be extracted by a greater and greater expenditure of labor and capital. As a mine does not reproduce the coal or ore taken from it, not only are all mines at last exhausted, but even when they as yet show no signs of exhaustion they must be worked at a continually increasing cost; shafts must be sunk deeper, galleries driven farther, greater power applied to keep them clear of water; the produce must be lifted from a greater depth, or conveyed a greater distance. The law of diminishing return applies therefore to mining in a still more unqualified sense than to agriculture; but the antagonizing agency, that of improvements in production, also applies in a still greater degree. Mining operations are more susceptible of mechanical improvements than agricultural: the first great application of the steam-engine was to mining; and there are unlimited possibilities of improvement in the chemical processes by which the metals are extracted. There is another contingency, of no unfrequent occurrence, which avails to counterbalance the progress of all existing mines toward exhaustion: this is, the discovery of new ones, equal or superior in richness.

> Professor Jevons has applied this economic law to the industrial situation of England.[139] While explaining that the supply of cheap coal is the basis of English manufacturing prosperity, yet he insists that, if the demand for coal is constantly increasing, the point must inevitably be reached in the future when the increased supply can be obtained only at a higher cost. When coal costs England as much as it does any other nation, then her exclusive industrial advantage will cease to exist. In the United States the outlying iron deposits of Lake Superior, Lake Champlain, and Pennsylvania, so geologists tell us, will find competition arising from the new grades of greater productiveness in the richer deposits of States like Alabama. In that case we shall be going from poorer to better grades of iron-mines, but after the change is

made a series of different grades of productiveness will be established as before.

To resume: all natural agents which are limited in quantity are not only limited in their ultimate productive power, but, long before that power is stretched to the utmost, they yield to any additional demands on progressively harder terms. This law may, however, be suspended, or temporarily controlled, by whatever adds to the general power of mankind over nature, and especially by any extension of their knowledge, and their consequent command, of the properties and powers of natural agents.

Chapter X. Consequences Of The Foregoing Laws.

§ 1. Remedies for Weakness of the Principle of Accumulation.

From the preceding exposition it appears that the limit to the increase of production is twofold: from deficiency of capital, or of land. Production comes to a pause, either because the effective desire of accumulation is not sufficient to give rise to any further increase of capital, or because, however disposed the possessors of surplus income may be to save a portion of it, the limited land at the disposal of the community does not permit additional capital to be employed with such a return as would be an equivalent to them for their abstinence.

In countries where the principle of accumulation is as weak as it is in the various nations of Asia, the desideratum economically considered is an increase of industry, and of the effective desire of accumulation. The means are, first, a better government: more complete security of property; moderate taxes, and freedom from arbitrary exaction under the name of taxes; a more permanent and more advantageous tenure of land, securing to the cultivator as far as possible the undivided benefits of the industry, skill, and economy he may exert. Secondly, improvement of the public intelligence. Thirdly, the introduction of foreign arts, which raise the returns derivable from additional capital to a rate corresponding to the low strength of the desire of accumulation.

> An excellent example of what might be done by this process is to be seen under our very eyes in the present development of Mexico, to which American capital and enterprise have been so prominently drawn of late. All these proposed remedies, if put into use in Mexico, would undoubtedly result in a striking increase of wealth.

§ 2. Even where the Desire to Accumulate is Strong, Population must be Kept within the Limits of Population from Land.

But there are other countries, and England [and the United States are] at the head of them, in which neither the spirit of industry nor the effective desire of accumulation need any encouragement. In these countries there would never be any deficiency of capital, if its increase were never checked or brought to a stand by too great a diminution of its returns. It is the tendency of the returns to a progressive diminution which causes the increase of production to be often attended with a deterioration in the condition of the producers; and this tendency, which would in time put an end to increase of production altogether, is a result of the necessary and inherent conditions of production from the land.

> This, of course, is based on the supposition that no new lands, such as those of the United States, can be opened for cultivation. If there is no prohibition to the importation of cheaper food, new and richer land in any part of the world, within reach of the given country, is an influence which works against the tendency. Yet the tendency, or economic law, is there all the same, forever working.

In all countries which have passed beyond a very early stage in the progress of agriculture, every increase in the demand for food, occasioned by increased population, will always, unless there is a simultaneous improvement in production, diminish the share which on a fair division would fall to each individual. An increased production, in default of unoccupied tracts of fertile land, or of fresh improvements tending to cheapen commodities, can never be obtained but by increasing the labor in more than the same proportion. The population must either work harder or eat less, or obtain their usual food by sacrificing a part of their other customary comforts. Whenever this necessity is postponed, it is because the improvements which facilitate production continue progressive; because the contrivances of mankind for making their labor more effective keep up an equal struggle with Nature, and extort fresh resources from her reluctant powers as fast as human necessities occupy and engross the old.

From this results the important corollary, that the necessity of restraining population is not, as many persons believe, peculiar to a condition of great inequality of property. A greater number of people can not, in any given state of civilization, be collectively so well provided for as a smaller. The niggardliness of nature,[140] not the injustice of society, is the cause of the penalty attached to over-population. An unjust distribution of wealth does not even aggravate the evil, but, at most, causes it to be somewhat earlier felt. It is in vain to say that all mouths which the increase of mankind calls into existence bring with them hands. The new mouths require as much food as the old ones, and the hands do not produce as much.

After a degree of density has been attained, sufficient to allow the principal benefits of combination of labor, all further increase tends in itself to mischief, so far as regards the average condition of the people; but the progress of improvement has a counteracting operation, and allows of increased numbers without any deterioration, and even consistently with a higher average of comfort. Improvement must here be understood in a wide sense, including not only new industrial inventions, or an extended use of those already known, but improvements in institutions, education, opinions, and human affairs generally, provided they tend, as almost all improvements do, to give new motives or new facilities to production.

> The increase in the population of the United States has been enormous, as already seen, but the increase of production has been still greater, owing to the fertility of our land, to improvements in the arts, and to our great genius for invention, as may be seen by the following table (amounts in the second column are given in millions).[141] The steady increase of the valuation of our wealth goes on faster than the increase of population, so that it manifests itself in a larger average wealth to each inhabitant.

Decades.	Valuation.	Per cent of increase.	Population.	Per cent of increase.	Per capital valuation.
1800	$1,742	..	5,308,483	..	$328
1810	2,382	37	7,239,881	36	329
1820	3,734	57	9,633,882	33	386
1830	4,328	16	12,866,020	34	336
1840	6,124	41	17,069,453	33	359
1850	8,800	44	23,191,876	36	379

1860	16,160	84	31,443,321	35	514
1870	30,068	86	38,558,371	23	780
1880	40,000	33	50,155,783	30	798

If the productive powers of the country increase as rapidly as advancing numbers call for an augmentation of produce, it is not necessary to obtain that augmentation by the cultivation of soils more sterile than the worst already under culture, or by applying additional labor to the old soils at a diminished advantage; or at all events this loss of power is compensated by the increased efficiency with which, in the progress of improvement, labor is employed in manufactures. In one way or the other, the increased population is provided for, and all are as well off as before. But if the growth of human power over nature is suspended or slackened, and population does not slacken its increase; if, with only the existing command over natural agencies, those agencies are called upon for an increased produce; this greater produce will not be afforded to the increased population, without either demanding on the average a greater effort from each, or on the average reducing each to a smaller ration out of the aggregate produce.

Ever since the great mechanical inventions of Watt, Arkwright, and their contemporaries, the return to labor has probably increased as fast as the population; and would even have outstripped it, if that very augmentation of return had not called forth an additional portion of the inherent power of multiplication in the human species. During the twenty or thirty years last elapsed, so rapid has been the extension of improved processes of agriculture [in England], that even the land yields a greater produce in proportion to the labor employed; the average price of corn had become decidedly lower, even before the repeal of the corn laws had so materially lightened, for the time being, the pressure of population upon production. But though improvement may during a certain space of time keep up with, or even surpass, the actual increase of population, it assuredly never comes up to the rate of increase of which population is capable: and nothing could have prevented a general deterioration in the condition of the human race, were it not that population has in fact been restrained. Had it been restrained still more, and the same improvements taken place, there would have been a larger dividend than there now is, for the nation or the species at large. The new ground wrung from nature by the improvements would not have been all tied up in the support of mere numbers. Though the gross produce would not have been so great, there would have been a greater produce per head of the population.

§ 3. Necessity of Restraining Population not superseded by Free Trade in Food.

When the growth of numbers outstrips the progress of improvement, and a country is driven to obtain the means of subsistence on terms more and more unfavorable, by the inability of its land to meet additional demands except on more onerous conditions, there are two expedients, by which it may hope to mitigate that disagreeable necessity, even though no change should take place in the habits of the people with respect to their rate of increase. One of these expedients is the importation of food from abroad. The other is emigration.

The admission of cheaper food from a foreign country is equivalent to an agricultural invention by which food could be raised at a similarly diminished cost at home. It equally increases the productive power of labor. The return was before, so much food for so much labor employed in the growth of food: the return is now, a greater quantity of food for the same labor employed in producing cottons or hardware, or some other commodity to be given in exchange for food. The one improvement, like the other, throws back the decline of the productive power of labor by a certain distance: but in the one case, as in the other, it immediately resumes its course; the tide which has receded, instantly begins to readvance. It might seem, indeed, that, when a country draws its supply of food from so wide a surface as the whole habitable globe, so little impression can be produced on that great expanse by any increase of mouths in one small corner of it that the inhabitants of the country may double and treble their numbers without feeling the effect in any increased tension of the springs of production, or any enhancement of the price of food throughout the world. But in this calculation several things are overlooked.

In the first place, the foreign regions from which corn can be imported do not comprise the whole globe, but those parts of it almost alone which are in the immediate neighborhood of coasts or navigable rivers; and of such there is not, in the productive regions of the earth, so great a multitude as to suffice during an indefinite time for a rapidly growing demand, without an increasing strain on the productive powers of the soil.

In the next place, even if the supply were drawn from the whole instead of a small part of the surface of the exporting countries, the quantity of food would still be limited, which could be obtained from them without an increase of the proportional cost. The countries which export food may be divided into two classes: those in which the effective desire of accumulation is strong, and those in which it is weak. In Australia and the United States of America, the effective desire of accumulation is strong; capital increases fast, and the production of food might be very rapidly extended. But in such countries population also increases with extraordinary rapidity. Their agriculture has to provide for their own expanding numbers, as well as for those of the importing countries. They must, therefore, from the nature of the case, be rapidly driven, if not to less fertile, at least what is equivalent, to remoter and less accessible lands, and to modes of cultivation like those of old countries, less productive in proportion to the labor and expense.

> The extraordinary resources of the United States are scarcely understood even by Americans. Chart No. XVIII (see Book IV, Chap. III) may give some idea of the agricultural possibilities of our land. It will be seen from this that the quantity of fertile land in but one of our States—Texas—is greater than that of Austria-Hungary.

But the countries which have at the same time cheap food and great industrial prosperity are few, being only those in which the arts of civilized life have been transferred full-grown to a rich and uncultivated soil. Among old countries, those which are able to export food, are able only because their industry is in a very backward state, because capital, and hence population, have never increased sufficiently to make food rise to a higher price. Such countries are Russia, Poland, and Hungary.

The law, therefore, of diminishing return to industry, whenever population makes a more rapid progress than improvement, is not solely applicable to countries which are fed from their own soil, but in substance applies quite as much to those which are willing to draw their food from any accessible quarter that can afford it cheapest.

§ 4. —Nor by Emigration.

Besides the importation of corn, there is another resource which can be invoked by a nation whose increasing numbers press hard, not against their capital, but against the productive capacity of their land: I mean Emigration, especially in the form of Colonization. Of this remedy the efficacy as far as it goes is real, since it consists in seeking elsewhere those unoccupied tracts of fertile land which, if they existed at home, would enable the demand of an increasing population to be met without any falling off in the productiveness of labor. Accordingly, when the region to be colonized is near at hand, and the habits and tastes of the people sufficiently migratory, this remedy is completely effectual. The migration from the older parts of the American Confederation to the new Territories, which is to all intents and purposes colonization, is what enables population to go on unchecked throughout the Union without having yet diminished the return to industry, or increased the difficulty of earning a subsistence.

> How strictly true this is may be seen by examining the map given in the last census returns,[142] showing the residence of the natives of the State of New York. The greater or less frequency of natives of New York, residing in other States, is shown by different degrees of shading on the map. A large district westward as far as the Mississippi shows a density of natives of New York of from two to six to a square mile, and a lesser density from Minnesota to Indian Territory, on the other side of the Mississippi. The same is shown of other older States. The explanation of the movement can not be anything else than the same as that for the larger movement from Europe to America.

There is no probability that even under the most enlightened arrangements (in older countries) a permanent stream of emigration could be kept up, sufficient to take off, as in America, all that portion of the annual increase (when proceeding at its greatest rapidity) which, being in excess of the progress made during the same short period in the arts of life, tends to render living more difficult for every averagely situated individual in the community. And, unless this can be done, emigration can not, even in an economical point of view, dispense with the necessity of checks to population.

The influence of immigration to the United States from European countries, in lessening the tension in the relation between food and numbers, is one of the most marked events in this century. The United States has received about one fourth of its total population in 1880 from abroad since the foundation of the republic, as will be seen by this table:

Total Immigration Into The United States.

Periods.	Numbers.
From 1789-1820	250,000[143]
1820-1830	151,824
1831-1840	599,125
1841-1850	1,713,251
1851-1860	2,598,214
1861-1870	2,491,451
1871-1880	2,812,191
1881-1883	2,061,745
Total	12,677,801

Of this number, 5,333,991 came from the British Isles, of which 3,367,624 were Irish.

There came 3,860,624 Germans, 593,021 Scandinavians, and 334,064 French. (See United States "Statistical Abstract," 1878, 1880, 1883.)

The causes operating on this movement of men—a movement unequaled in history—are undoubtedly economic. Like the migration of the early Teutonic races from the Baltic to Southern Europe, it is due to the pressure of numbers on subsistence.

A still more interesting study is that of the causes which attempt to explain the direction of this stream after it has reached our shores. It is a definite fact that the old slave States have hitherto received practically none of this vast foreign immigration.[144] The actual distribution of the foreign born in the United States is to be seen in a most interesting way by aid of the colored map, Chart No. VIII, giving the different densities of foreign-born population in different parts of the Union. It seems almost certain that the general belief hitherto in the insecurity of life and property in the old slave States has worked against the material prosperity of that section.

The different ages of the native- and foreign-born inhabitants of the United States may be seen from the accompanying diagrams[145] comparing the aggregate population of the United States with the foreign-born. This may profitably be compared with a similar diagram relating to the Chinese in the United States (Book II, Chap. III, § 3).

Aggregate: 1870. The figures give the number of thousands of each sex.

Decade of Life.	Males.	Females.
1	136	132
2	115	114
3	87	90
4	62	63
5	47	44
6	31	27
7	17	15
8	7	7
9	2	2

Foreign: 1870.

Decade of Life.	Males.	Females.
1	24	23
2	48	49
3	128	114
4	134	113
5	107	84
6	60	44
7	27	23
8	9	9
9	2	2

Book II. Distribution.

Chapter I. Of Property.

§ 1. Individual Property and its opponents.

The laws and conditions of the Production of Wealth partake of the character of physical truths. There is nothing optional or arbitrary in them. It is not so with the Distribution of Wealth. That is a matter of human institution solely. The things once there, mankind, individually or collectively, can do with them as they like. They can place them at the disposal of whomsoever they please, and on whatever terms. The Distribution of Wealth depends on the laws and customs of society. The rules by which it is determined are what the opinions and feelings of the ruling portion of the community make them, and are very different in different ages and countries; and might be still more different, if mankind so chose. We have here to consider, not the causes, but the consequences, of the rules according to which wealth may be distributed. Those, at least, are as little arbitrary, and have as much the character of physical laws, as the laws of production.

We proceed, then, to the consideration of the different modes of distributing the produce of land and labor, which have been adopted in practice, or may be conceived in theory. Among these, our attention is first claimed by that primary and fundamental institution, on which, unless in some exceptional and very limited cases, the economical arrangements of society have always rested, though in its secondary features it has varied, and is liable to vary. I mean, of course, the institution of individual property.

Private property, as an institution, did not owe its origin to any of those considerations of utility which plead for the maintenance of it when established. Enough is known of rude ages, both from history and from analogous states of society in our own time, to show that tribunals (which always precede laws) were originally established, not to determine rights, but to repress violence and terminate quarrels. With this object chiefly in view, they naturally enough gave legal effect to first occupancy, by treating as the aggressor the person who first commenced violence, by turning, or attempting to turn, another out of possession.

In considering the institution of property as a question in social philosophy, we must leave out of consideration its actual origin in any of the existing nations of Europe. We may suppose a community unhampered by any previous possession; a body of colonists, occupying for the first time an uninhabited country. (1.) If private property were adopted, we must presume that it would be accompanied by none of the initial inequalities and injustice which obstruct the beneficial operation of the principle in old society. Every full-grown man or woman, we must suppose, would be secured in the unfettered use and disposal of his or her bodily and mental faculties; and the instruments of production, the land and tools, would be divided fairly among them, so that all might start, in respect to outward appliances, on equal terms. It is possible also to conceive that, in this original apportionment, compensation might be made for the injuries of nature, and the balance redressed by assigning to the less robust members of the community advantages in the distribution, sufficient to put them on a par with the rest. But the division, once made, would not again be interfered with; individuals would be left to their own exertions and to the ordinary chances for making an advantageous use of what was assigned to them. (2.) If individual property, on the contrary, were excluded, the plan which must be adopted would be to hold the land and all instruments of production as the joint property of the community, and to carry on the operations of industry on the common account. The direction of the labor of the community would devolve upon a magistrate or magistrates, whom we may suppose elected by the suffrages of the community, and whom we must assume to be voluntarily obeyed by them. The division of the produce would in like manner be a public act. The principle might either be that of complete equality, or of apportionment to the necessities or deserts of individuals, in whatever manner might be conformable to the ideas of justice or policy prevailing in the community.

The assailants of the principle of individual property may be divided into two classes: (1) those whose scheme implies absolute equality in the distribution of the physical means of life and enjoyment, and (2) those who admit inequality, but grounded on some principle, or supposed principle, of justice or general expediency, and not, like so many of the existing social inequalities, dependent on accident alone. The characteristic name for this [first] economical system is Communism, a word of Continental origin, only of late introduced into this country. The word Socialism, which originated among the English Communists, and was assumed by them as a name to designate their own doctrine, is now, on the Continent, employed in a larger sense; not necessarily implying Communism, or the entire abolition of private property, but applied to any system which requires that the land and the instruments of production should be the property, not of individuals, but of communities, or associations, or of the government.

It should be said, moreover, that Socialism is to-day used in the distinct sense of a system which abolishes private property, and places the control of the capital, labor, and combined industries of the country in the hands of the state. The essence of modern socialism is the appeal to state-help and the weakening of individual self-help. Collectivism is also a term now used by German and French writers to describe an organization of the industries of a country under a collective instead of an individual management. Collectivism is but the French expression for the system of state socialism.

§ 2. The case for Communism against private property presented.

The objection ordinarily made to a system of community of property and equal distribution of the produce, that each person would be incessantly occupied in evading his fair share of the work, points, undoubtedly, to a real difficulty. But those who urge this objection forget to how great an extent the same difficulty exists under the system on which nine tenths of the business of society is now conducted. And though the "master's eye," when the master is vigilant and intelligent, is of proverbial value, it must be remembered that, in a Socialist farm or manufactory, each laborer would be under the eye, not of one master, but of the whole community. If Communistic labor might be less vigorous than that of a peasant proprietor, or a workman laboring on his own account, it would probably be more energetic than that of a laborer for hire, who has no personal interest in the matter at all.

Another of the objections to Communism is that if every member of the community were assured of subsistence for himself and any number of children, on the sole condition of willingness to work, prudential restraint on the multiplication of mankind would be at an end, and population would start forward at a rate which would reduce the community through successive stages of increasing discomfort to actual starvation. But Communism is precisely the state of things in which opinion might be expected to declare itself with greatest intensity against this kind of selfish intemperance. An augmentation of numbers which diminished the comfort or increased the toil of the mass would then cause (which now it does not) immediate and unmistakable inconvenience to every individual in the association; inconvenience which could not then be imputed to the avarice of employers, or the unjust privileges of the rich.

A more real difficulty is that of fairly apportioning the labor of the community among its members. There are many kinds of work, and by what standard are they to be measured one against another? Who is to judge how much cotton-spinning, or distributing goods from the stores, or brick-laying, or chimney-sweeping, is equivalent to so much plowing? Besides, even in the same kind of work, nominal equality of labor would be so great a real inequality that the feeling of justice would revolt against its being enforced. All persons are not equally fit for all labor; and the same quantity of labor is an unequal burden on the weak and the strong, the hardy and the delicate, the quick and the slow, the dull and the intelligent.[146]

If, therefore, the choice were to be made between Communism with all its chances and the present state of society with all its sufferings and injustices, all the difficulties, great or small, of Communism, would be but as dust in the balance. But, to make the comparison applicable, we must compare Communism at its best with the *régime* of individual property, not as it is, but as it might be made. The laws of property have never yet conformed to the principles on which the justification of private property rests. They have made property of things which never ought to be property, and absolute property where only a qualified property ought to exist. Private property, in every defense made of it, is supposed to mean the guarantee to individuals of the fruits of their own labor and abstinence. The guarantee to them of the fruits of the labor and abstinence of others, transmitted to them without any merit or exertion of their own, is not of the essence of the institution, but a mere incidental consequence, which, when it reaches a certain height, does not promote, but conflicts with the ends which render private property legitimate. To judge of the final destination of the institution of property, we must suppose everything rectified which causes the institution to work in a manner opposed to that equitable principle, of proportion between remuneration and exertion, on which, in every vindication of it that will bear the light, it is assumed to be grounded. We must also suppose two conditions realized, without which neither Communism nor any other laws or institutions could make the condition of the mass of mankind other than degraded and miserable. One of these conditions is, universal education; the other, a due limitation of the numbers of the community. With these, there could be no poverty, even under the present social institutions: and, these being supposed, the question of socialism is not, as generally stated by Socialists, a question of flying to the sole refuge against the evils which now bear down humanity, but a mere question of comparative advantages, which futurity must determine. We are too ignorant either of what individual agency in its best form, or socialism in its best form, can accomplish, to be qualified to decide which of the two will be the ultimate form of human society.

If a conjecture may be hazarded, the decision will probably depend mainly on one consideration, viz., which of the two systems is consistent with the greatest amount of human liberty and spontaneity. It is yet to be ascertained whether the communistic scheme would be consistent with that multiform development of human nature, those manifold unlikenesses, that diversity of tastes and talents, and variety of intellectual points of view, which not only form a great part of the interest of human life, but, by bringing intellects into stimulating collision and by presenting to each innumerable notions that he would not have conceived of himself, are the mainspring of mental and moral progression.

§ 3. The Socialists who appeal to state-help.

> For general purposes, a clearer understanding of the various schemes may be gained by observing that (1) one class of socialists intend to include the state itself within their plan, and (2) another class aim to form separate communities inside the state, and under its protection.
>
> Of this first system there are no present examples; but the object of most of the socialistic organizations in the United States and Europe is to strive for the assumption by the state of the production and distribution of wealth.[147] At present the most active Socialists are to be found in Germany. The origin of this influence, however, is to be traced to France.[148] Louis Blanc,[149] in his "Organisation du Travail," considers property the great scourge of society. The Government, he asserts, should regulate production; raise money to be appropriated without interest for creating state workshops, in which the workmen should elect their own overseers, and all receive the same wages; and the sums needed should be raised from the abolition of collateral inheritance. The important practical part of his scheme was that the great state workshops, aided by the Government, would make private competition in those industries

impossible, and thus bring about the change from the private to the socialistic system.

The founder of modern German socialism was Karl Marx,[150] and almost the only Socialist who pretended to economic knowledge. He aimed his attack on the present social system against the question of value, by asserting that the amount of labor necessary for the production of an article is the sole measure of its exchange value. It follows from this that the right of property in the article vests wholly in the laborer, while the capitalist, if he claims a share of the product, is nothing less than a robber. No just system, he avers, can properly exist so long as the rate of wages is fixed by free contract between the employer and laborer; therefore the only remedy is the nationalization of all the elements of production, land, tools, materials, and all existing appliances, which involves, of course, the destruction of the institution of private property. An obvious weakness in this scheme is the provision that the Government should determine what goods are to be produced, and that every one is bound to perform that work which is assigned by the state. In this there is no choice of work, and the tyranny of one master would be supplanted by the tyranny of a greater multiplex master in the officers of Government. Moreover, it can not be admitted that exchange value is determined by the quantity of labor alone. Every one knows that the result of ten days' labor of a skilled watch-maker does not exchange for the result of ten days' labor of an unskilled hodman. Of two men making shoes, one may produce a good the other a poor article, although both may work the same length of time; so that their exchange value ought not to be determined by the mere quantity of labor expended. Above all, Marx would extend the equality of wages for the same time to the manager and superintendent also. In other words, he proposes to take away all the incentives to the acquirement or exercise of superior and signal ability in every work of life, the result of which would inevitably lead to a deadening extension of mediocrity.

This system gained an undue attention because it was made the instrument of a socialist propaganda under the leadership of Ferdinand Lassalle.[151] This active leader, in 1863, founded the German "Workingmen's Union," a year earlier than the "International[152] Association." In 1869 Liebknecht and his friends established the "Social Democratic Workingmen's Party," which after some difficulties absorbed the followers of Lassalle in a congress at Gotha in 1875, and form the present Socialist party in Germany. Their programme,[153] as announced at Gotha, is as follows:

I. Labor is the source of all riches and of all culture. As general profitable labor can only be done by the human society, the whole product of labor belongs to society—i.e., to all its members—who have the same duties and the same right to work, each according to his reasonable wants.

In the present society the means of work are the monopoly of the class of capitalists. The class of workingmen thus become dependent on them, and consequently are given over to all degrees of misery and servitude.

In order to emancipate labor it is requisite that the means of work be transformed into the common property of society, that all production be regulated by associations, and that the entire product of labor be turned over to society and justly distributed for the benefit of all.

None but the working-class itself can emancipate labor, as in relation to it all other classes are only a reactionary mass.

II. Led by these principles, the German Social Workingmen's party, by all legal means, strives for a free state and society, the breaking down of the iron laws of wages by abolishing the system of hired workingmen, by abolishing exploitation in every shape, and doing away with all social and political inequality.

The German Social Workingmen's party, although first working within its national confines, is fully conscious of the international character of the general workingmen's movement, and is resolved to fulfill all duties which it imposes on each workingman in order to realize the fraternity of all men.

The German Social Workingmen's party, for the purpose of preparing the way, and for the solution of the social problem, demands the creation of social productive associations, to be supported by the state government, and under the control of the working-people. The productive associations are to be founded in such numbers that the social organization of the whole production can be effected by them.

The German Social Workingmen's party requires as the basis of state government:

1. Universal, equal, direct, and secret suffrage, which, beginning with the twentieth year, obliges all citizens to vote in all State, county, and town elections. Election-day must be a Sunday or a holiday.

2. Direct legislation by the people; decision as to war and peace by the people.

3. General capability of bearing arms; popular defense in place of standing armies.

4. Abolition of all exceptional laws, especially those relating to the press, public meetings, and associations—in short, of all laws which hinder the free expression of ideas and thought.

5. Gratuitous administration of justice by the people.

6. General and equal, popular and gratuitous education by the Government in all classes and institutes of learning; general duty to attend school; religion to be declared a private affair.

The German Social Workingmen's party insists on realizing in the present state of society:

1. The largest possible extension of political rights and freedom in conformity to the above six demands.

2. A single progressive income-tax for State, counties, and towns, instead of those which are imposed at

present, and in place of indirect taxes, which unequally burden the people.

3. Unlimited right of combination.

4. A normal working-day corresponding with the wants of society; prohibition of Sunday labor.

5. Prohibition of children's work and of women's work, so far as it injures their health and morality.

6. Protective laws for the life and health of workingmen; sanitary control of their dwellings; superintendence of mines, factories, industry, and home work by officers chosen by the workingmen; an effectual law guaranteeing the responsibility of employers.

7. Regulation of prison-work.

8. Unrestricted self-government of all banks established for the mutual assistance of workingmen.

The above scheme also represents very well the character of the Socialist agitators in the United States, who are themselves chiefly foreigners, and have foreign conceptions of socialism. On this form of socialism it is interesting to have Mr. Mill's later opinions[154] in his own words.

"Among those who call themselves Socialists, two kinds of persons may be distinguished. There are, in the first place, (1) those whose plans for a new order of society, in which private property and individual competition are to be superseded and other motives to action substituted, are on the scale of a village community or township, and would be applied to an entire country by the multiplication of such self-acting units; of this character are the systems of Owen, of Fourier, and the more thoughtful and philosophic Socialists generally. The other class (2) who are more a product of the Continent than of Great Britain, and may be called the revolutionary Socialists, propose to themselves a much bolder stroke. Their scheme is the management of the whole productive resources of the country by one central authority, the general Government. And with this view some of them avow as their purpose that the working-classes, or somebody in their behalf, should take possession of all the property of the country, and administer it for the general benefit. The aim of that is to substitute the new rule for the old at a single stroke, and to exchange the amount of good realized under the present system, and its large possibilities of improvement, for a plunge without any preparation into the most extreme form of the problem of carrying on the whole round of the operations of social life without the motive power which has always hitherto worked the social machinery. It must be acknowledged that those who would play this game on the strength of their own private opinion, unconfirmed as yet by any experimental verification, must have a serene confidence in their own wisdom on the one hand, and a recklessness of people's sufferings on the other, which Robespierre and St. Just, hitherto the typical instances of those united attributes, scarcely came up to."

§ 4. Of various minor schemes, Communistic and Socialistic.

[Of the schemes to be tried within a state], the two elaborate forms of non-communistic Socialism known as Saint-Simonism and Fourierism are totally free from the objections usually urged against Communism. The Saint-Simonian[155] scheme does not contemplate an equal, but an unequal division of the produce; it does not propose that all should be occupied alike, but differently, according to their vocation or capacity; the function of each being assigned, like grades in a regiment, by the choice of the directing authority, and the remuneration being by salary, proportioned to the importance, in the eyes of that authority, of the function itself, and the merits of the person who fulfills it. But to suppose that one or a few human beings, howsoever selected, could, by whatever machinery of subordinate agency, be qualified to adapt each person's work to his capacity, and proportion each person's remuneration to his merits, is a supposition almost too chimerical to be reasoned against.[156]

The most skillfully combined, and with the greatest foresight of objections, of all the forms of Socialism is that commonly known as Fourierism.[157] This system does not contemplate the abolition of private property, nor even of inheritance: on the contrary, it avowedly takes into consideration, as an element in the distribution of the produce, capital as well as labor. It proposes that the operations of industry should be carried on by associations of about two thousand members, combining their labor on a district of about a square league in extent, under the guidance of chiefs selected by themselves (the "phalanstery"). In the distribution a certain minimum is first assigned for the subsistence of every member of the community, whether capable or not of labor. The remainder of the produce is shared in certain proportions, to be determined beforehand, among the three elements, Labor, Capital, and Talent. The capital of the community may be owned in unequal shares by different members, who would in that case receive, as in any other joint-stock company, proportional dividends. The claim of each person on the share of the produce apportioned to talent is estimated by the grade or rank which the individual occupies in the several groups of laborers to which he or she belongs, these grades being in all cases conferred by the choice of his or her companions. The remuneration, when received, would not of necessity be expended or enjoyed in common; there would be separate *ménages* for all who preferred them, and no other community of living is contemplated than that all the members of the association should reside in the same pile of buildings; for saving of labor and expense, not only in building, but in every branch of domestic economy; and in order that, the whole buying and selling operations of the community being performed by a single agent, the enormous portion of the produce of industry now carried off by the profits of mere distributors might be reduced to the smallest amount possible.

> Fourierism was tried in West Virginia by American disciples, and it was advocated by Horace Greeley. A modified form appeared in the famous community at Brook Farm (near Dedham, Massachusetts), which drew there George Ripley, Margaret Fuller, and even George William Curtis and Nathaniel Hawthorne.
>
> There have been many smaller communities established in the United States, but it can not be said that they have been successful from the point of view either of numbers or material prosperity. The followers of Rapp, or the Harmonists, in Pennsylvania and Indiana; the Owenites,[158] in Indiana; the community of Zoar, in Ohio; the Inspirationists, in New York and Iowa; the Perfectionists, at Oneida and Wallingford— are all evidently suffering from the difficulties due to the absence of family life, from the increasing spirit of personal independence which carries away the younger members of the organizations,[159] and the want of that executive ability which distinguishes the successful manager in private enterprises.

§ 5. The Socialist objections to the present order of Society examined.

"The attacks[160] on the present social order are vigorous and earnest, but open to the charge of exaggeration.

"In the first place, it is unhappily true that the wages of ordinary labor, in all the countries of Europe, are wretchedly insufficient to supply the physical and moral necessities of the population in any tolerable measure. But when it is further alleged that even this insufficient remuneration has a tendency to diminish; that there is, in the words of M. Louis Blanc, *une baisse continue des salaires*; the assertion is in opposition to all accurate information, and to many notorious facts. It has yet to be proved that there is any country in the civilized world where the ordinary wages of labor, estimated either in money or in articles of consumption, are declining; while in many they are, on the whole, on the increase; and an increase which is becoming, not slower, but more rapid. There are, occasionally, branches of industry which are being gradually superseded by something else, and in those, until production accommodates itself to demand, wages are depressed.

"M. Louis Blanc appears to have fallen into the same error which was at first committed by Malthus and his followers, that of supposing because population has a greater power of increase than subsistence, its pressure upon subsistence must be always growing more severe. It is a great point gained for truth when it comes to be seen that the tendency to over-population is a fact which Communism, as well as the existing order of society, would have to deal with. However this may be, experience shows that in the existing state of society the pressure of population on subsistence, which is the principal cause of low wages, though a great, is not an increasing evil; on the contrary, the progress of all that is called civilization has a tendency to diminish it, partly by the more rapid increase of the means of employing and maintaining labor, partly by the increased facilities opened to labor for transporting itself to new countries and unoccupied fields of employment, and partly by a general improvement in the intelligence and prudence of the population. It is, of course, open to discussion what form of society has the greatest power of dealing successfully with the pressure of population on subsistence, and on this question there is much to be said for Socialism; but it has no just claim to be considered as the sole means of preventing the general and growing degradation of the mass of mankind through the peculiar tendency of poverty to produce over-population.

"Next, it must be observed that Socialists generally, and even the most enlightened of them, have a very imperfect and one-sided notion of the operation of competition. They see half its effects, and overlook the other half. They forget that competition is a cause of high prices and values as well as of low; that the buyers of labor and of commodities compete with one another as well as the sellers; and that, if it is competition which keeps the prices of labor and commodities as low as they are, it is competition which keeps them from falling still lower. To meet this consideration, Socialists are reduced to affirm that, when the richest competitor has got rid of all his rivals, he commands the market and can demand any price he pleases. But in the ordinary branches of industry no one rich competitor has it in his power to drive out all the smaller ones. Some businesses show a tendency to pass out of the hands of small producers or dealers into a smaller number of larger ones; but the cases in which this happens are those in which the possession of a larger capital permits the adoption of more powerful machinery, more efficient by more expensive processes, or a better organized and more economical mode of carrying on business, and this enables the large dealer legitimately and permanently to supply the commodity cheaper than can be done on the small scale; to the great advantage of the consumers, and therefore of the laboring-classes, and diminishing, *pro tanto*, that waste of the resources of the community so much complained of by Socialists, the unnecessary multiplication of mere distributors, and of the various other classes whom Fourier calls the parasites of industry.

"Another point on which there is much misapprehension on the part of Socialists, as well as of trades-unionists and other partisans of labor against capital, relates to the proportion in which the produce of the country is really shared and the amount of what is actually diverted from those who produce it, to enrich other persons. When, for instance, a capitalist invests £20,000 in his business, and draws from it an income of (suppose) £2,000 a year, the common impression is as if he were the beneficial owner both of the £20,000 and of the £2,000, while the laborers own nothing but their wages. The truth, however, is that he only obtains the £2,000 on condition of applying no part of the £20,000 to his own use. He has the legal control over it, and might squander it if he chose, but if he did he would not have the £2,000 a year also. For all personal purposes they have the capital and he has but the profits, which it only yields to him on condition that the capital itself is employed in satisfying not his own wants, but those of laborers. Even of his own share a small part only belongs to him as the owner of capital. The portion of the produce which falls to capital merely as capital is measured by the interest of money, since that is all that the owner of capital obtains when he contributes to production nothing except the capital itself.

"The result of our review of the various difficulties of Socialism has led us to the conclusion that the various schemes for managing the productive resources of the country by public instead of private agency have a case for a trial, and some of them may eventually establish their claims to preference over the existing order of things, but that they are at present workable only by the *élite* of mankind, and have yet to prove their power of training mankind at large to the state of improvement which they presuppose."

§ 6. Property in land different from property in Movables.

It is next to be considered what is included in the idea of private property and by what considerations the application of the principle should be bounded.

The institution of property, when limited to its essential elements, consists in the recognition, in each person, of a right to the exclusive disposal of what he or she have produced by their own exertions, or received either by gift or by fair agreement, without force or fraud, from those who produced it. The foundation of the whole is, the right of producers to what they themselves have produced. Nothing is implied in property but the right of each to his (or her) own faculties, to what he can produce by them, and to whatever he can get for them in a fair market: together with his right to give this to any other person if he chooses, and the right of that other to receive and enjoy it.

It follows, therefore, that although the right of bequest, or gift after death, forms part of the idea of private property, the right of inheritance, as distinguished from bequest, does not. That the property of persons who have made no disposition of it during their lifetime should pass first to their children, and, failing them, to the nearest relations, may be a proper arrangement or not, but is no consequence of the principle of private property. I see no reason why collateral inheritance should exist at all. Mr. Bentham long ago proposed, and other high authorities have agreed in the opinion, that, if there are no heirs either in the descending or in the ascending line, the property, in case of intestacy, should escheat to the state. The parent owes to society to endeavor to make the child a good and valuable member of it, and owes to the children to provide, so far as depends on him, such education, and such appliances and means, as will enable them to start with a fair chance of achieving by their own exertions a successful life. To this every child has a claim; and I can not admit that as a child he has a claim to more.

The essential principle of property being to assure to all persons what they have produced by their labor and accumulated by their abstinence, this principle can not apply to what is not the produce of labor, the raw material of the earth. If the land derived its productive power wholly from nature, and not at all from industry, or if there were any means of discriminating what is derived from each source, it not only would not be necessary, but it would be the height of injustice, to let the gift of nature be engrossed by individuals. [But] the use of the land in agriculture must indeed, for the time being, be of necessity exclusive; the same person who has plowed and sown must be permitted to reap.

But though land is not the produce of industry, most of its valuable qualities are so. Labor is not only requisite for using, but almost equally so for fashioning, the instrument. Considerable labor is often required at the commencement, to clear the land for cultivation. In many cases, even when cleared, its productiveness is wholly the effect of labor and art. One of the barrenest soils in the world, composed of the material of the Goodwin Sands, the Pays de Waes in Flanders, has been so fertilized by industry as to have become one of the most productive in Europe. Cultivation also requires buildings and fences, which are wholly the produce of labor. The fruits of this industry can not be reaped in a short period. The labor and outlay are immediate, the benefit is spread over many years, perhaps over all future time. A holder will not incur this labor and outlay when strangers and not himself will be benefited by it. If he undertakes such improvements, he must have a sufficient period before him in which to profit by them; and he is in no way so sure of having always a sufficient period as when his tenure is perpetual.

These are the reasons which form the justification, in an economical point of view, of property in land. It is seen that they are only valid in so far as the proprietor of land is its improver. Whenever, in any country, the proprietor, generally speaking, ceases to be the improver, political economy has nothing to say in defense of landed property, as there established.

When the "sacredness of property" is talked of, it should always be remembered that any such sacredness does not belong in the same degree to landed property. No man made the land. It is the original inheritance of the whole species. Its appropriation is wholly a question of general expediency. When private property in land is not expedient, it is unjust. The reverse is the case with property in movables, and in all things the product of labor: over these, the owner's power both of use and of exclusion should be absolute, except where positive evil to others would result from it; but, in the case of land, no exclusive right should be permitted in any individual which can not be shown to be productive of positive good. To be allowed any exclusive right at all, over a portion of the common inheritance, while there are others who have no portion, is already a privilege. No quantity of movable goods which a person can acquire by his labor prevents others from acquiring the like by the same means; but, from the very nature of the case, whoever owns land keeps others out of the enjoyment of it. When land is not intended to be cultivated, no good reason can in general be given for its being private property at all. Even in the case of cultivated land, a man whom, though only one among millions, the law permits to hold thousands of acres as his single share, is not entitled to think that all this is given to him to use and abuse, and deal with as if it concerned nobody but himself. The rents or profits which he can obtain from it are at his sole disposal; but with regard to the land, in everything which he does with it, and in everything which he abstains from doing, he is morally bound, and should, whenever the case admits, be legally compelled to make his interest and pleasure consistent with the public good.

Chapter II. Of Wages.

§ 1. Of Competition and Custom.

Political economists generally, and English political economists above others, have been accustomed to lay almost exclusive stress upon the first of [two] agencies [competition and custom]; to exaggerate the effect of competition, and to take into little account the other and conflicting principle. They are apt to express themselves as if they thought that competition actually does, in all cases, whatever it can be shown to be the tendency of competition to do. This is partly intelligible, if we consider that only through the principle of competition has political economy any pretension to the character of a science. So far as rents, profits, wages, prices, are determined by competition, laws may be assigned for them. Assume competition to be their exclusive regulator, and principles of broad generality and scientific precision may be laid down, according to which they will be regulated. The political economist justly deems this his proper business: and, as an abstract or hypothetical science, political economy can not be required to do, and indeed can not do, anything more. But it would be a great misconception of the actual course of human affairs to suppose that competition exercises in fact this unlimited sway. I am not speaking of monopolies, either natural or artificial, or of any interferences of authority with the liberty of production or exchange. Such disturbing causes have always been allowed for by political economists. I speak of cases in which there is nothing to restrain competition; no hindrance to it either in the nature of the case or in artificial obstacles; yet in which the result is not determined by competition, but by custom or usage; competition either not taking place at all, or producing its effect in quite a different manner from that which is ordinarily assumed to be natural to it.

> As stated by Mr. Cairnes,[161] political economy is a science just as is any recognized physical science—astronomy, chemistry, physiology. The economic "facts we find existing are the results of causes, between which and them the connection is constant and invariable. It is, then, the constant relations exhibited in economic phenomena that we have in view when we

speak of the laws of the phenomena of wealth; and in the exposition of these laws consists the science of political economy." It is to be remembered that economic laws are *tendencies*, not actual descriptions of any given conditions in this or that place.

Competition, in fact, has only become in any considerable degree the governing principle of contracts, at a comparatively modern period. The further we look back into history, the more we see all transactions and engagements under the influence of fixed customs. The relations, more especially between the land-owner and the cultivator, and the payments made by the latter to the former, are, in all states of society but the most modern, determined by the usage of the country. The custom of the country is the universal rule; nobody thinks of raising or lowering rents, or of letting land, on other than the customary conditions. Competition, as a regulator of rent, has no existence.

Prices, whenever there was no monopoly, came earlier under the influence of competition, and are much more universally subject to it, than rents. The wholesale trade, in the great articles of commerce, is really under the dominion of competition. But retail price, the price paid by the actual consumer, seems to feel very slowly and imperfectly the effect of competition; and, when competition does exist, it often, instead of lowering prices, merely divides the gains of the high price among a greater number of dealers. The influence of competition is making itself felt more and more through the principal branches of retail trade in the large towns.

All professional remuneration is regulated by custom. The fees of physicians, surgeons, and barristers, the charges of attorneys, are nearly invariable. Not certainly for want of abundant competition in those professions, but because the competition operates by diminishing each competitor's chance of fees, not by lowering the fees themselves.

These observations must be received as a general correction to be applied whenever relevant, whether expressly mentioned or not, to the conclusions contained in the subsequent portions of this treatise. Our reasonings must, in general, proceed as if the known and natural effects of competition were actually produced by it, in all cases in which it is not restrained by some positive obstacle. Where competition, though free to exist, does not exist, or where it exists, but has its natural consequences overruled by any other agency, the conclusions will fail more or less of being applicable. To escape error, we ought, in applying the conclusions of political economy to the actual affairs of life, to consider not only what will happen supposing the maximum of competition, but how far the result will be affected if competition falls short of the maximum.

§ 2. The Wages-fund, and the Objections to it Considered.

Under the head of Wages are to be considered, first, the causes which determine or influence the wages of labor generally, and secondly, the differences that exist between the wages of different employments. It is convenient to keep these two classes of considerations separate; and in discussing the law of wages, to proceed in the first instance as if there were no other kind of labor than common unskilled labor, of the average degree of hardness and disagreeableness.

Competition, however, must be regarded, in the present state of society, as the principal regulator of wages, and custom or individual character only as a modifying circumstance, and that in a comparatively slight degree.

Wages, then, depend mainly upon the demand and supply of labor; or, as it is often expressed, on the proportion between population and capital. By population is here meant the number only of the laboring-class, or rather of those who work for hire; and by capital, only circulating capital, and not even the whole of that, but the part which is expended in the direct purchase of labor. To this, however, must be added all funds which, without forming a part of capital, are paid in exchange for labor, such as the wages of soldiers, domestic servants, and all other unproductive laborers. There is unfortunately no mode of expressing, by one familiar term, the aggregate of what may be called the wages-fund of a country: and, as the wages of productive labor form nearly the whole of that fund, it is usual to overlook the smaller and less important part, and to say that wages depend on population and capital. It will be convenient to employ this expression, remembering, however, to consider it as elliptical, and not as a literal statement of the entire truth.

With these limitations of the terms, wages not only depend upon the relative amount of capital and population, but can not, under the rule of competition, be affected by anything else. Wages (meaning, of course, the general rate) can not rise, but by an increase of the aggregate funds employed in hiring laborers, or a diminution in the number of the competitors for hire; nor fall, except either by a diminution of the funds devoted to paying labor, or by an increase in the number of laborers to be paid.

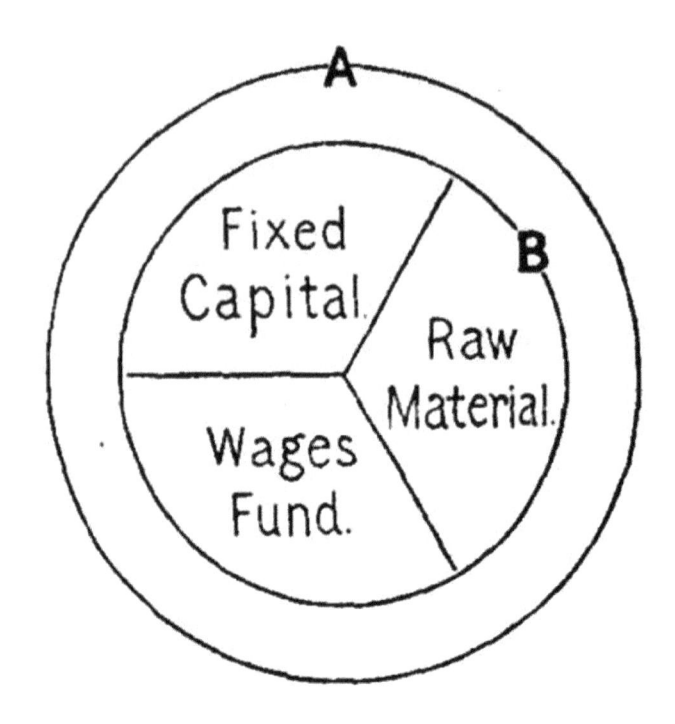

[Diagram: A circle labeled A (outer) containing an inner circle labeled B, divided into three sections: "Fixed Capital", "Raw Material", and "Wages Fund".]

This is the simple statement of the well-known Wages-Fund Theory, which has given rise to no little animated discussion. Few economists now assent to this doctrine when stated as above, and without changes. The first attack on this explanation of the rate of wages came from what is now a very scarce pamphlet, written by F. D. Longe, entitled "A Refutation of the Wage-Fund Theory of Modern Political Economy" (1866). Because laborers do not really compete with each other, he regarded the idea of average wages as absurd as the idea of an average price of ships and cloth; he declared that there was no predetermined wages-fund necessarily expended on labor; and that "demand for commodities" determined the amount of wealth devoted to paying wages (p. 46). While the so-called wages-fund limits the total amount which the laborers *can* receive, the employer would try to get his workmen at as much less than that amount as possible, so that the aggregate fund would have no bearing on the actual amount paid in wages. The quantity of work to be done, he asserts, determines the quantity of labor to be employed. About the same time (but unknown to Mr. Longe), W. T. Thornton was studying the same subject, and attracted considerable attention by his publication, "On Labor" (1868), which in Book II, Chap. I, contained an extended argument to show that demand and supply (i.e., the proportion between wages-fund and laborers) did not regulate wages, and denied the existence of a predetermined wages-fund fixed in amount. His attack, however, assumes a very different conception of an economic law from that which we think right to insist upon. The character of mankind being what it is, it will be for their interest to invest so much and no more in labor, and we must believe that in this sense there is a predetermination of wealth to be paid in wages. In order to make good investments, a certain amount must, if capitalists follow their best interests, go to the payment of labor.[162] Mr. Thornton's argument attracted the more attention because Mr. Mill[163] admitted that Mr. Thornton had induced him to abandon his Wages-Fund Theory. The subject was, however, taken up, re-examined by Mr. Cairnes,[164] and stated in a truer form. (1.) The total wealth of a country (circle A in the diagram) is the outside limit of its capital. How much capital will be saved out of this depends upon the effective desire of accumulation in the community (as set forth in Book I, Chap. VIII). The size of circle B within circle A, therefore, depends on the character of the people. The wages-fund, then, depends ultimately on the extent of A, and proximately on the extent of B. It can never be larger than B. So far, at least, its amount is "predetermined" in the economic sense by general laws regarding the accumulation of capital and the expectation of profit. Circle B contracts and expands under influences which have nothing to do with the immediate bargains between capitalists and laborers. (2.) Another influence now comes in to affect the amount of capital actually paid as wages, one also governed by general causes outside the reach of laborer or capitalist, that is, the state of the arts of production. In production, the particular conditions of each industry will determine how much capital is to be set apart for raw material, how much for machinery, buildings, and all forms of fixed capital, and how many laborers will be assigned to a given machine for a given amount of material. With some kinds of hand-made goods the largest share of capital goes to wages, a less amount for materials, and a very small proportion for machinery and tools. In many branches of agriculture and small farming this holds true. The converse, however, is true in many manufactures, where machinery is largely used. No two industries will maintain the same proportion between the three elements. The nature of the industry, therefore, will determine whether a greater or a less share of capital will be spent in wages. It is needless to say that this condition of things is not one to be changed at the demand of either of the two parties to production, Labor and Capital; it responds only to the advance of mechanical science or general intelligence. It is impossible, then, to escape the conclusion that general causes restrict the amount which will, under any normal investment, go to the payment of wages. Only within the limits set by these forces can any further expansion or contraction take place. (3.) Within these limits, of course, minor changes may take place, so that the fund can not be said to be "fixed" or "absolutely predetermined"; but these changes must take place within such narrow limits that they do not much affect the practical side of the question. How these changes act, may be seen in a part of the following illustration of the above principles:

Suppose a cotton-mill established in one of the valleys of Vermont, for the management of which the owner has $140,000 of capital. Of this, $100,000 is given for buildings, machinery, and plant. If he turns over his remaining capital ($40,000) each month, we will suppose that $28,000 spent in raw materials will keep five hundred men occupied at a monthly expenditure of $12,000. The present state of cotton-manufacture itself settles the relation between a given quantity of raw cotton and a certain amount of machinery. A fixed amount of cotton, no more, no less, can be spun by each spindle and woven by each loom; and the nature of the process determines the number of laborers to each machine. This proportion is something which an owner must obey, if he expects to compete with other manufacturers: the relationship is fixed for, not by, him. Now, each of the five hundred laborers being supposed to receive on an average $1.00 a day, imagine an influx of a body of French Canadians who offer to work, on an average, for eighty cents a day.[165] The five hundred men will now receive but $9,600 monthly instead of $12,000, as before, as a wages-fund; the monthly payment for wages now is nearly seven per cent, while formerly it was nearly nine per cent of the total capital invested ($140,000). Thus it will be seen that the wages-fund can change with a change in the supply of labor: but the point to be noticed is that it is a change in the subdivision, $12,000, of the total $140,000. That is, this alteration can take place only within the limits set by the nature of the industry. Now, if this $2,400 (i.e., $12,000 less $9,600) saved out of the wages-fund were to be reinvested, it must necessarily be divided between raw materials, fixed capital, and wages in the existing relations, that is, only seven per cent of the new $2,400 would be added to the wages-fund. It is worth while calling attention to this, if for no other reason than to show that in this way a change can be readily made in the wages-fund by natural movements; and that no one can be so absurd as to say that it is absolutely fixed in amount. But it certainly is "predetermined" in the economic sense, in that any reinvestments, as well as former funds, must necessarily be distributed according to the above general principles, independent of the "higgling" in the labor market. The following is Mr. Cairnes's statement of the amount and "predetermination" of the wages-fund:

"I believe that, in the existing state of the national wealth, the character of Englishmen being what it is, a certain prospect of profit will 'determine' a certain proportion of this wealth to productive investment; that the amount thus 'determined' will increase as the field for investment is extended, and that it will not increase beyond what this field can find employment for at that rate of profit which satisfies English commercial expectation. Further, I believe that, investment thus taking place, the form which it shall assume will be 'determined' by the nature of the national industries—'determined,' not under acts of Parliament, or in virtue of any physical law, but through the influence of the investor's interests; while this, the form of the investment, will again 'determine' the proportion of the whole capital which shall be paid as wages to laborers."[166] In this excellent and masterly conception, the doctrine of a wages-fund is not open to the objections usually urged against it. Indeed, with the exception of Professor Fawcett, scarcely any economist believes in an absolutely fixed wages-fund. In this sense, then, and in view of the above explanation, it will be understood what is meant by saying that wages depend upon the proportion of the wages-fund to the number of the wage-receivers.[167]

In applying these principles to the question of strikes, it is evident enough that if they result in an actual expansion of the whole circle B, by forcing saving from unproductive expenditure, a real addition, of some extent, may be made to the wages-fund; but only by increasing the total capital. If, however, they attempt to increase one of the elements of capital, the wages-fund, without also adding to the other elements, fixed capital and materials, in the proportion fixed by the nature of the industry, they will destroy all possibility of continuing that production in the normal way, and the capitalist must withdraw from the enterprise.

Francis A. Walker[168] has also offered a solution of this problem in his "Wages Question" (1876), in which he holds that "wages are, in a philosophical view of the subject, paid out of the product of present industry, and hence that production furnishes the true measure of wages" (p. 128). "It is the prospect of a profit in production which determines the employer to hire laborers; it is the anticipated value of the product which determines how much he can pay him" (p. 144). No doubt wages *can* be (and often are) paid out of the current product; but *what* amount? What is the principle of distribution? Wherever the incoming product is a moral certainty (and, unless this is true, in no case could wages be paid out of the future product), saving is as effective upon it as upon the actual accumulations of the past; and the amount of the coming product which will be saved and used as capital is determined by the same principles which govern the saving of past products. An increase of circle A by a larger production makes possible an increase of circle B, but whether it will be enlarged or not depends on the principle of accumulation. The larger the total production of wealth, the greater the *possible* wages, all must admit; but it does not seem clear that General Walker has given us a solution of the real question at issue. The larger the house you build, the larger the rooms may be; but it does not follow that the rooms will be necessarily large—as any inmate of a summer hotel will testify.

§ 3. Examination of some popular Opinions respecting Wages.

There are, however, some facts in apparent contradiction to this [the Wages-Fund] doctrine, which it is incumbent on us to consider and explain.

1. For instance, it is a common saying that wages are high when trade is good. The demand for labor in any particular employment is more pressing, and higher wages are paid, when there is a brisk demand for the commodity produced; and the contrary when there is what is called a stagnation: then work-people are dismissed, and those who are retained must submit to a reduction of wages; though in these cases there is neither more nor less capital than before. This is true; and is one of those complications in the concrete phenomena which obscure and disguise the operation of general causes; but it is not really inconsistent with the principles laid down. Capital which the owner does not employ in purchasing labor, but keeps idle in his hands, is the same thing to the laborers, for the time being, as if it did not exist. All capital is, from the variations of trade, occasionally in this state. A manufacturer, finding a slack demand for his commodity, forbears to employ laborers in increasing a stock which he finds it difficult to dispose of; or if he goes on until all his capital is locked up in unsold goods, then at least he must of necessity pause until he can get paid for some of them. But no one expects either of these states to be permanent; if he did, he would at the first opportunity remove his capital to some other occupation, in which it would still continue to employ labor. The capital remains unemployed for a time, during which the labor market is overstocked, and wages fall. Afterward the demand revives, and perhaps becomes unusually brisk, enabling the manufacturer to sell his commodity even faster than he can

produce it; his whole capital is then brought into complete efficiency, and, if he is able, he borrows capital in addition, which would otherwise have gone into some other employment. These, however, are but temporary fluctuations: the capital now lying idle will next year be in active employment, that which is this year unable to keep up with the demand will in its turn be locked up in crowded warehouses; and wages in these several departments will ebb and flow accordingly: but nothing can permanently alter general wages, except an increase or a diminution of capital itself (always meaning by the term, the funds of all sorts, destined for the payment of labor) compared with the quantity of labor offering itself to be hired.

2. Again, it is another common notion that high prices make high wages; because the producers and dealers, being better off, can afford to pay more to their laborers. I have already said that a brisk demand, which causes temporary high prices, causes also temporary high wages. But high prices, in themselves, can only raise wages if the dealers, receiving more, are induced to save more, and make an addition to their capital, or at least to their purchases of labor. Wages will probably be temporarily higher in the employment in which prices have risen, and somewhat lower in other employments: in which case, while the first half of the phenomenon excites notice, the other is generally overlooked, or, if observed, is not ascribed to the cause which really produced it. Nor will the partial rise of wages last long: for, though the dealers in that one employment gain more, it does not follow that there is room to employ a greater amount of savings in their own business: their increasing capital will probably flow over into other employments, and there counterbalance the diminution previously made in the demand for labor by the diminished savings of other classes.

> A clear distinction must be made between real wages and money wages; the former is of importance to the laborer as being his real receipts. The quantity of commodities satisfying his desires which the laborer receives for his exertion constitutes his real wages. The mere amount of money he receives for his exertions, irrespective of what the money will exchange for, forms his money wages. Since the functions of money have not yet been explained, it is difficult to discuss the relation between prices and money wages here. But, as the total value of the products in a certain industry is the sum out of which both money wages and profits are paid, this total will rise or fall (efficiency of labor remaining the same) with the price of the particular

article. If the price rises, profits will be greater than elsewhere, and more capital will be invested in that one business; that is, the capital will be a demand for more labor, and, until equalization is accomplished in all trades between wages and profits, money wages will be higher in some trades than in others.[162]

When reference is had to the connection between real wages and prices, the question is a different one. General high prices would not change general *real wages*. But if high prices cause higher money wages in particular branches of trade, then, because the movement is not general, there will accrue, to those receiving more money, the means to buy more of real wages. And, as in practice, changes in prices which arise from an increased demand are partial, and not general, it often happens that high prices produce high real wages (not general high wages) in some, not in all employments. (For a further study of this relation between prices and wages the reader is advised to recall this discussion in connection with that in a later part of the volume, Book III, Chaps. XX and XXI.)

3. Another opinion often maintained is, that wages (meaning of course money wages) vary with the price of food; rising when it rises, and falling when it falls. This opinion is, I conceive, only partially true; and, in so far as true, in no way affects the dependence of wages on the proportion between capital and labor: since the price of food, when it affects wages at all, affects them through that law. Dear or cheap food caused by variety of seasons does not affect wages (unless they are artificially adjusted to it by law or charity): or rather, it has some tendency to affect them in the contrary way to that supposed; since in times of scarcity people generally compete more violently for employment, and lower the labor market against themselves. But dearness or cheapness of food, when of a permanent character, and capable of being calculated on beforehand, may affect wages. (1.) In the first place, if the laborers have, as is often the case, no more than enough to keep them in working condition and enable them barely to support the ordinary number of children, it follows that, if food grows permanently dearer without a rise of wages, a greater number of the children will prematurely die; and thus wages will ultimately be higher, but only because the number of people will be smaller, than if food had remained cheap. (2.) But, secondly, even though wages were high enough to admit of food's becoming more costly without depriving the laborers and their families of

necessaries; though they could bear, physically speaking, to be worse off, perhaps they would not consent to be so. They might have habits of comfort which were to them as necessaries, and sooner than forego which, they would put an additional restraint on their power of multiplication; so that wages would rise, not by increase of deaths but by diminution of births. In these cases, then, wages do adapt themselves to the price of food, though after an interval of almost a generation.[170] If wages were previously so high that they could bear reduction, to which the obstacle was a high standard of comfort habitual among the laborers, a rise of the price of food, or any other disadvantageous change in their circumstances, may operate in two ways: (*a*) it may correct itself by a rise of wages, brought about through a gradual effect on the prudential check to population; or (*b*) it may permanently lower the standard of living of the class, in case their previous habits in respect of population prove stronger than their previous habits in respect of comfort. In that case the injury done to them will be permanent, and their deteriorated condition will become a new minimum, tending to perpetuate itself as the more ample minimum did before. It is to be feared that, of the two modes in which the cause may operate, the last (*b*) is the most frequent, or at all events sufficiently so to render all propositions, ascribing a self-repairing quality to the calamities which befall the laboring-classes, practically of no validity.

The converse case occurs when, by improvements in agriculture, the repeal of corn laws, or other such causes, the necessaries of the laborers are cheapened, and they are enabled with the same [money] wages to command greater comforts than before. Wages will not fall immediately: it is even possible that they may rise; but they will fall at last, so as to leave the laborers no better off than before, unless during this interval of prosperity the standard of comfort regarded as indispensable by the class is permanently raised. Unfortunately this salutary effect is by no means to be counted upon: it is a much more difficult thing to raise, than to lower, the scale of living which the laborers will consider as more indispensable than marrying and having a family. According to all experience, a great increase invariably takes place in the number of marriages in seasons of cheap food and full employment.

> This is to be seen by some brief statistics of marriages in Vermont and Massachusetts.

Year.	Vermont	Massachusetts
1860	2,179	12,404
1861	2,188	10,972
1862	1,962	11,014
1863	2,007	10,873
1864	1,804	12,513
1865	2,569	13,052
1866	3,001	14,428
1867	2,857	14,451

In Vermont, while the average number of marriages was reached in 1860 and 1861, it fell off on the breaking out of the war; rose in 1863, under the fair progress of the Northern arms; again fell off in 1864, during the period of discouragement; and since 1865 has kept a steadily higher average. In manufacturing Massachusetts the number fell earlier than in agricultural Vermont, at the beginning of the difficulties.

1856, July to Jan.	6,418
1857, Jan. to July	5,803
1857, July to Jan.	5,936
1858, Jan. to July	4,917
1858, July to Jan.	5,610

The effects of the financial panic of 1857, in Massachusetts, show a similar movement in the number of marriages. The crisis came in October, 1857. In the three months following that date there were 400 less marriages.

To produce permanent advantage, the temporary cause operating upon them must be sufficient to make a great change in their condition—a change such as will be felt for many years, notwithstanding any stimulus which it may give during one generation to the increase of people. When, indeed, the improvement is of this signal character, and a generation grows up which has always been used to an improved scale of comfort, the habits of this new generation in respect to population become formed upon a higher minimum, and the improvement in their condition becomes permanent.

§ 4. *Certain rare Circumstances excepted, High Wages imply Restraints on Population.*

Wages depend, then, on the proportion between the number of the laboring population and the capital or other funds devoted to the purchase of labor; we will say, for shortness, the capital. If wages are higher at one time or place than at another, if the subsistence and comfort of the class of hired laborers are more ample, it is for no other reason than because capital bears a greater proportion to population. It is not the absolute amount of accumulation or of production that is of importance to the laboring-class; it is not the amount even of the funds destined for distribution among the laborers; it is the proportion between those funds and the numbers among whom they are shared. The condition of the class can be bettered in no other way than by altering that proportion to their advantage: and every scheme for their benefit which does not proceed on this as its foundation is, for all permanent purposes, a delusion.

In countries like North America and the Australian colonies, where the knowledge and arts of civilized life and a high effective desire of accumulation coexist with a boundless extent of unoccupied land, the growth of capital easily keeps pace with the utmost possible increase of population, and is chiefly retarded by the impracticability of obtaining laborers enough. All, therefore, who can possibly be born can find employment without overstocking the market: every laboring family enjoys in abundance the necessaries, many of the comforts, and some of the luxuries of life; and, unless in case of individual misconduct, or actual inability to work, poverty does not, and dependence need not, exist. [In England] so gigantic has been the progress of the cotton manufacture since the inventions of Watt and Arkwright, that the capital engaged in it has probably quadrupled in the time which population requires for doubling. While, therefore, it has attracted from other employments nearly all the hands which geographical circumstances and the habits or inclinations of the people rendered available; and while the demand it created for infant labor has enlisted the immediate pecuniary interest of the operatives in favor of promoting, instead of restraining, the increase of population; nevertheless wages in the great seats of the manufacture are still so high that the collective earnings of a family amount, on an average of years, to a very satisfactory sum; and there is as yet no sign of decrease, while the effect has also been felt in raising the general standard of agricultural wages in the counties adjoining.

But those circumstances of a country, or of an occupation, in which population can with impunity increase at its utmost rate, are rare and transitory. Very few are the countries presenting the needful union of conditions. Either the industrial arts are backward and stationary, and capital therefore increases slowly, or, the effective desire of accumulation being low, the increase soon reaches its limit; or, even though both these elements are at their highest known degree, the increase of capital is checked, because there is not fresh land to be resorted to of as good quality as that already occupied. Though capital should for a time double itself simultaneously with population, if all this capital and population are to find employment on the same land, they can not, without an unexampled succession of agricultural inventions, continue doubling the produce; therefore, if wages do not fall, profits must; and, when profits fall, increase of capital is slackened.

Except, therefore, in the very peculiar cases which I have just noticed, of which the only one of any practical importance is that of a new colony, or a country in circumstances equivalent to it, it is impossible that population should increase at its utmost rate without lowering wages. In no old country does population increase at anything like its utmost rate; in most, at a very moderate rate: in some countries, not at all. These facts are only to be accounted for in two ways. Either the whole number of births which nature admits of, and which happen in some circumstances, do not take place; or, if they do, a large proportion of those who are born, die. The retardation of increase results either from mortality or prudence; from Mr. Malthus's positive, or from his preventive check: and one or the other of these must and does exist, and very powerfully too, in all old societies. Wherever population is not kept down by the prudence either of individuals or of the state, it is kept down by starvation or disease.

§ 5. Due Restriction of Population the only Safeguard of a Laboring-Class.

Where a laboring-class who have no property but their daily wages, and no hope of acquiring it, refrain from over-rapid multiplication, the cause, I believe, has always hitherto been, either actual legal restraint, or a custom of some sort which, without intention on their part, insensibly molds their conduct, or affords immediate inducements not to marry. It is not generally known in how many countries of Europe direct legal obstacles are opposed to improvident marriages.

Where there is no general law restrictive of marriage, there are often customs equivalent to it. When the guilds or trade corporations of the middle ages were in vigor, their by-laws or regulations were conceived with a very vigilant eye to the advantage which the trade derived from limiting competition; and they made it very effectually the interest of artisans not to marry until after passing through the two stages of apprentice and journeyman, and attaining the rank of master.

Unhappily, sentimentality rather than common sense usually presides over the discussions of these subjects. Discussions on the condition of the laborers, lamentations over its wretchedness, denunciations of all who are supposed to be indifferent to it, projects of one kind or another for improving it, were in no country and in no time of the world so rife as in the present generation; but there is a tacit agreement to ignore totally the law of wages, or to dismiss it in a parenthesis, with such terms as "hard-hearted Malthusianism"; as if it were not a thousand times more hard-hearted to tell human beings that they may, than that they may not, call into existence swarms of creatures who are sure to be miserable, and most likely to be depraved!

I ask, then, is it true or not, that if their numbers were fewer they would obtain higher wages? This is the question, and no other: and it is idle to divert attention from it, by attacking any incidental position of Malthus or some other writer, and pretending that to refute that is to disprove the principle of population. Some, for instance, have achieved an easy victory over a passing remark of Mr. Malthus, hazarded chiefly by way of illustration, that the increase of food may perhaps be assumed to take place in an arithmetical ratio, while population increases in a geometrical: when every candid reader knows that Mr. Malthus laid no stress on this unlucky attempt to give numerical precision to things which do not admit of it, and every person capable of reasoning must see that it is wholly superfluous to his argument. Others have attached immense importance to a correction which more recent political economists have made in the mere language of the earlier followers of Mr. Malthus. Several writers had said that it is the tendency of population to *increase faster* than the means of subsistence. The assertion was true in the sense in which they meant it, namely, that population would in most circumstances increase faster than the means of subsistence, if it were not checked either by mortality or by prudence. But inasmuch as these checks act with unequal force at different times and places, it was possible to interpret the language of these writers as if they had meant that population is usually gaining ground upon subsistence, and the poverty of the people becoming greater. Under this interpretation of their meaning, it was urged that the reverse is the truth: that as civilization advances, the prudential check tends to become stronger, and population to slacken its rate of increase, relatively to subsistence; and that it is an error to maintain that population, in any improving community, tends to increase faster than, or even so fast as, subsistence.[171] The word tendency[172] is here used in a totally different sense from that of the writers who affirmed the proposition; but waiving the verbal question, is it not allowed, on both sides, that in old countries population presses too closely upon the means of subsistence?

Chapter III. Of Remedies For Low Wages.

§ 1. A Legal or Customary Minimum of Wages, with a Guarantee of Employment.

The simplest expedient which can be imagined for keeping the wages of labor up to the desirable point would be to fix them by law; and this is virtually the object aimed at in a variety of plans which have at different times been, or still are, current, for remodeling the relation between laborers and employers. No one, probably, ever suggested that wages should be absolutely fixed, since the interests of all concerned often require that they should be variable; but some have proposed to fix a minimum of wages, leaving the variations above that point to be adjusted by competition. Another plan, which has found many advocates among the leaders of the operatives, is that councils should be formed, which in England have been called local boards of trade, in France "conseils de prud'hommes," and other names; consisting of delegates from the work-people and from the employers, who, meeting in conference, should agree upon a rate of wages, and promulgate it from authority, to be binding generally on employers and workmen; the ground of decision being, not the state of the labor market, but natural equity; to provide that the workmen shall have *reasonable* wages, and the capitalist reasonable profits.

> The one expedient most suggested by politicians and labor-reformers in the United States is an eight-hour law, mandatory upon all employers. It is to be remembered, however, that in very many industries piece-work exists, and if a diminution of hours is enforced, that will mean a serious reduction in the amount of wages which can be possibly earned in a day. Even if all industries were alike in the matter of arranging their work, this plan means higher wages for the same work, or the same wages for less work, and so an increased cost of labor. This would, then, take its effect on profits at once; and the effects would be probably seen in a withdrawal of capital from many industries, where, as now, the profits are very low. It

> must be recalled, however, that in the United States there has been, under the influence of natural causes, unaided by legislation, a very marked reduction in the hours of labor, accompanied by an increase of wages. For example, in 1840, Rhode Island operatives in the carding-room of the cotton-mills worked fourteen hours a day for $3.28 a week, while in 1884 they work eleven hours and receive $5.40 a week. This result is most probably due to the gain arising from the invention of labor-saving machinery.

Others again (but these are rather philanthropists interesting themselves for the laboring-classes, than the laboring people themselves) are shy of admitting the interference of authority in contracts for labor: they fear that if law intervened, it would intervene rashly and ignorantly; they are convinced that two parties, with opposite interests, attempting to adjust those interests by negotiation through their representatives on principles of equity, when no rule could be laid down to determine what was equitable, would merely exasperate their differences instead of healing them; but what it is useless to attempt by the legal sanction, these persons desire to compass by the moral. Every employer, they think, *ought* to give *sufficient* wages; and if he does it not willingly, should be compelled to it by general opinion; the test of sufficient wages being their own feelings, or what they suppose to be those of the public. This is, I think, a fair representation of a considerable body of existing opinion on the subject.

I desire to confine my remarks to the principle involved in all these suggestions, without taking into account practical difficulties, serious as these must at once be seen to be. I shall suppose that by one or other of these contrivances wages could be kept above the point to which they would be brought by competition. This is as much as to say, above the highest rate which can be afforded by the existing capital consistently with employing all the laborers. For it is a mistake to suppose that competition merely keeps down wages. It is equally the means by which they are kept up. When there are any laborers unemployed, these, unless maintained by charity, become competitors for hire, and wages fall; but when all who were out of work have found employment, wages will not, under the freest system of competition, fall lower. There are strange notions afloat concerning the nature of competition. Some people seem to imagine that its effect is something indefinite; that the competition of sellers may lower prices, and the competition of laborers may lower wages, down to zero, or some unassignable minimum. Nothing can be more unfounded. Goods can only be lowered in price by competition to the point which calls forth buyers sufficient to take them off; and wages can only be lowered by competition until room is made to admit all the laborers to a share in the distribution of the wages-fund. If they fell below this point, a portion of capital would remain unemployed for want of laborers; a counter-competition would commence on the side of capitalists, and wages would rise.

> The assumption in the last chapter in regard to competition and custom should be kept in mind in all this reasoning. As a matter of fact, there is not that mobility of labor which insures so free an operation of competition that equality of payment always exists. In reality there is no competition at all between the lower grades of laborers and the higher classes of skilled labor. Of course, the *tendency* is as explained by Mr. Mill, and as time goes on there is a distinctly greater mobility of labor visible. Vast numbers pass from Scandinavia and other countries of Europe to the United States, or from England to Australia, urged by the desire to go from a community of low to one of higher wages.

Since, therefore, the rate of wages which results from competition distributes the whole wages-fund among the whole laboring population, if law or opinion succeeds in fixing wages above this rate, some laborers are kept out of employment; and as it is not the intention of the philanthropists that these should starve, they must be provided for by a forced increase of the wages-fund—by a compulsory saving. It is nothing to fix a minimum of wages unless there be a provision that work, or wages at least, be found for all who apply for it. This, accordingly, is always part of the scheme, and is consistent with the ideas of more people than would approve of either a legal or a moral minimum of wages. Popular sentiment looks upon it as the duty of the rich, or of the state, to find employment for all the poor. If the moral influence of opinion does not induce the rich to spare from their consumption enough to set all the poor at work at "reasonable wages," it is supposed to be incumbent on the state to lay on taxes for the purpose, either by local rates or votes of public money. The proportion between labor and the wages-fund would thus be modified to the advantage of the laborers, not by restriction of population, but by an increase of capital.

§ 2. —Would Require as a Condition Legal Measures for Repression of Population.

If this claim on society could be limited to the existing generation; if nothing more were necessary than a compulsory accumulation, sufficient to provide permanent employment at ample wages for the existing numbers of the people; such a proposition would have no more strenuous supporter than myself. Society mainly consists of those who live by bodily labor; and if society, that is, if the laborers, lend their physical force to protect individuals in the enjoyment of superfluities, they are entitled to do so, and have always done so, with the reservation of a power to tax those superfluities for purposes of public utility; among which purposes the subsistence of the people is the foremost. Since no one is responsible for having been born, no pecuniary sacrifice is too great to be made by those who have more than enough, for the purpose of securing enough to all persons already in existence.

But it is another thing altogether when those who have produced and accumulated are called upon to abstain from consuming until they have given food and clothing, not only to all who now exist, but to all whom these or their descendants may think fit to call into existence. Such an obligation acknowledged and acted upon, would suspend all checks, both positive and preventive; there would be nothing to hinder population from starting forward at its rapidest rate; and as the natural increase of capital would, at the best, not be more rapid than before, taxation, to make up the growing deficiency, must advance with the same gigantic strides. But let them work ever so efficiently, the increasing population could not, as we have so often shown, increase the produce proportionally; the surplus, after all were fed, would bear a less and less proportion to the whole produce and to the population: and the increase of people going on in a constant ratio, while the increase of produce went on in a diminishing ratio, the surplus would in time be wholly absorbed; taxation for the support of the poor would engross the whole income of the country; the payers and the receivers would be melted down into one mass.

It would be possible for the state to guarantee employment at ample wages to all who are born. But if it does this, it is bound in self-protection, and for the sake of every purpose for which government exists, to provide that no person shall be born without its consent. To give profusely to the people, whether under the name of charity or of employment, without placing them under such influences that prudential motives shall act powerfully upon them, is to lavish the means of benefiting mankind without attaining the object. But remove the regulation of their wages from their own control; guarantee to them a certain payment, either by law or by the feeding of the community; and no amount of comfort that you can give them will make either them or their descendants look to their own self-restraint as the proper means for preserving them in that state.

> The famous poor-laws of Elizabeth, enacted in 1601, were at first intended to relieve the destitute poor, sick, aged, and impotent, but in their administration a share was given to all who *begged* it. Employers, of course, found it cheaper to hire labor partly paid for by the parish, and the independent farm-laborer who would not go on the parish found his own wages lowered by this kind of competition. This continued a crying evil until it reached the proportions described by May: "As the cost of pauperism, thus encouraged, was increasing, the poorer rate-payers were themselves reduced to poverty. The soil was ill-cultivated by pauper labor, and its rental consumed by parish rates. In a period of fifty years, the poor-rates were quadrupled, and had reached, in 1833, the enormous amount of £8,600,000. In many parishes they were approaching the annual value of the land itself."[173] The old poor-laws were repealed, and there went into effect in 1834 the workhouse system, which, while not denying subsistence to all those born, required that the giving of aid should be made as disagreeable as possible, in order to stimulate among the poor a feeling of repugnance to all aid from the community. This is also the general idea of poor-relief in the United States.
>
> The cultivation of the principle of self-help in each laborer is certainly the right object at which to aim. In the United States voluntary charitable organizations have associated together, in some cities, in order to scrutinize all cases of poverty through a number of visitors in each district, who advise and counsel the unfortunate, but never give money. This system has been very successful, and, by basing its operations on the principle of self-help, has given the best proof of its right to an increasing influence.

§ 3. Allowances in Aid of Wages and the Standard of Living.

Next to the attempts to regulate wages, and provide artificially that all who are willing to work shall receive an adequate price for their labor, we have to consider another class of popular remedies, which do not profess to interfere with freedom of contract; which leave wages to be fixed by the competition of the market, but, when they are considered insufficient, endeavor by some subsidiary resource to make up to the laborers for the insufficiency. Of this nature was the allowance system. The principle of this scheme being avowedly that of adapting the means of every family to its necessities, it was a natural consequence that more should be given to the married than to the single, and to those who had large families than to those who had not: in fact, an allowance was usually granted for every child. It is obvious that this is merely another mode of fixing a minimum of wages.

There is a rate of wages, either the lowest on which the people can, or the lowest on which they will consent, to live. We will suppose this to be seven shillings a week. Shocked at the wretchedness of this pittance, the parish authorities humanely make it up to ten. But the laborers are accustomed to seven, and though they would gladly have more, will live on that (as the fact proves) rather than restrain the instinct of multiplication. Their habits will not be altered for the better by giving them parish pay. Receiving three shillings from the parish, they will be as well off as before, though they should increase sufficiently to bring down wages to four shillings. They will accordingly people down to that point; or, perhaps, without waiting for an increase of numbers, there are unemployed laborers enough in the workhouse to produce the effect at once. It is well known that the allowance system did practically operate in the mode described, and that under its influence wages sank to a lower rate than had been known in England before.

> The operation of a low standard upon the wages of those in the community who have a higher one, has been seen in the United States to a certain extent by the landing on our shores of Chinese laborers, who maintain a decidedly lower standard of living than either their American or Irish competitors. If they come in such numbers as to retain their lower standard by forming a group by themselves, and are thereby not assimilated into the body of laborers who have a higher standard of comfort, they can, to the extent of their ability to do work, drive other laborers out of employment. This, moreover, is exactly what was done by the Irish, who drove Americans out of the mills of

New England, and who are now being driven out, probably, by the French Canadians, with a standard lower than the Irish. The Chinese come here now without their families, as may be seen by the accompanying diagram, in which the shaded side represents the males on the left, and the unshaded the females on the right, of the perpendicular line.

Decade.	Males.	Females.
1	6	4
2	106	12
3	351	37
4	283	15
5	139	3
6	32	1
7	10	0
8	1	0
9	0	0

The horizontal lines show the ages, the largest number being about thirty years of age. It will be noted how many come in the prime of life, and how few children and females there are.

It need hardly be said that the economic side of a question is here discussed, which requires for its solution many ethical and political considerations besides.

§ 4. Grounds for Expecting Improvement in Public Opinion on the Subject of Population.

By what means, then, is poverty to be contended against? How is the evil of low wages to be remedied? If the expedients usually recommended for the purpose are not adapted to it, can no others be thought of? Is the problem incapable of solution? Can political economy do nothing, but only object to everything, and demonstrate that nothing can be done? Those who think it hopeless that the laboring-classes should be induced to practice a sufficient degree of prudence in regard to the increase of their families, because they have hitherto stopped short of that point, show an inability to estimate the ordinary principles of human action. Nothing more would probably be necessary to secure that result, than an opinion generally diffused that it was desirable.

But let us try to imagine what would happen if the idea became general among the laboring-class that the competition of too great numbers was the principal cause of their poverty. We are often told that the most thorough perception of the dependence of wages on population will not influence the conduct of a laboring-man, because it is not the children he himself can have that will produce any effect in generally depressing the labor market. True, and it is also true that one soldier's running away will not lose the battle; accordingly, it is not that consideration which keeps each soldier in his rank: it is the disgrace which naturally and inevitably attends on conduct by any one individual which, if pursued by a majority, everybody can see would be fatal. Men are seldom found to brave the general opinion of their class, unless supported either by some principle higher than regard for opinion, or by some strong body of opinion elsewhere.

If the opinion were once generally established among the laboring-class that their welfare required a due regulation of the numbers of families, the respectable and well-conducted of the body would conform to the prescription, and only those would exempt themselves from it who were in the habit of making light of social obligations generally; and there would be then an evident justification for converting the moral obligation against bringing children into the world, who are a burden to the community, into a legal one; just as in many other cases of the progress of opinion, the law ends by enforcing against recalcitrant minorities obligations which, to be useful, must be general, and which, from a sense of their utility, a large majority have voluntarily consented to take upon themselves.

The dependence of wages on the number of the competitors for employment is so far from hard of comprehension, or unintelligible to the laboring-classes, that by great bodies of them it is already recognized and habitually acted on. It is familiar to all trades-unions: every successful combination to keep up wages owes its success to contrivances for restricting the number of competitors; all skilled trades are anxious to keep down their own numbers, and many impose, or endeavor to impose, as a condition upon employers, that they shall not take more than a prescribed number of apprentices. There is, of course, a great difference between limiting their numbers by excluding other people, and doing the same thing by a restraint imposed on themselves; but the one as much as the other shows a clear perception of the relation between their numbers and their remuneration. The principle is understood in its application to any one employment, but not to the general mass of employment. For this there are several reasons: first, the operation of causes is more easily and distinctly seen in the more circumscribed field; secondly, skilled artisans are a more intelligent class than ordinary manual laborers; and the habit of concert, and of passing in review their general condition as a trade, keeps up a better understanding of their collective interests; thirdly and lastly, they are the most provident, because they are the best off, and have the most to preserve.

§ 5. Twofold means of Elevating the Habits of the Laboring-People; by Education, and by Foreign and Home Colonization.

For the purpose, therefore, of altering the habits of the laboring people, there is need of a twofold action, directed simultaneously upon their intelligence and their poverty. An effective national education of the children of the laboring-class is the first thing needful; and, coincidently with this, a system of measures which shall (as the Revolution did in France) extinguish extreme poverty for one whole generation. Without entering into disputable points, it may be asserted without scruple that the aim of all intellectual training for the mass of the people should be to cultivate common sense; to qualify them for forming a sound practical judgment of the circumstances by which they are surrounded. [But] education is not compatible with extreme poverty. It is impossible effectually to teach an indigent population. Toward effecting this object there are two resources available, without wrong to any one, without any of the liabilities of mischief attendant on voluntary or legal charity, and not only without weakening, but on the contrary strengthening, every incentive to industry, and every motive to forethought.

The first is a great national measure of colonization. I mean, a grant of public money, sufficient to remove at once, and establish in the colonies, a considerable fraction of the youthful agricultural population. It has been shown by others that colonization on an adequate scale might be so conducted as to cost the country nothing, or nothing that would not be certainly repaid; and that the funds required, even by way of advance, would not be drawn from the capital employed in maintaining labor, but from that surplus which can not find employment at such profit as constitutes an adequate remuneration for the abstinence of the possessor, and which is therefore sent abroad for investment, or wasted at home in reckless speculations.

The second resource would be to devote all common land, hereafter brought into cultivation, to raising a class of small proprietors. What I would propose is, that common land should be divided into sections of five acres or thereabout, to be conferred in absolute property on individuals of the laboring-class who would reclaim and bring them into cultivation by their own labor.

> This suggestion works to the same purpose as the proposal that our Government should retain its public lands and aid in the formation of a great number of small farmers, rather than, by huge grants, to foster large holdings in the Western States and Territories.[174]

The preference should be given to such laborers, and there are many of them, as had saved enough to maintain them until their first crop was got in, or whose character was such as to induce some responsible person to advance to them the requisite amount on their personal security. The tools, the manure, and in some cases the subsistence also, might be supplied by the parish, or by the state; interest for the advance, at the rate yielded by the public funds, being laid on as a perpetual quitrent, with power to the peasant to redeem it at any time for a moderate number of years' purchase. These little landed estates might, if it were thought necessary, be indivisible by law; though, if the plan worked in the manner designed, I should not apprehend any objectionable degree of subdivision. In case of intestacy, and in default of amicable arrangement among the heirs, they might be bought by government at their value, and re-granted to some other laborer who could give security for the price. The desire to possess one of these small properties would probably become, as on the Continent, an inducement to prudence and economy pervading the whole laboring population; and that great desideratum among a people of hired laborers would be provided, an intermediate class between them and their employers; affording them the double advantage of an object for their hopes, and, as there would be good reason to anticipate, an example for their imitation.

It would, however, be of little avail that either or both of these measures of relief should be adopted, unless on such a scale as would enable the whole body of hired laborers remaining on the soil to obtain not merely employment, but a large addition to the present wages—such an addition as would enable them to live and bring up their children in a degree of comfort and independence to which they have hitherto been strangers.

Chapter IV. Of The Differences Of Wages In Different Employments.

§ 1. Differences of Wages Arising from Different Degrees of Attractiveness in Different Employments.

In treating of wages, we have hitherto confined ourselves to the causes which operate on them generally, and *en masse*; the laws which govern the remuneration of ordinary or average labor, without reference to the existence of different kinds of work which are habitually paid at different rates, depending in some degree on different laws. We will now take into consideration these differences, and examine in what manner they affect or are affected by the conclusions already established.

The differences, says [Adam Smith], arise partly "from certain circumstances in the employments themselves, which either really, or at least in the imaginations of men, make up for a small pecuniary gain in some, and counterbalance a great one in others." These circumstances he considers to be: "First, the agreeableness or disagreeableness of the employments themselves; secondly, the easiness and cheapness, or the difficulty and expense of learning them; thirdly, the constancy or inconstancy of employment in them; fourthly, the small or great trust which must be reposed in those who exercise them; and, fifthly, the probability or improbability of success in them."

(1.) "The wages of labor vary with the ease or hardship, the cleanliness or dirtiness, the honorableness or dishonorableness of the employment. A journeyman blacksmith, though an artificer, seldom earns so much in twelve hours as a collier, who is only a laborer, does in eight. His work is not quite so dirty, is less dangerous, and is carried on in daylight and above ground. Honor makes a great part of the reward of all honorable professions. In point of pecuniary gain, all things considered," their recompense is, in his opinion, below the average. "Disgrace has the contrary effect. The trade of a butcher is a brutal and an odious business; but it is in most places more profitable than the greater part of common trades. The most detestable of all employments, that of the public executioner, is, in proportion to the quantity of work done, better paid than any common trade whatever."

(2.) "Employment is much more constant," continues Adam Smith, "in some trades than in others. In the greater part of manufactures, a journeyman may be pretty sure of employment almost every day in the year that he is able to work. A mason or brick-layer, on the contrary, can work neither in hard frost nor in foul weather, and his employment at all other times depends upon the occasional calls of his customers. He is liable, in consequence, to be frequently without any. What he earns, therefore, while he is employed, must not only maintain him while he is idle, but make him some compensation for those anxious and desponding moments which the thought of so precarious a situation must sometimes occasion."

"When (1) the inconstancy of the employment is combined with (2) the hardship, disagreeableness, and dirtiness of the work, it sometimes raises the wages of the most common labor above those of the most skillful artificers. A collier working by the piece is supposed, at Newcastle, to earn commonly about double, and in many parts of Scotland about three times, the wages of common labor. His high wages arise altogether from the hardship, disagreeableness, and dirtiness of his work. His employment may, upon most occasions, be as constant as he pleases. The coal-heavers in London exercise a trade which in hardship, dirtiness, and disagreeableness almost equals that of colliers; and from the unavoidable irregularity in the arrivals of coal-ships, the employment of the greater part of them is necessarily very inconstant. If colliers, therefore, commonly earn double and triple the wages of common labor, it ought not to seem unreasonable that coal-heavers should sometimes earn four or five times those wages. In the inquiry made into their condition a few years ago, it was found that, at the rate at which they were then paid, they could earn about four times the wages of common labor in London."

These inequalities of remuneration, which are supposed to compensate for the disagreeable circumstances of particular employments, would, under certain conditions, be natural consequences of perfectly free competition: and as between employments of about the same grade, and filled by nearly the same description of people, they are, no doubt, for the most part, realized in practice.

But it is altogether a false view of the state of facts to present this as the relation which generally exists between agreeable and disagreeable employments. The really exhausting and the really repulsive labors, instead of being better paid than others, are almost invariably paid the worst of all, because performed by those who have no choice. If the laborers in the aggregate, instead of exceeding, fell short of the amount of employment, work which was generally disliked would not be undertaken, except for more than ordinary wages. But when the supply of labor so far exceeds the demand that to find employment at all is an uncertainty, and to be offered it on any terms a favor, the case is totally the reverse. Partly from this cause, and partly from the natural and artificial monopolies, which will be spoken of presently, the inequalities of wages are generally in an opposite direction to the equitable principle of compensation, erroneously represented by Adam Smith as the general law of the remuneration of labor.

(3.) One of the points best illustrated by Adam Smith is the influence exercised on the remuneration of an employment by the uncertainty of success in it. If the chances are great of total failure, the reward in case of success must be sufficient to make up, in the general estimation, for those adverse chances. Put your son apprentice to a shoemaker, there is little doubt of his learning to make a pair of shoes; but send him to study the law, it is at least twenty to one if ever he makes such proficiency as will enable him to live by the business. In a perfectly fair lottery, those who draw the prizes ought to gain all that is lost by those who draw the blanks. In a profession where twenty fail for one that succeeds, that one ought to gain all that should have been gained by the unsuccessful twenty. How extravagant soever the fees of counselors-at-law may sometimes appear, their real retribution is never equal to this.

§ 2. Differences arising from Natural Monopolies.

The preceding are cases in which inequality of remuneration is necessary to produce equality of attractiveness, and are examples of the equalizing effect of free competition. The following are cases of real inequality, and arise from a different principle.

(4.) "The wages of labor vary according to the small or great trust which must be reposed in the workmen. The wages of goldsmiths and jewelers are everywhere superior to those of many other workmen, not only of equal but of much superior ingenuity, on account of the precious materials with which they are intrusted." The superiority of reward is not here the consequence of competition, but of its absence: not a compensation for disadvantages inherent in the employment, but an extra advantage; a kind of monopoly price, the effect not of a legal, but of what has been termed a natural monopoly. If all laborers were trustworthy, it would not be necessary to give extra pay to working goldsmiths on account of the trust. The degree of integrity required being supposed to be uncommon, those who can make it appear that they possess it are able to take advantage of the peculiarity, and obtain higher pay in proportion to its rarity.

This same explanation of a natural monopoly applies exactly to the causes which give able executive managers, who watch over productive operations, the usually high rewards for labor under the name of "wages of superintendence." If successful managers of cotton or woolen mills were as plentiful, in proportion to the demand for them, as ordinary artisans, in proportion to the demand for them, then the former would get no higher rewards than the latter. Able executive and business managers secure high wages solely on the ground—as explained above—of monopoly; that is, because their numbers, owing to natural causes, are few relatively to the demand for them in every industry in the land.

(5.) Some employments require a much longer time to learn, and a much more expensive course of instruction, than others; and to this extent there is, as explained by Adam Smith, an inherent reason for their being more highly remunerated. Wages, consequently, must yield, over and above the ordinary amount, an annuity sufficient to repay these sums, with the common rate of profit, within the number of years [the laborer] can expect to live and be in working condition.

But, independently of these or any other artificial monopolies, there is a natural monopoly in favor of skilled laborers against the unskilled, which makes the difference of reward exceed, sometimes in a manifold proportion, what is sufficient merely to equalize their advantages. But the fact that a course of instruction is required, of even a low degree of costliness, or that the laborer must be maintained for a considerable time from other sources, suffices everywhere to exclude the great body of the laboring people from the possibility of any such competition. Until lately, all employments which required even the humble education of reading and writing could be recruited only from a select class, the majority having had no opportunity of acquiring those attainments.

Here is found the germ of the idea, which has been elaborately worked out by Mr. Cairnes[175] in his theory of non-competing groups of laborers: "What we find, in effect, is not a whole population competing indiscriminately for all occupations, but a series of industrial layers superposed on one another, within each of which the various candidates for employment possess a real and effective power of selection, while those occupying the several strata are, for all purposes of effective competition, practically isolated from each other." (Mr. Mill certainly understood this fully, and stated it clearly again in Book III, Chap. II, § 2.)

The changes, however, now so rapidly taking place in usages and ideas, are undermining all these distinctions; the habits or disabilities which chained people to their hereditary condition are fast wearing away, and every class is exposed to increased and increasing competition from at least the class immediately below it. The general relaxation of conventional barriers, and the increased facilities of education which already are, and will be in a much greater degree, brought within the reach of all, tend to produce, among many excellent effects, one which is the reverse: they tend to bring down the wages of skilled labor.

§ 3. Effect on Wages of the Competition of Persons having other Means of Support.

A modifying circumstance still remains to be noticed, which interferes to some extent with the operation of the principles thus far brought to view. While it is true, as a general rule, that the earnings of skilled labor, and especially of any labor which requires school education, are at a monopoly rate, from the impossibility, to the mass of the people, of obtaining that education, it is also true that the policy of nations, or the bounty of individuals, formerly did much to counteract the effect of this limitation of competition, by offering eleemosynary instruction to a much larger class of persons than could have obtained the same advantages by paying their price.

[Adam Smith has pointed out that] "whenever the law has attempted to regulate the wages of workmen, it has always been rather to lower them than to raise them. But the law has upon many occasions attempted to raise the wages of curates, and, for the dignity of the Church, to oblige the rectors of parishes to give them more than the wretched maintenance which they themselves might be willing to accept of. And in both cases the law seems to have been equally ineffectual, and has never been either able to raise the wages of curates or to sink those of laborers to the degree that was intended, because it has never been able to hinder either the one from being willing to accept of less than the legal allowance, on account of the indigence of their situation and the multitude of their competitors, or the other from receiving more, on account of the contrary competition of those who expected to derive either profit or pleasure from employing them."

Although the highest pecuniary prizes of successful authorship are incomparably greater than at any former period, yet on any rational calculation of the chances, in the existing competition, scarcely any writer can hope to gain a living by books, and to do so by magazines and reviews becomes daily more difficult. It is only the more troublesome and disagreeable kinds of literary labor, and those which confer no personal celebrity, such as most of those connected with newspapers, or with the smaller periodicals, on which an educated person can now rely for subsistence. Of these, the remuneration is, on the whole, decidedly high; because, though exposed to the competition of what used to be called "poor scholars" (persons who have received a learned education from some public or private charity), they are exempt from that of amateurs, those who have other means of support being seldom candidates for such employments.

When an occupation is carried on chiefly by persons who derive the main portion of their subsistence from other sources, its remuneration may be lower almost to any extent than the wages of equally severe labor in other employments. The principal example of the kind is domestic manufactures. When spinning and knitting were carried on in every cottage, by families deriving their principal support from agriculture, the price at which their produce was sold (which constituted the remuneration of their labor) was often so low that there would have been required great perfection of machinery to undersell it. The amount of the remuneration in such a case depends chiefly upon whether the quantity of the commodity produced by this description of labor suffices to supply the whole of the demand. If it does not, and there is consequently a necessity for some laborers who devote themselves entirely to the employment, the price of the article must be sufficient to pay those laborers at the ordinary rate, and to reward, therefore, very handsomely the domestic producers. But if the demand is so limited that the domestic manufacture can do more than satisfy it, the price is naturally kept down to the lowest rate at which peasant families think it worth while to continue the production. Thus far, as to the remuneration of the subsidiary employment; but the effect to the laborers of having this additional resource is almost certain to be (unless peculiar counteracting causes intervene) a proportional diminution of the wages of their main occupation.

For the same reason it is found that, *cæteris paribus*, those trades are generally the worst paid in which the wife and children of the artisan aid in the work.

The income which the habits of the class demand, and down to which they are almost sure to multiply, is made up in those trades by the earnings of the whole family, while in others the same income must be obtained by the labor of the man alone. It is even probable that their collective earnings will amount to a smaller sum than those of the man alone in other trades, because the prudential restraint on marriage is unusually weak when the only consequence immediately felt is an improvement of circumstances, the joint earnings of the two going further in their domestic economy after marriage than before.

> This statement seems to be borne out by the statistics of wages[176] both in England and the United States. In our cotton-mills, where women do certain kinds of work equally well with men, the wages of the men are lower than in outside employments into which women can not enter.
>
> Blacksmiths, per week: $16.74
> Family of four: Drawers-in, cotton-mill—man, per week: $5.50
> Family of four: Drawers-in, cotton-mill—woman, per week: $5.50
> Family of four: Tenders, two boys: $4.50
> Total: $15.50
>
> In this case the family of four all together receive only about the same as the wages of the single blacksmith alone.

§ 4. Wages of Women, why Lower than those of Men.

Where men and women work at the same employment, if it be one for which they are equally fitted in point of physical power, they are not always unequally paid. Women in factories sometimes earn as much as men; and so they do in hand-loom weaving, which, being paid by the piece, brings their efficiency to a sure test. When the efficiency is equal, but the pay unequal, the only explanation that can be given is custom. But the principal question relates to the peculiar employments of women. The remuneration of these is always, I believe, greatly below that of employments of equal skill and equal disagreeableness carried on by men. In some of these cases the explanation is evidently that already given: as in the case of domestic servants, whose wages, speaking generally, are not determined by competition, but are greatly in excess of the market value of the labor, and in this excess, as in almost all things which are regulated by custom, the male sex obtains by far the largest share. In the occupations in which employers take full advantage of competition, the low wages of women, as compared with the ordinary earnings of men, are a proof that the employments are overstocked: that although so much smaller a number of women than of men support themselves by wages, the occupations which law and usage make accessible to them are comparatively so few that the field of their employment is still more overcrowded.

> Yet within the employments open to women, such as millinery and dress-making, certain women are able to charge excessively high prices for work, because, having obtained a reputation for especial skill and taste, they can exact in the high prices of their articles what is really their high wages. Within these employments women are unable to earn a living not so much by the lack of work, as by not bringing to their occupation that amount of skill and those business qualities (owing, of course, to their being brought up unaccustomed to business methods) which are requisite for the success of any one, either man or woman.

It must be observed that, as matters now stand, a sufficient degree of overcrowding may depress the wages of women to a much lower minimum than those of men. The wages, at least of single women, must be equal to their support, but need not be more than equal to it; the minimum, in their case, is the pittance absolutely requisite for the sustenance of one human being. Now the lowest point to which the most superabundant competition can permanently depress the wages of a man is always somewhat more than this. Where the wife of a laboring-man does not by general custom contribute to his earnings, the man's wages must be at least sufficient to support himself, a wife, and a number of children adequate to keep up the population, since, if it were less, the population would not be kept up.

§ 5. Differences of Wages Arising from Laws, Combinations, or Customs.

Thus far we have, throughout this discussion, proceeded on the supposition that competition is free, so far as regards human interference; being limited only by natural causes, or by the unintended effect of general social circumstances. But law or custom may interfere to limit competition. If apprentice laws, or the regulations of corporate bodies, make the access to a particular employment slow, costly, or difficult, the wages of that employment may be kept much above their natural proportion to the wages of common labor. In some trades, however, and to some extent, the combinations of workmen produce a similar effect. Those combinations always fail to uphold wages at an artificial rate unless they also limit the number of competitors. Putting aside the atrocities sometimes committed by workmen in the way of personal outrage or intimidation, which can not be too rigidly repressed, if the present state of the general habits of the people were to remain forever unimproved, these partial combinations, in so far as they do succeed in keeping up the wages of any trade by limiting its numbers, might be looked upon as simply intrenching round a particular spot against the inroads of over-population, and making the wages of the class depend upon their own rate of increase, instead of depending on that of a more reckless and improvident class than themselves.

To conclude this subject, I must repeat an observation already made, that there are kinds of labor of which the wages are fixed by custom, and not by competition. Such are the fees or charges of professional persons—of physicians, surgeons, barristers, and even attorneys.

Chapter V. Of Profits.

§ 1. Profits include Interest and Risk; but, correctly speaking, do not include Wages of Superintendence.

Having treated of the laborer's share of the produce, we next proceed to the share of the capitalist; the profits of capital or stock; the gains of the person who advances the expenses of production—who, from funds in his possession, pays the wages of the laborers, or supports them during the work; who supplies the requisite buildings, materials, and tools or machinery; and to whom, by the usual terms of the contract, the produce belongs, to be disposed of at his pleasure. After indemnifying him for his outlay, there commonly remains a surplus, which is his profit; the net income from his capital [and skill]; the amount which he can afford to expend in necessaries or pleasures, or from which by further saving he can add to his wealth.

As the wages of the laborer are the remuneration of labor, so [a part of] the profits of the capitalist are properly, according to Mr. Senior's well-chosen expression, the remuneration of abstinence. They are what he gains by forbearing to consume his capital for his own uses, and allowing it to be consumed by productive laborers for their uses. For this forbearance he requires a recompense.

Of the gains, however, which the possession of a capital enables a person to make, (1) a part only is properly an equivalent for the use of the capital itself; namely, as much as a solvent person would be willing to pay for the loan of it. This, which as everybody knows is called interest, is all that a person is enabled to get by merely abstaining from the immediate consumption of his capital, and allowing it to be used for productive purposes by others. The remuneration which is obtained in any country for mere abstinence is measured by the current rate of interest on the best security; such security as precludes any appreciable chance of losing the principal. What a person expects to gain, who superintends the employment of his own capital, is always more, and generally much more, than this. The rate of profit greatly exceeds the rate of interest. (2.) The surplus is partly compensation for risk. By lending his capital on unexceptionable security he runs little or no risk. But if he embarks in business on his own account, he always exposes his capital to some, and in many cases to very great, danger of partial or total loss. For this danger he must be compensated, otherwise he will not incur it. (3.) He must likewise be remunerated for the devotion of his time and labor. The control of the operations of industry usually belongs to the person who supplies the whole or the greatest part of the funds by which they are carried on, and who, according to the ordinary arrangement, is either alone interested, or is the person most interested (at least directly), in the result. To exercise this control with efficiency, if the concern is large and complicated, requires great assiduity, and often no ordinary skill. This assiduity and skill must be remunerated.

The gross profits from capital, the gains returned to those who supply the funds for production, must suffice for these three purposes; and the three parts into which profit may be considered as resolving itself may be described respectively as interest, insurance, and wages of superintendence.

> Inasmuch as risk is the cause affecting the rate of interest, it would be much simpler to consider the whole reward for abstinence as interest, the rate of which is affected by the risk; and to carefully exclude from the profits of capital the payment for "assiduity and skill," which is distinctly wages of labor. The "wages of superintendence," as every one on a moment's reflection must admit, have no necessary connection whatever with the possession of capital. The thing with which the laborer is occupied does not give the reason for associating his wages with the name of that thing; because a highly-qualified manager supervises the operations of capital, it does not follow that he has capital, or should be regarded as being paid for the possession of capital. The man who shovels ashes is not paid wages of ashes, any more than a man who superintends other people's capital is paid the reward of capital. The payment for services, in the one case as in the other, depends upon the skill of the manager, just as it does with an ordinary mechanic, rising or falling with his fitness for the peculiar work. Skill as a manager is the cause; the amount of the remuneration is the consequence. If so, then the wages of superintendence have no logical connection, in the economic sense, with capital as the thing which determines the amount of its reward, any more than it affects the wages of any and all labor. The payment for

the use of capital, simply as capital, may be seen by the amount which a widow who is not engaged in active business receives from her property invested as trust funds. Moreover, it is less and less true that the manager of the operations of industry is necessarily the capitalist. To see this, mark the executive managers (called "treasurers" by custom) of cotton and woolen mills, who receive a remuneration entirely distinct from any capital they may have invested in the shares of the corporation; and the officials of the great mutual insurance companies, who receive the wages of managers, but for managing the capital of others. A large—by far the largest—part of what is usually called profit, therefore, should be treated as wages, and the forces which govern its amount are the same as those affecting the amounts of all other kinds of wages, such as are discussed in the preceding chapter. The acknowledgment of this distinction is of extreme importance, and affects, in a profound way, the whole question of distribution. To include "wages of superintendence" in profits of capital is to unnecessarily complicate one of the most serious economic questions—namely, the relations of capital and labor.

§ 2. The Minimum of Profits; what produces Variations in the Amount of Profits.

The lowest rate of profit that can permanently exist is that which is barely adequate, at the given place and time, to afford an equivalent for the abstinence, risk, and exertion implied in the employment of capital. From the gross profit has first to be deducted as much as will form a fund sufficient on the average to cover all losses incident to the employment. Next, it must afford such an equivalent to the owner of the capital for forbearing to consume it as is then and there a sufficient motive to him to persist in his abstinence. How much will be required to form this equivalent depends on the comparative value placed, in the given society, upon the present and the future (in the words formerly used): on the strength of the effective desire of accumulation. Further, after covering all losses, and remunerating the owner for forbearing to consume, there must be something left to recompense the labor and skill of the person who devotes his time to the business.

Such, then, is the minimum of profits: but that minimum is exceedingly variable, and at some times and places extremely low, on account of the great variableness of two out of its three elements. That the rate of necessary remuneration for abstinence, or in other words the effective desire of accumulation, differs widely in different states of society and civilization, has been seen in a former chapter. There is a still wider difference in the element which consists in compensation for risk.

The remuneration of capital in different employments, much more than the remuneration of labor, varies according to the circumstances which render one employment more attractive or more repulsive than another. The profits, for example, of retail trade, in proportion to the capital employed, exceed those of wholesale dealers or manufacturers, for this reason among others, that there is less consideration attached to the employment. The greatest, however, of these differences, is that caused by difference of risk. The profits of a gunpowder-manufacturer must be considerably greater than the average, to make up for the peculiar risks to which he and his property are constantly exposed. When, however, as in the case of marine adventure, the peculiar risks are capable of being, and commonly are, commuted for a fixed payment, the premium of insurance takes its regular place among the charges of production, and the compensation which the owner of the ship or cargo receives for that payment does not appear in the estimate of his profits, but is included in the replacement of his capital.

> The minimum of profits can not properly include wages of superintendence, nor is it so included, practically, in Mr. Mill's discussions on the minimum of profits in a later part of this volume. The operation of the various elements in changing the amount of profits might be expressed as follows: As between different countries and communities, who have a different effective desire of accumulation, profits may vary with the element of interest and risk; within the same district, where interest is generally the same on the same security, profits may vary with the risk attached to different industries; and, within the same occupations, interest and risk being given, the wages of superintendence may make a greater variation than either of the other two causes—since a skillful manager may make a large return, a poor one none at all. Or between two employments, interest and risk remaining the same, wages of superintendence sometimes produce a wide difference.

The portion, too, of the gross profit, which forms the remuneration for the labor and skill of the dealer or producer, is very different in different employments. This is the explanation always given of the extraordinary rate of apothecaries' profit. There are cases, again, in which a considerable amount of labor and skill is required to conduct a business necessarily of limited extent. In such cases a higher than common rate of profit is necessary to yield only the common rate of remuneration.

All the natural monopolies (meaning thereby those which are created by circumstances, and not by law) which produce or aggravate the disparities in the remuneration of different kinds of labor, operate similarly between different employments of capital.

> In this passage Mr. Mill points out distinctly that the movement up and down in the wages of a manager are governed by the same laws as those which regulate differences in the different rewards of labor, but yet he connects it improperly with capital. It will be seen that Mr. Mill uses the term "gross profit" on the next page in order to avoid the difficulty, which rises unconsciously in his mind, of the anomalous presence of the wages of the manager in the question of profit.

§ 3. General Tendency of Profits to an Equality.

After due allowance is made for these various causes of inequality, namely, difference in the risk or agreeableness of different employments, and natural or artificial monopolies [which give greater or less wages of superintendence], the rate of profit on capital in all employments tends to an equality. That portion of profit which is properly interest, and which forms the real remuneration for abstinence, is strictly the same at the same time and place, whatever be the employment. The rate of interest, on equally good security, does not vary according to the destination of the principal, though it does vary from time to time very much, according to the circumstances of the market.

It is far otherwise with gross profit, which, though (as will presently be seen) it does not vary much from employment to employment, varies very greatly from individual to individual, and can scarcely be in any two cases the same. It depends on the knowledge, talents, economy, and energy of the capitalist himself, or of the agents whom he employs; on the accidents of personal connection; and even on chance. Hardly any two dealers in the same trade, even if their commodities are equally good and equally cheap, carry on their business at the same expense, or turn over their capital in the same time. That equal capitals give equal profits, as a general maxim of trade, would be as false as that equal age or size gives equal bodily strength, or that equal reading or experience gives equal knowledge. The effect depends as much upon twenty other things as upon the single cause specified. On an average (whatever may be the occasional fluctuations) the various employments of capital are on such a footing as to hold out, not equal profits, but equal expectations of profit, to persons of average abilities and advantages. By equal, I mean after making compensation for any inferiority in the agreeableness or safety of an employment. If the case were not so; if there were, evidently, and to common experience, more favorable chances of pecuniary success in one business than in others, more persons would engage their capital in the business. If, on the contrary, a business is not considered thriving; if the chances of profit in it are thought to be inferior to those in other employments; capital gradually leaves it, or at least new capital is not attracted to it; and by this change in the distribution of capital between the less profitable and the more profitable employments, a sort of balance is restored.

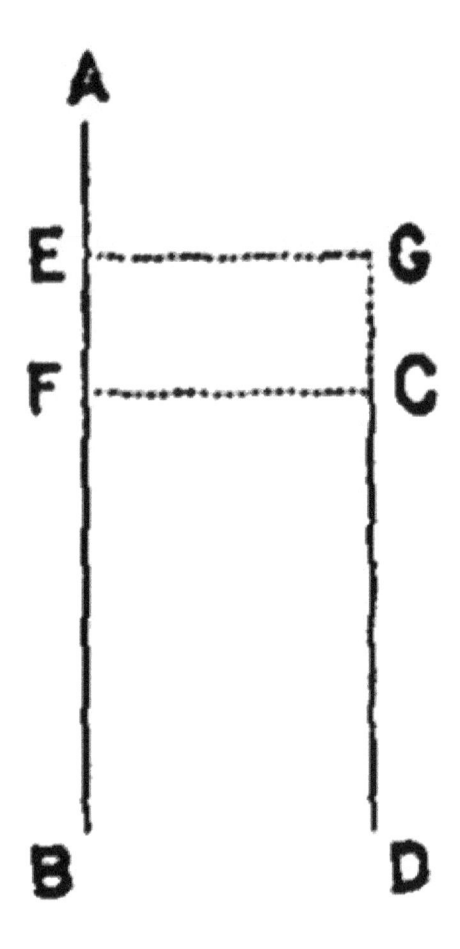

This may be easily shown by a diagram in which the capital in one employment is represented by *A B*, and which exceeds *C D*, that in another employment, by the amount of *A F*. It is not necessary that the whole of the excess, *A F* should be transferred to *C D* to make the two capitals equal, but only *A E*, which, added to *C D*, brings *C D* to an equality with *E B*.

This equalizing process, commonly described as the transfer of capital from one employment to another, is not necessarily the onerous, slow, and almost impracticable operation which it is very often represented to be. In the first place, it does not always imply the actual removal of capital already embarked in an employment. In a rapidly progressive state of capital, the adjustment often takes place by means of the new accumulations of each year, which direct themselves in preference toward the more thriving trades. Even when a real transfer of capital is necessary, it is by no means implied that any of those who are engaged in the unprofitable employment relinquish business and break up their establishments. The numerous and multifarious channels of credit through which, in commercial nations, unemployed capital diffuses itself over the field of employment, flowing over in greater abundance to the lower levels, are the means by which the equalization is accomplished. The process consists in a limitation by one class of dealers or producers and an extension by the other of that portion of their business which is carried on with borrowed capital.

> "Political economists say that capital sets toward the most profitable trades, and that it rapidly leaves the less profitable and non-paying trades. But in ordinary countries this is a slow process, and some persons, who want to have ocular demonstrations of abstract truths, have been inclined to doubt it because they could not see it. The process would be visible enough if you could only see the books of the bill-brokers and the bankers. If the iron-trade ceases to be as profitable as usual, less iron is sold; the fewer the sales the fewer the bills; and in consequence the number of iron bills [at the banks] is diminished. On the other hand, if, in consequence of a bad harvest, the corn trade becomes on a sudden profitable, immediately 'corn bills' are created in large numbers, and, if good, are discounted [at the banks]. Thus capital runs as surely and instantly where it is most wanted, and where there is most to be made of it, as water runs to find its level."[177]

In the case of an altogether declining trade, in which it is necessary that the production should be, not occasionally varied, but greatly and permanently diminished, or perhaps stopped altogether, the process of extricating the capital is, no doubt, tardy and difficult, and almost always attended with considerable loss; much of the capital fixed in machinery, buildings, permanent works, etc., being either not applicable to any other purpose, or only applicable after expensive alterations; and time being seldom given for effecting the change in the mode in which it would be effected with least loss, namely, by not replacing the fixed capital as it wears out. There is besides, in totally changing the destination of a capital, so great a sacrifice of established connection, and of acquired skill and experience, that people are always very slow in resolving upon it, and hardly ever do so until long after a change of fortune has become hopeless.

In general, then, although profits are very different to different individuals, and to the same individual in different years, there can not be much diversity at the same time and place in the average profits of different employments (other than the standing differences necessary to compensate for difference of attractiveness), except for short periods, or when some great permanent revulsion has overtaken a particular trade. It is true that, to persons with the same amount of original means, there is more chance of making a large fortune in some employments than in others. But it would be found that in those same employments bankruptcies also are more frequent, and that the chance of greater success is balanced by a greater probability of complete failure.

§ 4. The Cause of the Existence of any Profit; the Advances of Capitalists consist of Wages of Labor.

The preceding remarks have, I hope, sufficiently elucidated what is meant by the common phrase, "the ordinary rate of profit," and the sense in which, and the limitations under which, this ordinary rate has a real existence. It now remains to consider what causes determine its amount.

The cause of profit is, that labor produces more than is required for its support; the reason why capital yields a profit is, because food, clothing, materials, and tools last longer than the time which is required to produce them; so that if a capitalist supplies a party of laborers with these things, on condition of receiving all they produce, they will, in addition to reproducing their own necessaries and instruments, have a portion of their time remaining, to work for the capitalist. We thus see that profit arises, not from the incident of exchange, but from the productive power of labor; and the general profit of the country is always what the productive power of labor makes it, whether any exchange takes place or not. I proceed, in expansion of the considerations thus briefly indicated, to exhibit more minutely the mode in which the rate of profit is determined.

I assume, throughout, the state of things which, where the laborers and capitalists are separate classes, prevails, with few exceptions, universally; namely, that the capitalist advances the whole expenses, including the entire remuneration of the laborer. That he should do so is not a matter of inherent necessity; the laborer might wait until the production is complete for all that part of his wages which exceeds mere necessaries, and even for the whole, if he has funds in hand sufficient for his temporary support. But in the latter case the laborer is to that extent really a capitalist, investing capital in the concern, by supplying a portion of the funds necessary for carrying it on; and even in the former case he may be looked upon in the same light, since, contributing his labor at less than the market price, he may be regarded as lending the difference to his employer, and receiving it back with interest (on whatever principle computed) from the proceeds of the enterprise.

The capitalist, then, may be assumed to make all the advances and receive all the produce. His profit consists of the excess of the produce above the advances; his *rate* of profit is the ratio which that excess bears to the amount advanced.

> For example, if A advances 8,000 bushels of corn to laborers in return for 10,000 yards of cloth (and if one bushel of corn sells for the same sum as one yard of cloth), his profit consists of 2,000 yards of cloth. The ratio of the excess, 2,000, to 8,000, the outlay, or 25 per cent, is the *rate* of profit. It is not the ratio of 2,000 to 10,000.

But what do the advances consist of? It is, for the present, necessary to suppose that the capitalist does not pay any rent; has not to purchase the use of any appropriated natural agent. The nature of rent, however, we have not yet taken into consideration; and it will hereafter appear that no practical error, on the question we are now examining, is produced by disregarding it.

If, then, leaving rent out of the question, we inquire in what it is that the advances of the capitalist, for purposes of production, consist, we shall find that they consist of wages of labor.

A large portion of the expenditure of every capitalist consists in the direct payment of wages. What does not consist of this is composed of materials and implements, including buildings. But materials and implements are produced by labor; and as our supposed capitalist is not meant to represent a single employment, but to be a type of the productive industry of the whole country, we may suppose that he makes his own tools and raises his own materials. He does this by means of previous advances, which, again, consist wholly of wages. If we suppose him to buy the materials and tools instead of producing them, the case is not altered: he then repays to a previous producer the wages which that previous producer has paid. It is true he repays it to him with a profit; and, if he had produced the things himself, he himself must have had that profit on this part of his outlay as well as on every other part. The fact, however, remains, that in the whole process of production, beginning with the materials and tools and ending with the finished product, all the advances have consisted of nothing but wages, except that certain of the capitalists concerned have, for the sake of general convenience, had their share of profit paid to them before the operation was completed.

> This idea may be more clear, perhaps, if we imagine a large corporation, not only making woolen cloth, but owning sheep-ranches, where the raw materials are produced; the shops where all machinery is made; and who even produce on their own property all the food, clothing, shelter, and consumption of the laborers employed by them. A line of division may be passed through the returns in all these branches of the industry, separating what is wages from what is profit. Then it can be easily imagined that all the returns on one side, representing profits, go to capitalists, no matter whether they are thousands in number, or only one capitalist typifying the rest, or a single corporation acting for many small capitalists.

§ 5. The Rate of Profit depends on the Cost of Labor.

It thus appears that the two elements on which, and which alone, the gains of the capitalists depend, are, first, the magnitude of the produce, in other words, the productive power of labor; and secondly, the proportion of that produce obtained by the laborers themselves; the ratio which the remuneration of the laborers bears to the amount they produce.

We thus arrive at the conclusion of Ricardo and others, that the rate of profits depends upon wages; rising as wages fall, and falling as wages rise. In adopting, however, this doctrine, I must insist upon making a most necessary alteration in its wording. Instead of saying that profits depend on wages, let us say (what Ricardo really meant) that they depend on the *cost of labor*.

> This is an entirely different question from that concerning the rate of wages before discussed (Book II, Chap. II). That had to do with the amount of the capital which each laborer, on an average, received as real wages, and this average rate was affected by the number of competitors for labor, as compared with the existing capital, taking into account the nature of the industries in a country. An increase of population, bringing more laborers to compete for employment, will lower the average amount of real wages received by each one; and a decrease of population will bring about the reverse. The rate of wages, however, now that we are considering the matter from the point of view of the capitalist, is but one of the things to be considered affecting *cost of labor*. The former question was one as to the distribution of capital; the latter is one as to the amount by which the total production is greater than the total capital advanced. Since all capital consists of advances to labor, the present inquiry is one in regard to the quantity of advances compared with the quantity returned; that is, the relation of the total capital to the total production arising from the use of that capital. In the diagram before used (p. 179) the question is not how the contents of circle B are to be distributed, but the relative size of circle B to circle A. In order to produce circle A, it is necessary to advance what is represented by circle B.

Wages and the cost of labor; what labor brings in to the laborer and what it costs to the capitalist are ideas quite distinct, and which it is of the utmost importance to keep so. For this purpose it is essential not to designate them, as is almost always done, by the same name. Wages, in public discussions, both oral and printed, being looked upon from the same point of view of the payers, much oftener than from that of the receivers, nothing is more common than to say that wages are high or low, meaning only that the cost of labor [to the capitalist] is high or low. The reverse of this would be oftener the truth: the cost of labor is frequently at its highest where wages are lowest. This may arise from two causes. (1.) In the first place, the labor, though cheap, may be inefficient.

> The facts presented by Mr. Brassey[178] very fully illustrate this principle. Although French workmen in their ship-yards receive less wages for the same kind of work than the English workmen in English yards, yet it costs less per ton to build ships in England than in France. The same correspondence between high wages and efficient work was found to be true of railway construction in different parts of the world. With different character, varying amounts of industrial energy, varying intelligence, and endurance, different people do not have the same efficiency of labor. It is ascertained that inefficiency is, as a rule, accompanied by low wages. Even though wages paid for ordinary labor in constructing railways were in India only from nine to twelve cents a day, and in England from seventy-five to eighty-seven cents a day, yet it cost as much to build a mile of railway in India as in England. The English laborer gave a full equivalent for his higher wages. Moreover, while an English weaver tends from two to three times as many looms as his Russian competitor, the workman in the United States, it is said, will tend even more than the Englishman. In American sailing-vessels, also, a less number of sailors, relatively to the tonnage, is required than in English sailing-ships. Mr. Brassey, besides, came to the conclusion that the working power, or efficiency, of ordinary English laborers was to the French as five to three.

(2.) The other cause which renders wages and the cost of labor no real criteria of one another is the varying costliness of the articles which the laborer consumes. If these are cheap, wages, in the sense which is of importance to the laborer, may be high, and yet the cost of labor may be low; if dear, the laborer may be wretchedly off, though his labor may cost much to the capitalist. This last is the condition of a country over-peopled in relation to its land; in which, food being dear, the poorness of the laborer's real reward does not prevent labor from costing much to the purchaser, and low wages and low profits coexist. The opposite case is exemplified in the United States of America. The laborer there enjoys a greater abundance of comforts than in any other country of the world, except some of the newest colonies; but owing to the cheap price at which these comforts can be obtained (combined with the great efficiency of the labor), the cost of labor to the capitalist is considerably lower than in Europe. It must be so, since the rate of profit is higher; as indicated by the rate of interest, which is six per cent at New York when it is three or three and a quarter per cent in London.

The cost of labor, then, is, in the language of mathematics, a function of three variables: (1) the efficiency of labor; (2) the wages of labor (meaning thereby the real reward [or real wages] of the laborer); and (3) the greater or less cost[179] at which the articles composing that real reward can be produced or purchased. It is plain that the cost of labor to the capitalist must be influenced by each of these three circumstances, and by no others. These, therefore, are also the circumstances which determine the rate of profit; and it can not be in any way affected except through one or other of them.

> The efficiency of labor, in this connection, is highly important in its practical aspects, and as affecting the labor question, because as a function of cost of labor, that is, as an element affecting the quantity of things advanced to the laborers in comparison with the quantity of things returned to the employer, it includes the whole influence of machinery, labor-saving devices, and the results of invention. The quantity of produce depends, for a given advance, on the kind of machinery, the speed with which it is run, and on the general state of the arts and industrial inventions. The extent to which the productive capacity of a single laborer has been increased in the United States has been almost incredible. Instead of weaving cloth by hand, as was done a hundred years ago, "one operative in Lowell, working one year, can produce the cotton fabric needed for the year's supply of 1,500 to 1,800 Chinese." Moreover, there is no question as to the fact that no nation in the world compares with ours in the power to invent, construct, and manage the most ingenious and complicated machinery. The inventive faculty belongs to every class in our country; and, in studying cost of labor, it must be well borne in mind that the efficiency of American labor, particularly as combined with mechanical appliances, is one of the

great causes of our enormous production. The result of this, for instance, has been that, without lowering profits, although the price of cloth has been greatly reduced, employers have been able to raise the wages of operatives, and shorten their hours of labor, because machinery has so vastly increased the production for a given outlay. As one of a few facts showing this tendency in the last fifty years, note the following table, taken from the books of the Namquit cotton-mill in Bristol, Rhode Island:

Kind Of Labor.	1841.	1884.
Card-room help, per week	$3.28	$5.40
Card-strippers, per week	4.98	6.00
Weavers, per week	4.75	6.00
Carding-room overseer, per week	7.00	13.50

The hours per week have decreased in the same time from 84 to 66, while the product of the mill in pounds has increased 25 per cent. It may be unnecessary, perhaps, to say that these figures represent the current wages in other mills at the same periods; and that these facts can be sustained by the records of other mills.

In its economic effect we must also consider, under efficiency, the whole question of natural advantages of soil, climate, and natural resources. Laborers of the same skill, paid the same real wages, of the same cost, will produce a vastly greater amount of wheat in Dakota than in Vermont or England. This is the chief reason why profits are so high in the United States. In many industries we have very marked natural advantages, which permits a high reward to labor, and yet yields a high profit to the capitalist. This applies not merely to agriculture, but to all the extractive industries, such as the production of petroleum, wood, copper, etc.

> In short, the whole matter of ease and difficulty of production, of high or low cost of production, taking it in the sense of great or little sacrifice (compare carefully Book III, Chap. II, § 4), comes in under the element of efficiency, in cost of labor. The reader can not be too strongly urged to connect different parts of the economic system together. And the questions of Cost of Labor and Cost of Production are of paramount importance to a proper understanding of political economy.

If labor generally became more efficient, without being more highly rewarded; if, without its becoming less efficient, its remuneration fell, no increase taking place in the cost of the articles composing that remuneration; or if those articles became less costly, without the laborers obtaining more of them; in any one of these three cases, profits would rise. If, on the contrary, labor became less efficient (as it might do from diminished bodily vigor in the people, destruction of fixed capital, or deteriorated education); or if the laborer obtained a higher remuneration, without any increased cheapness in the things composing it; or if, without his obtaining more, that which he did obtain became more costly; profits, in all these cases, would suffer a diminution. And there is no other combination of circumstances in which the general rate of profit of a country, in all employments indifferently, can either fall or rise.

> The connection of profit with the three constituents of cost of labor may probably be better seen by aid of the following illustration; it being premised that as yet money is not used, and that the laborers are paid in the articles which their money wages would have bought had money been used. For simplicity we will suppose that all articles of the laborer's consumption are represented by corn. Imagine a large woolen-mill employing 500 men, and paying them in corn; and suppose that one yard of woolen cloth exchanges for one bushel of corn in the open market. In the beginning, with a given condition of efficiency, suppose that each man produces on an average 1,200 yards of cloth, for which he is paid 1,000 bushels of corn:

500 men, each producing 1,200 yards, give a total product of 600,000 yards.
500 men, each paid 1,000 bushels, cause an outlay of 500,000 yards.
Profit: 100,000 yards.

(1.) Now suppose a change increasing the efficiency of labor to such an extent that each laborer produces 1,300 instead of 1,200 yards, then the account will stand, if the other elements remain unchanged:

500 men, each producing 1,300 yards, give a total product of 650,000 yards.
500 men, each paid 1,000 bushels, cause an outlay of 500,000 yards.
Profit: 150,000 yards.

(2.) If efficiency and the cost of producing food remain the same as at first, suppose a change to occur which raises the quantity of corn each laborer receives from 1,000 to 1,100, or, as it is called, increases his real wages—then the account will be:

500 men, each producing 1,200 yards, give a total product of 600,000 yards.
500 men, each paid 1,100 bushels, cause an outlay of 550,000 yards.
Profit: 50,000 yards.

(3.) If efficiency and real wages remain the same, suppose such an increase in the cost to the employers of obtaining corn that they are obliged to give one and one tenth yard of their goods for one bushel of corn (1,000 bushels of corn costing them 1,100 yards of cloth), then the statement will read:

500 men, each producing 1,200 yards, give a total product of 600,000 yards.
500 men, each paid 1,000 bushels, cause an outlay of 550,000 yards.
Profit: 50,000 yards.

Chapter VI. Of Rent.

§ 1. Rent the Effect of a Natural Monopoly.

The requisites of production being labor, capital, and natural agents, the only person, besides the laborer and the capitalist, whose consent is necessary to production, and who can claim a share of the produce as the price of that consent, is the person who, by the arrangements of society, possesses exclusive power over some natural agent. The land is the principal of the natural agents which are capable of being appropriated, and the consideration paid for its use is called rent. Landed proprietors are the only class, of any numbers or importance, who have a claim to a share in the distribution of the produce, through their ownership of something which neither they nor any one else have produced. If there be any other cases of a similar nature, they will be easily understood, when the nature and laws of rent are comprehended.

It is at once evident that rent is the effect of a monopoly. The reason why land-owners are able to require rent for their land is, that it is a commodity which many want, and which no one can obtain but from them. If all the land of the country belonged to one person, he could fix the rent at his pleasure. This case, however, is nowhere known to exist; and the only remaining supposition is that of free competition; the land-owners being supposed to be, as in fact they are, too numerous to combine.

> The ratio of the land to the cultivators shows the limited quantity of land. It is very desirable to keep the connection of one part of the subject with another wherever possible. "Agricultural rent, as it actually exists," says Mr. Cairnes,[180] truly, "is not a consequence of the *monopoly* of the soil, but of its diminishing productiveness." The doctrine of rent depends upon the law of diminishing returns; and it is only by the pressure of population upon land that the lessened productiveness of land, whether because of poorer qualities or poorer situations, is made apparent. Or, to take things in their natural sequence, an increase of population necessitates more food; and this implies a resort to more expensive methods, or poorer soils, so soon as land is pushed to the extent that it will not yield an increased crop for the same application of

labor and capital as formerly. Different qualities of land, then, being in cultivation at the same time, the better qualities must, of course, yield a greater return than the poorer, and the conditions then exist under which land pays rent. Those, therefore, who admit the law of diminishing returns are inevitably led to the doctrine of rent.

§ 2. No Land can pay Rent except Land of such Quality or Situation as exists in less Quantity than the Demand.

A thing which is limited in quantity, even though its possessors do not act in concert, is still a monopolized article. But even when monopolized, a thing which is the gift of nature, and requires no labor or outlay as the condition of its existence, will, if there be competition among the holders of it, command a price only if it exist in less quantity than the demand.

If the whole land of a country were required for cultivation, all of it might yield a rent. But in no country of any extent do the wants of the population require that all the land, which is capable of cultivation, should be cultivated. The food and other agricultural produce which the people need, and which they are willing and able to pay for at a price which remunerates the grower, may always be obtained without cultivating all the land; sometimes without cultivating more than a small part of it; the more fertile lands, or those in the more convenient situations, being of course preferred. There is always, therefore, some land which can not, in existing circumstances, pay any rent; and no land ever pays rent unless, in point of fertility or situation, it belongs to those superior kinds which exist in less quantity than the demand—which can not be made to yield all the produce required for the community, unless on terms still less advantageous than the resort to less favored soils. (1.) The worst land which can be cultivated as a means of subsistence is that which will just replace the seed and the food of the laborers employed on it, together with what Dr. Chalmers calls their secondaries; that is, the laborers required for supplying them with tools, and with the remaining necessaries of life. Whether any given land is capable of doing more than this is not a question of political economy, but of physical fact. The supposition leaves nothing for profits, nor anything for the laborers except necessaries: the land, therefore, can only be cultivated by the laborers themselves, or else at a pecuniary loss; and, *a fortiori*, can not in any contingency afford a rent. (2.) The worst land which can be cultivated as an investment for capital is that which, after replacing the seed, not only feeds the agricultural laborers and their secondaries, but affords them the current rate of wages, which may extend to much more than mere necessaries, and leaves, for those who have advanced the wages of these two classes of laborers, a surplus equal to the profit they could have expected from any other employment of their capital. (3.) Whether any given land can do more than this is not merely a physical question, but depends partly on the market value of agricultural produce. What the land can do for the laborers and for the capitalist, beyond feeding all whom it directly or indirectly employs, of course depends upon what the remainder of the produce can be sold for. The higher the market value of produce, the lower are the soils to which cultivation can descend, consistently with affording to the capital employed the ordinary rate of profit.

As, however, differences of fertility slide into one another by insensible gradations; and differences of accessibility, that is, of distance from markets do the same; and since there is land so barren that it could not pay for its cultivation at any price; it is evident that, whatever the price may be, there must in any extensive region be some land which at that price will just pay the wages of the cultivators, and yield to the capital employed the ordinary profit, and no more. Until, therefore, the price rises higher, or until some improvement raises that particular land to a higher place in the scale of fertility, it can not pay any rent. It is evident, however, that the community needs the produce of this quality of land; since, if the lands more fertile or better situated than it could have sufficed to supply the wants of society, the price would not have risen so high as to render its cultivation profitable. This land, therefore, will be cultivated; and we may lay it down as a principle that, so long as any of the land of a country which is fit for cultivation, and not withheld from it by legal or other factitious obstacles, is not cultivated, the worst land in actual cultivation (in point of fertility and situation together) pays no rent.

§ 3. The Rent of Land is the Excess of its Return above the Return to the worst Land in Cultivation.

If, then, of the land in cultivation, the part which yields least return to the labor and capital employed on it gives only the ordinary profit of capital, without leaving anything for rent, a standard [i.e., the "margin of cultivation"] is afforded for estimating the amount of rent which will be yielded by all other land. Any land yields just as much more than the ordinary profits of stock as it yields more than what is returned by the worst land in cultivation. The surplus is what the farmer can afford to pay as rent to the landlord; and since, if he did not so pay it, he would receive more than the ordinary rate of profit, the competition of other capitalists, that competition which equalizes the profits of different capitals, will enable the landlord to appropriate it. The rent, therefore, which any land will yield, is the excess of its produce, beyond what would be returned to the same capital if employed on the worst land in cultivation.

It has been denied that there can be any land in cultivation which pays no rent, because landlords (it is contended) would not allow their land to be occupied without payment. Inferior land, however, does not usually occupy, without interruption, many square miles of ground; it is dispersed here and there, with patches of better land intermixed, and the same person who rents the better land obtains along with it the inferior soils which alternate with it. He pays a rent, nominally for the whole farm, but calculated on the produce of those parts alone (however small a portion of the whole) which are capable of returning more than the common rate of profit. It is thus scientifically true that the remaining parts pay no rent.

> This point seems to need some illustration. Suppose that all the lands in a community are of five different grades of productiveness. When the price of agricultural produce was such that grades one, two, and three all came into cultivation, lands of poorer quality would not be cultivated. When a man rents a farm, he always gets land of varying degrees of fertility within its limits. Now, in determining what he ought to pay as rent, the farmer will agree to give that which will still leave him a profit on his working capital; if in his fields he finds land which would not enter into the question of rental, because it did not yield more than the profit on working it, after he rented the farm he would find it to his interest to cultivate it, simply because it yielded him a profit, and because he was not obliged to pay rent upon it; if required to pay rent for it, he would lose the ordinary rate of profit, would have no reason for cultivating it, of course, and would throw it out of cultivation. Moreover, suppose that lands down to grade three paid rent when A took the farm; now, if the price of produce rises slightly, grade four may pay something, but possibly not enough to warrant any rent going to a landlord. A will put capital on it for this return, but certainly not until the price warrants it; that is, not until the price will return him at least the cost of working the land, *plus* the profit on his outlay. But the community needed this land, or the price would not

have gone up to the point which makes possible its cultivation even for a profit, without rent. There must always be somewhere some land affected in just this way.

§ 4. —Or to the Capital employed in the least advantageous Circumstances.

Let us, however, suppose that there were a validity in this objection, which can by no means be conceded to it; that, when the demand of the community had forced up food to such a price as would remunerate the expense of producing it from a certain quality of soil, it happened nevertheless that all the soil of that quality was withheld from cultivation, the increase of produce, which the wants of society required, would for the time be obtained wholly (as it always is partially), not by an extension of cultivation, but by an increased application of labor and capital to land already cultivated.

Now we have already seen that this increased application of capital, other things being unaltered, is always attended with a smaller proportional return. The rise of price enables measures to be taken for increasing the produce, which could not have been taken with profit at the previous price. The farmer uses more expensive manures, or manures land which he formerly left to nature; or procures lime or marl from a distance, as a dressing for the soil; or pulverizes or weeds it more thoroughly; or drains, irrigates, or subsoils portions of it, which at former prices would not have paid the cost of the operation; and so forth. The farmer or improver will only consider whether the outlay he makes for the purpose will be returned to him with the ordinary profit, and not whether any surplus will remain for rent. Even, therefore, if it were the fact that there is never any *land* taken into cultivation, for which rent, and that too of an amount worth taking into consideration, was not paid, it would be true, nevertheless, that there is always some *agricultural capital* which pays no rent, because it returns nothing beyond the ordinary rate of profit: this capital being the portion of capital last applied—that to which the last addition to the produce was due; or (to express the essentials of the case in one phrase) that which is applied in the least favorable circumstances. But the same amount of demand and the same price, which enable this least productive portion of capital barely to replace itself with the ordinary profit, enable every other portion to yield a surplus proportioned to the advantage it possesses. And this surplus it is which competition enables the landlord to appropriate.

If land were all occupied, and of only one grade, the first installment of labor and capital produced, we will say, twenty bushels of wheat; when the price of wheat rose, and it became profitable to resort to greater expense on the soil, a second installment of the same amount of labor and capital when applied, however, only yielded fifteen bushels more; a third, ten bushels more; and a fourth, five bushels more. The soil now gives fifty bushels only under the highest pressure. But, if it was profitable to invest the same installment of labor and capital simply for the five bushels that at first had received a return of twenty bushels, the price must have gone up so that five bushels should sell for as much as the twenty did formerly; so, *mutatis mutandis*, of installments second and third. So that if the demand is such as to require all of the fifty bushels, the agricultural capital which produced the five bushels will be the standard according to which the rent of the capital, which grew twenty, fifteen, and ten bushels respectively, is measured. The principle is exactly the same as if equal installments of capital and labor were invested on four different grades of land returning twenty, fifteen, ten, and five bushels for each installment. Or, as if in the table on page 240, A, B, C, and D each represented different installments of the same amount of labor and capital put upon the same spot of ground, instead of being, as there, put upon different grades of land.

The rent of all land is measured by the excess of the return to the whole capital employed on it above what is necessary to replace the capital with the ordinary rate of profit, or, in other words, above what the same capital would yield if it were all employed in as disadvantageous circumstances as the least productive portion of it: whether that least productive portion of capital is rendered so by being employed on the worst soil, or by being expended in extorting more produce from land which already yielded as much as it could be made to part with on easier terms.

It will be true that the farmer requires the ordinary rate of profit on the whole of his capital; that whatever it returns to him beyond this he is obliged to pay to the landlord, but will not consent to pay more; that there is a portion of capital applied to agriculture in such circumstances of productiveness as to yield only the ordinary profits; and that the difference between the produce of this and of any other capital of similar amount is the measure of the tribute which that other capital can and will pay, under the name of rent, to the landlord. This constitutes a law of rent, as near the truth as such a law can possibly be; though of course modified or disturbed, in individual cases, by pending contracts, individual miscalculations, the influence of habit, and even the particular feelings and dispositions of the persons concerned.

>The law of rent, in the economic sense, operates in the United States as truly as elsewhere, although there is no separate class of landlords here. With us, almost all land is owned by the cultivator; so that two functions, those of the landlord and farmer, are both united in one person. Although one payment is made, it is still just as distinctly made up of two parts, one of which is a payment to the owner for the superior quality of his soil, and the other a payment (to the same person, if the owner is the cultivator) of profit on the farmer's working capital. Land which in the United States will only return enough to pay a profit on this capital can not pay any rent. And land which can pay more than a profit on this working capital, returns that excess as rent, even if the farmer is also the owner and landlord. The principle which regulates the amount of that excess—which is the essential point—is the principle which determines the amount of economic rent, and it holds true in the United States or Finland, provided only that different grades of land are called into cultivation. The governing principle is the same, no matter whether a payment is made to one man as profit and to another as rent, or whether the two payments are made to the same man in two capacities. It has been urged that the law of rent does not hold in the United States, because "the price of grain and other agricultural produce has not risen in proportion to the increase of our numbers, as it ought to have done if Ricardo's theory were true, but has fallen, since 1830, though since that time our population has been more than tripled."[181] This overlooks the fact that we have not even yet taken up all our best agricultural lands, so that for some products the law of diminishing productiveness has not yet shown itself. The reason is,

that the extension of our railway system has only of late years brought the really good grain-lands into cultivation. The fact that there has been no rise in agricultural products is due to the enormous extent of marvelously fertile grain-lands in the West, and to the cheapness of transportation from those districts to the seaboard.

For a general understanding of the law of rent the following table will show how, under constant increase of population (represented by four different advances of population, in the first column), first the best and then the poorer lands are brought into cultivation. We will suppose (1) that the most fertile land, A, at first pays no rent; then (2), when more food is wanted than land A can supply, it will be profitable to till land B, but which, as yet, pays no rent. But if eighteen bushels are a sufficient return to a given amount of labor and capital, then when an equal amount of labor and capital engaged on A returns twenty-four bushels, six of that are beyond the ordinary profit, and form the rent on land A, and so on; C will next be the line of comparison, and then D; as the poorer soils are cultivated, the rent of A increases:

Population Increase.	A		B		C		D	
	24 bushels		18 bushels		12 bushels		6 bushels	
	Total product	Rent in Bushels	Total product	Rent in Bushels	Total product	Rent in Bushels	Total product	Rent in Bushels
I.	24	0	..	..	..	..	..	..
II.	24	6	18	0	..	..	..	..
III.	24	12	18	6	12	0	..	..

| IV. | 24 | 18 | 18 | 12 | 12 | 6 | 6 | 0 |

§ 5. Opposing Views of the Law of Rent.

Under the name of rent, many payments are commonly included, which are not a remuneration for the original powers of the land itself, but for capital expended on it. The buildings are as distinct a thing from the farm as the stock or the timber on it; and what is paid for them can no more be called rent of land than a payment for cattle would be, if it were the custom that the landlord should stock the farm for the tenant. The buildings, like the cattle, are not land, but capital, regularly consumed and reproduced; and all payments made in consideration for them are properly interest.

But with regard to capital actually sunk in improvements, and not requiring periodical renewal, but spent once for all in giving the land a permanent increase of productiveness, it appears to me that the return made to such capital loses altogether the character of profits, and is governed by the principles of rent. It is true that a landlord will not expend capital in improving his estate unless he expects from the improvement an increase of income surpassing the interest of his outlay. Prospectively, this increase of income may be regarded as profit; but, when the expense has been incurred and the improvement made, the rent of the improved land is governed by the same rules as that of the unimproved.

> Mr. Carey (as well as Bastiat) has declared that there is a law of increasing returns from land. He points out that everything now existing could be reproduced to-day at a less cost than that involved in its original production, owing to our advance in skill, knowledge, and all the arts of production; that, for example, it costs less to make an axe now than it did five hundred years ago; so also with a farm, since a farm of a given amount of productiveness can be brought into cultivation at less cost to-day than that originally spent upon it. The gain of society has, we all admit, been such that we produce almost everything at a less cost now than long ago; but to class a farm and an axe together overlooks, in the most remarkable way, the

> fact that land can not be created by labor and capital, while axes can, and that too indefinitely. Nor can the *produce* from the land be increased indefinitely at a diminishing cost. This is sometimes denied by the appeal to facts: "It can be abundantly proved that, if we take any two periods sufficiently distant to afford a fair test, whether fifty or one hundred or five hundred years, the production of the land relatively to the labor employed upon it has progressively become greater and greater."[182] But this does not prove that an existing tendency to diminishing returns has not been more than offset by the progress of the arts and improvements. "The advance of a ship against wind and tide is [no] proof that there is no wind and tide."

In a work entitled "The Past, the Present, and the Future," Mr. Carey takes [a] ground of objection to the Ricardo theory of rent, namely, that in point of historical fact the lands first brought under cultivation are not the most fertile, but the barren lands. "We find the settler invariably occupying the high and thin lands requiring little clearing and no drainage. With the growth of population and wealth, other soils yielding a larger return to labor are always brought into activity, with a constantly increasing return to the labor expended upon them."

In whatever order the lands come into cultivation, those which when cultivated yield the least return, in proportion to the labor required for their culture, will always regulate the price of agricultural produce; and all other lands will pay a rent simply equivalent to the excess of their produce over this minimum. Whatever unguarded expressions may have been occasionally used in describing the law of rent, these two propositions are all that was ever intended by it. If, indeed, Mr. Carey could show that the return to labor from the land, agricultural skill and science being supposed the same, is not a diminishing return, he would overthrow a principle much more fundamental than any law of rent. But in this he has wholly failed.

> Another objection taken against the law of diminishing returns, and so against the law of rent, is that the potential increase of food, e.g., of a grain of wheat, is far greater than that of man.[183] No one disputes the fact that one grain of wheat can reproduce itself more times than man, and that too in a geometric increase; but not without land. A grain of wheat needs land in

> which it can multiply itself, and this necessary element of its increase is limited; and it is the very thing which limits the multiplication of the grains of wheat. On the same piece of land, one can not get more than what comes from one act of reproduction in the grain. If one grain produces 100 of its kind, doubling the capital will not repeatedly cause a geometric increase in the ratio of reproduction of each grain on this same land, so that one grain, by one process, produces of its kind 200, 400, 800, or 1,600, because you can not multiply the land in any such ratio as would accompany this potential reduplication of the grain. This objection would not seem worth answering, were it not that it furnishes some difficulty to really honest inquirers.

Others, again, allege as an objection against Ricardo, that if all land were of equal fertility it might still yield a rent. But Ricardo says precisely the same. It is also distinctly a portion of Ricardo's doctrine that, even apart from differences of situation, the land of a country supposed to be of uniform fertility would, all of it, on a certain supposition, pay rent, namely, if the demand of the community required that it should all be cultivated, and cultivated beyond the point at which a further application of capital begins to be attended with a smaller proportional return.

> This is simply the question, before discussed, whether, if only one class of land were cultivated, some agricultural capital would pay rent or not. It all depends on the fact whether population—and so the demand for food—has increased to the point where it calls out a recognition of the diminishing productiveness of the soil. In that case different capitals would be invested, so that there would be different returns to the same amount of capital; and the prior or more advantageous investments of capital on the land would yield more than the ordinary rate of profit, which could be claimed as rent.
>
> A. L. Perry[184] admits the law of diminishing returns, but holds that, "as land is capital, and as every form of capital may be loaned or rented, and thus become fruitful in the hands of another, the rent of land does not differ essentially in its nature from the rent of

buildings in cities, or from the interest of money." Henry George admits Ricardo's law of rent to its full extent, but very curiously says: "Irrespective of the increase of population, the effect of improvements in methods of production and exchange is to increase rent.... The effect of labor-saving improvements will be to increase the production of wealth. Now, for the production of wealth, two things are required, labor and land. Therefore, the effect of labor-saving improvements will be to *extend the demand for land*, and, wherever the limit of the quality of land in use is reached, to bring into cultivation lands of less natural productiveness, or to extend cultivation on the same lands to a point of lower natural productiveness. And thus, while the primary effect of labor-saving improvements is to increase the power of labor, the secondary effect is to extend cultivation, and, where this lowers the margin of cultivation, to increase rent."[185] Francis Bowen[186] rejects Ricardo's law, and says, "Rent depends, not on the increase, but on the distribution, of the population"—asserting that the existence of large cities and towns determines the amount of rent paid by neighboring land.[187]

§ 6. Rent does not enter into the Cost of Production of Agricultural Produce.

Rent does not really form any part of the expenses of [agricultural] production, or of the advances of the capitalist. The grounds on which this assertion was made are now apparent. It is true that all tenant-farmers, and many other classes of producers, pay rent. But we have now seen that whoever cultivates land, paying a rent for it, gets in return for his rent an instrument of superior power to other instruments of the same kind for which no rent is paid. The superiority of the instrument is in exact proportion to the rent paid for it. If a few persons had steam-engines of superior power to all others in existence, but limited by physical laws to a number short of the demand, the rent which a manufacturer would be willing to pay for one of these steam-engines could not be looked upon as an addition to his outlay, because by the use of it he would save in his other expenses the equivalent of what it cost him: without it he could not do the same quantity of work, unless at an additional expense equal to the rent. The same thing is true of land. The real expenses of production are those incurred on the worst land, or by the capital employed in the least favorable circumstances. This land or capital pays, as we have seen, no rent, but the expenses to which it is subject cause all other land or agricultural capital to be subjected to an equivalent expense in the form of rent. Whoever does pay rent gets back its full value in extra advantages, and the rent which he pays does not place him in a worse position than, but only in the same position as, his fellow-producer who pays no rent, but whose instrument is one of inferior efficiency.

> Soils are of every grade: some, which if cultivated, might replace the capital, but give no profit; some give a slight but not an ordinary profit; some, the ordinary profit. That is, "there is a point up to which it is profitable to cultivate, and beyond which it is not profitable to cultivate. The price of corn will not, for any long time, remain at a higher rate than is sufficient to cover with ordinary profit the cost of that portion of the general crop which is raised at greatest expense."[188] For similar reasons the price will not remain at a lower rate. If, then, the cost of production of grain is determined by that land which replaces the capital, yields only the ordinary profit, and pays no rent, rent forms no part of this cost, since that land does not and can not pay any rent. McLeod,[189] however, says it is not the cost of production which regulates the value of agricultural produce, but the value which regulates the cost.

Book III. Exchange.

Chapter I. Of Value.

§ 1. Definitions of Value in Use, Exchange Value, and Price.

It is evident that, of the two great departments of Political Economy, the production of wealth and its distribution, the consideration of Value has to do with the latter alone; and with that only so far as competition, and not usage or custom, is the distributing agency.

The use of a thing, in political economy, means its capacity to satisfy a desire, or serve a purpose. Diamonds have this capacity in a high degree, and, unless they had it, would not bear any price. Value in use, or, as Mr. De Quincey calls it, *teleologic* value, is the extreme limit of value in exchange. The exchange value of a thing may fall short, to any amount, of its value in use; but that it can ever exceed the value in use implies a contradiction; it supposes that persons will give, to possess a thing, more than the utmost value which they themselves put upon it, as a means of gratifying their inclinations.

The word Value, when used without adjunct, always means, in political economy, value in exchange.

Exchange value requires to be distinguished from Price. Writers have employed Price to express the value of a thing in relation to money—the quantity of money for which it will exchange. By the price of a thing, therefore, we shall henceforth understand its value in money; by the value, or exchange value of a thing, its general power of purchasing; the command which its possession gives over purchasable commodities in general. What is meant by command over commodities in general? The same thing exchanges for a greater quantity of some commodities, and for a very small quantity of others. A coat may exchange for less bread this year than last, if the harvest has been bad, but for more glass or iron, if a tax has been taken off those commodities, or an improvement made in their manufacture. Has the value of the coat, under these circumstances, fallen or risen? It is impossible to say: all that can be said is, that it has fallen in relation to one thing, and risen in respect to another. Suppose, for example, that an invention has been made in machinery, by which broadcloth could be woven at half the former cost. The effect of this would be to lower the value of a coat, and, if lowered by this cause, it would be lowered not in relation to bread only or to glass only, but to all purchasable things, except such as happened to be affected at the very time by a similar depressing cause. Those [changes] which originate in the commodities with which we compare it affect its value in relation to those commodities; but those which originate in itself affect its value in relation to all commodities.

There is such a thing as a general rise of prices. All commodities may rise in their money price. But there can not be a general rise of values. It is a contradiction in terms. A can only rise in value by exchanging for a greater quantity of B and C; in which case these must exchange for a smaller quantity of A. All things can not rise relatively to one another. If one half of the commodities in the market rise in exchange value, the very terms imply a fall of the other half; and, reciprocally, the fall implies a rise. Things which are exchanged for one another can no more all fall, or all rise, than a dozen runners can each outrun all the rest, or a hundred trees all overtop one another. A general rise or a general fall of prices is merely tantamount to an alteration in the value of money, and is a matter of complete indifference, save in so far as it affects existing contracts for receiving and paying fixed pecuniary amounts.

Before commencing the inquiry into the laws of value and price, I have one further observation to make. I must give warning, once for all, that the cases I contemplate are those in which values and prices are determined by competition alone. In so far only as they are thus determined, can they be reduced to any assignable law. The buyers must be supposed as studious to buy cheap as the sellers to sell dear.

> The reader is advised to study the definitions of value given by other writers. Cairnes[190] defines value as "the ratio in which commodities in open market are exchanged against each other." F. A. Walker[191] holds that "value is the power which an article confers upon its possessor, irrespective of legal authority or personal sentiments, of commanding, in exchange for itself, the labor, or the products of the labor, of others." Carey[192] says, "Value is the measure of the resistance to be overcome in obtaining those commodities or things required for our purposes—of the power of nature over man." Value is thus, with him, the antithesis of wealth, which is (according to Carey) the power of man over nature. In this school, value is the service rendered by any one who supplies the article for the use of another. This is also Bastiat's idea,[193] "*le rapport de deux services échangés.*" Following Bastiat, A. L. Perry[194] defines value as "always and everywhere the relation of

mutual purchase established between two services by their exchange." Roscher[195] explains exchange value as "the quality which makes them exchangeable against other goods." He also makes a distinction between utility and value in use: "Utility is a quality of things themselves, in relation, it is true, to human wants. Value in use is a quality imputed to them, the result of man's thought, or his view of them. Thus, for instance, in a beleaguered city, the stores of food do not increase in utility, but their value in use does." Levasseur[196] regards value as "the relation resulting from exchange"—*le rapport resultant de l'échange.* Cherbuliez[197] asserts that "the value of a product or of a service can be expressed only as the products or services which it obtains in exchange.... If I exchange the thing A against B, A is the value of B, B is the value of A." Jevons[198] defines value as "proportion in exchange."

§ 2. Conditions of Value: Utility, Difficulty of Attainment, and Transferableness.

That a thing may have any value in exchange, two conditions are necessary. 1. It must be of some use; that is (as already explained), it must conduce to some purpose, satisfy some desire. No one will pay a price, or part with anything which serves some of his purposes, to obtain a thing which serves none of them. 2. But, secondly, the thing must not only have some utility, there must also be some difficulty in its attainment.

The question is one as to the conditions essential to the existence of any value. Very justly Cairnes[199] adds also a third condition, "the possibility of transferring the possession of the articles which are the subject of the exchange." For instance, a cargo of wheat at the bottom of the sea has value in use and difficulty of attainment, but it is not transferable. Jevons (following J. B. Say) maintains that "value depends entirely on utility." If utility means the power to satisfy a desire, things which merely have utility and no difficulty of attainment could have no exchange value.[200] F. A. Walker[201] believes that "value depends wholly on the relation between demand and supply." Carey[202] holds

- 214 -

that value depends merely on the cost of reproduction of the given article. Roscher[203] finds that exchange value is "based on a combination of value in use with cost value." Cherbuliez[204] calls the conditions of value two, "the ability to give satisfaction, and inability of attainment without effort. The first element is subjective; it is determined wholly by the needs or desires of the parties to the exchange. The second is objective; it depends upon material considerations, which are the conditions of the existence of the thing, and upon which the needs of the persons exchanging have no influence whatever." It is, as usual, one of Cherbuliez's clear expositions. A. L. Perry[205] states that, "while value always takes its rise in the *desires* of men, it is never realized except through the *efforts* of men, and through these efforts as mutually exchanged."

The difficulty of attainment which determines value is not always the same kind of difficulty: (1.) It sometimes consists in an absolute limitation of the supply. There are things of which it is physically impossible to increase the quantity beyond certain narrow limits. Such are those wines which can be grown only in peculiar circumstances of soil, climate, and exposure. Such also are ancient sculptures; pictures by the old masters; rare books or coins, or other articles of antiquarian curiosity. Among such may also be reckoned houses and building-ground, in a town of definite extent.

De Quincey[206] has presented some ingenious diagrams to represent the operations of the two constituents of value in each of the three following cases: U represents the power of the article to satisfy some desire, and D difficulty of attainment. In the first case, exchange value is not hindered by D from going up to any height, and so it rises and falls entirely according to the force of U. D being practically infinite, the horizontal line, exchange value, is not kept down by D, but it rises just as far as U, the desires of purchasers, may carry it.

1.

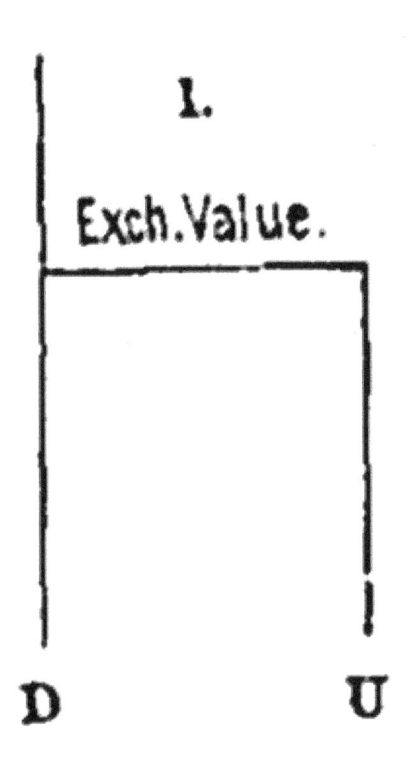

Exch.Value.

D   U

(2.) But there is another category (embracing the majority of all things that are bought and sold), in which the obstacle to attainment consists only in the labor and expense requisite to produce the commodity. Without a certain labor and expense it can not be had; but, when any one is willing to incur these, there needs be no limit to the multiplication of the product. If there were laborers enough and machinery enough, cottons, woolens, or linens might be produced by thousands of yards for every single yard now manufactured.

> In case (2) the horizontal line, representing exchange value, follows the force of D entirely. The utility of the article is very great, but the value is only limited by the difficulty of obtaining it. So far as U is concerned, exchange value can go up a great distance, but will go no higher than the point where the article can be obtained. The dotted lines underneath the horizontal

line indicate that the exchange value of articles in this class tend to fall in value.

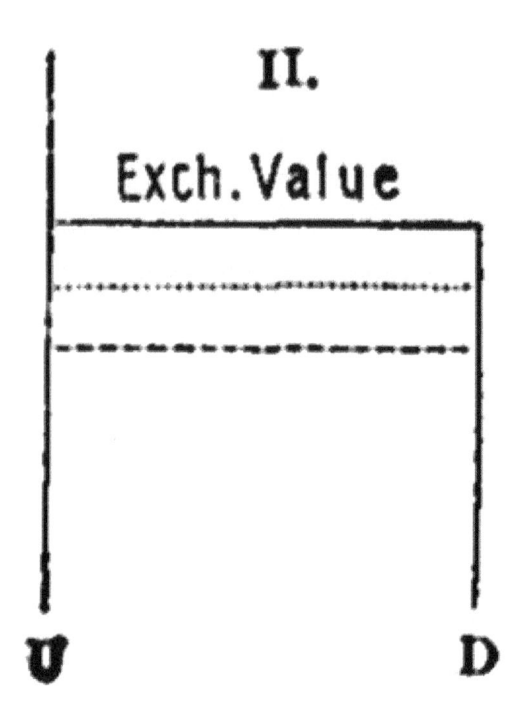

II.

Exch. Value

U   D

(3.) There is a third case, intermediate between the two preceding, and rather more complex, which I shall at present merely indicate, but the importance of which in political economy is extremely great. There are commodities which can be multiplied to an indefinite extent by labor and expenditure, but not by a fixed amount of labor and expenditure. Only a limited quantity can be produced at a given cost; if more is wanted, it must be produced at a greater cost. To this class, as has been often repeated, agricultural produce belongs, and generally all the rude produce of the earth; and this peculiarity is a source of very important consequences; one of which is the necessity of a limit to population; and another, the payment of rent.

In case (3) articles like agricultural produce have a very great power to satisfy desires, and if scarce would have a high value. So far as U is concerned, here also, as in case (2), exchange value might mount upward to almost any height, but it can go no higher than D permits. In commodities of this class, affected by the law of diminishing returns, the tendency is for D to increase, and so for exchange value to rise, as indicated by the dotted lines above that of the exchange value.

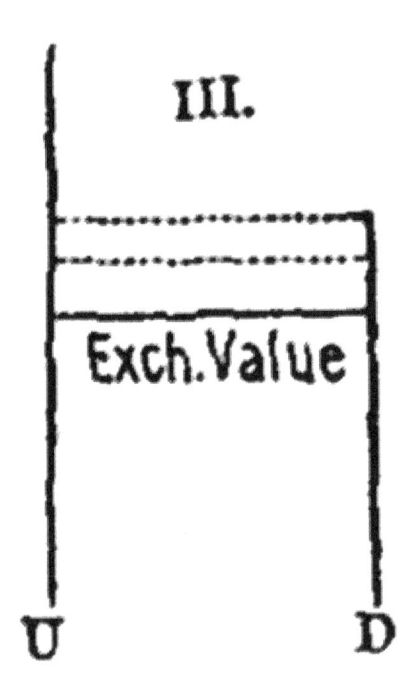

III.

Exch. Value

U   D

§ 3. Commodities limited in Quantity by the law of Demand and Supply: General working of this Law.

These being the three classes, in one or other of which all things that are bought and sold must take their place, we shall consider them in their order. And first, of things absolutely limited in quantity, such as ancient sculptures or pictures.

Of such things it is commonly said that their value depends on their scarcity; others say that the value depends on the demand and supply. But this statement requires much explanation. The supply of a commodity is an intelligible expression: it means the quantity offered for sale; the quantity that is to be had, at a given time and place, by those who wish to purchase it. But what is meant by the demand? Not the mere desire for the commodity. A beggar may desire a diamond; but his desire, however great, will have no influence on the price. Writers have therefore given a more limited sense to demand, and have defined it, the wish to possess, combined with the power of purchasing.[207] To distinguish demand in this technical sense from the demand which is synonymous with desire, they call the former *effectual* demand.

> General supply consists in the commodities offered in exchange for other commodities; general demand likewise, if no money exists, consists in the commodities offered as purchasing power in exchange for other commodities. That is, one can not increase the demand for certain things without increasing the supply of some articles which will be received in exchange for the desired commodities. Demand is based upon the production of articles having exchange value, in its economic sense; and the measure of this demand is necessarily the quantity of commodities offered in exchange for the desired goods. General demand and supply are thus reciprocal to each other. But as soon as money, or general purchasing power, is introduced, Mr. Cairnes[208] defines "demand as the desire for commodities or services, seeking its end by an offer of general purchasing power; and supply, as the desire for general purchasing power, seeking its end by an offer of specific commodities or services." But many persons find a difficulty because they insist upon separating the idea of supply from that of demand, owing to the fact that producers seem to be a distinct class in the community, different from consumers. That they are in reality the same persons can be easily explained by the following statement: "A certain number of people, A, B, C, D, E, F, etc., are engaged in industrial occupations—A produces for B, C, D, E, F; B for A, C, D, E, F; C for A, B, D, E, F, and so on. In each case the producer and the consumers are distinct, and hence, by a very natural fallacy, it is concluded that the whole body of consumers is distinct from the

whole body of producers, whereas they consist of precisely the same persons."

But in regard to demand and supply of particular commodities (not general demand and supply), the increase of the demand is not necessarily followed by an increased supply, or *vice versa*. Out of the total production (which constitutes general demand) a varying amount, sometimes more, sometimes less, may be directed by the desires of men to the purchase of some given thing. This should be borne in mind, in connection with the future discussion of over-production. The identity of general demand with general supply shows there can be no general over-production: but so long as there exists the possibility that the demand for a particular commodity may diminish without a corresponding effect being thereby produced on the supply of that commodity, by a necessary connection, we see that there may be over-production of particular commodities; that is, a production in excess of the demand.

The proper mathematical analogy [between demand and supply] is that of an *equation*. If unequal at any moment, competition equalizes them, and the manner in which this is done is by an adjustment of the value. If the demand increases, the value rises; if the demand diminishes, the value falls; again, if the supply falls off, the value rises; and falls, if the supply is increased. The rise or the fall continues until the demand and supply are again equal to one another: and the value which a commodity will bring in any market is no other than the value which, in that market, gives a demand just sufficient to carry off the existing or expected supply.

Mr. Cairnes[209] finally defined market value as the price "which is sufficient, and no more than sufficient, to carry the existing supply over, with such a surplus as circumstances may render advisable, to meet the new supplies forthcoming," which is nothing more than a paraphrase of the words "existing or expected supply" just used by Mr. Mill. It seems unnecessary, therefore, that Mr. Cairnes should have added: "According to Mr. Mill, the *actual market price* is the price which equalizes supply and demand in a given market; as I view the case, the 'proper market price' is the price which equalizes supply and demand, *not* as existing in the particular market, but in the larger sense which I have assigned to the terms. To this price the *actual market price* will, according to my view, approximate, in proportion to the intelligence and knowledge of the dealers."

Adam Smith, who introduced the expression "effectual demand," employed it to denote the demand of those who are willing and able to give for the commodity what he calls its natural price—that is, the price which will enable it to be permanently produced and brought to market.[210]

This, then, is the Law of Value, with respect to all commodities not susceptible of being multiplied at pleasure.

§ 4. Miscellaneous Cases falling under this Law.

There are but few commodities which are naturally and necessarily limited in supply. But any commodity whatever may be artificially so. The monopolist can fix the value as high as he pleases, short of what the consumer either could not or would not pay; but he can only do so by limiting the supply. Monopoly value, therefore, does not depend on any peculiar principle, but is a mere variety of the ordinary case of demand and supply.

Again, though there are few commodities which are at all times and forever unsusceptible of increase of supply, any commodity whatever may be temporarily so; and with some commodities this is habitually the case. Agricultural produce, for example, can not be increased in quantity before the next harvest; the quantity of corn already existing in the world is all that can be had for sometimes a year to come. During that interval, corn is practically assimilated to things of which the quantity can not be increased. In the case of most commodities, it requires a certain time to increase their quantity; and if the demand increases, then, until a corresponding supply can be brought forward, that is, until the supply can accommodate itself to the demand, the value will so rise as to accommodate the demand to the supply.

There is another case the exact converse of this. There are some articles of which the supply may be indefinitely increased, but can not be rapidly diminished. There are things so durable that the quantity in existence is at all times very great in comparison with the annual produce. Gold and the more durable metals are things of this sort, and also houses. The supply of such things might be at once diminished by destroying them; but to do this could only be the interest of the possessor if he had a monopoly of the article, and could repay himself for the destruction of a part by the increased value of the remainder. The value, therefore, of such things may continue for a long time so low, either from excess of supply or falling off in the demand, as to put a complete stop to further production; the diminution of supply by wearing out being so slow a process that a long time is requisite, even under a total suspension of production, to restore the original value. During that interval the value will be regulated solely by supply and demand, and will rise very gradually as the existing stock wears out, until there is again a remunerating value, and production resumes its course.

> The total value of gold and silver in the world is variously estimated at from $10,000,000,000 to $14,000,000,000; while the annual production of both gold and silver in the world during 1882[211] was only $212,000,000. The loss of gold by abrasion is about 1/1000 annually, and of silver about 1/700, but much depends on the size of the coin. A change in the annual production of the precious metals can have a perceptible effect on their value only after such a time as will permit the change to affect the existing quantity in a way somewhat comparable with its previous amount. The quantity, however, of wheat produced is nearly all consumed between harvests; and the annual supply bears a very large ratio to the existing quantity. Consequently the price of wheat will be very seriously affected by the quantity coming from the annual product.

Finally, there are commodities of which, though capable of being increased or diminished to a great and even an unlimited extent, the value never depends upon anything but demand and supply. This is the case, in particular, with the commodity Labor, of the value of which we have treated copiously in the preceding book; and there are many cases besides in which we shall find it necessary to call in this principle to solve difficult questions of exchange value. This will be particularly exemplified when we treat of International Values; that is, of the terms of interchange between things produced in different countries, or, to speak more generally, in distant places.

§ 5. Commodities which are Susceptible of Indefinite Multiplication without Increase of Cost. Law of their Value Cost of Production.

When the production of a commodity is the effect of labor and expenditure, whether the commodity is susceptible of unlimited multiplication or not, there is a minimum value which is the essential condition of its being permanently produced. The value at any particular time is the result of supply and demand, and is always that which is necessary to create a market for the existing supply. But unless that value is sufficient to repay the Cost of Production, and to afford, besides, the ordinary expectation of profit, the commodity will not continue to be produced. Capitalists will not go on permanently producing at a loss. When such profit is evidently not to be had, if people do not actually withdraw their capital, they at least abstain from replacing it when consumed. The cost of production, together with the ordinary profit, may, therefore, be called the *necessary* price or value of all things made by labor and capital. Nobody willingly produces in the prospect of loss.

When a commodity is not only made by labor and capital, but can be made by them in indefinite quantity, this Necessary Value, the minimum with which the producers will be content, is also, if competition is free and active, the maximum which they can expect. If the value of a commodity is such that it repays the cost of production not only with the customary but with a higher rate of profit, capital rushes to share in this extra gain, and, by increasing the supply of the article, reduces its value. This is not a mere supposition or surmise, but a fact familiar to those conversant with commercial operations. Whenever a new line of business presents itself, offering a hope of unusual profits, and whenever any established trade or manufacture is believed to be yielding a greater profit than customary, there is sure to be in a short time so large a production or importation of the commodity as not only destroys the extra profit, but generally goes beyond the mark, and sinks the value as much too low as it had before been raised too high, until the over-supply is corrected by a total or partial suspension of further production. As already intimated,[212] these variations in the quantity produced do not presuppose or require that any person should change his employment. Those whose business is thriving, increase their produce by availing themselves more largely of their credit, while those who are not making the ordinary profit, restrict their operations, and (in manufacturing phrase) work short time. In this mode is surely and speedily effected the equalization, not of profits, perhaps, but of the expectations of profit, in different occupations.

As a general rule, then, things tend to exchange for one another at such values as will enable each producer to be repaid the cost of production with the ordinary profit; in other words, such as will give to all producers the same rate of profit on their outlay. But in order that the profit may be equal where the outlay, that is, the cost of production, is equal, things must on the average exchange for one another in the ratio of their cost of production; things of which the cost of production is the same, must be of the same value.

> Mr. Mill has here used cost of production almost exactly in the sense of cost of labor, and as excluding profit (while in the next chapter he includes some part of profit in the analysis). It will be well, for the sake of definiteness, to collect the phrases above in which he describes cost of production: "Unless that value is sufficient to repay the cost of production, and to afford, *besides*, the ordinary expectation of profit, the commodity will not continue to be produced"; "the cost of production, *together with* the ordinary profit, may therefore be called the *necessary* price, or value"; "it repays the cost of production, not only *with* the customary, but *with* a higher rate of profit"; "the cost of production with the ordinary profit—in other words, such as will give to all producers the same rate of profit on their outlay"; "that the profit may be equal where *the outlay, that is, the cost of production*, is equal." This is a view which distinctly uses cost of production in the sense of the outlay to the capitalist, or cost of labor. In no other way can profit vary with "cost of production" than in the sense that it is what a given article "costs to the capitalist"; but that is Mr. Mill's definition of cost of labor (p. 227). It is, however, very puzzling when in the next section he speaks of "the natural value, that is, the cost of production." Above, value included cost of production and profit also. Having thus pointed out what is Mr. Mill's conception of cost of production, it will remain for us in the next chapter to consider whether any other view of it is more satisfactory.

Adam Smith and Ricardo have called that value of a thing which is proportional to its cost of production, its Natural Value (or its Natural

Price). They meant by this, the point about which the value oscillates, and to which it always tends to return; the center value, toward which, as Adam Smith expresses it, the market value of a thing is constantly gravitating; and any deviation from which is but a temporary irregularity which, the moment it exists, sets forces in motion tending to correct it. On an average of years sufficient to enable the oscillations on one side of the central line to be compensated by those on the other, the market value agrees with the natural value; but it very seldom coincides exactly with it at any particular time. The sea everywhere tends to a level, but it never is at an exact level; its surface is always ruffled by waves, and often agitated by storms. It is enough that no point, at least in the open sea, is permanently higher than another. Each place is alternately elevated and depressed; but the ocean preserves its level.

§ 6. The Value of these Commodities confirm, in the long run, to their Cost of Production through the operation of Demand and Supply.

The latent influence by which the values of things are made to conform in the long run to the cost of production is the variation that would otherwise take place in the supply of the commodity. The supply would be increased if the thing continued to sell above the ratio of its cost of production, and would be diminished if it fell below that ratio.

> If one dollar covers the expense of making one spade, then when a spade, by virtue of a sudden demand, rises in value to one dollar and ten cents, the manufacturers get an extra profit of ten cents. This could not long remain so, because other capital would enter this industry, and so increase the supply that one spade would sell for only one dollar; then all would receive the average profit. If, owing to a cessation of demand for spades, the price fell to ninety cents, then the manufacturers would lose ten cents on each one made and sold. Thereupon they would cease to do a losing business, capital would be withdrawn, and spades would not be made until the supply was suited to the necessary expense of making them (one dollar). In this way, whenever there is a departure of the value from the normal cost, there is set in motion *ipso facto* a series of forces which automatically restores the value to that cost. So here again we see the nature of an economic

> law: the value may not often correspond exactly with cost of production, but there is a *tendency* in all values to conform to that cost, and this tendency they irresistibly obey. A body possessing weight does not move downward under all circumstances (stones may be thrown upward), but the law of gravitation holds true, nevertheless.

There is no need that there should be any actual alteration of supply; and when there is, the alteration, if permanent, is not the cause but the consequence of the alteration in value. If, indeed, the supply *could* not be increased, no diminution in the cost of production would lower the value; but there is by no means any necessity that it *should*. The mere possibility often suffices; the dealers are aware of what would happen, and their mutual competition makes them anticipate the result by lowering the price.

> Before the electric light was yet known as a feasible means of lighting (in 1878), the mere rumor of Edison's invention, before it was made public, and long before it became practicable, caused a serious fall in the price of gas stocks.

It is, therefore, strictly correct to say that the value of things which can be increased in quantity at pleasure does not depend (except accidentally, and during the time necessary for production to adjust itself) upon demand and supply; on the contrary, demand and supply depend upon it. There is a demand for a certain quantity of the commodity at its natural or cost value, and to that the supply in the long run endeavors to conform.

> Mr. Cairnes[213] fitly says: "The supply of a commodity always tends to adapt itself to the demand at the normal price. I may here say briefly that by the normal price of a commodity I mean that price which suffices, and no more than suffices, to yield to the producers what is considered to be the average and usual remuneration on such sacrifices as they undergo."

When at any time it fails of so conforming, it is either from miscalculation, or from a change in some of the elements of the problem; either in the natural value, that is, in the cost of production, or in the demand, from an alteration in public taste, or in the number or wealth of the consumers. If a value different from the natural value be necessary to make the demand equal to the supply, the market value will deviate from the natural value; but only for a time, for the permanent tendency of supply is to conform itself to the demand which is found by experience to exist for the commodity when selling at its natural value. If the supply is either more or less than this, it is so accidentally, and affords either more or less than the ordinary rate of profit, which, under free and active competition, can not long continue to be the case.

To recapitulate: demand and supply govern the value of all things which can not be indefinitely increased; except that even for them, when produced by industry, there is a minimum value, determined by the cost of production. But in all things which admit of indefinite multiplication, demand and supply only determine the perturbations of value during a period which can not exceed the length of time necessary for altering the supply. While thus ruling the oscillations of value, they themselves obey a superior force, which makes value gravitate toward Cost of Production, and which would settle it and keep it there, if fresh disturbing influences were not continually arising to make it again deviate.

Chapter II. Ultimate Analysis Of Cost Of Production.

§ 1. Of Labor, the principal Element in Cost of Production.

The component elements of Cost of Production have been set forth in the First Part of this inquiry.[214] The principal of them, and so much the principal as to be nearly the sole, was found to be Labor. What the production of a thing costs to its producer, or its series of producers, is the labor expended in producing it. If we consider as the producer the capitalist who makes the advances, the word Labor may be replaced by the word Wages: what the produce costs to him, is the wages which he has had to pay. At the first glance, indeed, this seems to be only a part of his outlay, since he has not only paid wages to laborers, but has likewise provided them with tools, materials, and perhaps buildings. These tools, materials, and buildings, however, were produced by labor and capital; and their value, like that of the article to the production of which they are subservient, depends on cost of production, which again is resolvable into labor. The cost of production of broadcloth does not wholly consist in the wages of weavers; which alone are directly paid by the cloth-manufacturer. It consists also of the wages of spinners and wool-combers, and, it may be added, of shepherds, all of which the clothier has paid for in the price of yarn. It consists, too, of the wages of builders and brick-makers, which he has reimbursed in the contract price of erecting his factory. It partly consists of the wages of machine-makers, iron-founders, and miners. And to these must be added the wages of the carriers who transported any of the means and appliances of the production to the place where they were to be used, and the product itself to the place where it is to be sold.

> Confirmation is here given, in the above words, of the opinion that, in Mr. Mill's mind, Cost of Production was looked at wholly from the stand-point of the capitalist, and was identical with Cost of Labor to the capitalist.

The value of commodities, therefore, depends principally (we shall presently see whether it depends solely) on the quantity of labor required for their production, including in the idea of production that of conveyance to the market. But since the cost of production to the capitalist is not labor but wages, and since wages may be either greater or less, the quantity of labor being the same, it would seem that the value of the product can not be determined solely by the quantity of labor, but by the quantity together with the remuneration, and that values must partly depend on wages.

Now the relation of one thing to another can not be altered by any cause which affects them both alike. A rise or fall of general wages is a fact which affects all commodities in the same manner, and therefore affords no reason why they should exchange for each other in one rather than in another proportion. Though there is no such thing as a general rise of values, there is such a thing as a general rise of prices. As soon as we form distinctly the idea of values, we see that high or low wages can have nothing to do with them; but that high wages make high prices, is a popular and widely spread opinion. The whole amount of error involved in this proposition can only be seen thoroughly when we come to the theory of money; at present we need only say that if it be true, there can be no such thing as a real rise of wages; for if wages could not rise without a proportional rise of the price of everything, they could not, for any substantial purpose, rise at all. It must be remembered, too, that general high prices, even supposing them to exist, can be of no use to a producer or dealer, considered as such; for, if they increase his money returns, they increase in the same degree all his expenses. There is no mode in which capitalists can compensate themselves for a high cost of labor, through any action on values or prices. It can not be prevented from taking its effect in low profits. If the laborers really get more, that is, get the produce of more labor, a smaller percentage must remain for profit.

§ 2. Wages affect Values, only if different in different employments; "non-competing groups."

Although, however, *general* wages, whether high or low, do not affect values, yet if wages are higher in one employment than another, or if they rise or fall permanently in one employment without doing so in others, these inequalities do really operate upon values. Things, for example, which are made by skilled labor, exchange for the produce of a much greater quantity of unskilled labor, for no reason but because the labor is more highly paid. We have before remarked that the difficulty of passing from one class of employments to a class greatly superior has hitherto caused the wages of all those classes of laborers who are separated from one another by any very marked barrier to depend more than might be supposed upon the increase of the population of each class considered separately, and that the inequalities in the remuneration of labor are much greater than could exist if the competition of the laboring people generally could be brought practically to bear on each particular employment. It follows from this that wages in different employments do not rise or fall simultaneously, but are, for short and sometimes even for long periods, nearly independent of one another. All such disparities evidently alter the *relative* cost of production of different commodities, and will therefore be completely represented in their natural or average value.

> This is again a clear recognition of the influence of Mr. Cairnes's theory of "non-competing groups."[215]

Wages do enter into value. The relative *wages* of the labor necessary for producing different commodities affect their value just as much as the relative *quantities* of labor. It is true, the absolute wages paid have no effect upon values; but neither has the absolute quantity of labor. If that were to vary simultaneously and equally in all commodities, values would not be affected. If, for instance, the general efficiency of all labor were increased, so that all things without exception could be produced in the same quantity as before with a smaller amount of labor, no trace of this general diminution of cost of production would show itself in the values of commodities.

§ 3. Profits an element in Cost of Production.

Thus far of labor or wages as an element in cost of production. But in our analysis, in the First Book, of the requisites of production, we found that there is another necessary element in it besides labor. There is also capital; and this being the result of abstinence, the produce, or its value, must be sufficient to remunerate, not only all the labor required, but the abstinence of all the persons by whom the remuneration of the different classes of laborers was advanced. The return from abstinence is Profit. And profit, we have also seen, is not exclusively the surplus remaining to the capitalist after he has been compensated for his outlay, but forms, in most cases, no unimportant part of the outlay itself. The flax-spinner, part of whose expenses consists of the purchase of flax and of machinery, has had to pay, in their price, not only the wages of the labor by which the flax was grown and the machinery made, but the profits of the grower, the flax-dresser, the miner, the iron-founder, and the machine-maker. All these profits, together with those of the spinner himself, were again advanced by the weaver, in the price of his material—linen yarn; and along with them the profits of a fresh set of machine-makers, and of the miners and iron-workers who supplied them with their metallic material. All these advances form part of the cost of production of linen. Profits, therefore, as well as wages, enter into the cost of production which determines the value of the produce.

§ 4. Cost of Production properly represented by sacrifice, or cost, to the Laborer as well as to the Capitalist; the relation of this conception to the Cost of Labor.

> In discussing Cost of Labor (*supra*, pp. 225, 226), Mr. Mill found that the advances of the immediate producer consisted not only of wages, but also of tools, materials, etc., in the price of which he was including the profits of an auxiliary capitalist who advanced the capital for making these tools, etc. But, then, if a line of division were to be passed down through all these advances, separating wages from profits, he urged that, if all the capitalists (auxiliary and immediate both) were one, all the advances of the capitalist might be considered as wages. Profits did not form a part of the outlay to the capitalists in the former analysis. And this seems correct enough. Now, however, he suggests that the outlay of the immediate producers should include the profit of the auxiliary capitalist. More than this, Mr. Mill now includes in cost to the capitalist the profit of the immediate capitalist. For example, in his illustration of the manufacture of linen, he includes not merely the profit of the auxiliary capital engaged in spinning and weaving, but the profit of the immediate and last capitalist, the linen-manufacturer, also. This includes in the cost of producing an article a profit not realized until after the commodity is produced.
>
> It is now time to give a more correct idea of cost of production. Every one admits, for example, that the "cost of production" of wheat is less in the United

States than in England. If, for instance, three men with a capital of one hundred dollars may on a plot of ground, A, in the United States produce one hundred bushels of wheat, it will happen that the same men and capital will only produce sixty bushels on ground, B, in England.

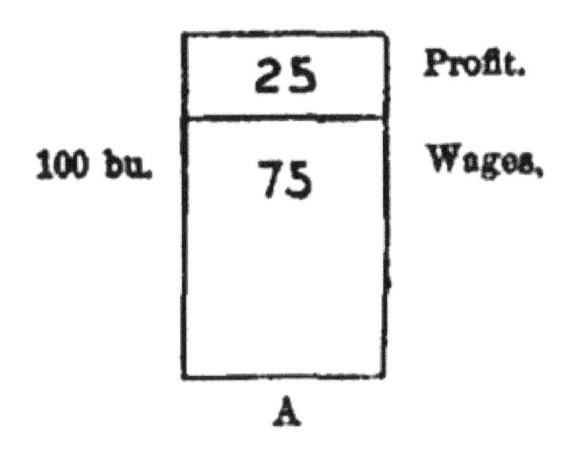

```
             ┌─────────────┐
             │     25      │  Profit.
             ├─────────────┤
  100 bu.    │     75      │  Wages,
             │             │
             │             │
             └─────────────┘
                    A
```

In ordinary language, then, we say that the cost of production is greater in England than in the United States, because the same labor and capital here produce one hundred bushels for sixty in England; or, what amounts to the same thing, that less labor and capital could produce sixty bushels in the United States than sixty bushels in England. If we suppose that one fourth of the crop is profit, and three fourths is assigned to wages in both countries, then in the United States the one hundred dollars of capital receives twenty-five bushels of profit, while in England it receives only fifteen; and the three men receive as wages in the United States twenty-five bushels each, while in England they receive only fifteen bushels each. The first important induction to be made is that where cost of production is low, wages and profits are high. The high productiveness of extractive industries in the United States is the reason why wages and profits are higher here than in older countries.

Now the second important question is, Is cost of production made up of wages and profits, and is it true that the cost rises with a rise of wages and profits? Certainly not. Wages and profits are both higher in the United States than in England, but no one is so absurd as to say that the cost of production of wheat (as above explained) is higher here than there. It is exactly because cost of production of wheat is lower in the United States that wages and profits measured in wheat are higher here than in England. Therefore, it can not be granted, as Mr. Mill expounds the doctrine, that cost of production is made up of wages and profits. When we speak of an increased cost of production of a given article, we mean that its production requires more labor and capital than before; and of a decrease in cost of production, that it requires less labor and capital than before; meaning by "more labor" that a given quality of labor is exerted for a longer or shorter time, and by "more capital" that a greater or less quantity of wealth abstained from is employed for a longer or shorter time; or, in other words, that laborers and capitalists undergo more or less sacrifice in exertion and abstinence, respectively, to attain a given result. This is the contribution to cost of production made by Mr. Cairnes, and briefly defined as follows: "In the case of labor, the cost of producing a given commodity will be represented by the number of average laborers employed in its production—regard at the same time being had to the severity of the work and the degree of risk it involves—multiplied by the duration of their labors. In that of abstinence, the principle is analogous; the sacrifice will be measured by the quantity of wealth abstained from, taken in connection with the risk incurred, and multiplied by the duration of the abstinence."[216]

This view of cost of production takes into consideration, in the act of production, what Mr. Mill does not include, the cost, or real sacrifice, to the laborer as well as to the capitalist. It may, then, be well to state the relations of cost of production, taken in this better sense, to value.

Within competing groups, where there is free choice for labor and capital to select the most remunerative occupations, the hardest and most disagreeable employments will be best paid, and the wages and profits will be in proportion to the sacrifice involved in each case. If so, the amount paid in wages and profits represents the sacrifices in each case. Now, the aggregate product of an industry is the source from which is drawn its wages and profits: the aggregate wages and profits, therefore, must vary with the value of the total product. If the total value depart from the sum hitherto sufficient to pay the given wages and profits, then some will be paid proportionally less than their sacrifice. The value of a commodity, therefore, within the competing group, must conform to the costs of production. If, for example (*a*), the value at any time were such as not to give the laborer the usual equivalent for his sacrifice, he would change his employment to another within the group where he could get it; if (*b*) the share of the capitalist were at any time insufficient to give him the usual reward for his abstinence, he would change the investment of his capital. Therefore, within such limits as allow a free competition of labor and capital, value must conform itself to cost of production.

Not so, however, with the products of non-competing industrial groups. As shown by Mr. Mill, labor does not pass freely from one employment to another; and it must be said that capital does not either, although vastly more ready to move than labor. In a large and thinly settled country capital does not move freely over the whole area of industry; if it did, different rates of profit would not prevail, as we all know they do, in the United States. Now, as before stated, the total value of the commodities resulting from the exertions of each group of producers is the source from which wages and profits are drawn. The aggregate wages and profits in each industry will vary with the value of the aggregate products. But this total value depends upon what it will exchange for of the products of other groups; that is, this value depends on the reciprocal demand of one group for the commodities of the other groups, as compared with the demand of the other groups for its products. For example, although cost of production is low in group A, if the demand from outside groups were to be strong, the exchange value of A's products would rise, and A would get more of other goods in exchange; that is, the total produce is large, but a second increment, arising from a higher exchange value, is to be shared among A's laborers and capitalists. A few years ago, about 1878-1879, the value of wheat in the United States rose because of the increased demand from Europe, where the harvests had been unusually deficient. There had been no falling off in the productiveness of the farming industry of the United States to cause the increased price; but the relative demand of other industrial groups for wheat, the product of the farming industry, raised the exchange value of wheat, and so increased the industrial rewards of those engaged as laborers and capitalists in farming. So it is to be concluded that since there is no free movement of labor and capital between non-competing groups, wages and profits may constantly remain at rates which are not in correspondence with the actual sacrifice, or cost, to labor and capital in different groups; hence, their products do not exchange for each other in proportion to their costs of production. Reciprocal demand is the law of their value.

It will be said, at once, that the foregoing conception of cost of production is entirely opposed to the language of practical men of affairs. They constantly speak of higher or lower wages as increasing their cost of production, or as affecting their ability to compete with foreigners. So universal a usage implies a foundation of truth which demands attention. Wages do represent cost to the capitalist, that is, the chief part of the outlay he makes in order to get a given return; but we have already seen this, and, in the language of Political Economy, termed it "cost of labor" to the capitalist. When the business world use the phrase cost of production, they use it in the sense of cost of labor, as hitherto explained. When they are obliged by strikers to pay more wages, they say that it increases their "cost of production," meaning the cost to them of getting their product, and that it affects their profits. This, then, will show that there is no objection to be urged, in its true sense, against the phrase cost of production, arising from its misuse in the common language of business.

The real connection between the proper conception of cost of production and cost of labor is, however, worth attention. It touches cost of labor through that one of its elements called "efficiency of labor." The more productive an industry is, the higher its wages and profits may be, and it is exactly at this point that more attention should be given to the relations of labor and capital. If productiveness can be increased, higher wages as well as higher profits are possible. The proper understanding of the idea that where cost of production is low wages and profits are high, throws a flood of light on many industrial questions in the United States. In the connection in which it stands, as I have shown, to cost of labor, it means that if commodities can be produced at a less sacrifice to labor and capital by the use of machinery and new processes, higher wages are consistent with a lower price of the given product. It explains the fact that, owing to skill or natural resources, labor, although paid much higher rates, can produce articles cheaper than laborers who are less highly paid. Mr. Brassey[217] has pointed out that English wages are higher than on the Continent; and yet England, through low cost of production, owing to skill, natural resources, etc., can produce so much more of commodities for a given outlay that (while keeping her usual rate of profit) she can generally undersell her competitors who employ cheaper labor. The same observations apply to the United States; but the question of foreign competition will be further discussed (Book III, Chap. XX) after we have studied international trade and values.

"And here it may be well to state precisely what is to be understood by a 'fluctuation of the market,' as distinguished from those changes of normal price which we have been considering. Normal price, as we have seen, is governed, according to the circumstances of the case [as to whether there is free industrial competition or not], by one or other of two causes—

cost of production and reciprocal demand. A change in normal price, therefore, is a change which is the consequence of an alteration in one or other of these conditions. So long as the determining condition—be it cost of production or reciprocal demand—remains constant, the normal price must be considered as remaining constant; but, the normal price remaining constant, the market price (which, as we have seen, depends on the opinion of dealers respecting the state of supply and demand in relation to the particular article) may undergo a change—may deviate, that is to say, either upward or downward from the normal level. Such changes of price, occurring while the permanent conditions of production remain unaffected, can only be temporary, calling into action, as they do, forces which at once tend to restore the normal state of things: they may therefore be properly described as 'fluctuations of the market.' "[218]

§ 5. When profits vary from Employment to Employment, or are spread over unequal lengths of Time, they affect Values accordingly.

Value, however, being purely relative, can not depend upon absolute profits, no more than upon absolute wages, but upon relative profits only. High general profits can not, any more than high general wages, be a cause of high values, because high general values are an absurdity and a contradiction. In so far as profits enter into the cost of production of all things, they can not affect the value of any. It is only by entering in a greater degree into the cost of production of some things than of others, that they can have any influence on value.

Profits, however, may enter more largely into the conditions of production of one commodity than of another, even though there be no difference in the *rate* of profit between the two employments. The one commodity may be called upon to yield a profit during a longer period of time than the other. The example by which this case is usually illustrated is that of wine. Suppose a quantity of wine and a quantity of cloth, made by equal amounts of labor, and that labor paid at the same rate. The cloth does not improve by keeping; the wine does. Suppose that, to attain the desired quality, the wine requires to be kept five years. The producer or dealer will not keep it, unless at the end of five years he can sell it for as much more than the cloth as amounts to five years' profit, accumulated at compound interest. The wine and the cloth were made by the same original outlay. Here, then, is a case in which the natural values, relatively to one another, of two commodities, do not conform to their cost of production alone, but to their cost of production *plus* something else—unless, indeed, for the sake of generality in the expression, we include the profit which the wine-merchant foregoes during the five years, in the cost of production of the wine, looking upon it as a kind of additional outlay, over and above his other advances, for which outlay he must be indemnified at last.

> Regarding cost of production as the amounts of labor and abstinence required in production, and not as Mr. Mill regards it, as the amounts of wages and profits, the above is simply a case where, in the production of wine, there is a longer *duration of the abstinence* than in the production of cloth. If there is a free movement of labor and capital between the two industries, they will exchange for each other in proportion to the sacrifices involved; so that the wine would exchange for more of cloth, because there was more sacrifice undergone. The same explanation also holds good in the following illustration:

All commodities made by machinery are assimilated, at least approximately, to the wine in the preceding example. In comparison with things made wholly by immediate labor, profits enter more largely into their cost of production. Suppose two commodities, A and B, each requiring a year for its production, by means of a capital which we will on this occasion denote by money, and suppose it to be £1,000. A is made wholly by immediate labor, the whole £1,000 being expended directly in wages. B is made by means of labor which cost £500 and a machine which cost £500, and the machine is worn out by one year's use. The two commodities will be of exactly the same value, which, if computed in money, and if profits are 20 per cent per annum, will be £1,200. But of this £1,200, in the case of A, only £200, or one sixth, is profit; while in the case of B there is not only the £200, but as much of £500 (the price of the machine) as consisted of the profits of the machine-maker; which, if we suppose the machine also to have taken a year for its production, is again one sixth. So that in the case of A only one sixth of the entire return is profit, while in B the element of profit comprises not only a sixth of the whole, but an additional sixth of a large part.

From the unequal proportion in which, in different employments, profits enter into the advances of the capitalist, and therefore into the returns required by him, two consequences follow in regard to value. (1). One is, that commodities do not exchange in the ratio simply of the quantities of labor required to produce them; not even if we allow for the unequal rates at which different kinds of labor are permanently remunerated.

(2.) A second consequence is, that every rise or fall of general profits will have an effect on values. Not, indeed, by raising or lowering them generally (which, as we have so often said, is a contradiction and an impossibility), but by altering the proportion in which the values of things are affected by the unequal lengths of time for which profit is due. When two things, though made by equal labor, are of unequal value because the one is called upon to yield profit for a greater number of years or months than the other, this difference of value will be greater when profits are greater, and less when they are less. The wine which has to yield five years' profit more than the cloth will surpass it in value much more if profits are forty per cent than if they are only twenty.

It follows from this that even a general rise of wages, when it involves a real increase in the cost of labor, does in some degree influence values. It does not affect them in the manner vulgarly supposed, by raising them universally; but an increase in the cost of labor lowers profits, and therefore lowers in natural values the things into which profits enter in a greater proportion than the average, and raises those into which they enter in a less proportion than the average. All commodities in the production of which machinery bears a large part, especially if the machinery is very durable, are lowered in their relative value when profits fall; or, what is equivalent, other things are raised in value relatively to them. This truth is sometimes expressed in a phraseology more plausible than sound, by saying that a rise of wages raises the value of things made by labor in comparison with those made by machinery. But things made by machinery, just as much as any other things, are made by labor—namely, the labor which made the machinery itself—the only difference being that profits enter somewhat more largely into the production of things for which machinery is used, though the principal item of the outlay is still labor.

§ 6. Occasional Elements in Cost of Production; taxes and ground-rent.

Cost of Production consists of several elements, some of which are constant and universal, others occasional. The universal elements of cost of production are the wages of the labor, and the profits of the capital. The occasional elements are taxes, and any extra cost occasioned by a scarcity value of some of the requisites. Besides the natural and necessary elements in cost of production—labor and profits—there are others which are artificial and casual, as, for instance, a tax. The taxes on hops and malt are as much a part of the cost of production of those articles as the wages of the laborers. The expenses which the law imposes, as well as those which the nature of things imposes, must be reimbursed with the ordinary profit from the value of the produce, or the things will not continue to be produced. But the influence of taxation on value is subject to the same conditions as the influence of wages and of profits. It is not general taxation, but differential taxation, that produces the effect. If all productions were taxed so as to take an equal percentage from all profits, relative values would be in no way disturbed. If only a few commodities were taxed, their value would rise; and if only a few were left untaxed, their value would fall.

But the case in which scarcity value chiefly operates in adding to cost of production is the case of natural agents. These, when unappropriated, and to be had for the taking, do not enter into the cost of production, save to the extent of the labor which may be necessary to fit them for use. Even when appropriated, they do not (as we have already seen) bear a value from the mere fact of the appropriation, but only from scarcity—that is, from limitation of supply. But it is equally certain that they often do bear a scarcity value.

No one can deny that rent sometimes enters into cost of production [of other than agricultural products]. If I buy or rent a piece of ground, and build a cloth-manufactory on it, the ground-rent forms legitimately a part of my expenses of production, which must be repaid by the product. And since all factories are built on ground, and most of them in places where ground is peculiarly valuable, the rent paid for it must, on the average, be compensated in the values of all things made in factories. In what sense it is true that rent does not enter into the cost of production or affect the value of *agricultural* produce will be shown in the succeeding chapter.

> These occasional elements in cost of production, such as taxes, insurance, ground-rent, etc., are to be considered as just so much of an increase in the quantity of capital required for the operation involved in the particular production, and, consequently, result in an increased cost of production, because there is either more abstinence, or abstinence for a longer time,

to be rewarded. These elements, therefore, if they are not universal (or common to all articles), will affect the exchange value of commodities, wherever there is a free competition.

Chapter III. Of Rent, In Its Relation To Value.

§ 1. Commodities which are susceptible of indefinite Multiplication, but not without increase of Cost. Law of their Value, Cost of Production in the most unfavorable existing circumstances.

We have investigated the laws which determine the value of two classes of commodities—the small class which, being limited to a definite quantity, have their value entirely determined by demand and supply, save that their cost of production (if they have any) constitutes a minimum below which they can not permanently fall; and the large class, which can be multiplied *ad libitum* by labor and capital, and of which the cost of production fixes the maximum as well as the minimum at which they can permanently exchange [if there be free competition]. But there is still a third kind of commodities to be considered—those which have, not one, but several costs of production; which can always be increased in quantity by labor and capital, but not by the same amount of labor and capital; of which so much may be produced at a given cost, but a further quantity not without a greater cost. These commodities form an intermediate class, partaking of the character of both the others. The principal of them is agricultural produce. We have already made abundant reference to the fundamental truth that in agriculture, the state of the art being given, doubling the labor does not double the produce; that, if an increased quantity of produce is required, the additional supply is obtained at a greater cost than the first. Where a hundred quarters of corn are all that is at present required from the lands of a given village, if the growth of population made it necessary to raise a hundred more, either by breaking up worse land now uncultivated, or by a more elaborate cultivation of the land already under the plow, the additional hundred, or some part of them, at least, might cost double or treble as much per quarter as the former supply.

If the first hundred quarters were all raised at the same expense (only the best land being cultivated), and if that expense would be remunerated with the ordinary profit by a price of 20*s.* the quarter, the natural price of wheat, so long as no more than that quantity was required, would be 20*s.*; and it could only rise above or fall below that price from vicissitudes of seasons, or other casual variations in supply. But if the population of the district advanced, a time would arrive when more than a hundred quarters would be necessary to feed it. We must suppose that there is no access to any foreign supply. By the hypothesis, no more than a hundred quarters can be produced in the district, unless by either bringing worse land into cultivation, or altering the system of culture to a more expensive one. Neither of these things will be done without a rise in price. This rise of price will gradually be brought about by the increasing demand. So long as the price has risen, but not risen enough to repay with the ordinary profit the cost of producing an additional quantity, the increased value of the limited supply partakes of the nature of a scarcity value. Suppose that it will not answer to cultivate the second best land, or land of the second degree of remoteness, for a less return than 25*s.* the quarter; and that this price is also necessary to remunerate the expensive operations by which an increased produce might be raised from land of the first quality. If so, the price will rise, through the increased demand, until it reaches 25*s.* That will now be the natural price; being the price without which the quantity, for which society has a demand at that price, will not be produced. At that price, however, society can go on for some time longer; could go on perhaps forever, if population did not increase. The price, having attained that point, will not again permanently recede (though it may fall temporarily from accidental abundance); nor will it advance further, so long as society can obtain the supply it requires without a second increase of the cost of production.

In the case supposed, different portions of the supply of corn have different costs of production. Though the twenty, or fifty, or one hundred and fifty quarters additional have been produced at a cost proportional to 25*s.*, the original hundred quarters per annum are still produced at a cost only proportional to 20*s.* This is self-evident, if the original and the additional supply are produced on different qualities of land. It is equally true if they are produced on the same land. Suppose that land of the best quality, which produced one hundred quarters at 20*s.*, has been made to produce one hundred and fifty by an expensive process, which it would not answer to undertake without a price of 25*s.* The cost which requires 25*s.* is incurred for the sake of fifty quarters alone: the first hundred might have continued forever to be produced at the original cost, and with the benefit, on that quantity, of the whole rise of price caused by the increased demand: no one, therefore, will incur the additional expense for the sake of the additional fifty, unless they alone will pay for the whole of it. The fifty, therefore, will be produced at their natural price, proportioned to the cost of their production; while the other hundred will now bring in 5*s.* a quarter more than their natural price—than the price corresponding to, and sufficing to remunerate, their lower cost of production.

If the production of any, even the smallest, portion of the supply requires as a necessary condition a certain price, that price will be obtained for all the rest. We are not able to buy one loaf cheaper than another because the corn from which it was made, being grown on a richer soil, has cost less to the grower. The value, therefore, of an article (meaning its natural, which is the same with its average value) is determined by the cost of that portion of the supply which is produced and brought to market at the greatest expense. This is the Law of Value of the third of the three classes into which all commodities are divided.

§ 2. Such commodities, when Produced in circumstances more favorable, yield a Rent equal to the difference of Cost.

If the portion of produce raised in the most unfavorable circumstances obtains a value proportioned to its cost of production; all the portions raised in more favorable circumstances, selling as they must do at the same value, obtain a value more than proportioned to their cost of production.

The owners, however, of those portions of the produce enjoy a privilege; they obtain a value which yields them more than the ordinary profit. The advantage depends on the possession of a natural agent of peculiar quality, as, for instance, of more fertile land than that which determines the general value of the commodity; and when this natural agent is not owned by themselves, the person who does own it is able to exact from them, in the form of rent, the whole extra gain derived from its use. We are thus brought by another road to the Law of Rent, investigated in the concluding chapter of the Second Book. Rent, we again see, is the difference between the unequal returns to different parts of the capital employed on the soil. Whatever surplus any portion of agricultural capital produces, beyond what is produced by the same amount of capital on the worst soil, or under the most expensive mode of cultivation, which the existing demands of society compel a recourse to, that surplus will naturally be paid as rent from that capital, to the owner of the land on which it is employed.

> The discussion of rent is here followed wholly from the point of view of value, while before (Book II, Chap. VI) the law of rent was reached through a limitation of the quantity of land due to the influence of population. In the former case the rent and produce were stated in bushels. By introducing price now (as the convenient symbol of value), instead of the separate increased demands of population in our

illustration than used (p. 240), it will be seen how the same operation, looking at it solely in respect to value, brings us to the same law:

Price per Bushel.	A	B		C		D	
	24 bushels	18 bushels		12 bushels		6 bushels	
	Total value of product.	Total value of product.	Rent.	Total value of product.	Rent.	Total value of product.	Rent.
$1.00	$24.00	$0.00	....	....		....	
$1.33	$32.00	$8.00	$24.00	$0.00	....	....	
$2.00	$48.00	$24.00	$36.00	$12.00	$24.00	$0.00	....
$4.00	$96.00	$72.00	$72.00	$48.00	$48.00	$24.00	$24.00

It was long thought by political economists, among the rest even by Adam Smith, that the produce of land is always at a monopoly value, because (they said), in addition to the ordinary rate of profit, it always yields something further for rent. This we now see to be erroneous. A thing can not be at a monopoly value when its supply can be increased to an indefinite extent if we are only willing to incur the cost. As long as there is any land fit for cultivation, which at the existing price can not be profitably cultivated at all, there must be some land a little better, which will yield the ordinary profit, but allow nothing for rent: and that land, if within the boundary of a farm, will be cultivated by the farmer; if not so, probably by the proprietor, or by some other person on sufferance. Some such land at least, under cultivation, there can scarcely fail to be.

Rent, therefore, forms no part of the cost of production which determines the value of agricultural produce. The land or the capital most unfavorably circumstanced among those actually employed, pays no rent, and that land or capital determines the cost of production which regulates the value of the whole produce. Thus rent is, as we have already seen, no cause of value, but the price of the privilege which the inequality of the returns to different portions of agricultural produce confers on all except the least favored portion.

Rent, in short, merely equalizes the profits of different farming capitals, by enabling the landlord to appropriate all extra gains occasioned by superiority of natural advantages. If all landlords were unanimously to forego their rent, they would but transfer it to the farmers, without benefiting the consumer; for the existing price of corn would still be an indispensable condition of the production of part of the existing supply, and if a part obtained that price the whole would obtain it. Rent, therefore, unless artificially increased by restrictive laws, is no burden on the consumer: it does not raise the price of corn, and is no otherwise a detriment to the public than inasmuch as if the state had retained it, or imposed an equivalent in the shape of a land-tax, it would then have been a fund applicable to general instead of private advantage.

> The nationalization of the land, consequently, would not benefit the laboring-classes a whit through lowering the price to them, or any consumer, of food or agricultural produce.

§ 3. Rent of Mines and Fisheries and ground-rent of Buildings, and cases of gain analogous to Rent.

Agricultural productions are not the only commodities which have several different costs of production at once, and which, in consequence of that difference, and in proportion to it, afford a rent. Mines are also an instance. Almost all kinds of raw material extracted from the interior of the earth—metals, coals, precious stones, etc.—are obtained from mines differing considerably in fertility—that is, yielding very different quantities of the product to the same quantity of labor and capital. There are, perhaps, cases in which it is impossible to extract from a particular vein, in a given time, more than a certain quantity of ore, because there is only a limited surface of the vein exposed, on which more than a certain number of laborers can not be simultaneously employed. But this is not true of all mines. In collieries, for example, some other cause of limitation must be sought for. In some instances the owners limit the quantity raised, in order not too rapidly to exhaust the mine; in others there are said to be combinations of owners, to keep up a monopoly price by limiting the production. Whatever be the causes, it is a fact that mines of different degrees of richness are in operation, and since the value of the produce must be proportional to the cost of production at the worst mine (fertility and situation taken together), it is more than proportional to that of the best. All mines superior in produce to the worst actually worked will yield, therefore, a rent equal to the excess. They may yield more; and the worst mine may itself yield a rent. Mines being comparatively few, their qualities do not graduate gently into one another, as the qualities of land do; and the demand may be such as to keep the value of the produce considerably above the cost of production at the worst mine now worked, without being sufficient to bring into operation a still worse. During the interval, the produce is really at a scarcity value.

Fisheries are another example. Fisheries in the open sea are not appropriated, but fisheries in lakes or rivers almost always are so, and likewise oyster-beds or other particular fishing-grounds on coasts. We may take salmon-fisheries as an example of the whole class. Some rivers are far more productive in salmon than others. None, however, without being exhausted, can supply more than a very limited demand. All others, therefore, will, if appropriated, afford a rent equal to the value of their superiority.

Both in the case of mines and of fisheries, the natural order of events is liable to be interrupted by the opening of a new mine, or a new fishery, of superior quality to some of those already in use. In this case, when things have permanently adjusted themselves, the result will be that the scale of qualities which supply the market will have been cut short at the lower end, while a new insertion will have been made in the scale at some point higher up; and the worst mine or fishery in use—the one which regulates the rents of the superior qualities and the value of the commodity—will be a mine or fishery of better quality than that by which they were previously regulated.

The ground-rent of a building, and the rent of a garden or park attached to it, will not be less than the rent which the same land would afford in agriculture, but may be greater than this to an indefinite amount; the surplus being either in consideration of beauty or of convenience, the convenience often consisting in superior facilities for pecuniary gain. Sites of remarkable beauty are generally limited in supply, and therefore, if in great demand, are at a scarcity value. Sites superior only in convenience are governed as to their value by the ordinary principles of rent. The ground-rent of a house in a small village is but little higher than the rent of a similar patch of ground in the open fields.

> Suppose the various kinds of land to be represented by the alphabet; that those below O pay no agricultural rent, and that all lands increase in fertility and situation as we approach the beginning of the alphabet, but which, as far up as K, are used in agriculture; that

higher than K all are more profitably used for building purposes, viz.:

A, B, C, ... | K, L, M, N, O, | ... X, Y, Z.

Now it will happen that land is chosen for building purposes irrespective of its fertility for agricultural purposes. It will not be true, as some may think, that no land will be used for building until it will pay a ground-rent greater than the greatest agricultural rent paid by any piece of land. It is not true, for example, if N be selected for a building-lot, that it must pay a ground-rent as high as the agricultural rent of K, the most fertile land cultivated in agriculture. It must pay a ground-rent higher only than it itself would pay, if cultivated. It is only necessary that it pay more than the same (not better) land would pay as rent if used only in agriculture.

The rents of wharfage, dock, and harbor room, water-power, and many other privileges, may be analyzed on similar principles. Take the case, for example, of a patent or exclusive privilege for the use of a process by which the cost of production is lessened. If the value of the product continues to be regulated by what it costs to those who are obliged to persist in the old process, the patentee will make an extra profit equal to the advantage which his process possesses over theirs. This extra profit is essentially similar to rent, and sometimes even assumes the form of it, the patentee allowing to other producers the use of his privilege in consideration of an annual payment.

The extra gains which any producer or dealer obtains through superior talents for business, or superior business arrangements, are very much of a similar kind. If all his competitors had the same advantages, and used them, the benefit would be transferred to their customers through the diminished value of the article; he only retains it for himself because he is able to bring his commodity to market at a lower cost, while its value is determined by a higher.[219]

§ 4. *Résumé* of the laws of value of each of the three classes of commodities.

A general *résumé* of the laws of value, where a free movement of labor and capital exists, may now be briefly made in the following form:

Exchange value has three conditions, viz.:
1. Utility, or ability to satisfy a desire (U).
2. Difficulty of attainment (D), according to which there are three classes of commodities.
3. Transferableness.

Of the second condition, there are three classes:
1. Those limited in supply—e.g., ancient pictures or monopolized articles.
2. Those whose supply is capable of indefinite increase by the use of labor and capital.
3. Those whose supply is gained at a gradually increasing cost, under the law of diminishing returns.

Of those limited in supply, their value is regulated by Demand and Supply. The only limit is U.

Of those whose supply is capable of indefinite increase, their normal and permanent value is regulated by Cost of Production, and their temporary or market value is regulated by Demand and Supply, oscillating around Cost of Production (which consists of the amount of labor and abstinence required).

Of those whose supply is gained at a gradually increasing cost, their normal value is regulated by the Cost of Production of that portion of the whole amount of the whole amount needed, which is brought to market at the greatest expense, and their market value is regulated by Demand and Supply (as in class 2).

If there be no free competition between industries, then the value of those commodities which has been said, in the above classification, to depend on cost of production, will be governed by the law of Reciprocal Demand.

Chapter IV. Of Money.

§ 1. The three functions of Money—a Common Denominator of Value, a Medium of Exchange, a "Standard of Value".

Having proceeded thus far in ascertaining the general laws of Value, without introducing the idea of Money (except occasionally for illustration), it is time that we should now superadd that idea, and consider in what manner the principles of the mutual interchange of commodities are affected by the use of what is termed a Medium of Exchange.

> As Professor Jevons[220] has pointed out, money performs three distinct services, capable of being separated by the mind, and worthy of separate definition and explanation:
>
> 1. A Common Measure, or Common Denominator, of Value.
>
> 2. A Medium of Exchange.
>
> 3. A Standard of Value.
>
> F. A. Walker,[221] however, says: "Money is the medium of exchange. Whatever performs this function, does this work, is money, no matter what it is made of.... That which does the money-work is the money-thing."

(1.) [If we had no money] the first and most obvious [inconvenience] would be the want of a *common measure for values* of different sorts. If a tailor had only coats, and wanted to buy bread or a horse, it would be very troublesome to ascertain how much bread he ought to obtain for a coat, or how many coats he should give for a horse. The calculation must be recommenced on different data every time he bartered his coats for a different kind of article, and there could be no current price or regular quotations of value. As it is much easier to compare different lengths by expressing them in a common language of feet and inches, so it is much easier to compare values by means of a common language of [dollars and cents].

The need of a common denominator of values (an excellent term, introduced by Storch), to whose terms the values of all other commodities may be reduced, and so compared, is as great as that the inhabitants of the different States of the United States should have a common language as a means by which ideas could be communicated to the whole nation. A man may have a horse, whose value he wishes to compare in some common term with the value of his house, although he might not wish to sell either. A valuation by the State for taxation could not exist but for this common denominator, or register, of value.

(2.) The second function is that of a medium of exchange. The distinction between this function and the common denominator of value is that the latter measures value, the former transfers value. The man owning the horse, after having measured its value by comparison with a given thing, may now wish to exchange it for other things. This discloses the need of another quality in money.

The inconveniences of barter are so great that, without some more commodious means of effecting exchanges, the division of employments could hardly have been carried to any considerable extent. A tailor, who had nothing but coats, might starve before he could find any person having bread to sell who wanted a coat: besides, he would not want as much bread at a time as would be worth a coat, and the coat could not be divided. Every person, therefore, would at all times hasten to dispose of his commodity in exchange for anything which, though it might not be fitted to his own immediate wants, was in great and general demand, and easily divisible, so that he might be sure of being able to purchase with it whatever was offered for sale. The thing which people would select to keep by them for making purchases must be one which, besides being divisible and generally desired, does not deteriorate by keeping. This reduces the choice to a small number of articles.

This need is well explained by the following facts furnished by Professor Jevons: "Some years since, Mademoiselle Zélie, a singer of the Théâtre Lyrique at Paris, made a professional tour round the world, and gave a concert in the Society Islands. In exchange for an air from 'Norma' and a few other songs, she was to receive a third part of the receipts. When counted, her share was found to consist of three pigs, twenty-three turkeys, forty-four chickens, five thousand cocoanuts, besides considerable quantities of bananas, lemons, and oranges. In the Society Islands, however, pieces of money were very scarce; and, as mademoiselle could not consume any considerable portion of the receipts herself, it became necessary in the mean time to feed the pigs and poultry with the fruit."[222]

(3.) The third function desired of money is what is usually termed a "standard of value." It is, perhaps, better expressed by F. A. Walker[223] as a "standard of deferred payments." Its existence is due to the desire to have a means of comparing the purchasing power of a commodity at one time with its purchasing power at another distant time; that is, that for long contracts, exchanges may be in unchanged ratios at the beginning and at the end of the contracts. There is no distinction between this function and the first, except one arising from the introduction of *time*. At the same time and place, the "standard of value" is given in the common denominator of value.

A Measure of Value,[224] in the ordinary sense of the word measure, would mean something by comparison with which we may ascertain what is the value of any other thing. When we consider, further, that value itself is relative, and that two things are necessary to constitute it, independently of the third thing which is to measure it, we may define a Measure of Value to be something, by comparing with which any two other things, we may infer their value in relation to one another.

In this sense, any commodity will serve as a measure of value at a given time and place; since we can always infer the proportion in which things exchange for one another, when we know the proportion in which each exchanges for any third thing. To serve as a convenient measure of value is one of the functions of the commodity selected as a medium of exchange. It is in that commodity that the values of all other things are habitually estimated.

But the desideratum sought by political economists is not a measure of the value of things at the same time and place, but a measure of the value of the same thing at different times and places: something by comparison with which it may be known whether any given thing is of greater or less value now than a century ago, or in this country than in America or China. To enable the money price of a thing at two different periods to measure the quantity of things in general which it will exchange for, the same sum of money must correspond at both periods to the same quantity of things in general—that is, money must always have the same exchange value, the same general purchasing power. Now, not only is this not true of money, or of any other commodity, but we can not even suppose any state of circumstances in which it would be true.

> It being very clear that money, or the precious metals, do not themselves remain absolutely stable in value for long periods, the only way in which a "standard of value" can be properly established is by the proposed "multiple standard of value," stated as follows:
>
> "A number of articles in general use—corn, beef, potatoes, wool, cotton, silk, tea, sugar, coffee, indigo, timber, iron, coal, and others—shall be taken, in a definite quantity of each, so many pounds, or bushels, or cords, or yards, to form a standard required. The value of these articles, in the quantities specified, and all of standard quality, shall be ascertained monthly or weekly by Government, and the total sum [in money] which would then purchase this bill of goods shall be, thereupon, officially promulgated. Persons may then, if they choose, make their contracts for future payments in terms of this multiple or tabular standard."[225] A, who had borrowed $1,000 of B in 1870 for ten years, would make note of the total money value of all these articles composing the multiple standard, which we will suppose is $125 in 1870. Consequently, A would promise to pay B eight multiple units in ten years (that is, eight times $125, or $1,000). But, if other things change in value relatively to money during these ten years, the same sum of money—$1,000—in 1880 will not return to B the same just amount of purchasing power which he parted with in 1870. Now, if, in 1880, when his note falls due, the government list is examined, and it is found that commodities in general have fallen in value relatively to gold, the multiple unit will not amount to as much gold as it did in 1870; perhaps each unit may be rated only at $100. In that

case, A is obliged to pay back but eight multiple units, which costs him only $800 in money, while B receives from A the same amount of purchasing power over other commodities which he loaned to him. B had no just claim to ten units, since the fall of all commodities relatively to gold was not due to his exertions. On the other hand, if, between 1870 and 1880, prices had risen, *mutatis mutandis*, the eight units would have cost A more than $1,000 in gold; but he would have been justly obliged to return the same amount of purchasing power to B which he received from him.

§ 2. Gold and Silver, why fitted for those purposes.

By a tacit concurrence, almost all nations, at a very early period, fixed upon certain metals, and especially gold and silver, to serve this purpose. No other substances unite the necessary qualities in so great a degree, with so many subordinate advantages. These were the things which it most pleased every one to possess, and which there was most certainty of finding others willing to receive in exchange for any kind of produce. They were among the most imperishable of all substances. They were also portable, and, containing great value in small bulk, were easily hid; a consideration of much importance in an age of insecurity. Jewels are inferior to gold and silver in the quality of divisibility; and are of very various qualities, not to be accurately discriminated without great trouble. Gold and silver are eminently divisible, and, when pure, always of the same quality; and their purity may be ascertained and certified by a public authority.

Jevons[226] has more fully stated the requisites for a perfect money as—

1. Value.
2. Portability.
3. Indestructibility.
4. Homogeneity.
5. Divisibility.
6. Stability of value.

7. Cognizability.

Accordingly, though furs have been employed as money in some countries, cattle in others, in Chinese Tartary cubes of tea closely pressed together, the shells called cowries on the coast of Western Africa, and in Abyssinia at this day blocks of rock-salt, gold and silver have been generally preferred by nations which were able to obtain them, either by industry, commerce, or conquest. To the qualities which originally recommended them, another came to be added, the importance of which only unfolded itself by degrees. Of all commodities, they are among the least influenced by any of the causes which produce fluctuations of value. No commodity is quite free from such fluctuations. Gold and silver have sustained, since the beginning of history, one great permanent alteration of value, from the discovery of the American mines.

In the present age the opening of new sources of supply, so abundant as the Ural Mountains, California, and Australia, may be the commencement of another period of decline, on the limits of which it would be useless at present to speculate. But, on the whole, no commodities are so little exposed to causes of variation. They fluctuate less than almost any other things in their cost of production. And, from their durability, the total quantity in existence is at all times so great in proportion to the annual supply, that the effect on value even of a change in the cost of production is not sudden: a very long time being required to diminish materially the quantity in existence, and even to increase it very greatly not being a rapid process. Gold and silver, therefore, are more fit than any other commodity to be the subject of engagements for receiving or paying a given quantity at some distant period.

> Since Mr. Mill wrote, two great changes in the production of the precious metals have occurred. The discoveries of gold, briefly referred to by him, have led to an enormous increase of the existing fund of gold (see chart No. IX, Chap. VI), and a fall in the value of gold within twenty years after the discoveries, according to Mr. Jevons's celebrated study,[227] of from nine to fifteen per cent. Another change took place, a change in the value, of silver, in 1876, which has resulted in a permanent fall of its value since that time (see chart No. X, Chap. VII). Before that date, silver sold at about 60*d.* per ounce in the central market of the world, London; and now it remains about 52*d.* per

ounce, although it once fell to 47*d*., in July, 1876. In spite of Mr. Mill's expressions of confidence in their stability of value—although certainly more stable than other commodities—the events of the last thirty-five years have fully shown that neither gold nor silver—silver far less than gold—can successfully serve as a perfect "standard of value" for any considerable length of time.

When gold and silver had become virtually a medium of exchange, by becoming the things for which people generally sold, and with which they generally bought, whatever they had to sell or to buy, the contrivance of coining obviously suggested itself. By this process the metal was divided into convenient portions, of any degree of smallness, and bearing a recognized proportion to one another; and the trouble was saved of weighing and assaying at every change of possessors—an inconvenience which, on the occasion of small purchases, would soon have become insupportable. Governments found it their interest to take the operation into their own hands, and to interdict all coining by private persons.

§ 3. Money a mere contrivance for facilitating exchanges, which does not affect the laws of value.

It must be evident, however, that the mere introduction of a particular mode of exchanging things for one another, by first exchanging a thing for money, and then exchanging the money for something else, makes no difference in the essential character of transactions. It is not with money that things are really purchased. Nobody's income (except that of the gold or silver miner) is derived from the precious metals. The [dollars or cents] which a person receives weekly or yearly are not what constitutes his income; they are a sort of tickets or orders which he can present for payment at any shop he pleases, and which entitle him to receive a certain value of any commodity that he makes choice of. The farmer pays his laborers and his landlord in these tickets, as the most convenient plan for himself and them; but their real income is their share of his corn, cattle, and hay, and it makes no essential difference whether he distributes it to them directly, or sells it for them and gives them the price. There can not, in short, be intrinsically a more insignificant thing, in the economy of society, than money; except in the character of a contrivance for sparing time and labor. It is a machine for doing quickly and commodiously what would be done, though less quickly and commodiously, without it; and, like many other kinds of machinery, it only exerts a distinct and independent influence of its own when it gets out of order.

The introduction of money does not interfere with the operation of any of the Laws of Value laid down in the preceding chapters. The reasons which make the temporary or market value of things depend on the demand and supply, and their average and permanent values upon their cost of production, are as applicable to a money system as to a system of barter. Things which by barter would exchange for one another will, if sold for money, sell for an equal amount of it, and so will exchange for one another still, though the process of exchanging them will consist of two operations instead of only one. The relations of commodities to one another remain unaltered by money; the only new relation introduced is their relation to money itself; how much or how little money they will exchange for; in other words, how the Exchange Value of money itself is determined. Money is a commodity, and its value is determined like that of other commodities, temporarily by demand and supply, permanently and on the average by cost of production.

Chapter V. Of The Value Of Money, As Dependent On Demand And Supply.

§ 1. Value of Money, an ambiguous expression.

The Value of Money is to appearance an expression as precise, as free from possibility of misunderstanding, as any in science. The value of a thing is what it will exchange for; the value of money is what money will exchange for, the purchasing power of money. If prices are low, money will buy much of other things, and is of high value; if prices are high, it will buy little of other things, and is of low value. The value of money is inversely as general prices; falling as they rise, and rising as they fall. When one person lends to another, as well as when he pays wages or rent to another, what he transfers is not the mere money, but a right to a certain value of the produce of the country, to be selected at pleasure; the lender having first bought this right, by giving for it a portion of his capital. What he really lends is so much capital; the money is the mere instrument of transfer. But the capital usually passes from the lender to the receiver through the means either of money, or of an order to receive money, and at any rate it is in money that the capital is computed and estimated. Hence, borrowing capital is universally called borrowing money; the loan market is called the money market; those who have their capital disposable for investment on loan are called the moneyed class; and the equivalent given for the use of capital, or, in other words, interest, is not only called the interest of money, but, by a grosser perversion of terms, the value of money.

§ 2. The Value of Money depends on its quantity.

The value or purchasing power of money depends, in the first instance, on demand and supply. But demand and supply, in relation to money, present themselves in a somewhat different shape from the demand and supply of other things.

The supply of a commodity means the quantity offered for sale. But it is not usual to speak of offering money for sale. People are not usually said to buy or sell money. This, however, is merely an accident of language. In point of fact, money is bought and sold like other things, whenever other things are bought and sold *for* money. Whoever sells corn, or tallow, or cotton, buys money. Whoever buys bread, or wine, or clothes, sells money to the dealer in those articles. The money with which people are offering to buy, is money offered for sale. The supply of money, then, is the quantity of it which people are wanting to lay out; that is, all the money they have in their possession, except what they are hoarding, or at least keeping by them as a reserve for future contingencies. The supply of money, in short, is all the money in *circulation* at the time.

The demand for money, again, consists of all the goods offered for sale. Every seller of goods is a buyer of money, and the goods he brings with him constitute his demand. The demand for money differs from the demand for other things in this, that it is limited only by the means of the purchaser.

> In this last statement Mr. Mill is misled by his former definition of demand as "quantity demanded." He has the true idea of demand in this case regarding money; but the demand for money does not, as he thinks, differ from the demand for other things, inasmuch as, in our corrected view of demand for other things (p. 255), it was found that the demand for other things than money was also limited by the means of the purchaser.[228]

As the whole of the goods in the market compose the demand for money, so the whole of the money constitutes the demand for goods. The money and the goods are seeking each other for the purpose of being exchanged. They are reciprocally supply and demand to one another. It is indifferent whether, in characterizing the phenomena, we speak of the demand and supply of goods, or the supply and the demand of money. They are equivalent expressions.

Supposing the money in the hands of individuals to be increased, the wants and inclinations of the community collectively in respect to consumption remaining exactly the same, the increase of demand would reach all things equally, and there would be a universal rise of prices. Let us rather suppose, therefore, that to every pound, or shilling, or penny in the possession of any one, another pound, shilling, or penny were suddenly added. There would be an increased money demand, and consequently an increased money value, or price, for things of all sorts. This increased value would do no good to any one; would make no difference, except that of having to reckon [dollars and cents] in higher numbers. It would be an increase of values only as estimated in money, a thing only wanted to buy other things with; and would not enable any one to buy more of them than before. Prices would have risen in a certain ratio, and the value of money would have fallen in the same ratio.

It is to be remarked that this ratio would be precisely that in which the quantity of money had been increased. If the whole money in circulation was doubled, prices would be doubled. If it was only increased one fourth, prices would rise one fourth. There would be one fourth more money, all of which would be used to purchase goods of some description. When there had been time for the increased supply of money to reach all markets, or (according to the conventional metaphor) to permeate all the channels of circulation, all prices would have risen one fourth. But the general rise of price is independent of this diffusing and equalizing process. Even if some prices were raised more, and others less, the average rise would be one fourth. This is a necessary consequence of the fact that a fourth more money would have been given for only the same quantity of goods. *General* prices, therefore, would in any case be a fourth higher.

So that the value of money, other things being the same, varies inversely as its quantity; every increase of quantity lowering the value, and every diminution raising it, in a ratio exactly equivalent. This, it must be observed, is a property peculiar to money. We did not find it to be true of commodities generally, that every diminution of supply raised the value exactly in proportion to the deficiency, or that every increase lowered it in the precise ratio of the excess. Some things are usually affected in a greater ratio than that of the excess or deficiency, others usually in a less; because, in ordinary cases of demand, the desire, being for the thing itself, may be stronger or weaker; and the amount of what people are willing to expend on it, being in any case a limited quantity, may be affected in very unequal degrees by difficulty or facility of attainment. But in the case of money, which is desired as the means of universal purchase, the demand consists of everything which people have to sell; and the only limit to what they are willing to give, is the limit set by their having nothing more to offer. The whole of the goods being in any case exchanged for the whole of the money which comes into the market to be laid out, they will sell for less or more of it, exactly according as less or more is brought.

§ 3. —Together with the Rapidity of Circulation.

It might be supposed that there is always in circulation in a country a quantity of money equal in value to the whole of the goods then and there on sale. But this would be a complete misapprehension. The money laid out is equal in value to the goods it purchases; but the quantity of money laid out is not the same thing with the quantity in circulation. As the money passes from hand to hand, the same piece of money is laid out many times before all the things on sale at one time are purchased and finally removed from the market; and each pound or dollar must be counted for as many pounds or dollars as the number of times it changes hands in order to effect this object.

If we assume the quantity of goods on sale, and the number of times those goods are resold, to be fixed quantities, the value of money will depend upon its quantity, together with the average number of times that each piece changes hands in the process. The whole of the goods sold (counting each resale of the same goods as so much added to the goods) have been exchanged for the whole of the money, multiplied by the number of purchases made on the average by each piece. Consequently, the amount of goods and of transactions being the same, the value of money is inversely as its quantity multiplied by what is called the rapidity of circulation. And the quantity of money in circulation is equal to the money value of all the goods sold, divided by the number which expresses the rapidity of circulation.

> This may be expressed in mathematical language, where V is the value of money, Q is the quantity in circulation, and R the number expressing the rapidity of circulation, as follows:
>
> $V = 1 / (Q \times R)$.

The phrase, rapidity of circulation, requires some comment. It must not be understood to mean the number of purchases made by each piece of money in a given time. Time is not the thing to be considered. The state of society may be such that each piece of money hardly performs more than one purchase in a year; but if this arises from the small number of transactions—from the small amount of business done, the want of activity in traffic, or because what traffic there is mostly takes place by barter—it constitutes no reason why prices should be lower, or the value of money higher. The essential point is, not how often the same money changes hands in a given time, but how often it changes hands in order to perform a given amount of traffic. We must compare the number of purchases made by the money in a given time, not with the time itself, but with the goods sold in that same time. If each piece of money changes hands on an average ten times while goods are sold to the value of a million sterling, it is evident that the money required to circulate those goods is £100,000. And, conversely, if the money in circulation is £100,000, and each piece changes hands, by the purchase of goods, ten times in a month, the sales of goods for money which take place every month must amount, on the average, to £1,000,000. [The essential point to be considered is] the average number of purchases made by each piece in order to affect a given pecuniary amount of transactions.

> "There is no doubt that the rapidity of circulation varies very much between one country and another. A thrifty people with slight banking facilities, like the French, Swiss, Belgians, and Dutch, hoard coin much more than an improvident people like the English, or even a careful people, with a perfect banking system, like the Scotch. Many circumstances, too, affect the rapidity of circulation. Railways and rapid steamboats enable coin and bullion to be more swiftly remitted than of old; telegraphs prevent its needless removal, and the acceleration of the mails has a like effect." "So different are the commercial habits of different peoples, that there evidently exists no proportion whatever between the amount of currency in a country and the aggregate of the exchanges which can be effected by it."[229]

§ 4. Explanations and Limitations of this Principle.

The proposition which we have laid down respecting the dependence of general prices upon the quantity of money in circulation must be understood as applying only to a state of things in which money—that is, gold or silver—is the exclusive instrument of exchange, and actually passes from hand to hand at every purchase, credit in any of its shapes being unknown. When credit comes into play as a means of purchasing, distinct from money in hand, we shall hereafter find that the connection between prices and the amount of the circulating medium is much less direct and intimate, and that such connection as does exist no longer admits of so simple a mode of expression. That an increase of the quantity of money raises prices, and a diminution lowers them, is the most elementary proposition in the theory of currency, and without it we should have no key to any of the others. In any state of things, however, except the simple and primitive one which we have supposed, the proposition is only true, other things being the same.

It is habitually assumed that whenever there is a greater amount of money in the country, or in existence, a rise of prices must necessarily follow. But this is by no means an inevitable consequence. In no commodity is it the quantity in existence, but the quantity offered for sale, that determines the value. Whatever may be the quantity of money in the country, only that part of it will affect prices which goes into the market of commodities, and is there actually exchanged against goods. Whatever increases the amount of this portion of the money in the country tends to raise prices.

> This statement needs modification, since the change in the amounts of specie in the bank reserves, particularly of England and the United States, determines the amount of credit and purchasing power granted, and so affects prices in that way; but prices are affected not by this specie being actually exchanged against goods.

It frequently happens that money to a considerable amount is brought into the country, is there actually invested as capital, and again flows out, without having ever once acted upon the markets of commodities, but only upon the market of securities, or, as it is commonly though improperly called, the money market.

A foreigner landing in the country with a treasure might very probably prefer to invest his fortune at interest; which we shall suppose him to do in the most obvious way by becoming a competitor for a portion of the stock, railway debentures, mercantile bills, mortgages, etc., which are at all times in the hands of the public. By doing this he would raise the prices of those different securities, or in other words would lower the rate of interest; and since this would disturb the relation previously existing between the rate of interest on capital in the country itself and that in foreign countries, it would probably induce some of those who had floating capital seeking employment to send it abroad for foreign investment, rather than buy securities at home at the advanced price. As much money might thus go out as had previously come in, while the prices of commodities would have shown no trace of its temporary presence. This is a case highly deserving of attention; and it is a fact now beginning to be recognized that the passage of the precious metals from country to country is determined much more than was formerly supposed by the state of the loan market in different countries, and much less by the state of prices.

If there be, at any time, an increase in the number of money transactions, a thing continually liable to happen from differences in the activity of speculation, and even in the time of year (since certain kinds of business are transacted only at particular seasons), an increase of the currency which is only proportional to this increase of transactions, and is of no longer duration, has no tendency to raise prices.

> For example, bankers in Eastern cities each year send in the autumn to the West, as the crops are gathered, very large sums of money, to settle transactions in the buying and selling of grain, wool, etc., but it again flows back to the great centers of business in a short time, in payment of purchases from Eastern merchants.

Chapter VI. Of The Value Of Money, As Dependent On Cost Of Production.

§ 1. The value of Money, in a state of Freedom, conforms to the value of the Bullion contained in it.

But money, no more than commodities in general, has its value definitely determined by demand and supply. The ultimate regulator of its value is Cost of Production.

We are supposing, of course, that things are left to themselves. Governments have not always left things to themselves. It was, until lately, the policy of all governments to interdict the exportation and the melting of money; while, by encouraging the exportation and impeding the importation of other things, they endeavored to have a stream of money constantly flowing in. By this course they gratified two prejudices: they drew, or thought that they drew, more money into the country, which they believed to be tantamount to more wealth; and they gave, or thought that they gave, to all producers and dealers, high prices, which, though no real advantage, people are always inclined to suppose to be one.

We are, however, to suppose a state, not of artificial regulation, but of freedom. In that state, and assuming no charge to be made for coinage, the value of money will conform to the value of the bullion of which it is made. A pound-weight of gold or silver in coin, and the same weight in an ingot, will precisely exchange for one another. On the supposition of freedom, the metal can not be worth more in the state of bullion than of coin; for as it can be melted without any loss of time, and with hardly any expense, this would of course be done until the quantity in circulation was so much diminished as to equalize its value with that of the same weight in bullion. It may be thought, however, that the coin, though it can not be of less, may be, and being a manufactured article will naturally be, of greater value than the bullion contained in it, on the same principle on which linen cloth is of more value than an equal weight of linen yarn. This would be true, were it not that Government, in this country and in some others, coins money gratis for any one who furnishes the metal. If Government, however, throws the expense of coinage, as is reasonable, upon the holder, by making a charge to cover the expense (which is done by giving back rather less in coin than has been received in bullion, and is called levying a seigniorage), the coin will rise, to the extent of the seigniorage, above the value of the bullion. If the mint kept back one per cent, to pay the expense of coinage, it would be against the interest of the holders of bullion to have it coined, until the coin was more valuable than the bullion by at least that fraction. The coin, therefore, would be kept one per cent higher in value, which could only be by keeping it one per cent less in quantity, than if its coinage were gratuitous.

> In the United States there was no charge for seigniorage on gold and silver to 1853, when one half of one per cent was charged as interest on the delay if coin was immediately delivered on the deposit of bullion; in 1873 it was reduced to one fifth of one per cent; and in 1875, by a provision of the Resumption Act, it was wholly abolished (the depositor, however, paying for the copper alloy). For the trade-dollars, as was consistent with their being only coined ingots and not legal money, a seigniorage was charged equal simply to the expense of coinage, which was one and a quarter per cent at Philadelphia, and one and a half per cent at San Francisco on the tale value.

§ 2. —Which is determined by the cost of production.

The value of money, then, conforms permanently, and in a state of freedom almost immediately, to the value of the metal of which it is made; with the addition, or not, of the expenses of coinage, according as those expenses are borne by the individual or by the state.

To the majority of civilized countries gold and silver are foreign products: and the circumstances which govern the values of foreign products present some questions which we are not yet ready to examine. For the present, therefore, we must suppose the country which is the subject of our inquiries to be supplied with gold and silver by its own mines [as in the case of the United States], reserving for future consideration how far our conclusions require modification to adapt them to the more usual case.

Of the three classes into which commodities are divided—those absolutely limited in supply, those which may be had in unlimited quantity at a given cost of production, and those which may be had in unlimited quantity, but at an increasing cost of production—the precious metals, being the produce of mines, belong to the third class. Their natural value, therefore, is in the long run proportional to their cost of production in the most unfavorable existing circumstances, that is, at the worst mine which it is necessary to work in order to obtain the required supply. A pound weight of gold will, in the gold-producing countries, ultimately tend to exchange for as much of every other commodity as is produced at a cost equal to its own; meaning by its own cost the cost in labor and expense at the least productive sources of supply which the then existing demand makes it necessary to work. The average value of gold is made to conform to its natural value in the same manner as the values of other things are made to conform to their natural value. Suppose that it were selling above its natural value; that is, above the value which is an equivalent for the labor and expense of mining, and for the risks attending a branch of industry in which nine out of ten experiments have usually been failures. A part of the mass of floating capital which is on the lookout for investment would take the direction of mining enterprise; the supply would thus be increased, and the value would fall. If, on the contrary, it were selling below its natural value, miners would not be obtaining the ordinary profit; they would slacken their works; if the depreciation was great, some of the inferior mines would perhaps stop working altogether: and a falling off in the annual supply, preventing the annual wear and tear from being completely compensated, would by degrees reduce the quantity, and restore the value.

When examined more closely, the following are the details of the process: If gold is above its natural or cost value—the coin, as we have seen, conforming in its value to the bullion—money will be of high value, and the prices of all things, labor included, will be low. These low prices will lower the expenses of all producers; but, as their returns will also be lowered, no advantage will be obtained by any producer, except the producer of gold; whose returns from his mine, not depending on price, will be the same as before, and, his expenses being less, he will obtain extra profits, and will be stimulated to increase his production. *E converso*, if the metal is below its natural value; since this is as much as to say that prices are high, and the money expenses of all producers unusually great; for this, however, all other producers will be compensated by increased money returns; the miner alone will extract from his mine no more metal than before, while his expenses will be greater: his profits, therefore, being diminished or annihilated, he will diminish his production, if not abandon his employment.

In this manner it is that the value of money is made to conform to the cost of production of the metal of which it is made. It may be well, however, to repeat (what has been said before) that the adjustment takes a long time to effect, in the case of a commodity so generally desired and at the same time so durable as the precious metals. Being so largely used, not only as money but for plate and ornament, there is at all times a very large quantity of these metals in existence: while they are so slowly worn out that a comparatively small annual production is sufficient to keep up the supply, and to make any addition to it which may be required by the increase of goods to be circulated, or by the increased demand for gold and silver articles by wealthy consumers. Even if this small annual supply were stopped entirely, it would require many years to reduce the quantity so much as to make any very material difference in prices. The quantity may be increased much more rapidly than it can be diminished; but the increase must be very great before it can make itself much felt over such a mass of the precious metals as exists in the whole commercial world. And hence the effects of all changes in the conditions of production of the precious metals are at first, and continue to be for many years, questions of quantity only, with little reference to cost of production. More especially is this the case when, as at the present time, many new sources of supply have been simultaneously opened, most of them practicable by labor alone, without any capital in advance beyond a pickaxe and a week's food, and when the operations are as yet wholly experimental, the comparative permanent productiveness of the different sources being entirely unascertained.

> For the facts in regard to the production of the precious metals, see the investigation by Dr. Adolf Soetbeer,[230] from which Chart IX has been taken. It is worthy of careful study. The figures in each period, at the top of the respective spaces, give the average annual production during those years. The last period has been added by me from figures taken from the reports of the Director of the United States Mint. Other accessible sources, for the production of the precious metals, are the tables in the appendices to the Report of the Committee to the House of Commons on the "Depreciation of Silver" (1876); the French official Procès-Verbaux of the International Monetary Conference of 1881, which give Soetbeer's figures to a later date than his publication above mentioned; the various papers in the British parliamentary documents; and the reports of the director of our mint. Since 1850 more gold has been produced than in the whole period preceding, from 1492 to 1850. Previous to 1849 the annual average product of gold, out of the total product of both gold and silver, was thirty-six per cent; for the twenty-six years ending in 1875, it has been

seventy and one half per cent. The result has been a rise in gold prices certainly down to 1862,[231] as shown by the following chart. It will be observed how much higher the prices rose during the depression after 1858 than it was during a period of similar conditions after 1848. The result, it may be said, was predicted by Chevalier.[232]

Chart IX.

Chart showing the Production of the Precious Metals, according to Value, from 1493 to 1879.

Years.	Silver.	Gold.	Total.
1493-1520	$2,115,000	$4,045,500	$6,160,500
1521-1544	4,059,000	4,994,000	9,053,000
1545-1560	14,022,000	5,935,500	19,957,500
1561-1580	13,477,500	4,770,750	18,248,250
1581-1600	18,850,500	5,147,500	23,998,000
1601-1620	19,030,500	5,942,750	24,973,250
1621-1640	17,712,000	5,789,250	23,501,250
1641-1660	16,483,500	6,117,000	22,600,500
1661-1680	15,165,000	6,458,750	21,623,750
1681-1700	15,385,500	7,508,500	22,894,000
1701-1720	16,002,000	8,942,000	24,944,000
1721-1740	19,404,000	13,308,250	32,712,250
1741-1760	23,991,500	17,165,500	41,157,000
1761-1780	29,373,250	14,441,750	43,815,000
1781-1800	39,557,750	12,408,500	51,966,250
1801-1810	40,236,750	12,400,000	52,636,750

1811-1820	24,334,750	7,983,000	32,317,750
1821-1830	20,725,250	9,915,750	30,641,000
1831-1840	26,840,250	14,151,500	40,991,750
1841-1850	35,118,750	38,194,250	73,313,000
1851-1855	39,875,250	137,766,750	177,642,000
1856-1860	40,724,500	143,725,250	184,449,750
1861-1865	49,551,750	129,123,250	178,675,000
1866-1870	60,258,750	133,850,000	194,108,750
1871-1875	88,624,000	119,045,750	207,669,750
1876-1879	110,575,000	119,710,000	230,285,000

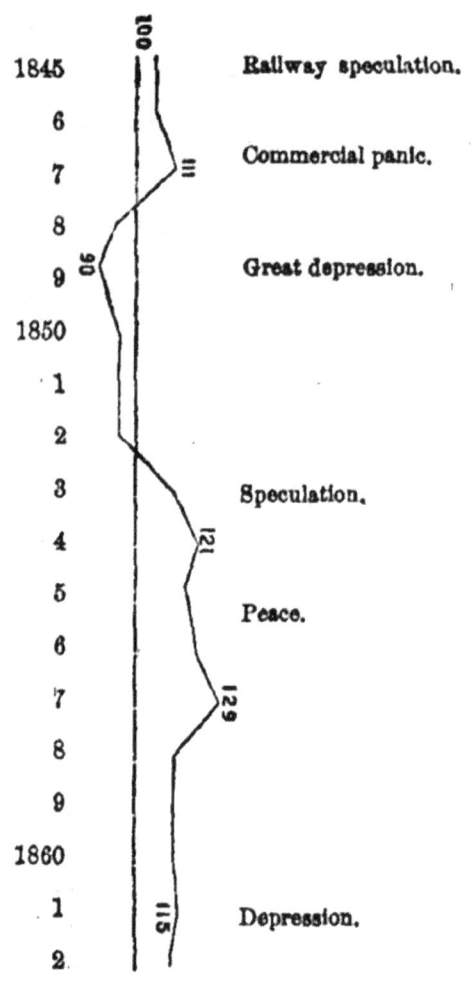

```
1845          100     Railway speculation.
   6           |
   7           |  =   Commercial panic.
   8           |
   9      90   |      Great depression.
1850           |
   1           |
   2           |
   3           |      Speculation.
   4       121 |
   5           |      Peace.
   6           |
   7       129 |
   8           |
   9           |
1860           |
   1       115 |      Depression.
   2           |
```

Chart showing rise of average gold prices after the gold discoveries of 1849 to 1862.

The fall of prices from 1873 to 1879, owing to the commercial panic in the former year, however, is regarded, somewhat unjustly, in my opinion, as an evidence of an appreciation of gold. Mr. Giffen's paper in the "Statistical Journal," vol. xlii, is the basis on which Mr. Goschen founded an argument in the "Journal of the Institute of Bankers" (London), May, 1883, and which attracted considerable attention. On the other side, see Bourne, "Statistical Journal," vol.

xlii. The claim that the value of gold has risen seems particularly hasty, especially when we consider that after the panics of 1857 and 1866 the value of money rose, for reasons not affecting gold, respectively fifteen and twenty-five per cent.

The very thing for which the precious metals are most recommended for use as the materials of money—their *durability*—is also the very thing which has, for all practical purposes, excepted them from the law of cost of production, and caused their value to depend practically upon the law of demand and supply. Their durability is the reason of the vast accumulations in existence, and this it is which makes the annual product very small in relation to the whole existing supply, and so prevents its value from conforming, except after a long term of years, to the cost of production of the annual supply.

§ 3. This law, how related to the principle laid down in the preceding chapter.

Since, however, the value of money really conforms, like that of other things, though more slowly, to its cost of production, some political economists have objected altogether to the statement that the value of money depends on its quantity combined with the rapidity of circulation, which, they think, is assuming a law for money that does not exist for any other commodity, when the truth is that it is governed by the very same laws. To this we may answer, in the first place, that the statement in question assumes no peculiar law. It is simply the law of demand and supply, which is acknowledged to be applicable to all commodities, and which, in the case of money, as of most other things, is controlled, but not set aside, by the law of cost of production, since cost of production would have no effect on value if it could have none on supply. But, secondly, there really is, in one respect, a closer connection between the value of money and its quantity than between the values of other things and their quantity. The value of other things conforms to the changes in the cost of production, without requiring, as a condition, that there should be any actual alteration of the supply: the potential alteration is sufficient; and, if there even be an actual alteration, it is but a temporary one, except in so far as the altered value may make a difference in the demand, and so require an increase or diminution of supply, as a consequence, not a cause, of the alteration in value. Now, this is also true of gold and silver, considered as articles of expenditure for ornament and luxury; but it is not true of money. If the permanent cost of production of gold were reduced one fourth, it might happen that there would not be more of it bought for plate, gilding, or jewelry, than before; and if so, though the value would fall, the quantity extracted from the mines for these purposes would be no greater than previously. Not so with the portion used as money: that portion could not fall in value one fourth unless actually increased one fourth; for, at prices one fourth higher, one fourth more money would be required to make the accustomed purchases; and, if this were not forthcoming, some of the commodities would be without purchasers, and prices could not be kept up. Alterations, therefore, in the cost of production of the precious metals do not act upon the value of money except just in proportion as they increase or diminish its quantity; which can not be said of any other commodity. It would, therefore, I conceive, be an error, both scientifically and practically, to discard the proposition which asserts a connection between the value of money and its quantity.

> There are cases, however, in which the *potential* change of the precious metals affects their value as money in the same way that it affects the value of other things. Such a case was the change in the value of silver in 1876. The usual causes assigned for that serious fall in value were the greatly increased production from the mines of Nevada; the demonetization of silver by Germany; and the decreased demand for export to India. It is true that the exports of silver from England to India fell off from about $32,000,000 in 1871-1872 to about $23,000,000 in 1874-1875; but none of the increased Nevada silver was exported from the United States to London, nor had Germany put more than $30,000,000 of her silver on the market;[233] and yet the price of silver so fell that the depreciation amounted to 20-¼ per cent as compared with the average price between 1867 and 1872. The change in value, however, took place without any corresponding change in the actual quantity in circulation. The relation between prices and the quantities of the precious metals is, therefore, not so exact, certainly as regards silver, as Mr. Mill would have us believe; and thus their values conform more nearly to the general law of Demand

and Supply in the same way that it affects things other than money.

It is evident, however, that the cost of production, in the long run, regulates the quantity; and that every country (temporary fluctuation excepted) will possess, and have in circulation, just that quantity of money which will perform all the exchanges required of it, consistently with maintaining a value conformable to its cost of production. The prices of things will, on the average, be such that money will exchange for its own cost in all other goods: and, precisely because the quantity can not be prevented from affecting the value, the quantity itself will (by a sort of self-acting machinery) be kept at the amount consistent with that standard of prices—at the amount necessary for performing, at those prices, all the business required of it.

Chapter VII. Of A Double Standard And Subsidiary Coins.

§ 1. Objections to a Double Standard.

Though the qualities necessary to fit any commodity for being used as money are rarely united in any considerable perfection, there are two commodities which possess them in an eminent and nearly an equal degree—the two precious metals, as they are called—gold and silver. Some nations have accordingly attempted to compose their circulating medium of these two metals indiscriminately.

There is an obvious convenience in making use of the more costly metal for larger payments, and the cheaper one for smaller; and the only question relates to the mode in which this can best be done. The mode most frequently adopted has been to establish between the two metals a fixed proportion [to decide by law, for example, that sixteen grains of silver should be equivalent to one grain of gold]; and it being left free to every one who has a [dollar] to pay, either to pay it in the one metal or in the other.

If [their] natural or cost values always continued to bear the same ratio to one another, the arrangement would be unobjectionable. This, however, is far from being the fact. Gold and silver, though the least variable in value of all commodities, are not invariable, and do not always vary simultaneously. Silver, for example, was lowered in permanent value more than gold by the discovery of the American mines; and those small variations of value which take place occasionally do not affect both metals alike. Suppose such a variation to take place—the value of the two metals relatively to one another no longer agreeing with their rated proportion—one or other of them will now be rated below its bullion value, and there will be a profit to be made by melting it.

Suppose, for example, that gold rises in value relatively to silver, so that the quantity of gold in a sovereign is now worth more than the quantity of silver in twenty shillings. Two consequences will ensue. No debtor will any longer find it his interest to pay in gold. He will always pay in silver, because twenty shillings are a legal tender for a debt of one pound, and he can procure silver convertible into twenty shillings for less gold than that contained in a sovereign. The other consequence will be that, unless a sovereign can be sold for more than twenty shillings, all the sovereigns will be melted, since as bullion they will purchase a greater number of shillings than they exchange for as coin. The converse of all this would happen if silver, instead of gold, were the metal which had risen in comparative value. A sovereign would not now be worth so much as twenty shillings, and whoever had a pound to pay would prefer paying it by a sovereign; while the silver coins would be collected for the purpose of being melted, and sold as bullion for gold at their real value—that is, above the legal valuation. The money of the community, therefore, would never really consist of both metals, but of the one only which, at the particular time, best suited the interest of debtors; and the standard of the currency would be constantly liable to change from the one metal to the other, at a loss, on each change, of the expense of coinage on the metal which fell out of use.

> This is the operation by which is carried into effect the law of Sir Thomas Gresham (a merchant of the time of Elizabeth) to the purport that "money of less value drives out money of more value," where both are legal payments among individuals. A celebrated instance is that where the clipped coins of England were received by the state on equal terms with new and perfect coin before 1695. They hanged men and women, but they did not prevent the operation of Gresham's law and the disappearance of the perfect coins. When the state refused the clipped coins at legal value, by no longer receiving them in payment of taxes, the trouble ceased.[234] Jevons gives a striking illustration of the same law: "At the time of the treaty of 1858 between Great Britain, the United States, and Japan, which partially opened up the last country to European traders, a very curious system of currency existed in Japan. The most valuable Japanese coin was the kobang, consisting of a thin oval disk of gold about two inches long, and one and a quarter inch wide, weighing two hundred grains, and ornamented in a very primitive manner. It was passing current in the towns of Japan for four silver itzebus, but was worth in English money about 18*s.* 5*d.*, whereas the silver itzebu was equal only to about 1*s.* 4*d.* [four itzebus being worth in English money 5*s.* 4*d.*]. The earliest European traders enjoyed a rare opportunity for making profit.

> By buying up the kobangs at the native rating they trebled their money, until the natives, perceiving what was being done, withdrew from circulation the remainder of the gold."[235]

It appears, therefore, that the value of money is liable to more frequent fluctuations when both metals are a legal tender at a fixed valuation than when the exclusive standard of the currency is either gold or silver. Instead of being only affected by variations in the cost of production of one metal, it is subject to derangement from those of two. The particular kind of variation to which a currency is rendered more liable by having two legal standards is a fall of value, or what is commonly called a depreciation, since practically that one of the two metals will always be the standard of which the real has fallen below the rated value. If the tendency of the metals be to rise in value, all payments will be made in the one which has risen least; and, if to fall, then in that which has fallen most.

> While liable to "more frequent fluctuations," prices do not follow the *extreme* fluctuations of both metals, as some suppose, and as is shown by the following diagram.[236] A represents the line of the value of gold, and B of silver, relatively to some third commodity represented by the horizontal line. Superposing these curves, C would show the line of *extreme* variations, while since prices would follow the metal which *falls* in value, D would show the actual course of variations. While the fluctuations are more frequent in D, they are less extreme than in C.

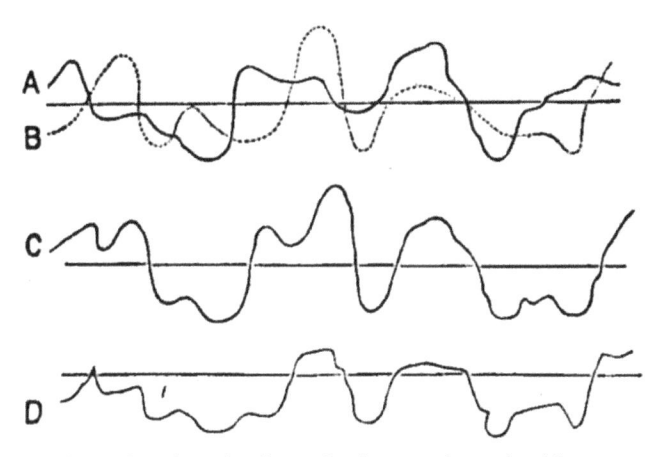

Chart showing the line of prices under a double standard.

§ 2. The use of the two metals as money, and the management of Subsidiary Coins.

The plan of a double standard is still occasionally brought forward by here and there a writer or orator as a great improvement in currency.

It is probable that, with most of its adherents, its chief merit is its tendency to a sort of depreciation, there being at all times abundance of supporters for any mode, either open or covert, of lowering the standard. [But] the advantage without the disadvantages of a double standard seems to be best obtained by those nations with whom one only of the two metals is a legal tender, but the other also is coined, and allowed to pass for whatever value the market assigns to it.

When this plan is adopted, it is naturally the more costly metal which is left to be bought and sold as an article of commerce. But nations which, like England, adopt the more costly of the two as their standard, resort to a different expedient for retaining them both in circulation, namely (1), to make silver a legal tender, but only for small payments. In England no one can be compelled to receive silver in payment for a larger amount than forty shillings. With this regulation there is necessarily combined another, namely (2), that silver coin should be rated, in comparison with gold, somewhat above its intrinsic value; that there should not be, in twenty shillings, as much silver as is worth a sovereign; for, if there were, a very slight turn of the market in its favor would make it worth more than a sovereign, and it would be profitable to melt the silver coin. The overvaluation of the silver coin creates an inducement to buy silver and send it to the mint to be coined, since it is given back at a higher value than properly belongs to it; this, however, has been guarded against (3) by limiting the quantity of the silver coinage, which is not left, like that of gold, to the discretion of individuals, but is determined by the Government, and restricted to the amount supposed to be required for small payments. The only precaution necessary is, not to put so high a valuation upon the silver as to hold out a strong temptation to private coining.

§ 3. The experience of the United States with a double standard from 1792 to 1883.

> The experience of the United States with a double standard, extending as it does from 1792 to 1873 without a break, and from 1878 to the present time, is a most valuable source of instruction in regard to the practical working of bimetallism. While we have nominally had a double standard, in reality we have either had one alone, or been in a transition from one to the other standard; and the history of our coinage strikingly illustrates the truth that the natural values of the two metals, in spite of all legislation, so vary relatively to each other that a constant ratio can not be maintained for any length of time; and that "the poor money drives out the good," according to Gresham's statement. For clearness, the period may be divided, in accordance with the changes of legislation, into four divisions:
>
> I. 1792-1834. Transition from gold to silver.
>
> II. 1834-1853. Transition from silver to gold.
>
> III. 1853-1878. Single gold currency (except 1862-1879, the paper period).
>
> IV. 1878-1884. Transition from gold to silver.
>
> I. With the establishment of the mint, Hamilton agreed upon the use of both gold and silver in our money, at a ratio of 15 to 1: that is, that the amount of pure silver in a dollar should be fifteen times the weight of gold in a dollar. So, while the various Spanish dollars then in

circulation in the United States seemed to contain on the average about 371-¼ grains of pure silver, and since Hamilton believed the relative market value of gold and silver to be about 1 to 15, he put 1/15 of 371-¼ grains, or 24-¾ grains of pure gold, into the gold dollar. It was the best possible example of the bimetallic system to be found, and the mint ratio was intended to conform to the market ratio. If this conformity could have been maintained, there would have been no disturbance. But a cause was already in operation affecting the supply of one of the metals—silver—wholly independent of legislation, and without correspondingly affecting gold.

Two periods of production of silver, in which the production of silver was great relatively to gold, stand out prominently in the history of that metal. (1) One was the enormous yield from the mines of the New World, continuing from 1545 to about 1640, and (2) the only other period of great production at all comparable with it (that is, as regards the production of silver relatively to gold) was that lasting from 1780 to 1820, due to the richness of the Mexican silver-mines. The first period of ninety-five years was longer than the second, which was only forty years; yet while about forty-seven times as much silver as gold was produced on an average during the first period, the average annual amount of silver produced relatively to gold was probably a little greater from 1780 to 1820. The effect of the first period in lowering the relation of silver to gold is well recognized in the history of the precious metals (see Chart X for the fall in the value of silver relatively to gold); that the effect of the second period on the value of silver has not been greater than was actually caused—it has not been small—is explicable only by the laws of the value of money. If you let the same amount of water into a small reservoir which you let into a large one, the level of the former will be raised more than the level of the latter. The great production of the first period was added to a very small existing stock of silver; that of the second period was added to a stock increased by the great previous production just mentioned. The smallness of the annual product relatively to the total quantity existing in the world requires some time, even for a production of silver forty-seven times greater than the gold production, to take its effect on the value of the total silver stock in existence. The effect of this process was beginning to be felt soon after the United States decided on a double standard. For this reason the value of silver was declining about 1800, and, although the annual silver product fell off seriously after 1820, the value of silver continued to decline even after that time, because the increased production, dating back to 1780, was just beginning to make itself felt. Thus we have the phenomenon—which seems very difficult for some persons to understand—of a falling off in the annual production of silver, accompanied by a decrease in its value relatively to gold.

This diminishing value of silver began to affect the coinage of the United States as early as 1811, and by 1820 the disappearance of gold was everywhere commented upon. The process by which this result is produced is a simple one, and is adopted as soon as a margin of profit is seen arising from a divergence between the mint and market ratios. In 1820 the market ratio of gold to silver was 1 to 15.7—that is, the amount of gold in a dollar (24-¾ grains) would exchange for 15.7 times as many grains of silver in the market, in the form of bullion; while at the mint, in the form of coin, it would exchange for only 15 times as many grains of silver. A broker having 1,000 gold dollars could buy with them in the market silver bullion enough (1,000 × 15.7 grains) to have coined, when presented at the mint, 1,000 dollars in silver pieces, and yet have left over as a profit by the operation 700 grains of silver. So long as this can be done, silver (the cheapest money) will be presented at the mint, and gold (the dearest money) will become an article of merchandise too valuable to be used as money when the cheaper silver is legally as good. The best money, therefore, disappears from circulation, as it did in the United States before 1820, owing to the fall in the value of silver. It is to be said, that it has been seriously urged by some writers that silver did not fall, but that gold rose, in value, owing to the demand of England for resumption in 1819.[237] Chronology kills this view;

for the change in the value of silver began too early to have been due to English measures, even if conclusive reasons have not been given above why silver should naturally have fallen in value.

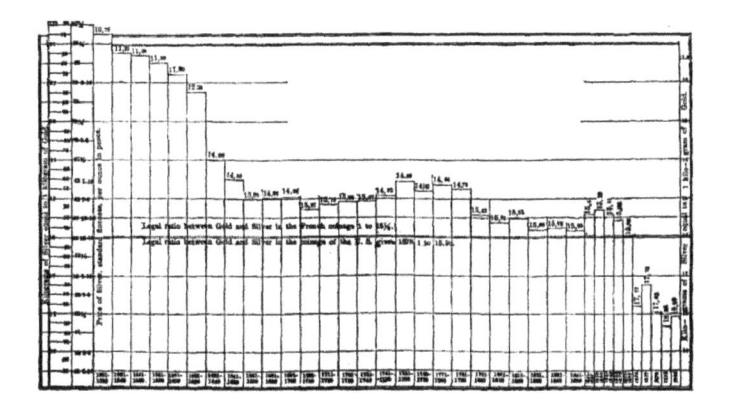

Chart X. Chart showing the Changes in the Relative Values of Gold and Silver from 1501 to 1880. From 1501 to 1680 a space is allotted to each 20 years; from 1681 to 1871, to each 10 years; from 1876 to 1880, to each year.

II. The change in the relative values of gold and silver finally forced the United States to change their mint ratio in 1834. Two courses were open to us: (1) either to increase the quantity of silver in the dollar until the dollar of silver was intrinsically worth the gold in the gold dollar; or (2) debase the gold dollar-piece until it was reduced in value proportionate to the depreciation of silver since 1792. The latter expedient, without any seeming regard to the effect on contracts and the integrity of our monetary standard, was adopted: 6.589 per cent was taken out of the gold dollar, leaving it containing 23.22 grains of pure gold; and as the silver dollar remained unchanged (371-¼ grains) the mint ratio established was 1 to 15.988, or, as commonly stated, 1 to 16. Did this correspond with the market ratio then existing? No. Having seen the former steady fall in silver, and believing that it would continue, Congress hoped to anticipate any further fall by making the mint ratio of gold to silver a little larger than the market ratio. This was done by establishing the mint ratio of 1 to 15.988, while the market ratio in 1834 was 1 to 15.73. Here, again, appeared the difficulty arising from the attempt to balance a ratio on a movable fulcrum. It will be seen that the act of 1834 set at work forces for another change in the coinage—forces of a similar kind, but working in exactly the opposite direction to those previous to 1834. A dollar of gold coin would now exchange for more grains of silver at the mint (15.98) than it would in the form of bullion in the market (15.73). Therefore it would be more profitable to put gold into coin than exchange it as bullion. Gold was sent to the mint, while silver began to be withdrawn from circulation, silver now being more valuable as bullion than as coin. By 1840 a silver dollar was worth 102 cents in gold.[238] This movement, which was displacing silver with gold, received a surprising and unexpected impetus by the gold discoveries of California and Australia in 1849, before mentioned, and made gold less valuable relatively to silver, by lowering the value of gold. Here, again, was another natural cause, independent of legislation, and not to be foreseen, altering the value of one of the precious metals, and in exactly the opposite direction from that in the previous period, when silver was lowered by the increase from the Mexican mines. In 1853 a silver dollar was worth 104 cents in gold (i.e., of a gold dollar containing 23.22 grains); but, some years before, all silver dollars had disappeared from use, and only gold was in circulation. For a large part of this period we had in reality a single standard of gold, the other metal not being able to stay in the currency.

III. After our previous experience, the impossibility of retaining both metals in the coinage together, on equal terms, now came to be generally recognized, and was accepted by Congress in the legislation of 1853. This act made no further changes intended to adapt the mint to the market ratios, but remained satisfied with the gold circulation. But hitherto no regard had been paid to the principles on which a subsidiary coinage is based, as explained by Mr. Mill in the last section (§ 2). The act of 1853, while acquiescing in the single gold standard, had for its purpose the readjustment of the subsidiary coins, which, together with silver dollar-pieces, had all gone out of circulation. Before this, two halves, four quarters, or ten dimes contained the same quantity of pure silver as the dollar-piece (371-¼ grains); therefore, when it became profitable to withdraw the dollar-pieces and substitute gold, it gave exactly the same profit to withdraw two halves or four quarters in silver. For this reason all the subsidiary silver had gone out of circulation, and there was no "small change" in the country. The legislation of 1853 rectified this error: (1) by reducing the quantity of pure silver in a dollar's worth of subsidiary coin to 345.6 grains. By making so much less an amount of silver equal to a dollar of small coins, it was more valuable in that shape than as bullion, and there was no reason for melting it, or withdrawing it (since even if gold and silver changed considerably in their relative values, 345.6 grains of silver could not easily rise sufficiently to become equal in value to a gold dollar, when 371-¼ grains were worth only 104 cents of the gold dollar); (2) this over-valuation of silver in subsidiary coin would cause a great flow of silver to the mint, since silver would be more valuable in subsidiary coin than as bullion; but this was prevented by the provision (section 4 of the act of 1853) that the amount or the small coinage should be limited according to the discretion of the Secretary of the Treasury; and, (3) in order that the overvalued small coinage might not be used for purposes other than for effecting change, its legal-tender power was restricted to payments not exceeding five dollars. This system, a single gold standard for large, and silver for small, payments, continued without question, and with great convenience, until the days of the war, when paper money (1862-1879) drove out (by its cheapness, again) both gold and silver. Paper was far cheaper than the cheapest of the two metals.

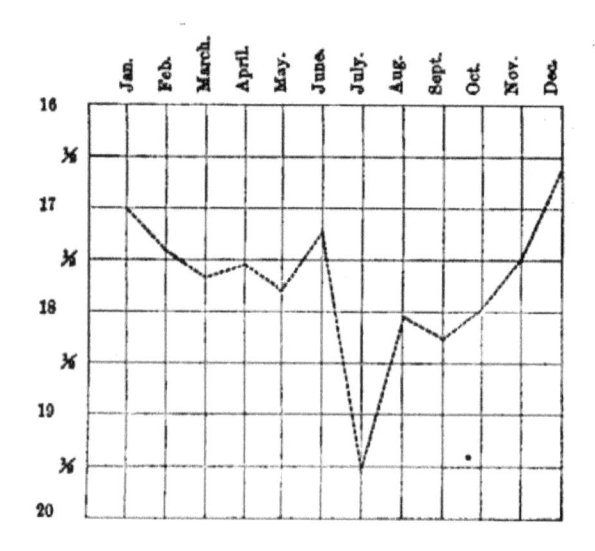

Relative values of gold and silver, by months, in 1876.

The mere fact that the silver dollar-piece had not circulated since even long before 1853 led the authorities to drop out the provisions for the coinage of silver dollars and in 1873 remove it from the list of legal coins (at the ratio of 1 to 15.98, the obsolete ratio fixed as far back as 1834). This is what is known as the "demonetization" of silver. It had no effect on the circulation of silver dollars, since none were in use, and had not been for more than twenty-five years. There had been no desire up to this time to use silver, since it was more expensive than gold; indeed, it is somewhat humiliating to our sense of national honor to reflect that it was not until silver fell so surprisingly in value (in 1876) that the agitation for its use in the coinage arose. When a silver dollar was worth 104 cents, no one wanted it as a means of liquidating debts; when it came to be worth 86 cents, it was capable of serving debtors even better than the then appreciating greenbacks. Thus, while from 1853 (and even before) we had legally two standards, of both gold and silver, but really only one, that of gold, from 1873 to 1878 we had both legally and really only one standard, that of gold.

It might be here added, that I have spoken of the silver dollar as containing 371-¼ grains of pure silver. Of course, alloy is mixed with the pure silver, sufficient, in 1792, to make the original dollar weigh 416 grains in all, its "standard" weight. In 1837 the amount of alloy was changed from 1/12 to 1/10 of the standard weight, which (as the 371-¼ grains of pure silver were unchanged) gave the total weight of the dollar as 412-½ grains, whence the familiar name assigned to this piece. In 1873, moreover, the mint was permitted to put its stamp and devices—to what was not money at all, but a "coined ingot"—on 378 grains of pure silver (420 grains, standard), known as the "trade-dollar." It was intended by this means to make United States silver more serviceable in the Asiatic trade. Oriental nations care almost exclusively for silver in payments. The Mexican silver dollar contained 377-¼ grains of pure silver; the Japanese yen, 374-4/10; and the United States dollar, 371-¼. By making the "trade-dollar" slightly heavier than any coin used in the Eastern world, it would give our silver a new market; and the United States Government was simply asked to certify to the fineness and weight by coining it, provided the owners of silver paid the expenses of coinage. Inadvertently the trade-dollar was included in the list of coins in the act of 1873 which were legal tender for payments of five dollars, but, when this was discovered, it was repealed in 1876. So that the trade-dollar was not a legal coin, in any sense (although it contained more silver than the 412-½-grains dollar). They ceased to be coined in 1878, to which time there had been made $35,959,360.

IV. In February, 1878, an indiscreet and unreasonable movement induced Congress to authorize the recoinage of the silver dollar-piece at the obsolete ratio of 1834 (1 to 15.98), while the market ratio was 1 to 17.87. So extraordinary a reversal of all sound principles and such blindness to our previous experience could be explained only by a desire to force this country to use a silver coinage only, and had its origin with the owners of silver-mines, aided by the desires of debtors for a cheap unit in which to absolve themselves from their indebtedness. There was no pretense of setting up a double standard about it; for it was evident to the most ignorant that so great a disproportion between the mint and market ratios must inevitably lead to the disappearance of gold entirely. This would happen, if owners could bring their silver freely, in any amounts, to the mint for coinage ("Free Coinage"), and so exchange silver against gold coin for the purpose of withdrawing gold, since gold would exchange for less as coin than as bullion. This immediate result was prevented by a provision in the law, which prevented the "free coinage" of silver, and required the Government itself to buy silver and coin at least $2,000,000 in silver each month. This retarded, but will not ultimately prevent, the change from the present gold to a single silver standard. At the rate of $24,000,000 a year, it is only a question of time when the Treasury will be obliged to pay out, for its regular disbursements on the public debt, silver in such amounts as will drive gold out of circulation. In February, 1884, it was feared that this was already at hand, and was practically reached in the August following. Unless a repeal of the law is reached very soon, the uncomfortable spectacle will be seen of a gradual disarrangement of prices, and consequently of trade, arising from a change of the standard.

In order that the alternate movements of silver and gold to the mint for coinage may be seen, there is appended a statement of the coinage[239] during the above periods, which well shows the effects of Gresham's law.

Ratio in the mint and in the market.	Period.	Gold coinage.	Silver dollars coined.
1:15 (silver lower in market)	1792-1834	$11,825,890	$36,275,077
1:15.98 (gold lower in market)	1834-1853	224,965,730	42,936,294

1:15.98 (gold lower in market)	1853-1873	544,864,921	5,538,948
Single gold standard.	1873-1878	166,253,816	....
1:15.98 (silver lower, but no free coinage)	1878-1883	354,019,865	147,255,899

From this it will be seen that there has been an enforced coinage by the Treasury, of almost twice as many silver dollars since 1878 as were coined in all the history of the mint before, since the establishment of the Government.

It may, perhaps, be asked why the silver dollar of 412-½ grains, being worth intrinsically only from 86 to 89 cents, does not depreciate to that value. The Government buys the silver, owns the coin, and holds all that it can not induce the public to receive voluntarily; so that but a part of the total coinage is out of the Treasury. And most of the coins issued are returned for deposit and silver certificates received in return. There being no free coinage, and no greater amount in circulation than satisfies the demand for change, instead of small bills, the dollar-pieces will circulate at their full value, on the principle of subsidiary coin, even though overvalued. And the silver certificates practically go through a process of constant redemption by being received for customs dues equally with gold. When they become too great in quantity to be needed for such purposes, then we may look for the depreciation with good reason.[240]

There are, then, the following kinds of legal tender in the United States in 1884: (1) Gold coins (if not below tolerance); (2) the silver dollar of 412-½ grains; (3) United States notes (except for customs and interest on the public debt); (4) subsidiary silver coinage, to the amount of five dollars; and (5) minor coins, to the amount of twenty-five cents.

The question of a double standard has provoked no little vehement discussion and has called forth a considerable literature since the fall of silver in 1876. A body of opinion exists, best represented in this country by F. A. Walker and S. D. Horton, that the relative values of gold and silver may be kept unchanged, in spite of all natural causes, by the force of law, which, provided that enough countries join in the plan, shall fix the ratio of exchange in the coinage for all great commercial countries, and by this means keep the coinage ratio equivalent to the bullion ratio. The difficulty with this scheme, even if it were wholly sufficient, has thus far been in the obstacles to international agreement. After several international monetary conferences, in 1867, 1878, and 1881, the project seems now to have been practically abandoned by all except the most sanguine. (For a fuller list of authorities on bimetallism, see Appendix I.)

Chapter VIII. Of Credit, As A Substitute For Money.

§ 1. Credit not a creation but a Transfer of the means of Production.

Credit has a great, but not, as many people seem to suppose, a magical power; it can not make something out of nothing. How often is an extension of credit talked of as equivalent to a creation of capital, or as if credit actually were capital! It seems strange that there should be any need to point out that, credit being only permission to use the capital of another person, the means of production can not be increased by it, but only transferred. If the borrower's means of production and of employing labor are increased by the credit given him, the lender's are as much diminished. The same sum can not be used as capital both by the owner and also by the person to whom it is lent; it can not supply its entire value in wages, tools, and materials, to two sets of laborers at once. It is true that the capital which A has borrowed from B, and makes use of in his business, still forms a part of the wealth of B for other purposes; he can enter into arrangements in reliance on it, and can borrow, when needful, an equivalent sum on the security of it; so that to a superficial eye it might seem as if both B and A had the use of it at once. But the smallest consideration will show that, when B has parted with his capital to A, the use of it as capital rests with A alone, and that B has no other service from it than in so far as his ultimate claim upon it serves him to obtain the use of another capital from a third person, C.

§ 2. In what manner it assists Production.

But, though credit is never anything more than a transfer of capital from hand to hand, it is generally, and naturally, a transfer to hands more competent to employ the capital efficiently in production. If there were no such thing as credit, or if, from general insecurity and want of confidence, it were scantily practiced, many persons who possess more or less of capital, but who from their occupations, or for want of the necessary skill and knowledge, can not personally superintend its employment, would derive no benefit from it: their funds would either lie idle, or would be, perhaps, wasted and annihilated in unskillful attempts to make them yield a profit. All this capital is now lent at interest, and made available for production. Capital thus circumstanced forms a large portion of the productive resources of any commercial country, and is naturally attracted to those producers or traders who, being in the greatest business, have the means of employing it to most advantage, because such are both the most desirous to obtain it and able to give the best security. Although, therefore, the productive funds of the country are not increased by credit, they are called into a more complete state of productive activity. As the confidence on which credit is grounded extends itself, means are developed by which even the smallest portions of capital, the sums which each person keeps by him to meet contingencies, are made available for productive uses. The principal instruments for this purpose are banks of deposit. Where these do not exist, a prudent person must keep a sufficient sum unemployed in his own possession to meet every demand which he has even a slight reason for thinking himself liable to. When the practice, however, has grown up of keeping this reserve not in his own custody, but with a banker, many small sums, previously lying idle, become aggregated in the banker's hands; and the banker, being taught by experience what proportion of the amount is likely to be wanted in a given time, and knowing that, if one depositor happens to require more than the average, another will require less, is able to lend the remainder, that is, the far greater part, to producers and dealers: thereby adding the amount, not indeed to the capital in existence, but to that in employment, and making a corresponding addition to the aggregate production of the community.

While credit is thus indispensable for rendering the whole capital of the country productive, it is also a means by which the industrial talent of the country is turned to better account for purposes of production. Many a person who has either no capital of his own, or very little, but who has qualifications for business which are known and appreciated by some possessors of capital, is enabled to obtain either advances in money, or, more frequently, goods on credit, by which his industrial capacities are made instrumental to the increase of the public wealth.

Such are, in the most general point of view, the uses of credit to the productive resources of the world. But these considerations only apply to the credit given to the industrious classes—to producers and dealers. Credit given by dealers to unproductive consumers is never an addition, but always a detriment, to the sources of public wealth. It makes over in temporary use, not the capital of the unproductive classes to the productive, but that of the productive to the unproductive.

§ 3. Function of Credit in economizing the use of Money.

But a more intricate portion of the theory of Credit is its influence on prices; the chief cause of most of the mercantile phenomena which perplex observers. In a state of commerce in which much credit is habitually given, *general prices at any moment depend much more upon the state of credit than upon the quantity of money.* For credit, though it is not productive power, is purchasing power; and a person who, having credit, avails himself of it in the purchase of goods, creates just as much demand for the goods, and tends quite as much to raise their price, as if he made an equal amount of purchases with ready money.

The credit which we are now called upon to consider, as a distinct purchasing power, independent of money, is of course not credit in its simplest form, that of money lent by one person to another, and paid directly into his hands; for, when the borrower expends this in purchases, he makes the purchases with money, not credit, and exerts no purchasing power over and above that conferred by the money. The forms of credit which create purchasing power are those in which no money passes at the time, and very often none passes at all, the transaction being included with a mass of other transactions in an account, and nothing paid but a balance. This takes place in a variety of ways, which we shall proceed to examine, beginning, as is our custom, with the simplest.

First: Suppose A and B to be two dealers, who have transactions with each other both as buyers and as sellers. A buys from B on credit. B does the like with respect to A. At the end of the year, the sum of A's debts to B is set against the sum of B's debts to A, and it is ascertained to which side a balance is due. This balance, which may be less than the amount of many of the transactions singly, and is necessarily less than the sum of the transactions, is all that is paid in money; and perhaps even this is not paid, but carried over in an account current to the next year. A single payment of a hundred pounds may in this manner suffice to liquidate a long series of transactions, some of them to the value of thousands.

But, secondly: The debts of A to B may be paid without the intervention of money, even though there be no reciprocal debts of B to A. A may satisfy B by making over to him a debt due to himself from a third person, C. This is conveniently done by means of a written instrument, called a bill of exchange, which is, in fact, a transferable order by a creditor upon his debtor, and when *accepted* by the debtor, that is, authenticated by his signature, becomes an acknowledgment of debt.

§ 4. Bills of Exchange.

Bills of exchange were first introduced to save the expense and risk of transporting the precious metals from place to place.

The trade between New York and Liverpool affords a constant illustration of the uses of a bill of exchange. Suppose that A in New York ships a cargo of wheat, worth $100,000, or £20,000, to B in Liverpool; also suppose that C in Liverpool (independently of the negotiations of A and B) ships, about the same time, a cargo of steel rails to D in New York, also worth £20,000. Without the use of bills of exchange, B would have been obliged to send £20,000 in gold across the Atlantic, and so would D, at the risk of loss to both. By the device of bills of exchange the goods are really bartered against each other, and all transmission of money saved.

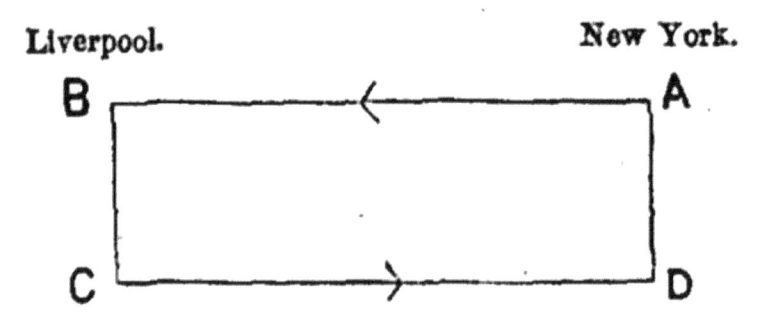

Liverpool.   **New York.**

B ←――――――――――― A

C ――――――――――→ D

A has money due to him in Liverpool, and he sells his claim to this money to any one who wants to make a payment in Liverpool. Going to his banker (the middle-man between exporters and importers and the one who deals in such bills) he finds there D, inquiring for some one who has a claim to money in Liverpool, since D owes C in Liverpool for his cargo of steel rails. A makes out a paper title to the £20,000 which B owes him (i.e., a bill of exchange) and by selling it to D gets immediately his £20,000 there in New York. The form in which this is done is as follows:

> NEW YORK, *January 1, 1884.*
>
> At sight [or sixty days after date] of this first bill of exchange (second and third unpaid), pay to the order of D [the importer of steel rails] £20,000, value received, and charge the same to the account of

[Signed] A [exporter of wheat].
To B [buyer of wheat],
Liverpool, Eng.

D has now paid $100,000, or £20,000, to A for a title to money across the Atlantic in Liverpool, and with this title he can pay his debt to C for the rails. D indorses the bill of exchange, as follows:

Pay to the order of C [the seller of steel rails], Liverpool, value in account. D [importer of steel rails].

To B [the buyer of wheat].

By this means D transfers his title to the £20,000 to C, sends the bill across by mail ("first" in one steamer, "second" in another, to insure certain transmission) to C, who then calls upon B to pay him the £20,000 instead of B sending it across the Atlantic to A; and all four persons have made their payments the more safely by the use of this convenient device. This is the simplest form of the transaction, and it does not change the principle on which it is based, when, as is the case, a banker buys the bills of A, and sells the bills to D—since A typifies all exporters and D all importers.

Bills of exchange having been found convenient as means of paying debts at distant places without the expense of transporting the precious metals, their use was afterward greatly extended from another motive. It is usual in every trade to give a certain length of credit for goods bought: three months, six months, a year, even two years, according to the convenience or custom of the particular trade. A dealer who has sold goods, for which he is to be paid in six months, but who desires to receive payment sooner, draws a bill on his debtor payable in six months, and gets the bill discounted by a banker or other money-lender, that is, transfers the bill to him, receiving the amount, minus interest for the time it has still to run. It has become one of the chief functions of bills of exchange to serve as a means by which a debt due from one person can thus be made available for obtaining credit from another.

Bills of exchange are drawn between the various cities of the United States. In the West, the factor who is purchasing grain or wool for a New York firm draws on his New York correspondents, and this bill (usually certified to by the bill of lading) is presented for discount at the Western banks; and, if there are many bills, funds are possibly sent westward to meet these demands. But the purchases of the West in New York will serve, even if a little later in time, somewhat to offset this drain; and the funds will again move eastward, as goods move westward, practically bartered against each other by the use of bills. There is, however, less movement of funds of late, now that Western cities have accumulated more capital of their own.

The notes given in consequence of a real sale of goods can not be considered as on that account *certainly* representing any actual property. Suppose that A sells £100 worth of goods to B at six months' credit, and takes a bill at six months for it; and that B, within a month after, sells the same goods, at a like credit, to C, taking a like bill; and again, that C, after another month, sells them to D, taking a like bill, and so on. There may then, at the end of six months, be six bills of £100 each existing at the same time, and every one of these may possibly have been discounted. Of all these bills, then, only one represents any actual property.

The extent of a man's actual sales forms some limit to the amount of his real notes; and, as it is highly desirable in commerce that credit should be dealt out to all persons in some sort of regular and due proportion, the measure of a man's actual sales, certified by the appearance of his bills drawn in virtue of those sales, is some rule in the case, though a very imperfect one in many respects. When a bill drawn upon one person is paid to another (or even to the same person) in discharge of a debt or a pecuniary claim, it does something for which, if the bill did not exist, money would be required: it performs the functions of currency. This is a use to which bills of exchange are often applied.

Many bills, both domestic and foreign, are at last presented for payment quite covered with indorsements, each of which represents either a fresh discounting, or a pecuniary transaction in which the bill has performed the functions of money.

§ 5. Promissory Notes.

A third form in which credit is employed as a substitute for currency is that of promissory notes.

The difference between a bill of exchange and a promissory note is, that the former is an order for the payment of money, while the latter is a promise to pay money. In a note the promissor is primarily liable; in a bill the drawer becomes liable only after an ineffectual resort to the drawee.

In the United States a Western merchant who buys $1,000 worth of cotton goods, for instance, of a Boston commission-house on credit, customarily gives his note for the amount, and this note is put upon the market, or presented at a bank for discount. This plan, however, puts all risk upon the one who discounted the note. In the United States such promissory notes are the forms of credit most used between merchants and buyers. The custom, however, is quite different in England and Germany (and generally, it is stated, on the Continent), where bills of exchange are employed in cases where we use a promissory note. A house in London sells $1,000 worth of cotton goods to A, in Carlisle, on a credit of sixty days, draws a bill of exchange on A, which is a demand upon A to pay in a given time (e.g., sixty days), and if "accepted" by him is a legal obligation. The London house takes this bill (perhaps adding its own firm name as indorsers to the paper), and presents it for discount at a London bank. This now explains why it is that, when a particular industry is prosperous and many goods are sold, there is more "paper" offered for discount at the banks (cf. p. 222), and why capital flows readily in that direction.

It is chiefly in the latter form [promissory notes] that it has become, in commercial countries, an express occupation to issue such substitutes for money. Dealers in money wish to lend, not their capital merely, but their credit, and not only such portion of their credit as consists of funds actually deposited with them, but their power of obtaining credit from the public generally, so far as they think they can safely employ it. This is done in a very convenient manner by lending their own promissory notes payable to bearer on demand—the borrower being willing to accept these as so much money, because the credit of the lender makes other people willingly receive them on the same footing, in purchases or other payments. These notes, therefore, perform all the functions of currency, and render an equivalent amount of money, which was previously in circulation, unnecessary. As, however, being payable on demand, they may be at any time returned on the issuer, and money demanded for them, he must, on pain of bankruptcy, keep by him as much money as will enable him to meet any claims of that sort which can be expected to occur within the time necessary for providing himself with more; and prudence also requires that he should not attempt to issue notes beyond the amount which experience shows can remain in circulation without being presented for payment.

The convenience of this mode of (as it were) coining credit having once been discovered, governments have availed themselves of the same expedient, and have issued their own promissory notes in payment of their expenses; a resource the more useful, because it is the only mode in which they are able to borrow money without paying interest.

§ 6. Deposits and Checks.

A fourth mode of making credit answer the purposes of money, by which, when carried far enough, money may be very completely superseded, consists in making payments by checks. The custom of keeping the spare cash reserved for immediate use, or against contingent demands, in the hands of a banker, and making all payments, except small ones, by orders on bankers, is in this country spreading to a continually larger portion of the public. If the person making the payment and the person receiving it keep their money with the same banker, the payment takes place without any intervention of money, by the mere transfer of its amount in the banker's books from the credit of the payer to that of the receiver. If all persons in [New York] kept their cash at the same banker's, and made all their payments by means of checks, no money would be required or used for any transactions beginning and terminating in [New York]. This ideal limit is almost attained, in fact, so far as regards transactions between [wholesale] dealers. It is chiefly in the retail transactions between dealers and consumers, and in the payment of wages, that money or bank-notes now pass, and then only when the amounts are small. As for the merchants and larger dealers, they habitually make all payments in the course of their business by checks. They do not, however, all deal with the same banker, and, when A gives a check to B, B usually pays it not into the same but into some other bank. But the convenience of business has given birth to an arrangement which makes all the banking-houses of [a] city, for certain purposes, virtually one establishment. A banker does not send the checks which are paid into his banking-house to the banks on which they are drawn, and demand money for them. There is a building called the Clearing-House, to which every [member of the association] sends, each afternoon, all the checks on other bankers which he has received during the day, and they are there exchanged for the checks on him which have come into the hands of other bankers, the balances only being paid in money; or even these not in money, but in checks.

> A clearing-house is simply a circular railing containing as many openings as there are banks in the association; a clerk from each bank presents, in the form of a bundle of checks, at his opening, all the claims of his bank against all others, and notes the total amount; a clerk inside takes the checks, distributes each check to the clerk of the bank against whom it is drawn, and all that are left at his opening constitute the total demands of all the other banks against itself; and this sum total is set off against the given bank's demands upon the others. The difference, for or against the bank, as the case may be, may then be settled by a check.[241]

> The total amount of exchanges made through the New York Clearing-House in 1883 was $40,293,165,258 (or about twenty-five times the total of our national debt in that year), and the balances paid in money were only 3.9 per cent of the exchanges.[242] For valuable explanations on this subject, consult Jevons, "Money and the Mechanism of Exchange," Chapters XIX-XXIII. The explanation of the functions of a bank, Chapter XX, is very good.

Chapter IX. Influence Of Credit On Prices.

§ 1. What acts on prices is Credit, in whatever shape given.

Having now formed a general idea of the modes in which credit is made available as a substitute for money, we have to consider in what manner the use of these substitutes affects the value of money, or, what is equivalent, the prices of commodities. It is hardly necessary to say that the permanent value of money—the natural and average prices of commodities—are not in question here. These are determined by the cost of producing or of obtaining the precious metals. An ounce of gold or silver will in the long run exchange for as much of every other commodity as can be produced or imported at the same cost with itself. And an order, or note of hand, or bill payable at sight, for an ounce of gold, while the credit of the giver is unimpaired, is worth neither more nor less than the gold itself.

It is not, however, with ultimate or average, but with immediate and temporary prices that we are now concerned. These, as we have seen, may deviate very widely from the standard of cost of production. Among other causes of fluctuation, one we have found to be the quantity of money in circulation. Other things being the same, an increase of the money in circulation raises prices; a diminution lowers them. If more money is thrown into circulation than the quantity which can circulate at a value conformable to its cost of production, the value of money, so long as the excess lasts, will remain below the standard of cost of production, and general prices will be sustained above the natural rate.

But we have now found that there are other things, such as bank-notes, bills of exchange, and checks, which circulate as money, and perform all the functions of it, and the question arises, Do these various substitutes operate on prices in the same manner as money itself? I apprehend that bank-notes, bills, or checks, as such, do not act on prices at all. What does act on prices is Credit, in whatever shape given, and whether it gives rise to any transferable instruments capable of passing into circulation or not.

§ 2. Credit a purchasing Power, similar to Money.

Money acts upon prices in no other way than by being tendered in exchange for commodities. The demand which influences the prices of commodities consists of the money offered for them. Money not in circulation has no effect on prices.

In the case, however, of payment by checks, the purchases are, at any rate, made, though not with the money in the buyer's possession, yet with money to which he has a right. But he may make purchases with money which he only expects to have, or even only pretends to expect. He may obtain goods in return for his acceptances payable at a future time, or on his note of hand, or on a simple book-credit—that is, on a mere promise to pay. All these purchases have exactly the same effect on price as if they were made with ready money. The amount of purchasing power which a person can exercise is composed of all the money in his possession or due to him, and of all his credit. For exercising the whole of this power he finds a sufficient motive only under peculiar circumstances, but he always possesses it; and the portion of it which he at any time does exercise is the measure of the effect which he produces on price.

Suppose that, in the expectation that some commodity will rise in price, he determines not only to invest in it all his ready money, but to take up on credit, from the producers or importers, as much of it as their opinion of his resources will enable him to obtain. Every one must see that by thus acting he produces a greater effect on price than if he limited his purchases to the money he has actually in hand. He creates a demand for the article to the full amount of his money and credit taken together, and raises the price proportionally to both. And this effect is produced, though none of the written instruments called substitutes for currency may be called into existence; though the transaction may give rise to no bill of exchange, nor to the issue of a single bank-note. The buyer, instead of taking a mere book-credit, might have given a bill for the amount, or might have paid for the goods with bank-notes borrowed for that purpose from a banker, thus making the purchase not on his own credit with the seller, but on the banker's credit with the seller, and his own with the banker. Had he done so, he would have produced as great an effect on price as by a simple purchase to the same amount on a book-credit, but no greater effect. The credit itself, not the form and mode in which it is given, is the operating cause.

§ 3. Great extensions and contractions of Credit. Phenomena of a commercial crisis analyzed.

The inclination of the mercantile public to increase their demand for commodities by making use of all or much of their credit as a purchasing power depends on their expectation of profit. When there is a general impression that the price of some commodity is likely to rise from an extra demand, a short crop, obstructions to importation, or any other cause, there is a disposition among dealers to increase their stocks in order to profit by the expected rise. This disposition tends in itself to produce the effect which it looks forward to—a rise of price; and, if the rise is considerable and progressive, other speculators are attracted, who, so long as the price has not begun to fall, are willing to believe that it will continue rising. These, by further purchases, produce a further advance, and thus a rise of price, for which there were originally some rational grounds, is often heightened by merely speculative purchases, until it greatly exceeds what the original grounds will justify. After a time this begins to be perceived, the price ceases to rise, and the holders, thinking it time to realize their gains, are anxious to sell. Then the price begins to decline, the holders rush into the market to avoid a still greater loss, and, few being willing to buy in a falling market, the price falls much more suddenly than it rose. Those who have bought at a higher price than reasonable calculation justified, and who have been overtaken by the revulsion before they had realized, are losers in proportion to the greatness of the fall and to the quantity of the commodity which they hold, or have bound themselves to pay for.

This is the ideal extreme case of what is called a commercial crisis. There is said to be a commercial crisis when a great number of merchants and traders at once either have, or apprehend that they shall have, a difficulty in meeting their engagements. The most usual cause of this general embarrassment is the recoil of prices after they have been raised by a spirit of speculation, intense in degree, and extending to many commodities. When, after such a rise, the reaction comes and prices begin to fall, though at first perhaps only through the desire of the holders to realize, speculative purchases cease; but, were this all, prices would only fall to the level from which they rose, or to that which is justified by the state of the consumption and of the supply. They fall, however, much lower; for as, when prices were rising, and everybody apparently making a fortune, it was easy to obtain almost any amount of credit, so now, when everybody seems to be losing, and many fail entirely, it is with difficulty that firms of known solidity can obtain even the credit to which they are accustomed, and which it is the greatest inconvenience to them to be without, because all dealers have engagements to fulfill, and, nobody feeling sure that the portion of his means which he has intrusted to others will be available in time, no one likes to part with ready money, or to postpone his claim to it. To these rational considerations there is superadded, in extreme cases, a panic as unreasoning as the previous over-confidence; money is borrowed for short periods at almost any rate of interest, and sales of goods for immediate payment are made at almost any sacrifice. Thus general prices, during a commercial revulsion, fall as much below the usual level as during the previous period of speculation they have risen above it; the fall, as well as the rise, originating not in anything affecting money, but in the state of credit.

> Professor Jevons seriously advanced a theory that, inasmuch as the harvests of the world were the causes of good or bad trade, and that their deficiency would regularly be followed by commercial distress, then a periodic cause of bad harvests, if found, would explain the constant recurrence of commercial crises. This cause he claimed to have found in the sun-spots, which periodically deprive the crops of that source of growth which is usually furnished by the sun when no spots appear.[243] It has not received general acceptance.
>
> In the United States financial disasters have occurred in 1814, 1819, 1825, 1837-1839, 1857, and 1873. Those of 1837 and 1873 seem to have been the most serious in their effects; but this field, so far as scientific study is concerned, has not been fully worked, and much remains to be learned about these crises in the United States. The crisis of 1873 was due to excessive railway-building. It was testified[244] concerning the New York banks in 1873 that "their capital needed for legitimate purposes was practically lent out on certain iron rails, railroad-ties, bridges, and rolling-stock, *called* railroads, many of them laid down in places where these materials were practically useless."
>
> Under the effects due to swift communication by steam, but especially to the electric telegraph, modern credit is a very different thing from what it was fifty years ago. Now, a shock on the Bourse at Vienna is felt the same day at Paris, London, and New York. A commercial crisis in one great money-center is felt at every other point in the world which has business connections with it. Moreover, as Cherbuliez[245] says: "A country is more subject to crises the more advanced is its economical development. There are certain

maladies which attack only grown-up persons who have reached a certain degree of vigor and maturity."

§ 4. Influence of the different forms of Credit on Prices.

It does not, indeed, follow that credit *will* be more used because it *can* be. When the state of trade holds out no particular temptation to make large purchases on credit, dealers will use only a small portion of the credit-power, and it will depend only on convenience whether the portion which they use will be taken in one form or in another. One single exertion of the credit-power in the form of (1) book-credit, is only the foundation of a single purchase; but, if (2) a bill is drawn, that same portion of credit may serve for as many purchases as the number of times the bill changes hands; while (3) every bank-note issued renders the credit of the banker a purchasing power to that amount in the hands of all the successive holders, without impairing any power they may possess of effecting purchases on their own credit. Credit, in short, has exactly the same purchasing power with money; and as money tells upon prices not simply in proportion to its amount, but to its amount multiplied by the number of times it changes hands, so also does credit; and credit transferable from hand to hand is in that proportion more potent than credit which only performs one purchase.

There is a form of credit transactions (4) by checks on bankers, and transfers in a banker's books, which is exactly parallel in every respect to bank-notes, giving equal facilities to an extension of credit, and capable of acting on prices quite as powerfully. A bank, instead of lending its notes to a merchant or dealer, might open an account with him, and credit the account with the sum it had agreed to advance, on an understanding that he should not draw out that sum in any other mode than by drawing checks against it in favor of those to whom he had occasion to make payments. These checks might possibly even pass from hand to hand like bank-notes; more commonly, however, the receiver would pay them into the hands of his own banker, and when he wanted the money would draw a fresh check against it; and hence an objector may urge that as the original check would very soon be presented for payment, when it must be paid either in notes or in coin, notes or coin to an equal amount must be provided as the ultimate means of liquidation. It is not so, however. The person to whom the check is transferred may perhaps deal with the same banker, and the check may return to the very bank on which it was drawn.

This is very often the case in country districts; if so, no payment will be called for, but a simple transfer in the banker's books will settle the transaction. If the check is paid into a different bank, it will not be presented for payment, but liquidated by set-off against other checks; and, in a state of circumstances favorable to a general extension of banking credits, a banker who has granted more credit, and has therefore more checks drawn on him, will also have more checks on other bankers paid to him, and will only have to provide notes or cash for the payment of balances; for which purpose the ordinary reserve of prudent bankers, one third of their liabilities, will abundantly suffice.

§ 5. On what the use of Credit depends.

The credit given to any one by those with whom he deals does not depend on the quantity of bank-notes or coin in circulation at the time, but on their opinion of his solvency. If any consideration of a more general character enters into their calculation, it is only in a time of pressure on the loan market, when they are not certain of being themselves able to obtain the credit on which they have been accustomed to rely; and even then, what they look to is the general state of the loan market, and not (preconceived theory apart) the amount of bank-notes. So far, as to the willingness to *give* credit. And the willingness of a dealer to *use* his credit depends on his expectations of gain, that is, on his opinion of the probable future price of his commodity; an opinion grounded either on the rise or fall already going on, or on his prospective judgment respecting the supply and the rate of consumption. When a dealer extends his purchases beyond his immediate means of payment, engaging to pay at a specified time, he does so in the expectation either that the transaction will have terminated favorably before that time arrives, or that he shall then be in possession of sufficient funds from the proceeds of his other transactions. The fulfillment of these expectations depends upon prices, but not specially upon the amount of bank-notes. It is obvious, however, that prices do not depend on money, but on purchases. Money left with a banker, and not drawn against, or drawn against for other purposes than buying commodities, has no effect on prices, any more than credit which is not used. Credit which *is* used to purchase commodities affects prices in the same manner as money. Money and credit are thus exactly on a par in their effect on prices.

> It is often seen, in our large cities, that money is very plentiful, but no one seems to wish its use (that is, no one with safe securities). Inability to find investments

and to find industries in which the rate of profit is satisfactory—all of which depends on the business character and activity of the people—will prevent credit from being used, no matter how many bank-notes, or greenbacks, or how much gold there is in the country. It is impossible to make people invest, simply by increasing the number of counters by which commodities are exchanged against each other; that is, by increasing the money. The reason why more credit is wanted is because men see that increased production is possible of a kind that will find other commodities ready to be offered (i.e., demand) in exchange for that production. Normal credit, therefore, on a healthy basis, increases and slackens with the activity or dullness of trade. Speculation, or the wild extension of credit, on the other hand, is apt to be begotten by a plethora of money, which has induced low rates for loans, and moves with the uncertain waves of popular impression. By normal credit we mean that the wealth represented by the credit is really at the disposal of the borrowers; in a crisis, the quantity of wealth supposed to be represented by credit is very much greater than that at the disposal of the lenders.[246]

§ 6. What is essential to the idea of Money?

There has been a great amount of discussion and argument on the question whether several of these forms of credit, and in particular whether bank-notes, ought to be considered as money. It seems to be an essential part of the idea of money that it be legal tender. An inconvertible paper which is legal tender is universally admitted to be money; in the French language the phrase *papier-monnaie* actually *means* inconvertibility, convertible notes being merely *billets à porteur*. An instrument which would be deprived of all value by the insolvency of a corporation can not be money in any sense in which money is opposed to credit. It either is not money, or it is money and credit too.

It would seem, from all study of the essentials of money (Book III, Chapter IV), that the necessary part of the idea of money is that it should have value in itself. No one parts with valuable commodities for a medium of exchange which does not possess value; and we have seen that Legislatures can not control the natural value of even the precious metals by giving them legal-tender power. Much less could it be done for paper money. Paper, therefore, may, as an instrument of credit, be a substitute for money; but, in accordance with the above test, it can not properly be considered as money in the full sense. Of course, paper money, checks, etc., perform some of the functions of money equally well with the precious metals. F. A. Walker holds that anything is money which performs money-work; but he excludes checks from his catalogue of things which may serve as money. It is practically of little importance, however, what we include under money, so long as its functions are well understood; it is merely a question of nomenclature, and need not disturb us.

Chapter X. Of An Inconvertible Paper Currency.

§ 1. What determines the value of an inconvertible paper money?

After experience had shown that pieces of paper, of no intrinsic value, by merely bearing upon them the written profession of being equivalent to a certain number of francs, dollars, or pounds, could be made to circulate as such, and to produce all the benefit to the issuers which could have been produced by the coins which they purported to represent, governments began to think that it would be a happy device if they could appropriate to themselves this benefit, free from the condition to which individuals issuing such paper substitutes for money were subject, of giving, when required, for the sign, the thing signified. They determined to try whether they could not emancipate themselves from this unpleasant obligation, and make a piece of paper issued by them pass for a pound, by merely calling it a pound, and consenting to receive it in payment of the taxes.

In the case supposed, the functions of money are performed by a thing which derives its power of performing them solely from convention; but convention is quite sufficient to confer the power; since nothing more is needful to make a person accept anything as money, and even at any arbitrary value, than the persuasion that it will be taken from him on the same terms by others. The only question is, what determines the value of such a currency, since it can not be, as in the case of gold and silver (or paper exchangeable for them at pleasure), the cost of production.

We have seen, however, that even in the case of metallic currency, the immediate agency in determining its value is its quantity. If the quantity, instead of depending on the ordinary mercantile motives of profit and loss, could be arbitrarily fixed by authority, the value would depend on the fiat of that authority, not on cost of production. The quantity of a paper currency not convertible into the metals at the option of the holder *can* be arbitrarily fixed, especially if the issuer is the sovereign power of the state. The value, therefore, of such a currency is entirely arbitrary.

> The value of paper money is, of course, primarily and mainly dependent on the quantity issued. The general

level of value depends on the *quantity*; but we also find that deviations from this general level, in the direction of further depreciation than could be due to quantity alone, is caused by any event which shakes the confidence of any one that he may get the existing value for his paper. The "convention" by which real value (the essential idea of money) was associated with this paper in the minds of all is thereby broken. *Fiat* money—that is, a piece of paper, not containing a promise to pay a dollar, but a simple declaration that this is a dollar—therefore, separates the paper from any connection with value. And yet we see that *fiat* money has some, although a fluctuating, value at certain times: if the State receives it for taxes, if it is a legal acquittal of obligations, then, to that extent, a certain quantity of it is given a value equal to the wealth represented by the taxes, or the debts. Jevons remarks on this point[247] that, if "the quantity of notes issued was kept within such moderate limits that any one wishing to realize the metallic value of the notes could find some one wanting to pay taxes, and therefore willing to give coin for notes," stability of value might be secured. If there is more in circulation than performs these functions, it will depreciate in the proportion of the *quantity* to the extent of the uses assigned to it; so that the relation of quantity to uses is the only thing which can give value to *fiat* money, but beyond a certain point in the issues other forces than mere quantity begin to affect the value. Although the paper is not even a promise to pay value, the form of expression on its face, or the term used as its designation, generally tends, under the force of convention and habit, to give a popular value to paper.

Although the State may not promise to pay a dollar, yet, wherever such paper money carries any purchasing power with it (which has very seldom happened, and then only for short periods), it will be found that there is a vague popular understanding that the State intends, at some time or other, to redeem the notes with value in coin to some amount. In the early cases of irredeemable money in our colonies, the income of taxes, or similar resources, were promised as a means of redemption. To some—although a slight—extent, the idea of value was associated with such paper. The actual quantity issued did not measure the depreciation. The paper did depreciate with increased issues. But only in so far as the increased issues proved to the community that there was less and less possibility of ever receiving value for them did they depreciate. In other words, we come to the familiar experience, known to many, of a paper money depending for its value on the opinions of men in the country. This was partially true, even of our own greenbacks, which were not *fiat* money, but promises to pay (although not then redeemable), as may be seen by the movement of the line in Chart XII (p. 359), which represents the fluctuations of our paper money during the civil war. The upward movement of the line, which indicates the premium on gold during our late war, of course represents correspondingly the depreciation of the paper. Every victory or defeat of the Union arms raised or lowered the premium on gold; it was the register of the opinion of the people as to the value to be associated with the paper. The second and third resorts to issues of greenbacks were regarded as confessions of financial distress; it was this which produced the effect on their value. It was not only the quantity but also that which caused the issue of the quantity. It is, of course, clear that the value of a paper money like the greenbacks, which were the promises to pay of a rich country, would bear a definite relation to the actual quantity issued; and this is to be seen by the generally higher level of the line on the chart, showing a steadily diminishing purchasing power as the issues increased. But the thing which weighed largely in people's minds was the possibility of ultimate redemption; and the premium on gold was practically a register of the "betting" on this possibility. In 1878, when Secretary Sherman's reserve was seen to be increasing to an effective amount, and when it became evident that he would have the means (i.e., the value represented by all the paper that was likely to be presented) to resume on the day set, January 1, 1879, the premium gradually faded away. The general shifting of the level to a lower stage in this later period was not due to any decrease in the quantity outstanding, because the contraction had been stopped in 1868, and that consequent on the resumption act in May, 1878.

Suppose that, in a country of which the currency is wholly metallic, a paper currency is suddenly issued, to the amount of half the metallic circulation; not by a banking establishment, or in the form of loans, but by the Government, in payment of salaries and purchase of commodities. The currency being suddenly increased by one half, all prices will rise, and, among the rest, the prices of all things made of gold and silver. An ounce of manufactured gold will become more valuable than an ounce of gold coin, by more than that customary difference which compensates for the value of the workmanship; and it will be profitable to melt the coin for the purpose of being manufactured, until as much has been taken from the currency by the subtraction of gold as had been added to it by the issue of paper. Then prices will relapse to what they were at first, and there will be nothing changed, except that a paper currency has been substituted for half of the metallic currency which existed before. Suppose, now, a second emission of paper; the same series of effects will be renewed; and so on, until the whole of the metallic money has disappeared [see Chart No. XIV, Chap. XV, for the exportation of gold from the United States after the issue of our paper money in 1862]: that is, if paper be issued of as low a denomination as the lowest coin; if not, as much will remain as convenience requires for the smaller payments. The addition made to the quantity of gold and silver disposable for ornamental purposes will somewhat reduce, for a time, the value of the article; and as long as this is the case, even though paper has been issued to the original amount of the metallic circulation, as much coin will remain in circulation along with it as will keep the value of the currency down to the reduced value of the metallic material; but the value having fallen below the cost of production, a stoppage or diminution of the supply from the mines will enable the surplus to be carried off by the ordinary agents of destruction, after which the metals and the currency will recover their natural value. We are here supposing, as we have supposed throughout, that the country has mines of its own, and no commercial intercourse with other countries; for, in a country having foreign trade, the coin which is rendered superfluous by an issue of paper is carried off by a much prompter method.

Mr. Mill's statement, that, if paper be not issued of as low a denomination as the lowest coin, "as much will remain as convenience requires for the smaller payments," will not hold true. During our recent experiment of depreciated paper, the depreciation was such as to drive out the subsidiary silver coins, by July, 1862, and we were forced to supply their place by a fractional paper currency. By an amendment inserted June 17, 1862, into the act authorizing a second issue of $150,000,000 of greenbacks, it was ordered "that no note shall be issued for the fractional part of a dollar, and not more than $35,000,000 shall be of lower denominations than five dollars" (act, finally passed July 11, 1862). Although there were no fractional notes, yet one-dollar notes drove out subsidiary silver, simply because the paper had depreciated to a value below that of the 345.6 grains of silver in two halves or four quarters of a dollar. By July 2d the disappearance of small coin was distinctly noted. Let the value of gold be represented by 100; and a dollar of small silver coin (345.6 grains), relatively to a gold dollar, by 96. Now, if paper depreciates to 90, relatively to gold, it will drive out the subsidiary silver at 96, in accordance with Gresham's law.

Up to this point the effects of a paper currency are substantially the same, whether it is convertible into specie or not. It is when the metals have been completely superseded and driven from circulation that the difference between convertible and inconvertible paper begins to be operative. When the gold or silver has all gone from circulation, and an equal amount of paper has taken its place, suppose that a still further issue is superadded. The same series of phenomena recommences: prices rise, among the rest the prices of gold and silver articles, and it becomes an object, as before, to procure coin, in order to convert it into bullion. There is no longer any coin in circulation; but, if the paper currency is convertible, coin may still be obtained from the issuers in exchange for notes. All additional notes, therefore, which are attempted to be forced into circulation after the metals have been completely superseded, will return upon the issuers in exchange for coin; and they will not be able to maintain in circulation such a quantity of convertible paper as to sink its value below the metal which it represents. It is not so, however, with an inconvertible currency. To the increase of that (if permitted by law) there is no check. The issuers may add to it indefinitely, lowering its value and raising prices in proportion; they may, in other words, depreciate the currency without limit.

Such a power, in whomsoever vested, is an intolerable evil. All variations in the value of the circulating medium are mischievous: they disturb existing contracts and expectations, and the liability to such changes renders every pecuniary engagement of long date entirely precarious. The person who buys for himself, or gives to another, an annuity of one [hundred dollars], does not know whether it will be equivalent to [two hundred or to fifty dollars] a few years hence. Great as this evil would be if it depended only on accident, it is still greater when placed at the arbitrary disposal of an individual or a body of individuals, who may have any kind or degree of interest to be served by an artificial fluctuation in fortunes, and who have at any rate a strong interest in issuing as much as possible, each issue being in itself a source of profit—not to add, that the issuers may have, and, in the case of a government paper, always have, a direct interest in lowering the value of the currency, because it is the medium in which their own debts are computed.

> The United States Supreme Court had decided in December, 1870, by the second legal-tender decision, that the issue of greenbacks (inconvertible from 1862 to 1879) was constitutional during a time of war; but it was thought that the reissue of these notes since the war, when no war emergency could be pleaded, was unconstitutional. This view, however, was met by the unfortunate decision of the Supreme Court, delivered by Justice Gray, March, 1884, which announced the doctrine that the expediency of an issue of legal-tender paper money was to be determined solely by Congress; and that, if Congress judged the issue expedient, it was within the limits of those provisions of the Constitution (section 8), which gave Congress the means to do whatever was "necessary and proper" to carry out the powers expressly granted to it. Nothing now can prevent Congress, should it choose to do so, from issuing paper money of any description whatever, even if of absolutely no value. The disaster that might be brought upon the country by a rising tide of repudiation among debtors, taking its effect through a facile and plastic Congress (as in the case of the silver coinage in 1878), is appalling to reflect upon.

§ 2. *If regulated by the price of Bullion, as inconvertible Currency might be safe, but not Expedient.*

In order that the value of the currency may be secure from being altered by design, and may be as little as possible liable to fluctuation from accident, the articles least liable of all known commodities to vary in their value, the precious metals, have been made in all civilized countries the standard of value for the circulating medium; and no paper currency ought to exist of which the value can not be made to conform to theirs. Nor has this fundamental maxim ever been entirely lost sight of, even by the governments which have most abused the power of creating inconvertible paper. If they have not (as they generally have) professed an intention of paying in specie at some indefinite future time, they have at least, by giving to their paper issues the names of their coins, made a virtual, though generally a false, profession of intending to keep them at a value corresponding to that of the coins. This is not impracticable, even with an inconvertible paper. There is not, indeed, the self-acting check which convertibility brings with it. But there is a clear and unequivocal indication by which to judge whether the currency is depreciated, and to what extent. That indication is the price of the precious metals. When holders of paper can not demand coin to be converted into bullion, and when there is none left in circulation, bullion rises and falls in price like other things; and if it is above the mint price—if an ounce of gold, which would be coined into the equivalent of [$18.60], is sold for [$20 or $25] in paper—the value of the currency has sunk just that much below what the value of a metallic currency would be. If, therefore, the issue of inconvertible paper were subjected to strict rules, one rule being that, whenever bullion rose above the mint price, the issues should be contracted until the market price of bullion and the mint price were again in accordance, such a currency would not be subject to any of the evils usually deemed inherent in an inconvertible paper.

But, also, such a system of currency would have no advantages sufficient to recommend it to adoption. An inconvertible currency, regulated by the price of bullion, would conform exactly, in all its variations, to a convertible one; and the only advantage gained would be that of exemption from the necessity of keeping any reserve of the precious metals, which is not a very important consideration, especially as a government, so long as its good faith is not suspected, need not keep so large a reserve as private issuers, being not so liable to great and sudden demands, since there never can be any real doubt of its solvency.

> The United States since 1879 finds that a reserve of from $130,000,000 to $140,000,000 is a sufficient reserve for outstanding notes to the amount of $346,000,000, and greenbacks are now at a par with gold.

Against this small advantage is to be set, in the first place, the possibility of fraudulent tampering with the price of bullion for the sake of acting on the currency, in the manner of the fictitious sales of corn, to influence the averages, so much and so justly complained of while the corn laws were in force. But a still stronger consideration is the importance of adhering to a simple principle, intelligible to the most untaught capacity. Everybody can understand convertibility; every one sees that what can be at any moment exchanged for five [dollars] is worth five [dollars]. Regulation by the price of bullion is a more complex idea, and does not recommend itself through the same familiar associations. There would be nothing like the same confidence, by the public generally, in an inconvertible currency so regulated, as in a convertible one: and the most instructed person might reasonably doubt whether such a rule would be as likely to be inflexibly adhered to. The grounds of the rule not being so well understood by the public, opinion would probably not enforce it with as much rigidity, and, in any circumstances of difficulty, would be likely to turn against it; while to the Government itself a suspension of convertibility would appear a much stronger and more extreme measure than a relaxation of what might possibly be considered a somewhat artificial rule. There is therefore a great preponderance of reasons in favor of a convertible, in preference to even the best regulated inconvertible, currency. The temptation to over-issue, in certain financial emergencies, is so strong, that nothing is admissible which can tend, in however slight a degree, to weaken the barriers that restrain it.

> The French Government, in the Franco-Prussian War (1870), issued inconvertible paper on this plan, as explained by Mr. Mill; but, acting through the Bank of France, they conducted their issues so successfully that the notes never depreciated more than about one half of one per cent. But this was a very rare management of inconvertible paper, since the issues were actually limited as the price of gold in paper rose above par.

§ 3. Examination of the doctrine that an inconvertible Current is safe, if representing actual Property.

Projectors every now and then start up, with plans for curing all the economical evils of society by means of an unlimited issue of inconvertible paper. There is, in truth, a great charm in the idea. To be able to pay off the national debt, defray the expenses of government without taxation, and, in fine, to make the fortunes of the whole community, is a brilliant prospect, when once a man is capable of believing that printing a few characters on bits of paper will do it. The philosopher's stone could not be expected to do more.[248]

As these projects, however often slain, always resuscitate, it is not superfluous to examine one or two of the fallacies by which the schemers impose upon themselves. One of the commonest is, that a paper currency can not be issued in excess so long as every note issued *represents* property, or has a *foundation* of actual property to rest on. These phrases, of representing and resting, seldom convey any distinct or well-defined idea; when they do, their meaning is no more than this—that the issuers of the paper must *have* property, either of their own, or intrusted to them, to the value of all the notes they issue, though for what purpose does not very clearly appear; for, if the property can not be claimed in exchange for the notes, it is difficult to divine in what manner its mere existence can serve to uphold their value. I presume, however, it is intended as a guarantee that the holders would be finally reimbursed, in case any untoward event should cause the whole concern to be wound up. On this theory there have been many schemes for "coining the whole land of the country into money" and the like.

In so far as this notion has any connection at all with reason, it seems to originate in confounding two entirely distinct evils, to which a paper currency is liable. One is, the insolvency of the issuers; which, if the paper is grounded on their credit—if it makes any promise of payment in cash, either on demand or at any future time—of course deprives the paper of any value which it derives from the promise. To this evil paper credit is equally liable, however moderately used; and against it, a proviso that all issues should be "founded on property," as for instance that notes should only be issued on the security of some valuable thing, expressly pledged for their redemption, would really be efficacious as a precaution. But the theory takes no account of another evil, which is incident to the notes of the most solvent firm, company, or government; that of being depreciated in value from being issued in excessive quantity. The assignats, during the French Revolution, were an example of a currency grounded on these principles. The assignats "represented" an immense amount of highly valuable property, namely, the lands of the crown, the church, the monasteries, and the emigrants; amounting possibly to half the territory of France. They were, in fact, orders or assignments on this mass of land. The revolutionary government had the idea of "coining" these lands into money; but, to do them justice, they did not originally contemplate the immense multiplication of issues to which they were eventually driven by the failure of all other financial resources. They imagined that the assignats would come rapidly back to the issuers in exchange for land, and that they should be able to reissue them continually until the lands were all disposed of, without having at any time more than a very moderate quantity in circulation. Their hope was frustrated: the land did not sell so quickly as they expected; buyers were not inclined to invest their money in possessions which were likely to be resumed without compensation if the revolution succumbed; the bits of paper which represented land, becoming prodigiously multiplied, could no more keep up their value than the land itself would have done if it had all been brought to market at once; and the result was that it at last required an assignat of five hundred francs to pay for a cup of coffee.

The example of the assignats has been said not to be conclusive, because an assignat only represented land in general, but not a definite quantity of land. To have prevented their depreciation, the proper course, it is affirmed, would have been to have made a valuation of all the confiscated property at its metallic value, and to have issued assignats up to, but not beyond, that limit; giving to the holders a right to demand any piece of land, at its registered valuation, in exchange for assignats to the same amount. There can be no question about the superiority of this plan over the one actually adopted. Had this course been followed, the assignats could never have been depreciated to the inordinate degree they were; for—as they would have retained all their purchasing power in relation to land, however much they might have fallen in respect to other things—before they had lost very much of their market value, they would probably have been brought in to be exchanged for land. It must be remembered, however, that their not being depreciated would presuppose that no greater number of them continued in circulation than would have circulated if they had been convertible into cash. However convenient, therefore, in a time of revolution, this currency convertible into land on demand might have been, as a contrivance for selling rapidly a great quantity of land with the least possible sacrifice, it is difficult to see what advantage it would have, as the permanent system of a country, over a currency convertible into coin; while it is not at all difficult to see what would be its disadvantages, since land is far more variable in value than gold and silver; and besides, land, to most persons, being rather an incumbrance than a desirable possession, except to be converted into money, people would submit to a much greater depreciation before demanding land, than they will before demanding gold or silver.[249]

It has been said that the assignats circulated without legal-tender power. They were received by the French treasury, and a law was passed condemning a man to six years in irons for exchanging gold or silver for assignats at a greater than the nominal or face value of the latter. The subsequent issues, called *mandats*, did not *represent* land, but were directly exchangeable for the land. Even that kind of money is no more valuable than a proportional amount of tax receipts for land. In a very short time *mandats* were worth 1/1000 of their face value, and assignats very much less. The assignats, moreover, were not limited in quantity to the money value of the lands they represented. By 1796, 45,000,000,000 francs of assignats had been issued.

§ 4. Experiments with paper Money in the United States.

The experience of the colonies before our Revolution is rich in warning examples of the over-issue of inconvertible paper money. Those of Rhode Island[250] and the Province of Massachusetts[251] are the most conspicuous, perhaps, because we have better knowledge of them, but other colonies suffered in as great a degree. The experience of the latter illustrates as well as any, perhaps, not only the general theory of inconvertible paper, but the device of supporting the paper by paying interest upon the notes. Although the issues since 1690 had depreciated, in 1702 £10,000 more notes were issued, because, as it was said, there was a scarcity of money. It is always noticeable that the more issues of paper money there are made, the more there is a cry of scarcity, much like the thirst of a hard drinker after the first exhilaration has passed off. On the new issues five per cent interest was paid, and even excises and imposts were set aside as security for their payment. The year 1709 saw a new expedition to Canada, and saw also the broken promises of the province, when £20,000 more notes were put out; the collection of the taxes with which to pay the notes was deferred in 1707 for two years; in 1709 deferred for four years; in 1710 for five years; in 1711 for six years. By 1712 they had depreciated thirty per cent, when the charm of legal tender was thrown around them, but to no purpose. The idea of value was not associated with them in people's minds, and they put no faith in promises. The usual result took place. People divided politically on the money question, and parties began to agitate for banks which should issue notes based on real estate, or for loans from the state to private persons at interest to be paid annually. Such facts show the train of evils following the first innocent departure from the maintenance of a currency equivalent to coin. The people forgot, or did not know, the nature of money, or the offices it performed. They did not understand that creating paper money did not create wealth. This experiment closed only in 1750 (March 31st), when the province had courage enough to resume specie payments. The effect was to transfer the West India trade from paper-issuing colonies to Massachusetts, and to produce a steady prosperity in her business interests.

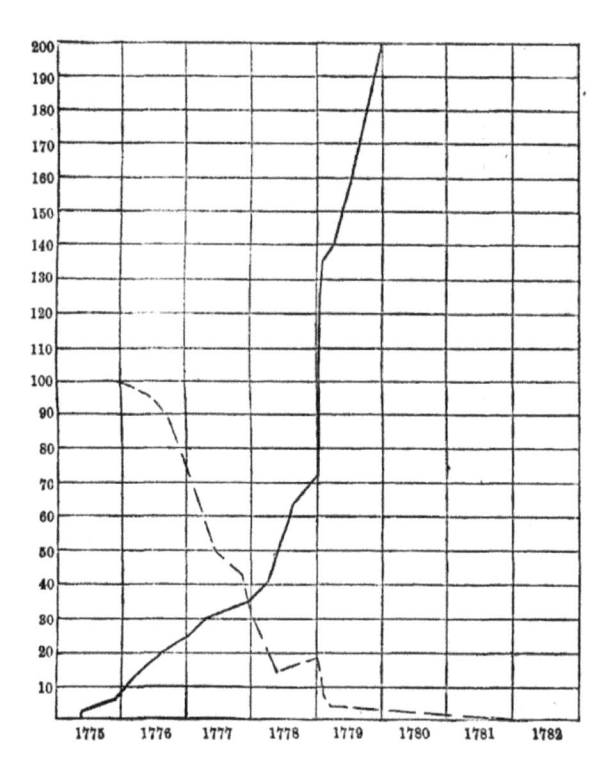

Chart XI. Continental Currency, Issue and Depreciation.

The issue of paper money as a means of making a forced loan from the people, when there seem to be no other means of getting funds, has been fully illustrated in our country by the Continental currency issued during our Revolution. It is not, however, considered that this is also accompanied by a process by which every debtor takes "a forced contribution from his creditor." Congress had no power to tax, and the separate States would not do it; and this has been considered as the excuse for making issues of that well-known paper money, which has given rise to the familiar by-word for absence of value, "not worth a Continental." Without going into details,[252] in one year, 1779, Congress issued $140,000,000, worth in coin only $7,000,000. They, however, bravely declared that paper had not depreciated, but that the price of coin had gone up! Legal attempts were made to repress the premium on silver; but resolutions do not create wealth as fast as money can be printed. The depreciation went on more rapidly than the issues (see Chart No. XI, in which the black line represents the amounts of issues, and the broken line the depreciation of paper, starting at 100); and, finally, March 18, 1780, Congress decided to admit a depreciation, and resumed in silver at the rate of one dollar in silver for forty in paper.

The question of government issues[253] of paper money again came up in the United States in 1862, during the civil war, and part of our present currency is the result of the policy then adopted. The first step—the one that generally costs—however, was taken July 17, 1861, when the Treasury issued $50,000,000 of "demand notes," not bearing interest. These notes, however, were not made legal tender. They could be used in payment of salaries and other dues from the United States. It may be well to state that the Treasury balanced the arguments for and against the issues of paper at the beginning of the experiment, and we can see how these views were realized as we go along. In favor of paper issues it was urged that we could borrow a large amount without interest, as in the case of the Continental currency; that there would be no expense beyond the coin necessary for keeping the paper at par; and that the country would gain a uniform currency. On the other hand, it was seen that there might be temptations to issue without provisions for redemption; that even if a fund were kept, a disturbance of the money market would precipitate a demand for coin, and all upon this single fund; and, lastly, that there were all the dangers of over-issue. Secretary Chase[254] then decided against paper issues. Government bonds, however, did not sell, and the attempt of the banks toward the end of 1861 to carry $150,000,000 of bonds brought on a suspension of specie payments, December 31, 1861. Without any taxation policy, the country drifted along, until in a spasm of dread at seeing an empty Treasury, Congress passed the legal-tender act (February 25, 1862), issuing $150,000,000 of paper in the form of promises to pay. A committee of bankers showed that the issue could have been avoided by selling bonds at their market price; but Congress would not sell them below par. No necessity for the issues of paper need have arrived. In four months another issue of $150,000,000 was authorized (July 11, 1862); and a third issue of a like amount (March 3, 1863), in all $450,000,000. The depreciation took place (see Chart No. XII), for, as Secretary Chase anticipated, no provision was made for redemption. They were made legal tender, but this "essential idea" did not preserve their value; nor did the provision that they be received for taxes (except customs), avail for this purpose.

The effects of the depreciation were as evil as can well be imagined. (1) The expenses of the Government were increased by the rise in prices, so that (2) our national debt became hundreds of millions larger than it need have been; (3) a vicious speculation in gold began, leading to the unsettling of legitimate trade and to greater variations in prices; (4) the existence of depreciated paper later gave rise to all the dishonest schemes for paying the coin obligations of the United States in cheap issues, to the ruin of its credit and honor; and (5) it has practically become a settled part of our circulation, and a possible source of danger.

Of the whole $450,000,000, $50,000,000 were set aside as a reserve for temporary deposits; but in July, 1864, $431,000,000 were in circulation. At this time (June 30, 1864) Congress, retaining distinctly the feeling that the issue of paper was but a temporary measure, forbade any further issues. Secretary McCulloch, immediately on the close of the war, began to contract, and, by a resolution of the lower branch in Congress (December 18, 1865), a cordial concurrence in the measures for contraction was manifested. Of course, the return from the path of inflated credit and high prices was painful, and Congress began to feel the pressure of its constituents. Had they not yielded, much of the severity of the crisis of 1873 might have been avoided; but (April 12, 1866) they forbade any greater contraction than $4,000,000 a month. Here was a lack of courage not foreseen by Secretary Chase. This was again shown (February 4, 1868) by a law which absolutely forbade the Secretary to further reduce the currency, which now stood at $356,000,000. This marks an important change in the attitude of the Government, as compared with 1862. After the panic of 1873, the paper evil produced its usual effect in the cry for more money, and, as in the Province of Massachusetts in 1712, parties divided on the question of inflation or contraction. A bill to expand the Government issues to $400,000,000 (and the national-bank notes also to $400,000,000) actually passed both Houses of Congress, and we were fortunately saved from it only by the veto of President Grant (April 22, 1874). This was another landmark in the history of our paper money. Secretary Richardson, however, had already, without authority, reissued $26,000,000 of the $44,000,000 withdrawn by Secretary McCulloch, and the amount outstanding was thus $382,000,000. A compromise measure was passed (June 20, 1874), which retained this amount in the circulation.

When the resumption act was passed (January 14, 1875), the provision that, for every $100 of new national-bank notes issued, $80 of United States notes should be retired, resulted in a contraction of the latter from $382,000,000 to $346,000,000. The reason of this was, that there was no provision for the increase of United States notes when national banks withdrew their own issues; and after the crisis many banks naturally did so. The culmination of the policy of Congress came in a law (May 31, 1878) which absolutely forbade all further retirement of United States notes, and we are now left at the present time with an inelastic limit of $346,000,000. Finally, in 1877 and 1878, Secretary Sherman, aided by a most fortunate state of foreign trade, began to accumulate gold in order to carry out the provisions of the resumption act, which required him to resume specie payments on January 1, 1879. He successfully collected $133,000,000 of gold, and on December 17, 1878, the premium on gold disappeared, and resumption was accomplished quietly on the day appointed, without a jar to business.

But it is a significant fact that even after all the evils inflicted on our country by over-issues, in spite of the temptation to misuse paper money if it is in any way permitted, in spite of all the warnings of history, there seems to be a dangerous acquiescence in the presence of government paper money in our currency. It is an open pitfall, tempting to evils whenever sudden emergencies arise. It ought not to be allowed to remain any longer.

§ 5. Examination of the gain arising from the increase and issue of paper Currency.

Another of the fallacies from which the advocates of an inconvertible currency derive support is the notion that an increase of the currency quickens industry. Mr. Attwood maintained that a rise of prices produced by an increase of paper currency stimulates every producer to his utmost exertions, and brings all the capital and labor of the country into complete employment; and that this has invariably happened in all periods of rising prices, when the rise was on a sufficiently great scale. I presume, however, that the inducement which, according to Mr. Attwood, excited this unusual ardor in all persons engaged in production must have been the expectation of getting more of commodities generally, more real wealth, in exchange for the produce of their labor, and not merely more pieces of paper. This expectation, however, must have been, by the very terms of the supposition, disappointed, since, all prices being supposed to rise equally, no one was really better paid for his goods than before. It calculates on finding the whole world persisting forever in the belief that more pieces of paper are more riches, and never discovering that, with all their paper, they can not buy more of anything than they could before. At the periods which Mr. Attwood mistook for times of prosperity, and which were simply (as all periods of high prices, under a convertible currency, must be) times of speculation, the speculators did not think they were growing rich because the high prices would last, but because they would not last, and because whoever contrived to realize while they did last would find himself, after the recoil, in possession of a greater number of [dollars], without their having become of less value.

Hume's version of the doctrine differed in a slight degree from Mr. Attwood's. He thought that all commodities would not rise in price simultaneously, and that some persons therefore would obtain a real gain, by getting more money for what they had to sell, while the things which they wished to buy might not yet have risen. And those who would reap this gain would always be (he seems to think) the first comers. It seems obvious, however, that, for every person who thus gains more than usual, there is necessarily some other person who gains less. The loser, if things took place as Hume supposes, would be the seller of the commodities which are slowest to rise; who, by the supposition, parts with his goods at the old prices, to purchasers who have already benefited by the new. This seller has obtained for his commodity only the accustomed quantity of money, while there are already some things of which that money will no longer purchase as much as before. If, therefore, he knows what is going on, he will raise his price, and then the buyer will not have the gain, which is supposed to stimulate his industry. But if, on the contrary, the seller does not know the state of the case, and only discovers it when he finds, in laying his money out, that it does not go so far, he then obtains less than the ordinary remuneration for his labor and capital; and, if the other dealer's industry is encouraged, it should seem that his must, from the opposite cause, be impaired.

An issue of notes is a manifest gain to the issuers, who, until the notes are returned for payment, obtain the use of them as if they were a real capital; and, so long as the notes are no permanent addition to the currency, but merely supersede gold or silver to the same amount, the gain of the issuer is a loss to no one; it is obtained by saving to the community the expense of the more costly material. But, if there is no gold or silver to be superseded—if the notes are added to the currency, instead of being substituted for the metallic part of it—all holders of currency lose, by the depreciation of its value, the exact equivalent of what the issuer gains. A tax is virtually levied on them for his benefit.

But besides the benefit reaped by the issuers, or by others through them, at the expense of the public generally, there is another unjust gain obtained by a larger class—namely, by those who are under fixed pecuniary obligations. All such persons are freed, by a depreciation of the currency, from a portion of the burden of their debts or other engagements; in other words, part of the property of their creditors is gratuitously transferred to them. On a superficial view it may be imagined that this is an advantage to industry; since the productive classes are great borrowers, and generally owe larger debts to the unproductive (if we include among the latter all persons not actually in business) than the unproductive classes owe to them, especially if the national debt be included. It is only thus that a general rise of prices can be a source of benefit to producers and dealers, by diminishing the pressure of their fixed burdens. And this might be accounted an advantage, if integrity and good faith were of no importance to the world, and to industry and commerce in particular.

§ 6. *Résumé* of the subject of money.

Before passing on to another branch of our subject, it may be a gain to clearer ideas to collect in the form of the following classification the main points discussed (in Chaps. IV to X) under money and credit, in continuance of a similar classification of value:

Money measures and transfers value.:

(1.) Hence best served by the precious metals, on account of their peculiar qualities.

(2.) Depends for its value, in the long run, on the cost of production at the worst mine worked (Class III); but practically on demand and supply (Class I). And (if no credit exists) its value changes exactly with the supply, which is expressed by $V = 1/(Q \times R)$

(3.) Under two legal standards, obeys Gresham's law— e.g., experience of Japan and the United States.

(4.) Substitutes for money, called *credit* (which is not capital, but calls out inactive capital).

Of these substitutes for money, (1) Use of credit depends not on quality of coin and notes, and (2) Various kinds of credit.

Of those various kinds of credit, there are (1) Book credits, (2) Bills of exchange, (3) Promissory notes, and (4) checks processed via clearing-house.

Of the promissory notes, they are of either (1) Individuals, (2) Banks (Coin Banks or Land Banks, etc.), or (3) Governments.

Of Government notes, there are (1) Convertible or (2) Inconvertible.

Chapter XI. Of Excess Of Supply.

§ 1. The theory of a general Over-Supply of Commodities stated.

After the elementary exposition of the theory of money contained in the last few chapters, we shall return to a question in the general theory of Value which could not be satisfactorily discussed until the nature and operations of Money were in some measure understood, because the errors against which we have to contend mainly originate in a misunderstanding of those operations.

Because the phenomenon of over-supply and consequent inconvenience or loss to the producer or dealer may exist in the case of any one commodity whatever, many persons, including some distinguished political economists,[255] have thought that it may exist with regard to all commodities; that there may be a general over-production of wealth; a supply of commodities in the aggregate surpassing the demand; and a consequent depressed condition of all classes of producers.

The doctrine appears to me to involve so much inconsistency in its very conception that I feel considerable difficulty in giving any statement of it which shall be at once clear and satisfactory to its supporters. They agree in maintaining that there may be, and sometimes is, an excess of productions in general beyond the demand for them; that when this happens, purchasers can not be found at prices which will repay the cost of production with a profit; that there ensues a general depression of prices or values (they are seldom accurate in discriminating between the two), so that producers, the more they produce, find themselves the poorer instead of richer; and Dr. Chalmers accordingly inculcates on capitalists the practice of a moral restraint in reference to the pursuit of gain, while Sismondi deprecates machinery and the various inventions which increase productive power. They both maintain that accumulation of capital may proceed too fast, not merely for the moral but for the material interest of those who produce and accumulate; and they enjoin the rich to guard against this evil by an ample unproductive consumption.

§ 2. The supply of commodities in general can not exceed the power of Purchase.

When these writers speak of the supply of commodities as outrunning the demand, it is not clear which of the two elements of demand they have in view—the desire to possess, or the means of purchase; whether their meaning is that there are, in such cases, more consumable products in existence than the public desires to consume, or merely more than it is able to pay for. In this uncertainty, it is necessary to examine both suppositions.

> It will be here noticed that Mr. Mill uses demand in the sense for which we contended it should be used (Book III, Chap. I, § 3), and not as "quantity demanded." The present discussion of over-production should also be connected by the student with the former reference to it, Book I, Chap. IV, § 2.

First, let us suppose that the quantity of commodities produced is not greater than the community would be glad to consume; is it, in that case, possible that there should be a deficiency of demand for all commodities for want of the means of payment? Those who think so can not have considered what it is which constitutes the means of payment for commodities. It is simply commodities. Each person's means of paying for the productions of other people consists of those which he himself possesses. All sellers are inevitably and *ex vi termini* buyers. Could we suddenly double the productive powers of the country, we should double the supply of commodities in every market; but we should, by the same stroke, double the purchasing power.

Everybody would bring a double demand as well as supply; everybody would be able to buy twice as much, because every one would have twice as much to offer in exchange. It is probable, indeed, that there would now be a superfluity of certain things. Although the community would willingly double its aggregate consumption, it may already have as much as it desires of some commodities, and it may prefer to do more than double its consumption of others, or to exercise its increased purchasing power on some new thing. If so, the supply will adapt itself accordingly, and the values of things will continue to conform to their cost of production. At any rate, it is a sheer absurdity that all things should fall in value, and that all producers should, in consequence, be insufficiently remunerated. If values remain the same, what becomes of prices is immaterial, since the remuneration of producers does not depend on how much money, but on how much of consumable articles, they obtain for their goods. Besides, money is a commodity; and, if all commodities are supposed to be doubled in quantity, we must suppose money to be doubled too, and then prices would no more fall than values would.

§ 3. There can never be a lack of Demand arising from lack of Desire to Consume.

A general over-supply, or excess of all commodities above the demand, so far as demand consists in means of payment, is thus shown to be an impossibility. But it may, perhaps, be supposed that it is not the ability to purchase, but the desire to possess, that falls short, and that the general produce of industry may be greater than the community desires to consume—the part, at least, of the community which has an equivalent to give.

This is much the most plausible form of the doctrine, and does not, like that which we first examined, involve a contradiction. There may easily be a greater quantity of any particular commodity than is desired by those who have the ability to purchase, and it is abstractedly conceivable that this might be the case with all commodities. The error is in not perceiving that, though all who have an equivalent to give *might* be fully provided with every consumable article which they desire, the fact that they go on adding to the production proves that this is not *actually* the case. Assume the most favorable hypothesis for the purpose, that of a limited community, every member of which possesses as much of necessaries and of all known luxuries as he desires, and, since it is not conceivable that persons whose wants were completely satisfied would labor and economize to obtain what they did not desire, suppose that a foreigner arrives and produces an additional quantity of something of which there was already enough. Here, it will be said, is over-production. True, I reply; over-production of that particular article. The community wanted no more of that, but it wanted something. The old inhabitants, indeed, wanted nothing; but did not the foreigner himself want something? When he produced the superfluous article, was he laboring without a motive? He has produced—but the wrong thing instead of the right. He wanted, perhaps, food, and has produced watches, with which everybody was sufficiently supplied. The new-comer brought with him into the country a demand for commodities equal to all that he could produce by his industry, and it was his business to see that the supply he brought should be suitable to that demand. If he could not produce something capable of exciting a new want or desire in the community, for the satisfaction of which some one would grow more food and give it to him in exchange, he had the alternative of growing food for himself, either on fresh land, if there was any unoccupied, or as a tenant, or partner, or servant of some former occupier, willing to be partially relieved from labor. He has produced a thing not wanted, instead of what was wanted, and he himself, perhaps, is not the kind of producer who is wanted—but there is no over-production; production is not excessive, but merely ill-assorted. We saw before that whoever brings additional commodities to the market brings an additional power of purchase; we now see that he brings also an additional desire to consume, since if he had not that desire he would not have troubled himself to produce. Neither of the elements of demand, therefore, can be wanting when there is an additional supply, though it is perfectly possible that the demand may be for one thing, and the supply may, unfortunately, consist of another.

> It is not sufficiently borne in mind, also, that the whole progress of civilization results in a differentiation of new wants and desires. To take but a single instance, with the growth of the artistic sense the articles of common use change their entire form; and the advances in the arts disclose new commodities which satisfy the world's desires, and for these new satisfactions people are willing to work and produce in order to attain them. With education also comes a wider horizon and a more refined perception of taste, which creates wants for new things for which the mind before had no desires. A little reflection, therefore, must inevitably lead us to see that no person, no community, ever had, or probably ever will have, all its wants satisfied. So far as we know man, it does not seem possible that there will ever be a falling off in demand, because of a satiety of all material satisfactions.

§ 4. Origin and Explanation of the notion of general Over-Supply.

I have already described the state of the markets for commodities which accompanies what is termed a commercial crisis. At such times there is really an excess of all commodities above the money demand: in other words, there is an under-supply of money. From the sudden annihilation of a great mass of credit, every one dislikes to part with ready money, and many are anxious to procure it at any sacrifice. Almost everybody, therefore, is a seller, and there are scarcely any buyers: so that there may really be, though only while the crisis lasts, an extreme depression of general prices, from what may be indiscriminately called a glut of commodities or a dearth of money. But it is a great error to suppose, with Sismondi, that a commercial crisis is the effect of a general excess of production. It is simply the consequence of an excess of speculative purchases. It is not a gradual advent of low prices, but a sudden recoil from prices extravagantly high: its immediate cause is a contraction of credit, and the remedy is, not a diminution of supply, but the restoration of confidence. It is also evident that this temporary derangement of markets is an evil only because it is temporary. The fall being solely of money prices, if prices did not rise again no dealer would lose, since the smaller price would be worth as much to him as the larger price was before. In no matter does this phenomenon answer to the description which these celebrated economists have given of the evil of over-production. That permanent decline in the circumstances of producers, for want of markets, which those writers contemplate, is a conception to which the nature of a commercial crisis gives no support.

The other phenomenon from which the notion of a general excess of wealth and superfluity of accumulation seems to derive countenance is one of a more permanent nature, namely, the fall of profits and interest which naturally takes place with the progress of population and production. The cause of this decline of profit is the increased cost of maintaining labor, which results from an increase of population and of the demand for food, outstripping the advance of agricultural improvement. This important feature in the economical progress of nations will receive full consideration and discussion in the succeeding book.[256] It is obviously a totally different thing from a want of market for commodities, though often confounded with it in the complaints of the producing and trading classes. The true interpretation of the modern or present state of industrial economy is, that there is hardly any amount of business which may not be done, if people will be content to do it on small profits; and this all active and intelligent persons in business perfectly well know: but even those who comply with the necessities of their time grumble at what they comply with, and wish that there were less capital,[257] or, as they express it, less competition, in order that there might be greater profits. Low profits, however, are a different thing from deficiency of demand, and the production and accumulation which merely reduce profits can not be called excess of supply or of production. What the phenomenon really is, and its effects and necessary limits, will be seen when we treat of that express subject.

Chapter XII. Of Some Peculiar Cases Of Value.

§ 1. Values of commodities which have a joint cost of production.

The general laws of value, in all the more important cases of the interchange of commodities in the same country, have now been investigated. We examined, first, the case of monopoly, in which the value is determined by either a natural or an artificial limitation of quantity, that is, by demand and supply: secondly, the case of free competition, when the article can be produced in indefinite quantity at the same cost; in which case the permanent value is determined by the cost of production, and only the fluctuations by supply and demand: thirdly, a mixed case, that of the articles which can be produced in indefinite quantity, but not at the same cost; in which case the permanent value is determined by the greatest cost which it is necessary to incur in order to obtain the required supply: and, lastly, we have found that money itself is a commodity of the third class; that its value, in a state of freedom, is governed by the same laws as the values of other commodities of its class; and that prices, therefore, follow the same laws as values.

From this it appears that demand and supply govern the fluctuations of values and prices in all cases, and the permanent values and prices of all things of which the supply is determined by any agency other than that of free competition: but that, under the *régime* of competition, things are, on the average, exchanged for each other at such values, and sold at such prices, as afford equal expectation of advantage to all classes of producers; which can only be when things exchange for one another in the ratio of their cost of production.

> Here, again, is a distinct recognition of the true meaning of cost of production, and its ruling influence within a competing group, which has been seen in its full significance by Mr. Cairnes.

It sometimes happens [however] that two different commodities have what may be termed a joint cost of production. They are both products of the same operation, or set of operations, and the outlay is incurred for the sake of both together, not part for one and part for the other. The same outlay would have to be incurred for either of the two, if the other were not wanted or used at all. There are not a few instances of commodities thus associated in their production. For example, coke and coal-gas are both produced from the same material, and by the same operation. In a more partial sense, mutton and wool are an example; beef, hides, and tallow; calves and dairy produce; chickens and eggs. Cost of production can have nothing to do with deciding the value of the associated commodities relatively to each other. It only decides their joint value. Cost of production does not determine their prices, but the sum of their prices. A principle is wanting to apportion the expenses of production between the two.

Since cost of production here fails us, we must revert to a law of value anterior to cost of production, and more fundamental, the law of demand and supply. The law is, that the demand for a commodity varies with its value, and that the value adjusts itself so that the demand shall be equal to the supply. This supplies the principle of repartition which we are in quest of.

Suppose that a certain quantity of gas is produced and sold at a certain price, and that the residuum of coke is offered at a price which, together with that of the gas, repays the expenses with the ordinary rate of profit. Suppose, too, that, at the price put upon the gas and coke respectively, the whole of the gas finds an easy market, without either surplus or deficiency, but that purchasers can not be found for all the coke corresponding to it. The coke will be offered at a lower price in order to force a market. But this lower price, together with the price of the gas, will not be remunerating; the manufacture, as a whole, will not pay its expenses with the ordinary profit, and will not, on these terms, continue to be carried on. The gas, therefore, must be sold at a higher price, to make up for the deficiency on the coke. The demand consequently contracting, the production will be somewhat reduced; and prices will become stationary when, by the joint effect of the rise of gas and the fall of coke, so much less of the first is sold, and so much more of the second, that there is now a market for all the coke which results from the existing extent of the gas-manufacture.

Or suppose the reverse case; that more coke is wanted at the present prices than can be supplied by the operations required by the existing demand for gas. Coke, being now in deficiency, will rise in price. The whole operation will yield more than the usual rate of profit, and additional capital will be attracted to the manufacture. The unsatisfied demand for coke will be supplied; but this can not be done without increasing the supply of gas too; and, as the existing demand was fully supplied already, an increased quantity can only find a market by lowering the price. Equilibrium will be attained when the demand for each article fits so well with the demand for the other, that the quantity required of each is exactly as much as is generated in producing the quantity required of the other.

When, therefore, two or more commodities have a joint cost of production, their natural values relatively to each other are those which will create a demand for each, in the ratio of the quantities in which they are sent forth by the productive process.

§ 2. Values of the different kinds of agricultural produce.

Another case of value which merits attention is that of the different kinds of agricultural produce. The case would present nothing peculiar, if different agricultural products were either grown indiscriminately and with equal advantage on the same soils, or wholly on different soils. The difficulty arises from two things: first, that most soils are fitter for one kind of produce than another, without being absolutely unfit for any; and, secondly, the rotation of crops.

For simplicity, we will confine our supposition to two kinds of agricultural produce; for instance, wheat and oats. If all soils were equally adapted for wheat and for oats, both would be grown indiscriminately on all soils, and their relative cost of production, being the same everywhere, would govern their relative value. If the same labor which grows three quarters of wheat on any given soil would always grow on that soil five quarters of oats, the three and the five quarters would be of the same value. The fact is, that both wheat and oats can be grown on almost any soil which is capable of producing either.

It is evident that each grain will be cultivated in preference on the soils which are better adapted for it than for the other; and, if the demand is supplied from these alone, the values of the two grains will have no reference to one another. But when the demand for both is such as to require that each should be grown not only on the soils peculiarly fitted for it, but on the medium soils which, without being specifically adapted to either, are about equally suited for both, the cost of production on those medium soils will determine the relative value of the two grains; while the rent of the soils specifically adapted to each will be regulated by their productive power, considered with reference to that one [grain] alone to which they are peculiarly applicable. Thus far the question presents no difficulty, to any one to whom the general principles of value are familiar.

```
Oats.                    Wheat.
 A                         a
  \                       /
   B                     b
    \                   /
     C                 c
      \               /
       D             d
        \           /
         \         /
            E
```

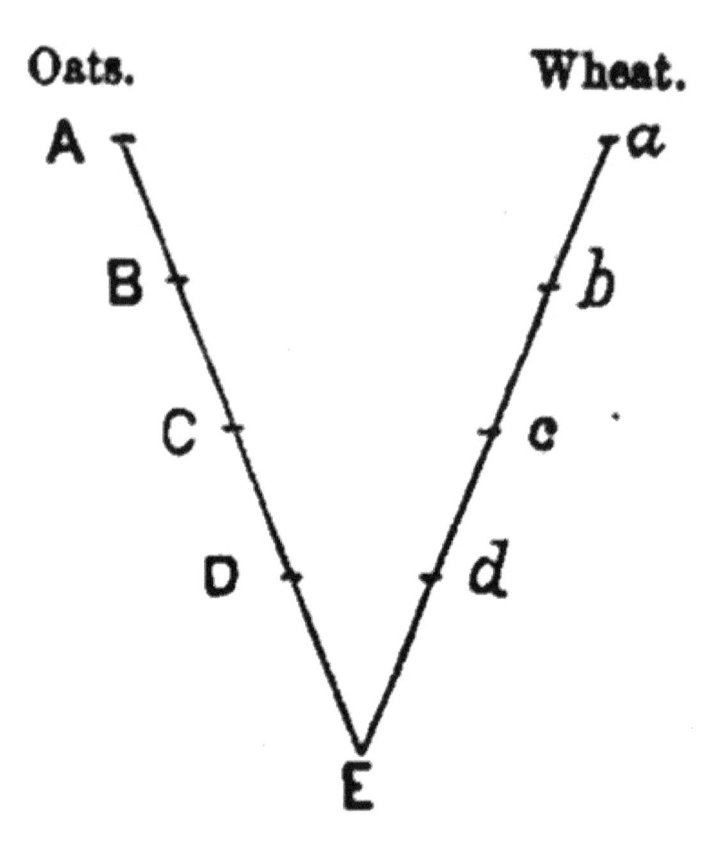

This may be easily shown by a diagram, in which A represents the grade of land best adapted for oats; B, C, D, respectively, lands of diminishing productiveness for oats, until E is reached, which is, perhaps, equally good for oats or wheat; *a, b, c, d*, and E likewise represent the wheat-lands, the best beginning with *a*. The rent of A, or B, is determined by a comparison with whatever grade of land planted in oats is cultivated at the least return, as E, for example. So, if all the wheat-lands are cultivated, land *a*, or *b*, is compared with E, but in regard to the capacity of E to produce wheat.

It may happen, however, that the demand for one of the two, as for example wheat, may so outstrip the demand for the other, as not only to occupy the soils specially suited for wheat, but to engross entirely those equally suitable to both, and even encroach upon those which are better adapted to oats. To create an inducement for this unequal apportionment of the cultivation, wheat must be relatively dearer, and oats cheaper, than according to the cost of their production on the medium land. Their relative value must be in proportion to the cost on that quality of land, whatever it may be, on which the comparative demand for the two grains requires that both of them should be grown. If, from the state of the demand, the two cultivations meet on land more favorable to one than to the other, that one will be cheaper and the other dearer, in relation to each other and to things in general, than if the proportional demand were as we at first supposed.

> As in the diagram just mentioned, if the demand for wheat forces its cultivation downward not only on to land E, suited to either indifferently, but, still farther on, to lands still less adapted for wheat (although good land for oats), wheat may be pushed down one stem of the V and up the other to D, or even to C. Then the value of wheat will be regulated by the cost of production on C, and the rent will be determined by a comparison between the productiveness of a, b, etc. (running downward through E), with C. The price of wheat will be high relatively to oats, which are now cultivated only on lands, A, B, better suited to growing oats, and whose cost of production on C is much less than on D or E.

Here, then, we obtain a fresh illustration, in a somewhat different manner, of the operation of demand, not as an occasional disturber of value, but as a permanent regulator of it, conjoined with, or supplementary to, cost of production.

Chapter XIII. Of International Trade.

§ 1. Cost of Production not a regulator of international values. Extension of the word "international."

Some things it is physically impossible to produce, except in particular circumstances of heat, soil, water, or atmosphere. But there are many things which, though they could be produced at home without difficulty, and in any quantity, are yet imported from a distance. The explanation which would be popularly given of this would be, that it is cheaper to import than to produce them: and this is the true reason. But this reason itself requires that a reason be given for it. Of two things produced in the same place, if one is cheaper than the other, the reason is that it can be produced with less labor and capital, or, in a word, at less cost. Is this also the reason as between things produced in different places? Are things never imported but from places where they can be produced with less labor (or less of the other element of cost, time) than in the place to which they are brought? Does the law, that permanent value is proportioned to cost of production, hold good between commodities produced in distant places, as it does between those produced in adjacent places?

We shall find that it does not. A thing may sometimes be sold cheapest, by being produced in some other place than that at which it can be produced with the smallest amount of labor and abstinence.

This could not happen between adjacent places. If the north bank of the Thames possessed an advantage over the south bank in the production of shoes, no shoes would be produced on the south side; the shoemakers would remove themselves and their capitals to the north bank, or would have established themselves there originally; for, being competitors in the same market with those on the north side, they could not compensate themselves for their disadvantage at the expense of the consumer; the amount of it would fall entirely on their profits; and they would not long content themselves with a smaller profit, when, by simply crossing a river, they could increase it. But between distant places, and especially between different countries, profits may continue different; because persons do not usually remove themselves or their capitals to a distant place without a very strong motive. If capital removed to remote parts of the world as readily, and for as small an inducement, as it moves to another quarter of the same town—if people would transport their manufactories to America or China whenever they could save a small percentage in their expenses by it—profits would be alike (or equivalent) all over the world, and all things would be produced in the places where the same labor and capital would produce them in greatest quantity and of best quality. A tendency may, even now, be observed toward such a state of things: capital is becoming more and more cosmopolitan; there is so much greater similarity of manners and institutions than formerly, and so much less alienation of feeling, among the more civilized countries, that both population and capital now move from one of those countries to another on much less temptation than heretofore. But there are still extraordinary differences, both of wages and of profits, between different parts of the world.

Between all distant places, therefore, in some degree, but especially between different countries (whether under the same supreme government or not), there may exist great inequalities in the return to labor and capital, without causing them to move from one place to the other in such quantity as to level those inequalities. The capital belonging to a country will, to a great extent, remain in the country, even if there be no mode of employing it in which it would not be more productive elsewhere. Yet even a country thus circumstanced might, and probably would, carry on trade with other countries. It would export articles of some sort, even to places which could make them with less labor than itself; because those countries, supposing them to have an advantage over it in all productions, would have a greater advantage in some things than in others, and would find it their interest to import the articles in which their advantage was smallest, that they might employ more of their labor and capital on those in which it was greatest.

> It might seem that a special theory of value is required for international trade, as compared with domestic trade, for the particular reason that in the former there exists *no free movement of labor and capital* from one trading country to another. But we shall see that no new theory is necessary. As before pointed out,[258] commodities exchange for each other at their relative costs wherever there is that free competition which insures perfect facility of movement for labor and capital. It has been usually assumed that capital and labor move freely as between different parts of the same country, but not between different countries. This, however, is not consistent with the facts. We saw that there were non-competing industrial groups within the same nation. Mr. Mill here, in a pointed way, suggests this, when he

speaks of "distant places." The addition, therefore, made to Mr. Mill's exposition by Mr. Cairns[259] is, that the word "international" (in default of a better term) should be applied to those conditions either within a country, or between two countries, which, because of the actual immobility of labor and capital from one occupation to another, furnishes a substantial interference with industrial competition. The obstacles to the free movement of labor and capital which produce the conditions called "international" are: 1. "Geographical distance; 2. Difference in political institutions; 3. Difference in language, religion, and social customs—in a word, in forms of civilization." These differences exist between Maine and Montana; or even between two adjoining States, Ohio and Kentucky, one a free and the other an old slave State. Labor and capital have not in the past moved freely even across Mason and Dixon's line. There is, therefore, no treatment of international trade and values separate from the laws of value already laid down concerning non-competing groups, since there is also no free competition between all the industrial groups within a country.

§ 2. Interchange of commodities between distance places determined by differences not in their absolute, but in the comparative, costs of production.

As I have said elsewhere[260] after Ricardo (the thinker who has done most toward clearing up this subject),[261] "it is not a difference in the *absolute* cost of production which determines the interchange, but a difference in the *comparative* cost. It may be to our advantage to procure iron from Sweden in exchange for cottons, even although the mines of England as well as her manufactories should be more productive than those of Sweden; for if we have an advantage of one half in cottons, and only an advantage of a quarter in iron, and could sell our cottons to Sweden at the price which Sweden must pay for them if she produced them herself, we should obtain our iron with an advantage [over Sweden] of one half, as well as our cottons. We may often, by trading with foreigners, obtain their commodities at a smaller expense of labor and capital than they cost to the foreigners themselves. The bargain is still advantageous to the foreigner, because the commodity which he receives in exchange, though it has cost us less, would have cost him more."

This may be illustrated as follows:

Articles interchanged.	England.	Sweden.
Cotton.	10 days' labor produces x yds.	15 days' labor produces x yds.
Iron.	12 days' labor produces y cwts.	15 days' labor produces y cwts.

Here England has the advantage over Sweden in both cotton and iron, since she can produce x yards of cotton in ten days' labor to fifteen days in Sweden, and y cwts. of iron in twelve days' labor to fifteen days in Sweden. The ship which takes x yards of cotton to Sweden, and there exchanges it, as may be done, for y cwts. of iron, brings back to England that which cost Sweden fifteen days' labor, while the cotton with which the iron was bought cost England only ten days' labor. So that England also got her iron at an advantage over Sweden of one half of ten days' labor; and yet England had an absolute advantage over Sweden in iron of a less amount (i.e., of one fourth of twelve days' labor). It is to be distinctly understood that by difference in *comparative cost* we mean a difference in the comparative cost of producing two or more articles in the *same country*, and not the difference of cost of the same article in the different trading countries. In this example, for instance, it is the difference in the comparative costs in England of both cotton and iron (not the different costs of cotton in England and

Sweden) which gives the reason for the existence of the foreign trade.

To illustrate the cases in which interchange of commodities will not, and those in which it will, take place between two countries, the supposition may be made that the United States has an advantage over England in the production both of iron and of corn. It may first be supposed that the advantage is of equal amount in both commodities; the iron and the corn, each of which required 100 days' labor in the United States, requiring each 150 days' labor in England. It would follow that the iron of 150 days' labor in England, if sent to the United States, would be equal to the iron of 100 days' labor in the United States; if exchanged for corn, therefore, it would exchange for the corn of only 100 days' labor. But the corn of 100 days' labor in the United States was supposed to be the same quantity with that of 150 days' labor in England. With 150 days' labor in iron, therefore, England would only get as much corn in the United States as she could raise with 150 days' labor at home; and she would, in importing it, have the cost of carriage besides. In these circumstances no exchange would take place. In this case the comparative costs of the two articles in England and in the United States were supposed to be the same, though the absolute costs were different; on which supposition we see that there would be no labor saved to either country by confining its industry to one of the two productions and importing the other.

It is otherwise when the comparative and not merely the absolute costs of the two articles are different in the two countries. If, while the iron produced with 100 days' labor in the United States was produced with 150 days' labor in England, the corn which was produced in the United States with 100 days' labor could not be produced in England with less than 200 days' labor, an adequate motive to exchange would immediately arise. With a quantity of iron which England produced with 150 days' labor, she would be able to purchase as much corn in the United States as was there produced with 100 days' labor; but the quantity which was there produced with 100 days' labor would be as great as the quantity produced in England with 200 days' labor. By importing corn, therefore, from the United States, and paying for it with iron, England would obtain for 150 days' labor what would otherwise cost her 200, being a saving of 50 days' labor on each repetition of the transaction; and not merely a saving to England, but a saving absolutely; for it is not obtained at the expense of the United States, who, with corn that cost her 100 days' labor, has purchased iron which, if produced at home, would have cost her the same. The United States, therefore, on this supposition, loses nothing; but also she derives no advantage from the trade, the imported iron costing her as much as if it were made at home. To enable the United States to gain anything by the interchange, something must be abated from the gain of England: the corn produced in the United States by 100 days' labor must be able to purchase from England more iron than the United States could produce by that amount of labor; more, therefore, than England could produce by 150 days' labor, England thus obtaining the corn which would have cost her 200 days at a cost exceeding 150, though short of 200. England, therefore, no longer gains the whole of the labor which is saved to the two jointly by trading with one another.[262]

The case in which both England and the United States would gain from the trade may be thus briefly shown:

Articles interchanged.	United States.	England.
Corn.	100 days' labor produces x bus.	200 days' labor produces x bus.
Iron.	125 days' labor produces y tons.	150 days' labor produces y tons.

The ship which carries x bushels of corn from the United States to England can there exchange it for at least y tons of iron (costing England 150 days' labor, since x bushels in England would cost 200 days' labor), and bring it home, gaining for the United States the difference between the 100 days' labor in corn, paid for the y tons of iron, and the 125 days which the iron would have cost here if produced at home. In this case the United States has an advantage over England in both corn and iron, but still an international trade will spring up, because the United States will derive a gain owing to the less cost of corn as compared with the cost of iron. Our *comparative* advantage is in corn. England, also, by sending to the United States y tons of iron, gets in return for it x bushels of corn. To produce the corn herself would have cost her 200 days' labor, but she bought that corn by only 150 days' labor spent on iron. England's *comparative* advantage is in iron. Then both countries will gain.

Mr. Bowen[263] gives an instance of international trade where one country has the advantage in both of the commodities entering into the exchange: "The inhabitants of Barbadoes, favored by their tropical climate and fertile soil, can raise provisions cheaper than we can in the United States. And yet Barbadoes buys nearly all her provisions from this country. Why is this so? Because, though Barbadoes has the advantage over us in the ability to raise provisions cheaply, she has a still greater advantage over us in her power to produce sugar and molasses. If she has an advantage of one fourth in raising provisions, she has an advantage of one half in regard to products exclusively tropical; and it is better for her to employ all her labor and capital in that branch of production in which her advantage is greatest. She can thus, by trading with us, obtain our breadstuffs and meat at a smaller expense of labor and capital than they cost ourselves. If, for instance, a barrel of flour costs ten days' labor in the United States and only eight days' labor in Barbadoes, the people of Barbadoes can still profitably buy the flour from this country, if they can pay for it with sugar which cost them only six days' labor; and the people of this country can profitably sell them the flour, or buy from them the sugar, provided the sugar, if raised in the United States, would cost eleven days' labor.... The United States receive sugar, which would have cost them eleven days' labor, by paying for it with flour which costs them but ten days. Barbadoes receives flour, which would have cost her eight days' labor, by paying for it with sugar which costs her but six days. If Barbadoes produced both commodities with greater facility, but greater in precisely the same degree, there would be no motive for interchange."

It may be said, however, that in practice no businessman considers the question of "comparative cost" in making shipments of goods abroad; that all he thinks of is whether the price here, for example, is less than it is in London. And yet the very fact that the prices are less here implies that gold is of high value relatively to the given commodity; while in London, if money is to be sent back in payment, and if prices are high there, that implies that gold is there of less comparative value than commodities, and consequently that gold is the cheapest article to send to the United States. The doctrine, then, is as true of gold, or the precious metals, as it is of other commodities.[264] It may be stated in the following language of Mr. Cairnes: "The proximate condition determining international exchange is the state of comparative prices in the exchanging countries as regards the commodities which form the subject of the trade. But comparative prices within the limits of each country are determined by two distinct principles—within the range of effective industrial competition, by cost of production; outside that range, by reciprocal demand."[265]

§ 3. The direct benefits of commerce consist in increased Efficiency of the productive powers of the World.

From this exposition we perceive in what consists the benefit of international exchange, or, in other words, foreign commerce. Setting aside its enabling countries to obtain commodities which they could not themselves produce at all, its advantage consists in a more efficient employment of the productive forces of the world. If two countries which traded together attempted, as far as was physically possible, to produce for themselves what they now import from one another, the labor and capital of the two countries would not be so productive, the two together would not obtain from their industry so great a quantity of commodities, as when each employs itself in producing, both for itself and for the other, the things in which its labor is relatively most efficient. The addition thus made to the produce of the two combined constitutes the advantage of the trade. It is possible that one of the two countries may be altogether inferior to the other in productive capacities, and that its labor and capital could be employed to greatest advantage by being removed bodily to the other. The labor and capital which have been sunk in rendering Holland habitable would have produced a much greater return if transported to America or Ireland. The produce of the whole world would be greater, or the labor less, than it is, if everything were produced where there is the greatest absolute facility for its production. But nations do not, at least in modern times, emigrate *en masse*; and, while the labor and capital of a country remain in the country, they are most beneficially employed in producing, for foreign markets as well as for its own, the things in which it lies under the least disadvantage, if there be none in which it possesses an advantage.

> The fundamental ground on which all trade, or all exchange of commodities, rests, is division of labor, or separation of employments. Beyond the ordinary gain from division of labor, arising from increased dexterity, there exist gains arising from the development of "the special capacities or resources possessed by particular individuals or localities." International exchanges call out chiefly the special advantages offered by particular *localities* for the prosecution of particular industries.
>
> "The only case, indeed, in which *personal aptitudes* go for much in the commerce of nations is where the nations concerned occupy different grades in the scale of civilization.... The most striking example which the world has ever seen of a foreign trade determined by the peculiar personal qualities of those engaged in ministering to it is that which was furnished by the Southern States of the American Union previous to the abolition of slavery. The effect of that institution was to give a very distinct industrial character to the laboring population of those States which unfitted them for all but a very limited number of occupations, but gave them a certain special fitness for these. Almost the entire industry of the country was consequently turned to the production of two or three crude commodities, in raising which the industry of slaves was found to be effective; and these were used, through an exchange with foreign countries, as the means of supplying the inhabitants with all other requisites.... In the main, however, it would seem that this cause [personal aptitudes] does not go for very much in international commerce."[266]
>
> In brief, then, international trade is but an extension of the principle of division of labor; and the gains to increased productiveness, arising from the latter, are exactly the same as those from the former.

§ 4. —Not in a Vent for exports, nor in the gains of Merchants.

According to the doctrine now stated, the only direct advantage of foreign commerce consists in the imports. A country obtains things which it either could not have produced at all, or which it must have produced at a greater expense of capital and labor than the cost of the things which it exports to pay for them. It thus obtains a more ample supply of the commodities it wants, for the same labor and capital; or the same supply, for less labor and capital, leaving the surplus disposable to produce other things. The vulgar theory disregards this benefit and deems the advantage of commerce to reside in the exports: as if not what a country obtains, but what it parts with, by its foreign trade, was supposed to constitute the gain to it. An extended market for its produce—an abundant consumption for its goods—a vent for its surplus—are the phrases by which it has been customary to designate the uses and recommendations of commerce with foreign countries. This notion is intelligible, when we consider that the authors and leaders of opinion on mercantile questions have always hitherto been the selling class. It is in truth a surviving relic of the Mercantile Theory, according to which, money being the only wealth, selling, or, in other words, exchanging goods for money, was (to countries without mines of their own) the only way of growing rich—and importation of goods, that is to say, parting with money, was so much subtracted from the benefit.

The notion that money alone is wealth has been long defunct, but it has left many of its progeny behind it. Adam Smith's theory of the benefit of foreign trade was, that it afforded an outlet for the surplus produce of a country, and enabled a portion of the capital of the country to replace itself with a profit. The expression, surplus produce, seems to imply that a country is under some kind of necessity of producing the corn or cloth which it exports; so that the portion which it does not itself consume, if not wanted and consumed elsewhere, would either be produced in sheer waste, or, if it were not produced, the corresponding portion of capital would remain idle, and the mass of productions in the country would be diminished by so much. Either of these suppositions would be entirely erroneous. The country produces an exportable article in excess of its own wants from no inherent necessity, but as the cheapest mode of supplying itself with other things. If prevented from exporting this surplus, it would cease to produce it, and would no longer import anything, being unable to give an equivalent; but the labor and capital which had been employed in producing with a view to exportation would find employment in producing those desirable objects which were previously brought from abroad; or, if some of them could not be produced, in producing substitutes for them. These articles would, of course, be produced at a greater cost than that of the things with which they had previously been purchased from foreign countries. But the value and price of the articles would rise in proportion; and the capital would just as much be replaced, with the ordinary profit, from the returns, as it was when employed in producing for the foreign market. The only losers (after the temporary inconvenience of the change) would be the consumers of the heretofore imported articles, who would be obliged either to do without them, consuming in lieu of them something which they did not like as well, or to pay a higher price for them than before.

If it be said that the capital now employed in foreign trade could not find employment in supplying the home market, I might reply that this is the fallacy of general over-production, discussed in a former chapter; but the thing is in this particular case too evident to require an appeal to any general theory. We not only see that the capital of the merchant would find employment, but we see what employment. There would be employment created, equal to that which would be taken away. Exportation ceasing, importation to an equal value would cease also, and all that part of the income of the country which had been expended in imported commodities would be ready to expend itself on the same things produced at home, or on others instead of them. Commerce is virtually a mode of cheapening production; and in all such cases the consumer is the person ultimately benefited; the dealer, in the end, is sure to get his profit, whether the buyer obtains much or little for his money.

> *E converso*, if for any reason, such as a removal of duties, capital should be withdrawn from the production of articles consumed at home, and imported commodities should entirely take their place, the very importation of the foreign commodities would imply that an increased corresponding production was going on in this country with which to pay for the imported goods. The capital thus thrown out of employment in an industry in which we had no comparative advantage (when competition became free) would necessarily be employed in the industries in which we had an advantage, and would supply—and the transferred capital would be the only means of supplying—the commodities which would be sent abroad to pay for those, which by the supposition are now imported, but were formerly produced at home. The result is a greater productiveness of industry, and so a greater sum from which both labor and capital

may be rewarded. Whenever capital, unrestrained by artificial support, leaves one employment as unprofitable, it means that that employment is naturally, and in itself, less productive than the usual run of other industries in the country, and so less profitable to both labor and capital than the majority of other occupations.

§ 5. Indirect benefits of Commerce, Economical and Moral; still greater than the Direct.

Such, then, is the direct economical advantage of foreign trade. But there are, besides, indirect effects, which must be counted as benefits of a high order. (1) One is, the tendency of every extension of the market to improve the processes of production. A country which produces for a larger market than its own can introduce a more extended division of labor, can make greater use of machinery, and is more likely to make inventions and improvements in the processes of production. Whatever causes a greater quantity of anything to be produced in the same place tends to the general increase of the productive powers of the world.[267] There is (2) another consideration, principally applicable to an early stage of industrial advancement. The opening of a foreign trade, by making them acquainted with new objects, or tempting them by the easier acquisition of things which they had not previously thought attainable, sometimes works a sort of industrial revolution in a country whose resources were previously undeveloped for want of energy and ambition in the people; inducing those who were satisfied with scanty comforts and little work to work harder for the gratification of their new tastes, and even to save, and accumulate capital, for the still more complete satisfaction of those tastes at a future time.

But (3) the economical advantages of commerce are surpassed in importance by those of its effects which are intellectual and moral. It is hardly possible to overrate the value, in the present low state of human improvement, of placing human beings in contact with persons dissimilar to themselves, and with modes of thought and action unlike those with which they are familiar. Commerce is now, what war once was, the principal source of this contact. Such communication has always been, and is peculiarly in the present age, one of the primary sources of progress. Finally, (4) commerce first taught nations to see with goodwill the wealth and prosperity of one another. Before, the patriot, unless sufficiently advanced in culture to feel the world his country, wished all countries weak, poor, and ill-governed but his own: he now sees in their wealth and progress a direct source of wealth and progress to his own country. It is commerce which is rapidly rendering war obsolete, by strengthening and multiplying the personal interests which are in natural opposition to it. And it may be said without exaggeration that the great extent and rapid increase of international trade, in being the principal guarantee of the peace of the world, is the great permanent security for the uninterrupted progress of the ideas, the institutions, and the character of the human race.

Chapter XIV. Of International Values.

§ 1. The values of imported commodities depend on the Terms of international interchange.

The values of commodities produced at the same place, or in places sufficiently adjacent for capital to move freely between them—let us say, for simplicity, of commodities produced in the same country—depend (temporary fluctuations apart) upon their cost of production. But the value of a commodity brought from a distant place, especially from a foreign country, does not depend on its cost of production in the place from whence it comes. On what, then, does it depend? The value of a thing in any place depends on the cost of its acquisition in that place; which, in the case of an imported article, means the cost of production of the thing which is exported to pay for it.

If, then, the United States imports wine from Spain, giving for every pipe of wine a bale of cloth, the exchange value of a pipe of wine in the United States will not depend upon what the production of the wine may have cost in Spain, but upon what the production of the cloth has cost in the United States. Though the wine may have cost in Spain the equivalent of only ten days' labor, yet, if the cloth costs in the United States twenty days' labor, the wine, when brought to the United States, will exchange for the produce of twenty days' American labor, *plus* the cost of carriage, including the usual profit on the importer's capital during the time it is locked up and withheld from other employment.[268]

The value, then, in any country, of a foreign commodity, depends on the quantity of home produce which must be given to the foreign country in exchange for it. In other words, the values of foreign commodities depend on the terms of international exchange. What, then, do these depend upon? What is it which, in the case supposed, causes a pipe of wine from Spain to be exchanged with the United States for exactly that quantity of cloth? We have seen that it is not their cost of production. If the cloth and the wine were both made in Spain, they would exchange at their cost of production in Spain; if they were both made in the United States, they would [possibly] exchange at their cost of production in the United States: but all the cloth being made in the United States, and all the wine in Spain, they are in circumstances to which we have already determined that the law of cost of production is not applicable. We must accordingly, as we have done before in a similar embarrassment, fall back upon an antecedent law, that of supply and demand; and in this we shall again find the solution of our difficulty.

§ 2. The values of foreign commodities depend, not upon Cost of Production, but upon Reciprocal Demand and Supply.

It has been previously explained that the conditions called. "international" are those, either within a nation, or those existing between two separate nations, which are such as to prevent the free movement of labor and capital from one group of industries to another, or from one locality to another distant one. Even if woolen cloth could be made cheaper in England than in the United States, we know that neither capital nor labor would easily leave the United States for England, although it might go from Rhode Island to Massachusetts under similar inducements. If shoes can be made with less advantage in Providence than in Lynn, the shoe industry will come to Lynn; but it does not follow that the English shoe industry would come to Lynn, even if the advantages of the latter were greater than those in England. If there be no obstacle to the free movement of labor and capital between places or occupations, and if some place or occupation can produce at a less cost than another place or occupation, then there will be a migration of the instruments of production. Since there is no free movement of labor and capital between one country and another, then two countries stand in the same relation as that of two "non-competing groups" within the same country, as before explained. When this fact is once fully grasped, the subject of international values becomes very simple. It does not differ from the question of those domestic values for which we found[262] that the dependence on cost of production would not hold, but that their values were governed by reciprocal demand and supply.

Attention should be drawn to the real nature of the present inquiry. It is not here a question as to what causes international *trade* between two countries: that has been treated in the preceding chapter, and has been found to be a difference in the comparative cost. The question now is one of *exchange value*, that is, for how much of other commodities a given commodity will exchange. The reasons for the trade are supposed to exist; but we now want to know what the law is which determines the proportions of the exchange. Why does one article exchange for more or less of another? Not, as we have seen, because one costs more or less to produce than the other.

In the trade between the United States and England in iron and corn, formerly referred to (p. 383), it was seen that a 100 days' labor of corn buys from England iron which would have cost the United States 125 days' labor. England sends 150 days' labor of iron and buys from the United States corn which would have cost her 200 days' labor. But what rule fixes the proportions between 100 and 125 for the United States, and between 150 and 200 for England, at which the exchanges will take place? The trade increases the productiveness of both countries, but in what ratio will the two countries share this gain? The answer is, briefly, in *the ratio set by reciprocal demand and supply*, that is, the relative strength, as compared with each other, of the demands of the two countries respectively for iron and corn. This, however, may be capable of explanation in a simple form.

A has spades, and B has oats, to dispose of; and each wishes to get the article belonging to the other. Will A give one spade for one bushel of oats, or for two? Will B give two bushels of oats for one spade? That depends upon how strong a desire A has for oats; the intensity of his demand may induce him to give two spades for one bushel. But the exchange also depends upon B. If he has no great need for spades, and A has a strong desire for oats, B will get more spades for oats than otherwise, possibly two spades for one bushel of oats; that is, oats will have a larger exchange value. If, on the other hand, A cares less for oats than B does for spades, then the exchange will result in an increased value of spades relatively to oats. When two commodities exchange against each other, their exchange values will depend entirely upon the relative intensity of the demand on each side for the other commodity. And this simple form of the statement of reciprocal demand and supply is also the law of international values.

If instead of spades and oats we substitute iron and corn, and let the trade be between England and the United States, the quantity of corn required to buy a given quantity of iron will depend upon the relative demands of England for corn and of the United States for iron. Something may cut off England's demand for our breadstuffs, and they will then have a less exchange value relatively to iron (if we keep up our demand), and their prices will fall. But if, on the other hand, England has poor harvests, and consequently a great demand for corn, and if our demand for iron is not excessive at the same time, then our breadstuffs will rise in value. And this was precisely what happened from 1877 to 1879. Now, in the above illustration of corn and iron, how can we know whether or not x bushels of corn (the produce of 100 days' labor in the United States) will exchange for exactly y tons of English iron? That, again, will depend upon the reciprocal demands of the two countries for corn and iron respectively. Moreover, it will have been already observed that the ratio of exchange is not capable of being ascertained exactly, since it varies with changing conditions, namely, the desires of the people of the two countries, together with their means of purchase.

But yet these variations are capable of ascertainment as regards their extreme limits. The reciprocal demand can not carry the exchange value in either country beyond the line set by the cost of production of the article. For instance, an urgent need in England for corn (if the United States has a light demand for English iron) can not carry the ratio of exchange to a point such that England will offer so much more than 150 days' labor in iron for x bushels of American corn that it will go beyond 200 days' labor in iron. It will be seen at once, then, if that were the case, that England would produce the corn herself; and that she would then have no gain whatever from the trade. The ratio of exchange will thus be limited by the reciprocal demand on one side to the cost of production (200 days' labor) of English corn. On the other hand, if the supposition were reversed, and the United States had a great demand for iron, but England had little need for our corn, then we would not offer more than 125 days' labor of corn for y tons of iron, because for that expenditure of labor we could produce the iron ourselves.

In the above examples we have considered the case of a trade in corn and iron only. If corn were to typify all our goods wanted by England, and iron all English goods wanted by the United States, the conclusions would be exactly the same. The ratios of a myriad of things, each governed by its particular reciprocal demand, exchanging against each other, give a general result by which the goods sent out exchange against the goods brought back at such rates as are fixed by the reciprocal demands acting on all the goods. Goods are payments for goods; the ratio of exchange depends on reciprocal demand and supply. If we now add more countries to the example, we simply increase the number of persons (although in different countries) wanting our goods, as set off against our demands for the goods of this greater number of persons. If France, Germany, and England all want our corn, we must have some demand for the goods of France, Germany, and England also; and the same law of reciprocal demand gives the ratio of interchange. That this explanation is consistent with the facts is to be seen when we notice how eagerly the exporters of American staples watch the conditions which increase or diminish the foreign demand for these commodities, looking at them as the causes which directly affect their exchange value, or price.

When cost of carriage is added, it will increase the price of corn to England and of iron to the United States. But, as every one knows, an increase of price affects the demand; and, as the demand on each side is affected, a new ratio of exchange will finally be reached consistent with the strength of desires on each side. Who, therefore, will pay the most of the cost of carriage England or the United States? That will, again, depend on whether England has the greatest relative demand for American goods, as compared with the demand of the United States for English goods.

No absolute rule, therefore, can be laid down for the division of the cost, no more than for the division of the advantage; and it does not follow that, in whatever ratio the one is divided, the other will be divided in the same. It is impossible to say, if the cost of carriage could be annihilated, whether the producing or the importing country would be most benefited. This would depend on the play of international demand.

Cost of carriage has one effect more. But for it, every commodity would (if trade be supposed free) be either regularly imported or regularly exported. A country would make nothing for itself which it did not also make for other countries. But in consequence of cost of carriage there are many things, especially bulky articles, which every, or almost every, country produces within itself. After exporting the things in which it can employ itself most advantageously, and importing those in which it is under the greatest disadvantage, there are many lying between, of which the relative cost of production in that and in other countries differs so little that the cost of carriage would absorb more than the whole saving in cost of production which would be obtained by importing one and exporting another. This is the case with numerous commodities of common consumption, including the coarser qualities of many articles of food and manufacture, of which the finer kinds are the subject of extensive international traffic.

§ 3. —As illustrated by trade in cloth and linen between England and Germany.

> Mr. Mill still further illustrates the operation of the law of reciprocal demand by the case of a trade between England and Germany in cloth and linen, as follows:

"Suppose that ten yards of broadcloth cost in England as much labor as fifteen yards of linen, and in Germany as much as twenty." This supposition then being made, it would be the interest of England to import linen from Germany, and of Germany to import cloth from England. "When each country produced both commodities for itself, ten yards of cloth exchanged for fifteen yards of linen in England, and for twenty in Germany. They will now exchange for the same number of yards of linen in both. For what number? If for fifteen yards, England will be just as she was, and Germany will gain all. If for twenty yards, Germany will be as before, and England will derive the whole of the benefit. If for any number intermediate between fifteen and twenty, the advantage will be shared between the two countries. If, for example, ten yards of cloth exchange for eighteen of linen, England will gain an advantage of three yards on every fifteen, Germany will save two out of every twenty. The problem is, what are the causes which determine the proportion in which the cloth of England and the linen of Germany will exchange for each other? Let us suppose, then, that by the effect of what Adam Smith calls the higgling of the market, ten yards of cloth, in both countries, exchange for seventeen yards of linen.

"The demand for a commodity, that is, the quantity of it which can find a purchaser, varies, as we have before remarked, according to the price. In Germany the price of ten yards of cloth is now seventeen yards of linen, or whatever quantity of money is equivalent in Germany to seventeen yards of linen. Now, that being the price, there is some particular number of yards of cloth, which will be in demand, or will find purchasers, at that price. There is some given quantity of cloth, more than which could not be disposed of at that price; less than which, at that price, would not fully satisfy the demand. Let us suppose this quantity to be 1,000 times ten yards.

"Let us now turn our attention to England. There the price of seventeen yards of linen is ten yards of cloth, or whatever quantity of money is equivalent in England to ten yards of cloth. There is some particular number of yards of linen which, at that price, will exactly satisfy the demand, and no more. Let us suppose that this number is 1,000 times seventeen yards.

"As seventeen yards of linen are to ten yards of cloth, so are 1,000 times seventeen yards to 1,000 times ten yards. At the existing exchange value, the linen which England requires will exactly pay for the quantity of cloth which, on the same terms of interchange, Germany requires. The demand on each side is precisely sufficient to carry off the supply on the other. The conditions required by the principle of demand and supply are fulfilled, and the two commodities will continue to be interchanged, as we supposed them to be, in the ratio of seventeen yards of linen for ten yards of cloth.

"But our suppositions might have been different. Suppose that, at the assumed rate of interchange, England had been disposed to consume no greater quantity of linen than 800 times seventeen yards; it is evident that, at the rate supposed, this would not have sufficed to pay for the 1,000 times ten yards of cloth which we have supposed Germany to require at the assumed value. Germany would be able to procure no more than 800 times ten yards at that price. To procure the remaining 200, which she would have no means of doing but by bidding higher for them, she would offer more than seventeen yards of linen in exchange for ten yards of cloth; let us suppose her to offer eighteen. At this price, perhaps, England would be inclined to purchase a greater quantity of linen. She would consume, possibly, at that price, 900 times eighteen yards. On the other hand, cloth having risen in price, the demand of Germany for it would probably have diminished. If, instead of 1,000 times ten yards, she is now contented with 900 times ten yards, these will exactly pay for the 900 times eighteen yards of linen which England is willing to take at the altered price; the demand on each side will again exactly suffice to take off the corresponding supply; and ten yards for eighteen will be the rate at which, in both countries, cloth will exchange for linen.

"The converse of all this would have happened if, instead of 800 times seventeen yards, we had supposed that England, at the rate of ten for seventeen, would have taken 1,200 times seventeen yards of linen. In this case, it is England whose demand is not fully supplied; it is England who, by bidding for more linen, will alter the rate of interchange to her own disadvantage; and ten yards of cloth will fall, in both countries, below the value of seventeen yards of linen. By this fall of cloth, or, what is the same thing, this rise of linen, the demand of Germany for cloth will increase, and the demand of England for linen will diminish, till the rate of interchange has so adjusted itself that the cloth and the linen will exactly pay for one another; and, when once this point is attained, values will remain without further alteration."

§ 4. The conclusion states in the Equation of International Demand.

"It may be considered, therefore, as established, that when two countries trade together in two commodities, the exchange value of these commodities relatively to each other will adjust itself to the inclinations and circumstances of the consumers on both sides, in such manner that the quantities required by each country, of the articles which it imports from its neighbor, shall be exactly sufficient to pay for one another. As the inclinations and circumstances of consumers can not be reduced to any rule, so neither can the proportions in which the two commodities will be interchanged. We know that the limits within which the variation is confined are the ratio between their costs of production in the one country and the ratio between their costs of production in the other. Ten yards of cloth can not exchange for more than twenty yards of linen, nor for less than fifteen. But they may exchange for any intermediate number. The ratios, therefore, in which the advantage of the trade may be divided between the two nations are various. The circumstances on which the proportionate share of each country more remotely depends admit only of a very general indication."

If, therefore, it be asked what country draws to itself the greatest share of the advantage of any trade it carries on, the answer is, the country for whose productions there is in other countries the greatest demand, and a demand the most susceptible of increase from additional cheapness. In so far as the productions of any country possess this property, the country obtains all foreign commodities at less cost. It gets its imports cheaper, the greater the intensity of the demand in foreign countries for its exports. It also gets its imports cheaper, the less the extent and intensity of its own demand for them. The market is cheapest to those whose demand is small. A country which desires few foreign productions, and only a limited quantity of them, while its own commodities are in great request in foreign countries, will obtain its limited imports at extremely small cost, that is, in exchange for the produce of a very small quantity of its labor and capital.

The law which we have now illustrated may be appropriately named the Equation of International Demand. It may be concisely stated as follows: The produce of a country exchanges for the produce of other countries at such values as are required in order that the whole of her exports may exactly pay for the whole of her imports. This law of International Values is but an extension of the more general law of Value, which we called the Equation of Supply and Demand.[270] We have seen that the value of a commodity always so adjusts itself as to bring the demand to the exact level of the supply. But all trade, either between nations or individuals, is an interchange of commodities, in which the things that they respectively have to sell constitute also their means of purchase: the supply brought by the one constitutes his demand for what is brought by the other. So that supply and demand are but another expression for reciprocal demand; and to say that value will adjust itself so as to equalize demand with supply, is, in fact, to say that it will adjust itself so as to equalize the demand on one side with the demand on the other.

> The *tendency* of imports to balance exports may be seen from Chart No. XIII, on the next page, which shows the relation between the exports and imports solely of merchandise, and exclusive of specie, to and from the United States. From 1850 to 1860, after the discoveries of the precious metals in this country, we sent great quantities of gold and silver out of the country, purely

as merchandise, so that, if we should include the precious metals among the exports in those years, the total exports would more nearly equal the total imports. The transmission of gold at that time was effected exactly as that of other merchandise; so that to the date of the civil war there was a very evident equilibrium between exports and imports. Then came the war, with the period of extravagance and speculation following, which led to great purchases abroad, and which was closed only by the panic of 1873. Since then more exports than imports were needed to pay for the great purchases of the former period; and the epoch of great exports, from 1875 to 1883, balanced the opposite conditions in the period preceding. It would seem, therefore, that we had reached a normal period about the year 1882.[271] A fuller statement as to the fluctuations of exports and imports about the equilibrium will be given when the introduction of money in international trade is made. The full statement must also include the financial account.

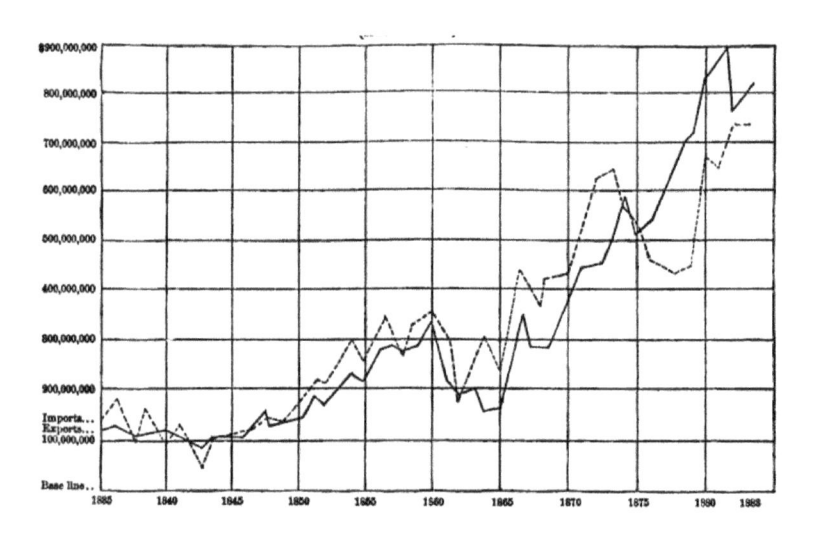

Chart XIII. *Value of Merchandise* IMPORTED *into (dotted line) and* EXPORTED *from (black line) the United States from 1835 to 1883.*

§ 5. The cost to a country of its imports depends not only on the ratio of exchange, but on the efficiency of its labor.

We now pass to another essential part of the theory of the subject. There are two senses in which a country obtains commodities cheaper by foreign trade: in the sense of value and in the sense of cost: (1.) It gets them cheaper in the first sense, by their falling in value relatively to other things; the same quantity of them exchanging, in the country, for a smaller quantity than before of the other produce of the country. To revert to our original figures [of the trade with Germany in cloth and linen]: in England, all consumers of linen obtained, after the trade was opened, seventeen or some greater number of yards for the same quantity of all other things for which they before obtained only fifteen. The degree of cheapness, in this sense of the term, depends on the laws of International Demand, so copiously illustrated in the preceding sections. (2.) But, in the other sense, that of cost, a country gets a commodity cheaper when it obtains a greater quantity of the commodity with the same expenditure of labor and capital. In this sense of the term, cheapness in a great measure depends upon a cause of a different nature: a country gets its imports cheaper, in proportion to the general productiveness of its domestic industry; to the general efficiency of its labor. The labor of one country may be, as a whole, much more efficient than that of another: all or most of the commodities capable of being produced in both may be produced in one at less absolute cost than in the other; which, as we have seen, will not necessarily prevent the two countries from exchanging commodities. The things which the more favored country will import from others are, of course, those in which it is least superior; but, by importing them, it acquires, even in those commodities, the same advantage which it possesses in the articles it gives in exchange for them. What her imports cost to her is a function of two variables: (1) the quantity of her own commodities which she gives for them, and (2) the cost of those commodities. Of these, the last alone depends on the efficiency of her labor; the first depends on the law of international values; that is, on the intensity and extensibility of the foreign demand for her commodities, compared with her demand for foreign commodities.

> The great productiveness of any industry in our country has thus two results: (1) it gives a larger total out of which labor and capital at home can receive

greater rewards; and (2) the commodities being cheaper in comparison than other commodities not so easily produced, furnish the very articles which are most likely to be sent abroad, in accordance with the doctrine of comparative cost. In the United States, those things in the production of which labor and capital are most efficient, and so earn the largest rewards, are precisely the articles entering most largely into our foreign trade. That is, we get foreign articles cheaper precisely because these exports cost us less in labor and capital. These, of course, since we inhabit a country whose natural resources are not yet fully worked, are largely the products of the extractive industries, as may be seen by the following table of the value of goods entering to the greatest extent into our foreign export trade in 1883:

Raw cotton	$247,328,721
Breadstuffs	208,040,850
Provisions and animals	118,177,555
Mineral oils	40,555,492
Wood	26,793,708
Tobacco	22,095,229

These six classes of commodities are arranged in the order in which they enter into our export trade, and are the six which come first and highest in the list.

Chapter XV. Of Money Considered As An Imported Commodity.

§ 1. Money imported on two modes; as a Commodity, and as a medium of Exchange.

The degree of progress which we have now made in the theory of foreign trade puts it in our power to supply what was previously deficient in our view of the theory of money; and this, when completed, will in its turn enable us to conclude the subject of foreign trade.

Money, or the material of which it is composed, is, in Great Britain, and in most other countries, a foreign commodity. Its value and distribution must therefore be regulated, not by the law of value which obtains in adjacent places, but by that which is applicable to imported commodities—the law of international values.

In the discussion into which we are now about to enter, I shall use the terms money and the precious metals indiscriminately. This may be done without leading to any error; it having been shown that the value of money, when it consists of the precious metals, or of a paper currency convertible into them on demand, is entirely governed by the value of the metals themselves: from which it never permanently differs, except by the expense of coinage, when this is paid by the individual and not by the state.

Money is brought into a country in two different ways. It is imported (chiefly in the form of bullion) like any other merchandise, as being an advantageous article of commerce. It is also imported in its other character of a medium of exchange, to pay some debt due to the country, either for goods exported or on any other account. The existence of these two distinct modes in which money flows into a country, while other commodities are habitually introduced only in the first of these modes, occasions somewhat more of complexity and obscurity than exists in the case of other commodities, and for this reason only is any special and minute exposition necessary.

§ 2. As a commodity, it obeys the same laws of Value as other imported Commodities.

In so far as the precious metals are imported in the ordinary way of commerce, their value must depend on the same causes, and conform to the same laws, as the value of any other foreign production. It is in this mode chiefly that gold and silver diffuse themselves from the mining countries into all other parts of the commercial world. They are the staple commodities of those countries, or at least are among their great articles of regular export; and are shipped on speculation, in the same manner as other exportable commodities. The quantity, therefore, which a country (say England) will give of its own produce, for a certain quantity of bullion, will depend, if we suppose only two countries and two commodities, upon the demand in England for bullion, compared with the demand in the mining country (which we will call the United States[272]) for what England has to give.

The bullion required by England must exactly pay for the cottons or other English commodities required by the United States. If, however, we substitute for this simplicity the degree of complication which really exists, the equation of international demand must be established not between the bullion wanted in England and the cottons or broadcloth wanted in the United States, but between the whole of the imports of England and the whole of her exports. The demand in foreign countries for English products must be brought into equilibrium with the demand in England for the products of foreign countries; and all foreign commodities, bullion among the rest, must be exchanged against English products in such proportions as will, by the effect they produce on the demand, establish this equilibrium.

There is nothing in the peculiar nature or uses of the precious metals which should make them an exception to the general principles of demand. So far as they are wanted for purposes of luxury or the arts, the demand increases with the cheapness, in the same irregular way as the demand for any other commodity. So far as they are required for money, the demand increases with the cheapness in a perfectly regular way, the quantity needed being always in inverse proportion to the value. This is the only real difference, in respect to demand, between money and other things.

Money, then, if imported solely as a merchandise, will, like other imported commodities, be of lowest value in the countries for whose exports there is the greatest foreign demand, and which have themselves the least demand for foreign commodities. To these two circumstances it is, however, necessary to add two others, which produce their effect through cost of carriage. The cost of obtaining bullion is compounded of two elements; the goods given to purchase it and the expense of transport; of which last, the bullion countries will bear a part (though an uncertain part) in the adjustment of international values. The expense of transport is partly that of carrying the goods to the bullion countries, and partly that of bringing back the bullion; both these items are influenced by the distance from the mines; and the former is also much affected by the bulkiness of the goods. Countries whose exportable produce consists of the finer manufactures obtain bullion, as well as all other foreign articles, *cæteris paribus*, at less expense than countries which export nothing but bulky raw produce.

To be quite accurate, therefore, we must say: The countries whose exportable productions (1) are most in demand abroad, and (2) contain greatest value in smallest bulk, (3) which are nearest to the mines, and (4) which have least demand for foreign productions, are those in which money will be of lowest value, or, in other words, in which prices will habitually range the highest. If we are speaking not of the value of money, but of its cost (that is, the quantity of the country's labor which must be expended to obtain it), we must add (5) to these four conditions of cheapness a fifth condition, namely, "whose productive industry is the most efficient." This last, however, does not at all affect the value of money, estimated in commodities; it affects the general abundance and facility with which all things, money and commodities together, can be obtained.[273]

> The accompanying Chart, No. XIV, on the next page, gives the excess of exports from the United States of gold and silver coin and bullion over imports, and the excess of imports over exports. The movement of the line above the horizontal baseline shows distinctly how largely we have been sending the precious metals abroad from our mines, simply as a regular article of export, like merchandise. From 1850 to 1879 the exports are clearly not in the nature of payments for trade balances; since it indicates a steady movement out of the country (with the exception of the first year of the war, when gold came to this country). The phenomenal increase of specie exports during the war, and until 1879, was due to the fact that we had a depreciated paper currency, which sent the metals out of the country as merchandise. This chart should be studied in connection with Chart No. XIII.

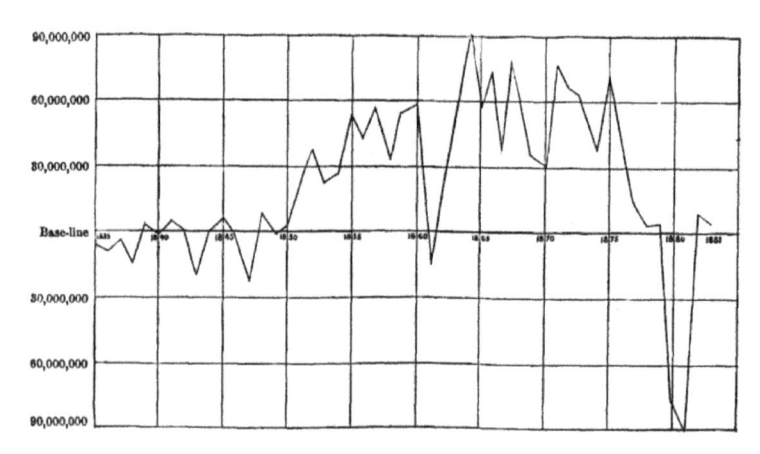

Chart XIV. *Chart showing the Excess of Exports and Imports of Gold and Silver Coin and Bullion, from and into the United States, from 1835 to 1883. The line when above the base-line shows the excess of exports; when below, the excess of imports.*

From the preceding considerations, it appears that those are greatly in error who contend that the value of money, in countries where it is an imported commodity, must be entirely regulated by its value in the countries which produce it; and can not be raised or lowered in any permanent manner unless some change has taken place in the cost of production at the mines. On the contrary, any circumstance which disturbs the equation of international demand with respect to a particular country not only may, but must, affect the value of money in that country—its value at the mines remaining the same. The opening of a new branch of export trade from England; an increase in the foreign demand for English products, either by the natural course of events or by the abrogation of duties; a check to the demand in England for foreign commodities, by the laying on of import duties in England or of export duties elsewhere; these and all other events of similar tendency would make the imports of England (bullion and other things taken together) no longer an equivalent for the exports; and the countries which take her exports would be obliged to offer their commodities, and bullion among the rest, on cheaper terms, in order to reestablish the equation of demand; and thus England would obtain money cheaper, and would acquire a generally higher range of prices. A country which, from any of the causes mentioned, gets money cheaper, obtains all its other imports cheaper likewise.

It is by no means necessary that the increased demand for English commodities, which enables England to supply herself with bullion at a cheaper rate, should be a demand in the mining countries. England might export nothing whatever to those countries, and yet might be the country which obtained bullion from them on the lowest terms, provided there were a sufficient intensity of demand in other foreign countries for English goods, which would be paid for circuitously, with gold and silver from the mining countries. The whole of its exports are what a country exchanges against the whole of its imports, and not its exports and imports to and from any one country.

Chapter XVI. Of The Foreign Exchanges.

§ 1. Money passes from country to country as a Medium of Exchange, through the Exchanges.

We have thus far considered the precious metals as a commodity, imported like other commodities in the common course of trade, and have examined what are the circumstances which would in that case determine their value. But those metals are also imported in another character, that which belongs to them as a medium of exchange; not as an article of commerce, to be sold for money, but as themselves money, to pay a debt, or effect a transfer of property.

Money is sent from one country to another for various purposes: the most usual purpose, however, is that of payment for goods. To show in what circumstances money actually passes from country to country for this or any of the other purposes mentioned, it is necessary briefly to state the nature of the mechanism by which international trade is carried on, when it takes place not by barter but through the medium of money.

In practice, the exports and imports of a country not only are not exchanged directly against each other, but often do not even pass through the same hands. Each is separately bought and paid for with money. We have seen, however, that, even in the same country, money does not actually pass from hand to hand each time that purchases are made with it, and still less does this happen between different countries. The habitual mode of paying and receiving payment for commodities, between country and country, is by bills of exchange.

A merchant in the United States, A, has exported American commodities, consigning them to his correspondent, B, in England. Another merchant in England, C, has exported English commodities, suppose of equivalent value, to a merchant, D, in the United States. It is evidently unnecessary that B in England should send money to A in the United States, and that D in the United States should send an equal sum of money to C in England. The one debt may be applied to the payment of the other, and the double cost and risk of carriage be thus saved. A draws a bill on B for the amount which B owes to him: D, having an equal amount to pay in England, buys this bill from A, and sends it to C, who, at the expiration of the number of days which the bill has to run, presents it to B for payment. Thus the debt due from England to the United States, and the debt due from the United States to England, are both paid without sending an ounce of gold or silver from one country to the other.[274]

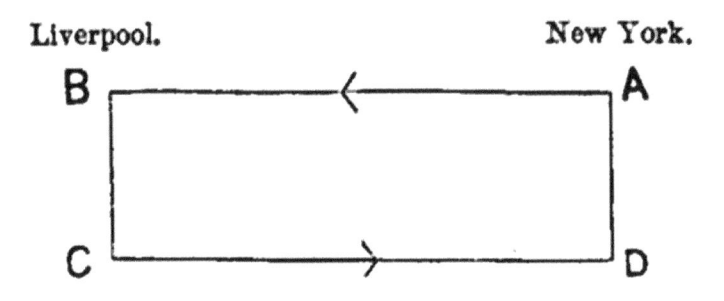

```
           Liverpool.                          New York.
           B ┌──────────────◄──────────────┐ A
             │                              │
             │                              │
             │                              │
           C └──────────────►──────────────┘ D
```

This implies (if we exclude for the present any other international payments than those occurring in the course of commerce) that the exports and imports exactly pay for one another, or, in other words, that the equation of international demand is established. When such is the fact, the international transactions are liquidated without the passage of any money from one country to the other. But, if there is a greater sum due from the United States to England than is due from England to the United States, or *vice versa*, the debts can not be simply written off against one another. After the one has been applied, as far as it will go, toward covering the other, the balance must be transmitted in the precious metals. In point of fact, the merchant who has the amount to pay will even then pay for it by a bill. When a person has a remittance to make to a foreign country, he does not himself search for some one who has money to receive from that country, and ask him for a bill of exchange. In this, as in other branches of business, there is a class of middle-men or brokers, who bring buyers and sellers together, or stand between them, buying bills from those who have money to receive, and selling bills to those who have money to pay. When a customer comes to a broker for a bill on Paris or Amsterdam, the broker sells to him perhaps the bill he may himself have bought that morning from a merchant, perhaps a bill on his own correspondent in the foreign city; and, to enable his correspondent to pay, when due, all the bills he has granted, he remits to him all those which he has bought and has not resold. In this manner these brokers take upon themselves the whole settlement of the pecuniary transactions between distant places, being remunerated by a small commission or percentage on the amount of each bill which they either sell or buy. Now, if the brokers find that they are asked for bills, on the one part, to a greater amount than bills are offered to them on the other, they do not on this account refuse to give them; but since, in that case, they have no means of enabling the correspondents on whom their bills are drawn to pay them when due, except by transmitting part of the amount in gold or silver, they require from those to whom they sell bills an additional price, sufficient to cover the freight and insurance of the gold and silver, with a profit sufficient to compensate them for their trouble and for the temporary occupation of a portion of their capital. This premium (as it is called) the buyers are willing to pay, because they must otherwise go to the expense of remitting the precious metals themselves, and it is done cheaper by those who make doing it a part of their especial business. But, though only some of those who have a debt to pay would have actually to remit money, all will be obliged, by each other's competition, to pay the premium; and the brokers are for the same reason obliged to pay it to those whose bills they buy. The reverse of all this happens, if, on the comparison of exports and imports, the country, instead of having a balance to pay, has a balance to receive. The brokers find more bills offered to them than are sufficient to cover those which they are required to grant. Bills on foreign countries consequently fall to a discount; and the competition among the brokers, which is exceedingly active, prevents them from retaining this discount as a profit for themselves, and obliges them to give the benefit of it to those who buy the bills for purposes of remittance.

When the United States had the same number of dollars to pay to England which England had to pay to her, one set of merchants in the United States would want bills, and another set would have bills to dispose of, for the very same number of dollars; and consequently a bill on England for $1,000 would sell for exactly $1,000, or, in the phraseology of merchants, the exchange would be at par. As England also, on this supposition, would have an equal number of dollars to pay and to receive, bills on the United States would be at par in England, whenever bills on England were at par in the United States.

If, however, the United States had a larger sum to pay to England than to receive from her, there would be persons requiring bills on England for a greater number of dollars than there were bills drawn by persons to whom money was due. A bill on England for $1,000 would then sell for more than $1,000, and bills would be said to be at a premium. The premium, however, could not exceed the cost and risk of making the remittance in gold, together with a trifling profit; because, if it did, the debtor would send the gold itself, in preference to buying the bill.

If, on the contrary, the United States had more money to receive from England than to pay, there would be bills offered for a greater number of dollars than were wanted for remittance, and the price of bills would fall below par: a bill for $1,000 might be bought for somewhat less than $1,000, and bills would be said to be at a discount.

When the United States has more to pay than to receive, England has more to receive than to pay, and *vice versa*. When, therefore, in the United States, bills on England bear a premium, then, in England, bills on the United States are at a discount; and, when bills on England are at a discount in the United States, bills on the United States are at a premium in England. If they are at par in either country, they are so, as we have already seen, in both.[275]

Thus do matters stand between countries, or places which have the same currency. So much of barbarism, however, still remains in the transactions of the most civilized nations, that almost all independent countries choose to assert their nationality by having, to their own inconvenience and that of their neighbors, a peculiar currency of their own. To our present purpose this makes no other difference than that, instead of speaking of *equal* sums of money, we have to speak of *equivalent* sums. By equivalent sums, when both currencies are composed of the same metal, are meant sums which contain exactly the same quantity of the metal, in weight and fineness.

> The quantity of gold in the English pound is equivalent to $4.8666+ of our gold coins. If the bills offered are about equal to those wanted, a claim to a pound in England will sell for $4.86. If many are wanted, and but few to be had, their price will go up, of course; but it can not go more than a small fraction beyond $4.90, since about 3-¼ cents is sufficient to cover the brokerage, insurance, and freight per pound sterling in a shipment of gold to London. Therefore, in order to get money to a creditor in London, no one will pay more for a pound in the form of a bill than he will be obliged to pay for sending it across in the form of bullion. Bills of exchange, then, can not rise in price beyond the point ($4.90 +) since, rather than pay a higher sum for a bill, gold will be sent. This point is called the "shipping-point" of gold. When the exchanges are at $4.90, it will be found that gold is going abroad. On the other hand, when the supply of bills is greater than the demand, their price will fall. A man having a bill on London to sell—i.e., a claim to a pound in London—will not sell it at a price here lower than $4.86, by more than the expense of bringing the

> gold itself across. Since this expense is about 3-¼ cents, bills can not fall below about $4.83. When exchange is at that price, it will be found that gold is coming to the United States from England. This price is the "shipping-point" for imports of gold. This, of course, applies to sight-bills only.
>
> Formerly, we computed exchange on a scale of percentages, the real par being about 109. This was given up after the war.

When bills on foreign countries are at a premium, it is customary to say that the exchanges are against the country, or unfavorable to it. In order to understand these phrases, we must take notice of what "the exchange," in the language of merchants, really means. It means the power which the money of the country has of purchasing the money of other countries. Supposing $4.86 to be the exact par of exchange, then when it requires more than $1,000 to buy a bill of £205, $1,000 of American money are worth less than their real equivalent of English money: and this is called an exchange unfavorable to the United States. The only persons in the United States, however, to whom it is really unfavorable are those who have money to pay in England, for they come into the bill market as buyers, and have to pay a premium; but to those who have money to receive in England the same state of things is favorable; for they come as sellers and receive the premium. The premium, however, indicates that a balance is due by the United States, which must be eventually liquidated in the precious metals; and since, according to the old theory, the benefit of a trade consisted in bringing money into the country, this prejudice introduced the practice of calling the exchange favorable when it indicated a balance to receive, and unfavorable when it indicated one to pay; and the phrases in turn tended to maintain the prejudice.

§ 2. Distinction between Variations in the Exchanges which are self-adjusting and those which can only be rectified through Prices.

It might be supposed at first sight that when the exchange is unfavorable, or, in other words, when bills are at a premium, the premium must always amount to a full equivalent for the cost of transmitting money. But a small excess of imports above exports, or any other small amount of debt to be paid to foreign countries, does not usually affect the exchanges to the full extent of the cost and risk of transporting bullion. The length of credit allowed generally permits, on the part of some of the debtors, a postponement of payment, and in the mean time the balance may turn the other way, and restore the equality of debts and credits without any actual transmission of the metals. And this is the more likely to happen, as there is a self-adjusting power in the variations of the exchange itself. Bills are at a premium because a greater money value has been imported than exported. But the premium is itself an extra profit to those who export. Besides the price they obtain for their goods, they draw for the amount and gain the premium. It is, on the other hand, a diminution of profit to those who import. Besides the price of the goods, they have to pay a premium for remittance. So that what is called an unfavorable exchange is an encouragement to export, and a discouragement to import. And if the balance due is of small amount, and is the consequence of some merely casual disturbance in the ordinary course of trade, it is soon liquidated in commodities, and the account adjusted by means of bills, without the transmission of any bullion. Not so, however, when the excess of imports above exports, which has made the exchange unfavorable, arises from a permanent cause. In that case, what disturbed the equilibrium must have been the state of prices, and it can only be restored by acting on prices. It is impossible that prices should be such as to invite to an excess of imports, and yet that the exports should be kept permanently up to the imports by the extra profit on exportation derived from the premium on bills; for, if the exports were kept up to the imports, bills would not be at a premium, and the extra profit would not exist. It is through the prices of commodities that the correction must be administered.

Disturbances, therefore, of the equilibrium of imports and exports, and consequent disturbances of the exchange, may be considered as of two classes: the one casual or accidental, which, if not on too large a scale, correct themselves through the premium on bills, without any transmission of the precious metals; the other arising from the general state of prices, which can not be corrected without the subtraction of actual money from the circulation of one of the countries, or an annihilation of credit equivalent to it.

It remains to observe that the exchanges do not depend on the balance of debts and credits with each country separately, but with all countries taken together. The United States may owe a balance of payments to England; but it does not follow that the exchange with England will be against the United States, and that bills on England will be at a premium; because a balance may be due to the United States from Holland or Hamburg, and she may pay her debts to England with bills on those places; which is technically called arbitration of exchange. There is some little additional expense, partly commission and partly loss of interest in settling debts in this circuitous manner, and to the extent of that small difference the exchange with one country may vary apart from that with others.

A common use of bills of exchange is that by which, when three countries are concerned, two of them may strike a balance through the third, if both countries have dealings with that third country. New York merchants may buy of China, but China may not be buying of New York, although both may have dealings with London.

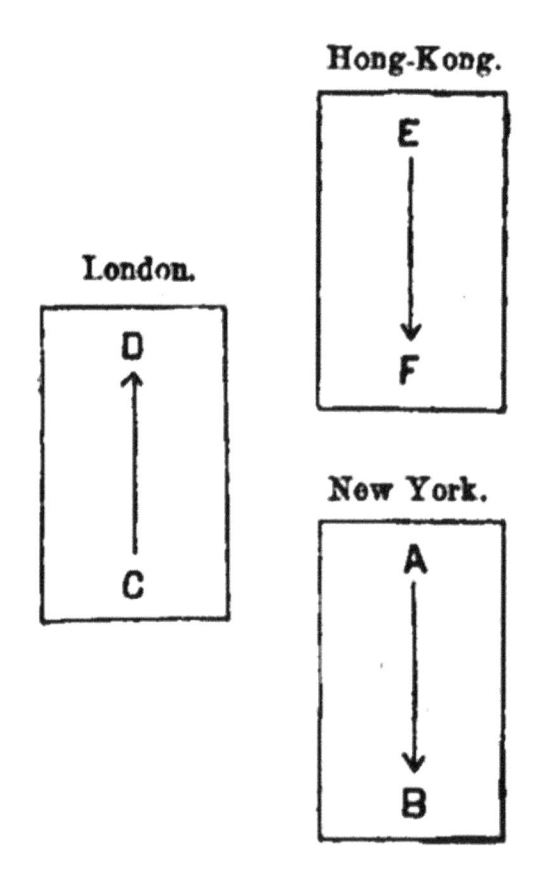

Hong-Kong.

E
↓
F

London.

D
↑
C

New York.

A
↓
B

A, we will suppose, is a buyer of £1,000 worth of tea from F, in Hong-Kong; B is an exporter of wheat

(£1,000) to C in London; D has sent £1,000 worth of cotton goods to E in Hong-Kong. A can now pay F through London without the transmission of coin. A buys B's claim on C for £1,000, and sends it to F. E wishes to pay D in London for the cotton goods he bought of him; therefore, he buys from F for £1,000 the claim he now holds (i.e., a bill of exchange on London) against C for £1,000. E sends it to D, and, when D collects it from C, the whole circle of exchanges is completed without the transmission of the precious metals.

Chapter XVII. Of The Distribution Of The Precious Metals Through The Commercial World.

§ 1. The substitution of money for barter makes no difference in exports and imports, nor in the Law of international Values.

Having now examined the mechanism by which the commercial transactions between nations are actually conducted, we have next to inquire whether this mode of conducting them makes any difference in the conclusions respecting international values, which we previously arrived at on the hypothesis of barter.

The nearest analogy would lead us to presume the negative. We did not find that the intervention of money and its substitutes made any difference in the law of value as applied to adjacent places. Things which would have been equal in value if the mode of exchange had been by barter are worth equal sums of money. The introduction of money is a mere addition of one more commodity, of which the value is regulated by the same laws as that of all other commodities. We shall not be surprised, therefore, if we find that international values also are determined by the same causes under a money and bill system as they would be under a system of barter, and that money has little to do in the matter, except to furnish a convenient mode of comparing values.

All interchange is, in substance and effect, barter; whoever sells commodities for money, and with that money buys other goods, really buys those goods with his own commodities. And so of nations: their trade is a mere exchange of exports for imports; and, whether money is employed or not, things are only in their permanent state when the exports and imports exactly pay for each other. When this is the case, equal sums of money are due from each country to the other, the debts are settled by bills, and there is no balance to be paid in the precious metals. The trade is in a state like that which is called in mechanics a condition of stable equilibrium.

But the process by which things are brought back to this state when they happen to deviate from it is, at least outwardly, not the same in a barter system and in a money system. Under the first, the country which wants more imports than its exports will pay for must offer its exports at a cheaper rate, as the sole means of creating a demand for them sufficient to re-establish the equilibrium. When money is used, the country seems to do a thing totally different. She takes the additional imports at the same price as before, and, as she exports no equivalent, the balance of payments turns against her; the exchange becomes unfavorable, and the difference has to be paid in money. This is, in appearance, a very distinct operation from the former. Let us see if it differs in its essence, or only in its mechanism.

Let the country which has the balance to pay be the United States,[276] and the country which receives it, England. By this transmission of the precious metals, the quantity of the currency is diminished in the United States, and increased in England. This I am at liberty to assume. We are now supposing that there is an excess of imports over exports, arising from the fact that the equation of international demand is not yet established: that there is at the ordinary prices a permanent demand in the United States for more English goods than the American goods required in England at the ordinary prices will pay for. When this is the case, if a change were not made in the prices, there would be a perpetually renewed balance to be paid in money. The imports require to be permanently diminished, or the exports to be increased, which can only be accomplished through prices; and hence, even if the balances are at first paid from hoards, or by the exportation of bullion, they will reach the circulation at last, for, until they do, nothing can stop the drain.

When, therefore, the state of prices is such that the equation of international demand can not establish itself, the country requiring more imports than can be paid for by the exports, it is a sign that the country has more of the precious metals, or their substitutes, in circulation, than can permanently circulate, and must necessarily part with some of them before the balance can be restored. The currency is accordingly contracted: prices fall, and, among the rest, the prices of exportable articles; for which, accordingly, there arises, in foreign countries, a greater demand: while imported commodities have possibly risen in price, from the influx of money into foreign countries, and at all events have not participated in the general fall. But, until the increased cheapness of American goods induces foreign countries to take a greater pecuniary value, or until the increased dearness (positive or comparative) of foreign goods makes the United States take a less pecuniary value, the exports of the United States will be no nearer to paying for the imports than before, and the stream of the precious metals which had begun to flow out of the United States will still flow on. This efflux will continue until the fall of prices in the United States brings within reach of the foreign market some commodity which the United States did not previously send thither; or, until the reduced price of the things which she did send has forced a demand abroad for a sufficient quantity to pay for the imports, aided perhaps by a reduction of the

American demand for foreign goods, through their enhanced price, either positive or comparative.

Now, this is the very process which took place on our original supposition of barter. Not only, therefore, does the trade between nations tend to the same equilibrium between exports and imports, whether money is employed or not, but the means by which this equilibrium is established are essentially the same. The country whose exports are not sufficient to pay for her imports offers them on cheaper terms, until she succeeds in forcing the necessary demand: in other words, the equation of international demand, under a money system as well as under a barter system, is the law of international trade. Every country exports and imports the very same things, and in the very same quantity, under the one system as under the other. In a barter system, the trade gravitates to the point at which the sum of the imports exactly exchanges for the sum of the exports: in a money system, it gravitates to the point at which the sum of the imports and the sum of the exports exchange for the same quantity of money. And, since things which are equal to the same thing are equal to one another, the exports and imports which are equal in money price would, if money were not used, precisely exchange for one another.[277]

§ 2. The preceding Theorem further illustrated.

Let us proceed to [examine] to what extent the benefit of an improvement in the production of an exportable article is participated in by the countries importing it.

The improvement may either consist in the cheapening of some article which was already a staple production of the country, or in the establishment of some new branch of industry, or of some process rendering an article exportable which had not till then been exported at all. It will be convenient to begin with the case of a new export, as being somewhat the simpler of the two.

The first effect is that the article falls in price, and a demand arises for it abroad. This new exportation disturbs the balance, turns the exchanges, money flows into the country (which we shall suppose to be the United States), and continues to flow until prices rise. This higher range of prices will somewhat check the demand in foreign countries for the new article of export; and will diminish the demand which existed abroad for the other things which the United States was in the habit of exporting. The exports will thus be diminished; while at the same time the American public, having more money, will have a greater power of purchasing foreign commodities. If they make use of this increased power of purchase, there will be an increase of imports; and by this, and the check to exportation, the equilibrium of imports and exports will be restored. The result to foreign countries will be, that they have to pay dearer than before for their other imports, and obtain the new commodity cheaper than before, but not so much cheaper as the United States herself does. I say this, being well aware that the article would be actually at the very same price (cost of carriage excepted) in the United States and in other countries. The cheapness, however, of the article is not measured solely by the money-price, but by that price compared with the money-incomes of the consumers. The price is the same to the American and to the foreign consumers; but the former pay that price from money-incomes which have been increased by the new distribution of the precious metals; while the latter have had their money-incomes probably diminished by the same cause. The trade, therefore, has not imparted to the foreign consumer the whole, but only a portion, of the benefit which the American consumer has derived from the improvement; while the United States has also benefited in the prices of foreign commodities. Thus, then, any industrial improvement which leads to the opening of a new branch of export trade benefits a country not only by the cheapness of the article in which the improvement has taken place, but by a general cheapening of all imported products.

Let us now change the hypothesis, and suppose that the improvement, instead of creating a new export from the United States, cheapens an existing one. Let the commodity in which there is an improvement be [cotton] cloth. The first effect of the improvement is that its price falls, and there is an increased demand for it in the foreign market. But this demand is of uncertain amount. Suppose the foreign consumers to increase their purchases in the exact ratio of the cheapness, or, in other words, to lay out in cloth the same sum of money as before; the same aggregate payment as before will be due from foreign countries to the United States; the equilibrium of exports and imports will remain undisturbed, and foreigners will obtain the full advantage of the increased cheapness of cloth. But if the foreign demand for cloth is of such a character as to increase in a greater ratio than the cheapness, a larger sum than formerly will be due to the United States for cloth, and when paid will raise American prices, the price of cloth included; this rise, however, will affect only the foreign purchaser, American incomes being raised in a corresponding proportion; and the foreign consumer will thus derive a less advantage than the United States from the improvement. If, on the contrary, the cheapening of cloth does not extend the foreign demand for it in a proportional degree, a less sum of debts than before will be due to the United States for cloth, while there will be the usual sum of debts due from the United States to foreign countries; the balance of trade will turn against the United States, money will be exported, prices (that of cloth included) will fall, and cloth will eventually be cheapened to the foreign purchaser in a still greater ratio than the improvement has cheapened it to the United States. These are the very conclusions which [would be] deduced on the hypothesis of barter.[278]

The result of the preceding discussion can not be better summed up than in the words of Ricardo.[279] "Gold and silver having been chosen for the general medium of circulation, they are, by the competition of commerce, distributed in such proportions among the different countries of the world as to accommodate themselves to the natural traffic which would take place if no such metals existed, and the trade between countries were purely a trade of barter." Of this principle, so fertile in consequences, previous to which the theory of foreign trade was an unintelligible chaos, Mr. Ricardo, though he did not pursue it into its ramifications, was the real originator.

> On the principles of trade which we have before explained, the same rule will apply to the distribution of money in different parts of the same country, especially of a large country with various kinds of production, like the United States. The medium of exchange will, by the competition of commerce, be distributed in such proportions among the different parts of the United States, by natural laws, as to accommodate itself to the number of transactions which would take place if no such medium existed. For this reason, we find more money in the so-called great financial centers, because there are more exchanges of goods there. In sparsely settled parts of the West there will be less money precisely because there are fewer transactions than in the older and more settled districts. So that there could be no worse folly than the following legislation of Congress to distribute the national-bank circulation: "That $150,000,000 of the entire amount of circulating notes authorized to be issued shall be apportioned to associations in the States, in the District of Columbia, and in the Territories, *according to representative population*" (act of March 3, 1865).

§ 3. The precious metals, as money, are of the same Value, and distribute themselves according to the same Law, with the precious metals as a Commodity.

It is now necessary to inquire in what manner this law of the distribution of the precious metals by means of the exchanges affects the exchange value of money itself; and how it tallies with the law by which we found that the value of money is regulated when imported as a mere article of merchandise.

The causes which bring money into or carry it out of a country (1) through the exchanges, to restore the equilibrium of trade, and which thereby raise its value in some countries and lower it in others, are the very same causes on which the local value of money would depend, if it were never imported except (2) as a merchandise, and never except directly from the mines. When the value of money in a country is permanently lowered (1) [as a medium of exchange] by an influx of it through the balance of trade, the cause, if it is not diminished cost of production, must be one of those causes which compel a new adjustment, more favorable to the country, of the equation of international demand—namely, either an increased demand abroad for her commodities, or a diminished demand on her part for those of foreign countries. Now, an increased foreign demand for the commodities of a country, or a diminished demand in the country for imported commodities, are the very causes which, on the general principles of trade, enable a country to purchase all imports, and consequently (2) the precious metals, at a lower value. There is, therefore, no contradiction, but the most perfect accordance, in the results of the two different modes [(1) as a medium of exchange; and (2) as merchandise] in which the precious metals may be obtained. When money [as a medium of exchange] flows from country to country in consequence of changes in the international demand for commodities, and by so doing alters its own local value, it merely realizes, by a more rapid process, the effect which would otherwise take place more slowly by an alteration in the relative breadth of the streams by which the precious metals [as merchandise] flow into different regions of the earth from the mining countries. As, therefore, we before saw that the use of money as a medium of exchange does not in the least alter the law on which the values of other things, either in the same country or internationally, depend, so neither does it alter the law of the value of the precious metals itself; and there is in the whole doctrine of international values, as now laid down, a unity and harmony which are a strong collateral presumption of truth.

§ 4. International payments entering into the "financial account."

Before closing this discussion, it is fitting to point out in what manner and degree the preceding conclusions are affected by the existence of international payments not originating in commerce, and for which no equivalent in either money or commodities is expected or received—such as a tribute, or remittances, or interest to foreign creditors, or a government expenditure abroad.

To begin with the case of barter. The supposed annual remittances being made in commodities, and being exports for which there is to be no return, it is no longer requisite that the imports and exports should pay for one another; on the contrary, there must be an annual excess of exports over imports, equal to the value of the remittance. If, before the country became liable to the annual payment, foreign commerce was in its natural state of equilibrium, it will now be necessary, for the purpose of effecting the remittances, that foreign countries should be induced to take a greater quantity of exports than before, which can only be done by offering those exports on cheaper terms, or, in other words, by paying dearer for foreign commodities. The international values will so adjust themselves that, either by greater exports or smaller imports, or both, the requisite excess on the side of exports will be brought about, and this excess will become the permanent state. The result is, that a country which makes regular payments to foreign countries, besides losing what it pays, loses also something more, by the less advantageous terms on which it is forced to exchange its productions for foreign commodities.

The same results follow on the supposition of money. Commerce being supposed to be in a state of equilibrium when the obligatory remittances begin, the first remittance is necessarily made in money. This lowers prices in the remitting country, and raises them in the receiving. The natural effect is, that more commodities are exported than before, and fewer imported, and that, on the score of commerce alone, a balance of money will be constantly due from the receiving to the paying country. When the debt thus annually due to the tributary country becomes equal to the annual tribute or other regular payment due from it, no further transmission of money takes place; the equilibrium of exports and imports will no longer exist, but that of payments will; the exchange will be at par, the two debts will be set off against one another, and the tribute or remittance will be virtually paid in goods. The result to the interests of the two countries will be as already pointed out—the paying country will give a higher price for all that it buys from the receiving country, while the latter, besides receiving the tribute, obtains the exportable produce of the tributary country at a lower price.

It has been seen, as in Chart No. XIII, that, considering the exports and imports merely as merchandise, there is, in fact, no actual equilibrium at any given time in accordance with the equation of International Demand. Another element, the "financial account" between the United States and foreign countries, must be considered before we can know all the factors necessary to bring about the equation. If we had been borrowing largely of England, Holland, and Germany, we should owe a regular annual sum as interest, and our exports must, as a rule, be exactly that much more (under right and normal conditions) than the imports. Or, take another case, if capital is borrowed in Europe for railways in the United States, this capital generally comes over in the form of imports of various kinds; but, if our exports are not sufficient at once to balance the increased imports, we go in debt for a time—or, in other words, in order to establish the balance, we send United States securities abroad instead of actual exports. This shipment of securities is not seen and recorded as among the exports; and so we find a period, like that during and after the war, from 1862 to 1873, of a vast excess of imports. Since 1873 the country has been practically paying the indebtedness incurred in the former period; and there has been a vast excess of exports over imports, and an apparent discrepancy in the equilibrium. But our government bonds and other securities have been coming back to us, producing a return current to balance the excessive exports.[280] In brief, the use of securities and various forms of indebtedness permits the period of actual payment to be deferred, so that an excess of imports at one time may be offset by an excess of exports at another, and generally a later, time. Moreover, the large expenses of people traveling in Europe will require us to remit abroad in the form of exports more than would ordinarily balance our imports by the amount spent by the travelers. The financial operations, therefore, between the United States and foreign countries, must be well considered in striking the equation between our exports and imports. As formulated by Mr. Cairnes,[281] the Equation of International Demand should be stated more broadly, as follows: "The state of international demand which results in commercial equilibrium is realized when the reciprocal demand of trading countries produces such a relation of exports and imports among them as enables each country by means of her exports to discharge *all her foreign liabilities.*" If we were a great lending instead of a great borrowing country, we should have, as a rule, a permanent excess of imports.

Chapter XVIII. Influence Of The Currency On The Exchanges And On Foreign Trade.

§ 1. Variations in the exchange, which originate in the Currency.

In our inquiry into the laws of international trade, we commenced with the principles which determine international exchanges and international values on the hypothesis of barter. We next showed that the introduction of money, as a medium of exchange, makes no difference in the laws of exchanges and of values between country and country, no more than between individual and individual: since the precious metals, under the influence of those same laws, distribute themselves in such proportions among the different countries of the world as to allow the very same exchanges to go on, and at the same values, as would be the case under a system of barter. We lastly considered how the value of money itself is affected by those alterations in the state of trade which arise from alterations either in the demand and supply of commodities or in their cost of production. It remains to consider the alterations in the state of trade which originate not in commodities but in money.

Gold and silver may vary like other things, though they are not so likely to vary as other things in their cost of production. The demand for them in foreign countries may also vary. It may increase by augmented employment of the metals for purposes of art and ornament, or because the increase of production and of transactions has created a greater amount of business to be done by the circulating medium. It may diminish, for the opposite reasons; or, from the extension of the economizing expedients by which the use of metallic money is partially dispensed with. These changes act upon the trade between other countries and the mining countries, and upon the value of the precious metals, according to the general laws of the value of imported commodities: which have been set forth in the previous chapters with sufficient fullness.

What I propose to examine in the present chapter is not those circumstances affecting money which alter the permanent conditions of its value, but the effects produced on international trade by casual or temporary variations in the value of money, which have no connection with any causes affecting its permanent value.

§ 2. Effect of a sudden increase of a metallic Currency, or of the sudden creation of Bank-Notes or other substitutes for Money.

Let us suppose in any country a circulating medium purely metallic, and a sudden casual increase made to it; for example, by bringing into circulation hoards of treasure, which had been concealed in a previous period of foreign invasion or internal disorder. The natural effect would be a rise of prices. This would check exports and encourage imports; the imports would exceed the exports, the exchanges would become unfavorable, and a newly acquired stock of money would diffuse itself over all countries with which the supposed country carried on trade, and from them, progressively, through all parts of the commercial world. The money which thus overflowed would spread itself to an equal depth over all commercial countries. For it would go on flowing until the exports and imports again balanced one another; and this (as no change is supposed in the permanent circumstances of international demand) could only be when the money had diffused itself so equally that prices had risen in the same ratio in all countries, so that the alteration of price would be for all practical purposes ineffective, and the exports and imports, though at a higher money valuation, would be exactly the same as they were originally. This diminished value of money throughout the world (at least if the diminution was considerable) would cause a suspension, or at least a diminution, of the annual supply from the mines, since the metal would no longer command a value equivalent to its highest cost of production. The annual waste would, therefore, not be fully made up, and the usual causes of destruction would gradually reduce the aggregate quantity of the precious metals to its former amount; after which their production would recommence on its former scale. The discovery of the treasure would thus produce only temporary effects; namely, a brief disturbance of international trade until the treasure had disseminated itself through the world, and then a temporary depression in the value of the metal below that which corresponds to the cost of producing or of obtaining it; which depression would gradually be corrected by a temporarily diminished production in the producing countries and importation in the importing countries.

The same effects which would thus arise from the discovery of a treasure accompany the process by which bank-notes, or any of the other substitutes for money, take the place of the precious metals. Suppose[282] that the United States possessed a currency, wholly metallic, of $200,000,000, and that suddenly $200,000,000 of bank-notes were sent into circulation. If these were issued by bankers, they would be employed in loans, or in the purchase of securities, and would therefore create a sudden fall in the rate of interest, which would probably send a great part of the $200,000,000 of gold out of the country as capital, to seek a higher rate of interest elsewhere, before there had been time for any action on prices. But we will suppose that the notes are not issued by bankers, or money-lenders of any kind, but by manufacturers, in the payment of wages and the purchase of materials, or by the Government [as, e.g., greenbacks] in its ordinary expenses, so that the whole amount would be rapidly carried into the markets for commodities. The following would be the natural order of consequences: All prices would rise greatly. Exportation would almost cease; importation would be prodigiously stimulated. A great balance of payments would become due, the exchanges would turn against the United States, to the full extent of the cost of exporting money; and the surplus coin would pour itself rapidly forth, over the various countries of the world, in the order of their proximity, geographically and commercially, to the United States.

> A study of Chart No. XIV will show how exactly this description fits the case of our country, when the rise of prices stimulated imports of merchandise (see Chart No. XIII) in 1862, and sent gold out of the country.

The efflux would continue until the currencies of all countries had come to a level; by which I do not mean, until money became of the same value everywhere, but until the differences were only those which existed before, and which corresponded to permanent differences in the cost of obtaining it. When the rise of prices had extended itself in an equal degree to all countries, exports and imports would everywhere revert to what they were at first, would balance one another, and the exchanges would return to par. If such a sum of money as $200,000,000, when spread over the whole surface of the commercial world, were sufficient to raise the general level in a perceptible degree, the effect would be of no long duration. No alteration having occurred in the general conditions under which the metals were procured, either in the world at large or in any part of it, the reduced value would no longer be remunerating, and the supply from the mines would cease partially or wholly, until the $200,000,000 were absorbed.[283]

Effects of another kind, however, will have been produced: $200,000,000, which formerly existed in the unproductive form of metallic money, have been converted into what is, or is capable of becoming, productive capital. This gain is at first made by the United States at the expense of other countries, who have taken her superfluity of this costly and unproductive article off her hands, giving for it an equivalent value in other commodities. By degrees the loss is made up to those countries by diminished influx from the mines, and finally the world has gained a virtual addition of

$200,000,000 to its productive resources. Adam Smith's illustration, though so well known, deserves for its extreme aptness to be once more repeated. He compares the substitution of paper in the room of the precious metals to the construction of a highway through the air, by which the ground now occupied by roads would become available for agriculture. As in that case a portion of the soil, so in this a part of the accumulated wealth of the country, would be relieved from a function in which it was only employed in rendering other soils and capitals productive, and would itself become applicable to production; the office it previously fulfilled being equally well discharged by a medium which costs nothing.

The value saved to the community by thus dispensing with metallic money is a clear gain to those who provide the substitute. They have the use of $200,000,000 of circulating medium which have cost them only the expense of an engraver's plate. If they employ this accession to their fortunes as productive capital, the produce of the country is increased and the community benefited, as much as by any other capital of equal amount. Whether it is so employed or not depends, in some degree, upon the mode of issuing it. If issued by the Government, and employed in paying off debt, it would probably become productive capital. The Government, however, may prefer employing this extraordinary resource in its ordinary expenses; may squander it uselessly, or make it a mere temporary substitute for taxation to an equivalent amount; in which last case the amount is saved by the tax-payers at large, who either add it to their capital or spend it as income. When [a part of the] paper currency is supplied, as in our own country, by banking companies, the amount is almost wholly turned into productive capital; for the issuers, being at all times liable to be called upon to refund the value, are under the strongest inducements not to squander it, and the only cases in which it is not forthcoming are cases of fraud or mismanagement. A banker's profession being that of a money-lender, his issue of notes is a simple extension of his ordinary occupation. He lends the amount to farmers, manufacturers, or dealers, who employ it in their several businesses. So employed, it yields, like any other capital, wages of labor, and profits of stock. The profit is shared between the banker, who receives interest, and a succession of borrowers, mostly for short periods, who, after paying the interest, gain a profit in addition, or a convenience equivalent to profit. The capital itself in the long run becomes entirely wages, and, when replaced by the sale of the produce, becomes wages again; thus affording a perpetual fund, of the value of $200,000,000, for the maintenance of productive labor, and increasing the annual produce of the country by all that can be produced through the means of a capital of that value. To this gain must be added a further saving to the country, of the annual supply of the precious metals necessary for repairing the wear and tear, and other waste, of a metallic currency.

The substitution, therefore, of paper for the precious metals should always be carried as far as is consistent with safety, no greater amount of metallic currency being retained than is necessary to maintain, both in fact and in public belief, the convertibility of the paper.

But since gold wanted for exportation is almost invariably drawn from the reserves of the banks, and is never likely to be taken directly from the circulation while the banks remain solvent, the only advantage which can be obtained from retaining partially a metallic currency for daily purposes is, that the banks may occasionally replenish their reserves from it.

§ 3. Effect of the increase of an inconvertible paper Currency. Real and nominal exchange.

When metallic money had been entirely superseded and expelled from circulation, by the substitution of an equal amount of bank-notes, any attempt to keep a still further quantity of paper in circulation must, if the notes are convertible [into gold], be a complete failure.

> This brings up the whole question at issue between the "Currency Principle" and the "Banking Principle." The latter, maintained by Fullerton, Wilson, Price, and Tooke (in his later writings), held that, if notes were convertible, the value of notes could not differ from the value of the metal into which they were convertible; while the former, advocated by Lord Overstone, G. W. Norman, Colonel Torrens, Tooke (in his earlier writings), and Sir Robert Peel, implied that even a convertible paper was liable to over-issues. This last school brought about the Bank Act of 1844.[284]

[A] new issue would again set in motion the same train of consequences by which the gold coin had already been expelled. The metals would, as before, be required for exportation, and would be for that purpose demanded from the banks, to the full extent of the superfluous notes, which thus could not possibly be retained in circulation. If, indeed, the notes were inconvertible, there would be no such obstacle to the increase in their quantity. An inconvertible paper acts in the same way as a convertible, while there remains any coin for it to supersede; the difference begins to manifest itself when all the coin is driven from circulation (except what may be retained for the convenience of small change), and the issues still go on increasing. When the paper begins to exceed in quantity the metallic currency which it superseded, prices of course rise; things which were worth $25 in metallic money become worth $30 in inconvertible paper, or more, as the case may be. But this rise of price will not, as in the cases before examined, stimulate import and discourage export. The imports and exports are determined by the metallic prices of things, not by the paper prices; and it is only when the paper is exchangeable at pleasure for the metals that paper prices and metallic prices must correspond.

Let us suppose that the United States is the country which has the depreciated paper. Suppose that some American production could be bought, while the currency was still metallic, for $25, and sold in England for $27.50, the difference covering the expense and risk, and affording a profit to the merchant. On account of the depreciation, this commodity will now cost in the United States $30, and can not be sold in England for more than $27.50, and yet it will be exported as before. Why? Because the $27.50 which the exporter can get for it in England is not depreciated paper, but gold or silver; and since in the United States bullion has risen in the same proportion with other things—if the merchant brings the gold or silver to the United States, he can sell his $27.50 [in coin] for $33 [in paper], and obtain as before 10 per cent for profit and expenses.

It thus appears that a depreciation of the currency does not affect the foreign trade of the country: this is carried on precisely as if the currency maintained its value. But, though the trade is not affected, the exchanges are. When the imports and exports are in equilibrium, the exchange, in a metallic currency, would be at par; a bill on England for the equivalent of $25 would be worth $25. But $25, or the quantity of gold contained in them, having come to be worth in the United States $30, it follows that a bill on England for $25 will be worth $30. When, therefore, the *real* exchange is at par, there will be a *nominal* exchange against the country of as much per cent as the amount of the depreciation. If the currency is depreciated 10, 15, or 20 per cent, then in whatever way the real exchange, arising from the variations of international debts and credits, may vary, the quoted exchange will always differ 10, 15, or 20 per cent from it. However high this nominal premium may be, it has no tendency to send gold out of the country for the purpose of drawing a bill against it and profiting by the premium; because the gold so sent must be procured, not from the banks and at par, as in the case of a convertible currency, but in the market, at an advance of price equal to the premium. In such cases, instead of saying that the exchange is unfavorable, it would be a more correct representation to say that the par has altered, since there is now required a larger quantity of American currency to be equivalent to the same quantity of foreign. The exchanges, however, continue to be computed according to the metallic par. The quoted exchanges, therefore, when there is a depreciated currency, are compounded of two elements or factors: (1) the real exchange, which follows the variations of international payments, and (2) the nominal exchange, which varies with the depreciation of the currency, but which, while there is any depreciation at all, must always be unfavorable. Since the amount of depreciation is exactly measured by the degree in which the market price of bullion exceeds the mint valuation, we have a sure criterion to determine what portion of the quoted exchange, being referable to depreciation, may be struck off as nominal, the result so corrected expressing the real exchange.

The same disturbance of the exchanges and of international trade which is produced by an increased issue of convertible bank-notes is in like manner produced by those extensions of credit which, as was so fully shown in a preceding chapter, have the same effect on prices as an increase of the currency. Whenever circumstances have given such an impulse to the spirit of speculation as to occasion a great increase of purchases on credit, money prices rise, just as much as they would have risen if each person who so buys on credit had bought with money. All the effects, therefore, must be similar. As a consequence of high prices, exportation is checked and importation stimulated; though in fact the increase of importation seldom waits for the rise of prices which is the consequence of speculation, inasmuch as some of the great articles of import are usually among the things in which speculative overtrading first shows itself. There is, therefore, in such periods, usually a great excess of imports over exports; and, when the time comes at which these must be paid for, the exchanges become unfavorable and gold flows out of the country. This efflux of gold takes effect on prices [by withdrawing gold from the reserves of the banks, and so by stopping loans and the use of credit, or purchasing power]: its effect is to make them recoil downward. The recoil once begun, generally becomes a total rout, and the unusual extension of credit is rapidly exchanged for an unusual contraction of it. Accordingly, when credit has been imprudently stretched, and the speculative spirit carried to excess, the turn of the exchanges and consequent pressure on the banks to obtain gold for exportation are generally the proximate cause of the catastrophe.

A glance at Chart No. XIII will give illustration to the situation here described. After the war, and until 1873, while the United States was under the influence of high prices and a speculation which has been seldom equaled in our history, the resulting great excess of imports became very striking. It was an unhealthy and abnormal condition of trade. The sudden reversal of the trade by the crisis in 1873 is equally striking, and, as prices fell, exports began to increase. The effect on international trade of a collapse of credit is thus clearly marked by the lines on the chart.

Chapter XIX. Of The Rate Of Interest.

§ 1. The Rate of Interest depends on the Demand and Supply of Loans.

The two topics of Currency and Loans, though in themselves distinct, are so intimately blended in the phenomena of what is called the money market, that it is impossible to understand the one without the other, and in many minds the two subjects are mixed up in the most inextricable confusion.

In the preceding book[285] we defined the relation in which interest stands to profit. We found that the gross profit of capital might be distinguished into three parts, which are respectively the remuneration for risk, for trouble, and for the capital itself, and may be termed insurance, wages of superintendence, and interest. After making compensation for risk, that is, after covering the average losses to which capital is exposed either by the general circumstances of society or by the hazards of the particular employment, there remains a surplus, which partly goes to repay the owner of the capital for his abstinence, and partly the employer of it for his time and trouble. How much goes to the one and how much to the other is shown by the amount of the remuneration which, when the two functions are separated, the owner of capital can obtain from the employer for its use. This is evidently a question of demand and supply. Nor have demand and supply any different meaning or effect in this case from what they have in all others. The rate of interest will be such as to equalize the demand for loans with the supply of them. It will be such that, exactly as much as some people are desirous to borrow at that rate, others shall be willing to lend. If there is more offered than demanded, interest will fall; if more is demanded than offered, it will rise; and in both cases, to the point at which the equation of supply and demand is re-established.

The desire to borrow and the willingness to lend are more or less influenced by every circumstance which affects the state or prospects of industry or commerce, either generally or in any of their branches. The rate of interest, therefore, on good security, which alone we have here to consider (for interest in which considerations of risk bear a part may swell to any amount), is seldom, in the great centers of money transactions, precisely the same for two days together; as is shown by the never-ceasing variations in the quoted prices of the funds and other negotiable securities.

Nevertheless, there must be, as in other cases of value, some rate which (in the language of Adam Smith and Ricardo) may be called the natural rate; some rate about which the market rate oscillates, and to which it always tends to return. This rate partly depends on the amount of accumulation going on in the hands of persons who can not themselves attend to the employment of their savings, and partly on the comparative taste existing in the community for the active pursuits of industry, or for the leisure, ease, and independence of an annuitant.

§ 2. Circumstances which Determine the Permanent Demand and Supply of Loans.

In [ordinary] circumstances, the more thriving producers and traders have their capital fully employed, and many are able to transact business to a considerably greater extent than they have capital for. These are naturally borrowers: and the amount which they desire to borrow, and can give security for, constitutes the demand for loans on account of productive employment. To these must be added the loans required by Government, and by land-owners, or other unproductive consumers who have good security to give. This constitutes the mass of loans for which there is an habitual demand.

Now, it is conceivable that there might exist, in the hands of persons disinclined or disqualified for engaging personally in business, (1) a mass of capital equal to, and even exceeding, this demand. In that case there would be an habitual excess of competition on the part of lenders, and the rate of interest would bear a low proportion to the rate of profit. Interest would be forced down to the point which would either tempt borrowers to take a greater amount of loans than they had a reasonable expectation of being able to employ in their business, or would so discourage a portion of the lenders as to make them either forbear to accumulate or endeavor to increase their income by engaging in business on their own account, and incurring the risks, if not the labors, of industrial employment.

> The low rates of interest, rather, tempt people to take some additional risk, and enter into investments which offer a higher rate of dividends; so that a period of low interest is a time when speculative enterprises find victims, and then by bad and worthless investments much of the loanable funds is actually lost; thereby

> reducing the total quantity of loans more nearly to that demand which will give an ordinary rate of interest.

(2.) On the other hand, the capital owned by persons who prefer lending it at interest, or whose avocations prevent them from personally superintending its employment, may be short of the habitual demand for loans. It may be in great part absorbed by the investments afforded by the public debt and by mortgages, and the remainder may not be sufficient to supply the wants of commerce. If so, the rate of interest will be raised so high as in some way to re-establish the equilibrium. When there is only a small difference between interest and profit, many borrowers may no longer be willing to increase their responsibilities and involve their credit for so small a remuneration: or some, who would otherwise have engaged in business, may prefer leisure, and become lenders instead of borrowers: or others, under the inducement of high interest and easy investment for their capital, may retire from business earlier, and with smaller fortunes, than they otherwise would have done.

Or, lastly, instead of [capital] being afforded by persons not in business, the affording it may itself become a business. A portion of the capital employed in trade may be supplied by a class of professional money-lenders. These money-lenders, however, must have more than a mere interest; they must have the ordinary rate of profit on their capital, risk and all other circumstances being allowed for. [For] it can never answer, to any one who borrows for the purposes of his business, to pay a full profit for capital from which he will only derive a full profit: and money-lending, as an employment, for the regular supply of trade, can not, therefore, be carried on except by persons who, in addition to their own capital, can lend their credit, or, in other words, the capital of other people. A bank which lends its notes lends capital which it borrows from the community, and for which it pays no interest.

> Of late years, however, banks are generally not permitted to issue notes on their simple credit. That privilege has been so often abused in this country that now, in the national banking system, a separate part of the resources are set aside for the security of the circulating notes (as is also true of the Bank of England since 1844). It is not generally true, then, that banks now create the means to make loans by issuing notes by which they borrow capital from the community

without paying interest. They do, however, depend almost entirely on deposits.

A bank of deposit lends capital which it collects from the community in small parcels, sometimes without paying any interest, and, if it does pay interest, it still pays much less than it receives; for the depositors, who in any other way could mostly obtain for such small balances no interest worth taking any trouble for, are glad to receive even a little. Having this subsidiary resource, bankers are enabled to obtain, by lending at interest, the ordinary rate of profit on their own capital. The disposable capital deposited in banks, together with the funds belonging to those who, either from necessity or preference, live upon the interest of their property, constitute the general loan fund of the country; and the amount of this aggregate fund, when set against the habitual demands of producers and dealers, and those of the Government and of unproductive consumers, determines the permanent or average rate of interest, which must always be such as to adjust these two amounts to one another.[286] But, while the whole of this mass of lent capital takes effect upon the *permanent* rate of interest, the *fluctuations* depend almost entirely upon the portion which is in the hands of bankers; for it is that portion almost exclusively which, being lent for short times only, is continually in the market seeking an investment. The capital of those who live on the interest of their own fortunes has generally sought and found some fixed investment, such as the public funds, mortgages, or the bonds of public companies, which investment, except under peculiar temptations or necessities, is not changed.

§ 3. Circumstances which Determine the Fluctuations.

Fluctuations in the rate of interest arise from variations either in the demand for loans or in the supply. The supply is liable to variation, though less so than the demand. The willingness to lend is greater than usual at the commencement of a period of speculation, and much less than usual during the revulsion which follows. In speculative times, money-lenders as well as other people are inclined to extend their business by stretching their credit; they lend more than usual (just as other classes of dealers and producers employ more than usual) of capital which does not belong to them. Accordingly, these are the times when the rate of interest is low; though for this too (as we shall immediately see) there are other causes. During the revulsion, on the contrary, interest always rises inordinately, because, while there is a most pressing need on the part of many persons to borrow, there is a general disinclination to lend.[287]

This disinclination, when at its extreme point, is called a panic. It occurs when a succession of unexpected failures has created in the mercantile, and sometimes also in the non-mercantile public, a general distrust in each other's solvency; disposing every one not only to refuse fresh credit, except on very onerous terms, but to call in, if possible, all credit which he has already given. Deposits are withdrawn from banks; notes are returned on the issuers in exchange for specie; bankers raise their rate of discount, and withhold their customary advances; merchants refuse to renew mercantile bills. At such times the most calamitous consequences were formerly experienced from the attempt of the law to prevent more than a certain limited rate of interest from being given or taken. Persons who could not borrow at five per cent had to pay, not six or seven, but ten or fifteen per cent, to compensate the lender for risking the penalties of the law; or had to sell securities or goods for ready money at a still greater sacrifice.

> The pernicious and hurtful custom exists in various States in this country of making any interest beyond a certain rate illegal. When it is remembered that legitimate business is often largely done on credit—until the proceeds of goods sold on credit are collected—the rate of interest from day to day is very important to trade. So, when there is a sudden demand for loans, a rate higher than the legal one will certainly be paid, and the law violated, if the getting of a loan is absolutely necessary to save the borrower from commercial ruin. The effect of a legal rate is to stop loans at the very time when loans are most essential to the business public. It would be far better to adopt such a sliding scale as exists at great European banks, which allows the rate of interest to rise with the demand. No one, then, with good security, need want loans if he is willing to pay the high rates; and those not really in need will defer their demand until the sudden emergency is past. Already in New York the legal penalty has been removed for loaning at higher than the legal rates when charged upon call-loans; and it has mitigated the extreme fluctuations of the rate in a market when financial necessity is contending against the law.

Except at such periods, the amount of capital disposable on loan is subject to little other variation than that which arises from the gradual process of accumulation; which process, however, in the great commercial countries, is sufficiently rapid to account for the almost periodical recurrence of these fits of speculation; since, when a few years have elapsed without a crisis, and no new and tempting channel for investment has been opened in the mean time, there is always found to have occurred in those few years so large an increase of capital seeking investment as to have lowered considerably the rate of interest, whether indicated by the prices of securities or by the rate of discount on bills; and this diminution of interest tempts the possessors to incur hazards in hopes of a more considerable return.

The demand for loans varies much more largely than the supply, and embraces longer cycles of years in its aberrations. A time of war, for example, is a period of unusual draughts on the loan market. The Government, at such times, generally incurs new loans, and, as these usually succeed each other rapidly as long as the war lasts, the general rate of interest is kept higher in war than in peace, without reference to the rate of profit, and productive industry is stinted of its usual supplies.

> The United States during the late war found that it could not borrow at even six or seven per cent. By receiving depreciated paper at par for its bonds it really agreed to pay six gold dollars on each loan of one hundred dollars in paper (worth, perhaps, at the worst only forty gold dollars), which was equivalent to fifteen per cent. This high rate was largely due to the weakened credit of the Government; but still it remains true that the rate was higher because the United States was in the market as a competitor for large loans. Now the Government can refund its bonds at three per cent.

Nor does the influence of these loans altogether cease when the Government ceases to contract others; for those already contracted continue to afford an investment for a greatly increased amount of the disposable capital of the country, which, if the national debt were paid off, would be added to the mass of capital seeking investment, and (independently of temporary disturbance) could not but, to some extent, permanently lower the rate of interest.

> The rapid payment of the public debt by the United States, $137,823,253 in 1882-1883, and more than $100,000,000 in 1883-1884, has taken away the former investment for enormous sums of loanable funds, and to the same extent increased the supply in the market. Without doubt this aids in making the present rate of interest a very low one. Whether the rate will remain "permanently lower," however, will depend upon whether the field of investment in the United States is already practically occupied. We believe it is not.

The same effect on interest which is produced by government loans for war expenditure is produced by the sudden opening of any new and generally attractive mode of permanent investment. The only instance of the kind in recent history, on a scale comparable to that of the war loans, is the absorption of capital in the construction of railways. This capital must have been principally drawn from the deposits in banks, or from savings which would have gone into deposit, and which were destined to be ultimately employed in buying securities from persons who would have employed the purchase-money in discounts or other loans at interest: in either case, it was a draft on the general loan fund. It is, in fact, evident that, unless savings were made expressly to be employed in railway adventure, the amount thus employed must have been derived either from the actual capital of persons in business or from capital which would have been lent to persons in business.

§ 4. The Rate of Interest not really Connected with the value of Money, but often confounded with it.

From the preceding considerations it would be seen, even if it were not otherwise evident, how great an error it is to imagine that the rate of interest bears any necessary relation to the quantity or value of the money in circulation. An increase of the currency has in itself no effect, and is incapable of having any effect, on the rate of interest. A paper currency issued by Government in the payment of its ordinary expenses, in however great excess it may be issued, affects the rate of interest in no manner whatever. It diminishes, indeed, the power of money to buy commodities, but not the power of money to buy money. If a hundred dollars will buy a perpetual annuity of four dollars a year, a depreciation which makes the hundred dollars worth only half as much as before has precisely the same effect on the four dollars, and therefore can not alter the relation between the two. Unless, indeed, it is known and reckoned upon that the depreciation will only be temporary; for people certainly might be willing to lend the depreciated currency on cheaper terms if they expected to be repaid in money of full value.

In considering the effect produced by the proceedings of banks in encouraging the excesses of speculation, an immense effect is usually attributed to their issues of notes, but until of late hardly any attention was paid to the management of their deposits, though nothing is more certain than that their imprudent extensions of credit take place more frequently by means of their deposits than of their issues. Says Mr. Tooke: "Supposing all the deposits received by a banker to be in coin, is he not, just as much as the issuing banker, exposed to the importunity of customers, whom it may be impolitic to refuse, for loans or discounts, or to be tempted by a high interest; and may he not be induced to encroach so much upon his deposits as to leave him, under not improbable circumstances, unable to meet the demands of his depositors?"

> In truth, the most difficult questions of banking center around the functions of discount and deposit. The separation of the Issue from the Banking Department by the act of 1844, which renewed the charter of the Bank of England, makes this perfectly clear. After entirely removing from their effect on credit all influences due to issues, England has had the same difficulties to encounter as before, which shows that the real question is concerned with the two essential functions of banking—discount and deposit. Since 1844, there have been the commercial disturbances of 1847, 1857, 1866, and 1873. Although no expansion of notes, without a corresponding deposit of specie, is possible.

§ 5. The Rate of Interest determines the price of land and of Securities.

Before quitting the general subject of this chapter, I will make the obvious remark that the rate of interest determines the value and price of all those salable articles which are desired and bought, not for themselves, but for the income which they are capable of yielding. The public funds, shares in joint-stock companies, and all descriptions of securities, are at a high price in proportion as the rate of interest is low. They are sold at the price which will give the market rate of interest on the purchase-money, with allowance for all differences in the risk incurred, or in any circumstance of convenience.

The price of land, mines, and all other fixed sources of income, depends in like manner on the rate of interest. Land usually sells at a higher price, in proportion to the income afforded by it, than the public funds, not only because it is thought, even in [England], to be somewhat more secure, but because ideas of power and dignity are associated with its possession. But these differences are constant, or nearly so; and, in the variations of price, land follows, *cæteris paribus*, the permanent (though, of course, not the daily) variations of the rate of interest. When interest is low, land will naturally be dear; when interest is high, land will be cheap.

> A lot of land, which fifty years ago gave an annual return of $100, if ten per cent was then the common rate of interest, would sell for $1,000. If the return from the land remains the same ($100) to-day, and if the usual rate of interest is now five per cent, the same piece of land, therefore, would sell for $2,000, since $100 is five per cent of $2,000.
>
> The price of a bond, it may be said, also varies with the time it has to run. At the same rate of interest, a bond running for a long term of years is better for an investment than one for a short term. The lumberman, who looks at two trees of *equal diameter* at the base, estimates the total value of each according to the *height* of the tree. Then, again, a bond running for a short term may be worth less than one for a long term, even though the first bears a higher rate of interest. That is, to resume the illustration, one tree, not rising very high, although *larger* at the bottom, may not contain so many square feet as another, with perhaps a *less* diameter at the bottom, but which stretches much higher up into the air.

Chapter XX. Of The Competition Of Different Countries In The Same Market.

§ 1. Causes which enable one Country to undersell another.

In the phraseology of the Mercantile System, there is no word of more frequent recurrence or more perilous import than the word *underselling*. To undersell other countries—not to be undersold by other countries—were spoken of, and are still very often spoken of, almost as if they were the sole purposes for which production and commodities exist.

> Nations may, like individual dealers, be competitors, with opposite interests, in the markets of some commodities, while in others they are in the more fortunate relation of reciprocal customers. The benefit of commerce does not consist, as it was once thought to do, in the commodities sold; but, since the commodities sold are the means of obtaining those which are bought, a nation would be cut off from the real advantage of commerce, the imports, if it could not induce other nations to take any of its commodities in exchange; and in proportion as the competition of other countries compels it to offer its commodities on cheaper terms, on pain of not selling them at all, the imports which it obtains by its foreign trade are procured at greater cost.

One country (A) can only undersell another (B) in a given market, to the extent of entirely expelling her from it, on two conditions: (1) In the first place, she (A) must have a greater advantage than the second country (B) in the production of the article exported by both; meaning by a greater advantage (as has been already so fully explained) not absolutely, but in comparison with other commodities; and (2) in the second place, such must be her (A's) relation with the customer-country in respect to the demand for each other's products, and such the consequent state of international values, as to give away to the customer-country more than the whole advantage possessed by the rival country (B); otherwise the rival will still be able to hold her ground in the market.

Let us suppose a trade between England and the United States, in iron and wheat. England being capable of producing ten cwts. of iron at the same cost as fifteen bushels of wheat, the United States at the same cost as twenty bushels, and the two commodities being exchanged between the two countries (cost of carriage apart) at some intermediate rate, say ten for seventeen. The United States could not be permanently undersold in the English market, and expelled from it, unless by a country (such as India) which offered not merely more than seventeen, but more than twenty bushels of wheat for ten cwts. of iron. Short of that, the competition would only oblige the United States to pay dearer for iron, but would not disable her from exporting wheat. The country, therefore, which could undersell the United States, must, in the first place, be able to produce wheat at less cost, compared with iron, than the United States herself; and, in the next place, must have such a demand for iron, or other English commodities, as would compel her, even when she became sole occupant of the market, to give a greater advantage to England than the United States could give by resigning the whole of hers; to give, for example, twenty-one bushels for ten cwts. For if not—if, for example, the equation of international demand, after the United States was excluded, gave a ratio of eighteen for ten—the United States would be now the underselling nation; and there would be a point, perhaps nineteen for ten, at which both countries would be able to maintain their ground, and to sell in England enough wheat to pay for the iron, or other English commodities, for which, on these newly adjusted terms of interchange, they had a demand. In like manner, England, as an exporter of iron, could only be driven from the American market by some rival whose superior advantages in the production of iron enabled her, and the intensity of whose demand for American produce compelled her, to offer ten cwts. of iron, not merely for less than seventeen bushels of

> wheat, but for less than fifteen. In that case, England could no longer carry on the trade without loss; but, in any case short of this, she would merely be obliged to give to the United States more iron for less wheat than she had previously given.[288]

It thus appears that the alarm of being permanently undersold may be taken much too easily; may be taken when the thing really to be anticipated is not the loss of the trade, but the minor inconvenience of carrying it on at a diminished advantage; an inconvenience chiefly falling on the consumers of foreign commodities, and not on the producers or sellers of the exported article. It is no sufficient ground of apprehension to the [American] producers, to find that some other country can sell [wheat] in foreign markets, at some particular time, a trifle cheaper than they can themselves afford to do in the existing state of prices in [the United States]. Suppose them to be temporarily unsold, and their exports diminished; the imports will exceed the exports, there will be a new distribution of the precious metals, prices will fall, and, as all the money expenses of the [American] producers will be diminished, they will be able (if the case falls short of that stated in the preceding paragraph) again to compete with their rivals.

The loss which [the United States] will incur will not fall upon the exporters, but upon those who consume imported commodities; who, with money incomes reduced in amount, will have to pay the same or even an increased price for all things produced in foreign countries.

> But the business world would regard what was going on under economic laws as a great and dreaded disaster, if it meant that prices were to fall, and gold leave the country. Those holding large stocks of goods would for that time suffer; and so, at first, it might really happen that "exporters," in the sense of exporting agents (not the producers, perhaps, of the exportable article), would incur a loss. In the end, of course, the consumers of imports suffer. But, temporarily, and on the face of it, exporters do lose.

§ 2. High wages do not prevent one Country from underselling another.

According to the preceding doctrine, a country can not be undersold in any commodity, unless the rival country has a stronger inducement than itself for devoting its labor and capital to the production of the commodity; arising from the fact that by doing so it occasions a greater saving of labor and capital, to be shared between itself and its customers—a greater increase of the aggregate produce of the world. The underselling, therefore, though a loss to the undersold country, is an advantage to the world at large; the substituted commerce being one which economizes more of the labor and capital of mankind, and adds more to their collective wealth, than the commerce superseded by it. The advantage, of course, consists in being able to produce the commodity of better quality, or with less labor (compared with other things); or perhaps not with less labor, but in less time; with a less prolonged detention of the capital employed. This may arise from greater natural advantages (such as soil, climate, richness of mines); superior capability, either natural or acquired, in the laborers; better division of labor, and better tools, or machinery. But there is no place left in this theory for the case of lower wages. This, however, in the theories commonly current, is a favorite cause of underselling. We continually hear of the disadvantage under which the [American] producer labors, both in foreign markets and even in his own, through the lower wages paid by his foreign rivals. These lower wages, we are told, enable, or are always on the point of enabling, them to sell at lower prices, and to dislodge the [American] manufacturer from all markets in which he is not artificially protected.

> It will be remembered that, as we have before seen, international trade, in actual practice, depends on comparative prices within the same country (even though the exporter may not consciously make a comparison). We send wheat abroad, because it is low in price relatively to certain manufactured goods; that is, we send the wheat, but we do not send the manufactured goods. But, so far, this is considering only the comparative prices in the same country. Yet we shall fail to realize in actual practice the application of the above principles, when we use the terms prices and money, if we do not admit that there is in the matter of underselling a comparison, also, between the absolute price of the goods in one country and the absolute price of the same goods in the competing country. For example, wheat is not shipped to England unless the price is lower here than there. If India or Morocco were to send wheat into the English market in close competition with the United States, and the

price were to fall in London, it would mean that, if we continued our shipments of wheat to England, we must part with our wheat at a less advantage in the international exchange. In the illustration already used, we must, for example, offer more than seventeen bushels of wheat for ten cwts. of iron. The fall in the price of wheat, without any change in that of iron, implies the necessity of offering a greater quantity of wheat for the same quantity of iron, perhaps nineteen or twenty bushels for ten cwts. of iron. If the price went so low as to require twenty-one bushels to pay for ten cwts. of iron, then we should be entirely undersold; and the price here as compared with the price in London would be an indication of the fact. So that the comparison of prices here with prices abroad is merely a register of the terms at which our international exchanges are performed; but not the cause of the existence of the international trade. If the price falls so low in a foreign market that we can not sell wheat there, it simply means that we have reached in the exchange ratios the limit of our comparative advantages in wheat and iron; so that we are obliged to offer twenty or more bushels of wheat for ten cwts. of iron.

But in all this it must be noted that this price must include the return to capital also, and that it must be equal to the usual reward for capital in other competing industries, that is, the ordinary rate of profit. In exporting wheat from the United States the capital engaged will insist on getting the rate of profit to be found in other occupations to which the capital can go, in the United States. Now, the price, if it stands for the value (which is supposed to be governed by cost of production in this case), is the sum out of which wages and profits are paid. If the price were to fall in the foreign market, then there might not be the means with which to pay the usual rate of wages and the usual rate of profit also. Then we should probably hear of complaints by the shippers that there is no profit in the exportation of wheat, and of a falling off in the trade. In other words, as the capitalist is the one who manages the operation, and is the one first affected, the diminution of advantage in foreign trade arising from competition, generally shows itself first in lessened profits. The price, then, is the means by which we determine whether a certain article gives us that comparative advantage which will insure a gain from international trade.

An exportable article whose price in this country is low—since it is for this reason selected as an export—is one whose cost is low. If the cost be low, it means that the industry is very productive; that the same capital and labor produce more for their exertion in this than in other industries. And yet it is precisely in the most productive industries that higher wages and profits can be, and are, paid. Although each article is sold at a low price, the great quantity produced makes the total sum, or value, out of which the industrial rewards, profits, and wages, are paid, large. That is, the price may be very low (lower, also, in direct comparison with prices abroad) and yet pay the rate of wages and profits current in this country. Consequently, although wages and profits may be very high (relatively to older countries) in those industries of the United States whose productiveness is great, yet the very fact of this low cost, and consequently this low price (where competition is effective), is that which fits the commodity for exportation. We are, therefore, inevitably led to a position in which we see that high wages and low prices naturally go together in an exportable commodity. In practice, certainly, the high wages do not, by raising the price, prevent us, by comparing our price with English prices, from sending goods abroad—because we send goods abroad from our most productive employments. As an illustration of this principle, it is found that the leading exports of the United States, in 1883, were cotton, breadstuffs, provisions, tobacco, mineral oils, and wood.

But, since a direct comparison is in practice made between prices here and prices in England (for example), in order to determine whether the trade can be a profitable one, we constantly hear it said that we can not send goods abroad because our labor is so dear. It need scarcely be observed that we do not hear this from those engaged in any of the extractive industries just mentioned as furnishing large exports, which are admittedly very productive; it is generally heard in regard to certain kinds of manufactured goods. The difficulty arises not with regard to articles in which we have the greatest advantage in productiveness, but those in which we have a less advantage. If the majority of occupations are so productive as to assure a generally high reward to labor and capital throughout the country, these less advantageously situated industries—not being so productive as others (either from lack of skill or good management, or high cost of machinery and materials, or peculiarities of climate, or heavy taxation)—can not pay the usual high reward to labor, and at the same time get for the capitalist the same high reward he can everywhere else receive at home. For, at a price low enough to warrant an exportation, the quantity made by a given amount of labor and capital does not yield a total value so great as is given in the majority of other occupations to the same amount of labor and capital, and out of which the usual high wages and profits can be paid. The less productiveness of an industry, compared with other industries in the same country, then, is the real cause which prevents it from competing with foreign countries consistently with receiving the ordinary rate of profit. It is the high rate of profits as well as the high rate of wages common in the country which prevents selling abroad. It is absurd to say that it is only high wages: it is just as much high profits. Of course, if the less productive industries wish to compete with England, and if they pay—as we know they must—the high rate of wages due to the general productiveness of our country's industries, they must submit to less profits for the pleasure of having that particular desire. It is not possible that we should produce everything equally well here; nor is it possible that England should produce everything equally well. If we wish to send any goods at all to England, we must receive some goods from her. In order to get the gain arising from our productiveness, we must earnestly wish that England should have some commodity also in which she has a comparative advantage, in order that any trade whatever may exist. It is not, however, worth while, in my opinion, to go on in this discussion to consider the position of those who would shut us off from any and all foreign trade.

Our present high wages should be a cause for congratulation, because they are due to the generally high productiveness of our resources, or, in other words, due to low cost; and it is to be hoped that they may long continue high. We do not seem to be in imminent danger of not having goods which we can export in quantities which will buy for us all we may wish to import from abroad. (See Chart No. XIII, and note the vast increase of exports at the same time that wages are known to be higher in this country than abroad.) So long as wages continue high, we may possibly be unwilling to see gratified that false and ignorant desire which leads some people to think that we ought to produce, equally well with any competitor in the world, everything that is made. If, as was pointed out under the discussion on cost of labor,[289] we must necessarily connect with efficiency of labor all natural advantages under which labor works, it is easy to see that high wages are entirely consistent with low prices; and that high wages do not prevent us to-day from having an hitherto unequaled export trade. Even if all wages and all profits were lower, it would, however, affect all industries alike, and some would still be more productive relatively to others, and the same inequality would remain. If, however, we learn to use our materials better, use machinery with more effect on the quantity produced, adapt our industries to our climate, get the raw products more cheaply, free ourselves from excessive and unreasonable taxation, it would be difficult to say what commodities we might not be able eventually to manufacture in competition with the rest of the world. For we have scarcely ever, as a country, had the advantage of such conditions to aid us in our foreign trade.

Mr. Mill now goes on to consider the suggestive fact that wages are higher in England than on the Continent, and yet that the English have no difficulty in underselling their Continental rivals.

Before examining this opinion on grounds of principle, it is worth while to bestow a moment's consideration upon it as a question of fact. Is it true that the wages of manufacturing labor are lower in foreign countries than in England, in any sense in which low wages are an advantage to the capitalist? The artisan of Ghent or Lyons may earn less wages in a day, but does he not do less work? Degrees of efficiency considered, does his labor cost less to his employer? Though wages may be lower on the Continent, is not the Cost of Labor, which is the real element in the competition, very nearly the same? That it is so seems the opinion of competent judges, and is confirmed by the very little difference in the rate of profit between England and the Continental countries. But, if so, the opinion is absurd that English producers can be undersold by their Continental rivals from this cause. It is only in America that the supposition is *prima facie* admissible. In America wages are much higher than in England, if we mean by wages the daily earnings of a laborer; but the productive power of American labor is so great—its efficiency, combined with the favorable circumstances in which it is exerted, makes it worth so much to the purchaser—that the Cost of Labor is lower in America than in England; as is proved by the fact that the general rate of profits and of interest is very much higher.

§ 3. Low wages enable a Country to undersell another, when Peculiar to certain branches of Industry.

But is it true that low wages, even in the sense of low Cost of Labor, enable a country to sell cheaper in the foreign market? I mean, of course, low wages which are common to the whole productive industry of the country.

If wages, in any of the departments of industry which supply exports, are kept, artificially or by some accidental cause, below the general rate of wages in the country, this is a real advantage in the foreign market. It lessens the *comparative* cost of production of those articles in relation to others, and has the same effect as if their production required so much less labor. Take, for instance, the case of the United States in respect to certain commodities. In that country tobacco and cotton, two great articles of export, are produced by slave-labor, while food and manufactures generally are produced by free laborers, who either work on their own account or are paid by wages. In spite of the inferior efficiency of slave-labor, there can be no reasonable doubt that, in a country where the wages of free labor are so high, the work executed by slaves is a better bargain to the capitalist. To whatever extent it is so, this smaller cost of labor, being not general, but limited to those employments, is just as much a cause of cheapness in the products, both in the home and in the foreign market, as if they had been made by a less quantity of labor. If the slaves in the Southern States were emancipated, and their wages rose to the general level of the earnings of free labor in America, that country might be obliged to erase some of the slave-grown articles from the catalogue of its exports, and would certainly be unable to sell any of them in the foreign market at the present price. Their cheapness is partly an artificial cheapness, which may be compared to that produced by a bounty on production or on exportation; or, considering the means by which it is obtained, an apter comparison would be with the cheapness of stolen goods.

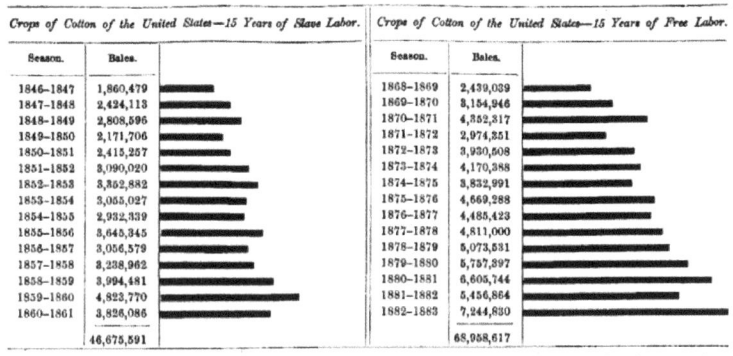

| Crops of Cotton of the United States—15 Years of Slave Labor. || Crops of Cotton of the United States—15 Years of Free Labor. ||
Season.	Bales.	Season.	Bales.
1846-1847	1,860,479	1868-1869	2,439,039
1847-1848	2,424,113	1869-1870	3,154,946
1848-1849	2,808,596	1870-1871	4,352,317
1849-1850	2,171,706	1871-1872	2,974,351
1850-1851	2,415,257	1872-1873	3,930,508
1851-1852	3,090,020	1873-1874	4,170,388
1852-1853	3,352,882	1874-1875	3,832,991
1853-1854	3,055,027	1875-1876	4,669,288
1854-1855	2,932,339	1876-1877	4,485,423
1855-1856	3,645,345	1877-1878	4,811,000
1856-1857	3,056,579	1878-1879	5,073,531
1857-1858	3,238,962	1879-1880	5,757,397
1858-1859	3,994,481	1880-1881	6,605,744
1859-1860	4,823,770	1881-1882	5,456,854
1860-1861	3,826,086	1882-1883	7,244,830
	46,675,591		68,958,617

Excess of 15 free-labor crops, 22,283,026, or nearly one-half the total of 15 crops by slave-labor. Represented on the same scale by this line: ▬▬▬▬▬▬

Chart XV.

How far Mr. Mill was in error may be seen by Chart No. XV, which shows the enormous increase of cotton production under the *régime* of free labor as compared with that of slave-labor in the United States. The abolition of slavery has been an economic gain to the South. Moreover, the exports of raw cotton have increased from 644,327,921 pounds in 1869, to 2,288,075,062 pounds in 1883; while for corresponding years the exports of tobacco increased from 181,527,630 to 235,628,360 pounds. In other words, exports of tobacco were increased by 30 per cent, and those of raw cotton by no less than 255 per cent. Besides, the prices of cotton and tobacco are no higher now than before 1850.

An advantage of a similar economical, though of a very different moral character, is that possessed by domestic manufactures; fabrics produced in the leisure hours of families partially occupied in other pursuits, who, not depending for subsistence on the produce of the manufacture, can afford to sell it at any price, however low, for which they think it worth while to take the trouble of producing. The workman of Zürich is to-day a manufacturer, to-morrow again an agriculturist, and changes his occupations with the seasons in a continual round. Manufacturing industry and tillage advance hand in hand, in inseparable alliance, and in this union of the two occupations the secret may be found why the simple and unlearned Swiss manufacturer can always go on competing and increasing in prosperity in the face of those extensive establishments fitted out with great economic and (what is still more important) intellectual resources.

In the case of these domestic manufactures, the comparative cost of production, on which the interchange between countries depends, is much lower than in proportion to the quantity of labor employed. The workpeople, looking to the earnings of their loom for a part only, if for any part, of their actual maintenance, can afford to work for a less remuneration than the lowest rate of wages which can permanently exist in the employments by which the laborer has to support the whole expense of a family. Working, as they do, not for an employer but for themselves, they may be said to carry on the manufacture at no cost at all, except the small expense of a loom and of the material; and the limit of possible cheapness is not the necessity of living by their trade, but that of earning enough by the work to make that social employment of their leisure hours not disagreeable.

§ 4. —But not when common to All.

These two cases, of slave-labor and of domestic manufactures, exemplify the conditions under which low wages enable a country to sell its commodities cheaper in foreign markets, and consequently to undersell its rivals, or to avoid being undersold by them. But no such advantage is conferred by low wages when common to all branches of industry. General low wages never caused any country to undersell its rivals, nor did general high wages ever hinder it from doing so.

To demonstrate this, we must turn to an elementary principle which was discussed in a former chapter.[290] General low wages do not cause low prices, nor high wages high prices, within the country itself. General prices are not raised by a rise of wages, any more than they would be raised by an increase of the quantity of labor required in all production. Expenses which affect all commodities equally have no influence on prices. If the maker of broadcloth or cutlery, and nobody else, had to pay higher wages, the price of his commodity would rise, just as it would if he had to employ more labor; because otherwise he would gain less profit than other producers, and nobody would engage in the employment. But if everybody has to pay higher wages, or everybody to employ more labor, the loss must be submitted to; as it affects everybody alike, no one can hope to get rid of it by a change of employment; each, therefore, resigns himself to a diminution of profits, and prices remain as they were. In like manner, general low wages, or a general increase in the productiveness of labor, does not make prices low, but profits high. If wages fall (meaning here by wages the cost of labor), why, on that account, should the producer lower his price? He will be forced, it may be said, by the competition of other capitalists who will crowd into his employment. But other capitalists are also paying lower wages, and by entering into competition with him they would gain nothing but what they are gaining already. The rate, then, at which labor is paid, as well as the quantity of it which is employed, affects neither the value nor the price of the commodity produced, except in so far as it is peculiar to that commodity, and not common to commodities generally.

> However, without there being any change in the productiveness of any industry, if the price of the article should rise, for instance, from an increased demand, that would make the total value arising from the products of the industry larger in its purchasing power, and so there would be a larger sum to be divided among labor and capital. If there be free competition, more capital would move into this one industry under the hope of larger profits, and so wages would rise. Therefore, it is possible that high wages and high prices may go together, but not as cause and effect. In fact, the change in price generally precedes the change in wages. On the other hand, while low wages are not the cause of low prices nor high wages of high prices, yet the two may be found together, as both due to a common cause, viz., the small or great value of the total product.[291]

Since low wages are not a cause of low prices in the country itself, so neither do they cause it to offer its commodities in foreign markets at a lower price. It is quite true that, if the cost of labor is lower in America than in England, America could sell her cottons to Cuba at a lower price than

England, and still gain as high a profit as the English manufacturer. But it is not with the profit of the English manufacturer that the American cotton-spinner will make his comparison; it is with the profits of other American capitalists. These enjoy, in common with himself, the benefit of a low cost of labor, and have accordingly a high rate of profit. This high profit the cotton-spinner must also have: he will not content himself with the English profit. It is true he may go on for a time at that lower rate, rather than change his employment; and a trade may be carried on, sometimes for a long period, at a much lower profit than that for which it would have been originally engaged in. Countries which have a low cost of labor and high profits do not for that reason undersell others, but they do oppose a more obstinate resistance to being undersold, because the producers can often submit to a diminution of profit without being unable to live, and even to thrive, by their business. But this is all which their advantage does for them; and in this resistance they will not long persevere when a change of times which may give them equal profits with the rest of their countrymen has become manifestly hopeless.

§ 5. Low profits as affecting the carrying Trade.

It is worth while also to notice a third class of small, but in this case mostly independent communities, which have supported and enriched themselves almost without any productions of their own (except ships and marine equipments), by a mere carrying-trade, and commerce of entrepot; by buying the produce of one country, to sell it at a profit in another. Such were Venice and the Hanse Towns.

When the Venetians became the agents of the general commerce of Southern Europe, they had scarcely any competitors: the thing would not have been done at all without them, and there was really no limit to their profits except the limit to what the ignorant feudal nobility could and would give for the unknown luxuries then first presented to their sight. At a later period competition arose, and the profit of this operation, like that of others, became amenable to natural laws. The carrying-trade was taken up by Holland, a country with productions of its own and a large accumulated capital. The other nations of Europe also had now capital to spare, and were capable of conducting their foreign trade for themselves: but Holland, having, from the variety of circumstances, a lower rate of profit at home, could afford to carry for other countries at a smaller advance on the original cost of the goods than would have been required by their own capitalists; and Holland, therefore, engrossed the greatest part of the carrying-trade of all those countries which did not keep it to themselves by navigation laws,[292] constructed, like those of England, for the express purpose.

> In the United States, early in the century, a retaliatory policy against England gave us a body of navigation laws copied after the mediæval statutes of England and the Continent, which still remain on the statute-book. They do not permit an American to buy a vessel abroad and sail it under our flag without paying enormous duties; a provision which is intended to foster ship-building in the United States. Even with this legislation, ships, as a fact, are not built here for the foreign trade; and our ship-builders practically supply the coasting-trade only (which is not open to foreigners). The ability to buy ships anywhere, and enter them to registry under our flag free of duty, is what is meant by the demand for "free ships." This, however, has to do with ship-building. But ship-owning or ship-sailing, is quite distinct from it. The ability to get as great a return from capital and labor invested in a ship as from other occupations open to Americans is another thing. Even if we had "free ships," the higher returns in other industries in our country, particularly as regards profits, might cause capitalists naturally to neglect a less for a more productive business. In 1884 Congress has very properly taken away many vexatious restrictions upon ships, which diminished the returns from ship-sailing, and it remains to be seen whether we can thereby regain any of our foreign carrying-trade. At present we have a very small tonnage even in that part of the shipping engaged in carrying our own goods.

Chapter XXI. Of Distribution, As Affected By Exchange.

§ 1. Exchange and money make no Difference in the law of Wages.

The division of the produce among the three classes, laborers, capitalists, and landlords, when considered without any reference to exchange, appeared to depend on certain general laws. It is fit that we should now consider whether these same laws still operate, when the distribution takes place through the complex mechanism of exchange and money; or whether the properties of the mechanism interfere with and modify the presiding principles.

The primary division of the produce of human exertion and frugality is, as we have seen, into three shares—wages, profits, and rents; and these shares are portioned out, to the persons entitled to them, in the form of money and by a process of exchange; or, rather, the capitalist, with whom in the usual arrangements of society the produce remains, pays in money, to the other two sharers, the market value of their labor and land. If we examine on what the pecuniary value of labor and the pecuniary value of the use of land depend, we shall find that it is on the very same causes by which we found that wages and rent would be regulated if there were no money and no exchange of commodities.

It is evident, in the first place, that the law of wages is not affected by the existence or non-existence of exchange or money. Wages depend on the ratio between population and capital [taking into account the nature of a country's industries]; and would do so if all the capital in the world were the property of one association, or if the capitalists among whom it is shared maintained each an establishment for the production of every article consumed in the community, exchange of commodities having no existence. As the ratio between capital and population, everywhere but in new colonies, depends on the strength of the checks by which the too rapid increase of population is restrained, it may be said, popularly speaking, that wages depend on the checks to population; that, when the check is not death by starvation or disease, wages depend on the prudence of the laboring people; and that wages in any country are habitually at the lowest rate to which in that country the laborer will suffer them to be depressed rather than put a restraint upon multiplication.

What is here meant, however, by wages, is the laborer's real scale of comfort; the quantity he obtains of the things which nature or habit has made necessary or agreeable to him: wages in the sense in which they are of importance to the receiver. In the sense in which they are of importance to the payer, they do not depend exclusively on such simple principles. Wages in the first sense, the wages on which the laborer's comfort depends, we will call real wages, or wages in kind. Wages in the second sense we may be permitted to call, for the present, money wages; assuming, as it is allowable to do, that money remains for the time an invariable standard, no alteration taking place in the conditions under which the circulating medium itself is produced or obtained. If money itself undergoes no variation in cost, the money price of labor is an exact measure of the cost of labor, and may be made use of as a convenient symbol to express it [if the efficiency of labor also be supposed to remain the same].

The money wages of labor are a compound result of two elements: first, real wages, or wages in kind, or, in other words, the quantity which the laborer obtains of the ordinary articles of consumption; and, secondly, the money prices of those articles. In all old countries—all countries in which the increase of population is in any degree checked by the difficulty of obtaining subsistence—the habitual money price of labor is that which will just enable the laborers, one with another, to purchase the commodities without which they either can not or will not keep up the population at its customary rate of increase. Their standard of comfort being given (and by the standard of comfort in a laboring class is meant that rather than forego which they will abstain from multiplication), money wages depend on the money price, and therefore on the cost of production, of the various articles which the laborers habitually consume: because, if their wages can not procure them a given quantity of these, their increase will slacken and their wages rise. Of these articles, food and other agricultural produce are so much the principal as to leave little influence to anything else.

It is at this point that we are enabled to invoke the aid of the principles which have been laid down in this Third Part. The cost of production of food and agricultural produce has been analyzed in a preceding chapter. It depends on the productiveness of the least fertile land, or of the least productively employed portion of capital, which the necessities of society have as yet put in requisition for agricultural purposes. The cost of production of the food grown in these least advantageous circumstances determines, as we have seen, the exchange value and money price of the whole. In any given state, therefore, of the laborers' habits, their money wages depend on the productiveness of the least fertile land, or least productive agricultural capital: on the point which cultivation has reached in its downward progress—in its encroachments on the barren lands, and its gradually increased strain upon the powers of the more fertile. Now, the force which urges cultivation in this downward course is the increase of people; while the counter-force, which checks the descent, is the improvement of agricultural science and practice, enabling the same soil to yield to the same labor more ample returns. The costliness of the most costly part of the produce of cultivation is an exact expression of the state, at any given moment, of the race which population and agricultural skill are always running against each other.

> It will be noted, in this exposition, that Mr. Mill has in view an old country, with a population so dense that numbers are always pressing close upon subsistence; that their wages are so low as to give the laborers little more than the necessary wants of life. That these are not the economic conditions in the United States goes without saying. First of all, the margin of cultivation is high: only soils of high productiveness are in cultivation, and the returns to labor and capital are, consequently, very large. High wages are found together with low prices of food. The existing population is not so numerous as to require for the cultivation of food any but lands of a very high grade of fertility. The ability to command a high reward for labor (as compared with European industries), owing to the general prevalence of high returns in the United States, has resulted in the establishment of a higher standard for our laborers. The standard being relatively so high, there is no intimate connection between the increase of population here and the price of food; for, as a rule, wages are not so low that any change in the cost of producing food would require checks upon population. There is a considerable margin above necessaries, in the laborer's real wages in the United States, which may go for comforts, decencies, and amusements.

§ 2. In the law of Rent.

The degree of productiveness of this extreme margin is an index to the existing state of the distribution of the produce among the three classes, of laborers, capitalists, and landlords. When the demand of an increasing population for more food can not be satisfied without extending cultivation to less fertile land, or incurring additional outlay, with a less proportional return, on land already in cultivation, it is a necessary condition of this increase of agricultural produce that the value and price of that produce must first rise. The price of food will always on the average be such that the worst land, and the least productive installment of the capital employed on the better lands, shall just replace the expenses with the ordinary profit. If the least favored land and capital just do thus much, all other land and capital will yield an extra profit, equal to the proceeds of the extra produce due to their superior productiveness; and this extra profit becomes, by competition, the prize of the landlords. Exchange and money, therefore, make no difference in the law of rent: it is the same as we originally[293] found it. Rent is the extra return made to agricultural capital when employed with peculiar advantages; the exact equivalent of what those advantages enable the producers to economize in the cost of production: the value and price of the produce being regulated by the cost of production to those producers who have no advantages; by the return to that portion of agricultural capital the circumstances of which are the least favorable.

§ 3. —Nor in the law of Profits.

Wages and rent being thus regulated by the same principles when paid in money, as they would be if apportioned in kind, it follows that Profits are so likewise. For the surplus, after replacing wages and paying rent, constitutes Profits.

We found, in the last chapter of the Second Book, that the advances of the capitalist, when analyzed to their ultimate elements, consist either in the purchase or maintenance of labor, or in the profits of former capitalists; and that, therefore, profits in the last resort depend upon the Cost of Labor, falling as that rises, and rising as it falls. Let us endeavor to trace more minutely the operation of this law.

There are two modes in which the Cost of Labor, which is correctly represented (money being supposed invariable as well as efficiency) by the money wages of the laborer, may be increased. The laborer may obtain greater comforts; wages in kind—real wages—may rise. Or the progress of population may force down cultivation to inferior soils and more costly processes; thus raising the cost of production, the value, and the price, of the chief articles of the laborer's consumption. On either of these suppositions the rate of profit will fall.

If the laborer obtains more abundant commodities only by reason of their greater cheapness, if he obtains a greater quantity, but not on the whole a greater cost, real wages will be increased, but not money wages, and there will be nothing to affect the rate of profit. But, if he obtains a greater quantity of commodities of which the cost of production is not lowered, he obtains a greater cost; his money wages are higher. The expense of these increased money wages falls wholly on the capitalist. There are no conceivable means by which he can shake it off. It may be said—it used formerly to be said—that he will get rid of it by raising his price. But this opinion we have already, and more than once, fully refuted.[294]

The doctrine, indeed, that a rise of wages causes an equivalent rise of prices, is, as we formerly observed, self-contradictory: for, if it did so, it would not be a rise of wages; the laborer would get no more of any commodity than he had before, let his money wages rise ever so much; a rise of real wages would be an impossibility. This being equally contrary to reason and to fact, it is evident that a rise of money wages does not raise prices; that high wages are not a cause of high prices. A rise of general wages falls on profits. There is no possible alternative.

Having disposed of the case in which the increase of money wages, and of the Cost of Labor, arises from the laborer's obtaining more ample wages in kind, let us now suppose it to arise from the increased cost of production of the things which he consumes, owing to an increase of population unaccompanied by an equivalent increase of agricultural skill. The augmented supply required by the population would not be obtained, unless the price of food rose sufficiently to remunerate the farmer for the increased cost of production. The farmer, however, in this case sustains a twofold disadvantage. He has to carry on his cultivation under less favorable conditions of productiveness than before. For this, as it is a disadvantage belonging to him only as a farmer, and not shared by other employers, he will, on the general principles of value, be compensated by a rise of the price of his commodity; indeed, until this rise has taken place, he will not bring to market the required increase of produce. But this very rise of price involves him in another necessity, for which he is not compensated. He must pay higher money wages to his laborers [if they retain the same quantity of real wages]. This necessity, being common to him with all other capitalists, forms no ground for a rise of price. The price will rise, until it has placed him in as good a situation, in respect of profits, as other employers of labor; it will rise so as to indemnify him for the increased labor which he must now employ in order to produce a given quantity of food; but the increased wages of that labor are a burden common to all, and for which no one can be indemnified. It will be paid wholly from profits.

Thus we see that increased wages, when common to all descriptions of productive laborers, and when really representing a greater Cost of Labor, are always and necessarily at the expense of profits. And by reversing the cases, we should find in like manner that diminished wages, when representing a really diminished Cost of Labor, are equivalent to a rise of profits. But the opposition of pecuniary interest thus indicated between the class of capitalists and that of laborers is to a great extent only apparent. Real wages are a very different thing from the Cost of Labor, and are generally highest at the times and places where, from the easy terms on which the land yields all the produce as yet required from it, the value and price of food being low, the cost of labor to the employer, notwithstanding its ample remuneration, is comparatively cheap, and the rate of profit consequently high, as at present in the United States. We thus obtain a full confirmation of our original theorem that Profits depend on the Cost of Labor: or, to express the meaning with still greater accuracy, the rate of profit and the cost of labor vary inversely as one another, and are joint effects of the same agencies or causes.

Book IV. Influence Of The Progress Of Society On Production And Distribution.

Chapter I. Influence Of The Progress Of Industry And Population On Values And Prices.

§ 1. Tendency of the progress of society toward increased Command over the powers of Nature; increased Security, and increased Capacity of Co-Operation.

In the leading countries of the world, and in all others as they come within the influence of those leading countries, there is at least one progressive movement which continues with little interruption from year to year and from generation to generation—a progress in wealth; an advancement in what is called material prosperity. All the nations which we are accustomed to call civilized increase gradually in production and in population: and there is no reason to doubt that not only these nations will for some time continue so to increase, but that most of the other nations of the world, including some not yet founded, will successively enter upon the same career. It will, therefore, be our first object to examine the nature and consequences of this progressive change, the elements which constitute it, and the effects it produces on the various economical facts of which we have been tracing the laws, and especially on wages, profits, rents, values, and prices.

Of the features which characterize this progressive economical movement of civilized nations, that which first excites attention, through its intimate connection with the phenomena of Production, is the perpetual, and, so far as human foresight can extend (1), the unlimited, growth of man's power over nature. Our knowledge of the properties and laws of physical objects shows no sign of approaching its ultimate boundaries: it is advancing more rapidly, and in a greater number of directions at once, than in any previous age or generation, and affording such frequent glimpses of unexplored fields beyond as to justify the belief that our acquaintance with nature is still almost in its infancy.

Another change, which has always hitherto characterized, and will assuredly continue to characterize, the progress of civilized society, is (2) a continual increase of the security of person and property. Of this increased security, one of the most unfailing effects is a great increase both of production and of accumulation. Industry and frugality can not exist where there is not a preponderant probability that those who labor and spare will be permitted to enjoy.

One of the changes which most infallibly attend the progress of modern society is, (3) an improvement in the business capacities of the general mass of mankind. I do not mean that the practical sagacity of an individual human being is greater than formerly. What is lost in the separate efficiency of each is far more than made up by the greater capacity of united action. Works of all sorts, impracticable to the savage or the half-civilized, are daily accomplished by civilized nations, not by any greatness of faculties in the actual agents, but through the fact that each is able to rely with certainty on the others for the portion of the work which they respectively undertake. The peculiar characteristic, in short, of civilized beings, is the capacity of co-operation; and this, like other faculties, tends to improve by practice, and becomes capable of assuming a constantly wider sphere of action.

[This progress affords] space and scope for an indefinite increase of capital and production, and for the increase of population which is its ordinary accompaniment. That the growth of population will overpass the increase of production, there is not much reason to apprehend. It is, however, quite possible that there might be a great progress in industrial improvement, and in the signs of what is commonly called national prosperity; a great increase of aggregate wealth, and even, in some respects, a better distribution of it; that not only the rich might grow richer, but many of the poor might grow rich, that the intermediate classes might become more numerous and powerful, and the means of enjoyable existence be more and more largely diffused, while yet the great class at the base of the whole might increase in numbers only, and not in comfort nor in cultivation. We must, therefore, in considering the effects of the progress of industry, admit as a supposition, however greatly we deprecate as a fact, an increase of population as long-continued, as indefinite, and possibly even as rapid, as the increase of production and accumulation.

§ 2. Tendency to a Decline of the Value and Cost of Production of all Commodities.

The changes which the progress of industry causes or presupposes in the circumstances of production are necessarily attended with changes in the values of commodities.

The permanent values of all things which are neither under a natural nor under an artificial monopoly depend, as we have seen, on their cost of production. (1.) But the increasing power which mankind are constantly acquiring over nature increases more and more the efficiency of human exertion, or, in other words, diminishes cost of production. All inventions by which a greater quantity of any commodity can be produced with the same labor, or the same quantity with less labor, or which abridge the process, so that the capital employed needs not be advanced for so long a time, lessen the cost of production of the commodity. As, however, value is relative, if inventions and improvements in production were made in all commodities, and all in the same degree, there would be no alteration in values.

As for prices, in these circumstances they would be affected or not, according as the improvements in production did or did not extend to the precious metals. If the materials of money were an exception to the general diminution of cost of production, the values of all other things would fall in relation to money—that is, there would be a fall of general prices throughout the world. But if money, like other things, and in the same degree as other things, were obtained in greater abundance and cheapness, prices would be no more affected than values would.

> As regards the precious metals, it is to be said that since 1850 there has been a vast increase in their amount, and probably in greater proportion than the need arising from increased transactions. This is certainly true of silver; and it is admitted to be true of gold as late as about 1865. It has been asserted by Mr. Goschen that since then, especially since 1873, gold has not existed in a quantity that would permit it to keep its former proportions to commodities, and that it had appreciated. An appreciation, of course, would show itself in lower gold prices. On the other hand, gold has, as I think, not appreciated. Prices, even in the collapse of credit after the panic of 1873 down to 1879, were not quite so low as in 1845-1850, as is seen by the following table taken from the London "Economist"—2,200 indicating the price of a given number of articles in 1845-1850, as the basis of the table with which the prices of other years are compared:

Year.	Index numbers.
1845-1850	2,200

1857, July 1	2,996
1858, January 1	2,612
1865	3,575
1866	3,564
1867	3,024
1868	2,682
1869	2,666
1870	2,689
1871	2,590
1872	2,835
1873	2,947
1874 (Depression)	2,891
1875 (Depression)	2,778
1876 (Depression)	2,711
1877 (Depression)	2,723
1878 (Depression)	2,529
1879 (Depression)	2,202
1880	2,538
1881	2,376
1882	2,435
1883	2,343

But the progress of society, particularly in the direction of improved and cheapened processes of manufacturing, has vastly lowered the cost of a great number of articles of common consumption. The process has been already seen in the diminished charge for railway transportation (see Chart No. V). Moreover, the years of a depression are exactly those in which there is always a forced economy, and generally form a period in which cheapening goes on at its best. Hence, if prices have had a tendency to fall, owing to the lowered cost of production consequent on improvements—and if they are not, as a rule, lower than in 1850—it shows that they are still supported by the high tide of the great gold production of this century. And even the access to more fertile land in the world has acted to prevent an increase in the prices of agricultural products such as would offset the fall of manufactured goods. That is, the fact that prices have not fallen as much as might be expected, indicates that the gold has prevented the lower costs due to the progress of industry from being fully seen.

Improvements in production are not the only circumstance accompanying the progress of industry, which tends to diminish the cost of producing, or at least of obtaining, commodities. (2.) Another circumstance is the increase of intercourse between different parts of the world. As commerce extends, and the ignorant attempts to restrain it by tariffs become obsolete, commodities tend more and more to be produced in the places in which their production can be carried on at the least expense of labor and capital to mankind. (3.) Much will also depend on the increasing migration of labor and capital to unoccupied parts of the earth, of which the soil, climate, and situation are found, by the ample means of exploration now possessed, to promise not only a large return to industry, but great facilities of producing commodities suited to the markets of old countries. Much as the collective industry of the earth is likely to be increased in efficiency by the extension of science and of the industrial arts, a still more active source of increased cheapness of production will be found, probably, for some time to come, in the gradually unfolding consequences of Free Trade, and in the increasing scale on which Emigration and Colonization will be carried on.

From the causes now enumerated, unless counteracted by others, the progress of things enables a country to obtain, at less and less of real cost, not only its own productions but those of foreign countries. Indeed, whatever diminishes the cost of its own productions, when of an exportable character, enables it, as we have already seen, to obtain its imports at less real cost.

§ 3. —except the products of Agriculture and Mining, which have a tendency to Rise.

Are no causes of an opposite character, brought into operation by the same progress, sufficient in some cases not only to neutralize but to overcome the former, and convert the descending movement of cost of production into an ascending movement? We are already aware that there are such causes, and that, in the case of the most important classes of commodities, food, and materials, there is a tendency diametrically opposite to that of which we have been speaking. The cost of production of these commodities tends to increase.

This is not a property inherent in the commodities themselves. If population were stationary, and the produce of the earth never needed to be augmented in quantity, there would be no cause for greater cost of production.[295] The only products of industry which, if population did not increase, would be liable to a real increase of cost of production, are those which, depending on a material which is not renewed, are either wholly or partially exhaustible, such as coal, and most if not all metals; for even iron, the most abundant as well as most useful of metallic products, which forms an ingredient of most minerals and of almost all rocks, is susceptible of exhaustion so far as regards its richest and most tractable ores.

When, however, population increases, as it has never yet failed to do, then comes into effect that fundamental law of production from the soil on which we have so frequently had occasion to expatiate, the law that increased labor, in any given state of agricultural skill, is attended with a less than proportional increase of produce. The cost of production of the fruits of the earth increases, *cæteris paribus*, with every increase of the demand.

> Mr. Cairnes has made some essential contributions to the discussion of changes of value arising from the progress of society:[296] "When a colony establishes itself in a new country, the course of its industrial development naturally follows the character of the opportunities offered to industrial enterprise by the environment. These will, of course, vary a good deal, according to the part of the world in which the new society happens to be placed; but, speaking broadly, they will be such as to draw the bulk of the industrial activity of the new people into some one or more of those branches of industry which have been conveniently designated 'extractive.' Agriculture, pastoral and mining pursuits, and the cutting of lumber, are among the principal of such industries." To these pursuits apply "that law of Political Economy, or, more properly, of physical nature, which Mr. Mill has rightly characterized as the most important proposition in economic science—the law, as he phrased it, of 'diminishing productiveness.' It

may be thus briefly stated: In any given state of the arts of production, the returns to human industry employed upon natural agents will, up to a certain point, be the maximum which those natural agents, cultivated with the degree of skill brought to bear upon them, are capable of yielding; but, after this point has been passed, though an increased application of labor and capital will obtain an increased return, it will not obtain a proportionally increased return; on the contrary, every further increase of outlay—always assuming that the skill employed in applying it continues the same as before—will be attended with a return constantly diminishing.... What I am now concerned to show is the manner in which, with the progress of society, the law in question affects the course of normal[297] values in all commodities coming under its influence.

"The class of commodities in the production of which the facilities possessed by new communities, as compared with old, attain their greatest height, are those of which timber and meat may be taken as the type, and comprises such articles as wool, game, furs, hides, horns, pitch, resin, etc. The circumstance which most powerfully affects the course of values in the products of extractive industry, and in the commodities just referred to among the rest, is the degree in which they admit of being transported from place to place—that is to say, their *portableness*—depending, as it does, partly on their durability and partly on their bulk." It is found that, taking timber and meat as a type—one possessing portableness in a vastly greater degree than the other—in the early settlement of a new country, the portable article, like timber, at once rises in price "to a level lower than that prevailing in old countries only by the cost of transport"; on the other hand, perishable articles like meat are "confined for a market, if not to the immediate locality where it is produced, at least to the bordering countries; and, being raised in new countries at very low cost, their value during the early stages of their growth is necessarily low. But, as population advances, and agriculture encroaches on the natural pasture-lands originally available for the rearing of cattle, still more as it becomes necessary to cultivate land for the purpose of pasture, the cost of meat constantly rises." As population increases there will be an increased demand for dairy-products, eggs, small fruits, fresh vegetables, milk, etc., and thereby it becomes more profitable to employ land near populous centers for such perishable products than for the products of large farming. Almost every one, who knows the high prices of butter, eggs, and vegetables in large cities as compared with their prices in country districts, is familiar with the phenomena which illustrate this principle. Moreover, as a denser population settles on our Western prairies, now given over to ranches and vast pasturing-grounds for cattle—since cattle in general require a large extent of land—the cost of meat will rise. The prices of perishable articles, therefore, will rise without any limit except that set by increasing numbers, and can not be kept down by the force of competition from other distant places, as is the case with such easily transportable things as timber and wool. What has been said of the transportableness of meat, however, is to be modified somewhat by the introduction of improved processes of transporting meat in refrigerator-cars; but there still exist commodities of which meat was only taken as a type.

No tendency of a like kind exists with respect to manufactured articles. The tendency is in the contrary direction. The larger the scale on which manufacturing operations are carried on, the more cheaply they can in general be performed. As manufactures, however, depend for their materials either upon agriculture, or mining, or the spontaneous produce of the earth, manufacturing industry is subject, in respect of one of its essentials, to the same law as agriculture. But the crude material generally forms so small a portion of the total cost that any tendency which may exist to a progressive increase in that single item is much overbalanced by the diminution continually taking place in all the other elements; to which diminution it is impossible at present to assign any limit.

It follows that the exchange values of manufactured articles, compared with the products of agriculture and of mines, have, as population and industry advance, a certain and decided tendency to fall. Money being a product of mines, it may also be laid down as a rule that manufactured articles tend, as society advances, to fall in money price. The industrial history of modern nations, especially during the last hundred years, fully bears out this assertion.

> In regard to manufactures, as opposed to raw products, it is to be remarked "that, as the course of price in the field of raw products is, on the whole, upward, so in that of manufactured goods the course is, not less strikingly, in the opposite direction. The reasons of this are exceedingly plain. In the first place, *division of labor*—the first and most powerful of all cheapeners of production, but for which there is in extractive industry but very limited scope—finds in manufacturing industry an almost unbounded range for its application; and, secondly, it is in manufacturing industry also that *machinery*, the other great cheapener of production, admits of being employed on the largest scale, and has, in fact, been employed with the most signal success. It follows at once from these facts, taken in connection with the further fact that industrial invention does not take place *per saltum*, but gradually—one invention ever treading on the heels of another—and that its advance seems to be subject to no limitation; it follows, I say, from these considerations, that that portion of the cost of manufactured goods which properly belongs to the manufacturing process must, with the progress of society, undergo constant diminution.... In all the great branches of manufacturing industry the portion of the cost incurred in the manufacturing process bears in general a large proportion to that represented by the raw material, while the influence of industrial invention, in reducing this portion of the cost, is, as every one knows, great and unremitting in its action."

> As has been said, "the two great cheapeners of production are division of labor and machinery, and the degree in which these admit of being applied to manufacture is mainly dependent upon the scale on which the manufacturing process is carried on. Those manufactures, therefore, that are produced upon a large scale are the sort of manufactures in which we

may expect the greatest reduction in cost; in which, therefore, the fall in price, with the progress of society, will be most marked. But the manufactures which are produced upon the largest scale are those for which there exists the largest demand—that is to say, are those which enter most extensively into the consumption of the great mass of people. They are also, I may add, those in which a fall in price is apt to stimulate a great increase of demand. All the common kinds of clothing, furniture, and utensils fall within the scope of this remark; and it is in these, rather than in the commodities consumed exclusively or mainly by the richer classes, that we should, accordingly, expect to find the greatest marvels of cheapening." But the articles of common consumption are those in which "the amount of manufacture bestowed upon them bears a smaller proportion to the raw material than is the case with the more elaborate manufactures. Such coarser manufactures, therefore, would feel the effects of the advancing cost of the raw material more sensibly than the refined sorts. Nevertheless, it can not be supposed to compensate the advantages due to the causes I have pointed out which fall to the share of the commoner sorts. It is in this class of goods that the most remarkable reductions in price have been accomplished in the past, and it is in them, probably, that we shall witness in the future the greatest results of the same kind."

§ 4. —that tendency from time to time Counteracted by Improvements in Production.

Whether agricultural produce increases in absolute as well as comparative cost of production depends on the conflict of the two antagonist agencies—increase of population and improvement in agricultural skill. In some, perhaps in most, states of society (looking at the whole surface of the earth), both agricultural skill and population are either stationary, or increase very slowly, and the cost of production of food, therefore, is nearly stationary. In a society which is advancing in wealth, population generally increases faster than agricultural skill, and food consequently tends to become more costly; but there are times when a strong impulse sets in toward agricultural improvement. Such an impulse has shown itself in Great Britain during the last fifteen or twenty years [before 1847]. In England and Scotland agricultural skill has of late increased considerably faster than population, insomuch that food and other agricultural produce, notwithstanding the increase of people, can be grown at less cost than they were thirty years ago; and the abolition of the Corn Laws has given an additional stimulus to the spirit of improvement. In some other countries, and particularly in France, the improvement of agriculture gains ground still more decidedly upon population, because though agriculture, except in a few provinces, advances slowly, population advances still more slowly, and even with increasing slowness, its growth being kept down, not by poverty, which is diminishing, but by prudence.

> Moreover, the cheapened cost of transportation has admitted to England and the Continent the wheat supplies of our Western States at a low price even after having been carried to transatlantic markets. New methods of getting food-supplies from foreign countries act equally with improvements at home.

§ 5. Effect of the Progress of Society in moderating fluctuations of Value.

Thus far, of the effect of the progress of society on the permanent or average values and prices of commodities. It remains to be considered in what manner the same progress affects their fluctuations. Concerning the answer to this question there can be no doubt. It tends in a very high degree to diminish them.

In poor and backward societies, as in the East, and in Europe during the middle ages, extraordinary differences in the price of the same commodity might exist in places not very distant from each other, because the want of roads and canals, the imperfection of marine navigation, and the insecurity of communications generally, prevented things from being transported from the places where they were cheap to those where they were dear. The things most liable to fluctuations in value, those directly influenced by the seasons, and especially food, were seldom carried to any great distances. In most years, accordingly, there was, in some part or other of any large country, a real dearth; while a deficiency at all considerable, extending to the whole world, is [now] a thing almost unknown. In modern times, therefore, there is only dearth, where there formerly would have been famine, and sufficiency everywhere when anciently there would have been scarcity in some places and superfluity in others.

The same change has taken place with respect to all other articles of commerce. The safety and cheapness of communications, which enable a deficiency in one place to be supplied from the surplus of another, at a moderate or even a small advance on the ordinary price, render the fluctuations of prices much less extreme than formerly. This effect is much promoted by the existence of large capitals, belonging to what are called speculative merchants, whose business it is to buy goods in order to resell them at a profit. These dealers naturally buying things when they are cheapest, and storing them up to be brought again into the market when the price has become unusually high, the tendency of their operations is to equalize price, or at least to moderate its inequalities. The prices of things are neither so much depressed at one time, nor so much raised at another, as they would be if speculative dealers did not exist.

> Mr. Mill uses the term "speculative" in a different sense from that which is customary in this country. Merchants who buy outright and store up grain are not speculators in the sense in which the word is used with us; but those gamblers who purchase, "for future delivery," grain which they never see, and which they sell in the same way, are here known as speculators.

It appears, then, that the fluctuations of values and prices arising from variations of supply, or from alterations in real (as distinguished from speculative) demand, may be expected to become more moderate as society advances. With regard to those which arise from miscalculation, and especially from the alternations of undue expansion and excessive contraction of credit, which occupy so conspicuous a place among commercial phenomena, the same thing can not be affirmed with equal confidence. Such vicissitudes, beginning with irrational speculation and ending with a commercial crisis, have not hitherto become either less frequent or less violent with the growth of capital and extension of industry. Rather they may be said to have become more so, in consequence, as is often said, of increased competition, but, as I prefer to say, of a lower rate of profits and interest, which makes capitalists dissatisfied with the ordinary course of safe mercantile gains. The connection of this low rate of profit with the advance of population and accumulation is one of the points to be illustrated in the ensuing chapters.

Mr. Cairnes also adds some investigations as to the fluctuations of value: "Hitherto I have examined the derivative laws of value in so far only as they are exemplified in the movements of *normal* prices. It will be interesting now to consider whether it is possible to discover in the movements of *market* prices any corresponding phenomena.

"Taking manufactures first, it is evident at once that, as regards conditions of protection, the circumstances of the case are such as to secure, in general, (1.) great rapidity and great certainty in bringing commodities to market. A deal table may be made in a few hours, a piece of cloth in a few weeks, and a moderate-sized house in a month or little more. Tables, cloth, and houses may be produced with certainty in any quantity required. It results from this that it is scarcely possible that, under ordinary circumstances, the selling price of a product of manufacture should for any long time much exceed its normal price. (2.) The nature of manufactures is, in general, such as to fit them admirably for distant transport. Any considerable elevation of price, therefore, is pretty certain to attract supplies from remote sources. (3.) Further, considered in their relation to human needs, I think it may be said of manufactured goods, that either the need for them is not very urgent, or, where it happens to be so, substitutes ... may easily be found. From all these circumstances it results that an advance in the price ... either attracts supplies, or deters purchasers, ... preventing any great departure from the usual terms of the market.

"Turning now to the products of agricultural, pastoral, or, more generally, 'extractive' industry, we find the circumstances under which this class of goods is brought to market in all respects extremely different from those which we have just examined, and such as to permit a much wider margin of deviation for the market from the normal price. Here the period of production is longer, the result of the process much more uncertain, the commodity at once more perishable and less portable, and human requirements in relation to it are mostly of a more urgent kind: (1.)

The shortest period within which additions can be made to the supply of food and raw material of the vegetable kind is in general a year, and, if the commodity be of animal origin, the minimum is considerably larger. (2.) Again, the farmer may decide upon the breadth of ground to be devoted to a particular crop, or upon the number of cattle he will maintain; but the actual returns will vary according to the season, and may prove far in excess or far in defect of his calculations. These circumstances all present obstacles to the adjustment of supply and demand, and consequently tend to produce frequent and extensive deviations of the market from the normal price. Nor are the other conditions of the case such as to neutralize the influence of such disturbing agencies. (3.) The nature, indeed, of some of the principal agricultural products fits them sufficiently well for distant transport, and so far tends to correct fluctuations of price. But, on the other hand, (4.) the relation of these products to human wants is such as greatly to enhance that tendency to violent fluctuation incident to the conditions of their production. More especially is this the case with the commodity, whatever it may be, which forms the staple food of a people. For observe the peculiar nature of human requirements with reference to such a commodity. They are of this kind, that, given the number of a population, the quantity of the staple food required is nearly a fixed quantity, and this almost irrespective of price. Except among the poorest, increased cheapness will not stimulate a larger consumption; while, on the other hand, all, at any cost within the range of their means, will obtain their usual supply. The consequence is that, when even a moderate deficiency or excess occurs in the supply of the staple food of a people, in the one case (*a*), the competition of consumers for their usual quantum of food rapidly forces up the price far out of proportion to the diminution in the supply; in the other (*b*), no one being inclined to increase his usual consumption, the competition of sellers, in their eagerness to find a market for the superfluous portion of the supply, is equally powerful to depress it."

Chapter II. Influence Of The Progress Of Industry And Population On Rents, Profits, And Wages.

§ 1. Characteristic features of industrial Progress.

Continuing the inquiry into the nature of the economical changes taking place in a society which is in a state of industrial progress, we shall next consider what is the effect of that progress on the distribution of the produce among the various classes who share in it. We may confine our attention to the system of distribution which is the most complex, and which virtually includes all others—that in which the produce of manufactures is shared between two classes, laborers and capitalists, and the produce of agriculture among three, laborers, capitalists, and landlords.

The characteristic features of what is commonly meant by industrial progress resolve themselves mainly into three, increase of capital, increase of population, and improvements in production; understanding the last expression, in its widest sense, to include the process of procuring commodities from a distance, as well as that of producing them. It will be convenient to set out by considering each of the three causes, as operating separately; after which we can suppose them combined in any manner we think fit.[298]

§ 2. First two cases, Population and Capital increasing, the arts of production stationary.

For the sake of clearness we will form two general groups of these causes:

A. *The Influence of Population and Capital (Improvements remaining stationary).*

B. *The Influence of Improvements (Population and Capital remaining stationary).*

We will first take up A, and under this division make for convenience two separate suppositions:

I. The first is that, while Population is advancing, Capital is stationary. By this means we can study separately the operation of one of the factors of societary progress, Population, and see its influence on rents, profits, and wages. There being only the same given quantity of wealth in the form of capital to be now distributed among more laborers (1), real wages must fall; whereupon, if the same capital purchases more labor, and obtains more produce (2), profits rise. Now, if the laborers were so well off before as to suffer the reduction of wages to take place not in their food, but in their other comforts, then, if each laborer uses as much food as before, and if, as by the supposition, there are more laborers, an increased quantity of food will be required from the soil. This supply can be produced only at a greater cost, and, as inferior soils are called into cultivation (3), rents will rise. This last action (3), however, will have an influence on the rise of profits (2). For it was only by a reduction of real wages that profits rose; but if the cost of food, that is, the real wages, have since risen, then one of the elements entering into cost of labor has risen, and in so far will offset the fall of real wages; so that profits will not gain so much as if rents had not risen. The result of this first supposition, then, is, that the landlord is the chief gainer:

I. (1.) Wages fall.
(2.) Profits rise (less if rents rise).
(3.) Rents rise.

II. We will now take up the second supposition under A, that while Capital is advancing Population remains stationary. Then, of course (1), wages will rise; and, as there is no improvement to cheapen the cost of their real wages, there will be an increase in cost of labor to the capitalist, and (2) profits will fall. If, now, the laborers, being better off, demand more food, the new food would cost more, as the margin of cultivation was pushed down, and (3) rents would inevitably rise. But not only have the laborers received more real wages, but since that change the cost, as just described, of these real wages has increased. Therefore (2), profits would fall still more than by the rise of real wages. In this supposition, consequently, while the laborer gains, so does the landlord:

II. (1.) Wages rise.
(2.) Profits fall (more if rents rise).
(3.) Rents rise.

A. It is easy for us now to take into our view the total effects under A, and see what the combined action of I and II would be. That is, if both Capital and Population (improvements remaining stationary) increase, what will be the effect on Wages, Profits, and Rent? Of course, we must suppose that Capital and Population just keep pace with each other; and in that case (1) real wages remain the same, each laborer receiving the same quantity and same quality of commodities as before. Hence, if each laborer receives the same quantity as before, and there are many more laborers, there will be an increased demand put upon the soil for food, poorer soils will be cultivated, and the cost of the products will rise. So (3) rents rise. But if each laborer receives the same quantity of real wages as before, and the cost of them has risen, as just explained, an increased cost of labor will result which must come out of profits. (2) Profits will fall. So that the results of A upon distribution, taken separately from B, are that the owner of capital loses; but the owner of land again gains.

A. (1.) Wages the same.
(2.) Profits fall.
(3.) Rents rise.

§ 3. The arts of production advancing, capital and population stationary.

Now, let us go back to our first general group of causes, B—an advance in the arts of production (while capital and population remain stationary). We can now study by themselves the effect of improvements on wages, profits, and rent. The general effects arising from the extended introduction of machinery into agriculture and manufactures, the lowered cost of transportation by steam, have been to lessen the value of articles consumed chiefly by the laboring-classes. For the sake of clearness, imagine that the improvement comes suddenly. The first effect will be to lower the value and price of articles entering into the real wages of the laborers; and, if those consist mostly of food, there will be a rise in the margin of cultivation and a fall in rents (3). It has been previously shown[299] that improvements retard, or put back, the law of diminishing returns from land (or in manufactures compensate for it), and so lower rents. The poorest soil cultivated is now of a better grade than before, and the produce is yielded at a less cost and value; so that the land with which the best grades are compared, to determine the rent, is not separated from the best grades by so wide a gap. It would at first blush seem, then, that the interests of the landlord were antagonistic to improvements, since they lower rents; but, in practice, it is not so, as we shall soon see.

We have seen that improvements cheapen the price of articles entering into the real wages of the laborer. Having had a given sum as money wages before the change, then, when the sudden change of improvements came, it lowered prices to the laborer, and the same money wages bought more (1) real wages. If nothing more happened, we could see that improvements raised real wages—without lowering (2) profits (because cost of labor remains the same, since the lowered cost of the articles consumed was exactly in proportion to the increase of real wages). And, if the laborers chose to retain this higher standard, this would be the situation. Sadly enough, however, in practice they are apt to be satisfied with the old standard; and the amount of real wages to give the old standard of living can be had now for less money wages. While only the same number, without any increase, can live at the new (higher) standard, a larger number can live at the old (lower) standard. In short, the obstacles to an increase of population will be removed by the possession of higher money wages. After a generation, it is very probable that a larger number of laborers will be in existence living at the same (or possibly a slightly higher) standard of real wages, and money wages will have fallen.

Now we can understand better than before what would be the practical result of the causes under B. (3.) Rent has fallen; money wages have fallen (even if (2) real wages have not); and, since real wages have not fallen in the proportion that their cost has been reduced, (2) profits will have risen. The general result of the causes under B alone, acting as just described, will then be:

B. (1.) Real wages remain the same; money wages less.
(2.) Profits rise.
(3.) Rents fall.

§ 4. Theoretical results, if all three Elements progressive.

We have considered, on the one hand, under A, the manner in which the distribution of the produce into rent, profits, and wages is affected by the ordinary increase of Population and Capital; and on the other, under B, how it is affected by improvements in production, and more especially in agriculture, as follows:

A. (1.) Wages the same. B. (1.) Real wages the same, money wages less.
A. (2.) Profits fall. B. (2.) Profits rise.
A. (3.) Rents rise. B. (3.) Rents fall.

The effects are clearly contrasted. Under A, we see a tendency to a rise of rents (3), an increased cost of labor, and a fall of profits (2); under B, a fall of rents (3), a diminished cost of labor, and a rise of profits (2). We have, therefore, analyzed the forces belonging to the progress of industry, and found two distinct and antagonistic forces, working against each other. If, at any period, improvements (B) advance faster than population and capital (A), rent and money wages will tend downward and profits upward. If, on the other hand, population advances faster than improvements (B) either the laborers will submit to a reduction in the quantity or quality of their food, or, if not, rent and money wages will progressively rise, and profits will fall.

§ 5. Practical Results.

This, however, is not the final and practical result. We have hitherto supposed that improvements, B, come suddenly. In point of fact, agricultural skill is slowly diffused, and inventions and discoveries are, in general, only occasional, not continuous in their action, as is the increase of capital and population. Inasmuch as it seldom happens that improvement has so much the start of population and capital as actually to lower rent, or raise the rate of profits, population almost everywhere "treads close on the heels of agricultural improvement," and effaces its effects as fast as they are produced.

The reason why agricultural improvement seldom lowers rent is, that it seldom cheapens food, but only prevents it from growing dearer; and seldom, if ever, throws land out of cultivation, but only enables worse and worse land to be taken in for the supply of an increasing demand. What is sometimes called the natural state of a country which is but half cultivated, namely, that the land is highly productive, and food obtained in great abundance by little labor, is only true of unoccupied countries colonized by a civilized people. In the United States the worst land in cultivation is of a high quality (except sometimes in the immediate vicinity of markets or means of conveyance, where a bad quality is compensated by a good situation); and even if no further improvements were made in agriculture or locomotion, cultivation would have many steps yet to descend, before the increase of population and capital would be brought to a stand; but in Europe five hundred years ago, though so thinly peopled in comparison to the present population, it is probable that the worst land under the plow was, from the rude state of agriculture, quite as unproductive as the worst land now cultivated, and that cultivation had approached as near to the ultimate limit of profitable tillage in those times as in the present. What the agricultural improvements since made have really done is, by increasing the capacity of production of land in general, to enable tillage to extend downward to a much worse natural quality of land than the worst which at that time would have admitted of cultivation by a capitalist for profit; thus rendering a much greater increase of capital and population possible, and removing always a little and a little further off the barrier which restrains them; population meanwhile always pressing so hard against the barrier that there is never any visible margin left for it to seize, every inch of ground made vacant for it by improvement being at once filled up by its advancing columns. Agricultural improvement may thus be considered to be not so much a counter-force conflicting with increase of population as a partial relaxation of the bonds which confine that increase.

> Now, since improvements enable a much poorer quality of land to be ultimately cultivated, under the constant pressure of the increase of population and capital, improvements enable rent (3) in the end to rise gradually to a much higher limit than it could otherwise have attained.

If a great agricultural improvement were suddenly introduced, it might throw back rent for a considerable space, leaving it to regain its lost ground by the progress of population and capital, and afterward to go on further. But taking place, as such improvement always does, very gradually, it causes no retrograde movement of either rent or cultivation; it merely enables the one to go on rising, and the other extending, long after they must otherwise have stopped.

> Inasmuch as, in point of fact, B never gets the start of A, but follows along with A, the general result will be that which we found true under A—a rise of rents (3), and increased cost of labor to the capitalist, arising from an increased cost of laborers' subsistence and a fall of profits (2). The effect of a more rapid advance of improvements, at any one time, will temporarily better the condition of the laborers and also raise profits; but, if it is followed immediately by an increase of population, the land-owners will reap the benefits of the improvement in the rise of rent. The final result, then, is as follows:

(1.) Real wages, probably higher.
(2.) Profits fall.
(3.) Rents rise.

It is possible that a different combination from the above may sometimes occur in the causes which underlie the progress of society: (1.) There may be a period in which capital is increasing more rapidly than population, and when there seems to be an era of industrial improvements also. Then both wages and profits will be high, and it will be a period of general satisfaction. (2.) If capital goes on increasing, but improvements are few, wages will rise; but profits must suffer a fall. In this country, where population has not yet increased so as to press seriously against subsistence, and where capital increases with incredible swiftness, these cases are often exemplified. The extraordinary resources of the newer States have permitted an unlimited increase of population, and capital has found no difficulty in finding an investment. But yet those States which have been burdened with the disabilities of the old slave *régime* are far behind the others. The changes in the rank of the States, in respect of population, at each decade, as seen in Chart No. XVI, are suggestive.

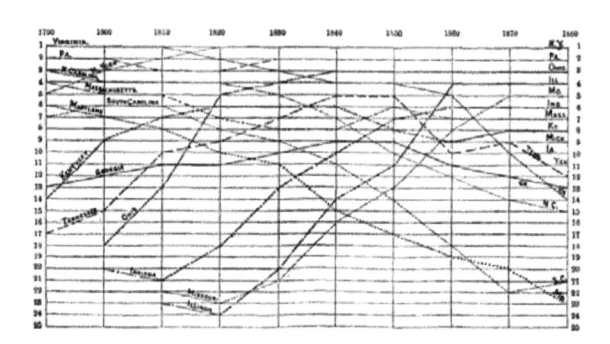

Chart XVI. *Changes of the Rank of the States in the Scale of Relative Population, from 1790 to 1880.*

Chapter III. Of The Tendency Of Profits To A Minimum.

§ 1. Different Theories as to the fall of Profits.

The tendency of profits to fall as society advances, which has been brought to notice in the preceding chapter, was early recognized by writers on industry and commerce; but, the laws which govern profits not being then understood, the phenomenon was ascribed to a wrong cause. Adam Smith considered profits to be determined by what he called the competition of capital. In Adam Smith's opinion, the manner in which the competition of capital lowers profits is by lowering prices; that being usually the mode in which an increased investment of capital in any particular trade lowers the profits of that trade. But, if this was his meaning, he overlooked the circumstance that the fall of price, which, if confined to one commodity, really does lower the profits of the producer, ceases to have that effect as soon as it extends to all commodities; because, when all things have fallen, nothing has really fallen, except nominally; and, even computed in money, the expenses of every producer have diminished as much as his returns. Unless, indeed, labor be the one commodity which has not fallen in money price, when all other things have: if so, what has really taken place is a rise of wages; and it is that, and not the fall of prices, which has lowered the profits of capital. There is another thing which escaped the notice of Adam Smith; that the supposed universal fall of prices, through increased competition of capitals, is a thing which can not take place. Prices are not determined by the competition of the sellers only, but also by that of the buyers; by demand as well as supply. The demand which affects money prices consists of all the money in the hands of the community destined to be laid out in commodities; and, as long as the proportion of this to the commodities is not diminished, there is no fall of general prices. Now, howsoever capital may increase, and give rise to an increased production of commodities, a full share of the capital will be drawn to the business of producing or importing money, and the quantity of money will be augmented in an equal ratio with the quantity of commodities. For, if this were not the case, and if money, therefore, were, as the theory supposes, perpetually acquiring increased purchasing power, those who produced or imported it would obtain constantly increasing profits; and this could not happen without attracting labor and capital to that occupation from other employments. If a general fall of prices and increased value of money were really to occur, it could only be as a consequence of increased cost of production, from the gradual exhaustion of the mines.

It is not tenable, therefore, in theory, that the increase of capital produces, or tends to produce, a general decline of money prices. Neither is it true that any general decline of prices, as capital increased, has manifested itself in fact. The only things observed to fall in price with the progress of society are those in which there have been improvements in production, greater than have taken place in the production of the precious metals; as, for example, all spun and woven fabrics. Other things, again, instead of falling, have risen in price, because their cost of production, compared with that of gold and silver, has increased. Among these are all kinds of food, comparison being made with a much earlier period of history. The doctrine, therefore, that competition of capital lowers profits by lowering prices, is incorrect in fact, as well as unsound in principle.

Mr. Wakefield, in his Commentary on Adam Smith, and his important writings on Colonization, takes a much clearer view of the subject, and arrives, through a substantially correct series of deductions, at practical conclusions which appear to me just and important. Mr. Wakefield's explanation of the fall of profits is briefly this: Production is limited not solely by the quantity of capital and of labor, but also by the extent of the "field of employment." The field of employment for capital is twofold: the land of the country, and the capacity of foreign markets to take its manufactured commodities. On a limited extent of land, only a limited quantity of capital can find employment at a profit. As the quantity of capital approaches this limit, profit falls; when the limit is attained, profit is annihilated, and can only be restored through an extension of the field of employment, either by the acquisition of fertile land, or by opening new markets in foreign countries, from which food and materials can be purchased with the products of domestic capital.[300]

§ 2. What determines the minimum rate of Profit?

There is at every time and place some particular rate of profit which is the lowest that will induce the people of that country and time to accumulate savings, and to employ those savings productively. This minimum rate of profit varies according to circumstances. It depends on two elements: One is the strength of the effective desire of accumulation; the comparative estimate, made by the people of that place and era, of future interests when weighed against present. This element chiefly affects the inclination to save. The other element, which affects not so much the willingness to save as the disposition to employ savings productively, is the degree of security of capital engaged in industrial operations. In employing any funds which a person may possess as capital on his own account, or in lending it to others to be so employed, there is always some additional risk over and above that incurred by keeping it idle in his own custody. This extra risk is great in proportion as the general state of society is insecure: it may be equivalent to twenty, thirty, or fifty per cent, or to no more than one or two; something however, it must always be; and for this the expectation of profit must be sufficient to compensate.

There would be adequate motives for a certain amount of saving, even if capital yielded no profit. There would be an inducement to lay by in good times a provision for bad; to reserve something for sickness and infirmity, or as a means of leisure and independence in the latter part of life, or a help to children in the outset of it. Savings, however, which have only these ends in view, have not much tendency to increase the amount of capital permanently in existence. The savings by which an addition is made to the national capital usually emanate from the desire of persons to improve what is termed their condition in life, or to make a provision for children or others, independent of their exertions. Now, to the strength of these inclinations it makes a very material difference how much of the desired object can be effected by a given amount and duration of self-denial; which again depends on the rate of profit. And there is in every country some rate of profit below which persons in general will not find sufficient motive to save for the mere purpose of growing richer, or of leaving others better off than themselves. Any accumulation, therefore, by which the general capital is increased, requires as its necessary condition a certain rate of profit—a rate which an average person will deem to be an equivalent for abstinence, with the addition of a sufficient insurance against risk.

I have already observed that this minimum rate of profit, less than which is not consistent with the further increase of capital, is lower in some states of society than in others; and I may add that the kind of social progress characteristic of our present civilization tends to diminish it: (1.) In the first place, one of the acknowledged effects of that progress is an increase of general security. Destruction by wars and spoliation by private or public violence are less and less to be apprehended. The risks attending the investment of savings in productive employment require, therefore, a smaller rate of profit to compensate for them than was required a century ago, and will hereafter require less than at present. (2.) In the second place, it is also one of the consequences of civilization that mankind become less the slaves of the moment, and more habituated to carry their desires and purposes forward into a distant future. This increase of providence is a natural result of the increased assurance with which futurity can be looked forward to; and is, besides, favored by most of the influences which an industrial life exercises over the passions and inclinations of human nature. In proportion as life has fewer vicissitudes, as habits become more fixed, and great prizes are less and less to be hoped for by any other means than long perseverance, mankind become more willing to sacrifice present indulgence for future objects. But, though the minimum rate of profit is liable to vary, and though to specify exactly what it is would at any given time be impossible, such a minimum always exists; and, whether it be high or low, when once it is reached, no further increase of capital can for the present take place. The country has then attained what is known to political economists under the name of the stationary state.

§ 3. In old and opulent countries, profits habitually near to the minimum.

We now arrive at the fundamental proposition which this chapter is intended to inculcate. When a country has long possessed a large production, and a large net income to make savings from, and when, therefore, the means have long existed of making a great annual addition to capital (the country not having, like America, a large reserve of fertile land still unused), it is one of the characteristics of such a country that the rate of profit is habitually within, as it were, a hand's breadth of the minimum, and the country, therefore, on the very verge of the stationary state. My meaning is, that it would require but a short time to reduce profits to the minimum, if capital continued to increase at its present rate, and no circumstances having a tendency to raise the rate of profit occurred in the mean time.

In England, the ordinary rate of interest on government securities, in which the risk is next to nothing, may be estimated at a little more than three per cent: in all other investments, therefore, the interest or profit calculated upon (exclusively of what is properly a remuneration for talent or exertion) must be as much more than this amount as is equivalent to the degree of risk to which the capital is thought to be exposed. Let us suppose that in England even so small a net profit as one per cent, exclusive of insurance against risk, would constitute a sufficient inducement to save, but that less than this would not be a sufficient inducement. I now say that the mere continuance of the present annual increase of capital, if no circumstance occurred to counteract its effect, would suffice in a small number of years to reduce the rate of net profit to one per cent.

To fulfill the conditions of the hypothesis, we must suppose an entire cessation of the exportation of capital for foreign investment. We must suppose the entire savings of the community to be annually invested in really productive employment within the country itself, and no new channels opened by industrial inventions, or by a more extensive substitution of the best-known processes for inferior ones.

The difficulty in finding remunerative employment every year for so much new capital would not consist in any want of a market. If the new capital were duly shared among many varieties of employment, it would raise up a demand for its own produce, and there would be no cause why any part of that produce should remain longer on hand than formerly. What would really be, not merely difficult, but impossible, would be to employ this capital without submitting to a rapid reduction of the rate of profit.

As capital increased, population either would also increase, or it would not. If it did not, wages would rise, and a greater capital would be distributed in wages among the same number of laborers. There being no more labor than before, and no improvements to render the labor more efficient, there would not be any increase of the produce; and, as the capital, however largely increased, would only obtain the same gross return, the whole savings of each year would be exactly so much subtracted from the profits of the next and of every following year.

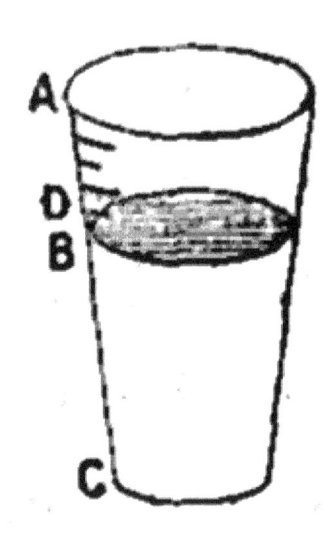

This can be illustrated by supposing that the whole capital is handed out to the producers in a vessel which

- 448 -

is returned full at the end of the period of production with the original outlay, plus an advance called profit. B C represents the total outlay, A C the total produce, and A B the profit on B C. Now, since the conditions of production remain the same, the same number of laborers can produce, as before, no more than A C; even though in the second year some of last year's profit, represented by D B, is saved and added to the outlay by the capitalist. If D C is now the outlay of capital, the profit can only be A C, minus D C, or A D; that is, the profit of the second year is diminished by D B, exactly the amount of savings of the year before. And this would be repeated each successive year, each saving added to B C being "exactly so much subtracted from the profits of the next and of every following year."

It is hardly necessary to say that in such circumstances profits would very soon fall to the point at which further increase of capital would cease. An augmentation of capital, much more rapid than that of population, must soon reach its extreme limit, unless accompanied by increased efficiency of labor (through inventions and discoveries, or improved mental and physical education), or unless some of the idle people, or of the unproductive laborers, became productive.

If population did increase with the increase of capital and in proportion to it, the fall of profits would still be inevitable. Increased population implies increased demand for agricultural produce. In the absence of industrial improvements, this demand can only be supplied at an increased cost of production, either by cultivating worse land, or by a more elaborate and costly cultivation of the land already under tillage. The cost of the laborer's subsistence is therefore increased, and, unless the laborer submits to a deterioration of his condition, profits must fall. In an old country like England, if, in addition to supposing all improvement in domestic agriculture suspended, we suppose that there is no increased production in foreign countries for the English market, the fall of profits would be very rapid. If both these avenues to an increased supply of food were closed, and population continued to increase, as it is said to do, at the rate of a thousand a day, all waste land which admits of cultivation in the existing state of knowledge would soon be cultivated, and the cost of production and price of food would be so increased that, if the laborers received the increased money wages necessary to compensate for their increased expenses, profits would very soon reach the minimum. The fall of profits would be retarded if money wages did not rise, or rose in a less degree; but the margin which can be gained by a deterioration of the laborers' condition is a very narrow one: in general, they *can not* bear much reduction; when they can, they have also a higher standard of necessary requirements, and *will* not. On the whole, therefore, we may assume that in such a country as England, if the present annual amount of savings were to continue, without any of the counteracting circumstances which now keep in check the natural influence of those savings in reducing profit, the rate of profit would speedily attain the minimum, and all further accumulation of capital would for the present cease.

> Mr. Carey, on the other hand, asserts the existence of a law of increasing returns from land, and that, while wages are constantly increasing with the progress of society, there is a diminution in the rate of profit, although the increasing returns permit an increase of absolute, if not of proportional, profit. That is, although wages increase more in proportion than profit, there is still a larger gross amount to be divided among capitalists as profit, out of a larger product.

§ 4. —prevented from reaching it by commercial revulsions.

What, then, are these counteracting circumstances which, in the existing state of things, maintain a tolerably equal struggle against the downward tendency of profits, and prevent the great annual savings which take place in this country from depressing the rate of profit much nearer to that lowest point to which it is always tending, and which, left to itself, it would so promptly attain? The resisting agencies are of several kinds.

First among them is the waste of capital in periods of overtrading and rash speculation, and in the commercial revulsions by which such times are always followed. Mines are opened, railways or bridges made, and many other works of uncertain profit commenced, and in these enterprises much capital is sunk which yields either no return, or none adequate to the outlay. Factories are built and machinery erected beyond what the market requires, or can keep in employment. Even if they are kept in employment, the capital is no less sunk; it has been converted from circulating into fixed capital, and has ceased to have any influence on wages or profits. Besides this, there is a great unproductive consumption of capital during the stagnation which follows a period of general overtrading. Establishments are shut up, or kept working without any profit. Such are the effects of a commercial revulsion; and that such revulsions are almost periodical is a consequence of the very tendency of profits which we are considering. By the time a few years have passed over without a crisis, so much additional capital has been accumulated that it is no longer possible to invest it at the accustomed profit; all public securities rise to a high price, the rate of interest on the best mercantile security falls very low, and the complaint is general among persons in business that no money is to be made. But the diminished scale of all safe gains inclines persons to give a ready ear to any projects which hold out, though at the risk of loss, the hope of a higher rate of profit; and speculations ensue, which, with the subsequent revulsions, destroy, or transfer to foreigners, a considerable amount of capital, produce a temporary rise of interest and profit, make room for fresh accumulations, and the same round is recommenced.

This, doubtless, is one considerable cause which arrests profits in their descent to the minimum, by sweeping away from time to time a part of the accumulated mass by which they are forced down. But this is not, as might be inferred from the language of some writers, the principal cause. If it were, the capital of the country would not increase; but in England it does increase greatly and rapidly. This is shown by the increasing productiveness of almost all taxes, by the continual growth of all the signs of national wealth, and by the rapid increase of population, while the condition of the laborers certainly is not on the whole declining.[301]

§ 5. —by improvements in Production.

This brings us to the second of the counter-agencies, namely, improvements in production. These evidently have the effect of extending what Mr. Wakefield terms the field of employment, that is, they enable a greater amount of capital to be accumulated and employed without depressing the rate of profit; provided always that they do not raise, to a proportional extent, the habits and requirements of the laborer. If the laboring-class gain the full advantage of the increased cheapness, in other words, if money wages do not fall, profits are not raised, nor their fall retarded. But, if the laborers people up to the improvement in their condition, and so relapse to their previous state, profits will rise. All inventions which cheapen any of the things consumed by the laborers, unless their requirements are raised in an equivalent degree, in time lower money wages, and, by doing so, enable a greater capital to be accumulated and employed, before profits fall back to what they were previously.

Improvements which only affect things consumed exclusively by the richer classes do not operate precisely in the same manner. The cheapening of lace or velvet has no effect in diminishing the cost of labor; and no mode can be pointed out in which it can raise the rate of profit, so as to make room for a larger capital before the minimum is attained. It, however, produces an effect which is virtually equivalent; it lowers, or tends to lower, the minimum itself. In the first place, increased cheapness of articles of consumption promotes the inclination to save, by affording to all consumers a surplus which they may lay by, consistently with their accustomed manner of living. In the next place, whatever enables people to live equally well on a smaller income inclines them to lay by capital for a lower rate of profit. If people can live on an independence of [$1,000] a year in the same manner as they formerly could on one of [$2,000], some persons will be induced to save in hopes of the one, who would have been deterred by the more remote prospect of the other. All improvements, therefore, in the production of almost any commodity tend in some degree to widen the interval which has to be passed before arriving at the stationary state.

§ 6. —by the importation of cheap Necessaries and Implements.

Equivalent in effect to improvements in production is the acquisition of any new power of obtaining cheap commodities from foreign countries. If necessaries are cheapened, whether they are so by improvements at home or importation from abroad, is exactly the same thing to wages and profits. Unless the laborer obtains and, by an improvement of his habitual standard, keeps the whole benefit, the cost of labor is lowered and the rate of profit raised. As long as food can continue to be imported for an increasing population without any diminution of cheapness, so long the declension of profits through the increase of population and capital is arrested, and accumulation may go on without making the rate of profit draw nearer to the minimum. And on this ground it is believed by some that the repeal of the corn laws has opened to [England] a long era of rapid increase of capital with an undiminished rate of profit.

Before inquiring whether this expectation is reasonable, one remark must be made, which is much at variance with commonly received notions. Foreign trade does not necessarily increase the field of employment for capital. When foreign trade makes room for more capital at the same profit, it is by enabling the necessaries of life, or the habitual articles of the laborer's consumption, to be obtained at smaller cost. It may do this in two ways: by the importation either of those commodities themselves, or of the means and appliances for producing them. Cheap iron has, in a certain measure, the same effect on profits and the cost of labor as cheap corn, because cheap iron makes cheap tools for agriculture and cheap machinery for clothing. But a foreign trade, which neither directly nor by any indirect consequence increases the cheapness of anything consumed by the laborers, does not, any more than an invention or discovery in the like case, tend to raise profits or retard their fall; it merely substitutes the production of goods for foreign markets in the room of the home production of luxuries, leaving the employment for capital neither greater nor less than before.

It must, of course, be supposed that, with the increase of capital, population also increases; for, if it did not, the consequent rise of wages would bring down profits, in spite of any cheapness of food. Suppose, then, that the population of Great Britain goes on increasing at its present rate, and demands every year a supply of imported food considerably beyond that of the year preceding. This annual increase in the food demanded from the exporting countries can only be obtained either by great improvements in their agriculture, or by the application of a great additional capital to the growth of food. The former is likely to be a very slow process, from the rudeness and ignorance of the agricultural classes in the food-exporting countries of Europe, while the British colonies and the United States are already in possession of most of the improvements yet made, so far as suitable to their circumstances. There remains, as a resource, the extension of cultivation. And on this it is to be remarked that the capital by which any such extension can take place is mostly still to be created. In Poland, Russia, Hungary, Spain, the increase of capital is extremely slow. In America it is rapid, but not more rapid than the population. The principal fund at present available for supplying this country with a yearly increasing importation of food is that portion of the annual savings of America which has heretofore been applied to increasing the manufacturing establishments of the United States, and which free trade in corn may possibly divert from that purpose to growing food for our market. This limited source of supply, unless great improvements take place in agriculture, can not be expected to keep pace with the growing demand of so rapidly increasing a population as that of Great Britain; and, if our population and capital continue to increase with their present rapidity, the only mode in which food can continue to be supplied cheaply to the one is by sending the other abroad to produce it.

Chart XVII. *Grain-Crops of the United States.*

Year.	Bushels.
1865	1,127,499,187
1866	1,343,027,868
1867	1,329,729,400
1868	1,450,789,000
1869	1,491,412,100
1870	1,629,027,600
1871	1,528,776,100
1872	1,664,331,600
1873	1,538,892,891
1874	1,455,180,200
1875	2,032,235,300
1876	1,962,821,600
1877	2,178,934,646
1878	2,302,254,950
1879	2,434,884,541
1880	2,448,079,181
1881	2,699,394,496
1882	2,699,394,496
1883	2,623,319,089

Not even Americans have any adequate knowledge of the productive capacity of the United States. The grainfields are not yet all occupied; and we can easily produce the total cotton consumption of the world on that quantity of land in Texas alone by which the whole cultivable area of that State exceeds the corresponding area of the empire of Austria-Hungary (see Chart No. XVIII, which shows the remarkable proportion of land possessed by the United States as compared with European countries); and the exports of agricultural food from the United States are now six times what they were in 1850, about the time when Mr. Mill made the above statements. Immense areas of our soil have not yet been broken by the plow, and the quantities of cereals grown in the United States seem to be steadily increasing. In fact, the greatest grain-crop yet grown in this country was that of 1882. The comparison of the crops of late years with those just succeeding the war (as seen in Chart No. XVII) shows a very suggestive increase; since it indicates where employment has been given to vast numbers of laborers, and where investment has been found for our rapidly growing capital.[302]

§ 7. —by the emigration of Capital.

This brings us to the last of the counter-forces which check the downward tendency of profits in a country whose capital increases faster than that of its neighbors, and whose profits are therefore nearer to the minimum. This is, the perpetual overflow of capital into colonies or foreign countries, to seek higher profits than can be obtained at home. I believe this to have been for many years one of the principal causes by which the decline of profits in England has been arrested. It has a twofold operation: In the first place, it does what a fire, or an inundation, or a commercial crisis would have done—it carries off a part of the increase of capital from which the reduction of profits proceeds; secondly, the capital so carried off is not lost, but is chiefly employed either in founding colonies, which become large exporters of cheap agricultural produce, or in extending and perhaps improving the agriculture of older communities.

In countries which are further advanced in industry and population, and have therefore a lower rate of profit, than others, there is always, long before the actual minimum is reached, a practical minimum, viz., when profits have fallen so much below what they are elsewhere that, were they to fall lower, all further accumulations would go abroad. As long as there are old countries where capital increases very rapidly, and new countries where profit is still high, profits in the old countries will not sink to the rate which would put a stop to accumulation: the fall is stopped at the point which sends capital abroad.

Chapter IV. Consequences Of The Tendency Of Profits To A Minimum, And The Stationary State.

§ 1. Abstraction of Capital not necessarily a national loss.

The theory of the effect of accumulation on profits must greatly abate, or rather, altogether destroy, in countries where profits are low, the immense importance which used to be attached by political economists to the effects which an event or a measure of government might have in adding to or subtracting from the capital of the country. We have now seen that the lowness of profits is a proof that the spirit of accumulation is so active, and that the increase of capital has proceeded at so rapid a rate, as to outstrip the two counter-agencies, improvements in production and increased supply of cheap necessaries from abroad. A sudden abstraction of capital, unless of inordinate amount, [would not] have any real effect in impoverishing the country. After a few months or years, there would exist in the country just as much capital as if none had been taken away. The abstraction, by raising profits and interest, would give a fresh stimulus to the accumulative principle, which would speedily fill up the vacuum. Probably, indeed, the only effect that would ensue would be that for some time afterward less capital would be exported, and less thrown away in hazardous speculation.

In the first place, then, this view of things greatly weakens, in a wealthy and industrious country, the force of the economical argument against the expenditure of public money for really valuable, even though industriously unproductive, purposes. In poor countries, the capital of the country requires the legislator's sedulous care; he is bound to be most cautious of encroaching upon it, and should favor to the utmost its accumulation at home, and its introduction from abroad. But in rich, populous, and highly cultivated countries, it is not capital which is the deficient element, but fertile land; and what the legislator should desire and promote, is not a greater aggregate saving, but a greater return to savings, either by improved cultivation, or by access to the produce of more fertile lands in other parts of the globe.

The same considerations enable us to throw aside as unworthy of regard one of the common arguments against emigration as a means of relief for the laboring-class. Emigration, it is said, can do no good to the laborers, if, in order to defray the cost, as much must be taken away from the capital of the country as from its population. If one tenth of the laboring people of England were transferred to the colonies, and along with them one tenth of the circulating capital of the country, either wages, or profits, or both, would be greatly benefited, by the diminished pressure of capital and population upon the fertility of the land. The landlords alone would sustain some loss of income; and even they, only if colonization went to the length of actually diminishing capital and population, but not if it merely carried off the annual increase.

§ 2. In opulent countries, the extension of machinery not detrimental but beneficial to Laborers.

From the same principles we are now able to arrive at a final conclusion respecting the effects which machinery, and generally the sinking of capital for a productive purpose, produce upon the immediate and ultimate interests of the laboring-class. The characteristic property of this class of industrial improvements is the conversion of circulating capital into fixed: and it was shown in the first book[303] that, in a country where capital accumulates slowly, the introduction of machinery, permanent improvements of land, and the like, might be, for the time, extremely injurious; since the capital so employed might be directly taken from the wages fund, the subsistence of the people and the employment for labor curtailed, and the gross annual produce of the country actually diminished. But in a country of great annual savings and low profits no such effects need be apprehended. It merely draws off at one orifice what was already flowing out at another; or, if not, the greater vacant space left in the reservoir does but cause a greater quantity to flow in. Accordingly, in spite of the mischievous derangements of the money market which have been occasioned by the great sums in process of being sunk in railways, I can not agree with those who apprehend any mischief, from this source, to the productive resources of the country. Not on the absurd ground (which to any one acquainted with the elements of the subject needs no confutation) that railway expenditure is a mere transfer of capital from hand to hand, by which nothing is lost or destroyed. This is true of what is spent in the purchase of the land; a portion too of what is paid to agents, counsels, engineers, and surveyors, is saved by those who receive it, and becomes capital again: but what is laid out in the *bona fide* construction of the railway itself is lost and gone; when once expended, it is incapable of ever being paid in wages or applied to the maintenance of laborers again; as a matter of account, the result is, that so much food and clothing and tools have been consumed, and the country has got a railway instead.

It already appears, from these considerations, that the conversion of circulating capital into fixed, whether by railways, or manufactories, or ships, or machinery, or canals, or mines, or works of drainage and irrigation, is not likely, in any rich country, to diminish the gross produce or the amount of employment for labor. There is hardly any increase of fixed capital which does not enable the country to contain eventually a larger circulating capital than it otherwise could possess and employ within its own limits; for there is hardly any creation of fixed capital which, when it proves successful, does not cheapen the articles on which wages are habitually expended.

> As regards the effects upon the material condition of the wages-receiving class, since it seems clear that capital increases faster than improvements, and probably faster even than population, it follows that in countries where the laboring-classes are evidently growing in intelligence, they gain in wages with the progress of society. Such certainly seems to be the teaching of Mr. Giffen's late studies (see Book IV, Chap. III, § 5).

§ 3. Stationary state of wealth and population dreaded by some writers, but not in itself undesirable.

Toward what ultimate point is society tending by its industrial progress? When the progress ceases, in what condition are we to expect that it will leave mankind?

It must always have been seen, more or less distinctly, by political economists, that the increase of wealth is not boundless; that at the end of what they term the progressive state lies the stationary state, that all progress in wealth is but a postponement of this, and that each step in advance is an approach to it. We have now been led to recognize that this ultimate goal is at all times near enough to be fully in view; that we are always on the verge of it, and that, if we have not reached it long ago, it is because the goal itself flies before us. The richest and most prosperous countries would very soon attain the stationary state, if no further improvements were made in the productive arts, and if there were a suspension of the overflow of capital from those countries into the uncultivated or ill-cultivated regions of the earth. Adam Smith always assumes that the condition of the mass of the people, though it may not be positively distressed, must be pinched and stinted in a stationary condition of wealth, and can only be satisfactory in a progressive state. The doctrine that, to however distant a time incessant struggling may put off our doom, the progress of society must "end in shallows and in miseries," far from being, as many people still believe, a wicked invention of Mr. Malthus, was either expressly or tacitly affirmed by his most distinguished predecessors, and can only be successfully combated on his principles.

Even in a progressive state of capital, in old countries, a conscientious or prudential restraint on population is indispensable, to prevent the increase of numbers from outstripping the increase of capital, and the condition of the classes who are at the bottom of society from being deteriorated. Where there is not, in the people, or in some very large proportion of them, a resolute resistance to this deterioration—a determination to preserve an established standard of comfort—the condition of the poorest class sinks, even in a progressive state, to the lowest point which they will consent to endure. The same determination would be equally effectual to keep up their condition in the stationary state, and would be quite as likely to exist.

I can not, therefore, regard the stationary state of capital and wealth with the unaffected aversion so generally manifested toward it by political economists of the old school. I am inclined to believe that it would be, on the whole, a very considerable improvement on our present condition.

It is only in the backward countries of the world that increased production is still an important object; in those most advanced, what is economically needed is a better distribution, of which one indispensable means is a stricter restraint on population. On the other hand, we may suppose this better distribution of property attained, by the joint effect of the prudence and frugality of individuals, and of a system of legislation favoring equality of fortunes, so far as is consistent with the just claim of the individual to the fruits, whether great or small, of his or her own industry. We may suppose, for instance (according to the suggestion thrown out in a former chapter[304]), a limitation of the sum which any one person may acquire by gift or inheritance, to the amount sufficient to constitute a moderate independence. Under this twofold influence, society would exhibit these leading features: a well-paid and affluent body of laborers; no enormous fortunes, except what were earned and accumulated during a single lifetime; but a much larger body of persons than at present, not only exempt from the coarser toils, but with sufficient leisure, both physical and mental, from mechanical details, to cultivate freely the graces of life, and afford examples of them to the classes less favorably circumstanced for their growth. This condition of society, so greatly preferable to the present, is not only perfectly compatible with the stationary state, but, it would seem, more naturally allied with that state than with any other.

There is room in the world, no doubt, and even in old countries, for a great increase of population, supposing the arts of life to go on improving, and capital to increase. But even if innocuous, I confess I see very little reason for desiring it. The density of population necessary to enable mankind to obtain, in the greatest degree, all the advantages both of co-operation and of social intercourse, has, in all the most populous countries, been attained. If the earth must lose that great portion of its pleasantness which it owes to things that the unlimited increase of wealth and population would extirpate from it, for the mere purpose of enabling it to support a larger but not a better or a happier population, I sincerely hope, for the sake of posterity, that they will be content to be stationary, long before necessity compels them to it.

It is scarcely necessary to remark that a stationary condition of capital and population implies no stationary state of human improvement. Even the industrial arts might be as earnestly and as successfully cultivated, with this sole difference, that instead of serving no purpose but the increase of wealth, industrial improvements would produce their legitimate effect, that of abridging labor. Hitherto it is questionable if all the mechanical inventions yet made have lightened the day's toil of any human being. They have enabled a greater population to live the same life of drudgery and imprisonment, and an increased number of manufacturers and others to make fortunes. They have increased the comforts of the middle classes.

> The statement that inventions have not "lightened the day's toil of any human being" has been persistently misquoted by many persons and has been taken out of its connection. Mr. Mill distinctly holds that the laborer's lot could have been improved had there been any limitation of population; that it is the constant growth of population as society progresses which destroys the gains afforded to the laboring-classes by improvements. But it is quite certain that the material facts of Mr. Mill's statement are no longer true. In the United States wages have risen, with an additional gain in lower prices; and Mr. Giffen shows the same progress in England. Moreover, travelers on the Continent speak of a similar movement already noticeable there. Mr. Giffen's statement in his comparison[305] with fifty years ago, is as follows:

"While the money wages have increased as we have seen, the hours of labor have diminished. It is difficult to estimate what the extent of this diminution has been, but collecting one or two scattered notices I should be inclined to say very nearly 20 per cent. There has been at least this reduction in the textile, engineering, and house-building trades. The workman gets from 50 to 100 per cent more money for 20 per cent less work; in round figures he has gained from 70 to 120 per cent in fifty years in money return. It is just possible, of course, that the workman may do as much, or nearly as much, in the shorter period as he did in his longer hours. Still, there is the positive gain in his being less time at his task, which many of the classes still tugging lengthily day by day at the oar would appreciate."

Chapter V. On The Possible Futurity Of The Laboring-Classes.

§ 1. The possibility of improvement while Laborers remain merely receivers of Wages.

There has probably never been a time when more attention has been called to the material and social conditions of the working-classes than in the last few years. The great increase of literature and the extension of the newspaper has brought to every reader, even where public and private charities have not sent eye-witnesses into direct contact with distress, a more explicit knowledge of the working-classes than ever before. The revelation of existing poverty and misery is, often wrongly, taken to be a proof of the increasing degradation of the working-men, and the cause has been ascribed to the grasping cruelty of capitalists. Instances of injustice arising from the relations of employers and employed will occur so long as human nature remains imperfect. But the world hopes that some other relation than that of master and workman may be evolved in which not only many admitted wrongs may be avoided, but also new forces may be applied to raise the laborer out of his dependence on other classes in the community.

We are, at present, living under a *régime* of private property and competition. But certainly the progress of the laborer is not that which can excite enthusiastic hopes for the future, so long as he remains a mere receiver of wages. The progress of industrial improvements has resulted, says Mr. Cairnes, in "a temporary improvement of the laborer's condition, followed by an increase of population and an enlarged demand for the cheapened commodity.... Laborers' commodities, however, are for the most part commodities of raw produce, or in which the raw material constitutes the chief element of the value (clothing is, in truth, the only important exception); and of all such commodities it is the well-known law that an augmentation of quantity can only be obtained, other things being the same, at an increasing proportional cost. Thus, it has happened that the gain in productiveness obtained by improved processes has, after a generation, to a great extent been lost—lost, that is to say, for any benefit that can be derived from it in favor of wages and profits.... The large addition to the wealth of the country has gone neither to profits nor to wages, nor yet to the public at large [as consumers], but to swell a fund ever growing even while its proprietors sleep—the rent-roll of the owners of the soil.... The aggregate return from the land has immensely increased; but the cost of the costliest portion of the produce, which is that which determines the price of the whole, remains pretty nearly as it was. Profits, therefore, have not risen at all, and the real remuneration of the laborer, taking the whole field of labor, in but a slight degree—at all events in a degree very far from commensurate with the general progress of industry."[306]

Under these conditions, it seems that the only hope of an improvement for the laboring-classes lies in the limitation of population—or at least in an increase of numbers less than the increase of capital and improvements. It is possible, however, that Mr. Cairnes, with many others, has failed to recognize the full extent of the improvement which is taking place in the wages of the laborer under the existing social order. Although we hear much of the wrongs of the working-men—and they no doubt exist—yet it is unquestionable that their condition has vastly improved within the last fifty years; largely, in my opinion, because improvements have outstripped population, and because wide areas of fertile land in new and peaceful countries have drawn off the surplus population in the older countries, and because the available spots in the newer countries like the United States have not yet been covered over with a population sufficiently dense to keep real wages

- 463 -

anything below a relatively high standard. The facts to substantiate this opinion, so far as regards Great Britain, are to be found in a recent investigation[307] by Mr. Giffen, the statistician of the English Board of Trade. For a very considerable reduction in hours of daily labor, the workman now receives wages on an average about 70 per cent higher than fifty years ago, as may be seen by the following table:

Occupation.	Place.	Wages fifty years ago, per week.	Wages, present time, per week.	Increase or decrease, amount, per cent.
Carpenters	Manchester	24 0	34 0	10 0 (+) 42
	Glasgow	14 0	26 0	12 0 (+) 85
Bricklayers	Manchester[308] 24 0	36 0	12 0 (+) 50
	Glasgow	15 0	27 0	12 0 (+) 80
Masons	Manchester[309] 24 0	29 10	5 10 (+) 24
	Glasgow	14 0	23 8	9 8 (+) 69
Miners	Staffordshire	2 8[310]	4 0[311]	1 4 (+) 50
Pattern-weavers	Huddersfield	16 0	25 0	9 0 (+) 55
Wool-scourers	"	17 0	22 0	5 0 (+) 30
Mule-spinners	"	25 6	30 0	4 6 (+) 20
Weavers	"	12 0	26 0	14 0 (+) 115
Warpers and beamers	"	17 0	27 0	10 0 (+) 58
Winders and reelers	"	6 0	11 0	5 0 (+) 83
Weavers (men)	Bradford	8 3	20 6	12 3 (+) 150

Reeling and warping	"	7 9	15 6	7 9 (+) 100
Spinning (children)	"	4 5	11 6	7 1 (+) 160

With increased wages, prices are not much higher than fifty years ago. But the clearest evidence as to their bettered material condition is to be found in the following table, which shows the amount of food consumed per head by the total population of Great Britain:

Articles.	1840.	1881.
Bacon and hams, Pounds.	0.01	13.93
Butter, Pounds.	1.05	6.36
Cheese, Pounds.	0.92	5.77
Currants and raisins, Pounds.	1.45	4.34
Eggs, No.	3.63	21.65
Potatoes, Pounds.	0.01	12.5
Rice, Pounds.	0.90	16.32
Cocoa, Pounds.	0.08	0.31
Coffee, Pounds.	1.08	0.89
Corn, wheat, and wheat-flour, Pounds.	42.47	216.92
Raw sugar, Pounds.	15.20	58.92
Refined sugar, Pounds.	Nil.	8.44
Tea, Pounds.	1.22	4.58
Tobacco, Pounds.	0.86	1.41
Wine, Gallons.	0.25	0.45
Spirits, Gallons.	0.97	1.08

Malt, Bushels.   1.59   1.91[312]

The question then at once arises, whether capital has been shown by the statistics to have gained accordingly, or whether there has been a proportionally less increase than in wages. Says Mr. Giffen: "If the return to capital had doubled, as the wages of the working-classes appear to have doubled, the aggregate income of the capitalist classes returned to the income-tax would now be £800,000,000 instead of £400,000,000.... The capitalist, as such, gets a low interest for his money, and the aggregate returns to capital is not a third part of the aggregate income of the country, which may be put at not less than £1,200,000,000." It is found, moreover—as a suggestion that property is more generally diffused—that while there were 25,368 estates entered to probate in 1838, of an average value of £2,160 each, there were 55,359 estates in 1882 of an average value of £2,500 each.

But yet the vast increase of wealth made possible by improvements and the growth of capital would have bettered the condition of all still more had population been somewhat more limited. As it is, the material gain has been large in spite of an increase in the population from 16,500,000 in 1831 to nearly 30,000,000 in 1881. In other words, the landlords have been great gainers, while the laborers have intercepted much more than Mr. Cairnes supposed.

There are at hand some very striking data relating to the United States which point in the same direction as those of Mr. Giffen. Charts No. XIX and XX show vividly how far the increased productiveness of an industry, arising from greater skill and greater efficiency of labor in the connection of improved machinery, has enabled manufacturers to steadily lower the price of their goods, and yet increase the wages paid to their operatives. What was true of these two cotton-mills was true of others within New England; for the rate of wages paid by these mills was the rate current in the country in 1830 and in 1884. While each spindle and loom has become vastly more effective, we see by Chart No. XIX that the average production of each operative constantly increased from 4,321 yards per year in 1830, to 28,032 yards in 1884; and this it was which made possible the corresponding increase in the rate of wages from $164 in 1830, to $290 in 1884. The sum of $290 a year as an average for each operative, is a stipend too small to cause any general satisfaction; but he must be gloomy indeed who does not see that $290 is a cheerful possession as compared with $164. There is, then, abundant ground for believing that in the past fifty years the condition of the working-classes in the United States has been materially improved. The diminishing proportion of the price which goes to the capital is a significant fact, and illustrates the tendency of profits to fall with the increase of capital.[313] The same truth seems to be seen in the table given in a previous chapter,[314] where the wages have been increased, but the hours have fallen per day from thirteen to eleven since 1840.

§ 2.—through small holdings, by which the landlord's gain is shared.

So far we have considered the chances for improvement in an industrial order in which the present separation of capitalists from laborers is maintained. But this does not take into account that future time when cultivation in the United States shall be forced down upon inferior land, and no more remains to be occupied, and when capital may no longer increase as fast as population. What must be the ultimate outlook for wages-receivers? Or, more practically, what is the outlook now for those who are wages-receivers, and for whom a more equitable distribution of the product seems desirable? How can they escape the thralldom of dependence on the accumulations of others?

In this connection, and of primary importance, is the avenue opened to all holders of small properties to share in the increase which goes to owners of land. It has been seen that owners of the soil constantly gain from the inevitable tendencies of industrial progress. If one large owner gains, why should not the increment be the same if ten owners held the property instead of one? The more the land is subdivided, the more the vast increase arising from rent will be shared by a larger number. This, in my opinion, is the strongest reason for the encouragement of small holdings in every country. The greater the extension of small properties among the working-class, the more will they gain a share of that part of the product which goes to the owner of land by the persistent increase of population. If, then, the gain arising from improvements is largely passed to the credit of land-owners, as Mr. Cairnes believes, it should be absolutely necessary to spread among the working-classes the doctrine that if they own their own homes, and buy the land they live on, to that extent will they "grow rich while they sleep," independently of their other exertions. Land worth $500 to-day when bought by the savings of a laborer, besides the self-respect[315] it gives him, will increase in value with the density of population, and become worth $600 or more without other sacrifice of his.

§ 3. —through co-operation, by which the manager's wages are shared.

It will be found, however, that, of the various industrial rewards, profits tend to diminish, meaning by "profits" only the interest and insurance given for abstinence and risk in the use of capital; but that the manager's wages (wages of superintendence) are larger than is commonly supposed in relation to other industrial rewards, owing to the position of monopoly practically held by such executive ability as is competent to successfully manage large business interests. To the laborer this large payment to the manager seems to be paid for the possession of capital. This we now know to be wrong. The manager's wages are payments of exactly the same nature as any laborer's wages. It makes no difference whether wages are paid for manual or mental labor. The payment to capital, purely as such, known as interest (with insurance for risk), is unmistakably decreasing, even in the United States. And yet we see men gain by industrial operations enormous rewards; but these returns are in their essence solely manager's wages. For in many instances, as hitherto discussed, we have seen that the manager is not the owner of the capital he employs. To what does this lead us? Inevitably to the conclusion that the laborer, if he would become something more than a receiver of wages, in the ordinary sense, must himself move up in the scale of laborers until he reaches the skill and power also to command manager's wages. The importance of this principle to the working-man can not be exaggerated, and there flows from it important consequences to the whole social condition of the lower classes. It leads us directly to the means by which the lower classes may raise themselves to a higher position—the actual details of which, of course, are difficult, but, as they are not included in political economy, they must be left to sociology—and forms the essential basis of hope for any proper extension of productive co-operation. In short, co-operation owes its existence to the possibility of dividing the manager's wages, to a greater or less degree, among the so-called wages-receivers, or the "laboring-class." And it is from this point of view that co-operation is seen more truly and fitly than in any other way. For it is to be said that in some of its forms co-operation gives the most promising economic results as regards the condition of the laborer which have yet been reached in the long discussion upon the relations of labor and capital.

§ 4. Distributive Co-operation.

It will be my object, then, to describe the chief forms in which the co-operative principle has manifested itself. These may be said, in general, to be four: (1) distributive co-operation, by which goods already produced are bought and sold to members without the aid of retail dealers; (2) productive co-operation, by which associations are formed for producing and manufacturing goods for the market; (3) partial productive co-operation in the form of industrial partnerships between laborers and employers, without dispensing with the latter; and (4) co-operative, or People's, banks. There are, of course, many other forms in which the principle of co-operation has been applied; but these four are probably the most characteristic.

Distributive co-operation is at once the simplest and the most successful form, not merely because it requires less for capital than any other for its inception, but also because it calls for less business and executive capacity. The number of persons capable of managing a small retail store is vastly greater than the class fit to assume control of the very complex duties involved in the care of wholesale houses—or, at all events, of mills and factories. Distributive co-operation has its origin in the fact that the expenses of a middle-man between the producer and consumer may be entirely dispensed with, and in the fact that more capital had collected in the business of distribution than could economically be so employed. Its educating power on the men concerned in teaching them to save, in showing the need of business methods, and in instilling the elements of industrial management, is of no little importance. It is, therefore, the best gateway to any further or more difficult co-operative experiments—such experiments as can be attempted only after the proper capital is saved, and the necessary executive capacity is discovered, or developed by training. In England co-operation began its history in distributive stores, and has finally led to such a stimulus of self-help in the laborer, that now co-operative gymnasiums, libraries, gardens, and other results have proved the wisdom of calling upon the laborers for their own exertions. Under the system which separates employers and the employed, high wages are not found to be the only boon which the receivers could wish; for it is sometimes found that the best-paid workmen are the most unwise and intemperate.[316] For the most ignorant and unskilled of the workmen in the lowest strata the object would seem to be to give not merely more wages, but give more in such a way as might excite new and better motives, a desire as well as a possibility of improvement. Self-help must be stimulated, not deadened by stifling dependence on a class of superiors, or on the state. The extraordinary growth of co-operation is one of the most cheering signs of modern times. Distributive co-operation originated in Rochdale, in England, about 1844, with a few laborers desirous of saving themselves from the high prices paid for poor provisions. By uniting, they purchased tea by the chest, sugar by the hogshead, which they sold to each member at market prices. They were surprised to find a large profit by the operation, which they divided proportionally to the capital subscribed. Others soon joined them; they took a store-room, and in 1882 there were 10,894 members, with a share capital of $1,576,215, and with realized profits in that year of $162,885. They have erected expensive steam flour-mills, and the society occupies eighteen branch establishments in Rochdale. Libraries containing more than 15,000 volumes, and classes in science, language, and the technical arts, attended by 500 students, have been maintained. The extension of the Rochdale store led to the necessity of a wholesale establishment of their own. It is now a large institution with branches in London and Newcastle. "It owns manufactories in London, Manchester, Newcastle, Leicester, Durham, and Crumpsall; and it has depots in Cork, Limerick, Kilmallock, Waterford, Tipperary, Tralee, and Armagh, for the purchase of butter, potatoes, and eggs. It has buyers in New York and Copenhagen, and it owns two steamships. It has a banking department with a turn-over of more than £12,000,000 annually."[317]

The following figures for England and Wales tell their own story as to the progress of co-operation:[318]

1862. 1881.

Number of members 90,000   525,000

Capital: Share	428,000	5,881,000
Capital: Loan	55,000	1,267,000
Sales	2,333,000	20,901,000
Net profit	165,000	1,617,000

Several persons each subscribe a sum to make up the share capital of a store, and a person is selected to take charge of the purchase and care of the goods. The advantages of the plan are: (1) A division among the co-operators of all the net profits of the retail trade; (2) a saving in advertisements, since members are always purchasers without solicitation; (3) no loss by bad debts, since only cash sales are permitted; and (4) security against fraud as to the character of the goods, because there is no inducement to make gains by adulterations. It is often found that the capital is turned over ten times in the course of a year; while the cost of management in the wholesale Rochdale stores does not amount to one per cent on the returns.

The arrangement of obligations in due order of their priority, which has been recommended by Mr. Holyoake,[319] is as follows: of funds in the store, payment should be made, (1) of the expenses of management; (2) of interest due on all loans; (3) of an amount equivalent to ten per cent of the value of the fixed stock to cover the annual depreciation from wear and tear; (4) of dividends on the subscribed capital of the members;[320] (5) of such a sum as may be necessary for an extension of the business; (6) of two and a half per cent of the remaining profit, after all the above items are provided for, for educational purposes; (7) of the residue, and that only, among all the persons employed, and members of the store, in proportion to the amount of their wages, or of their respective purchases during the quarter.[321] The payment of dividends to customers on their purchases seems now to be considered an essential element of success.

§ 5. Productive Co-Operation.

Productive co-operation presents many serious difficulties, the chief of which is the need of managing ability. Some one in the association must know the wholesale markets well, the expectation of crops connected with his materials used, the proper time to buy; he must know the processes of the special production thoroughly, the best machinery, the best adaptation of labor to the given end; he must know the whims of purchasers, and be ready to change his products accordingly—in short, a man eminently fitted for success in his own factory is essential to the profitable management of one belonging to a body of co-operators. It has been already seen how large a variation in profit is due to manager's wages; and it is very often only his skill, prudence, and experience that make the difference between a failure and a success in business. Unless co-operators are willing to pay as large a sum for the services of a good manager as he could get in his own establishment, they can not secure the talent which will make their venture succeed.[322]

In France the national workshops of Louis Blanc, established in 1848, were a failure. Nowhere has it been more clearly seen that state help has been disastrous than in France, where the Constituent Assembly voted 3,000,000 francs for co-operative experiments, all of which failed. Curiously enough, distributive co-operation has not succeeded in France, because, owing to a wide-spread dislike of the wages system, workmen will try nothing less than productive schemes. And their success in this has been no greater than might be expected, when inexperience is put to a task beyond its powers.[323]

In Great Britain and the United States there have been some successful experiments in production; and Mr. Holyoake[324] holds that, although workmen certainly do begrudge the manager's salary, productive associations are possible when managed by a board of elected directors. He urges, moreover, that, as in distributive co-operation, if profits are shared with customers, there will be insured both popularity and continuity of custom without the cost of advertising, and such expenses as those of travelers and commissions. The plan of actual operations upon which successes have been reached in England seems to be briefly this: (1) To save capital, chiefly through co-operative associations; (2) to purchase or lease premises; (3) to engage managers, accountants, and officers at the ordinary salaries which such men can command in the market according to their ability; (4) to borrow capital on the credit of the association; (5) to pay upon capital subscribed by members the same rate of interest as that upon borrowed capital; (6) to regard as profit only that which remains after making payment for rent, materials, wages, all business outlays, and interest on capital; and (7) to divide the profits according to the salaries of all officers, wages of workmen, and purchases of customers. Those mills and factories which have sprung out of the extension of distributive associations, as at Rochdale, seem, and naturally so, to have been most successful. They have gradually trained themselves somewhat for the work, and their customers were beforehand secured. That is, where the difficulties of the manager's function have been lessened, they have a better chance of success. And yet it must be said that productive associations will gain largely from the efficiency of the labor when working for its own interest; and this is an important consideration to be urged in favor of such associations.

The Sun Mill,[325] at Oldham, England, was established for spinning cotton in 1861 by the exertions of some co-operative bodies. Beginning with a share capital of $250,000, and a loan capital of a like amount, it set 80,000 spindles in operation. In 1874 they had a share capital of $375,000 (all subscribed except $1,000), and an equal amount of loan capital, while the whole plant was estimated as worth $615,000. Two and a half per cent per annum has been set apart for the depreciation in the value of the mill, and seven and a half per cent for the machinery; so that in the first ten years a total sum of $160,000 was set aside for depreciation of the property. The profits have varied from two to forty per cent; and, while only five per cent interest was paid on the loan capital, large dividends were made on the share capital. During the last few years the Sun Mill has on an average realized a profit of 12-½ per cent, although it is known that the cotton trade has suffered during this time from a serious depression.

Many experiments, however, have proved failures; and sometimes, when they are successful (as in the case of the Hatters' Association in Newark, New Jersey[326]), the workmen have no desire to share their benefits with others, and practically form a corporation by themselves. The mere fact that they do sometimes succeed is an important thing. Then, too, they have an opportunity of securing by salaries that executive ability in the community which exists separate from the possession of capital. And in these days, in large corporations, the manager is not necessarily (although he often is) a large owner of capital. The last annual report of the Co-operative Congress (1882) shows the existence in England and Scotland of productive associations for the manufacture of cloth, flannel, fustian, hosiery, quilts, worsted, nails, watches, linen, and silk, as well as those for engineering, printing, and quarrying; and these were but a few of them.[327]

In the United States there have been some successes as well as failures. In January, 1872, a number of machinists and other working-men organized in the town of Beaver Falls, Pennsylvania, a Co-operative Foundry Association for the manufacture of stoves, hollow-ware, and fine castings. On a small capital of only $4,000 they have steadily prospered, paid the market rate of wages, and also paid annual dividends, over and above all expenses and interest on the plant, of from twelve to fifteen per cent. In 1867 thirty workmen started a co-operative foundry in Somerset, Massachusetts, with a capital of about $14,000. In the years 1874-1875 the company spent $5,400 for new flasks and patterns, and yet showed a net gain of $11,914. In 1876 it had a capital of $30,000, and a surplus fund of $28,924.[328]

§ 6. Industrial Partnership.

The difficulties of productive co-operation arising from the need of skilled management, together with the existing unsatisfactory relation between employers and laborers when wholly separate from each other, have led to a most promising plan of industrial partnership by which the manager retains the control of the business operations, but shares his profits with the workmen. The gain through increased efficiency, greater economy, and superior workmanship, recoups the manager for the voluntary subtraction from his share, and yet the laborers receive an additional share; but more than this, it educates the laborer in industrial methods, discloses the difficulties of management, and stimulates him to saving habits and greater regularity of work. This system is particularly adapted to reaching those laborers who would not themselves rise to the demands of productive co-operation.

The principle was tried on one of the Belgian railways. "Ninety-five kilogrammes of coke were consumed for every league of distance run, but this was known to be more than necessary; but how to remedy the evil was the problem. A bonus of 3-½d. on every hectolitre of coke saved on this average of ninety-five to the league was offered to the men concerned, and this trifling bonus worked the miracle. The work was done equally well, or better, with forty-eight kilogrammes of coke instead of ninety-five; just one half, or nearly, saved by careful work, at an expense of probably less than one tenth of the saving."[329]

The experiment which has attracted most attention in the past has been that of the Messrs. Briggs, at their collieries in Yorkshire, England.[330] The relations between the owners and the laborers were as bad as they could well be. "All coal-masters is devils, and Briggs is the prince of devils," ran the talk of the miners, when they did not choose to send letters threatening to shoot the owners. In 1865 Messrs. Briggs tried the plan of an industrial partnership with their men, purely from business considerations.

Seventy per cent of the cost of raising coal consisted of wages, and fully fifteen per cent of materials which were habitually wasted. The whole property was valued, and divided into shares of $50 each, of which the owners retained two thirds, together with the control of the business. The remaining one third of the shares was offered to the employés. If any subscriber was too poor to pay $50 for a share, the subsequent dividends and payments were to be applied to purchasing the share. After reserving a fair allowance for expenses, like the redemption of capital, whenever the remaining profits exceeded ten per cent on the capital, that excess was to be divided into two equal parts, one of which was to be distributed among all persons employed by the company in proportion to their wages, and the other was to be retained by the capital. In previous years but once had they made ten per cent profit on their capital, and twice only five per cent. In the first year after the new system came into operation, the total profits were fourteen per cent, and the four per cent of excess was divided, two to the laborers' bonus, and two to the capital, so that capital received twelve per cent. In the second year the profits were sixteen per cent, in the third year seventeen per cent; the first year the work-people received in addition to their wages $9,000, in the second $13,500, in the third $15,750. The moral effect was striking. Work was done regularly, forbearance was exercised, habits improved, and the faces of the men were set toward improvement in life. The scheme worked successfully for years, but was finally ended by the pressure of the outside trades-unions, who compelled the workmen to give up the arrangement.

A similar experiment was tried by the Messrs. Brewster, carriage-manufacturers, of New York. They offered to their workmen ten per cent of their profits, before any allowance was made for interest on the capital invested, or before any payment was made for the services of the firm as managers. In one year as much as $11,000 was divided among the laborers. Again, as in the case of the Briggs colliery, the experiment was brought to an end by an unreasoning submission to the pressure of outside workmen during a strike.[331]

But, all in all, industrial partnership[332] offers a great field for that kind of improvement which is worth more than a mere increase of wages, and seems to make it possible to reach the heavy weight of sluggishness among the lower and more hopeless strata of society. And it is possible that it will stir in them the powers which may afterward find employment in the harder problems of productive co-operation.[333]

§ 7. People's Banks.

In Germany the struggle between the two theories—self-help and state-help—was fought out by Schultze-Delitsch—that is, Schultze of Delitsch, a town in Saxony—and Lasalle, and the victory given to the former. Schultze-Delitsch, as a consequence, was successful in directing the co-operative principle in Germany to giving workmen credit in purchasing tools, etc., when he had no security but his character. This form of co-operation works to give the energetic and industrious workmen a lever by which, through the possession of credit, they can raise themselves to the position of small capitalists, and thus widen the field of possible improvement. While the former schemes of co-operation described above have given the wages-receivers a share of the unearned increment from land, and tend to give them a share of the manager's wages, the plan of Schultze was to assist them to gain a share in the advantages belonging to the possession of capital. The capital was to be accumulated by their own exertions, and, in his scheme depended on the principle of self-help. The following is the plan of banks adopted:

"Every member is obliged to make a certain weekly payment into the common stock. As soon as it reaches a certain sum he is allowed to raise a loan exceeding his share in the inverse ratio of the amount of his deposit. For instance, after he has deposited one dollar, he is allowed to borrow five or six; but, if he had deposited twenty dollars, he is allowed only to borrow thirty. The security he is compelled to offer is his own and that of two other members of the association, who become jointly and severally liable. He may have no assets whatever beyond the amount of his deposits, nor may his guarantors; the bank relies simply on the character of the three, and the two securities rely on the character of their principal; and the remarkable fact is, that the security has been found sufficient, that the interest of the men in the institutions and the fear of the opinion of their fellows has produced a display of honesty and punctuality such as perhaps is not to be found in the history of any other banking institutions. Such is the confidence inspired by these institutions that they hold on deposit, or as loans from third parties, an amount exceeding by more than three fourths the total amount of their own capital. The monthly contributions of the members may be as low as ten cents, but the amount which each member is allowed to have in some banks is not more than seven or eight dollars, in none more than three hundred dollars. He has a right to borrow to the full amount of his deposit without giving security; if he desires to borrow a larger sum, he must furnish security in the manner we have described. The liability of the members is unlimited. The plan of limiting the liability to the amount of the capital deposited was tried at first, but it inspired no confidence, and the enterprise did not succeed till every member was made generally liable. Each member, on entering, is obliged to pay a small fee, which goes toward forming or maintaining a reserve fund, apart from the active capital. The profits are derived from the interest paid by borrowers, which amounts to from eight to ten per cent, which may not sound very large in our ears, but in Germany is very high. Not over five per cent is paid on capital borrowed from outsiders. All profits are distributed in dividends among the members of the association, in the proportion of the amount of their deposits—after the payment of the expenses of management, of course—and the apportionment of a certain percentage to the reserve-fund. Every member, as we have said, has a right to borrow to the extent of his deposit without security; but then, if he seeks to borrow more, whether he shall obtain any loan, and, if so, how large a one, is decided by the board of management, who are guided in making their decision just as all bank officers are—by a consideration of the circumstances of the bank as well as those of the borrower. All the affairs of the association are discussed and decided in the last resort by a general assembly composed of all the members."[334] The main part of the capital loaned by the banks is obtained from outside sources on the credit of the associations. In 1865 there were 961 of these institutions in Germany; in 1877 there were 1,827, with over 1,000,000 members, owning $40,000,000 of capital, with $100,000,000 more on loan, and doing a business of $550,000,000.[335]

Book V. On The Influence Of Government.

Chapter I. On The General Principles Of Taxation.

§ 1. Four fundamental rules of Taxation.

One of the most disputed questions, both in political science and in practical statesmanship at this particular period, relates to the proper limits of the functions and agency of governments.

We shall first consider the economical effects arising from the manner in which governments perform their necessary and acknowledged functions.

We shall then pass to certain governmental interferences of what I have termed the optional kind (i.e., overstepping the boundaries of the universally acknowledged functions) which have heretofore taken place, and in some cases still take place, under the influence of false general theories.

The first of these divisions is of an extremely miscellaneous character: since the necessary functions of government, and those which are so manifestly expedient that they have never or very rarely been objected to, are too various to be brought under any very simple classification. We commence, [under] the first head, with the theory of Taxation.

The qualities desirable, economically speaking, in a system of taxation, have been embodied by Adam Smith in four maxims or principles, which, having been generally concurred in by subsequent writers, may be said to have become classical, and this chapter can not be better commenced than by quoting them:[336]

"1. The subjects of every state ought to contribute to the support of the government, as nearly as possible in proportion to their respective abilities: that is, in proportion to the revenue which they respectively enjoy under the protection of the state. In the observation or neglect of this maxim consists what is called the equality or inequality of taxation.

"2. The tax which each individual is bound to pay ought to be certain, and not arbitrary. The time of payment, the manner of payment, the quantity to be paid, ought all to be clear and plain to the contributor, and to every other person. The certainty of what each individual ought to pay is, in taxation, a matter of so great importance, that a very considerable degree of inequality, it appears, I believe, from the experience of all nations, is not near so great an evil as a very small degree of uncertainty.

"3. Every tax ought to be levied at the time, or in the manner, in which it is most likely to be convenient for the contributor to pay it. Taxes upon such consumable goods as are articles of luxury are all finally paid by the consumer, and generally in a manner that is very convenient to him. He pays them little by little, as he has occasion to buy the goods. As he is at liberty, too, either to buy or not to buy, as he pleases, it must be his own fault if he ever suffers any considerable inconvenience from such taxes.

"4. Every tax ought to be so contrived as both to take out and to keep out of the pockets of the people as little as possible over and above what it brings into the public treasury of the state. A tax may either take out or keep out of the pockets of the people a great deal more than it brings into the public treasury in the four following ways: First, the levying of it may require a great number of officers, whose salaries may eat up the greater part of the produce of the tax, and whose perquisites may impose another additional tax upon the people." Secondly, it may divert a portion of the labor and capital of the community from a more to a less productive employment. "Thirdly, by the forfeitures and other penalties which those unfortunate individuals incur who attempt unsuccessfully to evade the tax it may frequently ruin them, and thereby put an end to the benefit which the community might have derived from the employment of their capitals. An injudicious tax offers a great temptation to smuggling. Fourthly, by subjecting the people to the frequent visits and the odious examination of the tax-gatherers it may expose them to much unnecessary trouble, vexation, and oppression": to which may be added that the restrictive regulations to which trades and manufactures are often subjected, to prevent evasion of a tax, are not only in themselves troublesome and expensive, but often oppose insuperable obstacles to making improvements in the processes.

§ 2. Grounds of the principle of Equality of Taxation.

The first of the four points, equality of taxation, requires to be more fully examined, being a thing often imperfectly understood, and on which many false notions have become to a certain degree accredited, through the absence of any definite principles of judgment in the popular mind.

For what reason ought equality to be the rule in matters of taxation? For the reason that it ought to be so in all affairs of government. A government ought to make no distinction of persons or classes in the strength of their claims on it. If any one bears less than his fair share of the burden, some other person must suffer more than his share. Equality of taxation, therefore, as a maxim of politics, means equality of sacrifice. It means apportioning the contribution of each person toward the expenses of government, so that he shall feel neither more nor less inconvenience from his share of the payment than every other person experiences from his. There are persons, however, who regard the taxes paid by each member of the community as an equivalent for value received, in the shape of service to himself; and they prefer to rest the justice of making each contribute in proportion to his means upon the ground that he who has twice as much property to be protected receives, on an accurate calculation, twice as much protection, and ought, on the principles of bargain and sale, to pay twice as much for it. Since, however, the assumption that government exists solely for the protection of property is not one to be deliberately adhered to, some consistent adherents of the *quid pro quo* principle go on to observe that protection being required for persons as well as property, and everybody's person receiving the same amount of protection, a poll-tax of a fixed sum per head is a proper equivalent for this part of the benefits of government, while the remaining part, protection to property, should be paid for in proportion to property. But, in the first place, it is not admissible that the protection of persons and that of property are the sole purposes of government. In the second place, the practice of setting definite values on things essentially indefinite, and making them a ground of practical conclusions, is peculiarly fertile in the false views of social questions. It can not be admitted that to be protected in the ownership of ten times as much property is to be ten times as much protected. If we wanted to estimate the degrees of benefit which different persons derive from the protection of government, we should have to consider who would suffer most if that protection were withdrawn: to which question, if any answer could be made, it must be, that those would suffer most who were weakest in mind or body, either by nature or by position.

§ 3. Should the same percentage be levied on all amounts of Income?

Setting out, then, from the maxim that equal sacrifices ought to be demanded from all, we have next to inquire whether this is in fact done, by making each contribute the same percentage on his pecuniary means. Many persons maintain the negative, saying that a tenth part taken from a small income is a heavier burden than the same fraction deducted from one much larger; and on this is grounded the very popular scheme of what is called a graduated property-tax, viz., an income-tax in which the percentage rises with the amount of the income.

On the best consideration I am able to give to this question, it appears to me that the portion of truth which the doctrine contains arises principally from the difference between a tax which can be saved from luxuries and one which trenches, in ever so small a degree, upon the necessaries of life. To take a thousand a year from the possessor of ten thousand would not deprive him of anything really conducive either to the support or to the comfort of existence; and, if such *would* be the effect of taking five pounds from one whose income is fifty, the sacrifice required from the last is not only greater than, but entirely incommensurable with, that imposed upon the first. The mode of adjusting these inequalities of pressure which seems to be the most equitable is that recommended by Bentham, of leaving a certain minimum of income, sufficient to provide the necessaries of life, untaxed. Suppose [$250] a year to be sufficient to provide the number of persons ordinarily supported from a single income with the requisites of life and health, and with protection against habitual bodily suffering, but not with any indulgence. This then should be made the minimum, and incomes exceeding it should pay taxes not upon their whole amount, but upon the surplus. If the tax be ten per cent, an income of [$300] should be considered as a net income of [$50], and charged with [$5] a year, while an income of [$5,000] should be charged as one of [$4,750]. An income not exceeding [$250] should not be taxed at all, either directly or by taxes on necessaries; for, as by supposition this is the smallest income which labor ought to be able to command, the government ought not to be a party to making it smaller.

Both in England and on the Continent a graduated property-tax (*l'impôt progressif*) has been advocated, on the avowed ground that the state should use the instrument of taxation as a means of mitigating the inequalities of wealth. I am as desirous as any one that means should be taken to diminish those inequalities, but not so as to relieve the prodigal at the expense of the prudent. To tax the larger incomes at a higher percentage than the smaller is to lay a tax on industry and economy; to impose a penalty on people for having worked harder and saved more than their neighbors. It is not the fortunes which are earned, but those which are unearned, that it is for the public good to place under limitation. With respect to the large fortunes acquired by gift or inheritance, the power of bequeathing is one of those privileges of property which are fit subjects for regulation on grounds of general expediency; and I have already suggested,[337] as the most eligible mode of restraining the accumulation of large fortunes in the hands of those who have not earned them by exertion, a limitation of the amount which any one person should be permitted to acquire by gift, bequest, or inheritance. I conceive that inheritances and legacies, exceeding a certain amount, are highly proper subjects for taxation; and that the revenue from them should be as great as it can be made without giving rise to evasions, by donation *inter vivos* or concealment of property, such as it would be impossible adequately to check. The principle of graduation (as it is called), that is, of levying a larger percentage on a larger sum, though its application to general taxation would be in my opinion objectionable, seems to me both just and expedient as applied to legacy and inheritance duties.

The objection to a graduated property-tax applies in an aggravated degree to the proposition of an exclusive tax on what is called "realized property," that is, property not forming a part of any capital engaged in business, or rather in business under the superintendence of the owner; as land, the public funds, money lent on mortgage, and shares in stock companies. Except the proposal of applying a sponge to the national debt, no such palpable violation of common honesty has found sufficient support in this country, during the present generation, to be regarded as within the domain of discussion. It has not the palliation of a graduated property-tax, that of laying the burden on those best able to bear it; for "realized property" includes the far larger portion of the provision made for those who are unable to work, and consists, in great part, of extremely small fractions. I can hardly conceive a more shameless pretension than that the major part of the property of the country, that of merchants, manufacturers, farmers, and shopkeepers, should be exempted from its share of taxation; that these classes should only begin to pay their proportion after retiring from business, and if they never retire should be excused from it altogether. But even this does not give an adequate idea of the injustice of the proposition. The burden thus exclusively thrown on the owners of the smaller portion of the wealth of the community would not even be a burden on that *class* of persons in perpetual succession, but would fall exclusively on those who happened to compose it when the tax was laid on. As land and those particular securities would thenceforth yield a smaller net income, relatively to the general interest of capital and to the profits of trade, the balance would rectify itself by a permanent depreciation of those kinds of property. Future buyers would acquire land and securities at a reduction of price, equivalent to the peculiar tax, which tax they would, therefore, escape from paying; while the original possessors would remain burdened with it even after parting with the property, since they would have sold their land or securities at a loss of value equivalent to the fee-simple of the tax. Its imposition would thus be tantamount to the confiscation for public uses of a percentage of their property equal to the percentage laid on their income by the tax.

> The above proposition has been extended, by those in the United States who appeal to class prejudice, to a proposal to tax the incomes of those who hold

government bonds. It so happened that, for example, the six dollars income on a one-hundred-dollar bond of the United States was not, in the war period, deemed a sufficient equivalent for the risk of loaning one hundred dollars to the state; and Congress, therefore, agreed to relieve them of taxation. It is the same thing to a lender if he receive six per cent directly from the Government, or if he receive seven per cent, and is obliged to pay back one per cent to the treasury in the form of taxation; but to the Government it is another thing, because if it sell a taxed bond at seven per cent interest, it does not receive back the whole of the one per cent tax, but the one per cent tax less the expense of levying it. In other words the Government, in the latter case, pays six per cent interest plus the cost of levying the tax; and consequently borrowed more cheaply in the form of an untaxed bond, as was the hope when the provision was made. If, then, a tax were now to be put upon the bonds, it would fall exclusively on the present holders of them; for, since it diminishes the net income from the bond, it lowers the selling price of the bond itself, as before explained.[338]

§ 4. Should the same percentage be levied on Perpetual and on Terminable Incomes?

Whether the profits of trade may not rightfully be taxed at a lower rate than incomes derived from interest or rent is part of the more comprehensive question whether life-incomes should be subjected to the same rate of taxation as perpetual incomes; whether salaries, for example, or annuities, or the gains of professions, should pay the same percentage as the income from inheritable property.

The existing tax [in England] treats all kinds of incomes exactly alike,[339] taking its [fivepence] in the pound as well from the person whose income dies with him as from the landholder, stockholder, or mortgagee, who can transmit his fortune undiminished to his descendants. This is a visible injustice; yet it does not arithmetically violate the rule that taxation ought to be in proportion to means. When it is said that a temporary income ought to be taxed less than a permanent one, the reply is irresistible that it is taxed less: for the income which lasts only ten years pays the tax only ten years, while that which lasts forever pays forever. The claim in favor of terminable incomes does not rest on grounds of arithmetic, but of human wants and feelings. It is not because the temporary annuitant has smaller means, but because he has greater necessities, that he ought to be assessed at a lower rate.

In spite of the nominal equality of income, A, an annuitant of £1,000 a year, can not so well afford to pay £100 out of it as B, who derives the same annual sum from heritable property; A having usually a demand on his income which B has not, namely, to provide by saving for children or others; to which, in the case of salaries or professional gains, must generally be added a provision for his own later years; while B may expend his whole income without injury to his old age, and still have it all to bestow on others after his death. If A, in order to meet these exigencies, must lay by £300 of his income, to take £100 from him as income-tax is to take £100 from £700, since it must be retrenched from that part only of his means which he can afford to spend on his own consumption. Were he to throw it ratably on what he spends and on what he saves, abating £70 from his consumption and £30 from his annual saving, then indeed his immediate sacrifice would be proportionally the same as B's; but then his children or his old age would be worse provided for in consequence of the tax. The capital sum which would be accumulated for them would be one tenth less, and on the reduced income afforded by this reduced capital they would be a second time charged with income-tax; while B's heirs would only be charged once.

The principle, therefore, of equality of taxation, interpreted in its only just sense, equality of sacrifice, requires that a person who has no means of providing for old age, or for those in whom he is interested, except by saving from income, should have the tax remitted on all that part of his income which is really and *bona fide* applied to that purpose.

If, indeed, reliance could be placed on the conscience of the contributors, or sufficient security taken for the correctness of their statements by collateral precautions, the proper mode of assessing an income-tax would be to tax only the part of income devoted to expenditure, exempting that which is saved. For when saved and invested (and all savings, speaking generally, are invested) it thenceforth pays income-tax on the interest or profit which it brings, notwithstanding that it has already been taxed on the principal. Unless, therefore, savings are exempted from income-tax, the contributors are twice taxed on what they save, and only once on what they spend. To tax the sum invested, and afterward tax also the proceeds of the investment, is to tax the same portion of the contributor's means twice over.

No income-tax is really just from which savings are not exempted; and no income-tax ought to be voted without that provision, if the form of the returns and the nature of the evidence required could be so arranged as to prevent the exemption from being taken fraudulent advantage of, by saving with one hand and getting into debt with the other, or by spending in the following year what had been passed tax-free as saving in the year preceding. But, if no plan can be devised for the exemption of actual savings, sufficiently free from liability to fraud, it is necessary, as the next thing in point of justice, to take into account, in assessing the tax, what the different classes of contributors *ought* to save. In fixing the proportion between the two rates, there must inevitably be something arbitrary; perhaps a deduction of one fourth in favor of life-incomes would be as little objectionable as any which could be made.

Of the net profits of persons in business, a part, as before observed, may be considered as interest on capital, and of a perpetual character, and the remaining part as remuneration for the skill and labor of superintendence. The surplus beyond interest depends on the life of the individual, and even on his continuance in business, and is entitled to the full amount of exemption allowed to terminable incomes.

§ 5. The increase of the rent of land from natural causes a fit subject of peculiar Taxation.

Suppose that there is a kind of income which constantly tends to increase, without any exertion or sacrifice on the part of the owners: those owners constituting a class in the community, whom the natural course of things progressively enriches, consistently with complete passiveness on their own part. In such a case it would be no violation of the principles on which private property is grounded, if the state should appropriate this increase of wealth, or part of it, as it arises. This would not properly be taking anything from anybody; it would merely be applying an accession of wealth, created by circumstances, to the benefit of society, instead of allowing it to become an unearned appendage to the riches of a particular class.

Now, this is actually the case with rent. The ordinary progress of a society which increases in wealth is at all times tending to augment the incomes of landlords; to give them both a greater amount and a greater proportion of the wealth of the community, independently of any trouble or outlay incurred by themselves. They grow richer, as it were, in their sleep, without working, risking, or economizing. What claim have they, on the general principle of social justice, to this accession of riches? In what would they have been wronged if society had, from the beginning, reserved the right of taxing the spontaneous increase of rent, to the highest amount required by financial exigencies? The only admissible mode of proceeding would be by a general measure. The first step should be a valuation of all the land in the country. The present value of all land should be exempt from the tax; but after an interval had elapsed, during which society had increased in population and capital, a rough estimate might be made of the spontaneous increase which had accrued to rent since the valuation was made. Of this the average price of produce would be some criterion: if that had risen, it would be certain that rent had increased, and (as already shown) even in a greater ratio than the rise of price. On this and other data, an approximate estimate might be made how much value had been added to the land of the country by natural causes; and in laying on a general land-tax, which for fear of miscalculation should be considerably within the amount thus indicated, there would be an assurance of not touching any increase of income which might be the result of capital expended or industry exerted by the proprietor.

With reference to such a tax, perhaps a safer criterion than either a rise of rents or a rise of the price of corn, would be a general rise in the price of land. It would be easy to keep the tax within the amount which would reduce the market value of land below the original valuation; and up to that point, whatever the amount of the tax might be, no injustice would be done to the proprietors.

> In 1870 Mr. Mill became President of the Land Tenure Association, one of whose objects was: "To claim for the benefit of the State the Interception by Taxation of the Future Unearned Increase of the Rent of Land (so far as the same can be ascertained), or a great part of that increase, which is continually taking place, without any effort or outlay by the proprietors, merely through the growth of population and wealth; reserving to owners the option of relinquishing their property to the state at the market value which it may have acquired at the time when this principle may be adopted by the Legislature." It is urged against this plan that, if the Government take for itself the increase from rent, it should also make compensation for loss arising from declining rents, whenever there happens to be any readjustment of values in land.[340]

§ 6. Taxes falling on Capital not necessarily objectionable.

In addition to the preceding rules, another general rule of taxation is sometimes laid down—namely, that it should fall on income and not on capital.

To provide that taxation shall fall entirely on income, and not at all on capital, is beyond the power of any system of fiscal arrangements. There is no tax which is not partly paid from what would otherwise have been saved; no tax, the amount of which, if remitted, would be wholly employed in increased expenditure, and no part whatever laid by as an addition to capital. All taxes, therefore, are in some sense partly paid out of capital; and in a poor country it is impossible to impose any tax which will not impede the increase of the national wealth. But, in a country where capital abounds and the spirit of accumulation is strong, this effect of taxation is scarcely felt. To take from capital by taxation what emigration would remove, or a commercial crisis destroy, is only to do what either of those causes would have done—namely, to make a clear space for further saving.

I can not, therefore, attach any importance, in a wealthy country, to the objection made against taxes on legacies and inheritances, that they are taxes on capital. It is perfectly true that they are so. As Ricardo observes, if £100 are taken from any one in a tax on houses or on wine, he will probably save it, or a part of it, by living in a cheaper house, consuming less wine, or retrenching from some other of his expenses; but, if the same sum be taken from him because he has received a legacy of £1,000, he considers the legacy as only £900, and feels no more inducement than at any other time (probably feels rather less inducement) to economize in his expenditure. The tax, therefore, is wholly paid out of capital; and there are countries in which this would be a serious objection. But, in the first place, the argument can not apply to any country which has a national debt and devotes any portion of revenue to paying it off, since the produce of the tax, thus applied, still remains capital, and is merely transferred from the tax-payer to the fund-holder. But the objection is never applicable in a country which increases rapidly in wealth.

Chapter II. Of Direct Taxes.

§ 1. Direct taxes either on income or expenditure.

Taxes are either direct or indirect. A direct tax is one which is demanded from the very persons who, it is intended or desired, should pay it. Indirect taxes are those which are demanded from one person in the expectation and intention that he shall indemnify himself at the expense of another: such as the excise or customs. The producer or importer of a commodity is called upon to pay tax on it, not with the intention to levy a peculiar contribution upon him, but to tax through him the consumers of the commodity, from whom it is supposed that he will recover the amount by means of an advance in price.

Direct taxes are either on income or on expenditure. Most taxes on expenditure are indirect, but some are direct, being imposed, not on the producer or seller of an article, but immediately on the consumer. A house-tax, for example, is a direct tax on expenditure, if levied, as it usually is, on the occupier of the house. If levied on the builder or owner, it would be an indirect tax. A window-tax is a direct tax on expenditure; so are the taxes on horses and carriages.

The sources of income are rent, profits, and wages. This includes every sort of income, except gift or plunder. Taxes may be laid on any one of the three kinds of income, or a uniform tax on all of them. We will consider these in their order.

§ 2. Taxes on rent.

A tax on rent falls wholly on the landlord. There are no means by which he can shift the burden upon any one else. It does not affect the value or price of agricultural produce, for this is determined by the cost of production in the most unfavorable circumstances, and in those circumstances, as we have so often demonstrated, no rent is paid.

This, however, is, in strict exactness, only true of the rent which is the result either of natural causes, or of improvements made by tenants. When the landlord makes improvements which increase the productive power of his land, he is remunerated for them by an extra payment from the tenant; and this payment, which to the landlord is properly a profit on capital, is blended and confounded with rent. A tax on rent, if extending to this portion of it, would discourage landlords from making improvements; but whatever hinders improvements from being made in the manner in which people prefer to make them, will often prevent them from being made at all; and on this account a tax on rent would be inexpedient unless some means could be devised of excluding from its operation that portion of the nominal rent which may be regarded as landlord's profit.

§ 3. —on profits.

A tax on profits, like a tax on rent, must, at least in its immediate operation, fall wholly on the payer. All profits being alike affected, no relief can be obtained by a change of employment. If a tax were laid on the profits of any one branch of productive employment, the tax would be virtually an increase of the cost of production, and the value and price of the article would rise accordingly; by which the tax would be thrown upon the consumers of the commodity, and would not affect profits. But a general and equal tax on all profits would not affect general prices, and would fall, at least in the first instance, on capitalists alone.

There is, however, an ulterior effect, which, in a rich and prosperous country, requires to be taken into account. It may operate in two different ways: (1.) The curtailment of profit, and the consequent increased difficulty in making a fortune or obtaining a subsistence by the employment of capital, may act as a stimulus to inventions, and to the use of them when made. If improvements in production are much accelerated, and if these improvements cheapen, directly or indirectly, any of the things habitually consumed by the laborer, profits may rise, and rise sufficiently to make up for all that is taken from them by the tax. In that case the tax will have been realized without loss to any one, the produce of the country being increased by an equal, or what would in that case be a far greater, amount. The tax, however, must even in this case be considered as paid from profits, because the receivers of profits are those who would be benefited if it were taken off.

But (2.) though the artificial abstraction of a portion of profits would have a real tendency to accelerate improvements in production, no considerable improvements might actually result, or only of such a kind as not to raise general profits at all, or not to raise them so much as the tax had diminished them. If so, the rate of profit would be brought closer to that practical minimum to which it is constantly approaching. At its first imposition the tax falls wholly on profits; but the amount of increase of capital, which the tax prevents, would, if it had been allowed to continue, have tended to reduce profits to the same level; and at every period of ten or twenty years there will be found less difference between profits as they are and profits as they would in that case have been, until at last there is no difference, and the tax is thrown either upon the laborer or upon the landlord. The real effect of a tax on profits is to make the country possess at any given period a smaller capital and a smaller aggregate production, and to make the stationary state be attained earlier, and with a smaller sum of national wealth.

Even in countries which do not accumulate so fast as to be always within a short interval of the stationary state, it seems impossible that, if capital is accumulating at all, its accumulation should not be in some degree retarded by the abstraction of a portion of its profit; and, unless the effect in stimulating improvements be a full counterbalance, it is inevitable that a part of the burden will be thrown off the capitalist, upon the laborer or the landlord. One or other of these is always the loser by a diminished rate of accumulation. If population continues to increase as before, the laborer suffers; if not, cultivation is checked in its advance, and the landlords lose the accession of rent which would have accrued to them. The only countries in which a tax on profits seems likely to be permanently a burden on capitalists exclusively are those in which capital is stationary, because there is no new accumulation. In such countries the tax might not prevent the old capital from being kept up through habit, or from unwillingness to submit to impoverishment, and so the capitalists might continue to bear the whole of the tax.

§ 4. —on Wages.

We now turn to Taxes on Wages. The incidence of these is very different, according as the wages taxed as those of ordinary unskilled labor, or are the remuneration of such skilled or privileged employments, whether manual or intellectual, as are taken out of the sphere of competition by a natural or conferred monopoly.

I have already remarked that, in the present low state of popular education, all the higher grades of mental or educated labor are at a monopoly price, exceeding the wages of common workmen in a degree very far beyond that which is due to the expense, trouble, and loss of time required in qualifying for the employment. Any tax levied on these gains, which still leaves them above (or not below) their just proportion, falls on those who pay it; they have no means of relieving themselves at the expense of any other class.

The same thing is true of ordinary wages, in cases like that of the United States, or of a new colony, where, capital increasing as rapidly as population can increase, wages are kept up by the increase of capital, and not by the adherence of the laborers to a fixed standard of comforts. In such a case, some deterioration of their condition, whether by a tax or otherwise, might possibly take place without checking the increase of population. The tax would in that case fall on the laborers themselves, and would reduce them prematurely to that lower state to which, on the same supposition with regard to their habits, they would in any case have been reduced ultimately, by the inevitable diminution in the rate of increase of capital, through the occupation of all the fertile land.

Some will object that, even in this case, a tax on wages can not be detrimental to the laborers, since the money raised by it, being expended in the country, comes back to the laborers again through the demand for labor. Without, however, reverting to general principles, we may rely on an obvious *reductio ad absurdum*. If to take money from the laborers and spend it in commodities is giving it back to the laborers, then, to take money from other classes, and spend it in the same manner, must be giving it to the laborers; consequently, the more a government takes in taxes, the greater will be the demand for labor, and the more opulent the condition of the laborers—a proposition the absurdity of which no one can fail to see.

In the condition of most communities, wages are regulated by the habitual standard of living to which the laborers adhere, and on less than which they will not multiply. Where there exists such a standard, a tax on wages will indeed for a time be borne by the laborers themselves; but, unless this temporary depression has the effect of lowering the standard itself, the increase of population will receive a check, which will raise wages, and restore the laborers to their previous condition. On whom, in this case, will the tax fall? A rise of wages occasioned by a tax must, like any other increase of the cost of labor, be defrayed from profits. To attempt to tax day-laborers, in an old country, is merely to impose an extra tax upon all employers of common labor; unless the tax has the much worse effect of permanently lowering the standard of comfortable subsistence in the minds of the poorest class.

We find in the preceding considerations an additional argument for the opinion, already expressed, that direct taxation should stop short of the class of incomes which do not exceed what is necessary for healthful existence. These very small incomes are mostly derived from manual labor; and, as we now see, any tax imposed on these, either permanently degrades the habits of the laboring-class, or falls on profits, and burdens capitalists with an indirect tax, in addition to their share of the direct taxes; which is doubly objectionable, both as a violation of the fundamental rule of equality, and for the reasons which, as already shown, render a peculiar tax on profits detrimental to the public wealth, and consequently to the means which society possesses of paying any taxes whatever.

§ 5. —on Income.

We now pass, from taxes on the separate kinds of income, to a tax attempted to be assessed fairly upon all kinds; in other words, an Income-Tax. The discussion of the conditions necessary for making this tax consistent with justice has been anticipated in the last chapter. We shall suppose, therefore, that these conditions are complied with. They are, first, that incomes below a certain amount should be altogether untaxed. This minimum should not be higher than the amount which suffices for the necessaries of the existing population. The second condition is, that incomes above the limit should be taxed only in proportion to the surplus by which they exceed the limit. Thirdly, that all sums saved from income and invested should be exempt from the tax; or, if this be found impracticable, that life-incomes and incomes from business and professions should be less heavily taxed than inheritable incomes.

An income-tax, fairly assessed on these principles, would be, in point of justice, the least exceptionable of all taxes. The objection to it, in the present state of public morality, is the impossibility of ascertaining the real incomes of the contributors. Notwithstanding, too, what is called the inquisitorial nature of the tax, no amount of inquisitorial power which would be tolerated by a people the most disposed to submit to it could enable the revenue officers to assess the tax from actual knowledge of the circumstances of contributors. Rents, salaries, annuities, and all fixed incomes, can be exactly ascertained. But the variable gains of professions, and still more the profits of business, which the person interested can not always himself exactly ascertain, can still less be estimated with any approach to fairness by a tax-collector. The main reliance must be placed, and always has been placed, on the returns made by the person himself. The tax, therefore, on whatever principles of equality it may be imposed, is in practice unequal in one of the worst ways, falling heaviest on the most conscientious.

It is to be feared, therefore, that the fairness which belongs to the principle of an income-tax can not be made to attach to it in practice. This consideration would lead us to concur in the opinion which, until of late, has usually prevailed—that direct taxes on income should be reserved as an extraordinary resource for great national emergencies, in which the necessity of a large additional revenue overrules all objections.

The difficulties of a fair income-tax have elicited a proposition for a direct tax of so much per cent, not on income but on expenditure; the aggregate amount of each person's expenditure being ascertained as the amount of income now is, from statements furnished by the contributors themselves. The only security would still be the veracity of individuals, and there is no reason for supposing that their statements would be more trustworthy on the subject of their expenses than on that of their revenues. The taxes on expenditure at present in force, either in this or in other countries, fall only on particular kinds of expenditure, and differ no otherwise from taxes on commodities than in being paid directly by the person who consumes or uses the article, instead of being advanced by the producer or seller, and reimbursed in the price. The taxes on horses and carriages, on dogs, on servants, are of this nature. They evidently fall on the persons from whom they are levied—those who use the commodity taxed. A tax of a similar description, and more important, is a house-tax, which must be considered at somewhat greater length.

§ 6. A House-Tax.

The rent of a house consists of two parts, the ground-rent, and what Adam Smith calls the building-rent. The first is determined by the ordinary principles of rent. It is the remuneration given for the use of the portion of land occupied by the house and its appurtenances; and varies from a mere equivalent for the rent which the ground would afford in agriculture to the monopoly rents paid for advantageous situations in populous thoroughfares. The rent of the house itself, as distinguished from the ground, is the equivalent given for the labor and capital expended on the building. The fact of its being received in quarterly or half-yearly payments makes no difference in the principles by which it is regulated. It comprises the ordinary profit on the builder's capital, and an annuity, sufficient at the current rate of interest, after paying for all repairs chargeable on the proprietor, to replace the original capital by the time the house is worn out, or by the expiration of the usual term of a building-lease.

A tax of so much per cent on the gross rent falls on both those portions alike. The more highly a house is rented, the more it pays to the tax, whether the quality of the situation or that of the house itself is the cause. The incidence, however, of these two portions of the tax must be considered separately.

As much of it as is a tax on building-rent must ultimately fall on the consumer, in other words, the occupier. For, as the profits of building are already not above the ordinary rate, they would, if the tax fell on the owner and not on the occupier, become lower than the profits of untaxed employments, and houses would not be built. It is probable, however, that for some time after the tax was first imposed, a great part of it would fall, not on the renter, but on the owner of the house. A large proportion of the consumers either could not afford, or would not choose, to pay their former rent with the tax in addition, but would content themselves with a lower scale of accommodation. Houses, therefore, would be for a time in excess of the demand. The consequence of such excess, in the case of most other articles, would be an almost immediate diminution of the supply; but so durable a commodity as houses does not rapidly diminish in amount. New buildings, indeed, of the class for which the demand had decreased, would cease to be erected, except for special reasons; but in the mean time the temporary superfluity would lower rents, and the consumers would obtain, perhaps, nearly the same accommodation as formerly, for the same aggregate payment, rent and tax together. By degrees, however, as the existing houses wore out, or as increase of population demanded a greater supply, rents would again rise; until it became profitable to recommence building, which would not be until the tax was wholly transferred to the occupier. In the end, therefore, the occupier bears that portion of a tax on rent which falls on the payment made for the house itself, exclusively of the ground it stands on.

The case is partly different with the portion which is a tax on ground-rent. As taxes on rent, properly so called, fall on the landlord, a tax on ground-rent, one would suppose, must fall on the ground-landlord, at least after the expiration of the building-lease. It will not, however, fall wholly on the landlord, unless with the tax on ground-rent there is combined an equivalent tax on agricultural rent. The lowest rent of land let for building is very little above the rent which the same ground would yield in agriculture: since it is reasonable to suppose that land, unless in case of exceptional circumstances, is let or sold for building as soon as it is decidedly worth more for that purpose than for cultivation. If, therefore, a tax were laid on ground-rents without being also laid on agricultural rents, it would, unless of trifling amount, reduce the return from the lowest ground-rents below the ordinary return from land, and would check further building quite as effectually as if it were a tax on building-rents, until either the increased demand of a growing population, or a diminution of supply by the ordinary causes of destruction, had raised the rent by a full equivalent for the tax. But whatever raises the lowest ground-rents raises all others, since each exceeds the lowest by the market value of its peculiar advantages. If, therefore, the tax on ground-rents were a fixed sum per square foot, the more valuable situations paying no more than those least in request, this fixed payment would ultimately fall on the occupier. Suppose the lowest ground-rent to be $50 per acre, and the highest $5,000, a tax of $5 per acre on ground-rents would ultimately raise the former to $55, and the latter consequently to $5,005, since the difference of value between the two situations would be exactly what it was before: the annual $5, therefore, would be paid by the occupier. But a tax on ground-rent is supposed to be a portion of a house-tax which is not a fixed payment, but a percentage on the rent. The cheapest site, therefore, being supposed as before to pay $5, the dearest would pay $500, of which only the $5 could be thrown upon the occupier, since the rent would still be only raised to $5,005. Consequently, $495 of the $500 levied from the expensive site would fall on the ground-landlord.[341] A house-tax thus requires to be considered in a double aspect, as a tax on all occupiers of houses, and a tax on ground-rents.

In the vast majority of houses the ground-rent forms but a small proportion of the annual payment made for the house, and nearly all the tax falls on the occupier. It is only in exceptional cases, like that of the favorite situations in large towns, that the predominant element in the rent of the house is the ground-rent; and, among the very few kinds of income which are fit subjects for peculiar taxation, these ground-rents hold the principal place, being the most gigantic example extant of enormous accessions of riches acquired rapidly, and in many cases unexpectedly, by a few families, from the mere accident of their possessing certain tracts of land without their having themselves aided in the acquisition by the smallest exertion, outlay, or risk. So far, therefore, as a house-tax falls on the ground-landlord, it is liable to no valid objection.

In so far as it falls on the occupier, if justly proportioned to the value of the house, it is one of the fairest and most unobjectionable of all taxes. No part of a person's expenditure is a better criterion of his means, or bears, on the whole, more nearly the same proportion to them. The equality of this tax can only be seriously questioned on two grounds. The first is, that a miser may escape it. This objection applies to all taxes on expenditure; nothing but a direct tax on income can reach a miser. The second objection is, that a person may require a larger and more expensive house, not from having greater means, but from having a larger family. Of this, however, he is not entitled to complain, since having a large family is at a person's own choice; and, so far as concerns the public interest, is a thing rather to be discouraged than promoted.[342]

A valuation should be made of the house, not at what it would sell for, but at what would be the cost of rebuilding it, and this valuation might be periodically corrected by an allowance for what it had lost in value by time, or gained by repairs and improvements. The amount of the amended valuation would form a principal sum, the interest of which, at the current price of the public funds, would form the annual value at which the building should be assessed to the tax.

As incomes below a certain amount ought to be exempt from income-tax, so ought houses below a certain value from house-tax, on the universal principle of sparing from all taxation the absolute necessaries of healthful existence. In order that the occupiers of lodgings, as well as of houses, might benefit, as in justice they ought, by this exemption, it might be optional with the owners to have every portion of a house which is occupied by a separate tenant valued and assessed separately.

Chapter III. Of Taxes On Commodities, Or Indirect Taxes.

§ 1. A Tax on all commodities would fall on Profits.

By taxes on commodities are commonly meant those which are levied either on the producers, or on the carriers or dealers who intervene between them and the final purchasers for consumption; the phrase being, by custom, confined to indirect taxes—those which are advanced by one person, to be, as is expected and intended, reimbursed by another.

Taxes on commodities are either on production within the country, or on importation into it, or on conveyance or sale within it, and are classed respectively as excise, customs, or tolls and transit duties. To whichever class they belong, and at whatever stage in the progress of the community they may be imposed, they are equivalent to an increase of the cost of production; using that term in its most enlarged sense, which includes the cost of transport and distribution, or, in common phrase, of bringing the commodity to market.

When the cost of production is increased artificially by a tax, the effect is the same as when it is increased by natural causes. If only one or a few commodities are affected, their value and price rise, so as to compensate the producer or dealer for the peculiar burden; but if there were a tax on all commodities, exactly proportioned to their value, no such compensation would be obtained; there would neither be a general rise of values, which is an absurdity, nor of prices, which depend on causes entirely different. There would, however, as Mr. McCulloch has pointed out, be a disturbance of values, some falling, others rising, owing to a circumstance, the effect of which on values and prices we formerly discussed—the different durability of the capital employed in different occupations. The gross produce of industry consists of two parts; one portion serving to replace the capital consumed, while the other portion is profit. Now, equal capital in two branches of production must have equal expectations of profit; but if a greater portion of the one than of the other is fixed capital, or if that fixed capital is more durable, there will be a less consumption of capital in the year, and less will be required to replace it, so that the profit, if absolutely the same, will form a greater proportion of the annual returns. To derive from a capital of $1,000 a profit of $100, the one producer may have to sell produce to the value of $1,100, the other only to the value of $500. If on these two branches of industry a tax be imposed of five per cent *ad valorem*, the last will be charged only with $25, the first with $55; leaving to the one $75 profit, to the other only $45. To equalize, therefore, their expectation of profit, the one commodity must rise in price, or the other must fall, or both.[343] Commodities made chiefly by immediate labor must rise in value, as compared with those which are chiefly made by machinery. It is unnecessary to prosecute this branch of the inquiry any further.

§ 2. Taxes on particular commodities fall on the consumer.

A tax on any one commodity, whether laid on its production, its importation, its carriage from place to place, or its sale, and whether the tax be a fixed sum of money for a given quantity of the commodity, or an *ad valorem* duty, will, as a general rule, raise the value and price of the commodity by at least the amount of the tax. There are few cases in which it does not raise them by more than that amount. In the first place, there are few taxes on production on account of which it is not found or deemed necessary to impose restrictive regulations on the manufacturers or dealers, in order to check evasions of the tax. These regulations are always sources of trouble and annoyance, and generally of expense, for all of which, being peculiar disadvantages, the producers or dealers must have compensation in the price of their commodity. These restrictions also frequently interfere with the processes of manufacture, requiring the producer to carry on his operations in the way most convenient to the revenue, though not the cheapest or most efficient for purposes of production. Any regulations whatever, enforced by law, make it difficult for the producer to adopt new and improved processes. Further, the necessity of advancing the tax obliges producers and dealers to carry on their business with larger capitals than would otherwise be necessary, on the whole of which they must receive the ordinary rate of profit, though a part only is employed in defraying the real expenses of production or importation. The price of the article must be such as to afford a profit on more than its natural value, instead of a profit on only its natural value. Neither ought it to be forgotten that whatever renders a larger capital necessary in any trade or business limits the competition in that business, and, by giving something like a monopoly to a few dealers, may enable them either to keep up the price beyond what would afford the ordinary rate of profit, or to obtain the ordinary rate of profit with a less degree of exertion for improving and cheapening their commodity. In these several modes, taxes on commodities often cost to the consumer, through the increased price of the article, much more than they bring into the treasury of the state. There is still another consideration: the higher price necessitated by the tax almost always checks the demand for the commodity; and, since there are many improvements in production which, to make them practicable, require a certain extent of demand, such improvements are obstructed, and many of them prevented altogether. It is a well-known fact that the branches of production in which fewest improvements are made are those with which the revenue-officer interferes; and that nothing, in general, gives a greater impulse to improvements in the production of a commodity than taking off a tax which narrowed the market for it.

§ 3. Peculiar effects of taxes on Necessaries.

Such are the effects of taxes on commodities, considered generally; but, as there are some commodities (those composing the necessaries of the laborer) of which the values have an influence on the distribution of wealth among different classes of the community, it is requisite to trace the effects of taxes on those particular articles somewhat further. If a tax be laid, say on corn, and the price rises in proportion to the tax, the rise of price may operate in two ways: First, it may lower the condition of the laboring-classes; temporarily, indeed, it can scarcely fail to do so. If it diminishes their consumption of the produce of the earth, or makes them resort to a food which the soil produces more abundantly, and therefore more cheaply, it to that extent contributes to throw back agriculture upon more fertile lands or less costly processes, and to lower the value and price of corn; which therefore ultimately settles at a price, increased not by the whole amount of the tax, but by only a part of its amount. Secondly, however, it may happen that the dearness of the taxed food does not lower the habitual standard of the laborer's requirements, but that wages, on the contrary, through an action on population, rise, in shorter or longer periods, so as to compensate the laborers for their portion of the tax, the compensation being of course at the expense of profits. Taxes on necessaries must thus have one of two effects: either they lower the condition of the laboring-classes, or they exact from the owners of capital, in addition to the amount due to the state on their own necessaries, the amount due on those consumed by the laborers. In the last case, the tax on necessaries, like a tax on wages, is equivalent to a peculiar tax on profits; which is, like all other partial taxation, unjust, and is specially prejudicial to the increase of the national wealth.

It remains to speak of the effect on rent. Assuming (what is usually the fact) that the consumption of food is not diminished, the same cultivation as before will be necessary to supply the wants of the community; the margin of cultivation, to use Dr. Chalmers's expression, remains where it was; and the same land or capital, which, as the least productive, already regulated the value and price of the whole produce, will continue to regulate them. The effect which a tax on agricultural produce will have on rent depends on its affecting or not affecting the difference between the return to this least productive land or capital and the returns to other lands and capitals. Now, this depends on the manner in which the tax is imposed. If it is an *ad valorem* tax, or, what is the same thing, a fixed proportion of the produce, such as tithe for example, it evidently lowers corn-rents. For it takes more corn from the better lands than from the worse, and exactly in the degree in which they are better, land of twice the productiveness paying twice as much to the tithe. Whatever takes more from the greater of two quantities than from the less, diminishes the difference between them. The imposition of a tithe on corn would take a tithe also from corn-rent: for, if we reduce a series of numbers by a tenth each, the differences between them are reduced one tenth.

For example, let there be five qualities of land, which severally yield, on the same extent of ground and with the same expenditure, 100, 90, 80, 70, and 60 bushels of wheat, the last of these being the lowest quality which the demand for food renders it necessary to cultivate. The rent of these lands will be as follows:

The land producing 100 bushels will yield a rent of 100-60, or 40 bushels.
That producing 90 bushels, a rent of 90-60, or 30 bushels.
That producing 80 bushels, a rent of 80-60, or 20 bushels.
That producing 70 bushels, a rent of 70-60, or 10 bushels.
That producing 60 bushels, will yield no rent.

Now let a tithe be imposed, which takes from these five pieces of land 10, 9, 8, 7, and 6 bushels respectively, the fifth quality still being the one which regulates the price, but returning to the farmer, after payment of tithe, no more than 54 bushels:

The land producing 100 bushels reduced to 90 will yield a rent of 90-54, or 36 bushels.
That producing 90 bushels reduced to 81, a rent of 81-54, or 27 bushels.
That producing 80 bushels reduced to 72, a rent of 72-54, or 18 bushels.
That producing 70 bushels reduced to 63, a rent of 63-54, or 9 bushels.

and that producing 60 bushels, reduced to 54, will yield, as before, no rent. So that the rent of the first quality of land has lost four bushels; of the second, three; of the third, two; and of the fourth, one: that is, each has lost exactly one tenth. A tax, therefore, of a fixed proportion of the produce lowers, in the same proportion, corn-rent.

But it is only corn-rent that is lowered, and not rent estimated in money, or in any other commodity. For, in the same proportion as corn-rent is reduced in quantity, the corn composing it is raised in value. Under the tithe, 54 bushels will be worth in the market what 60 were before; and nine tenths will in all cases sell for as much as the whole ten tenths previously sold for. The landlords will therefore be compensated in value and price for what they lose in quantity, and will suffer only so far as they consume their rent in kind, or, after receiving it in money, expend it in agricultural produce; that is, they only suffer as consumers of agricultural produce, and in common with all the other consumers. Considered as landlords, they have the same income as before; the tithe, therefore, falls on the consumer, and not on the landlord.

The same effect would be produced on rent if the tax, instead of being a fixed proportion of the produce, were a fixed sum per quarter or per bushel. A tax which takes a shilling for every bushel takes more shillings from one field than from another, just in proportion as it produces more bushels; and operates exactly like tithe, except that tithe is not only the same proportion on all lands, but is also the same proportion at all times, while a fixed sum of money per bushel will amount to a greater or less proportion, according as corn is cheap or dear.

There are other modes of taxing agriculture, which would affect rent differently. A tax proportioned to the rent would fall wholly on the rent, and would not at all raise the price of corn, which is regulated by the portion of the produce that pays no rent. A fixed tax of so much per cultivated acre, without distinction of value, would have effects directly the reverse. Taking no more from the best qualities of land than from the worst, it would leave the differences the same as before, and consequently the same corn-rents, and the landlords would profit to the full extent of the rise of price. To put the thing in another manner: the price must rise sufficiently to enable the worst land to pay the tax, thus enabling all lands which produce more than the worst to pay not only the tax, but also an increased rent to the landlords. These, however, are not so much taxes on the produce of land as taxes on the land itself. Taxes on the produce, properly so called, whether fixed or *ad valorem*, do not affect rent, but fall on the consumer, profits, however, generally bearing either the whole or the greatest part of the portion which is levied on the consumption of the laboring-classes.

§ 4. —how modified by the tendency of profits to a minimum.

The preceding is, I apprehend, a correct statement of the manner in which taxes on agricultural produce operate when first laid on. When, however, they are of old standing, their effect may be different. Now, the effect of accumulation, when attended by its usual accompaniment, an increase of population, is to increase the value and price of food, to raise rent, and to lower profits; that is, to do precisely what is done by a tax on agricultural produce, except that this does not raise rent. The tax, therefore, merely anticipates the rise of price and fall of profits which would have taken place ultimately through the mere progress of accumulation, while it at the same time prevents, or at least retards, that progress. If the rate of profit was such that the effect of the tithe reduces it to the practical minimum, after a lapse of time which would have admitted of a rise of one tenth from the natural progress of wealth, the consumer will be paying no more than he would have paid if the tithe had never existed; he will have ceased to pay any portion of it, and the person who will really pay it is the landlord, whom it deprives of the increase of rent which would by that time have accrued to him. At every successive point in this interval of time, less of the burden will rest on the consumer, and more of it on the landlord; and, in the ultimate result, the minimum of profits will be reached with a smaller capital and population and a lower rental than if the course of things had not been disturbed by the imposition of the tax. If, on the other hand, the tithe or other tax on agricultural produce does not reduce profits to the minimum, but to something above the minimum, accumulation will not be stopped, but only slackened; and, if population also increases, the twofold increase will continue to produce its effects—a rise of the price of corn and an increase of rent. These consequences, however, will not take place with the same rapidity as if the higher rate of profit had continued. At the end of twenty years the country will have a smaller population and capital than, but for the tax, it would by that time have had; the landlords will have a smaller rent, and the price of corn, having increased less rapidly than it would otherwise have done, will not be so much as a tenth higher than what, if there had been no tax, it would by that time have become. A part of the tax, therefore, will already have ceased to fall on the consumer and devolved upon the landlord, and the proportion will become greater and greater by lapse of time.

But though tithes and other taxes on agricultural produce, when of long standing, either do not raise the price of food and lower profits at all, or, if at all, not in proportion to the tax, yet the abrogation of such taxes, when they exist, does not the less diminish price, and, in general, raise the rate of profit. The abolition of a tithe takes one tenth from the cost of production, and consequently from the price, of all agricultural produce; and, unless it permanently raises the laborer's requirements, it lowers the cost of labor and raises profits. Rent, estimated in money or in commodities, generally remains as before; estimated in agricultural produce, it is raised. The country adds as much, by the repeal of a tithe, to the margin which intervenes between it and the stationary state as was cut off from that margin by the tithe when first imposed. Accumulation is greatly accelerated, and, if population also increases, the price of corn immediately begins to recover itself and rent to rise, thus gradually transferring the benefit of the remission from the consumer to the landlord.

§ 5. Effects of discriminating Duties.

We have hitherto inquired into the effects of taxes on commodities, on the assumption that they are levied impartially on every mode in which the commodity can be produced or brought to market. Another class of considerations is opened, if we suppose that this impartiality is not maintained, and that the tax is imposed, not on the commodity, but on some particular mode of obtaining it.

Suppose that a commodity is capable of being made by two different processes—as a manufactured commodity may be produced either by hand or by steam-power—sugar may be made either from the sugar-cane or from beet-root, cattle fattened either on hay and green crops or on oil-cake and the refuse of breweries. It is the interest of the community that, of the two methods, producers should adopt that which produces the best article at the lowest price. This being also the interest of the producers, unless protected against competition, and shielded from the penalties of indolence, the process most advantageous to the community is that which, if not interfered with by Government, they ultimately find it to their advantage to adopt. Suppose, however, that a tax is laid on one of the processes, and no tax at all, or one of smaller amount, on the other. If the taxed process is the one which the producers would not have adopted, the measure is simply nugatory. But if the tax falls, as it is of course intended to do, upon the one which they would have adopted, it creates an artificial motive for preferring the untaxed process, though the inferior of the two. If, therefore, it has any effect at all, it causes the commodity to be produced of worse quality, or at a greater expense of labor; it causes so much of the labor of the community to be wasted, and the capital employed in supporting and remunerating that labor to be expended as uselessly as if it were spent in hiring men to dig holes and fill them up again. This waste of labor and capital constitutes an addition to the cost of production of the commodity, which raises its value and price in a corresponding ratio, and thus the owners of the capital are indemnified. The loss falls on the consumers; though the capital of the country is also eventually diminished, by the diminution of their means of saving, and, in some degree, of their inducements to save.

The kind of tax, therefore, which comes under the general denomination of a discriminating duty, transgresses the rule that taxes should take as little as possible from the taxpayer beyond what they bring into the treasury of the state. A discriminating duty makes the consumer pay two distinct taxes, only one of which is paid to the Government, and that frequently the less onerous of the two. If a tax were laid on sugar produced from the cane, leaving the sugar from beet-root untaxed, then in so far as cane-sugar continued to be used, the tax on it would be paid to the treasury, and might be as unobjectionable as most other taxes; but if cane-sugar, having previously been cheaper than beet-root sugar, was now dearer, and beet-root sugar was to any considerable amount substituted for it, and fields laid out and manufactories established in consequence, the Government would gain no revenue from the beet-root sugar, while the consumers of it would pay a real tax. They would pay for beet-root sugar more than they had previously paid for cane-sugar, and the difference would go to indemnify producers for a portion of the labor of the country actually thrown away, in producing by the labor of (say) three hundred men what could be obtained by the other process with the labor of two hundred.

> An interesting illustration, in late years, of the operation of a discriminating duty is to be found in the case of different grades of sugar imported into the United States. Our tariff levied certain duties on different grades of sugar classified by color, on the theory that color was a test of saccharine strength. Cargoes were examined and compared with graded sugars hermetically sealed in glass bottles and distributed by the Dutch authorities, whence came the name of "Dutch standard." Grades from No. 1 (melado) to No. 10 must go to the refiner before consumption; but the grades to No. 13, although some might have gone into immediate consumption, were usually sent to be manufactured into the highest grades of soft and hard sugars. So long as the sugar was secured by evaporation in open coppers, or by passing the molasses through a layer of clay, saccharine strength and color went fairly well together. But with the invention of the vacuum-pan and the centrifugal

wheel, by which the sugar is reduced through a shorter and more effective process, sugar of a certain grade of color by the Dutch standard contained a much greater degree of sweetness than that produced by the old methods. Cuban planters, therefore, were permitted to send sugar into this country at a duty which was really levied on grades much inferior, and so paid a less duty than other sugars. The products of one country were discriminated against in favor of another. The difficulty was settled by using the polariscope, which gave an absolute chemical test of the sweetness, irrespective of color.

One of the commonest cases of discriminating duties is that of a tax on the importation of a commodity capable of being produced at home, unaccompanied by an equivalent tax on the home production. A commodity is never permanently imported, unless it can be obtained from abroad at a smaller cost of labor and capital, on the whole, than is necessary for producing it. If, therefore, by a duty on the importation, it is rendered cheaper to produce the article than to import it, an extra quantity of labor and capital is expended, without any extra result. The labor is useless, and the capital is spent in paying people for laboriously doing nothing. All custom duties which operate as an encouragement to the home production of the taxed article are thus an eminently wasteful mode of raising a revenue.

This character belongs in a peculiar degree to custom duties on the produce of land, unless countervailed by excise duties on the home production. Such taxes bring less into the public treasury, compared with what they take from the consumers, than any other imposts to which civilized nations are usually subject. If the wheat produced in a country is twenty millions of quarters, and the consumption twenty-one millions, a million being annually imported, and if on this million a duty is laid which raises the price ten shillings per quarter, the price which is raised is not that of the million only, but of the whole twenty-one millions. Taking the most favorable but extremely improbable supposition, that the importation is not at all checked, nor the home production enlarged, the state gains a revenue of only half a million, while the consumers are taxed ten millions and a half, the ten millions being a contribution to the home growers, who are forced by competition to resign it all to the landlords. The consumer thus pays to the owners of land an additional tax, equal to twenty times that which he pays to the state. Let us now suppose that the tax really checks importation. Suppose importation stopped altogether in ordinary years; it being found that the million of quarters can be obtained, by a more elaborate cultivation, or by breaking up inferior land, at a less advance than ten shillings upon the previous price—say, for instance, five shillings a quarter. The revenue now obtains nothing, except from the extraordinary imports which may happen to take place in a season of scarcity. But the consumers pay every year a tax of five shillings on the whole twenty-one millions of quarters, amounting to £5,250,000 sterling. Of this the odd £250,000 goes to compensate the growers of the last million of quarters for the labor and capital wasted under the compulsion of the law. The remaining £5,000,000 go to enrich the landlords as before.

Such is the operation of what are technically termed corn laws, when first laid on; and such continues to be their operation so long as they have any effect at all in raising the price of corn. The difference between a country without corn laws and a country which has long had corn laws is not so much that the last has a higher price or a larger rental, but that it has the same price and the same rental with a smaller aggregate capital and a smaller population. The imposition of corn laws raises rents, but retards that progress of accumulation which would in no long period have raised them fully as much. The repeal of corn laws tends to lower rents, but it unchains a force which, in a progressive state of capital and population, restores and even increases the former amount.

What we have said of duties on importation generally is equally applicable to discriminating duties which favor importation from one place, or in one particular manner, in contradistinction to others; such as the preference given to the produce of a colony, or of a country with which there is a commercial treaty; or the higher duties formerly imposed by our navigation laws on goods imported in other than British shipping. Whatever else may be alleged in favor of such distinctions, whenever they are not nugatory, they are economically wasteful. They induce a resort to a more costly mode of obtaining a commodity in lieu of one less costly, and thus cause a portion of the labor which the country employs in providing itself with foreign commodities to be sacrificed without return.

§ 6. Effects produced on international Exchange by Duties on Exports and on Imports.

There is one more point, relating to the operation of taxes on commodities conveyed from one country to another, which requires notice: the influences which they exert on international exchanges. Every tax on a commodity tends to raise its price, and consequently to lessen the demand for it in the market in which it is sold. All taxes on international trade tend, therefore, to produce a disturbance, and a readjustment of what we have termed the equation of international demand.

Taxes on foreign trade are of two kinds—taxes on imports and on exports. On the first aspect of the matter it would seem that both these taxes are paid by the consumers of the commodity; that taxes on exports consequently fall entirely on foreigners, taxes on imports wholly on the home consumer. The true state of the case, however, is much more complicated.

"By taxing exports we may, in certain circumstances, produce a division of the advantage of the trade more favorable to ourselves. In some cases we may draw into our coffers, at the expense of foreigners, not only the whole tax, but more than the tax; in other cases we should gain exactly the tax; in others, less than the tax. In this last case a part of the tax is borne by ourselves; possibly the whole, possibly even, as we shall show, more than the whole."

Reverting to the supposititious case employed of a trade between England and the United States in iron and corn, suppose that the United States taxes her export of corn, the tax not being supposed high enough to induce England to produce corn for herself. The price at which corn can be sold in England is augmented by the tax. This will probably diminish the quantity consumed. It may diminish it so much that, even at the increased price, there will not be required so great a money value as before. Or it may not diminish it at all, or so little that, in consequence of the higher price, a greater money value will be purchased than before. In this last case, the United States will gain, at the expense of England, not only the whole amount of the duty, but more; for, the money value of her exports to England being increased, while her imports remain the same, money will flow into the United States from England. The price of corn will rise in the United States, and consequently in England; but the price of iron will fall in England, and consequently in the United States. We shall export less corn and import more iron, till the equilibrium is restored. It thus appears (what is at first sight somewhat remarkable) that, by taxing her exports, the United States would, in some conceivable circumstances, not only gain from her foreign customers the whole amount of the tax, but would also get her imports cheaper. She would get them cheaper in two ways, for she would obtain them for less money, and would have more money to purchase them with. England, on the other hand, would suffer doubly: she would have to pay for her corn a price increased not only by the duty, but by the influx of money into the United States, while the same change in the distribution of the circulating medium would leave her less money to purchase it with.[344]

This, however, is only one of three possible cases. If, after the imposition of the duty, England requires so diminished a quantity of corn that its total value is exactly the same as before, the balance of trade would be undisturbed; the United States will gain the duty, England will lose it, and nothing more. If, again, the imposition of the duty occasions such a falling off in the demand that England requires a less pecuniary value than before, our exports will no longer pay for our imports; money must pass from the United States into England; and England's share of the advantage of the trade will be increased. By the change in the distribution of money, corn will fall in the United States, and therefore it will, of course, fall in England. Thus England will not pay the whole of the tax. From the same cause, iron will rise in England, and consequently in the United States. When this alteration of prices has so adjusted the demand that the corn and the iron again pay for one another, the result is that England has paid only a part of the tax, and the remainder of what has been received into our treasury has come indirectly out of the pockets of our own consumers of iron, who pay a higher price for that imported commodity in consequence of the tax on our exports, while at the same time they, in consequence of the efflux of money and the fall of prices, have smaller money incomes wherewith to pay for the iron at that advanced price.

It is not an impossible supposition that by taxing our exports we might not only gain nothing from the foreigner, the tax being paid out of our own pockets, but might even compel our own people to pay a second tax to the foreigner. Suppose, as before, that the demand of England for corn falls off so much on the imposition of the duty that she requires a smaller money value than before, but that the case is so different with iron in the United States that when the price rises the demand either does not fall off at all, or so little that the money value required is greater than before. The first effect of laying on the duty is, as before, that the corn exported will no longer pay for the iron imported.

Money will therefore flow out of the United States into England. One effect is to raise the price of iron in England, and consequently in the United States. But this, by the supposition, instead of stopping the efflux of money, only makes it greater; because, the higher the price, the greater the money value of the iron consumed. The balance, therefore, can only be restored by the other effect, which is going on at the same time, namely, the fall of corn in the American and consequently in the English market. Even when corn has fallen so low that its price with the duty is only equal to what its price without the duty was at first, it is not a necessary consequence that the fall will stop; for the same amount of exportation as before will not now suffice to pay the increased money value of the imports; and although the English consumers have now not only corn at the old price, but likewise increased money incomes, it is not certain that they will be inclined to employ the increase of their incomes in increasing their purchases of corn. The price of corn, therefore, must perhaps fall, to restore the equilibrium, more than the whole amount of the duty; England may be enabled to import corn at a lower price when it is taxed than when it was untaxed; and this gain she will acquire at the expense of the American consumers of iron, who, in addition, will be the real payers of the whole of what is received at their own custom-house under the name of duties on the export of corn.

In general, however, there could be little doubt that a country which imposed such taxes would succeed in making foreign countries contribute something to its revenue; but, unless the taxed article be one for which their demand is extremely urgent, they will seldom pay the whole of the amount which the tax brings in.[345]

> The result of this investigation may, then, be generally formulated as follows: That country which has the strongest demand for the commodities of other countries as compared with the demand of other countries for its own commodities will pay the burden of the export duty.

Thus far of duties on exports. We now proceed to the more ordinary case of duties on imports: "We have had an example of a tax on exports, that is, on foreigners, falling in part on ourselves. We shall therefore not be surprised if we find a tax on imports, that is, on ourselves, partly falling upon foreigners.

"Instead of taxing the corn which we export, suppose that we tax the iron which we import. The duty which we are now supposing must not be what is termed a protecting duty, that is, a duty sufficiently high to induce us to produce the article at home. If it had this effect, it would destroy entirely the trade both in corn and in iron, and both countries would lose the whole of the advantage which they previously gained by exchanging those commodities with one another. We suppose a duty which might diminish the consumption of the article, but which would not prevent us from continuing to import, as before, whatever iron we did consume.

"The equilibrium of trade would be disturbed if the imposition of the tax diminished, in the slightest degree, the quantity of iron consumed. For, as the tax is levied at our own custom-house, the English exporter only receives the same price as formerly, though the American consumer pays a higher one. If, therefore, there be any diminution of the quantity bought, although a larger sum of money may be actually laid out in the article, a smaller one will be due from the United States to England: this sum will no longer be an equivalent for the sum due from England to the United States for corn, the balance therefore must be paid in money. Prices will fall in England and rise in the United States; iron will fall in the English market; corn will rise in the American. The English will pay a higher price for corn, and will have smaller money incomes to buy it with; while the Americans will obtain iron cheaper, that is, its price will exceed what it previously was by less than the amount of the duty, while their means of purchasing it will be increased by the increase of their money incomes.

"If the imposition of the tax does not diminish the demand, it will leave the trade exactly as it was before. We shall import as much, and export as much; the whole of the tax will be paid out of our own pockets.

"But the imposition of a tax on a commodity almost always diminishes the demand more or less; and it can never, or scarcely ever, increase the demand. It may, therefore, be laid down as a principle that a tax on imported commodities, when it really operates as a tax, and not as a prohibition either total or partial, almost always falls in part upon the foreigners who consume our goods; and that this is a mode in which a nation may appropriate to itself, at the expense of foreigners, a larger share than would otherwise belong to it of the increase in the general productiveness of the labor and capital of the world, which results from the interchange of commodities among nations."

Those are, therefore, in the right who maintain that taxes on imports are partly paid by foreigners; but they are mistaken when they say that it is by the foreign producer. It is not on the person from whom we buy, but on all those who buy from us, that a portion of our custom duties spontaneously falls. It is the foreign consumer of our exported commodities who is obliged to pay a higher price for them because we maintain revenue duties on foreign goods.

There are but two cases in which duties on commodities can in any degree, or in any manner, fall on the producer. One is, when the article is a strict monopoly, and at a scarcity price. The price in this case being only limited by the desires of the buyer—the sum obtained for the restricted supply being the utmost which the buyers would consent to give rather than go without it—if the treasury intercepts a part of this, the price can not be further raised to compensate for the tax, and it must be paid from the monopoly profits. A tax on rare and high-priced wines will fall wholly on the growers, or rather, on the owners of the vineyards. The second case, in which the producer sometimes bears a portion of the tax, is more important: the case of duties on the produce of land or of mines. These might be so high as to diminish materially the demand for the produce, and compel the abandonment of some of the inferior qualities of land or mines. Supposing this to be the effect, the consumers, both in the country itself and in those which dealt with it, would obtain the produce at smaller cost; and a part only, instead of the whole, of the duty would fall on the purchaser, who would be indemnified chiefly at the expense of the landowners or mine-owners in the producing country.

Duties on importation may, then, be divided "into two classes: (1) those which have the effect of encouraging some particular branch of domestic industry [protective duties], (2) and those which have not [revenue duties]. The former are purely mischievous, both to the country imposing them and to those with whom it trades. They prevent a saving of labor and capital, which, if permitted to be made, would be divided in some proportion or other between the importing country and the countries which buy what that country does or might export.

"The other class of duties are those which do not encourage one mode of procuring an article at the expense of another, but allow interchange to take place just as if the duty did not exist, and to produce the saving of labor which constitutes the motive to international as to all other commerce. Of this kind are duties on the importation of any commodity which could not by any possibility be produced at home, and duties not sufficiently high to counterbalance the difference of expense between the production of the article at home and its importation. Of the money which is brought into the treasury of any country by taxes of this last description, a part only is paid by the people of that country; the remainder by the foreign consumers of their goods.

"Nevertheless, this latter kind of taxes are in principle as ineligible as the former, though not precisely on the same ground. A protecting duty can never be a cause of gain, but always and necessarily of loss, to the country imposing it, just so far as it is efficacious to its end. A non-protecting duty, on the contrary, would in most cases be a source of gain to the country imposing it, in so far as throwing part of the weight of its taxes upon other people is a gain; but it would be a means which it could seldom be advisable to adopt, being so easily counteracted by a precisely similar proceeding on the other side.

"If the United States, in the case already supposed, sought to obtain for herself more than her natural share of the advantage of the trade with England, by imposing a duty upon iron, England would only have to impose a duty upon corn sufficient to diminish the demand for that article about as much as the demand for iron had been diminished in the United States by the tax. Things would then be as before, and each country would pay its own tax—unless, indeed, the sum of the two duties exceeded the entire advantage of the trade, for in that case the trade and its advantage would cease entirely.

"There would be no advantage, therefore, in imposing duties of this kind with a view to gain by them in the manner which has been pointed out. But, when any part of the revenue is derived from taxes on commodities, these may often be as little objectionable as the rest. It is evident, too, that considerations of reciprocity, which are quite unessential when the matter in debate is a protecting duty, are of material importance when the repeal of duties of this other description is discussed. A country can not be expected to renounce the power of taxing foreigners unless foreigners will in return practice toward itself the same forbearance. The only mode in which a country can save itself from being a loser by the revenue duties imposed by other countries on its commodities is, to impose corresponding revenue duties on theirs. Only it must take care that those duties be not so high as to exceed all that remains of the advantage of the trade, and put an end to importation altogether, causing the article to be either produced at home, or imported from another and a dearer market."

> By "reciprocity" is meant that, when one country admits goods free of duty from a second country, this latter country will also admit the commodities of the former free of duty; or, as is often the case, if not free of duty, at a less than the usual rate. Until the last few years we have had a reciprocity treaty with Canada, but it is not now in force; and an arrangement for closer commercial relations with Mexico is now under consideration.

Chapter IV. Comparison Between Direct And Indirect Taxation.

§ 1. Arguments for and against direct Taxation.

Are direct or indirect taxes the most eligible? A man dislikes not so much the payment as the act of paying. He dislikes seeing the face of the tax-collector, and being subjected to his peremptory demand. Perhaps, too, the money which he is required to pay directly out of his pocket is the only taxation which he is quite sure that he pays at all. That a tax of two shillings per pound on tea, or of three shillings per bottle on wine, raises the price of each pound of tea and bottle of wine which he consumes, by that and more than that amount, can not, indeed, be denied; it is the fact, and is intended to be so, and he himself, at times, is perfectly aware of it; but it makes hardly any impression on his practical feelings and associations, serving to illustrate the distinction between what is merely known to be true and what is felt to be so. The unpopularity of direct taxation, contrasted with the easy manner in which the public consent to let themselves be fleeced in the prices of commodities, has generated in many friends of improvement a directly opposite mode of thinking to the foregoing. They contend that the very reason which makes direct taxation disagreeable makes it preferable. Under it every one knows how much he really pays; and, if he votes for a war, or any other expensive national luxury, he does so with his eyes open to what it costs him. If all taxes were direct, taxation would be much more perceived than at present, and there would be a security, which now there is not, for economy in the public expenditure.

Although this argument is not without force, its weight is likely to be constantly diminishing. The real incidence of indirect taxation is every day more generally understood and more familiarly recognized. The mere distinction between paying money directly to the tax-collector and contributing the same sum through the intervention of the tea-dealer or the wine-merchant no longer makes the whole difference between dislike or opposition and passive acquiescence.

If our present revenue [of $400,000,000 in 1883] were all raised by direct taxes, an extreme dissatisfaction would certainly arise at having to pay so much; but while men's minds are so little guided by reason, as such a change of feeling from so irrelevant a cause would imply, so great an aversion to taxation might not be an unqualified good. Of the [$400,000,000] in question, nearly [$60,000,000] are pledged, under the most binding obligations, to those whose property has been borrowed and spent by the state; and, while this debt remains unredeemed, a greatly increased impatience of taxation would involve no little danger of a breach of faith. That part, indeed, of the public expenditure which is devoted to the maintenance of civil and military establishments [$206,000,000] (that is, all except the interest of the national debt), affords, in many of its details, ample scope for retrenchment. If so great an addition were made to the public dislike of taxation as might be the consequence of confining it to the direct form, the classes who profit by the misapplication of public money might probably succeed in saving that by which they profit, at the expense of that which would only be useful to the public.

There is, however, a frequent plea in support of indirect taxation, which must be altogether rejected as grounded on a fallacy. We are often told that taxes on commodities are less burdensome than other taxes, because the contributor can escape from them by ceasing to use the taxed commodity. He certainly can, if that be his object, deprive the Government of the money; but he does so by a sacrifice of his own indulgences, which (if he chose to undergo it) would equally make up to him for the same amount taken from him by direct taxation. Suppose a tax laid on wine, sufficient to add [$25] to the price of the quantity of wine which he consumes in a year. He has only (we are told) to diminish his consumption of wine by [$25], and he escapes the burden. True, but if the [$25], instead of being laid on wine, had been taken from him by an income-tax, he could, by expending [$25] less in wine, equally save the amount of the tax, so that the difference between the two cases is really illusory. If the Government takes from the contributor [$25] a year, whether in one way or another, exactly that amount must be retrenched from his consumption to leave him as well off as before; and in either way the same amount of sacrifice, neither more nor less, is imposed on him.

On the other hand, it is some advantage on the side of indirect taxes that what they exact from the contributor is taken at a time and in a manner likely to be convenient to him. It is paid at a time when he has at any rate a payment to make; it causes, therefore, no additional trouble, nor (unless the tax be on necessaries) any inconvenience but what is inseparable from the payment of the amount. He can also, except in the case of very perishable articles, select his own time for laying in a stock of the commodity, and consequently for payment of the tax. The producer or dealer who advances these taxes is, indeed, sometimes subjected to inconvenience; but, in the case of imported goods, this inconvenience is reduced to a minimum by what is called the Warehousing System, under which, instead of paying the duty at the time of importation, he is only required to do so when he takes out the goods for consumption, which is seldom done until he has either actually found, or has the prospect of immediately finding, a purchaser.

The strongest objection, however, to raising the whole or the greater part of a large revenue by direct taxes, is the impossibility of assessing them fairly without a conscientious co-operation on the part of the contributors, not to be hoped for in the present low state of public morality. In the case of an income-tax, we have already seen that, unless it be found practicable to exempt savings altogether from the tax, the burden can not be apportioned with any tolerable approach to fairness upon those whose incomes are derived from business or professions; and this is in fact admitted by most of the advocates of direct taxation who, I am afraid, generally get over the difficulty by leaving those classes untaxed, and confining their projected income-tax to "realized property," in which form it certainly has the merit of being a very easy form of plunder. But enough has been said in condemnation of this expedient. We have seen, however, that a house-tax is a form of direct taxation not liable to the same objections as an income-tax, and indeed liable to as few objections of any kind as perhaps any of our indirect taxes. But it would be impossible to raise, by a house-tax alone, the greatest part of the revenue, without producing a very objectionable overcrowding of the population, through the strong motive which all persons would have to avoid the tax by restricting their house accommodation.

A certain amount of revenue may, as we have seen, be obtained without injustice by a peculiar tax on rent. Besides (1) the land-tax,[346] and (2) an equivalent for the revenue derived from stamp duties on the conveyance of land, some further taxation might, I have contended, at some future period be imposed, (3) to enable the state to participate in the progressive increase of the incomes of landlords from natural causes. (4) Legacies and inheritances, we have also seen, ought to be subjected to taxation sufficient to yield a considerable revenue. With these taxes, and (5) a house-tax of suitable amount, we should, I think, have reached the prudent limits of direct taxation. The remainder of the revenue would have to be provided by taxes on consumption, and the question is, which of these are the least objectionable.

§ 2. What forms of indirect taxation are most eligible?

There are some forms of indirect taxation which must be peremptorily excluded. (1.) Taxes on commodities, for revenue purposes, must not operate as protecting duties, but must be levied impartially on every mode in which the articles can be obtained, whether produced in the country itself, or imported. (2.) An exclusion must also be put upon all taxes on the necessaries of life, or on the materials or instruments employed in producing those necessaries. Such taxes are always liable to encroach on what should be left untaxed, the incomes barely sufficient for healthful existence; and on the most favorable supposition, namely, that wages rise to compensate the laborers for the tax, it operates as a peculiar tax on profits, which is at once unjust and detrimental to national wealth.[347] What remain are taxes on luxuries. And these have some properties which strongly recommend them. In the first place, they can never, by any possibility, touch those whose whole income is expended on necessaries; while they do reach those by whom what is required for necessaries is expended on indulgences. In the next place, they operate in some cases as a useful, and the only useful, kind of sumptuary law. A great portion of the expense of the higher and middle classes in most countries is not incurred for the sake of the pleasure afforded by the things on which the money is spent, but from regard to opinion, and an idea that certain expenses are expected from them, as an appendage of station; and I can not but think that expenditure of this sort is a most desirable subject of taxation. When a thing is bought, not for its use but for its costliness, cheapness is no recommendation.

§ 3. Practical rules for indirect taxation.

In order to reduce as much as possible the inconveniences, and increase the advantages, incident to taxes on commodities, the following are the practical rules which suggest themselves: 1. To raise as large a revenue as conveniently may be, from those classes of luxuries which have most connection with vanity, and least with positive enjoyment; such as the more costly qualities of all kinds of personal equipment and ornament. But with regard to horses and carriages, as there are many persons to whom, from health or constitution, these are not so much luxuries as necessaries, the tax paid by those who have but one riding-horse, or but one carriage, especially of the cheaper descriptions, should be low; while taxation should rise very rapidly with the number of horses and carriages, and with their costliness. 2. Whenever possible, to demand the tax, not from the producer, but directly from the consumer, since, when levied on the producer, it raises the price always by more, and often by much more, than the mere amount of the tax. 3. But as the only indirect taxes which yield a large revenue are those which fall on articles of universal or very general consumption, and as it is therefore necessary to have some taxes on real luxuries, that is, on things which afford pleasure in themselves, and are valued on that account rather than for their cost, these taxes should, if possible, be so adjusted as to fall with the same proportional weight on small, on moderate, and on large incomes. This is not an easy matter; since the things which are the subjects of the more productive taxes are in proportion more largely consumed by the poorer members of the community than by the rich. Tea, coffee, sugar, tobacco, fermented drinks, can hardly be so taxed that the poor shall not bear more than their due share of the burden. Something might be done by making the duty on the superior qualities, which are used by the richer consumers, much higher in proportion to the value; but in some cases the difficulty of at all adjusting the duty to the value, so as to prevent evasion, is said, with what truth I know not, to be insuperable; so that it is thought necessary to levy the same fixed duty on all the qualities alike. 4. As far as is consistent with the preceding rules, taxation should rather be concentrated on a few articles than diffused over many, in order that the expenses of collection may be smaller, and that as few employments as possible may be burdensomely and vexatiously interfered with. 5. Among luxuries of general consumption, taxation should by preference attach itself to stimulants, because these, though in themselves as legitimate indulgences as any others, are more liable than most others to be used in excess, so that the check to consumption, naturally arising from taxation, is on the whole better applied to them than to other things. 6. As far as other considerations permit, taxation should be confined to imported articles, since these can be taxed with a less degree of vexatious interference, and with fewer incidental bad effects, than when a tax is levied on the field or on the workshop. Custom duties are, *cæteris paribus*, much less objectionable than excise: but they must be laid only on things which either can not, or at least will not, be produced in the country itself; or else their production there must be prohibited (as in England is the case with tobacco), or subjected to an excise duty of equivalent amount. 7. No tax ought to be kept so high as to furnish a motive to its evasion, too strong to be counteracted by ordinary means of prevention; and especially no commodity should be taxed so highly as to raise up a class of lawless characters—smugglers, illicit distillers, and the like.

> The experience of the United States is pregnant with lessons in this direction. During the war we imposed an internal-revenue tax on distilled spirits of so large an amount that it not only produced less revenue than a smaller tax would have done, but it created gigantic

frauds, public corruption, and infinite devices to escape the payment. The following table will show how the production, as indicated by the tax, fell off when the tax was excessive. It forced evasions by distillers. It has been found by various experiences that with a less rate the revenue is largely increased.

Year.	Revenue.	Production indicated by the tax (gallons).	Amount of tax.
1862-1863	$3,200,000	16,000,000	July, 1862, 20 c. per gallon.
1867-1868	14,200,000	7,000,000	Jan., 1865, $2 per gallon.
1868-1869	34,200,000	16,000,000	July, 1868, 50 c. per gallon.
1869-1870	39,200,000	18,000,000	

The actual amount reached by taxation is very much less than that known to be actually used by from ten to fifteen millions of gallons, or nearly one half the product. The openness of the frauds can be judged by the fact that proof spirits were "openly sold in the market, and even quoted in price-currents, at from five to fifteen cents less per gallon than the rate of tax and the average cost of manufacture."[348]

In what manner the finer articles of manufacture, consumed by the rich, might most advantageously be taxed, I must leave to be decided by those who have the requisite practical knowledge. The difficulty would be, to effect it without an inadmissible degree of interference with production. In countries which, like the United States, import the principal part of the finer manufactures which they consume, there is little difficulty in the matter; and, even where nothing is imported but the raw material, that may be taxed, especially the qualities of it which are exclusively employed for the fabrics used by the richer class of consumers. Thus, in England a high custom duty on raw silk would be consistent with principle; and it might perhaps be practicable to tax the finer qualities of cotton or linen yarn, whether spun in the country itself or imported.

§ 4. Taxation systems of the United States and other Countries.

It will now well repay study to examine Chart No. XXI, which shows in what manner the United States have raised their revenues, and to consider how far the right rules of taxation have been followed.

I. For means of comparison, I shall give the last annual budget of the United States in order to make clear from what sources the country derives its revenues:

Chart XXI.

United States Budget, Year Ending June 30, 1883.

[In millions and tenths of millions.]

Receipts:

Customs	$214.7
Internal revenue	144.7
Direct tax	.1
Sale of public lands	7.9
Miscellaneous	30.8
Net ordinary receipts	$398.2

Expenditures:

War Department	$48.9
Navy Department	15.3
Indians	7.3

Pensions	66.0
Miscellaneous	68.7
Net ordinary expenditures	$206.2
Interest on public debt	59.2
Total	$265.4

This leaves a surplus of $132,839,444 above all expenditures, and our problem is now where to reduce taxation. The annual interest charge is lessening with the payment of the public debt, having fallen from its highest figure of $143,781,591 in 1867, to $59,160,131 in 1883.[349] Our national taxation is practically all indirect, that of internal taxation being chiefly levied on tobacco and distilled spirits, and our customs falling on almost all articles which can be imported, materials as well as manufactures.

In the United States direct taxation on real and personal property is very generally levied for State, county, and municipal purposes. In fact, nearly all the perceptible taxation is the property tax, and, inasmuch as the State and county tax is very light, the burden is almost always owing to municipal and town expenditures. People do not seem to be aware of the enormous national burden, because the taxes are indirect, and only increase the prices of commodities. Other countries, it will be seen, make a greater use of direct taxation than the United States. In fact, the comparison of the ways by which different countries collect their revenues may naturally show us where we may gain by their experience.

II. The English system is especially interesting, because, after having had an extended scheme of customs duties, they abandoned it, and raised their revenue, some on imported articles, it is true (generally on those which could not be produced in England), but by the income-tax, and other forms.[350]

In 1842 Sir Robert Peel found 1,200 articles subject to customs-duties. He began (1) by removing all prohibitions; (2) by reducing duties on raw materials to 5 per cent or less; (3) by limiting the rates on partially manufactured goods to 12 per cent; and (4) those on wholly manufactured goods to 20 per cent. Now customs-duties are levied only on beer, cards, chiccory, chocolate, cocoa, coffee, dried fruit, plate, spirits, tea, tobacco, and wine. The following budget gives the sources of revenue for Great Britain:[351]

Budget Of Great Britain, 1883.

[In millions and tenths of millions.]

Receipts:

Customs	$98.4
Excise (such as on tobacco and spirits)	134.9
Stamps	58.5
Land tax	5.2
House duty	8.9
Income tax	60.9
Post-Office	36.5
Telegraph	8.6
Crown lands	2.0
Interest (on loans, Suez Canal, etc.)	6.1
Miscellaneous	26.4
Total	$446.4

Expenditures:

Interest on national debt	$148.4
Army, navy, etc.	157.1

Cost of revenue departments	45.1
Public works	9.1
Public departments, salaries, etc.	12.5
Law and justice	35.7
Education, science, and art	22.9
Colonial and consular	3.4
Civil list	2.0
Pensions	2.0
Miscellaneous	6.8
Total expenditures	$445.0

From this it will be seen that in the land, income, and house taxes, Great Britain raises by direct taxation about $75,000,000, and in customs and excise, by indirect taxation, about $233,000,000.

III. The following is the system adopted by Germany (Prussia):

German Budget, 1881-1882.

[In millions and tenths of millions.]

Receipts:

(1.) Property income from domains and forests	$11.7
From mines and salt-works	2.5
From railways	22.5
Miscellaneous	5.0
	$41.7
(2.) Royal Lottery	1.0
(3.) Bureau of Justice	$12.7
Harbors and bridges	.5

		13.2
(4.) Direct taxes		$35.5
(5.) Indirect taxes (for Prussia)		12.3
Total receipts		$103.6

Expenditures:

(1.) Civil list	3.0
(2.) Debt	25.0
(3.) Various ministries, schools, etc.	49.5
(4.) Pensions	4.0
(5.) Miscellaneous	19.5
Total expenditures[352]	$101.0

The Prussian *direct* taxes include (1) a land-tax, (2) a house-tax, (3) an income-tax, (4) a class-tax, (5) a trade-tax, and (6) miscellaneous taxes.

IV. How the French supply themselves may be seen by the following statement:[353]

French Budget, 1881.

[In millions and tenths of millions.]

Receipts:

Direct taxes	$75.9
Similar taxes	4.7
Registry, stamps, etc	135.1
Forests	7.6
Customs (and salt duty $3.5)	65.4
Indirect taxes (including tobacco)	209.7
Post-Office and telegraph	27.2

Miscellaneous	29.8	
Total receipts	$555.4	

Expenditures:

Public debt, etc.	$249.0
General functions of the ministries	243.7
Administrative expenses, cost of revenue collections, etc.	58.5
Miscellaneous	3.5
Total expenditures	$554.7

The direct taxes are (1) on property; (2) one nearly like our poll-tax together with a species of income-tax; (3) a tax on doors and windows; and (4) one on licenses.

§ 5. A *Résumé* of the general principles of taxation.

After the manner of our classification and *résumé* of the subject of value and money, it may be convenient to here insert a recapitulation of the various principles under the treatment of taxation.[354]

Comparison Between Direct And Indirect Taxation.

Adam Smith's "Canons of Taxation."—A tax should be: I. *Equal* (in amount of *sacrifice* entailed). II. *Certain.* III. *Timely.* IV. *All for the state.*

A Tax is either:
Direct.
Indirect (on commodities.)

Direct taxes are:
On Income.
On Expenditure.

Taxes on Income are:
General.
Special.

General income taxes. The best of taxes, if people were all honest. As it is, it falls most heavily on the conscientious. Should be reserved for emergency. All *savings* and a fixed amount in *all* incomes should be exempt.

Special taxes are on:
Rent.
Wages.
Profits.

Taxes on Rent. Agricultural rent is meant. It falls entirely on the landlord, and, if not balanced by taxes on other classes, is unjust. May be blended with a tax on profits, if on rent due to landlord's improvements.

Taxes on Wages are:
On Skilled.
On Unskilled.

Skilled wages are at a monopoly price, and taxes on them are paid by the laborers, so long as wages are not reduced below their just proportion.

Unskilled wages. (1) *Population diminished by it.* Paid by profits. (2) *Population left stationary.* Shared between profits and wages. (3) *Population increasing in spite of it.* Falls entirely on wages.

Taxes on Profits. May possible stimulate production, and is then a good all round, contributing to the state, and leaving no one any poorer. If not, if profits are really diminished by the tax, capital may be diminished also. This (a) may, or (b) may not diminish population. If (a), then the margin of cultivation ceases to be extended, and part of the tax, *pro tanto*, falls on the landlords. If (b), then wages fall, and part of the tax falls on the laborer. Total result is a nearer approach to the stationary state.

Taxes on Expenditure are open to the same objections as the general income-tax. They may be:
Assessed taxes.
House-tax.

Assessed taxes, such as on servants, dogs, etc. These are rigidly *direct*.

House-taxes are:
On building-rent.
On ground-rent.

House-taxes on building-rent are paid by occupier. This tax is *indirect*.

House-taxes on ground-rent are (1.) with, or (2.) without an equivalent tax on agricultural rent. (1.) Are paid by ground landlord wholly, and therefore *direct*. (2.) Are part by occupier, and therefore *indirect*.

Indirect taxes are: Excise,
Customs, or
Tolls.

Indirect taxes may be on (1.) Long or (2.) Short investments of capital.

Indirect taxes on Long investments are always unadvisable, in view of Canon IV.

Indirect taxes on Short investments are subject to the laws of indirect taxation. 1. Tax vanities rather than positive enjoyments (e.g., liveries rather than servants). 2. The consumer and not the producer should pay the tax collector (Canon IV). That is, collect the tax as near the actual consumer as possible. 3. Taxes on real enjoyments to be kept as equal as possible for large and small means. 4. Tax as few articles as possible. England taxes only a very small number of imports. The United States taxes nearly everything imported. 5. Tax stimulants freely. The United States collect $91,000,000 from spirits and liquors, and $42,000,000 from tobacco (1883). 6. Tax imports of commodities not made at home, or whose home production is under an excise (internal revenue) duty equal to the customs tax. 7. Keep the rate of tax low, in order to get most revenue.

Chapter V. Of A National Debt.

§ 1. Is it desirable to defray extraordinary public expenses by loans?

The question must now be considered, how far it is right or expedient to raise money for the purposes of government, not by laying on taxes to the amount required, but by taking a portion of the capital of the country in the form of a loan, and charging the public revenue with only the interest.

This question has already been touched upon in the First Book.[355] We remarked, that if the capital taken in loans is abstracted from funds either engaged in production, or destined to be employed in it, their diversion from that purpose is equivalent to taking the amount from the wages of the laboring-classes. Borrowing, in this case, is not a substitute for raising the supplies within the year. A government which borrows does actually take the amount within the year, and that too by a tax exclusively on the laboring-classes, than which it could have done nothing worse, if it had supplied its wants by avowed taxation; and in that case the transaction, and its evils, would have ended with the emergency; while, by the circuitous mode adopted, the value exacted from the laborers is gained, not by the state, but by the employers of labor, the state remaining charged with the debt besides, and with its interest in perpetuity. The system of public loans, in such circumstances, may be pronounced the very worst which, in the present state of civilization, is still included in the catalogue of financial expedients.

We, however, remarked that there are other circumstances in which loans are not chargeable with these pernicious consequences: namely, first, when what is borrowed is foreign capital, the overflowings of the general accumulation of the world; or, secondly, when it is capital which either would not have been saved at all, unless this mode of investment had been open to it, or, after being saved, would have been wasted in unproductive enterprises, or sent to seek employment in foreign countries. When the progress of accumulation has reduced profits either to the ultimate or to the practical minimum—to the rate less than which would either put a stop to the increase of capital, or send the whole of the new accumulations abroad—government may annually intercept these new accumulations, without trenching on the employment or wages of the laboring-classes in the country itself, or perhaps in any other country. To this extent, therefore, the loan system may be carried, without being liable to the utter and peremptory condemnation which is due to it when it overpasses this limit. What is wanted is an index to determine whether, in any given series of years, as during the last great war, for example, the limit has been exceeded or not.

Such an index exists, at once a certain and an obvious one. Did the Government, by its loan operations, augment the rate of interest? If it only opened a channel for capital which would not otherwise have been accumulated, or which, if accumulated, would not have been employed within the country, this implies that the capital, which the Government took and expended, could not have found employment at the existing rate of interest. So long as the loans do no more than absorb this surplus, they prevent any tendency to a fall of the rate of interest, but they can not occasion any rise. [But] To the full extent to which the loans of government, during the war, caused the rate of interest to exceed what it was before, and what it has been since, those loans are chargeable with all the evils which have been described. If it be objected that interest only rose because profits rose, I reply that this does not weaken, but strengthens, the argument. If the Government loans produced the rise of profits by the great amount of capital which they absorbed, by what means can they have had this effect, unless by lowering the wages of labor? It will, perhaps, be said that what kept profits high during the war was not the drafts made on the national capital by the loans, but the rapid progress of industrial improvements. This, in a great measure, was the fact; and it, no doubt, alleviated the hardship to the laboring-classes, and made the financial system which was pursued less actively mischievous, but not less contrary to principle. These very improvements in industry made room for a larger amount of capital; and the Government, by draining away a great part of the annual accumulations, did not indeed prevent that capital from existing ultimately (for it started into existence with great rapidity after the peace), but prevented it from existing at the time, and subtracted just so much, while the war lasted, from distribution among productive laborers. If the Government had abstained from taking this capital by loan, and had allowed it to reach the laborers, but had raised the supplies which it required by a direct tax on the laboring-classes, it would have produced (in every respect but the expense and inconvenience of collecting the tax) the very same economical effects which it did produce, except that we should not now have had the debt. The course it actually took was therefore worse than the very worst mode which it could possibly have adopted of raising the supplies within the year; and the only excuse, or justification, which it admits of (so far as that excuse could be truly pleaded) was hard necessity; the impossibility of raising so enormous an annual sum by taxation, without resorting to taxes which from their odiousness, or from the facility of evasion, it would have been found impracticable to enforce.[356]

When government loans are limited to the overflowings of the national capital, or to those accumulations which would not take place at all unless suffered to overflow, they are at least not liable to this grave condemnation. In this case, therefore, the question really is, what it is commonly supposed to be in all cases—namely, a choice between a great sacrifice at once, and a small one indefinitely prolonged. On this matter it seems rational to think that the prudence of a nation will dictate the same conduct as the prudence of an individual; to submit to as much of the privation immediately as can easily be borne, and, only when any further burden would distress or cripple them too much, to provide for the remainder by mortgaging their future income. It is an excellent maxim to make present resources suffice for present wants; the future will have its own wants to provide for. On the other hand, it may reasonably be taken into consideration that, in a country increasing in wealth, the necessary expenses of government do not increase in the same ratio as capital or population; any burden, therefore, is always less and less felt; and, since those extraordinary expenses of government which are fit to be incurred at all are mostly beneficial beyond the existing generation, there is no injustice in making posterity pay a part of the price, if the inconvenience would be extreme of defraying the whole of it by the exertions and sacrifices of the generation which first incurred it.

§ 2. Not desirable to redeem a national Debt by a general Contribution.

When a country, wisely or unwisely, has burdened itself with a debt, is it expedient to take steps for redeeming that debt? In principle it is impossible not to maintain the affirmative.

Two modes have been contemplated of paying off a national debt: either at once by a general contribution, or gradually by a surplus revenue. The first would be incomparably the best, if it were practicable; and it would be practicable if it could justly be done by assessment on property alone. If property bore the whole interest of the debt, property might, with great advantage to itself, pay it off; since this would be merely surrendering to a creditor the principal sum, the whole annual proceeds of which were already his by law, and would be equivalent to what a land-owner does when he sells part of his estate, to free the remainder from a mortgage. But property, it need hardly be said, does not pay, and can not justly be required to pay, the whole interest of the debt. Whatever is the fitting contribution from property to the general expenses of the state, in the same, and in no greater proportion, should it contribute toward either the interest or the repayment of the national debt. This, however, if admitted, is fatal to any scheme for the extinction of the debt by a general assessment on the community. Persons of property could pay their share of the amount by a sacrifice of property, and have the same net income as before.

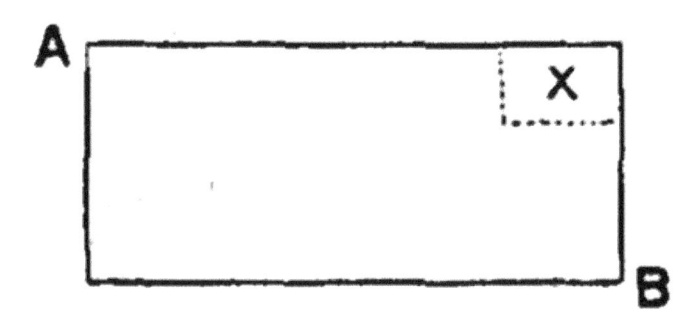

If a person owns a property, A B, which returns him $1,000 income, and if he pays $10 a year in taxes as his share of interest on the public debt, suppose that part of his estate represented by X, which returns him annually $10 (and which return he has annually handed over to the state), to be carved out of it, and that he is to be hereafter relieved of his share of taxes. He would then, after having paid the capitalized value (X) of that which was his share of the annual tax to the state on account of the public debt, have the same net income as before; for he was never able to enjoy the income of X.

If those who have no accumulations, but only incomes, were required to make up by a single payment the equivalent of the annual charge laid on them by the taxes maintained to pay the interest of the debt, they could only do so by incurring a private debt equal to their share of the public debt; while, from the insufficiency, in most cases, of the security which they could give, the interest would amount to a much larger annual sum than their share of that now paid by the state. Besides, a collective debt defrayed by taxes has, over the same debt parceled out among individuals, the immense advantage that it is virtually a mutual insurance among the contributors. If the fortune of a contributor diminishes, his taxes diminish; if he is ruined, they cease altogether, and his portion of the debt is wholly transferred to the solvent members of the community. If it were laid on him as a private obligation, he would still be liable to it, even when penniless.

When the state possesses property, in land or otherwise, which there are not strong reasons of public utility for its retaining at its disposal, this should be employed, as far as it will go, in extinguishing debt. Any casual gain, or god-send, is naturally devoted to the same purpose. Beyond this, the only mode which is both just and feasible, of extinguishing or reducing a national debt, is by means of a surplus revenue.

§ 3. In what cases desirable to maintain a surplus revenue for the redemption of Debt.

The desirableness, *per se*, of maintaining a surplus for this purpose does not, I think, admit of a doubt.

It is not, however, advisable in all cases to maintain a surplus revenue for the extinction of debt. The advantage of paying off the national debt is, that it would enable us to get rid of the worst half of our taxation. But of this worst half some portions must be worse than others, and to get rid of those would be a greater benefit proportionally than to get rid of the rest. If renouncing a surplus revenue would enable us to dispense with a tax, we ought to consider the very worst of all our taxes as precisely the one which we are keeping up for the sake of ultimately abolishing taxes not so bad as itself. In a country advancing in wealth, whose increasing revenue gives it the power of ridding itself from time to time of the most inconvenient portions of its taxation, I conceive that the increase of revenue should rather be disposed of by taking off taxes, than by liquidating debt, as long as any very objectionable imposts remain. In the present state of England, therefore, I hold it to be good policy in the Government, when it has a surplus of an apparently permanent character, to take off taxes, provided these are rightly selected. Even when no taxes remain but such as are not unfit to form part of a permanent system, it is wise to continue the same policy by experimental reductions of those taxes, until the point is discovered at which a given amount of revenue can be raised with the smallest pressure on the contributors. After this, such surplus revenue as might arise from any further increase of the produce of the taxes should not, I conceive, be remitted, but applied to the redemption of debt. Eventually, it might be expedient to appropriate the entire produce of particular taxes to this purpose; since there would be more assurance that the liquidation would be persisted in, if the fund destined to it were kept apart, and not blended with the general revenues of the state. The succession duties would be peculiarly suited to such a purpose, since taxes paid as they are, out of capital, would be better employed in reimbursing capital than in defraying current expenditure. If this separate appropriation were made, any surplus afterward arising from the increasing produce of the other taxes, and from the saving of interest on the successive portions of debt paid off, might form a ground for a remission of taxation.

> The relative amount of the United States public debt may be seen, by Chart No. XXII, from an early date down to 1880. Since the war, the surplus revenue of the United States has been constantly appropriated for the payment of the public debt incurred during the late war, until, what with the reduction of debt and the fall in the interest charge, our income is now so much greater than expenditure that we are (1884) actually in difficulties owing to the surplus. To the present time the Treasury has been able to use its excess of receipts in redeeming matured debt; but the rapidity of the payment has been such that in two years or more no matured debt will exist to be redeemed: $250,000,000 of 4-½ per cent bonds remain, but they do not fall due until 1891; and the 4 per cent bonds to the amount of $737,620,700 do not mature until 1907. Having once raised a large revenue under war pressure, it seems very difficult for people to understand now why heavy duties were originally levied, and the extraordinary suggestion is often made that the surplus should remain, and new channels of expenditure should be made (such as enormous pensions), simply in order to keep up the heavy taxation. The difficulty is, however, that the unnecessary surplus exists because of customs duties levied for war purposes. But the heavy burden of war taxation ought not to be continued, adding to the cost of production in all industries, without doing a greater wrong than would be done by the passing—and only possible—trouble of a redistribution of capital in a few cases; especially since that distribution of capital will be one from less productive to more productive industries; otherwise, no change would be made.

The condition of foreign debts, and the progress made in their reduction, may be studied in Chart No. XXIII. That of the United States is exceptional. The interest-bearing debt, as given by the last report of the Secretary of the Treasury, 1883, has been reduced to $1,312,446,050, and the reduction is more striking than is indicated in the chart for the year 1880.

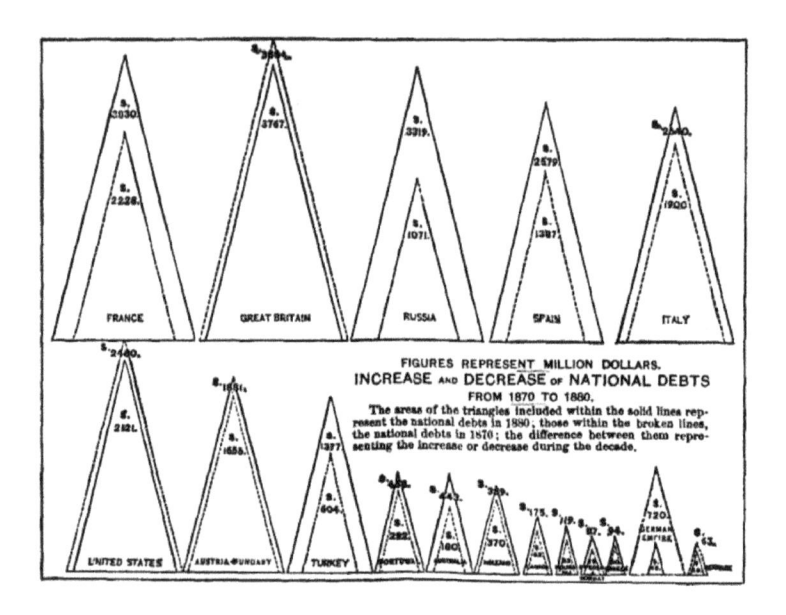

Chart XXIII. Reduction of National Debts in Various Countries.

Chapter VI. Of An Interference Of Government Grounded On Erroneous Theories.

§ 1. The doctrine of Protection to Native Industry.

We proceed to the functions of government which belong to what I have termed, for want of a better designation, the optional class; those which are sometimes assumed by governments and sometimes not, and which it is not unanimously admitted that they ought to exercise. We will begin by passing in review false theories which have from time to time formed the ground of acts of government more or less economically injurious.

Of these false theories, the most notable is the doctrine of Protection to Native Industry—a phrase meaning the prohibition, or the discouragement by heavy duties, of such foreign commodities as are capable of being produced at home. If the theory involved in this system had been correct, the practical conclusions grounded on it would not have been unreasonable. The theory was that, to buy things produced at home was a national benefit, and the introduction of foreign commodities generally a national loss. It being at the same time evident that the interest of the consumer is to buy foreign commodities in preference to domestic whenever they are either cheaper or better, the interest of the consumer appeared in this respect to be contrary to the public interest; he was certain, if left to his own inclinations, to do what according to the theory was injurious to the public.

It was shown, however, in our analysis of the effects of international trade, as it had been often shown by former writers, that the importation of foreign commodities, in the common course of traffic, never takes place except when it is, economically speaking, a national good, by causing the same amount of commodities to be obtained at a smaller cost of labor and capital to the country. To prohibit, therefore, this importation, or impose duties which prevent it, is to render the labor and capital of the country less efficient in production than they would otherwise be, and compel a waste of the difference between the labor and capital necessary for the home production of the commodity and that which is required for producing the things with which it can be purchased from abroad. The amount of national loss thus occasioned is measured by the excess of the price at which the commodity is produced over that at which it could be imported.

In the case of manufactured goods the whole difference between the two prices is absorbed in indemnifying the producers for waste of labor, or of the capital which supports that labor. Those who are supposed to be benefited, namely, the makers of the protected articles (unless they form an exclusive company, and have a monopoly against their own countrymen as well as against foreigners), do not obtain higher profits than other people. All is sheer loss to the country as well as to the consumer.

> Of the industries in a country some are said to "need protection" and others not—that is, those industries which are carried on at a relative disadvantage are the only ones which need protection in order that they may continue in operation. By relative disadvantage is meant a greater relative cost, or sacrifice, to the same amount of labor and capital. Those industries which can not yield so great a value for the labor and capital engaged in them as other more profitable industries are those which are said to "need protection." Wherever protective duties exist it is implied by those who lay them on that there production is carried on under more onerous conditions than in other competing places or occupations. After duties are thus supposed to have protected the less advantageously situated occupations, it may be said that all industries will then have an equal chance. "No doubt," as Mr. Cairnes says, "they would be equalized just as by compelling every one to move about with a weight attached to his leg. The weight would, indeed, be an impediment to locomotion, but, provided it were in each case exactly proportioned to the strength of the limb which drew it, no one ... would have any reason to complain. No one would walk as fast as if his limbs were free, but then his neighbor would be equally fettered, and, if it took him twice as long to reach his destination as before, he would at least have company on his journey."[357]

§ 2. —had its origin in the Mercantile System.

The restrictive and prohibitory policy was originally grounded on what is called the Mercantile System, which, representing the advantage of foreign trade to consist solely in bringing money into the country, gave artificial encouragement to exportation of goods, and discountenanced their importation. The only exceptions to the system were those required by the system itself. The materials and instruments of production were the subject of a contrary policy, directed, however, to the same end; they were freely imported, and not permitted to be exported, in order that manufacturers, being more cheaply supplied with the requisites of manufacture, might be able to sell cheaper, and therefore to export more largely. For a similar reason importation was allowed and even favored, when confined to the productions of countries which were supposed to take from the country still more than it took from them, thus enriching it by a favorable balance of trade. As part of the same system colonies were founded, for the supposed advantage of compelling them to buy our commodities, or at all events not to buy those of any other country: in return for which restriction we were generally willing to come under an equivalent obligation with respect to the staple productions of the colonists. The consequences of the theory were pushed so far that it was not unusual even to give bounties on exportation, and induce foreigners to buy from [England] rather than from other countries by a cheapness which [England] artificially produced, by paying part of the price for them out of [their] own taxes. This is a stretch beyond the point yet reached by any private tradesman in his competition for business. No shopkeeper, I should think, ever made a practice of bribing customers by selling goods to them at a permanent loss, making it up to himself from other funds in his possession.

The principle of the Mercantile Theory is now given up even by writers and governments who still cling to the restrictive system. Whatever hold that system has over men's minds, independently of the private interests exposed to real or apprehended loss by its abandonment, is derived from fallacies other than the old notion of the benefits of heaping up money in the country. The most effective of these is the specious plea of employing our own countrymen and our national industry, instead of feeding and supporting the industry of foreigners. The answer to this, from the principles laid down in former chapters, is evident. Without reverting to the fundamental theorem discussed in an early part of the present treatise,[358] respecting the nature and sources of employment for labor, it is sufficient to say, what has usually been said by the advocates of free trade, that the alternative is not between employing our own people and foreigners, but between employing one class and another of our own people. The imported commodity is always paid for, directly or indirectly, with the produce of our own industry: that industry being, at the same time, rendered more productive, since, with the same labor and outlay, we are enabled to possess ourselves of a greater quantity of the article. Those who have not well considered the subject are apt to suppose that our exporting an equivalent in our own produce, for the foreign articles we consume, depends on contingencies—on the consent of foreign countries to make some corresponding relaxation of their own restrictions, or on the question whether those from whom we buy are induced by that circumstance to buy more from us; and that, if these things, or things equivalent to them, do not happen, the payment must be made in money. Now, in the first place, there is nothing more objectionable in a money payment than in payment by any other medium, if the state of the market makes it the most advantageous remittance; and the money itself was first acquired, and would again be replenished, by the export of an equivalent value of our own products. But, in the next place, a very short interval of paying in money would so lower prices as either to stop a part of the importation, or raise up a foreign demand for our produce, sufficient to pay for the imports. I grant that this disturbance of the equation of international demand would be in some degree to our disadvantage, in the purchase of other imported articles; and that a country which prohibits some foreign commodities, does, *cæteris paribus*, obtain those which it does not prohibit at a less price than it would otherwise have to pay. To express the same thing in other words: a country which destroys or prevents altogether certain branches of foreign trade, thereby annihilating a general gain to the world, which would be shared in some proportion between itself and other countries, does, in some circumstances, draw to itself, at the expense of foreigners, a larger share than would else belong to it of the gain arising from that portion of its foreign trade which it suffers to subsist. But even this it can only be enabled to do, if foreigners do not maintain equivalent prohibitions or restrictions against its commodities. In any case, the justice or expediency of destroying one of two gains, in order to engross a rather larger share of the other, does not require much discussion; the gain, too, which is destroyed, being, in proportion to the magnitude of the transactions, the larger of the two, since it is the one which capital, left to itself, is supposed to seek by preference.

§ 3. —supported by pleas of national subsistence and national defense.

Defeated as a general theory, the Protectionist doctrine finds support in some particular cases from considerations which, when really in point, involve greater interests than mere saving of labor—the interests of national subsistence and of national defense.[359] The discussions on the Corn Laws have familiarized everybody with the plea that we ought to be independent of foreigners for the food of the people; and the Navigation Laws were grounded, in theory and profession, on the necessity of keeping up a "nursery of seamen" for the navy. On this last subject I at once admit that the object is worth the sacrifice; and that a country exposed to invasion by sea, if it can not otherwise have sufficient ships and sailors of its own to secure the means of manning on an emergency an adequate fleet, is quite right in obtaining those means, even at an economical sacrifice in point of cheapness of transport. When the English navigation laws were enacted, the Dutch, from their maritime skill and their low rate of profit at home, were able to carry for other nations, England included, at cheaper rates than those nations could carry for themselves: which placed all other countries at a great comparative disadvantage in obtaining experienced seamen for their ships of war. The navigation laws, by which this deficiency was remedied, and at the same time a blow struck against the maritime power of a nation with which England was then frequently engaged in hostilities, were probably, though economically disadvantageous, politically expedient. But English ships and sailors can now navigate as cheaply as those of any other country, maintaining at least an equal competition with the other maritime nations even in their own trade. The ends which may once have justified navigation laws require them no longer, and afford no reason for maintaining this invidious exception to the general rule of free trade.

> Since the introduction of steamships and the advance of invention in naval contrivances, the plea for navigation laws on the ground that they keep up a "nursery of seamen" for the navy is practically obsolete. The "seaman" employed on the modern naval ships more nearly resembles the artisan in a manufacturing establishment; he need have but comparatively little knowledge of the sea, since the days of sailing-vessels have passed by, so far as naval warfare is concerned. Steam and mechanical appliances now do what was before done by wind and sail.
>
> While Mr. Mill thinks navigation laws were economically—that is, so far as increase of wealth is concerned—disadvantageous, yet he believes that they may have been "politically expedient." It is possible, for example, that retaliation by the United States and other countries against England early in this century brought about the remission of the English restrictions on foreign shipping. But it is quite another thing to say that such laws produced an ability to sail ships more cheaply. That the English navigation acts of 1651 built up English shipping is not supported by many proofs; whereas it is very distinctly shown that English shipping languished and suffered under them.[360]

Moreover, under the *régime* of steam and iron (which drew out England's peculiar advantages in iron and coal), in all its history English shipping never prospered more than it has since the abolition in 1849 of the navigation laws—events which have taken place since Mr. Mill wrote.

The United States is still weighed down by navigation laws adapted to mediæval conditions, and the relics of a time when retaliation was the cause of their enactment. So long as wooden vessels did the carrying-trade, the natural advantages of the United States gave us a proud position on the ocean. Now, however, when it is a question of cheaper iron, steel, and coal for vessels of iron and steel, we are at a possible disadvantage, and the bulk of navigation laws proposed in these days are intended to draw capital either by raising prices through duties on ships and materials, or by outright bounties and subsidies from industries in which we have advantages, to building ships. And until of late no distinction has been made between ship-building and ship-owning (or ship-sailing). Within the last year (1884) many burdens on ship-sailing have been removed; but even when we are permitted to sail ships on equal terms with foreigners, we can not yet build them with as small a cost as England (which is proved by the very demand of the builders of iron vessels for the retention of protective duties), and our laws do not as yet allow us to buy ships abroad and sail them under our own flag.[361]

With regard to subsistence, the plea of the Protectionists has been so often and so triumphantly met, that it requires little notice here. That country is the most steadily as well as the most abundantly supplied with food which draws its supplies from the largest surface. It is ridiculous to found a general system of policy on so improbable a danger as that of being at war with all the nations of the world at once; or to suppose that, even if inferior at sea, a whole country could be blockaded like a town, or that the growers of food in other countries would not be as anxious not to lose an advantageous market as we should be not to be deprived of their corn.

In countries in which the system of Protection is declining, but not yet wholly given up, such as the United States, a doctrine has come into notice which is a sort of compromise between free trade and restriction, namely, that protection for protection's sake is improper, but that there is nothing objectionable in having as much protection as may incidentally result from a tariff framed solely for revenue. Even in England regret is sometimes expressed that a "moderate fixed duty" was not preserved on corn, on account of the revenue it would yield. Independently, however, of the general impolicy of taxes on the necessaries of life, this doctrine overlooks the fact that revenue is received only on the quantity imported, but that the tax is paid on the entire quantity consumed. To make the public pay much, that the treasury may receive a little, is no eligible mode of obtaining a revenue. In the case of manufactured articles the doctrine involves a palpable inconsistency. The object of the duty as a means of revenue is inconsistent with its affording, even incidentally, any protection. It can only operate as protection in so far as it prevents importation, and to whatever degree it prevents importation it affords no revenue.

§ 4. —on the ground of encouraging young industries; colonial policy.

The only case in which, on mere principles of political economy, protecting duties can be defensible, is when they are imposed temporarily (especially in a young and rising nation) in hopes of naturalizing a foreign industry, in itself perfectly suitable to the circumstances of the country. The superiority of one country over another in a branch of production often arises only from having begun it sooner. There may be no inherent advantage on one part, or disadvantage on the other, but only a present superiority of acquired skill and experience. A country which has this skill and experience yet to acquire may in other respects be better adapted to the production than those which were earlier in the field; and, besides, it is a just remark of Mr. Rae that nothing has a greater tendency to promote improvements in any branch of production than its trial under a new set of conditions. But it can not be expected that individuals should, at their own risk, or rather to their certain loss, introduce a new manufacture, and bear the burden of carrying it on, until the producers have been educated up to the level of those with whom the processes are traditional. A protecting duty, continued for a reasonable time, will sometimes be the least inconvenient mode in which the nation can tax itself for the support of such an experiment. But the protection should be confined to cases in which there is good ground of assurance that the industry which it fosters will after a time be able to dispense with it; nor should the domestic producers ever be allowed to expect that it will be continued to them beyond the time necessary for a fair trial of what they are capable of accomplishing.

The great difficulty with this proposal is that it introduces (what is inconsistent with Mr. Mill's general system) the Socialistic basis of state-help, instead of self-help. If industries will never support themselves, then, of course, it is a misappropriation of the property of its citizens whenever a government takes a slice by taxation from productive industries and gives it to a less productive one to make up its deficiencies. The only possible theory of protection to young industries is that, if protected for a season, the industries may soon grow strong and stand alone. Mr. Mill never contemplated anything else. But the difficulty is constantly met with, in putting this theory into practice, that the industry, once that it has learned to depend on the help of the state, never reaches a stage when it is willing to give up the assistance of the duties. Dependence on legislation begets a want of self-reliance, and destroys the stimulus to progress and good management. It is said: "There has never been an instance in the history of the country where the representatives of such industries, who have enjoyed protection for a long series of years, have been willing to submit to a reduction of the tariff, or have proposed it. But, on the contrary, their demands for still higher and higher duties are insatiable, and never intermitted."[362] The question of fact, as to whether or not the United States is indebted for its present manufacturing position to protection when our industries were young, seems to be capable of answer, and an answer which shows that protection was imposed generally after the industries got a foothold, and that very little assistance was derived from the duties on imports.[363]

The following explanation by Mr. Mill[364] of the meaning put upon his argument of protection to young industries by those who have applied it to the United States will be of no slight interest:

"The passage has been made use of to show the inapplicability of free trade to the United States, and for similar purpose in the Australian colonies, erroneously in my opinion, but certainly with more plausibility than can be the case in the United States, for Australia really is a new country whose capabilities for carrying on manufactures can not yet be said to have been tested; but the manufacturing parts of the United States—New England and Pennsylvania—are no longer new countries; they have carried on manufactures on a large scale, and with the benefit of high protecting duties, for at least two generations; their operatives have had full time to acquire the manufacturing skill in which those of England had preceded them; there has been ample experience to prove that the alleged inability of their manufactures to compete in the American market with those of Great Britain does not arise merely from the more recent date of their establishment, but from the fact that American labor and capital can, in the present circumstances of America, be employed with greater return, and greater advantage to the national wealth, in the production of other articles. I have never for a moment recommended or countenanced any protecting industry except for the purpose of enabling the protected branch of industry, in a very moderate time, to become independent of protection. That moderate time in the United States has been exceeded, and if the cotton and iron of America still need protection against those of the other hemisphere, it is in my eyes a complete proof that they aught not to have it, and that the longer it is continued the greater the injustice and the waste of national resources will be."

There is only one part of the protectionist scheme which requires any further notice: its policy toward colonies and foreign dependencies; that of compelling them to trade exclusively with the dominant country. A country which thus secures to itself an extra foreign demand for its commodities, undoubtedly gives itself some advantage in the distribution of the general gains of the commercial world. Since, however, it causes the industry and capital of the colony to be diverted from channels which are proved to be the most productive, inasmuch as they are those into which industry and capital spontaneously tend to flow, there is a loss, on the whole, to the productive powers of the world, and the mother-country does not gain so much as she makes the colony lose. If, therefore, the mother-country refuses to acknowledge any reciprocity of obligations, she imposes a tribute on the colony in an indirect mode, greatly more oppressive and injurious than the direct.

§ 5. —on the ground of high wages.

> The discussion by Mr. Cairnes on the question of wages as affected by the tariff is such that I have quoted it as fully as possible: "The position taken in the

United States is that protection is only needed and only asked for where American industry is placed under a disadvantage, as compared with the industry of foreign countries.... The rates of wages measured in money are higher in the United States than in Europe, and, therefore, it is argued, the cost of producing commodities is higher.... The high rates of wages in the United States are not peculiar to any branch of industry, but are universal throughout its whole range. If, therefore, a high rate of wages proves a high cost of production, and a high cost of production proves a need of protection, it follows that the farmers of Illinois and the cotton-planters of the Southern States stand in as much need of fostering legislation as the cotton-spinners of New England or the iron-masters of Pennsylvania! A criterion which leads to such results must, I think, be regarded as sufficiently condemned. The fallacy is, in truth, ... that all industries are not in each country equally favored or disfavored by nature, and have not, therefore, equal need of this protecting care. If American protectionists are not prepared to demand protective duties in favor of the Illinois farmer against the competition of his English rival, they are bound to admit either that a high cost of production is not incompatible with effective competition, or else that a high rate of wages does not prove a high cost of production; and if this is not so in Illinois, then I wish to know why the case should be different in Pennsylvania or in New England. If a high rate of wages in the first of these States be consistent with a low cost of production, why may not a high rate of wages in Pennsylvania be consistent with a low cost of producing coal and iron?

"The rate of wages, whether measured in money or in the real remuneration of the laborer, affords an approximate criterion of the cost of production,[365] either of money, or of the commodities that enter into the laborer's real remuneration, *but in a sense the inverse of that in which it is understood in the argument under consideration*: in other words, a high rate of wages indicates not a high but a low cost of production.[366] ... Thus in the United States the rate of wages is high, whether measured in gold or in the most important articles of the laborer's consumption—a fact which proves that the cost of producing gold, as well as that of producing those other commodities, is low in the United States.... I would ask [objectors] to consider what are the true causes of the high remuneration of American industry. It will surely be admitted that, in the last resort, these resolve themselves into the one great fact of its high productive power.... I must, therefore, contend that the high scale of industrial remuneration in America, instead of being evidence of a high cost of production in that country, is distinctly evidence of a low cost of production—of a low cost of production, that is to say, in the first place, of gold, and, in the next, of the commodities which mainly constitute the real wages of labor—a description which embraces at once the most important raw materials of industry and the most important articles of general consumption. As regards commodities not included in this description, the criterion of wages stands in no constant relation of any kind to their cost, and is, therefore, simply irrelevant to the point at issue. And now we may see what this claim for protection to American industry, *founded on the high scale of American remuneration*, really comes to: it is a demand for special legislative aid in consideration of the possession of special industrial facilities—a complaint, in short, against the exceptional bounty of nature.

"Perhaps I shall here be asked, How, if the case be so—if the high rate of industrial remuneration in America be only evidence of a low cost of production—the fact is to be explained, since fact it undoubtedly is, that the people of the United States are unable to compete in neutral markets, in the sale of certain important wares, with England and other European countries?[367] No one will say that the people of New England, New York, and Pennsylvania, are deficient in any industrial qualities possessed by the workmen of any country in the world. How happens it, then, that, enjoying industrial advantages superior to other countries, they are yet unable to hold their own against them in the general markets of commerce? I shall endeavor to meet this objection fairly, and, in the first place, let me state what my contention is with regard to the cost of production in America. I do not contend that it is low in the case of all commodities capable of being produced in the country, but only in that of a large, very important, but still limited group. With regard to commodities lying outside this group, I hold that the rate of wages is simply no evidence as to the cost of their production, one way or the other. But, secondly, I beg the reader to consider what is meant by the alleged 'inability' of New England and Pennsylvania to compete, let us say, with Manchester and Sheffield, in the manufacture of calico and cutlery. What it means, and what it only can mean, is that they are unable to do so *consistently with obtaining that rate of remuneration on their industry which is current in the United States*. If only American laborers and capitalists would be content with the wages and profits current in Great Britain, there is nothing that I know of to prevent them from holding their own in any markets to which Manchester and Sheffield can send their wares. And this brings us to the heart of the question. Over a large portion of the great field of industry the people of the United States enjoy, as compared with those of Europe, (1) advantages of a very exceptional kind; over the rest (2) the advantage is less decided, or (3) they stand on a par with Europeans, or (4) possibly they are, in some instances, at a disadvantage. Engaging in the branches of industry in which their advantage over Europe is great, they reap industrial returns proportionally great; and, so long as they confine themselves to these occupations, they can compete in neutral markets against all the world, and still secure the high rewards accruing from their exceptionally rich resources. But the people of the Union decline to confine themselves within these liberal bounds. They would cover the whole domain of industrial activity, and think it hard that they should not reap the same rich harvests from every part of the field. They must descend into the arena with Sheffield and Manchester, and yet secure the rewards of Chicago and St. Louis. They must employ European conditions of production, and obtain American results. What is this but to quarrel with the laws of nature? These laws have assigned to an extensive range of industries carried on in the United

States a high scale of return, far in excess of what Europe can command, to a few others a return on a scale not exceeding the European proportion. American enterprise would engage in all departments alike, and obtain upon all the high rewards which nature has assigned only to some. Here we find the real meaning of the 'inability' of Americans to compete with the 'pauper labor' of Europe. They can not do so, and at the same time secure the American rate of return on their work. The inability no doubt exists, but it is one created, not by the drawbacks, but by the exceptional advantages of their position. It is as if a skilled artisan should complain that he could not compete with the hedger and ditcher. Let him only be content with the hedger and ditcher's rate of pay, and there will be nothing to prevent him from entering the lists even against this rival."[368]

It is often said that wages are kept at a high rate in the United States by the existence of protected industries. On the other hand, the truth is that the protected industries must pay the current high rate of wages fixed by the general productiveness of all industries in the country. When the facts are investigated, it is surprising how small a portion of the laborers of the United States are employed in occupations which owe their existence to the tariff. A general view of the relative numbers engaged in different occupations may be seen by reference to Chart No. XXIV, based on the returns for the census of 1880. The data are well worth examination:[369]

(1.) Agriculture 7,670,493

(2.) Manufacturing, mechanical, and mining 3,837,112

(3.) Trade and transportation 1,810,256

(4.) Professional and personal services 4,074,238

All occupations 17,392,099

(1.) Engaged in agriculture............................. 7,670,493
(2.) " manufactures and mining.................. 3,837,112
(3.) " trade and transportation.... 1,810,256
(4.) " professional and personal services.......... 4,074,238
                                                            17,392,099
Not so engaged...................................... 19,369,508
Total population over ten years of age................ 36,761,607

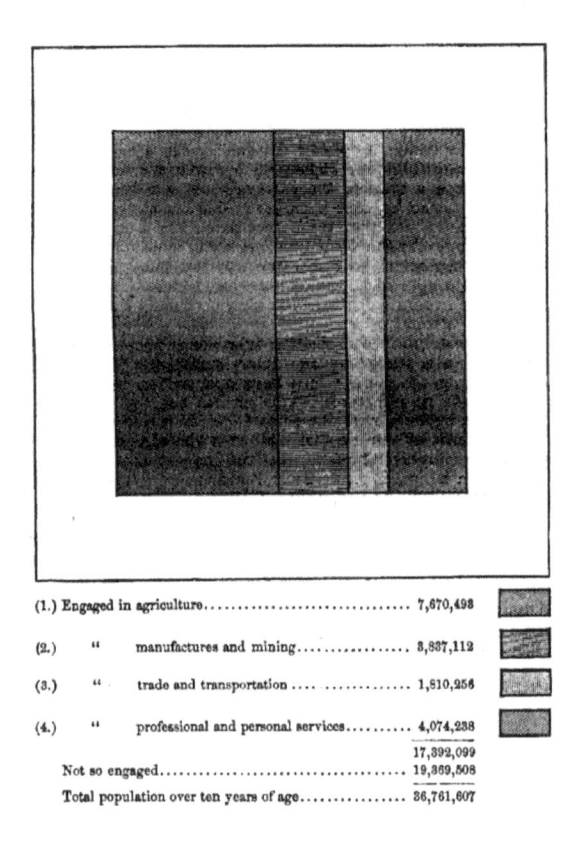

Chart XXIV. *Chart showing for the United States, in 1880, the ratio between the total population over ten years of age and the number of persons reported as engaged in each principal class of gainful occupations. Compiled from the returns of the Tenth Census, by the Editor.* NOTE.—The interior square represents the proportion of the population which is accounted for as engaged in gainful occupations. The unshaded space between the inner and outer squares represents the proportion of the population not so accounted for.

Of the second class, less than 450,000 work-people are engaged in the chief protected industries—cotton, woolen, and iron and steel, combined. This class, it is to be noted, in the census returns, includes bakers, blacksmiths, brick-makers, builders, butchers, cabinet-makers, carpenters, carriage-makers, and so on through the whole list of similar occupations practically unaffected by the tariff (so far as protection to them is concerned). So that, at the most, there are less than a million laborers engaged in industries directly dependent on the tariff, and the number is undoubtedly very much less than a million. When some writers assert, therefore, that the existence of customs-duties allows industries (even including all those employed in producing cotton, wool, iron, and steel) to employ less than a million laborers in such a way that the remuneration is fixed for the remaining 16,000,000 laborers in the United States, keeping wages high for 16,000,000 by paying current wages for less than a million, the extravagance and ignorance of the statement are at once apparent; while, on the other hand, it is distinctly seen that the causes fixing the generally high rates of wages for the 16,000,000 are those governing the majority of occupations, and that the less than one million must be paid the wages which can be obtained elsewhere in the more productive industries. The facts thus strikingly bear out the principles as stated above.

Confirmation—if confirmation now seems necessary—may be found in a study[370] by our ablest statistician, Francis A. Walker, upon the causes which have operated on the growth of American manufactures. This growth has not been commensurate, he finds, with the remarkable inventive and industrial capacity of our people, and with the richness of our national resources: "I answer that the cause of that comparative failure is found, primarily and principally, in the extraordinary success of our agriculture, as already intimated in what has been said of the investment of capital. The enormous profits of cultivating a virgin soil without the need of artificial fertilization; the advantages which a sparse population derives from the privilege of selecting for tillage only the choicest spots,[371] those most accessible, most fertile, most easily brought under the plow; and the consequent abundance of food and other necessaries enjoyed by the agricultural class, have tended continually to disparage mechanical industries, in the eyes alike of the capitalist, looking to the most remunerative investment of his savings, and of the laborer, seeking that avocation which should promise the most liberal and constant support.

"It has been the competition of the farm with the shop which, throughout the entire century of our national independence, has most effectually hindered the growth of manufactures. A people who are privileged to cultivate a reasonably fertile soil, under the conditions indicated above, can secure for themselves subsistence up to the highest limit of physical well-being. If that people possess the added advantage of great skill in the use of tools, and great adroitness in meeting the large and the little exigencies of the occupation and cultivation of the soil, the fruits of their labor will include not only everything which is essential to health and comfort, but much that is of the nature of luxury."

It remains to be said in this connection that workmen are already discerning the practical and real causes at work affecting their wages—affecting them more directly than any tariff system possibly could—by showing no small alarm at the immigration of foreigners, such as the Hungarian miners and Italian laborers, who willingly underbid them. In other words, they are beginning to realize, in a practical way, the truth that increasing numbers are far more potent than anything else in reducing wages. So long as immigration is free to any race or nationality, there is no such thing as "protection to home laborers"; the only protection to them—not that I am urging the desirability of such measures—can come solely from forces which limit the number of workmen who enter into competition with them. Any other protection to laboring-men than the prohibition of immigration—which no one thinks of (except for the Chinese)—is an economic delusion. Instead of "protecting" them to the extent of affording higher wages, the tariff increases the cost of woolen clothing and other articles of their consumption, in addition to forcing capital into employments which yield a less return, and so insure lower wages.

§ 6. —on the ground of creating a diversity of industries.

It must be kept in mind that Political Economy deals only with the phenomena of material wealth; it does not supply ethical or political grounds of action. It is quite conceivable that a legislator, in coming to a decision, may have to balance economic gains against moral or political losses, and may choose to give up the former to prevent the latter. But the economic truth remains unchanged. Political economy, for instance, to the question, Is there any gain in international trade? answers, unequivocally, yes. Would it be a loss of wealth to the community to have the goods formerly bought abroad now produced at home? The answer is, certainly it would. But here it has been ably urged by intelligent writers that a state has other ends to gain than the accumulation of mere riches; that it must aim to secure the greatest moral, social, and elevating influences possible for the working-classes; and that while free exchange of goods may add to wealth, it may injure the social and political well-being of a nation. So far as these are social and political questions they do not belong to Political Economy. But the commonest form of argument is that, under free exchange, the United States would become purely an "agricultural" country, its social horizon would become narrowed, and a lower standard of industrial activity would then ensue; instead of which, it is said, we should, by protection, keep in existence diversified industries by which the national mind may be better stimulated, and greater enterprise may be encouraged in all branches of industry. This argument for "diversity of industries," however, is not merely a sociological question; it can only be fully discussed from an economic stand-point, and deserves even more than the brief attention we can give it here.

In the first place, as soon as any purely agricultural country gains even a slight density of population—a density only such as to warrant the introduction of the principle of division of labor—there comes an inevitable differentiation of pursuits, wholly outside of legislation, and through the operation of natural causes. Not all of any population is required in agriculture to provide the whole with food. By a division of labor, one man in agriculture can produce the sustenance of himself and many others. "The United States have at the present time but five persons engaged in agriculture for each square mile of settled area." By the side of the farm must early spring up a wide circle of industries—the shoemaker, the carpenter, the blacksmith, the wagon-maker, the painter, the builder, the mason, and all the ordinary employments which arise in any small community from the earliest division of labor. Moreover, "agriculture" is often used in a too limited sense as confined to producing food alone (although even in that limited sense employing nearly one half of the total number of our laborers). In a new country the natural field of employment is found in the "extractive industries," which include the preparation for the market not only of food, but also of all ores, coal, minerals, oils, hides, leather, wool, lumber, and the industries intimately connected with them; all the employments which transport these from one part of the country to another (employing at present over one ninth of all our laborers); and professional and personal services of an extended variety. Even, therefore, if we were obliged to forego manufactures entirely, the "extractive industries" would necessarily involve a very extensive diversity of employments.

The real question, however, for most persons, centers in the next stage of the industrial evolution—that of the manufactures of these above-mentioned products of the "extractive industries." It will be remembered, here, that a country does not possess an equal ability in producing each of these or any commodities: the timber formerly near great rivers may vanish into the interior; the oil-sources may be more or less fertile; or the ore-deposits may be more or less rich, more or less accessible, than those of other countries. This being understood, then, as soon as the demand in the country calls for an increased quantity of a particular article, the cost may increase under the law of diminishing returns until a foreign country—having inferior agents of production as compared with our best—may be able to send supplies into our markets. It all depends on whether the United States wants more articles than can be produced on grades of natural agents superior to those possessed by foreigners, taking cost of carriage to this country into consideration. Even though foreign competition appears when we reach poorer grades of natural agents, it does not follow that some of the particular articles will not be produced. What ought to be clear is, that untrammeled exchange between countries will not prevent the existence of various industries, but only limit production to those grades of agents which are its best. This may be better seen by a simple diagram:

Iron and Coal: England   7654321

Iron and Coal: United States 4321

Wheat: England   4321

Wheat: United States   7654321

England may have seven different grades of productiveness in her iron and coal supplies, of which her grades 1, 2, and 3 are superior to the best grade of the United States, while grades 1, 2, 3, and 4 in the United States may compare only with grades 4, 5, 6, 7 of England. So long as England can supply herself and the United States also with coal and iron from the three superior grades, the United States can not work grade 1 at home. But if the supply for England and the world requires grade 5 to be worked, then the United States can begin the industry on her best grade, although that is far inferior to the best grade in England. Likewise, if the United States has three grades of wheat-land superior to England's best grade, the ability of England to grow wheat depends on whether the United States can, or can not, supply both herself and England from grades 1, 2, and 3. If we must resort to grade 4, then England can begin to grow wheat as well as we. In short, under a system of free exchange, as great a diversity as under protection is probably possible, but only in such a way that the best possible advantages in each particular industry are employed. Smaller amounts in some branches, and greater amounts in others, may be produced under a free than under a restrictive system, but with all the greater gain which arises from a proper and healthy adjustment of trade. The most poorly endowed enterprises in each occupation would be given up, but not the whole industry itself. No class of persons feel the competition of rivals more than English farmers since American wheat has come into English markets, and yet it does not follow that England can not grow a bushel of wheat. The fact is, merely, that some kinds of lands were thrown out of cultivation, and a readjustment made, to the benefit of those wanting cheaper food. So with us: we should not, by the free exchange, be forced to give up the iron and coal industries entirely; for the best mines would still keep that occupation in existence to "diversify" the others.

So far the explanation covers the "extractive industries" only, or those industries affected by the law of diminishing returns when a larger quantity is demanded. The real question arises as to the manufactures of these materials. But we count upon larger industrial rewards, in the form of wages, and profits, here than in England; we must get more from an industry than England in order to satisfy us. Our grades of occupations, therefore, must be more productive to a certain extent, grade for grade, than English grades, in order to allow of their remaining free from competition. But we have this superiority, as regards our home market, owing to natural causes: (1) cheap raw materials (if we except wool and other commodities whose price is raised by the tariff); (2) advantage over England in cost of transportation of raw products; and (3) in the cost of transportation, again, of the finished goods in reaching our markets.

Now, the processes of manufacture which do not put much labor upon the materials, especially where the articles are bulky, are conducted in this country without fear of foreign competition. And the range of this class of manufactures is surprisingly large. It includes the manufactures of iron, such as stoves, and the common utensils of every-day life; of hides, such as leather, harnesses, etc.; and of wood, such as all the furniture of common use. The list is too long to be fully stated here. These industries are not kept in existence by the tariff; and a diversity as wide as this would arise under a system of free exchange, as well as of restriction. Indeed, if duties were removed from so-called "raw materials," it is altogether probable that a wider diversity would exist than ever before.

And yet, it will be said, there are some things we can not produce in free competition with England. Of course there are; and it is to be hoped it will long continue so. If there are not some kinds of commodities which foreigners can produce to better advantage than we, then there will be no possibility of any foreign trade whatever; since, if they can send us nothing, they can take nothing from us. To deny this position, is to say that the export and import trade of the United States (amounting in 1883 to more than $1,500,000,000) is of no profit, and had best be entirely destroyed, in order that a few industries in which we have no natural advantages (and which employ less than one seventeenth of the laborers in the United States) should be continued at a loss to the general productiveness of our labor and capital, and so to a general diminution of wages and profits.

§ 7. —on the ground that it lowers prices.

The argument—heard less frequently now than formerly—has been advanced, drawn inductively from statistics, that protection does not raise prices; because, after duties are put on, a larger quantity is produced, the advantages of large production are reaped, and then the price of the manufactured commodity falls lower here than it was before the duty was imposed. The position is then held that protection does not raise prices. It is, of course, understood to mean the prices of protected commodities—a necessary precaution, because we find our own agricultural (unprotected) commodities cited to show that prices are lower here than in England.

No one, however, will deny that there has been a fall in the prices of textile fabrics and manufactured goods. That is the result of a general law of value, and of the tendencies of a progressive state of industry.[372] The causes of this acknowledged fall would be at work, no matter whether tariffs existed or not. It is the result of the general forward march of improvements, as evidenced in the application of new inventions and the display of skill and ingenuity in new processes. To say that it comes because of a tariff, is a complete *non sequitur*. How true this is may be seen by observing that a country like England, without tariffs, shares in the general fall of prices of manufactured goods equally with the country which has heavy customs-duties. The causes must be wider than tariffs, if they are seen working alike in tariff and non-tariff countries.

But the fact itself can not be gainsaid that protection does raise the prices of the protected goods in the home market. The comparison is not to be made between prices as they now are in this country and as they were twenty or forty years ago also in this country, for this would show only the general march of improvements in this country; but a comparison is to be made between prices in this country to-day and present prices in foreign countries. Does, for instance, the tariff increase the price of woolen goods and clothing to every consumer far beyond what the price would be if the duty on imported woolens were removed? The very existence of a protecting duty is the answer to this. If the duty does not raise the price, then why does the woolen industry wish a continuance of the duties? If goods can be sold as cheaply here as the foreign goods, why do protectionists want any duties?

The duties are intended to keep foreign goods out of our markets; and they would be unnecessary if our goods could be sold as cheaply as the foreign wares.

The facts, however, are at hand to show that the statement of principle as made above is corroborated by the statistics. In 1883, although average weekly wages in Massachusetts were over 77 per cent higher than in England, the American laborer had to pay more for the articles entering into his real wages; and to that extent lost the advantage of his higher reward in this country. This is to be seen in the following figures,[373] which show, in percentages, whether prices are higher or lower here than in England:

Classes of Articles.	Higher Percent.	Lower Percent.
Groceries	16	
Provisions, including meat, eggs, butter, and potatoes		23
Dry goods (all grades)	13	
Boots, shoes, and slippers	62	
Clothing	45	

And yet, in spite of the high prices, 31 per cent of the Massachusetts workman's expenditure represents more comfort and better home surroundings than is enjoyed by the English workman. If the American could purchase at English prices, he would have no less than 37 per cent of a surplus for additional enjoyments (after making due allowance for the higher rents paid here than in England). In other words, higher prices cut off the American laborer from reaping all the superiority in comfort which might be expected from knowing that he had an advantage over the English laborer of 77 per cent in the money wages received.

In order that the reader may easily find the arguments of the protectionists, he is referred to the following books:

Carey's "Principles of Social Science" (3 vols.). The form of argument is, briefly, that all industries should be kept going within the bounds of a country so as to avoid foreign trade. The change of form into the finished commodity should, he holds, take place near the spot where the raw materials are produced, so that not so great a share should go to the mere middle-men, or transporters.

Bowen's "Political Economy," Chap. XX, advocates protection on the ground that it is needed to secure diversity of industries, and that it lowers the prices of imported goods.

Sir J. B. Byles's "Sophisms of Free Trade" is an answer to Bastiat's "Sophisms of Protection," the latter having been translated into English by Horace White.

Erastus B. Bigelow's "The Tariff Question." This is one of the ablest discussions, from the protectionist point of view, based on statistical tables and comparisons of the policy of England and the United States.

Stebbins's "Protectionists' Manual" is a brief and handy statement.

Ellis H. Roberts's "Government Revenue" is the form into which he has thrown his lectures at Cornell University (1884) on protection, and is the latest statement emanating from that side of the discussion. He goes at length into the history of taxes in various countries; holds that wages are higher here than in England because of protection; that our manufactures are more flourishing than our agriculture, etc.

Frederick List's "National Economy" is the German statement of protection, much on Carey's own grounds.

"The Congressional Globe" contains numerous speeches of members of Congress on the tariff; and the

Iron and Steel Association of Philadelphia send out pamphlets explaining the protectionist position.

The free-trade arguments may be found also in W. M. Grosvenor's "Does Protection Protect?" He studies the results of the various tariffs of the United States, and gives many very valuable tables and collections of statistics bearing upon this question.

W. G. Sumner's "History of Protection in the United States" is a very vigorous account of the evils of the various tariffs and the protective system.

D. A. Wells's "Reports" as Special Commissioner of the Revenue, and his numerous pamphlets (see Putnams' publisher's catalogue), are full of facts, and give the results of special study of the subject as affecting the United States.

A. L. Perry's "Political Economy" gives a radical free-trade view.

Henry Fawcett's "Free Trade and Protection" explains the causes which have retarded the more general adoption of free trade.

J. E. Cairnes's "Leading Principles of Political Economy" gives the ablest discussion of the economic principles involved in the question which has yet been offered to the reader. Moreover, almost all our systematic writers on political economy (excepting, perhaps, Bowen and R. E. Thompson) give the system of free exchange their support on economic grounds.

Appendix I. Bibliographies.

A Brief Bibliography Of The Tariffs Of The United States.

I. *General Works.*—Young's "Special Report on the Customs-Tariff Legislation of the United States" contains useful extracts from debates of Congress, and also valuable tables of duties; in the Index, p. cciii, under "Tariff Act," will be found references to, and dates of, all acts to 1870. See, also, Sumner's "History of American Currency," and his "Lectures on Protection in the United States"; A. L. Perry's "Political Economy," chap. xiii; Grosvenor's "Does Protection Protect?" A valuable study is E. J. James's "Studien über den Amerikanischen Zoll tariff." For different views, see Carey's "Social Science"; Bolles's "Financial History of the United States," vol. ii, Bk. i, chap. v, Bk. iii, chaps. iii to x; and Stebbins's "American Protectionists' Manual."

II. *Earlier Periods.*—H. C. Adams's "Taxation in the United States, 1789-1816"; F. W. Taussig's "Protection to Young Industries"; the works of Hamilton, Madison, Jefferson, Webster, and Clay; "The Statesman's Manual"; and of course the Debates in Congress, etc. See, also, Bristed's "Resources of the United States"; Pitkin's "Statistical View of the Commerce of the United States"; Seybert's "Statistical Annals" (1818); and the "American Almanac."

III. *Noteworthy Documents.*—Hamilton's Reports: "Report on Manufactures," Works, ii, pp. 192-284, or American State Papers, Finance, i, 123-144. Dallas, Treasury Report of 1816, American State Papers, Finance, iii, 87-91.

A report which is of the greatest importance and weight is Albert Gallatin's "Memorial in Favor of Tariff Reform" (1832). Printed separately. Unfortunately, not in his collected works.

Walker's Report, see Finance Report, December 3, 1845.

J. Q. Adams's Report of 1832, Congressional Documents, 1831-1832, H. R. No. 481.

D. A. Wells's "Reports as Special Commissioner of the Revenue," 1866, Senate Documents, second session, Thirty-ninth Congress, vol. i, No. 2; 1868, House Executive Documents, second session, Fortieth Congress, vol. ix, No. 81; 1869, House Executive Documents, third session, Fortieth Congress, vol. vii, No. 16; 1869, House Executive Documents, second session, Forty-first Congress, vol. v, No. 27; and his paper in the Cobden Club Essays (second series).

W. D. Kelley's "Speeches, Addresses, and Letters."

"Report of the Tariff Commission," 1882 (two vols). H. R. Miscellaneous Documents, No. 6, Part I, Forty-seventh Congress, second session.

IV. *Pauper-Labor Argument.*—See Taussig, "Protection to Young Industries," p. 69, note 1; Calhoun's speech, Works, iv, pp. 201-212; Greeley's speech of 1843; Cooper's "Politics," pp. 99-109; Webster's Works, v, pp. 161-235; Cairnes, "Leading Principles," pp. 382-388. Fifteenth Annual Report of the Massachusetts Bureau of Statistics (1884), by Carroll D. Wright. D. A. Wells, "Princeton Review," November, 1883, p. 261; Schoenhof, "Wages and Trade."

V. *View of Early Manufactures.*—Bishop, "History of American Manufactures"; Batchelder's "Introduction and Early Progress of the Cotton Manufacture in the United States"; N. Appleton, "Origin of Lowell"; G. S. White, "Memoir of Samuel Slater"; B. F. French, "History of the Rise and Progress of the Iron Trade of the United States for 1621-1857"; H. Scrivenor, "History of the Iron Trade"; "Bulletin of the National Association of Woolen Manufactures," ii, pp. 479-488. Tench Coxe, "Statement of the Arts and Manufactures of the United States for 1810" (1814).

VI. *Later View of Manufactures:*

(1.) THE IRON MANUFACTURE.—See Swank's "Reports of Iron and Steel Association," 1882; ibid., "Census Report," 1880; ibid., "Iron Trade," 1876; J. S. Newberry, for an excellent article in "International Review," i, pp. 768-780.

For Bessemer steel, Swank, "Census Report," 1880, pp. 149-153; and Schoenhof, "Destructive Influences of the Tariff," chap. vii. A. S. Hewett, Speech in Congress, May 16, 1882. Separately printed.

(2.) WOOL, WOOLENS, AND COTTONS.—Production and importation of wool, see "United States Statistical Abstract"; "Tariff Commission Report," i, pp. 1782-1785; ii, p. 2432.

Production and importation of woolens, see "Bulletin of Woolen Manufacturers," vii, p. 359; "Commerce and Navigation Reports."

Prosperity of woolen manufacturers after 1867, see Wells, "Wool and the Tariff" (a letter to the "New York Tribune," March 20, 1873); R. W. Robinson, article of December, 1872, in "Bulletin of Woolen Manufacturers," iii, p. 354. Edward Harris, "Memorial of the Manufacturers of Woolen Goods to the Committee of Ways and Means," Washington, 1872. John L. Hayes, "The Fleece and the Loom."

Production and importation of cottons, see "Commerce and Navigation Reports"; Census Report of 1880.

(3.) SILK.—Manufacture since 1860, see "Silk Association Reports"; Wyckoff, "Silk Manufacture in the United States" (1883) for recent history, pp. 42-51. Wyckoff, "The Silk Goods of America" (1880), on methods of manufacture, chaps. ii, iv, vi.

(4.) SUGAR DUTIES.—D. A. Wells, "Princeton Review," vi (November, 1880), pp. 319-335; and "The Sugar Industry of the United States and the Tariff" (1878).

VII. *Present Tariff.*—Heyl's "United States Duties on Imports" (1881) contains all acts in force to date of publication, and gives all acts since the year 1861 in full. It is used by the United States officials.

"Imports Duties from 1867 to 1883 inclusive" (House of Representatives, Miscellaneous Documents, No. 49, Forty-eighth Congress, first session) gives duties on each article by years, and reduces specific to *ad valorem* rates.

"The Existing Tariff on Imports into the United States," 1884 (Senate Document, Report, No. 12, Forty-eighth Congress, first session).

A Brief Bibliography Of Bimetallism.

"The Report of the International Monetary Conference, 1878" (p. 754), contains an extended bibliography on money, by S. Dana Horton. Chevalier's third volume of his "Cours d'Économie politique," entitled "Monnaie," also gives a bibliography.

I. *Standard of Value.*—See Jevons, "Money and the Mechanism of Exchange," chaps iii, xxv; S. Dana Horton, "Gold and Silver," chap. iv, p. 36; F. A. Walker, "Political Economy," pp. 363-368, "Money, Trade, and Industry," pp. 56-77; Wolowski, "L'Or et l'Argent," pp. 7, 22, 207; Mill, "Principles of Political Economy," book iii, chap. xv; Walras, "Journal des Économistes," October, 1882, pp. 5-13.

II. *Bimetallic Theory.*—Horton, "Gold and Silver," p. 29; F. A. Walker, "Money, Trade, and Industry," p. 157, "Political Economy," p. 408; Giffen, "Fortnightly Review," vol. xxxii (1879), p. 279; Wolowski, "L'Or et l'Argent," p. 35; Jevons, ibid., chap, xii; A. J. Wilson, "Reciprocity, Bimetallism, and Land Reform," p. 107; S. Bourne, "Trade, Population, and Food," p. 227; Seyd, "The Decline of Prosperity," and the various pamphlets of Cernuschi.

III. *Operation of Gresham's Law.*—Macaulay, chap. xxi for clipped coin of 1695; Jevons, ibid., pp. 80-85, also gives an example taken from the Japanese currency; for the case of France, see "Report of the Select Committee of the House of Commons on the Depreciation of Silver, 1876," p. xlii, and Appendix, pp. 86, 148; for the United States, see *supra*, book iii, chap. vii, § 3. See, also, Lord Liverpool's "Treatise on the Coins of the Realm," chap. xii, for changes in the coin of England.

IV. *Compensatory Effect of Two Standards.*—Jevons, ibid., pp. 139, 140; F. A. Walker, "Political Economy," pp. 411-416; Wolowski, "L'Or et l'Argent," p. 28; Mannequin, "Journal des Économistes," August, 1878, p. 202.

V. *Effect of a League of States, or Law, on the Relative Value of Gold and Silver.*—Giffen, "Fortnightly Review," vol. xxxii (1879), pp. 285-290; Wolowski, "L'Or et l'Argent," pp. 23, 24, 31; F. A. Walker, "Political Economy," p. 410, "Report of the International Monetary Conference, 1878," p. 74; Sumner, "Princeton Review," vol. iv, p. 563; S. Dana Horton, "Report of the International Monetary Conference, 1878," p. 741; Bourne, "Trade, Population, and Food," pp. 228, 230; Jevons, "Contemporary Review," vol. xxxix (1881), p. 750; S. Newcomb, "International Review" (1879), p. 314.

VI. *Production of Gold and Silver; Relative Value of the Two Metals.*—Ad. Soetbeer, Petermann's "Mittheilungen," No. 57; "House of Commons Report on Depreciation of Silver," 1876, Appendix, pp. 11, 12, 24; Bourne, "Statistical Journal," vol. xlii, p. 409, gives Sir H. Hay's figures corrected by him to 1878; Spofford's "American Almanac," 1878, gives tables from the "Journal des Économistes"; the figures of Seyd, Hay, Jacob, and Tooke and Newmarch are in the "House of Commons Report," above. Also see, *supra*, book iii, chap. vi, for references.

The relative values of gold and silver since 1834, as given in Pixley and Abell's (London) tables, are trustworthy. Previous to 1834 there is much uncertainty. Soetbeer, ibid., gives Hamburg quotations since 1687. Another table, probably incorrect in places, is that of White, see "Report of the International Monetary Conference," 1878, p. 647.

VII. *Demonetization of Silver by Germany.*—For copy of laws of 1871 and 1873, see "Report of Directors of the United States Mint, 1873," p. 82; "House of Commons Report on Depreciation of Silver," 1876, p. 18; "Conférence Monétaire Internationale," 1881, index, p. 215 for "Allemagne."

VIII. *Latin Union.*—For treaty, see "Journal des Économistes," May, 1866; "House of Commons Report," ibid, xxxviii, Appendix, pp. 92, 98, 106-109, 116; "Report of Monetary Conference," 1878, pp. 779-787.

IX. *Flow of Silver to the East.*—The figures of Sir Hector Hay after 1851, "House of Commons Report," ibid., App., p. 24, are fullest, and should be combined with Pixley and Abell's figures for years before 1851, ibid., Appendix, p. 21. See also Bourne, "Statistical Journal," 1879, p. 422; Waterfield, "House of Commons Report," ibid., Appendix, pp. 171, 172, 174; Quetteville, ibid., p. 184; "Conférence Monétaire Internationale," 1881, p. 197; London "Economist," February 24, 1883, Supplement, p. 7; "Parliamentary Documents," 1881, vol. xciii; "Report of the Director of the United States Mint," 1880 (in the Finance Report, 1880, p. 194); J. B. Robertson, "Westminster Review," vol. cxv, p. 200.

X. *Depreciation of Silver, 1876.*—Causes, Bourne, ibid., pp. 206, 212, 222, 233; Wilson, ibid., p. 128; "House of Commons Report," ibid.; Sumner, "Princeton Review," vol. iv., p. 570; S. Newcomb, "International Review," vol. vi (1879), p. 326; Cochut, "Revue des Deux Mondes," i, December, 1883, p. 514; Cairnes, "Essays"; F. Bowen, "Minority Report of the United States Silver Commission," 1878.

Supposed cause of panic of 1873, see Williamson, "Contemporary Review," April 1879; Seyd, "Decline of Prosperity"; Bourne, ibid., pp. 226, 227.

XI. *Appreciation of Gold.*—Giffen, "Statistical Journal," vol. xlii, p. 36, started the theory for the period 1873-1879. Also see Bourne, "Statistical Journal," vol. xlii, p. 406; S. Newcomb, "International Review," 1879, p. 329; Wolowski, ibid., pp. 29, 30; Goschen, "Journal of the Institute of Bankers" (London), vol. iv, part vi, May, 1883; Patterson, "Statistical Journal," vol. xliii, p. 1; for table of prices see London "Economist" (e.g., December 28, 1878).

XII. *Bimetallism in the United States.*—See *supra*, book iii, chap. vii; for a vast array of materials, see "Report of the International Monetary Conference," 1878; Linderman's "Money and Legal Tender"; the Finance Reports of the United States; and Congressional Documents. For the coinage laws of 1792, 1834, 1853, 1873, 1878, see pamphlet, "Extracts from the Laws of the United States relating to Currency and Finance," by C. F. Dunbar. For detailed account of passage of Act of 1873, see "Report of the Comptroller of the Currency," 1876, p. 170. Present situation, "Atlantic Monthly," May, 1884, "The Silver Danger."

A Brief Bibliography Of American Shipping.

I. *English Navigation Acts.*—Macpherson's "Annals," ii, pp. 442, 484; Scobell, "Collection of Acts," p. 176; Ruffhead, "Statutes at Large," iii, p. 182; Roger Coke, "Treatise on Trade" (1671), p. 36; Sir Josiah Child, "New Discourse on Trade" (1671); Sir Matthew Decker, "Essay on the Causes of the Decline of Foreign Trade" (1744); Joshua Gee, "Trade and Navigation of Great Britain" (1730); Lindsay, "History of Merchant Shipping and Ancient Commerce"; McCulloch, "Dictionary of Commerce" (new edition), articles "Navigation" and "Colonial Trade"; ibid., edition of Adam Smith, note xii, p. 534; Huskisson, speeches, iii, 13, 351; Levi, "History of British Commerce," p. 158.

II. *Navigation Laws of the United States.*—"United States Statutes at Large," i, 27, 287, 305; Act of 1817, Statutes, iii, 351; Revised Statutes (1878), "Commerce and Navigation," p. 795; Lord Sheffield, "Observations on the Commerce of the United States"; Pitkin, "Statistical View of the Commerce of the United States," chap. i; D. A. Wells, "Our Merchant Marine," chap. v; Seybert's "Statistical Annals"; Macgregor, "Commercial Statistics of America."

III. *Growth of American Shipping.*—Rapid growth, 1840-1856. Levi, "History of British Commerce," p. 582; Bigelow, "Tariff Question," Appendix No. 57; "Harper's Magazine," January, 1884, p. 217; Lindsay, "History of Merchant Shipping," iii, p. 187; for ship-building, see Report of the United States Bureau of Statistics, "Commerce and Navigation," 1881, p. 927; for tonnage, ibid., pp. 928-930; also, see "United States Statistical Abstract"; Dingley's Report to House of Representatives, December 15, 1882, No. 1,827, Forty-seventh Congress, second session, pp. 5, 8, 254.

IV. *Steam and Iron Ships.*—Preble, "History of Steam Navigation"; Colden, "Life of Fulton"; Porter, "Progress of the Nation," section 3, chap. iv; Nimmo, "Report to the Secretary of the Treasury in Relation to the Foreign Commerce of the United States and the Decadence of American Shipping" (1870); Dingley's Report, pp. 4, 23; Kelley, "The Question of Ships," Appendix ii, p. 208.

V. *Decline of American Shipping.*—"Report on Commerce and Navigation" (1881), pp. 927, 928; Lindsay, ibid., iii, pp. 83, 187, 593, 645; ibid., iv, pp. 163-180, 292, 316, 376; "North American Review," October, 1864, p. 489; "Report on Commerce and Navigation," 1881, lxv, pp. 915, 916, 922, 934; Lynch, Report to House of Representatives on "Causes of the Reduction of American Tonnage," February 17, 1878, pp. ix, 80, 176, 195-213; remission of duties, Revised Statutes of the United States (edition of 1878), section 2,513; Report on "Commerce and Navigation," xi, 83, 210; Dingley's Report; Nimmo, "Decadence of American Shipping" (which gives several charts), p. 17, "The Practical Workings of our Relations of Maritime Reciprocity" (1871); Kelley, ibid.; Reports of the New York Chamber of Commerce; Sumner, "Shall Americans own Ships?" in "North American Review," June, 1880; Codman, "Free Ships"; for high-rate profit in the United States, Dingley's Report, p. 4.

VI. *Burdens on Ship-Owners.*—Tonnage duties, Wells, p. 179; sailors' wages, Revised Statutes, sections 4,561, 4,578, 4,580-4,584, 4,600; consular fees, Dingley's Report, p. 9; pilotage, taxation, Wells, p. 172, *et seq.*; see also Act of 1884, abolishing many of these burdens.

Appendix II. Examination Questions.

The following problems and questions have been arranged to indicate to the reader the character of examinations set by English[374] and American universities. They have been taken in each case from papers actually given. It is hardly necessary to state, perhaps, that these questions do not exhaust the subject, and are only some of a kind of which many more might be added:

DEFINITIONS.

1. Define briefly, Fixed Capital; Unproductive Consumption; Law of Diminishing Returns; Effective Desire of Accumulation; Law of Increase of Labor; Communism; Wages Fund; Wages of Superintendence; Real Wages; Value; Price; Demand; Medium of Exchange; Gresham's Law.

2. Explain carefully the following terms: Productive Consumption, Effectual Demand, Margin of Cultivation, Cost of Production, Value of Money, Cost of Labor, Wealth, and Abstinence.

3. Explain the following terms: Real Wages, Fixed Capital, Allowance System, Margin of Cultivation, Price, Demand, Medium of Exchange, Seignorage, Value of Money, and Bill of Exchange.

4. Define Supply, Value of Money, Productive Consumption, Cost of Production, Cost of Labor, Exchange Value, Law of Production from Land, Rate of Profit, Capital, and Gresham's Law.

5. Define Political Economy: State the parts into which it may be divided, and show how they are mutually related.

LABOR.

6. Distinguish between direct and indirect labor, and give an illustration of the distinction.

7. Apply the distinction between productive and unproductive labor, and productive and unproductive consumption, respectively, to each of the following persons: a tailor, an architect, an annuitant, a sailor, and a bricklayer.

8. Is an actor to be classed as a productive laborer? The inventor of a machine? A confectioner?

9. In which of the two classes of laborers, productive and unproductive, would you place the following?

(1.) The officers of our Government.

(2.) The maker of an organ.

(3.) An organist.

(4.) A schoolmaster.

(5.) An artist.

(6.) He who makes an article for which there is no use.

10. Classify as productive or unproductive the following laborers: a clergyman, musical-instrument maker, actor, soldier, and lace-maker.

CAPITAL.

11. Explain fully what you understand by capital, and what function it discharges in production. Consider whether or not the following ought to be included in capital: (1) the original and acquired powers of the laborer, (2) the original properties of the soil, (3) improvements on land, (4) credit, (5) unsold stock in the hands of a merchant, (6) articles purchased but still in the consumer's hands.

12. Does a national loan add to the capital of a country?

13. Inquire how far, or in what cases, or in what sense, it may be said that a common dwelling-house, an hotel, a school-house, a police-station, a theatre, and a fortification, constitute part of the capital of the country.

14. Discuss carefully the question whether money lying in a bank (or corn lying in a granary) is always capital, or whether its economic nature depends upon the intentions of the owner.

15. Are railway-shares, stocks of wine, wheat, munitions of war, and land, to be considered capital, or not?

16. Explain fully whether you consider that United States bonds are capital or not.

17. Is an investment in government funds capital, or not? Give your reasons.

18. In what manner does a large expenditure for military purposes affect the operations of capital and labor?

19. Distinguish between wealth and capital. Show that there is no assignable limit to the employment of capital in bettering the condition of the members of a community.

20. "If there are human beings capable of work, and food to feed them, they may always be employed in producing something." Explain the meaning of this fully.

21. What is meant by saying wealth can only perform the functions of capital by being wholly or partially consumed?

22. Explain and illustrate the statement that demand for commodities is not demand for labor.

23. Show that expenditure of money does not necessarily increase the demand for labor.

24. In what way would a general demand for luxuries affect productive laborers and the wealth of the community?

25. In a community where capital is all employed, what would be the effect if one employer gradually withdrew some of his capital, and spent this for personal luxuries?

26. It is contended that "the demand for commodities, which can only be got by labor, is as much a demand for labor as a demand for beef is a demand for bullocks." Criticise this position.

27. "It is often said that, though employment is withdrawn from labor in one department, an exactly equivalent employment is opened for it in others, because what the consumers save in the increased cheapness of one particular article enables them to augment their consumption of others, thereby increasing the demand for other kinds of labor." Point out the fallacy.

28. A college undergraduate, with the applause of shopkeepers, bought twenty waistcoats, under the plea that he was doing good to trade. Examine the economical soundness of his act.

29. A man invested a portion of his capital in a loan to a state which subsequently repudiated its debts. The man thereupon gave up his carriage, discharged superfluous gardeners, and reduced the number of his domestic servants. Examine the effect of these changes on the employment of labor in the district where he resides.

30. In the sixteenth century a great change in the mode of expenditure took place. Retainers were dismissed, households were reduced and a demand for commodities was substituted for a demand for labor. How would this change affect wages, and why?

31. It is supposed by some persons that expenditure by the rich in costly entertainments is good for trade. What is your opinion on the subject?

32. A is an absentee who spends his income abroad. B spends his income chiefly on American pictures and other works of art. C spends most of his income on American servants. D saves and buys United States bonds. E employs most of his income in the production of manufactures. Explain the various effects of these different modes of expenditure on the amount of wealth in the United States, and on the working-classes of the country.

33. Compare the economic effects of defraying war expenditure (1) by loans, (2) by increased taxation.

34. Define the term capital, and distinguish between fixed and circulating capital, giving instances of each.

35. Distinguish between fixed and circulating capital, and point out how far, or in what manner, each of the following articles belongs to one kind or the other: a dwelling-house, a crop of corn, a wagon, a load of coal, an ingot of gold, a railway-engine, a bale of cotton goods.

36. Of the following, which would you class under fixed and which under circulating capital: cash in the hands of a merchant, a cotton-mill, a plow, diamonds in a jeweler's shop, a locomotive, a nursery-gardener's seeds, greenhouses, manures; a carpenter's tools, woods, nails?

37. If in a country like this a large amount of capital becomes fixed in the building of railroads, what effect will this change taken by itself have upon the laboring-class, supposing the capital to be (1) domestic, or (2) borrowed wholly or in part from abroad?

38. What conclusion is reached by Mr. Mill respecting the objections to the use of labor-saving machinery?

39. Is the extension of machinery beneficial to laborers?

40. What is "the conclusive answer to the objections against machinery"?

EFFICIENCY OF PRODUCTION.

41. Explain briefly the chief causes on which the productiveness of labor depends.

42. What are the principal ways in which advantage arises from the division of labor?

43. What are the principal advantages of division of labor? In what cases and why is it better to carry on a productive enterprise on a large scale?

44. Under what circumstances, and in what callings, can the division of employment be carried out to the fullest extent?

45. Show how the amount of available capital and the extent of the market for products limit division of labor.

POPULATION.

46. Give a brief statement of Malthus's theory of population, explaining the different checks on population in different stages of civilization.

47. Enunciate Malthus's law of population, and give an outline of the reasoning by which he established it. Give an account of any objections that have been brought against Malthus's position, and criticise those objections.

48. When the growth of population outstrips the progress of improvements, what are the means of relief for the laborer?

49. Does the increased facility of emigration nullify the Malthusian law of population in your opinion or not, and why?

50. Explain the law of diminishing return and the Malthusian doctrine of population; and trace the connection between them.

INCREASE OF PRODUCTION.

51. Compare the motives to saving in the case of savages, and of a country like the United States. State the causes of diversity in the strength of the effective desire of accumulation.

52. Capital is said to be accumulated by saving; what is saving? Is hoarded money a saving while hoarded?

53. How far does the increasing productiveness of manufacturing industry tend to neutralize the effect on profits of the diminishing productiveness of agricultural industry?

54. What conclusion as to the limit to the increase of production does Mr. Mill deduce from his investigation of the laws of the various requisites of production?

PROPERTY.

55. What are the essential elements of property? Are the grounds of property in land the same as those of property in movables?

56. Give what you conceive to be the chief arguments in favor of the institution of private property, as opposed to common ownership.

57. What arguments does Mr. Mill suggest in favor of some redistribution of landed property?

58. What are the economic arguments for and against Communism?

59. In what way, and by what means, do Socialists want to alter the present distribution of wealth?

60. Sketch the principal forms of Communistic and Non-communistic Socialism.

61. Should the power of bequest be limited?

WAGES.

62. On what, according to Mill, does the rate of wages depend? Hence, show the fallacy of the popularly proposed remedies for low wages.

63. State and examine the principal theories which have been put forward as to the circumstances which regulate the general rate of wages, saying which you deem to be correct, and why so.

64. Mr. Thornton argues that the wages-fund is neither "determined" nor "limited": not "determined," because there is no "law" to compel capitalists to devote any portion of their wealth to the payment of labor, nor are they morally "bound" to do so; and not "limited," because there is nothing to prevent them from adding to the portion of their wealth so applied. Criticise this argument, and, if you dissent from Mr. Thornton's view, state the causes which "determine" and "limit" the fund in question.

65. State precisely what you mean by the "wages-fund," and explain the conditions on which its growth depends.

66. Explain generally the circumstances which determine the rate of wages. Mention some of the reasons why wages should be higher in one occupation than in another.

67. In what way does dearness or cheapness of food affect money wages?

68. What determines—

(1.) The general rate of wages in a country?

(2.) The relative rates of wages in different employments?

69. What causes different rates of wages in different employments, and by what methods might wages be raised?

70. How do you explain the fact that some of the most disagreeable kinds of labor are the most badly paid?

71. What, according to Mr. Mill, are the most promising means for the improvement of the laboring-classes?

72. In the Island of Laputa a law was passed compelling each workman to work with his left hand tied behind his back, and the law was justified on the ground that the demand for labor was more than doubled by it. Examine this argument.

73. Some coal-workers are calling for a diminution of the output of coal, so as to keep up their wages. Examine how far, if at all, this result would follow from their proposed action.

74. Discuss any remedies for low wages that have been or might be suggested.

75. Why are the wages of women habitually lower than those of men?

PROFITS.

76. What is the cause of the existence of profits? And what, according to Mr. Mill, are the circumstances which determine the respective shares of the laborer and the capitalist?

77. (1.) What is the lowest rate of profit which can permanently exist? (2.) Why is this minimum variable?

78. Analyze the remuneration received by any of the following: (1) the proprietor of a cotton-mill managing his own mill; (2) a merchant conducting his own business; (3) a railway shareholder; (4) a holder of government funds.

79. Into what portions may we divide the return which is usually called profit? Which of these portions would be received by a merchant carrying on business with borrowed capital?

80. Analyze the payment called profits into its various elements. Point out in what respects the earnings of the employer differ from or resemble the wages paid to other classes of laborers.

81. It is asserted that "profits tend to an equality." What conditions must be satisfied before this position can be maintained?

82. How is the alleged tendency of profits to equivalence in different employments to be reconciled with the notorious difference in the profit of different individuals?

83. Which one of the elements in profit has the greatest effect on its amount? Explain by comparing the causes which regulate each element.

84. How does Mill reconcile the high wages in America with Ricardo's law of profits?

85. Explain the proposition that the rate of profits depends on the cost of labor, stating carefully what elements are included in cost of labor.

86. Explain what connection there may be between an increase of population and any of the elements entering into cost of labor.

87. What effect would an increase or diminution of population have upon cost of labor?

88. Explain Mill's view as to the cost of labor being a function of three variables, considering the passages in which he says, 1. "If without labor becoming less efficient its remuneration fell, *no increase taking place in the cost of the articles composing that remuneration;*" 2. "If the laborer obtained a higher remuneration, *without any increased cheapness in the things composing it*; or if, without his obtaining more, *that which he did obtain would become more costly*": profits in the last two cases would suffer a diminution; and discussing—Firstly, if the remuneration of labor falls, what can the cost of the articles composing that remuneration signify to the capitalist? Secondly, if the laborer gets a higher remuneration, what can the increased cheapness of the things composing it signify to the capitalist?

89. Is the contest between capital and labor permanent and fundamental? If not, give your reasons for your answer.

90. What is the effect on wages and profits of the introduction of machinery?

RENT.

91. What connection exists between the law of Malthus and Ricardo's doctrine of rent?

92. What is the reason why land-owners can demand rent?

93. Explain and illustrate the distinction between rent and profits. In what cases are they nearly indistinguishable?

94. It has often been observed that in America land is much less highly cultivated than in England. Explain the economic reasons for this.

95. How does the theory of rent apply in a country like the United States, where the farmer owns his land instead of hiring it?

96. How is it that some agricultural capital pays rent, even if resort is not had to different grades of land?

97. Give a brief description of the theory of rent, and point out to what payments not usually called rent the theory may be applied.

98. State briefly Ricardo's theory of rent, and show that, if it be true, the following statements of Adam Smith must be false:

"The most fertile coal-mine regulates the price of coals at all the other mines in the neighborhood."

"In the price of corn one part pays the rent of the landlord, another pays the wages, and another the profit of the farmer."

99. Why does the farming business pay rent, and the cotton business (ground-rent excluded) pay none? Define rent.

100. "As population increases, rents estimated in corn increase, and the price of corn rises; rents, therefore, doubly tend to increase." Prove this.

101. Professor Rogers adduces, in refutation of the common theory of rent, the fact that land near New York pays a high rent, while land of the same natural fertility in the Western States pays no rent. How far do you admit the force of this objection?

102. Examine the following doctrine:

> "If invention and improvement still go on, the efficiency of labor will be further increased, and the amount of labor and capital necessary to produce a given result further diminished. The same causes will lead to the utilization of this new gain in productive power for the production of more wealth; the margin of cultivation will be again extended, and rent will increase, both in proportion and amount, without any increase in wages and interest. And so, ... will ... rent constantly increase, though population should remain stationary."—Henry George, "Progress and Poverty" (p. 226).

103. What answer is made to Mr. Carey's objection to Ricardo's theory of rent, that in point of fact the poorer, not the richer, lands are first brought under cultivation?

104. Explain how land, "even apart from differences of situation,... would all of it, on a certain supposition, pay rent."

105. Explain clearly how it is possible for the land of a country which is all of uniform fertility to pay rent.

106. "If the earth had a perfectly smooth surface the same everywhere, and if it were all tilled and cultivated in exactly the same way, there would be no such thing as rent." Examine this proposition.

107. Show that rent does not increase the price of bread.

108. How is it shown that "rent does not really form any part of the expenses of production or of the advances of the capitalist?"

109. (1.) What connection exists between the price of agricultural products and the amount of rent paid? (2.) Can rent affect the price?

110. "Rent is the effect and not the cause of price." Prove this.

111. Does rent enter into the cost of production of the following commodities or not, and why: Corn, cloth, the wine of the best vineyards?

112. "Rent arises from the difference between the least fertile and the most fertile soils, and from the fact that the former have been taken into cultivation.... Rent is the difference between the market price of produce and the cost of production." Harmonize these statements.

113. In order that the actual payments made by farmers to landlords should generally correspond with "economic rent," what conditions must be observed?

114. What is assumed, as to competition, in all Mr. Mill's reasoning on wages, profits, and rent? Explain its action in each case.

VALUE.

115. Enumerate, compare, and criticise any opinions known to you which have been held concerning the nature, origin, or measure of value in exchange.

116. Define precisely what it is which gives value to objects, and point out the causes which vary the value of the same object under differing circumstances.

117. Do men dive to the bottom of the sea to get pearls because they are valuable; or are pearls valuable because men must dive to the bottom of the sea to get them?

118. There are three forms of difficulty of attainment. State the law of value applicable to each.

119. Explain the exact economic meaning of the words supply and demand.

120. When it is said that the value of certain commodities depends upon supply and demand, what is meant by demand?

121. If the supply of all commodities were suddenly doubled, would any changes in their relative values ensue or not, and why?

122. State the laws which regulate the permanent and temporary values of agricultural products.

123. How far does the value of commodities depend on the quantity of labor required for their production?

124. Has the term exchange value any precise meaning when we are comparing times or places very remote from one another?

125. What is meant by the natural (or normal) price and the market price of commodities? To what extent can they differ?

126. Does a general rise of wages raise the prices of commodities in general or not, and why? Does it tend to cause any change in the relative prices of commodities or not, and why?

127. Suppose that wages were double, would the values of commodities be affected? What would be the effect on prices and profits of such an increase of wages?

128. Are wages and profits influenced by prices?

129. Can employers recoup themselves by a rise of prices for a rise of—

(a.) Wages in particular employments?

(b.) General wages?

How does this question bear on the efficacy of trades-unionism?

130. Do values depend on wages?

131. Explain the following statement: "It is true the absolute wages paid have no effect upon values; but neither has the absolute quantity of labor."

132. Explain the statement that "high general profits can not, any more than high general wages, be a cause of high values.... In so far as profits enter into the cost of production of all things, they can not affect the value of any."

133. Explain fully why it is that capitalists can not compensate themselves for a general high cost of labor through any action on values and prices.

134. "The value of a commodity depends on its cost of production." Under what conditions is this true, and what causes interfere with it?

135. Describe the hindrances which impede the free movement of capital to those fields which apparently offer the highest return for its employment.

136. Give J. S. Mill's analysis of the "cost of production," and also Professor Cairnes's, with the arguments for and against each.

137. Analyze cost of production. What is its connection with cost of labor?

138. Give an analysis of cost of production of any commodity.

139. Show carefully the distinction between wages, cost of labor, and cost of production.

140. Define clearly value, price, real wages, and cost of production.

141. Define real wages, money wages, cost of labor.

MONEY.

142. Point out the difference between the scientific and popular conceptions implied in the terms wealth and money.

143. Show the fallacy of confounding capital with money. Can there be a glut of capital?

144. What is money? To what sort of necessity does it owe its existence? What articles have been used for money? Enumerate the qualities which render a commodity fit to serve as money.

145. What are the qualities requisite in any commodity in order that it may serve as money?

146. Distinguish accurately between the functions of money.

147. How far is a fixed standard of value possible?

148. What effect does the great durability of gold and silver have upon the value of money?

149. How far does the law of demand and supply govern the value of money?

150. Explain fully how it is that the value of the precious metals is affected by "questions of quantity only, with little reference to cost of production."

151. What is to be said to the following: "Some political economists have objected altogether to the statement that the value of money depends on its quantity combined with the rapidity of circulation; which, they think, is assuming a law for money that does not exist for any other commodity"?

152. Under what conditions is it true that the "value of money is inversely as its quantity"?

153. Explain carefully the following: "The average value of gold is made to conform to its natural value in the same manner as the values of other things are made to conform to their natural value."

154. In what various meanings is the phrase "the value of money" used? How far does the value of money in each of these meanings depend on (1) the cost of production, (2) supply and demand?

155. Are the values of gold and silver subject to exactly the same natural laws as other commodities?

156. Give the explanations and qualifications required to render the following proposition true: "The quantity of coin in every country is regulated by the value of the commodities which are to be circulated by it."

157. Would the world be richer if every individual in it suddenly found the quantity of money in his possession doubled?

158. How far, or in what way, do you consider it correct to say that the general level of prices in a country depends upon the quantity of gold coin existing in that country?

159. A single good harvest causes a considerable fall in the value of *wheat*; but a great addition to the year's supply of *gold* from the mines produces little effect on its general value. How do you account for the difference?

160. Show the effect of establishing a double standard.

161. Show how Gresham's law is illustrated by the history of the currency in the United States between 1834 and 1873.

162. What effect had the discovery of gold in this century upon the coinage of the United States?

163. What is the system upon which the small silver currency of the United States is coined and issued?

164. State briefly the aim of the United States coinage act of 1853.

CREDIT.

165. How do you define credit? Form a classification of credit documents.

166. It has been said that "credit is capital." Is this so or not?

167. Define capital, and examine the meaning of the term in the following statements:

(*a.*) Demand for commodities can not create capital.

(*b.*) Credit is not a creation, but a transfer of capital.

(*c.*) Wages depend upon the proportion between population and capital.

168. State the law of the value of money which governs general prices. What change is to be made in the statement, if credit is to be taken into consideration?

169. What is the part which instruments of credit, other than bank-notes, play in the exchange of commodities?

170. Mention some of the principal features of a credit crisis.

171. What are inconvertible notes? What objections are there to currency of this description?

172. Can an inconvertible currency be made to maintain the same value as a convertible currency, and, if so, how? Supposing that it can, what objections are there, nevertheless, to it?

173. "Nothing is subject to more variation than paper money, even when it is limited, and has no guarantees; for this simple reason, that, having no value of its own, it depends on the idea that each person forms of those guarantees." Comment on this passage.

174. How is it that a bad dollar does the work of buying as well as a good one until it is found out? Is it that it makes no difference whether it is made of gold or not?

175. To what extent is a government capable of giving fictitious value to a paper or a metallic currency?

176. In a country with an inconvertible paper currency, how can it be determined whether the issues are excessive or not, and why?

177. What will be the effect if the circulating medium of a country is increased beyond its natural amount—

(1) when the medium is coin?

(2) when it is coin and convertible paper?

(3) when it is inconvertible paper?

178. What is the error involved in the assumption, frequently made by writers and public speakers, that the currency of a country ought to increase in like ratio with its wealth and population?

179. On what does the desire to use credit depend? What connection exists between the amount of notes and coin in circulation and the use of credit?

180. Compare the advantages and disadvantages of a metallic and paper currency.

181. A member of Congress advocated expansion of the paper currency by the following argument: "Our currency, as well as everything else, must keep pace with our growth as a nation.... France has a circulation *per capita* of thirty dollars; England, of twenty-five; and we, with our extent of territory and improvements, certainly require more than either." State your opinion of this argument.

182. Trace the effects, immediate and ultimate, on general prices of (*a*) an extended system of credit, (*b*) an enlarged issue of paper money, and (*c*) an addition to the stock of precious metals, respectively.

183. What is the error in the common notion that "a paper currency can not be issued in excess so long as every note *represents* property, or has a *foundation* of actual property to rest on"?

184. Explain the action of the check and clearing-house system, and state what is meant by the restoration of barter.

OVER-PRODUCTION.

185. State the relation between supply and demand as aggregates, e.g., between the aggregate supply of commodities in a given community and

the aggregate demand for them, and show the bearing of the principle involved on the doctrine of "general over-production."

186. Prove that the increase of capital and the extension of industry can not lead to a general over-production of commodities.

187. What is the error of those who believe in the danger of over-production?

188. Distinguish "excess of supply" from a "commercial crisis."

189. Give the substance of Mill's examination of the theories of excess of supply.

190. "When production is fully equal to consumption, every discovery in the arts, or in mechanics, is a calamity, because it only adds to the enjoyment of consumers the opportunity of obtaining commodities at a cheaper rate, while it deprives the producers of even life itself." Discuss this opinion of Sismondi.

191. Explain the difference in the theories of Dr. Chalmers and Mr. Mill on over-production, and the excess of supply.

PECULIAR CASES OF VALUE.

192. It costs as much to produce straw as to produce grain; how, then, do you explain the comparatively low value of straw?

193. Suppose a considerable rise in the price of wool to be foreseen, how should farmers expect the prices of mutton to be affected, and why?

194. Explain the operation of the laws of value by which the relative prices of wool and mutton are regulated.

INTERNATIONAL TRADE AND VALUES.

195. What is the meaning of the statement that "it is not a difference in the *absolute* cost of production which determines the interchange [of commodities between countries], but a difference in the *comparative* cost"?

196. What are the advantages which a country derives from foreign trade?

197. Explain clearly the following passage: "We may often, by trading with foreigners, obtain their commodities at a smaller expense of labor and capital than they cost to the foreigners themselves."

198. Is there any essential difference between trade between country and country, and trade between county and county, or even between man and man? What is the real nature of trade in all cases?

199. Why is it necessary to make any different statement of the laws of value for foreign than for domestic products? What is the cause for the existence of any international trade?

200. How would a serious decline in the efficiency of England, as compared with other countries, in the production of manufactures affect the scale of money incomes and prices in England, and why?

201. Mr. Mill refers the value of home products to the "cost of production"; of foreign products to the "cost of acquisition." Examine the truth of this distinction.

202. It is said that in the home market the value of commodities depends on the cost of production, in the foreign market on the cost of acquisition. Comment on this distinction.

203. Is the cost of production the regulator of international values?

204. Discuss the following statement: "International value is regulated just as inter-provincial or inter-parishional value is. Coals and hops are exchanged between Northumberland and Kent on absolutely the same principles as iron and wine between Lancashire and Spain."—Ruskin, "Munera Pulveris," p. 84.

205. What determines the value of imported commodities?

206. Why does cost of production fail to determine the value of commodities brought from a foreign country? Does it also fail in the case of commodities brought from distant parts of the same country?

207. It is on the matter of fact that there is not much migration of capital and labor from country to country that Mr. Mill has based his whole doctrine of "international trade and international values." Explain and comment on the above statement.

208. What are the causes which determine for a nation the cost of its imports?

209. It follows from the theory of international values, as laid down by Mill, that the permanent residence of Americans in Europe may enhance the cost of foreign imports to Americans residing at home. Explain in what way.

210. Suppose two countries, A and B, isolated from the rest of the world, and a trade established between them. In consequence of the labor of A becoming less effective, the cost of production of every article which can be produced in that country is greatly increased, but so that the relation between the costs of any two articles remains the same. What, if any, will be the effect of the change on the trade between A and B? Does your answer

depend upon your using the phrase "cost of production" in a sense different from that given to it by some economists?

211. Show that every country gets its imports at less cost in proportion to the efficiency of its labor.

FOREIGN EXCHANGES.

212. What is the ordinary limit to the premium on foreign bills of exchange, and why?

213. What are the chief effects on the foreign exchanges which are produced by the breaking out of a war? Account for the fact that in 1861 the exchanges on England in America fell considerably below specie point.

214. Suppose that the next harvest in England should be very defective, and extraordinary supplies of American grain needed. How would this probably affect the price of bills of exchange between England and America, and the profit on the exportation of English manufactures to the latter, and why?

215. Trace the process by which the precious metals spread from the mines over the world.

216. Suppose the exchange between England and the United States to be heavily against England, how will this fact affect the export and import trade between the two countries, and why?

217. What is meant by exchanges being against a country?

218. Enumerate the principal circumstances which affect the rate of exchange between two countries. How is the *par* of exchange ascertained?

219. In what way are gold and silver distributed among the different trading countries? Between different parts of the same country?

220. Trace the effects of large and continuous issues of inconvertible paper currency on the prices of commodities, on importation and exportation, and on the foreign exchanges.

221. State the conditions under which international trade can permanently exist. What will be the ultimate effect of a large movement of foreign gold upon prices, imports, and exports in the receiving country?

222. State the theory of the value of money (i.e., "metallic money"), and clear up any apparent inconsistencies between the following statements: (1.) The value of money depends on the cost of production at the worst mines; (2.) The value of money varies inversely as its quantity multiplied by its

rapidity of circulation; (3.) The countries whose products are most in demand abroad and contain the greatest value in the smallest bulk, which are nearest the mines and have the least demand for foreign productions, are those in which money will be of lowest value.

228. The effects of the depreciation of the paper currency in the United States are thus described by Mr. Wells: "It renders it impossible to sell abroad the products which have cost too much at home, and invites from other countries the products of a cheaper labor paid for in a sounder currency. It exaggerates imports, while destroying our ability to pay in kind." State how far you agree with the deductions here drawn, assigning your reasons where you differ.

224. When the foreign exchanges are manifestly against a country, and a balance of indebtedness is the cause, the equilibrium can be restored in two ways. State and explain the operation of each.

225. What are the conditions which determine for a country a high range of general prices? How far is this advantageous?

226. What is the effect of the imposition of a tribute by one country on another upon the course of trade between them, and the terms on which they exchange commodities; and why?

227. For what reasons may a nation's exports habitually exceed or fall short of its imports?

228. Explain the real and nominal exchange.

229. Expound Mr. Mill's theory of the influence which a convertible currency exercises on foreign trade.

230. What is the effect of a depreciated currency on (1) foreign trade, and (2) the exchanges?

INTEREST.

231. How does the general rate of interest determine the selling price of stocks and land?

232. Is there any relation between the rate of interest and the value of money?

233. What are the relations of interest and profit? On what causes does the rate of interest depend?

234. "High interest means bad security." Comment on this saying.

235. Is the rate of interest affected by the supply of the precious metals?

236. What determines the rate of interest on the loanable funds? Is the "current [or ordinary] rate of interest the measure of the relative abundance or scarcity of capital"?

237. What are the chief causes that determine the rate of interest?

238. If it be true that in America every man, however rich, is engaged in some business, but that in England many rich men have no trade or profession, how is the rate of interest in each country affected in consequence, and why?

239. How does a fall in the purchasing power of money tend to affect, if at all, and why, (1) the rate of interest, (2) the price of land, (3) the price of government bonds, (4) the price of gold and silver ornaments and plate?

FOREIGN COMPETITION.

240. Explain the grounds of Mr. Mill's proposition that general low wages never caused any country to undersell its rivals, nor did general high wages ever hinder it from doing so. If you think the proposition needs qualification, give your reason.

241. (1.) What is the true theory of one country underselling another in a foreign market? (2.) What weight should be attributed to the fact of generally higher or lower wages in one of the competing countries?

242. Discuss the question whether a high rate of wages necessarily lays the commerce of a country under a disadvantage with reference to a country where the rate of wages is lower.

243. What are the conditions under which one country can permanently undersell another in a foreign market?

244. Point out distinctly the connection between the money wages of laborers in the United States and the productiveness of the soil.

245. In the Eastern States iron-molders earn from fourteen to seventeen dollars a week; in California their wages run from twenty-one to twenty-seven dollars. Account for this variation.

PROGRESS OF SOCIETY.

246. What are the reasons for the change in the normal values of manufactured and of agricultural commodities, respectively, during the progress of society?

247. Wages and profits in different employments and neighborhoods are not uniformly proportional to the efforts of labor and abstinence of which

they are the respective rewards. Classify the circumstances which prevent this correspondence, and show how far their effect is likely to be reduced (*a*) by general economical progress, and (*b*) by the extension of the division of labor.

248. What is the law of diminishing returns? Can you point out any connection between this law and the following phenomena?—

(*a.*) Density of population.

(*b.*) Rate of wages.

(*c.*) Rate of profits in different countries.

249. Sketch the influence on rents and profits of an increase of population and capital concurrently with a stationary state of the arts of production.

250. Is there reason to believe that Mr. Mill has underrated the powers possessed by man of extending the area of production and facilitating the market of food? If such a statement has been made, to what extent is his theory of population modified, and the risks he had indicated rendered distant?

251. Compare the effects on rent, profits, and wages, of a sudden improvement in the production (*a*) of food, (*b*) of some manufactured articles largely consumed by the working-classes.

252. Trace the connection between Ricardo's theory of rent and the decline in the general rate of profits as a country increases in population. Explain clearly the connection which exists between wages and profits.

253. What effect is produced upon rents, profits, and wages, respectively, in a country like France, where population is stationary and capital advancing?

254. If capital continued to increase and population did not, explain the proposition that "the whole savings of each year would be exactly so much subtracted from the profits of the next and of every following year," if improvements were stationary.

255. How does social and industrial progress tend to affect the prices of land, raw produce, and manufactures, respectively, and why?

256. The capitalized value of land rises, in the progress of society, from two causes—from one which affects land in common with all investments; from another which is peculiar to land.

257. "The tendency of improved communications is to lower existing rents." How far is this true, and in what directions is it true?

258. What would be the effect on profits, wages, and rents of an improvement in a manufactured article consumed by the laboring-class?

259. Explain the doctrine of the tendency of profits to a minimum, the cause of that tendency, and the circumstances which counteract it.

260. What was Adam Smith's doctrine as to the decline of profit in progressive communities? Criticise his argument.

261. Mention some of the principal causes which, in the ordinary progress of society, respectively tend to increase or to reduce the current rate of profits.

262. Why do profits tend to fall as population increases, and how may this result be retarded or prevented?

263. What is the effect of a general rise of money wages, apart from the consideration of a greater efficiency of labor, in prices, profits, and rent? Give reasons for your answer.

264. How does the general progress of society in wealth and industrial efficiency tend to affect the rate of wages, the rate of profit, and the rate of rent, respectively?

265. What is the general effect of the progress of society on the land-owner, the capitalist, and the laborer?

FUTURE OF LABORING-CLASSES.

266. Examine the influences of machinery on the economic condition of the working-classes.

267. Mention and discuss some of the popular remedies for low wages, and especially the effect of the subdivision of landed property among peasant proprietors.

268. Explain briefly what is meant by co-operation, and indicate the more prominent forms assumed by the co-operative movement.

269. What is meant by the co-operative system of industry? Show ways in which this system may affect, for good or for evil, the productiveness of labor; and mention any moral benefits, or the opposite, in which it may be expected to issue.

270. What are the difficulties in the way of co-operation for the production of salable objects?

271. Explain the advantages of industrial partnership, in which the employés share, in proportion to the wages received, half the profits of the business beyond a certain fixed minimum which is assigned to the employers.

TAXATION.

272. How is the state justified in undertaking any manufacture or service which might be performed by private enterprise?

273. Enumerate Adam Smith's canons of taxation.

274. Examine the argument in favor of the resumption by the state of what is called the unearned increment in the value of land arising from the development of society.

275. A picture by Gainsborough and a house in Broadway are sold in the same year at the same price; at the end of fifty years each sells for five times its first cost. Is there any, and, if so, what, reason why the increase should be sequestrated for the public benefit in the one case and not in the other?

276. Explain the incidence of taxes laid on wages.

277. Why should a tax on profits, if no improvements follow, fall on the laborer and capitalist?

278. Explain what effect, if any, will be produced on the price of corn by—

(1) a tax upon rent;

(2) a tithe;

(3) a tax of so much per acre, irrespective of value;

(4) a tax of so much per bushel.

279. On whom does a tax of a fixed proportion of agricultural produce fall?

280. Discuss the question whether the income-tax ought to be a tax upon income and property, or upon expenditure.

281. Discuss the expediency of a graduated income-tax.

282. State the arguments which you think strongest both for and against exempting savings from the income-tax.

283. Explain the conditions which should be observed in imposing taxes on commodities.

284. What taxes does a tradesman get back in the price of the articles he sells, and what does he not?

285. Test by Adam Smith's four maxims of taxation the policy of indirect taxes on the necessaries of life.

286. All indirect taxation violates Adam Smith's fourth canon.

287. Discuss the following:

"A man with $100,000 in United States bonds comes to Boston, hires a house...; thus he lives in luxury.... I am in favor of taxing idle investments such as this, and allowing manufacturing investments to go untaxed."

288. Compare the advantages and disadvantages of direct and indirect taxation.

289. On what principles is this country now taxed?

290. Explain the arguments for and against the policy of maintaining a surplus for the purpose of redeeming a national debt.

291. In estimating the ability of the United States to pay its public debts, it is usual to include among the data of the question the increased productiveness of industry in that country. How far is this a pertinent consideration?

PROTECTION.

292. Mention some of the principal arguments brought forward in favor of protective tariffs.

293. Connect the principle of the division of employments (or labor) with the policy of free trade and the functions of government.

294. Sketch the effects of discriminating duties, including the operation of the corn laws.

295. Examine the following argument, emending, if you think it necessary, the free-trader's doctrine on the point raised: The free-trader's belief is that a customs duty is added to the price of the article upon which it is imposed. If the article is imported, according to his theory, the increase of the price goes into the public treasury; if the article is made in the country, the increase of the price goes into the pocket of the producer. But in the former case there is no protection; and competition will prevent the latter. Therefore protection does not increase the price of the protected article. If

a customs duty is imposed upon a commodity, and its price is not raised in consequence, what inference can you draw?

296. Under what circumstances did Mr. Mill think nascent states might be justified in adopting a policy of protection? Criticise his opinion, and, if you agree with it, give some examples of its application.

297. American protectionists allege that the high rate of wages prevailing in the United States disables them from competing with "the pauper labor" of Europe. Examine the grounds of this statement, and consider how far it forms a justification for protection to American industry.

298. A high rate of wages indicates, not a high, but a low cost of production for all commodities measured in which the rate of wages is high.

Explain and prove this proposition, and illustrate it from the circumstances of the United States.

299. State under what limitations the proposition is correct, that profits vary inversely with wages. Explain the circumstances which cause both a higher rate of wages and profits to prevail in a young country, such as the United States, than in England.

300. In America wages are much higher than in England, yet the general rate of profits is higher also, according to Mr. Mill. How do you reconcile the two facts?

301. Examine the following:

"It seems to me that protection is absolutely essential to the encouragement of capital, and equally necessary for the protection of the American laborer.... He must have good food, enough of it, good clothing, school-houses for his children, comforts for his home, and a fair chance to improve his condition. To this end I would protect him against competition with the half-paid laborers of European countries."—*Congressional Globe*.

302. An American newspaper has said of the burning of Chicago: "The money to replace what has been burned will not be sent abroad to enrich foreign manufacturers; but, thanks to the wise policy of protection which has built up American industries, it will stimulate our own manufactures, set our mills running faster, and give employment to thousands of idle working-men." Comment on this passage.

303. On whom does a tax on imports, if not prohibitory, fall?

304. In what cases would duties on imported commodities fall on the producers?

305. Are taxes on imports in any way paid by foreigners?

306. Discuss the effects of duties on exports.

307. Trace the effects of duties on the importation of raw materials, and distinguish, with examples, between duties that violate and duties which do not violate the principle of free trade.

308. Is it possible for any country by legislative enactments to engross a larger share of the advantages of foreign trade than it would naturally have? Discuss the question fully.

309. "Those are, therefore, in the right who maintain that taxes on imports are partly paid by foreigners; but they are mistaken when they say it is by the foreign producer. It is not on the person from whom we buy, but on all those who buy from us, that a portion of our customs duties spontaneously falls." Explain and examine the reasons for this conclusion.

310. State the principle which determines the relation between the amount of a country's imports and that of its exports, and show how this relation is affected by a system of protective duties.

THE END.

Footnotes

1.

Yet Blanqui diffusively gives nearly one half of his "History of Political Economy" to the period before the sixteenth century, when politico-economic laws had not yet been recognized. A. L. Perry, "Political Economy" (eighteenth edition, 1883), also devotes thirty-five out of eighty-seven pages to the period in which there was no systematic study of political economy.

2.

Xenophon, "Means of increasing the Revenues of Attika," ch. ix; also see his "Economics;" and Aristotle, "Politics," b. i, ch. vi, b. iii, ch. i.

3.

"Republic," b. ii.

4.

Roscher exhumed this book, entitled "De Origine, Natura, Jure et Mutationibus Monetarum," and it was reprinted in 1864 by Wolowski at Paris, together with the treatise of Copernicus, "De Monetae Cudendae Ratione."

5.

Sermon at St. Paul's Cross, 1549 (also see Jacob, "On the Precious Metals," pp. 244, 245).

6.

1530-1596. See II. Baudrillart's "J. Bodin et son temps" (Paris, 1853). Bodin wrote "Réponse aux paradoxes de M. de Malestroit touchant l'enchérissement de toutes les choses et des monnaies" (1568), and "Discours sur le rehaussement et la diminution des monnaies" (1578).

7.

"A Briefe Conceipte of English Policy" (1581). The book was published under the initials "W. S.," and was long regarded as the production of Shakespere.

8.

For information on this as well as a later period, consult Jacob "On the Precious Metals" (1832), a history of the production and influences of gold and silver from the earliest times. He is considered a very high authority. Humboldt's "Essay on New Spain" gives estimates and facts on the production of the precious metals in America. A very excellent study has been made by Levasseur in his "Histoire des classes ouvrières en France jusqu'à la Révolution." For pauperism and its history, Nicholl's "History of the Poor Laws" is, of course, to be consulted.

9.

See Cossa, "Guide," p. 119.

10.

See Antonio Serra, "Breve Trattato delle Cause che possono fare abbondare li Regni d' Oro e d' Argento," Naples, 1613.

11.

Thomas Mun, "England's Treasure by Foreign Trade" (published in 1640 and 1664); "Advice of the Council of Trade" (1660), in Lord Overstone's "Select Tracts on Money"; Sir William Petty, "Political Arithmetic," etc. (about 1680); Sir Josiah Child, "New Discourse of Trade" (1690); Sir Dudley North, "Discourse on Trade" (1691); Davenant's Works (1690-1711); Joshua Gee, "Trade and Navigation of Great Britain" (1730); Sir Matthew Decker (according to McCulloch, William Richardson), "Essay on the Causes of the Decline of Foreign Trade" (1744); Sir James Steuart, "An Inquiry into the Principles of Political Economy" (1767). For this period also consult Anderson's "History of Commerce" (1764), Macpherson's "Annals of Commerce" (1803), and Lord Sheffield's "Observations on the Commerce of the American States" (1783).

12.

The English Navigation Act of 1651 is usually described as the cause of the decline of Dutch shipping. The taxation necessitated by her wars is rather the cause, as history shows it to us. Sir Josiah Child (1668 and 1690) speaks of a serious depression in English commerce, and says the low rate of interest among the Dutch hurts the English trade. This does not show that the acts greatly aided English shipping. Moreover, Gee, a determined partisan of the mercantile theory, says, in 1730, that the ship-trade was languishing. Sir Matthew Decker (1744) confirms Gee's impressions. It looks very much as if the commercial supremacy of England was acquired by internal causes, and in spite of her navigation acts. The anonymous author of "Britannia Languens" confirms this view.

13.

This was, in substance, the whole teaching of one of the leading and most intelligent writers, Sir James Steuart (1767), "Principles of Political Economy." See also Held's "Carey's Socialwissenschaft und das Merkantilsystem" (1866), which places Carey among the mercantilists.

14.

Forbonnais, "Récherches sur les finances de la France" (1595-1721); Pierre Clément, "Histoire de Colbert et de son administration" (1874); "Lettres, instructions et mémoires de Colbert" (1861-1870); "Histoire du système protecteur en France" (1854); Martin, "Histoire de France," tome xiii.

15.

"Dîme royale" (1707).

16.

"Factum de la France" (1707).

17.

When Quesnay was sixty-one years old he wrote the article, "Fermiers," in the "Encyclopædia" (of Diderot and D'Alembert) in 1756; article "Grains," in the same, 1757; "Tableau économique," 1758; "Maximes générales du gouvernement économique d'un royaume"; "Problème économique"; "Dialogues sur le commerce et sur les travaux des artisans"; "Droit natural" (1768). "Collection des principaux économistes," edited by E. Daire (1846), is a collection containing the works of Quesnay, Turgot, and Dupont de Nemours. See also Lavergne, "Les économistes françaises du 18e siècle" (1870); and H. Martin, "Histoire de France." Quesnay's "Tableau économique" was the Koran of the school.

18.

From χράτησις τῆς φύσεως, as indicating a reverence for natural laws.

19.

The words were not invented by Quesnay, but formed the phrase of a merchant, Legendre, in addressing Colbert; although it was later ascribed, as by Perry, "Political Economy" (p. 46), and Cossa (p. 150), to one of the Economists, Gournay. (See Wolowski, in his Essay prefixed to "Roscher's Political Economy," p. 36, American translation.)

20.

The Margrave Karl Friedrich was the author of "Abrégé des principes de l'économie politique" (1775), and applied the physiocratic system of taxation to two of his villages with disastrous results.

21.

He published a first work on "Population" (1756); the "Théorie de l'impôt" (1760); and "Philosophie rurale" (1763). In this latter work Mirabeau adopted the "Tableau économique" as the key to the subject, and classed it with the discovery of printing and of money.

22.

In 1742 Turgot, when scarcely twenty, appeared as a sound writer on Paper Money in letters to Abbé Cicé. The physiocratic doctrines were presented in a more intelligible form in his greater work, "Réflexions sur la formation et la distribution des richesses" (1766). Three works of Turgot, on mining property, interest of money, and freedom in the corn-trade, bear a high reputation. For works treating of Turgot, see Batbie, "Turgot, philosophe, économiste et administrateur" (1861); Mastier, "Turgot, sa vie et sa doctrine" (1861); Tissot, "Turgot, sa vie, son administration et ses ouvrages" (1862).

23.

He was the editor of the works of Quesnay and Turgot, and wrote a "Mémoire de Turgot" (1817). He opposed the issue of assignats during the French Revolution, and, falling into disfavor, he barely escaped the scaffold. Having been a correspondent of Jefferson's, when Napoleon returned from Elba, he came to America, and settled in Delaware, where he died in 1817. The connection between the Economists and the framers of our Constitution is interesting, because it explains some peculiarities introduced into our system of taxation in that document. The only direct taxes recognized by the Supreme Court under our Constitution are the poll and land taxes; and it is in this connection that the constitutionality of the income-tax (a direct tax) is doubted.

24.

One of the earliest is that of Roger Coke (1675), in which he argues for free trade, and attacks the navigation acts. Sir Dudley North's "Discourse on Trade" (1691) urges that the whole world, as regards trade, is but one people, and explains that money is only merchandise.

25.

Joseph Harris, an official in the London Mint, published a very clear exposition of this subject in his "Essay upon Money and Coins" (1757); but, eighty years before, Rice Vaughan had given a satisfactory statement in his "Treatise of Money."

26.

"Contemporary Review," January, 1881, "Richard Cantillon." Adam Smith had quoted Cantillon on his discussion of the wages of labor, b. i, ch. viii, and evidently knew his book.

27.

Born in 1723, and died 1790; he was eleven years younger than Hume. A Professor of Logic (1751) and Moral Philosophy (1752) at Glasgow, he published a treatise on ethical philosophy, entitled the "Theory of Moral Sentiments" (1739). Dugald Stewart is the authority as to Smith's life, having received information from a contemporary of Smith's, Professor Miller (see Playfair's edition of Smith's works); for Adam Smith destroyed all his own papers in his last illness. His lectures on political economy at Glasgow outlined the results as they appeared in the "Wealth of Nations"; it was not until 1764 that he resigned his professorship, and spent two years on the Continent (twelve months of this in France). On his return home he immured himself for ten years of quiet study, and published the "Wealth of Nations" in 1776. (See also McCulloch's introduction to his edition of the "Wealth of Nations," and Bagehot's "Economic Studies," iii.)

28.

A glance at Sir James Steuart's treatise (1767) with the "Wealth of Nations" shows Adam Smith's great qualities; the former was a series of detached essays, although of wide range, but admittedly without any consistent plan.

29.

(*a.*) He went into a vague discussion upon labor as a measure of value. (*b.*) A legal rate of interest received his support, and his argument was answered effectually by Bentham ("Defense of Usury"). (*c.*) While not agreeing with the French school that agriculture is the only industry producing more than it consumes, and so land pays rent, yet he thinks that it produces more in proportion to the labor than other industries; that manufactures came next; and exportation and commerce after them. This error, however, did not modify his more important conclusions. Thorold Rogers and even Chevalier, however, claim that Adam Smith drew his inspiration from the French school. (*d.*) In the discussion of rent, he failed to follow out his ideas to a legitimate end, and did not get at the true doctrine. While hinting at the right connection between price and rent, he yet believed that rent formed a part of price. Of the fundamental principle in the doctrine of rent, the law of diminishing returns, he had no full knowledge, but came very close to it. He points out that in colonies, when the good soil has all been occupied, profits fall. (*e.*) In saying that every animal naturally multiplies in proportion to, and is limited by, the means of subsistence, Adam Smith just missed Malthus's law of population. In fact, Cantillon came quite as near it.

Book III in his "Wealth of Nations" is concerned with the policy of Europe in encouraging commerce at the expense of agriculture, and has less interest for us. Book V considers the revenue of the sovereign, and much of it is now obsolete; but his discussion of taxation is still highly important.

30.

Among the English Liberals carried away by the French Revolution, and by such theories as those of Condorcet, was William Godwin, the author of "Political Justice" (1793) and the "Inquirer" (1797), who advocated the abolition of government and even marriage, since by the universal practice of the golden rule there would come about a lengthening of life. Malthus tells us that his study was brought forward as an answer to the doctrines of the "Inquirer," and he applied his principles to Condorcet's and Godwin's ideas. It was a period when pauperism demanded attention from all. Malthus favored the repeal of the old poor-laws, as destroying independence of character among the poor.

Malthus also wrote "Principles of Political Economy" (1821) and "Definitions in Political Economy" (1827), but the former did not increase his reputation. He believed in taxing imported corn, and he gave in his adherence to the doctrine of over-production. But, on the other hand, he was one of several writers who, almost at the same time, discovered the true theory of rent. His father was a friend of Godwin, and a correspondent of Rousseau. (See Bagehot, "Economic Studies," p. 135.)

31.

See Cairnes, "Logical Method," Lecture VII, for the best modern statement of the question. Also, Roscher, "Principles of Political Economy," b. v, whose extended notes furnish information on facts and as to books. H. Carey, "Social Science" (edition of 1877), iii, pp. 263-312, opposes the doctrine, as also Bowen, "American Political Economy" (1870), ch. viii, and Henry George, "Progress and Poverty" (1880), pp. 81-134.

32.

J. Anderson, "An Inquiry into the Nature of the Corn Laws" (1777), "Agricultural Recreations," vol. v, p. 401 (1801); Sir Edward West, "Essay on the Application of Capital to Land" (1815); Rev. T. R. Malthus, "An Inquiry into the Nature and Progress of Rent" (1815). The last two appeared after Anderson's discoveries had been forgotten, but he has the honor of first discovery.

33.

Born in 1772 of Jewish parentage, Ricardo died in 1824. A rich banker, who made a fortune on the Stock Exchange, he early in life retired from business. The discussions on the Restriction Act and the corn laws led him to investigate the laws governing the subjects of money and rent. He gained notice first by his "Letters on the High Price of Bullion" (1810). The "Reply to Mr. Bosanquet" (1811), and "Inquiry into Rent" (1815), were followed by his greater work, "Principles of Political Economy and Taxation" (1817). He entered the House of Commons from Portarlington, a pocket borough in Ireland, and was influential in the discussions on resumption. Although he was not on the committee, his views on depreciated paper are practically embodied in the famous "Bullion Report" (1810). Tooke, "History of Prices," says the results of the restriction were not known until the time of Ricardo's contributions. Neither Mill nor Say has had so great an influence as Ricardo has gained, through the pages of his "Political Economy."

34.

Johann Heinrich von Thünen, a rich land-owner of Mecklenburg, in his "Der isolirte Staat in Beziehung auf Landwirthschaft und National-Oekonomie" (1826), worked entirely by himself, but reached practically the same law of rent as Ricardo's. In spreading the doctrines of Adam Smith he has influenced later German writers.

35.

The first distinct recognition of this important physical law, according to McCulloch (Introduction to "Wealth of Nations," lv), was in a fanciful work of two volumes, entitled "Principes de tout gouvernement," published in 1766: "Quand les cultivateurs, devenus nombreux, auront défriché toutes les bonnes terres; par leur augmentation successive, et par la continuité du défrichement, il se trouvera un point ou il sera plus avantageux à un nouveau colon de prendre à ferme des terres fécondes, que d'en défricher de nouvelles beaucoup moins bonnes" (I, p. 126). The author was, however, unaware of the importance of his discovery.

36.

Carey, "Social Science" (I, ch. iv, v), and Bowen, "American Political Economy" (ch. ix), have denied Ricardo's doctrine of rent. Thesupposed connection between free trade and Ricardo's teachings on rent has prejudiced protectionists against him. Free trade follows from the theory of international trade, and has nothing to do with Ricardo's main doctrines. It is true, Ricardo was a vigorous free-trader. Of opposing views on rent, Carey's argument is the most important.

37.

Say drew considerable attention by his theory of "gluts." He based his idea of value wholly on *utility*, which has lately been taken up again by Professor Jevons. Say was answered on this point by Ricardo in a later edition of his "Political Economy." See Cairnes, "Leading Principles," p. 17. As a free-trader and opponent of governmental interference, he went further than his master, Adam Smith. Napoleon did not like this part of Say's teaching, saying that it would destroy an empire of adamant, and tried to induce him to modify his position, but in vain. The second edition was not allowed to be published until 1815.

38.

Educated at Bologna, he went to Geneva in 1816, and was called (1833) by the French Government to succeed Say in the Collége de France. In 1845 he was sent as minister to Rome, led the revolutionary movement there, and was assassinated in 1848. His lectures were taken down in short-hand by one of his disciples, Porée, and later published.

39.

Malthus, who held that the unproductive consumption of the rich was desirable for the poor, supported Sismondi. The latter was answered by Say and McCulloch ("Edinburgh Review," March, 1821), to which Sismondi replied in his second edition, in 1827, and then withdrew from economic discussion.

40.

A native of Riga, educated in Germany, Storch was charged by the Czar Alexander with the duty of instructing his sons, the Grand Dukes Nicholas and Michael, and his treatise is the collection of his lectures. Knowing little of Malthus or Ricardo, he made a near approach to the doctrine of rent. His unsparing denunciation of Russian administrative corruption caused the Government to forbid the publication of the Russian translation.

41.

Cossa, "Guide" (p. 173), points out Sartorius, Lüder, Kraus, and Schlözer as teachers of Adam Smith, in Germany, followed later by G. Hufeland, J. F. E. Lotz, and L. H. von Jakob; Count Hogendorp and Gogel, in Holland; Count Szecheny, in Hungary, and (pp. 211-213) Cagnazzi, Bosellini, Ressi, Sanfilippo, and Scuderi (the last two protectionists), in Italy. Fuoco (1825-1827), in Italy, first saw the value of Ricardo's theory of rent, while Gioja opposed Adam Smith and Say. But K. H. Rau (died 1870), in his "Lehrbuch der politischen Oekonomie" (1826, fifth edition 1864), had the most extensive influence in Germany in expounding Adam Smith's system, with proper improvements. Another important writer of this school was F. B. W. von Hermann, "Staatswirthschaftliche Untersuchungen" (1832).

42.

From 1810 to 1840, political economy was a favorite study in England, and many writers deserve mention. There were Huskisson, a great financier; Thomas Tooke (1773-1858), who began his matchless "History of Prices" (1823); Lord Overstone (Samuel Jones Loyd), "Tracts and other Publications on Metallic and Paper Currency" (1858); Robert Torrens (1784-1864), "Essay on the Production of Wealth" (1821); Archbishop Whately, "Introductory Lectures" (1831), and "Easy Lessons on Money Matters"; Cobden and Sir Robert Peel; N. W. Senior (1790-1864), Professor of Political Economy at Oxford, article on "Political Economy" (1836) in the "Encyclopædia Metropolitana," and "Lectures on the Cost of obtaining Money" (1830). Senior showed great ability in analyzing cost of production, and stands far above McCulloch in real ability. J. R. McCulloch (1789-1864), who preceded Mill, wrote a good but dry textbook, "Principles of Political Economy" (1825), "A Treatise on the Principles, Practice, and History of Commerce" (1833), an excellent "Dictionary of Commerce" (last enlarged edition, 1882), "Literature of Political Economy" (1845). He edited Ricardo's works, with a biography, published a "Select Collection of Scarce and Valuable Tracts on Money" (1856), "A Treatise on the Principles and Practical Influence of Taxation and the Funding System" (1845). He contributed nothing practically new to the study. Miss Harriet Martineau (1802-1876) gave some admirable although somewhat extended stories in illustration of the various principles of political economy, entitled "Illustrations of Political Economy" (1859). This period in England was signalized by the abolition of the Corn Laws (1846), and the Navigation Laws (1849), the passage of the Bank Act (which separated the issue from the banking department, 1844), and the general abandonment of protective duties. Cf. Noble, "Fiscal Legislation, 1842-1865" (1867).

43.

Born in 1806, he died in 1873. For his extraordinary education see his "Autobiography." When thirteen years old, he began the study of political economy through lectures from his father while walking; he then (1819) read Ricardo and Adam Smith, and at fourteen he journeyed to France, where he lived for a time with J. B. Say. He entered the East India Office at seventeen, was occupied finally in conducting the correspondence for the directors, where he remained until 1858. When about twenty, Mill met twice a week in Threadneedle Street, from 8.30 to 10 A.M., with a political economy club, composed of Grote, Roebuck, Ellis,

Graham, and Prescott, where they discussed James Mill's and Ricardo's books, and also Bailey's "Dissertations on Value." In these discussions, chiefly with Graham, Mill elaborated his theory of international values. In 1865 he entered Parliament for Westminster, and for three years had a singular, characteristic, independent, but uninfluential career. His adherence to two radical reforms, woman suffrage and changes in the tenure of land, lost him any considerable influence.

44.

He (1773-1836) wrote the "History of India" (1817-1819), and "Elements of Political Economy" (1821). He was intimate with Ricardo, Bentham, Austin, and Zachary Macaulay.

45.

In his "infant industries" argument, and his statement on navigation laws (B. v, ch. x, §1), he conceded a great deal of free-trade ground; but in a private letter, 1866 (see New York "Nation," May 29, 1873), he denied that he intended the "infant industries" argument to apply to the United States. He did not consider New England and Pennsylvania any longer as young countries within the limits of his meaning. See also Taussig's "Protection to Young Industries" (1883).

46.

W. T. Thornton (1813-1880), in a volume "On Labor: its Wrongful Claims and Rightful Dues" (1869), attacked Mill's position on demand and supply, and on wages, so that Mill in consequence abandoned his doctrine of wages, in the "Fortnightly Review," May 1, 1869. Mr. Cairnes, however, rescued the Wages-Fund theory from Mr. Mill in his "Leading Principles" (1874). Thornton also wrote "Over-Population, and its Remedy" (1846), and an excellent book, "Plea for Peasant Proprietorship" (1848). See also "Nineteenth Century," August, 1879, for an answer by Thornton to Mr. Cairnes on the wages question.

47.

James Eliot Cairnes was born at Drogheda, 1824; was educated at Trinity College, Dublin, and made Whately Professor there in 1856. Having been Professor of Political Economy in Queen's College, Galway, he left Ireland in 1866 to accept the chair of Political Economy in University College, London. In that year, through an attack of inflammatory rheumatism, he fell under the power of a painful and growing malady which rendered him physically helpless, and portended certain death in the near future. The three years before his death, while working only in hopeless pain, was the period of his greatest literary activity. He collected his "Essays in Political Economy, Theoretical and Applied" (1873), in which he traced with great ability the effect of the gold-discoveries; brought out his "Leading Principles" (1874), and an enlarged edition of his "Logical Method" (second edition, 1875). The first edition of this last book was the result of lectures delivered in Dublin about 1858. In his earlier years the interest he felt in the United States led him into a very vigorous and masterly study of "The Slave Power; its Character, Career, and Probable Dangers" (1862); "The Revolution in America" (1862). He then wrote "Colonization and Colonial Government" (1864), and "Negro Suffrage" (1866). He finally succumbed to his fatal disease, and passed away prematurely, July 8, 1875. A short sketch of his personal character was written by Professor Fawcett, in the "Fortnightly Review," August 1, 1875, p. 149.

48.

Professor Jevons (1835-1882) was educated at University College, London, and spent the years from 1854 to 1859 in the Australian Royal Mint, where he became interested in the gold question. He wrote a study on "A Serious Fall in the Value of Gold ascertained" (1863), which attracted great attention. A fine metaphysician and mathematician, he did not give his whole time to economic work. In 1866 he became Professor of Logic and Cobden Lecturer on Political Economy in Owens College, Manchester, but later became Professor of Political Economy in University College, London. In 1881 he gave up academic teaching, to devote himself to literature. He investigated the permanence of the English coal-supply in "The Coal Question" (second edition, 1866). "The Theory of Political Economy" (1871) contains his application of the mathematical method, and a bibliography of similar attempts. "The Railways and the State" are to be found in his "Essays and Addresses" (1874). He prepared an elementary book, "Primer of Political Economy" (second edition, 1878). He was a contributor to the journals, and especially to the "London Statistical Journal." His last books were "The State in Relation to Labor" (1882), which deals with the question of state interference; and "Methods of Social Reform" (1883), containing a paper on industrial partnerships. He also advanced the theory that the presence of sun-spots affected agriculture unfavorably, and that, coming somewhat regularly, they produced a constant succession of commercial crises. (See "Nature," xix, 33, 588.) At the early age of forty-seven he was unfortunately drowned while bathing near Bexhill, England (1882).

49.

Like Cairnes, Thomas Edward Cliffe Leslie was a native of Ireland, and educated at Trinity College, Dublin. He was called to the bar, but gave up the law when offered the professorship of Political Economy in Queen's College, Belfast. Besides his discussion of land tenures, he published "Political and Moral Philosophy" (1874). He long suffered from bad health, and died January 28, 1882. His volume of "Land Systems" is now (1884) out of print, and scarce. He had also devoted himself to financial reform.

50.

See p. 33.

51.

Born 1826, died 1877. He was early made familiar with banking in connection with the Stuckey Banking Company, in Somersetshire; was educated at University College, London. In 1858 he married the daughter of James Wilson, the editor of the London "Economist," whom he succeeded. He was a political student of a rare kind, as is shown by his "English Constitution" (second edition, 1872), "Physics and Politics" (1872), "Literary Studies" (second edition, 1879). He also wrote "Depreciation of Silver" (1877).

52.

Established in 1848, and unquestionably the most useful economic publication for English questions.

53.

Born 1833. His eye-sight was lost by an accidental shot in 1858, but he was chosen Professor of Political Economy at Cambridge in 1863. His "Manual" and the "Economic Position of the British Laborer" (1865) gave him reputation, in 1865 he entered Parliament, and since 1880 he has been Postmaster-General in Mr. Gladstone's administration. He has published "Pauperism, its Causes and Remedies" (1871), "Speeches" (1878), "Free Trade and Protection" (1878). His wife (born 1847), Millicent Garret Fawcett, reduced his "Manual" into "Political Economy for Beginners"

(1869), and also wrote "Tales in Political Economy" (1874). Died November 13, 1884.

<u>54.</u>

He has also published "Social Economy" (1872); a small "Manual of Political Economy" (third edition, 1878); and a very considerable work, "Six Centuries of Work and Wages: the History of English Labor," 1250-1883 (1884). He has edited Adam Smith's "Wealth of Nations," and written "Cobden and Modern Political Opinion" (1873), and "The Colonial Question," in the Cobden Club Essays (1872).

<u>55.</u>

Of other books, mention should be made of G. J. Goschen's most admirable "Theory of Foreign Exchanges" (eighth edition, 1875); "Reports and Speeches on Local Taxation" (1872); T. Brassey's "Work and Wages" (third edition, 1883); E. Seyd, "Bullion and the Foreign Exchanges" (1868); H. D. McLeod, an eccentric writer, "Dictionary of Political Economy" (only one vol., A-C, 1863, published); and "Theory and Practice of Banking" (second edition, 1875-1876); H. Sidgwick, "Principles of Political Economy" (1883); J. Caird, "Landed Interest" (fourth edition, 1880); L. Levi, "History of British Commerce" (1872).

<u>56.</u>

Frédéric Bastiat (1801-1850) began life in a commercial house at Bayonne, but gained notice first by an article, "De l'influence des tarifs français et anglais sur l'avenir des deux peuples," in the "Journal des Économistes" of 1844, and consequently had a very short period of literary activity. The corn-law agitation in England and the revolutionary movement of 1848 led him to write chiefly against protection and socialism. He translated Cobden's speeches, "Cobden et la Ligue" (1845). His arguments against protection, "Sophismes économiques" (1846-1847), have been translated and published in this country; but the more extended exposition of his doctrine of value diminishing with the growth of civilization, and the harmony of all interests is in the "Harmonies économiques" (1850). In this his position is not much different from Carey's. His other books were "Capital et rente" (1849), directed against gratuitous loans; "Protectionisme et communisme" (1849), showing protection to be communism for the rich; "Propriété et loi" (1848), directed against socialism; and "Essais sur l'économie politique" (1853); "Le Libre-échange" (1855). "Œuvres complètes," 7 tom. (1855-1864).

57.

Carey, however, claimed, with probable truth, that Bastiat borrowed the idea from him, and Bastiat did not appear well in the controversy. Almost no one has followed the French writer in his theory except Professor A. L. Perry, of Williams College, Massachusetts, who has shaped his general argument according to this view of value. Also see Cairnes, "Essays in Political Economy," p. 312.

58.

Chevalier (1806-1879) first drew attention in an experiment of Saint-Simonism in 1830-1833. After traveling in the United States, and writing excellent books on the country and its railways, he became professor in the Collége de France, where his lectures were collected in a "Cours d'économie politique" (1842-1850; second edition, 1855-1866). His third volume, "La Monnaie," is a standard treatise on money, with an extensive bibliography. His treatise "Examen du système commerciale connu sous le nom de système protecteur" (1851) is now somewhat out of date. In his book "De la Baisse, probable de l'or" (1859), translated by Richard Cobden, he held that, unless prevented, gold would drive out the French currency, as against Faucher, who thought the fall temporary, and would progressively diminish. Other books are, "De l'industrie manufacturière en France," and "La liberté du travail" (1848).

59.

Émile Levasseur (born 1828) was professor at Alençon, 1852-1854, and elected a member of the Academy of Sciences in 1868. He has published "Récherches historiques sur le système de Law" (1854); "La question de l'or" (1858); "Histoire des classes ouvrières en France depuis la conquête de Jules César jusqu'à la révolution" (1859); the same history continued, "Depuis 1789 jusqu'à nos jours" (1867); "La France industriale" (1865); "Cours d'économie rurale, la France et ses colonies" (1868); "Précis d'économie politique" (fourth edition, 1883).

60.

Born in Berlin in 1816, but since 1821 living in France. He was long connected with the Bureau de Statistique Générale, and the Ministry of Agriculture and Commerce, but in 1861 he left office and gave himself wholly to private work. In this year he received the Montyon prize for statistics, not given since 1857. His chief books are: "Des charges de l'agriculture dans les divers pays de l'Europe" (1850), a work crowned by the Institute; "Statistique de la France, comparée avec les divers états de l'Europe" (1860); "Le dictionnaire de l'administration française" (second edition, 1878); "Les finances de la France depuis 1815" (1863); "Les théoriciens du socialisme en Allemagne" (1872); and in connection with M. Guillaumin, "L'annuaire de l'économie politique," since 1856.

61.

Jérôme-Adolphe Blanqui *aîné* (1798-1854) in 1833 succeeded to the chair of J. B. Say in the Conservatoire des Arts et Métiers, and was one of the founders of the "Journal des économistes." Besides his "Histoire de l'économie politique en l'Europe" (1837-1852), he published a "Résumé de l'histoire du commerce et de l'industrie" (1826); "Précis élémentaire d'économie politique" (1826); "Rapports, histoire de l'exposition des produits de l'industrie française en 1827" (1827); "Cours d'economie politique" (2 vols., 1837-1838), and notices of Huskisson and J. B. Say.

62.

Louis Wolowski (1810-1876), of Polish origin, was Chevalier's chief antagonist, and Professor of Legislation at the Conservatoire des Arts et Métiers (1839); founded the first Crédit Foncier of Paris, and was elected to the Institute in the place of Blanqui. In 1875 he was chosen senator. He was a fertile writer: "Mobilisation du Crédit Foncier" (1839); "De l'organisation du travail" (1846); "Études de l'économie politique et de statistique" (1848); "Henri IV, économiste, introduction de l'industrie de la soie en France" (1855); "Introduction de l'économie politique en Italie" (1859); "Les finances de la Russie" (1864); "La question des banques" (1864); his testimony in the "Enquête sur les principes et les faits généraux qui régissent la circulation monétaire et fiduciaire" (1866); "La banque d'Angleterre et les banques d'Écosse" (1867); "La liberté commerciale et les résultats du traité de commerce de 1860" (1868); "L'or et l'argent" (1870); "La change et la circulation"; and a translation of Roscher.

63.

Hippolyte-Philibert Passy (1793-1880) was educated for the army, and served at Waterloo. He was more prominent as a statesman than as an economist. In 1838 he entered the Academy in the place of Talleyrand, but politics left him unoccupied, and he wrote "Des systèmes de culture et de leur influence sur l'économie sociale" (1846), and "Des causes de l'inégalité des richesses" (1849).

64.

M. Léonce de Lavergne (1809-1880) came from Toulouse to Paris in 1840, elected deputy in 1846, a member of the Institute in 1855, and became professor in the Institut agronomique of Versailles. He was also the author of "L'économie rurale de l'Angleterre, de l'Écosse, et de l'Irlande" (1854), translated into English (1855); "L'agriculture et la population" (1857), a striking confirmation of Malthusianism; "Les économistes françaises du dixhuitième siècle" (1870). He also has contributed largely to the "Revue des Deux Mondes" and the "Journal des Économistes." For a personal sketch by Cliffe Leslie, see "Fortnightly Review," February, 1881.

65.

Born at Geneva, 1797, and died at Zurich, 1869. After studying law, he became an advocate, and in 1833 Professor of Law in the place of Rossi. In 1837 he was made Professor of Political Economy and Public Law at Geneva. He was also a member of the Swiss Grand Council. Besides his treatise, he wrote: "Richesse ou pauvreté" (1840); "Le socialisme, c'est la barbarie" (1848); "Études sur les causes de la misère" (1853); and aided in the "Dictionnaire de l'économie politique."

66.

J. G. Courcelle-Seneuil (born 1813) left a commercial career to become a writer, first for the journals, and later for the "Dictionnaire politique" (edited by Pagnerre). In 1848 he was connected with the Ministry of Finance, and called to a professorship of Political Economy in Santiago, Chili, 1853-1863. His chief work is a "Traité théorique et pratique d'économie politique" (1858), but he has also published "La crédit de banque" (1840), reforms for the bank of France; "Traité des opérations de banque" (1852; sixth edition, 1876); "Traité des entreprises industrielles, commerciales, et agricoles" (1854); "Études sur la science sociale" (1862); "Leçons élémentaires d'économie politique" (1864); "La banque libre" (1867); "Liberté et socialisme" (1868); and articles in the "Dictionnaire de l'économie politique."

67.

Died 1862; author of "De la liberté du travail" (1845).

68.

Professor of Political Economy at the Collége de France, author of an extended and able "Traité de la science des finances" (third edition, 1883). He has also published "De l'état moral et intellectual des populations ouvrières et de son influence sur le taux des salaires" (1868); "Récherches economiques, historiques, et statistiques sur les guerres contemporaines" (1869); "La question ouvrière au XIX siècle" (second edition, 1882); "L'administration locale en France et en Angleterre" (1872); "Le travail des femmes au XIX siècle" (1873); "Essai sur la répartition des richesses" (1880; second edition, 1883); and "De la colonisation chez les peuples modernes" (1882).

69.

He published two volumes on Socialism (see list of books p. 44). In several volumes on the "Régime des manufactures" he described the condition of the silk, woolen, cotton, and iron industries.

70.

The most vigorous advocate of monometallism in France. He also wrote well on taxation, "Traité des impôts" (4 vols., 1866-1867).

71.

His "Rapport sur l'indemnité du guerre" to the Corps Législatif gives the account of the most marvelous exchange operation of modern times, arising from the payment of the indemnity by France to Germany (1871-1873).

72.

An advocate of the mathematical method.

73.

Founded in 1863, published at Berlin, and edited by Dr. Eduard Wiss.

74.

Long Secretary to the Chamber of Commerce at Hamburg, and now honorary professor at Göttingen.

75.

Professor of Political Economy at Zürich in 1866, since 1875 director of statistics at Dresden, and editor of "Der

Arbeiterfreund." He made a valuable study of industrial partnerships, "Die Gewinnbetheiligung" (second edition 1878). He also wrote "Freiheit der Arbeit" (1858), and "Beiträge zur geschichte des Zunftwesens" (1861).

76.

His most important work is "Das Armenwesen und die Armengesetzebung in Europäischen Staaten" (1870). Selected essays from this have been translated into English by E. B. Eastwick, "Poor Relief in Different Parts of Europe" (1873).

77.

Max Wirth is at Vienna, and has devoted himself to a "Geschichte der Handelskrisen" (1874), including the crisis of 1873. Baron von Hock has written a history of the finances of France, and of the United States—"Die Finanzen und die Finanzgeschichte der vereinigten Staaten von Amerika" (1867).

78.

This book has been translated into English by G. A. Matile, with notes by Stephen Colwell (1856).

79.

Mohl on administration, and Rau and A. Wagner on finance, also deserve mention. Stein, besides other works, is the author of a handbook, "Die Verwaltungslehre" (1870).

80.

"Fortnightly Review" (1876).

81.

In Ely's "The Past and Present of Political Economy" (p. 9) it is clear the new school do not differ so much in reality as in seeming from the methods of the English writers, like Cairnes.

82.

The first division of Roscher's (born 1817) treatise, also known under the title of "Grundlagen der Nationalökonomie," has been translated here by J. J. Lalor, in two volumes, "Principles of Political Economy" (1878), with an essay by Wolowski on the historical method inserted. In 1840 he was made *Privat-Docent* at Göttingen, and professor extraordinary in 1843. In 1844 he was called to a chair at Erlangen, but since 1848 he has remained at Leipsic. A list of Roscher's works is as follows:

"Grundriss zu Vorlesungen über die Staatswirthschaft nach geschichtlicher Methode" (1843); "Kornhandel und Theuerungspolitik" (third edition, 1852); "Untersuchungen über das Colonialwesen"; "Verhältniss der Nationalökonomie zum klassischen Alterthume" (1849); "Geschichte der englischen Volkswirthschaftslehre im 16. und 17. Jahrhunderts"; "Ein nationalökonom. Princep der Forstwirthschaft"; "Ansichten der Volkswirthschaft aus dem geschichtlichen Standpunkte" (second edition, 1861); "Die deutsche Nationalökonomie an der Grenzscheide des 16. und 17. Jahrhunderts" (1862); "Gründungsgeschichte des Zollvereins" (1870); "Betrachtungen über die Währungsfrage der deutschen Müntzreform" (1872); "Geschichte der Nationalökonomie in Deutschland" (1874); "Nationalökonomie des Ackerbaues" (eighth edition, 1875). His histories of political economy in England and Germany are particularly valuable (see review by Cliffe Leslie, "Fortnightly Review," July, 1875). But he does not rightly estimate the English writers when he takes McLeod as a type; and Carey is the only American to whom he refers.

83.

Professor at Marburg, then at the University of Friedburg, in Breisgau, and now at Heidelberg. He has also studied railways (1853), and telegraphs (1857), and money and credit, "Geld und Credit" (1873-1879).

84.

Died 1878. He devoted himself mainly to criticism of other systems, and seems to be the least able of the three.

85.

"Catheder-Socialisten," or "Professional Socialists."

86.

By far the ablest is Adolph Wagner, of Berlin, editor of Rau's "Lehrbuch der politischen Oekonomie" (1872). He also published "Die russische Papierwährung" (1868); "Staatspapiergeld, Reichs-Kassen Scheine, und Banknoten" (1874); "Unsere Müntzreform" (1877); "Finanzwissenschaft" (1877); and "Die Communalsteuerfrage" (1878).

Dr. Eduard Engel was formerly the head of the Prussian Bureau of Statistics. Professor Gustav Schönberg, of Tübingen, with the assistance of twenty-one other economists, produced a large "Handbuch der politischen Oekonomie" (1882). The school have expressed their peculiar doctrines in the "Zeitschrift für die gesammte Staatswissenschaft" (quarterly, founded 1844, Tübingen), and the "Jahrbücher für Nationalökonomie" (established at Jena, 1863). Also, see A. Wagner's "Rede über die sociale Frage" (1872), H. v. Scheel's "Die Theorie der socialen Frage" (1871), and G. Schmoller's "Ueber einige Grundfrage des Rects und der Volkswirthschaft" (1875). A. E. F. Schäffle, once Minister of Commerce at Vienna, gained considerable reputation by "Das gesellschaftliche System der menschlichen Wirthschaft" (third edition, 1873).

87.

Émile de Laveleye (born 1822) studied law at Ghent, but since 1848 has given himself up to political economy and public questions. Through the pages of the "Revue des Deux Mondes" he gained attention in 1863, and the next year was made Professor of Political Economy at the University of Liége. In 1869 he received an election as corresponding member of the Academy of Sciences. While a fertile writer on political subjects, he has produced "La question d'or" (1860); "Essai sur l'économie rurale de la Belgique" (1863); a study on "Suisse," see "Revue des Deux Mondes," April 15, 1863; "Études d'économie rurale, la Neerlande" (1864); "La marché monetaire depuis cinquante ans" (1865); "Land Systems of Belgium and Holland," in the Cobden Club volume on "Land Tenures" (1870); "Bi-metallic Money," translated by G. Walker (1877); "La socialisme contemporaine" (1881); "Éléments d'économie politique" (1882), which satisfies a certain modern demand for "ethical political economy."

88.

Leslie found support in a well-known paper read before the Association for the Advancement of Science (see "London Statistical Journal," December, 1878; also see "Penn Monthly," 1879), by J. K. Ingram, who claimed that the old school isolated the study of economic from other social phenomena, and that Ricardo's system was not only too abstract, but that its conclusions were of so absolute a character that they were little adapted for real use. Robert Lowe (Lord Sherbrooke) replied to Leslie and Ingram ("Nineteenth Century," November, 1878). For most of this literature it will be necessary to consult the magazines. Cliffe Leslie, "Fortnightly Review" (November, 1870), placed Adam Smith among the inductive economists; D. Syme attacked the old methods, "Westminster Review," vol. xcvi (1871); Cairnes represented the old school, and discussed the new theories, "Political Economy and Comte," in the "Fortnightly Review," vol. xiii, p. 579 (1870), "Political Economy and Laissez Faire," vol. xvi, p. 80 (1871), and in 1872; see also his admirable "Logical Method"; F. Harrison discussed the limits of political economy, ibid. (1865), and answered Cairnes in an article on "Cairnes on Political Economy and M. Comte," "Fortnightly Review," vol. xiv, p. 39 (1870). W. Newmarch gave attention to Ingram's paper, "Statistical Journal" (1871). Leslie, "Fortnightly Review" (1875), and G. Cohn, ibid. (1873), wrote on political economy in Germany. Leslie also contributed an article on "Political Economy and Sociology," "Fortnightly Review," vol. xxxi, p. 25 (1879), and the "Bicentenary of Political Economy," in the "Bankers' Magazine," vol. xxxii, p. 29. Leslie examined the philosophical method, "Penn Monthly" (1877); Jevons saw the only hope for the future in the mathematical method, "Fortnightly Review" (1876); McLeod asks, "What is political economy?" in the "Contemporary Review" (1875); Maurice Block entered the discussion, "Penn Monthly" (1877), and "Bankers' Magazine," March and November, 1878. Henry Sidgwick answers Leslie in a paper on "Economic Method," in the "Fortnightly Review," vol. xxxi (1879), p. 301. See also essay by Wolowski prefixed to Roscher's "Political Economy" (English translation); Roscher's own statement in Chapters II and III of the Introduction to his "Political Economy," and Laveleye's "New Tendencies of Political Economy" (1879). See also "Penn Monthly," vol. vii, p. 190, and "Bankers' Magazine," vol. xxxiii, pp. 601, 698, 761; vol. xxxvi, pp. 349, 422; S. Newcomb for an admirable essay "On the Method and Province of Political Economy," "North American Review" (1875), vol. cxxi, p. 241, in which the "Orthodox" method is strongly supported; and an extreme position in favor of the historical method in a pamphlet, "The Past and Present of Political Economy," by R. T. Ely (1884).

89.

Daniel Raymond, "The Elements of Political Economy" (1820). Thomas Cooper, "Lectures on the Elements of Political Economy" (1826); "A Manual of Political Economy" (1834). Willard Phillips, "A Manual of Political Economy" (1828); "Propositions concerning Protection and Free Trade" (1860).

President Francis Wayland (1796-1865), "The Elements of Political Economy" (1837). Henry Vethake, "Principles of Political Economy" (1838). From 1840 to the civil war there appeared F. Bowen's "Principles of Political Economy" (1856), since changed to "American Political Economy" (1873), which opposed the Malthusian doctrine and defended protection; John Bascom's "Political Economy" (1859); and Stephen Colwell's "Ways and Means of Payment" (1859). After the war, "Science of Wealth" (1866), by Amasa Walker, a lecturer in Amherst College, and father of F. A. Walker.

90.

Prof. C. F. Dunbar, "North American Review," January, 1876, in an admirable review of economic science in America during the last century (1776-1876).

91.

See *supra*, p. 16.

92.

Carey (1793-1879) was the son of an Irish exile, and began a business career at the age of twelve. At twenty-eight he was the leading partner in the publishing firm of Carey & Lea, Philadelphia, from which he retired in 1835, to devote himself wholly to political economy. His leading works have been translated into French, Italian, Portuguese, German, Swedish, Russian, Magyar, and Japanese. He has written thirteen octavo volumes, three thousand pages in pamphlet form, and twice that amount for the newspaper press. See "Proceedings of the American Academy of Science" (1881-1882, p. 417), and W. Elder's "Memoir of Henry C. Carey" (January 5, 1880). The latter gives a list of his books.

93.

Bastiat's "Harmonies économiques" appeared in 1850, and the question of his indebtedness to Carey was discussed, rather unfavorably to Bastiat, in a series of letters in the "Journal des économistes" for 1851.

94.

See an able study, by Adolphe Held, "Carey's Socialwissenschaft und das Merkantilsystem" (1866).

95.

His system appears also in the books of disciples: E. Peshine Smith, "A Manual of Political Economy" (1853), William Elder's "Questions of the Day" (1871), and of Robert E. Thompson's "Social Science and National Economy" (1875). A condensation of Carey's "Social Science" has been made by Kate McKean, in one volume, octavo.

96.

The son of Amasa Walker, and formerly Professor of Political Economy and History in the Sheffield Scientific School of Yale College, he has become well known for his statistical work in connection with the United States census. His "Statistical Atlas of the United States" (1874) is unequaled. He has also published "Money" (1878); "Money, Trade, and Industry" (1879); "Political Economy" (1883); and "Land and Rent" (1884). The last book replies to various attacks on Ricardo's doctrine of rent, and particularly to Henry George's "Progress and Poverty." General Walker in 1883 became President of the Massachusetts Institute of Technology in Boston. He is also well known as an advocate of bimetallism.

97.

Professor of Political and Social Science in Yale College, and author of a "History of American Currency" (1874); "Lectures on the History of Protection in the United States" (1877); "What Social Classes owe to Each Other" (1883). He is a monometallist, and has devoted himself vigorously to the advocacy of free trade. His last book is a study in sociology, not in political economy.

98.

He has written "Political Economy" (eighteenth edition, 1883), and also "Introduction to Political Economy," an elementary work on the same basis as the former.

99.

Henry George was born in Philadelphia, 1839, ran away to sea, and in 1857 entered a printing-office in San Francisco. In 1871 he was one of the founders of the "San Francisco Post," which he gave up in 1875, and received a public office. He first began to agitate his views in a pamphlet entitled "Our Land and Land Policy" (1871), but not until the comparative leisure of his occupation (1875) gave him opportunity did he seriously begin the study which resulted in his "Progress and Poverty." This volume was begun in the summer of 1877, and finished in the spring of 1879. The sale of the book, it is needless to say, has been phenomenal. He has also applied his doctrine of land to Ireland, in a pamphlet entitled "The Irish Land Question" (1882). His last book is a collection of essays entitled "Social Problems" (1884). His home is now in New York.

100.

Cf. p. 4, *supra*.

101.

Bowen, "American Political Economy," p. 25.

102.

This is the beginning of Chapter II in the original treatise.

103.

This is his "sacrifice," which corresponds to the exertion of the laborer.

104.

See Roscher's note 1, section 42, for various definitions of capital.

105.

General Walker ("Political Economy," Part II, Chap. iv) adopts the same position, although seemingly inconsistent with his doctrine on the rate of wages. The "rate of wages" is, however, a different thing from the source of a laborer's subsistence. See Book II, Chapter II, § 2.

106.

The opinion mentioned above in the text is that of the believers in over-production, of whom the most distinguished are Mr. Malthus, Dr. Chalmers, and Sismondi.

107.

Page 371, English translation, N. Y. (1871).

108.

Edward Atkinson, "Labor and Capital, Allies not Enemies," p. 60.

109.

Cf. Bowen, "American Political Economy," p. 399.

110.

The functions of money are discussed later in the volume, and it is not proposed to unfold them here.

111.

See, for the argument that machinery necessarily injures labor, "Land and Labor," William Godwin Moody (1883); and for the answer, "North American Review," May, 1884, p. 510.

112.

Edward Atkinson, "Labor and Capital, Allies not Enemies," p. 33.

113.

See book iv, chap. iv.

114.

See Mr. Babbage's "Economy of Machinery and Manufactures."

115.

Book i, chap. iv, § 6.

116.

Constant use of the same muscles, as by gold-beaters or writers, very often produces paralysis.

117.

Hearn's "Plutology," p. 279.

118.

Cairnes, "Leading Principles," pp. 299, 300.

119.

"American Political Economy," p. 134. See also an article, "Malthusianism, Darwinism, and Pessimism," "North American Review," November, 1879.

120.

See Cairnes, "Logical Method," pp. 170-177.

121.

See also Walker's "Wages Question," chap. vi, and Roscher, "Political Economy," book v, chaps. i, ii, iii.

122.

See Galton's "Hereditary Genius," p. 131-135.

- 623 -

123.

> See also Edward Jarvis, "Atlantic Monthly," 1872, and F. A. Walker, "Social Science Journal," vol. v, 1873, p. 71. For other literature, see "Sketch of the History of Political Economy," p. 16.

124.

> This is the "preventive check" of Mr. Malthus, while the limitation through war, starvation, etc., is the "positive check."

125.

> This is fully confirmed by the inaugural address of Mr. Giffen as President of the London Statistical Society, November 20, 1883, *infra*, book iv, chap. v, § 1. (See the London "Statistical Journal," 1883.)

126.

> See Lavergne's "Agriculture et Population," pp. 305-316.

127.

> For tables of relative births and deaths, see "Statesman's Year-Book," p. 253.

128.

> This and the subsequent quotations are taken by Mr. Mill from Rae's "New Principles of Political Economy."

129.

> "International Review," article "Colonization," 1881, p. 88. See H. V. Redfield, "Homicide North and South," 1880.

130.

> "Letters from America," by John Robert Godley, vol. i. p. 42. See also Lyell's "Travels in America," vol. ii, p. 83.—Mill.

131.

> Cf. "American Agriculture," "Princeton Review," May, 1882, by F. A. Walker.

132.

> "Social Science," vol. iii, p. 19.

133.

> "Notes on North America," 1851, vol. ii, pp. 116, 117.

134.

See also Cairnes, "Logical Method," p. 35.

135.

I am indebted to Mr. Atkinson for advanced proofs of the annexed charts. See his paper in the "Journal of the American Agricultural Association," vol. i, Nos. 3 and 4, p. 154, and a later discussion in the supplement of the Boston "Manufacturers' Gazette," August 9, 1884, entitled "The Railway, the Farmer, and the Public." His figures are drawn mainly from Poor's "Railway Manual."

136.

Cf. Book IV, Chap. I.

137.

"Economy of Manufactures," pp. 163, 164.

138.

Cf. Book IV, Chap. I, § 4.

139.

"The Coal Question" (1866).

140.

Henry George, as well as the Socialists, thinks poverty arises from the injustice of society, and here takes issue with the present teaching. But the question can be better discussed under Distribution.

141.

Henry Gannet, "International Review," 1882, p. 503.

142.

Volume on Population, p. 481.

143.

Estimated.

144.

See article "Colonization," "International Review," 1881, p. 88.

145.

See F. A. Walker's "Statistical Atlas."

146.

For a further discussion of the difference between the motive powers under private property and under Communism, see Mr. Mill's posthumous "Chapters on Socialism," "Fortnightly Review," 1879 (vol. xxxi).

147.

For an exposition of the varying forms of modern state socialism, and that form of it which advocates the nationalization of land (in H. George's "Progress and Poverty," and Alfred Russel Wallace's "Land Nationalization, its Necessity and its Aims") see a chapter in Henry Fawcett's last (sixth) edition of his "Manual" (1884). For a general and valuable treatise on Socialism, but one which does not describe schemes much later than Owen's, see Louis Reybaud's "Études sur les reformateurs, ou socialistes modernes" (seventh edition, 1864). An excellent bibliography is given, vol. ii, pp. 453-470.

148.

Pierre Joseph Proudhon (born 1809) made a well-known attack on private property in his "Qu'est-ce que la Propriété," "What is Property?" (1840). His answer was, "It is robbery." See also Ely, "French and German Socialism" (1883), p. 140.

149.

Louis Blanc (born 1813, died 1882). His chief book, the "Organization of Labor," appeared in 1840, in the columns of the "Revue du Progrès."

150.

Karl Marx (born 1818, died 1883) published "The Criticism of Political Economy" (1859); and an extension of the same book under the new title of "Capital" (1867), of which only the first volume has appeared, on "The Process of the Production of Capital." This was again enlarged in 1872 to 822 pages. A large part of the work is filled with extracts from parliamentary reports on the condition of English workmen. Before the Revolution of 1848 he edited a communistic journal, and was obliged to leave the country afterward, by which he was led to London. He was an able writer on history and politics. Marx was assisted by Friedrich Engels, who wrote "The Condition of the Working Classes in England" (1845). See Ely, ibid., chap. x.

151.

Born 1825, the son of a rich Jewish merchant. In philosophy and jurisprudence he won the praise of Humboldt and Boeckh. But vanity and wild ambition checked the success due to great abilities and energy of character. He was finally shot in a duel in 1864. He appears as the antagonist of Schultze (of Delitzsch), advocating state-help against the self-help of the originator of the People's Banks.

152.

For an account of this society see Theodore D. Woolsey's "Communism and Socialism" (1880); "Nineteenth Century," July, 1878; and Ely, ibid., chap. xi.

153.

See New York "Nation," Nos. 684, 686.

154.

From his posthumous "Chapters on Socialism," "Fortnightly Review," 1879, p. 513 (vol. xxxi), and written in 1869.

155.

The Count de Saint-Simon served in our Revolutionary War in the French army, while very young, and ended a life of misfortune and poverty in 1825, a month after the publication of his "Nouveau Christianisme" (Woolsey's "Communism and Socialism," p. 107). For a fuller account, see R. T. Ely's "French and German Socialism," p. 53; A. J. Booth's "Saint-Simon and Saint-Simonism" (London, 1871); and Reybaud, ibid.

156.

This experiment when put on trial in France first brought up the question of the legal justice of giving an absolute right to inherited property, and numbered among its disciples the economists, Michel Chevalier and Adolphe Blanqui, and the philosopher, Auguste Comte.

157.

Fourier was born at Besançon in 1772. He wrote the "Theory of the Four Movements" (1808); "A Treatise on Domestic and Agricultural Association" (1822); "The Theory of Universal Unity" (1841). Died 1837. See Ely, ibid., p. 81; Victor Considérant's "La Destinée Sociale" (fourth edition, 1851); and Reybaud, ibid.

158.

Robert Owen (father of Robert Dale Owen), born 1771, in 1799 was engaged in the famous New Lanark Mills, of which Jeremy Bentham was one of the partners. In 1825 he purchased Harmony, in Indiana, from Mr. Rapp. He believed in a full community of property; that the Government should employ the surplus of labor for which there was no demand; and that, until the members became fully trained, affairs should be managed by one head (as in Saint-Simonism).

159.

For Brook Farm, see Noyes's "History of American Socialism," chapter xi, and the life of "George Ripley," by O. B. Frothingham (1882). In general, also, for American experiments see Charles Nordhoff's "The Communistic Societies of the United States"; W. A. Hinds's "American Communists" (1878); Woolsey's "Communism and Socialism" (1880); and Noyes's "American Socialism" (1870).

160.

The extracts in large type in this section are taken from Mr. Mill's "Chapters on Socialism" ("Fortnightly Review," 1879), being only the beginning of a larger work begun in 1869, and given to the public since his death. They are of interest because they give his conclusions twenty years after his "Political Economy" was written.

161.

"Logical Method," pp. 34, 36.

162.

Cf. Cairnes, "Leading Principles," pp. 180-188.

163.

In the "Fortnightly Review," May 1, 1869.

164.

"Leading Principles," pp. 149-189.

165.

Counting six days to a week and four weeks to a month.

166.

"Leading Principles," p. 185.

167.

Mr. Thornton replied to Mr. Cairnes ("Nineteenth Century," August, 1879). A succinct statement of the condition of the wages-fund controversy has been made by Henry Sidgwick, "Fortnightly Review," September 1, 1879. See also W. G. Sumner, "Princeton Review," "Wages," November, 1882.

168.

He advanced the same view in the "North American Review," vol. cxx, January, 1875. In his "Political Economy" (1883) he advances a more extensive theory of distribution. See "Atlantic Monthly," July, 1883, p. 129.

169.

See Cairnes, "Leading Principles," p. 209.

170.

This proposition needs to be kept in mind for the future discussion of the cost of production of food and its relation to cost of labor. Book II, Chap. V, § 5.

171.

Mr. Carey takes this ground.

172.

See the explanation of an economic law, Book II, Chap. II, § 1.

173.

"Constitutional History of England," vol. ii, p. 563. See also Nicholls's "History of the Poor Laws," vol. ii, p. 303.

174.

For further discussion of the advantages of small holdings, see Book IV, Chap. V, § 2.

175.

"Leading Principles," pp. 64-69.

176.

See Young, "Labor in Europe."

177.

178. Walter Bagehot, "Lombard Street," p. 13.

179. "Work and Wages."

180. The reader is advised to consider, in connection with this, the former discussion on the relation between wages and the price of food (pp. 185, 186).

181. "Logical Method," p. 206.

182. "American Political Economy," p. 164.

183. Rickards, "Population and Capital," p. 135.

184. Rickards, ibid., p. 75.

185. "Political Economy," p. 288.

186. "Progress and Poverty," pp. 220, 221.

187. "American Political Economy," p. 164.

188. For other writers opposed to the doctrine of Rent as maintained by Ricardo and Mill, see Bonamy Price, "Practical Political Economy," chap. x; McLeod, "Principles of Economic Philosophy," chap. x; and J. E. T. Rogers, "Manual of Political Economy," chap. xii.

189. Cairnes, "Logical Method," p. 199.

"Theory and Practice of Banking," vol. i, p. 13. Cf. Cairnes, "Logical Method," p. 106.

190.
"Leading Principles," p. 11.

191.
"Political Economy," p. 5.

192.
"Social Science," vol. i, p. 158.

193.
"Harmonies," p. 171.

194.
"Political Economy," p. 126.

195.
"Political Economy," Introduction, Chap. I, § 5.

196.
"Précis d'Économie politique," p. 175.

197.
"Précis de la Science économique," vol. i, p. 202.

198.
"Political Economy Primer," p. 98.

199.
"Leading Principles," p. 15.

200.
"Theory of Political Economy," pp. 82-91. See Cairnes, ibid., pp. 17-19.

201.
"Political Economy," p. 92.

202.
"Social Science," vol. ii, p. 335.

203.
"Political Economy," Introduction, Chap. I, § 5.

204.

205. "Précis," p. 206.

206. "Political Economy," p. 165.

207. "Logic of Political Economy."

208. Although here using demand in its proper sense, a little later Mr. Mill defines it as the "quantity demanded." As he again uses it in the proper sense in discussing excess of money (Book III, Chap. V), supply (Book III, Chap. XI), and foreign trade (Book III, Chap. XIV), I have omitted from his present exposition his evidently inconsistent use of the word.

209. "Leading Principles," p. 25.

210. "Leading Principles," p. 108.

211. See his chapter on "Natural and Market Price," book i, chap. vii.

212. "Report of the Director of the Mint," 1883, p. 69.

213. *Supra*, p. 222.

214. "Leading Principles," p. 41.

215. Book I, Chap. I, § 2.

216. See *supra*, p. 210.

217. "Leading Principles," part i, chap. iii, p. 87.

218. "Work and Wages."

219. "Leading Principles," p. 136.

220. F. A. Walker ("Political Economy," pp. 248-259) expands this idea, and makes it the pivotal part of his whole theory of distribution among laborers, capitalists, and landlords.

221. "Money and the Mechanism of Exchange," chap. iii.

222. "Political Economy," p. 127.

223. "Money and the Mechanism of Exchange," p. 1.

224. "Political Economy," p. 144.

225. The substance of Mr. Mill's former chapter, XV (Book III), is here inserted in its direct connection with the functions of money.

226. F. A. Walker, "Political Economy," p. 363. A German, Count Soden (1805), Joseph Lowe (1822), and G. Poulett Scrope (1833), proposed this scheme. See Jevons, "Money and the Mechanism of Exchange," chap. xxv.

227. "Money and the Mechanism of Exchange," p. 31.

228. "A Serious Fall in the Value of Gold" (1863).

F. A. Walker defines the demand for money as "the occasion for the use of money in effecting exchanges; in other words, it is the amount of money-work to be done" ("Political Economy," p. 133); and the supply of money as "the money-force available to do the money-work which the demand for money indicates as required to be done, in the given community, at the given time. The supply of money is measured by ... the amount of money and the rapidity of circulation" (ibid., p. 136).

229.

Jevons, "Money and the Mechanism of Exchange," pp. 336, 339.

230.

"Edelmetall-Production," in Petermann's "Mittheilungen," Ergänzungsheft, No. 57.

231.

See Jevons's "A Serious Fall in the Value of Gold."

232.

In his book "De la Baisse probable de l'Or" (1859). See also Cairnes's "Essays." For authorities on the new gold, see Robinson's "California" (Larkin's and Mason's Reports, pp. 17, 33); Executive Documents of United States, 1848, I, 1; Westgarth's "Colony of Victoria," pp. 122, 315; Wood, "Sixteen Months in the Gold Diggings," p. 125; Lalor's "Cyclopædia," II, p. 851; Walker, "Money," part i, chaps. vii, viii. For the probable effects, see "North American Review," October, 1852; Tooke's "History of Prices," vi, p. 224; "Statistical Journal," 1878, p. 230; Levasseur, "Question de l'Or." As to how far the value of gold was lowered, Jevons, "Serious Fall," etc.; "Statistical Journal," 1865; ibid., 1869, p. 445; and Giffen's "Essays in Finance," p. 82.

233.

"Report of the House of Commons on Depreciation of Silver," 1876, p. v.

234.

See Macaulay, "History of England," chap. xxi.

235.

"Money and the Mechanism of Exchange," p. 84.

236.

Jevons, ibid., p. 138.

237.

238. See S. Dana Horton, "Gold and Silver," 1877, p. 84, *et seq*.

239. See Linderman, "Money and Legal Tender," p. 161.

240. Director of the Mint, Report, 1883, p. 49, and Linderman, ibid., p. 173.

241. See "Atlantic Monthly," "The Silver Danger," May, 1884.

242. See "International Review," September, 1876; and for some further explanation of banks, see "Atlantic Monthly," 1882, pp. 196, 695, 696.

243. "Report of the Comptroller of the Currency," 1883, p. 34.

244. See "Nature," xix, 33, 588.

245. See Walker's "Money," p. 473.

246. Vol. i, p. 302. See Sumner's "History of American Currency" and Walker's "Money" for much valuable material.

247. See Cherbuliez, vol. i, p. 299.

248. "Money and the Mechanism of Exchange," p. 232.

For John Law's famous scheme (1718-1720) in France, called the "Mississippi Bubble," the best authority is Levasseur's "Système de Law" (1854). Also consult M. Thiers's "The Mississippi Bubble" (translated by F. F. Fiske, 1859); Steuart's "Political Economy" (1767); and McLeod's "Dictionary of Political Economy," article on "Banking in France."

249.

For the best brief account of the issues of assignats, see President A. D. White's "Paper Money Inflation in France." See also F. A. Walker, "Money," pp. 336-347; Bazot's "Assignats"; and Alison's "History of the French Revolution," vol. ii, p. 606.

250.

See "Some Account of the Bills of Credit or Paper Money of Rhode Island, 1710-1786," in "Rhode Island Historical Tracts," No. 8 (1880), by E. S. Potter and S. S. Rider.

251.

See Felt's "History of Massachusetts Currency." Consult also Minot, Hutchinson, and Gouge. Walker, "Money," and Sumner, "History of American Currency," have given considerable accounts of paper experiments in the United States, and should be well studied.

252.

See Walker, "Money," p. 329.

253.

See J. J. Knox's "United States Notes" (1884); the Finance Reports during and since the war to 1879; Spaulding's "Financial History of the War" (1869); Bowen's "American Political Economy," chap. xv; "Chapters of Erie," by H. Adams and F. A. Walker; and the voluminous pages of the "Congressional Globe." For the decisions in the legal-tender cases, see "Banker's Magazine," 1869-1870, p. 712, and 1871-1872, pp. 752, 780. A collection of statutes affecting United States finance, especially since 1860, has been made in a small pamphlet, by Professor C. F. Dunbar (published by Sever, Cambridge, Massachusetts).

254.

Report of 1861.

255.

Mr. Malthus, Dr. Chalmers, M. de Sismondi, and various minor writers. It is especially likely that, in times of commercial depression, the journals of the day will contain arguments to show a general over-production.

256.

257.

Book IV, Chap. II.

258.

This is practically the argument of a little book, "Excessive Saving a Cause of Commercial Distress" (1884), by Uriel H. Crocker.

259.

Book III, Chap. II, § 4.

260.

"Leading Principles," pp. 302-307.

261.

"Essays on some Unsettled Questions of Political Economy," Essay I.

262.

I at one time believed Mr. Ricardo to have been the sole author of the doctrine now universally received by political economists, on the nature and measure of the benefit which a country derives from foreign trade. But Colonel Torrens, by the republication of one of his early writings, "The Economists refuted," has established at least a joint claim with Mr. Ricardo to the origination of the doctrine, and an exclusive one to its earliest publication.— MILL.

263.

I have in this illustration retained almost the exact words quoted by Mr. Mill from his father's book, James Mill's "Elements of Political Economy," but altered it by changing the trade from Poland to the United States, and by speaking of iron instead of cloth.

264.

"American Political Economy," p. 481.

265.

For a fuller discussion of this question see Cairnes, "Leading Principles," p. 319, ff.

266.

"Leading Principles," p. 323.

266.

Cairnes, "Leading Principles," p. 301.

267.

Book I, chap. VI, § 4.

268.

I have changed the illustration from England to the United States in this example.

269.

Book III, Chap. II, § 4.

270.

Book III, Chap. I, § 3.

271.

See "Statistical Abstract," 1883, pp. 32, 33.

272.

This substitution has been made for Brazil.

273.

See close of last chapter.

274.

I have also changed the illustrations in this chapter so as to apply to the United States.

275.

The examples in this and the next section have been altered so as to apply to the United States.

276.

I have changed the names of the countries in the illustrations contained in this chapter, but have not further altered the language beyond the occasional change of a pronoun.

277.

The subjoined extract from the separate essay ["Some Unsettled Questions of Political Economy"] previously referred to will give some assistance in following the course of the phenomena. It is adapted to the imaginary case used for illustration throughout that essay, the case of a trade between England and Germany in cloth and linen.

"We may, at first, make whatever supposition we will with respect to the value of money. Let us suppose, therefore, that, before the opening of the trade, the price of cloth is the same in both countries, namely, six shillings per yard. As ten yards of cloth were supposed to exchange in England for fifteen yards of linen, in Germany for twenty, we must suppose that linen is sold in England at four shillings per yard, in Germany at three. Cost of carriage and importer's profit are left, as before, out of consideration.

"In this state of prices, cloth, it is evident, can not yet be exported from England into Germany; but linen can be imported from Germany into England. It will be so; and, in the first instance, the linen will be paid for in money.

"The efflux of money from England and its influx into Germany will raise money prices in the latter country, and lower them in the former. Linen will rise in Germany above three shillings per yard, and cloth above six shillings. Linen in England, being imported from Germany, will (since cost of carriage is not reckoned) sink to the same price as in that country, while cloth will fall below six shillings. As soon as the price of cloth is lower in England than in Germany, it will begin to be exported, and the price of cloth in Germany will fall to what it is in England. As long as the cloth exported does not suffice to pay for the linen imported, money will continue to flow from England into Germany, and prices generally will continue to fall in England and rise in Germany.

"By the fall, however, of cloth in England, cloth will fall in Germany also, and the demand for it will increase. By the rise of linen in Germany, linen must rise in England also, and the demand for it will diminish. As cloth fell in price and linen rose, there would be some particular price of both articles at which the cloth exported and the linen imported would exactly pay for each other. At this point prices would remain, because money would then cease to move out of England into Germany. What this point might be would entirely depend upon the circumstances and inclinations of the purchasers on both sides. If the fall of cloth did not much increase the demand for it in Germany, and the rise of linen did not diminish very rapidly the demand for it in England, much money must pass before the equilibrium is restored; cloth would fall very much, and linen would rise, until England, perhaps, had to pay nearly as much for it as when she produced it for herself. But, if, on the contrary, the fall of cloth caused a very rapid increase of the demand for it in Germany, and the rise of linen in Germany reduced very rapidly the demand in England from what it was under the influence of the first cheapness produced by the opening of the trade, the cloth would very soon suffice to pay for the linen, little money would pass between the two countries, and England would derive a large portion of the benefit of the trade. We have thus arrived at precisely the same conclusion, in supposing the employment of money, which we found to hold under the supposition of barter.

"In what shape the benefit accrues to the two nations from the trade is clear enough. Germany, before the commencement of the trade, paid six shillings per yard for broadcloth; she now obtains it at a lower price. This, however, is not the whole of her advantage. As the money-prices of all her other commodities have risen, the money-incomes of all her producers have increased. This is no advantage to them in buying from each other, because the price of what they buy has risen in the same ratio with their means of paying for it: but it is an advantage to them in buying anything which has not risen, and, still more, anything which has fallen. They, therefore, benefit as consumers of cloth, not merely to the extent to which cloth has fallen, but also to the extent to which other prices have risen. Suppose that this is one tenth. The same proportion of their money-incomes as before will suffice to supply their other wants; and the remainder, being increased one tenth in amount, will enable them to purchase one tenth more cloth than before, even though cloth had not fallen: but it has fallen; so that they are doubly gainers. They purchase the same quantity with less money, and have more to expend upon their other wants.

"In England, on the contrary, general money-prices have fallen. Linen, however, has fallen more than the rest, having been lowered in price by importation from a country where it was cheaper; whereas the others have fallen only from the consequent efflux of money. Notwithstanding, therefore, the general fall of money-prices, the English producers will be exactly as they were in all other respects, while they will gain as purchasers of linen.

"The greater the efflux of money required to restore the equilibrium, the greater will be the gain of Germany, both by the fall of cloth and by the rise of her general prices. The less the efflux of money requisite, the greater will be the gain of England; because the price of linen will continue lower, and her general prices will not be reduced so much. It must not, however, be imagined that high money-prices are a good, and low money-prices an evil, in themselves. But, the higher the general money-prices in any country, the greater will be that country's means of purchasing those commodities, which, being imported from abroad, are independent of the causes which keep prices high at home."

"In practice, the cloth and the linen would not, as here supposed, be at the same price in England and in Germany: each would be dearer in money-price in the country which imported than in that which produced it, by the amount of the cost of carriage, together with the ordinary profit on the importer's capital for the average length of time which elapsed before the commodity could be disposed of. But it does not follow that each country pays the cost of carriage of the commodity it imports; for the addition of this item to the price may operate as a greater check to demand on one side than on the other; and the equation of international demand, and consequent equilibrium of payments, may not be maintained. Money would then flow out of one country into the other, until, in the manner already illustrated, the equilibrium was restored: and, when this was effected, one country would be paying more than its own cost of carriage, and the other less."—MILL.

278.

See Book III, Chap. XVIII, § 5, of Mill's original work.

279.

"Principles of Political Economy and Taxation," third edition, p. 143.

280.

For an exceedingly good study on the conditions of our foreign trade down to 1873, and a prophecy of the panic of 1873, see Cairnes, "Leading Principles," pp. 364-374.

281.

"Leading Principles," p. 357.

282.

The illustrations in this chapter have also been changed, but only so far as to make them apply to the United States.

283.

I am here supposing a state of things in which gold and silver mining are a permanent branch of industry, carried on under known conditions; and not the present state of uncertainty, in which gold-gathering is a game of chance, prosecuted (for the present) in the spirit of an adventure, not in that of a regular industrial pursuit.—MILL. It is, however, worth recalling that gold and silver mining have not been—for large effects on the value of the metals—anything like a permanent branch of industry, but that, in the main, great additions have been obtained suddenly and by chance discoveries.—J. L. L.

284.

See Walker, "Money," Chap. XIX.

285.

Book II, Chap. V, § 1.

286.

I do not include in the general loan fund of the country the capitals, large as they sometimes are, which are habitually employed in speculatively buying and selling the public funds and other securities.—MILL.

287.

The rate of interest at such crises in New York has several times risen to 400 or 500 per cent per annum.

288.

In this illustration I have retained as nearly as possible the form of that given by Mr. Mill for the trade between England and Germany in cloth and linen.

289.

Book II, Chap. V, § 5.

290.

Book II, Chap. II, § 3.

291.

Cf. Cairnes, "Leading Principles," p. 209.

292.

293.

For a brief bibliography on our own Navigation Laws and the Shipping Question, see Appendix I.

294.

Book III, Chap. III, § 1.

295.

Supra, Book III, Chap. II, § 2, and Chap. XX, § 4.

296.

Henry George, however, asserts that, "irrespective of the increase of population, the effect of improvements in methods of production and exchange is to increase rent" ("Progress and Poverty," p. 220).

297.

"Leading Principles," Part I, chap. v.

298.

For the distinction between normal and market values, see *supra*, Book III, Chap. II, § 4, and p. 269.

299.

Before beginning this discussion the reader is advised to review the relation of profits to cost of labor, and the dependence of the latter on its three factors, Book II, Chap. V, § 5.

300.

Book I, Chap. IX

301.

Mr. Mill commended, as the most scientific treatment of the subject with which he had met, an "Essay on the Effects of Machinery," by William Ellis, "Westminster Review," January, 1826.

302.

Although their needs now attract more attention through the extension of newspapers and cheap books, the condition of the laboring-class is certainly better than it was fifty years ago. See Mr. Robert Giffen's "Progress of the Working-Classes in the Last Half-Century" (1884), referred to in Book IV, Chap. V, § 1.

A comparison of Chart No. XVII with Chart No. VI will furnish some means of learning whether the building of railways has gone on faster than is warranted by the increase of our crops (see *supra*, pp. 138).

303.

Book I, Chap. V, § 2.

304.

Book II, Chap. I, § 6.

305.

"Progress of the Working-Classes in the Last Half-Century" (1884), page 8.

306.

"Leading Principles," pp. 278-280.

307.

"Progress of the Working-Classes in the Last Half-Century" (1884), being his inaugural address as President of the London Statistical Society, November 20, 1883.

308.

1825.

309.

1825.

310.

Wages per day.

311.

Wages per day.

312.

Year 1878.

313.

These mills have not been able to pay ten per cent regularly, as mentioned in Chart No. XIX, but it has merely been supposed that ten per cent were demanded by capital, in order to show that, for such a dividend, it required a diminishing proportion of the price to meet that estimate.

314.

Book II, Chap. V, § 5; see also "North American Review," May, 1884, p. 517.

315.

For the influences of small properties in restraining an undue increase of population, see *supra*, p. 119. For a more general account of the benefits arising from such holdings, consult Mill's original work, Book II, Chaps. VI and VII, and T. E. Cliffe Leslie's "Land Systems."

316.

Cf. E. L. Godkin, "North American Review," 1868, p. 150.

317.

Fawcett, "Manual of Political Economy" (last edition), chapter on Co-operation.

318.

Giffen, "Progress of the Working-Classes in the Last Half-Century," p. 19.

319.

"History of Co-operation in England" (2 vols., 1879), p. 105.

320.

Mr. Holyoake ("History of Co-operation in England," p. 99) quotes as follows from another's experience: "My own pass-book shows that I paid on November 3d, of last year (1860), £1 to become a member of a co-operative store. I have paid nothing since, and I am now credited with £3 16*s.* 6*d.*, nearly three hundred per cent on my capital in a single year. Of course, that arises from my purchases having been large in proportion to my investment. In a co-operative store you get five per cent upon the money which you invest as a shareholder; and, if the store be well conducted, you will get seven and a half per cent addition."

321.

321.

For a full account of the proper steps to be taken in establishing a store, with many practical details, see Charles Barnard's "Co-operation as a Business," p. 119.

322.

Cf. Walker, "Wages Question," p. 276.

323.

Godkin, "North American Review," 1868.

324.

"History of Co-operation," vol. ii, chap. ix.

325.

Holyoake, "History of Co-operation," p. 131.

326.

Godkin, "North American Review," 1868.

327.

Pp. 27, 31, 32.

328.

Barnard, "Co-operation as a Business," pp. 150-152.

329.

Holyoake, "History of Co-operation," p. 235.

330.

See Thornton, "On Labor," p. 370. Also see "Parliamentary Documents," 1868, 1869, xxxi; "Trades-Unions of England," by the Count de Paris; Brassey's "Work and Wages," chap. xiii.

331.

See Walker, "Wages Question," p. 283. Also see Mill, Book IV, Chap. VII, § 5, for an account of M. Leclaire's experiments in France with house-painters.

332.

See also Von Böhmert, "Gewinnbetheiligung," second edition, 1878, and Jevons's "Methods of Social Reform" (1883). Professor Jevons ("The State in Relation to Labor," pp. 146, 147) has given a brief bibliography, which I reproduce here:

Charles Babbage, "Economy of Manufactures," chap. xxvi; H. C. Briggs, "Social Science Association," 1869; H. C. and A. Briggs, "Evidence before the Trades-Union Commission," March 4, 1868, Questions 12,485 to 12,753 [Parliamentary Documents]; "The Industrial Partnerships Record"; Pare, "Co-operative Agriculture" (Longmans) 1870; Jean Billon, "Participation des Ouvriers aux Bénéfices des Patrons," Genève, 1877; Fougerousse, "Patrons et Ouvriers de Paris" (Chaix), 1880; Sedley Taylor, "Society of Arts Journal," February 18, 1881, vol. xxix, pp. 260-270; also in "Nineteenth Century," May, 1881, pp. 802-811, "On Profit-Sharing"; J. C. Van Marken, "La Question Ouvrière: Essai de Solution Pratique" (Chaix) 1881.

333.

In his last edition of his "Manual," Professor Fawcett thus describes a co-operative experiment in agriculture: "The one that has attracted the most attention was made nearly forty years since by Mr. Gurdon, on his estate at Assington, near Sudbury, in Suffolk. Mr. Gurdon was so much impressed with the miserable condition of the agricultural laborers who were employed on his estate, that he was prompted to do something on their behalf. When, therefore, one of his farms became vacant, he offered to let it at the ordinary rent, £150 a year, to the laborers who worked upon it. As they, of course, had not sufficient capital to cultivate it, he in the first instance loaned them the requisite stock and implements. The laborers were, in fact, formed into a company in which there were eleven shares, and no laborer was permitted to hold more than one share. The plan was so eminently successful that in a few years sufficient had been saved out of the profits to repay all that had been advanced, and the stock and implements became the property of the laborers. Each share greatly increased in value. Mr. Gurdon was so much encouraged, not only by the pecuniary advantages secured to the laborers, but also by the general improvement effected in their condition, that some years afterward he let another and a larger farm on similar terms. Although no statement of accounts has ever been published, the remarkable pecuniary advantages secured to the laborers is proved by the fact that, after enjoying at least as high wages as were paid in the district, they were able in a few years to become the owners of a valuable property, consisting of the stock and implements on the farms. One of the most significant and hopeful circumstances connected with the experiment is, that it was not carried out by a picked body of men; and if so much could be done by laborers who were probably among the worst educated in the country, it maybe fairly concluded, that when the intelligence of our rural population has been better developed, co-operation may be applied in a more complete form to agriculture, and with even more striking results than were obtained at Assington.... In the description which has been frequently given of the system of peasant proprietorship, it is shown how powerfully the industry of the laborer is stimulated by the feeling of property. When he cultivates his own plot of ground, he exerts himself to the utmost, because he knows that he will enjoy all that is yielded by his labor. Each year, with the extended use of machinery in agriculture, it is becoming more advantageous to carry on farming on a large scale. When, therefore, co-operative agriculture becomes practicable, land may be cultivated by associations of laborers, and thus many of the advantages associated with the system of peasant proprietorship may be secured, while at the same time the disadvantages of small farming may be avoided. The progress toward co-operative agriculture will no doubt be slow and gradual."

334.

Godkin, "North American Review," 1868. Also see Hermann Schultze-Delitsch, "Die Entwickelung des Genossenschaftswesens in Deutschland" (1870). This eminent philanthropist died April 29, 1883. For other forms of co-operation, building associations, etc., see Barnard, "Co-operation as a Business"; Pajot, "Du Progrès par les Sociétés de Secours Mutuels" (1878).

335.

See "Economics of Industry," by Mr. and Mrs. Marshall, p. 223.

336.

"Wealth of Nations," Book V, chap. ii.

337.

Book II, Chap. I, § 6.

338.

Book III, Chap. XIX, § 5.

339.

A higher rate is now imposed on landed than on professional incomes.

<u>340.</u>

>Cf. Walker, "Land and Rent," page 134.

<u>341.</u>

>I have changed the sums mentioned in this illustration into our own money.

<u>342.</u>

>Another common objection is that large and expensive accommodation is often required, not as a residence, but for business. But it is an admitted principle that buildings, or portions of buildings, occupied exclusively for business, such as shops, warehouses, or manufactories, ought to be exempted from house-tax.

>It has been also objected that house-rent in the rural districts is much lower than in towns, and lower in some towns and in some rural districts than in others; so that a tax proportioned to it would have a corresponding inequality of pressure. To this, however, it may be answered that, in places where house-rent is low, persons of the same amount of income usually live in larger and better houses, and thus expend in house-rent more nearly the same proportion of their incomes than might at first sight appear. Or, if not, the probability will be that many of them live in those places precisely because they are too poor to live elsewhere, and have, therefore, the strongest claim to be taxed lightly. In some cases it is precisely because the people are poor that house-rent remains low.—MILL.

<u>343.</u>

>I have here also changed the amounts into our own money.

<u>344.</u>

>This illustration has also been changed, but only so far as to fit the trade between England and the United States.

<u>345.</u>

>Probably the strongest known instance of a large revenue raised from foreigners by a tax on exports is the opium-trade with China. The high price of the article under the Government monopoly (which is equivalent to a high export duty) has so little effect in discouraging its consumption that it is said to have been

occasionally sold in China for as much as its weight in silver.—MILL.

346.

A land-tax is, to its extent, an evidence that the state claims a certain right in the soil, and that it stands to the contributor, as it were, in the place of a landlord. This tax, however, is generally so small that it does not materially diminish the rent of land. So far as it goes, it is a tax on rent.

347.

Some argue that the materials and instruments of all production should be exempt from taxation; but these, when they do not enter into the production of necessaries, seem as proper subjects of taxation as the finished article. It is chiefly with reference to foreign trade that such taxes have been considered injurious. Internationally speaking, they may be looked upon as export duties, and, unless in cases in which an export duty is advisable, they should be accompanied with an equivalent drawback on exportation. But there is no sufficient reason against taxing the materials and instruments used in the production of anything which is itself a fit object of taxation.—MILL.

348.

See Lalor's "Cyclopædia," article "Distilled Spirits," by David A. Wells.

349.

"United States Statistical Abstract," 1883, pp. 2, 3.

350.

The old condition of things was well described by Sydney Smith: "We must pay taxes upon every article which enters into the mouth or covers the back, or is placed under the foot. Taxes upon everything which is pleasant to see, hear, feel, smell, and taste. Taxes upon warmth, light, and locomotion. Taxes upon everything upon earth and the waters under the earth. On everything that comes from abroad or is grown at home. Taxes on raw material. Taxes on every value that is added to it by the industry of man. Taxes on the sauce which pampers man's appetite and the drug which restores him to health. On the ermine which decorates the judge and the rope which hangs the criminal. On the brass nails of the coffin and on the ribbons of the bride. At bed or at board, couchant or levant, we must pay. The beardless youth manages his taxed horse with a taxed bridle on a taxed road, and the dying Englishman, pouring his medicine (which has paid 7 per cent) into a spoon (which has paid 30 per cent), throws himself back upon his chintz bed (which has paid 22 per cent), makes his will, and expires in the arms of the apothecary (who has paid £100 for the privilege of putting him to death). His whole property is then taxed from 2 to 10 per cent; besides the probate, large fees are demanded for burying him in the chancel: his virtues are handed down to posterity on taxed marble, and he is then gathered to his fathers to be taxed no more."

351.

"Financial Reform Almanac," 1883, pp. 107-109.

352.

"Handbuch der Verfassung und Verwaltung in Preussen und dem Deutschen Reich," by Graf Hue de Grais (second edition, 1882), p. 138.

353.

"Le Budget. Revenus et Dépenses de la France," by M. Block (1881), pp. 57, 82.

354.

Taken, with modifications, from Milnes's "Problems in Political Economy," p. 377.

355.

Book I, Chap. IV, § 5.

356.

Although Mr. Mill had reference to the French wars in the beginning of this century, his words apply also to the circumstances of our own late war, 1861-1865.

357.

Cairnes, "Leading Principles," pp. 381, 382.

358.

Book I, Chap. IV.

359.

Mr. Mill here takes up political considerations, which are not properly to be included in a purely economic treatment. (See the beginning of § 6.)

360.

See "Sketch of the History of Political Economy," *supra*, p. 6, note 1.

361.

For bibliography of the United States shipping question, see Appendix I.

362.

D. A. Wells, "Cobden Club Essays," second series, p. 533.

363.

See F. W. Taussig's "Protection to Young Industries as applied in the United States" (1883).

364.

In a letter written February 26, 1866, to Mr. Horace White, published in the Chicago "Tribune," an d reprinted in the New York "Nation," May 29, 1873.

365.

Business men constantly use the term "cost of production" when in reality they mean that which to the economist is expressed by "cost of labor." If cost of labor becomes higher, it takes from profits—the place where they feel the difficulties of competition—but they say that the cost of production has risen: the cost, to them, only has risen, that is, the "cost of labor," not "cost of production."

366.

Cf. Cairnes, "Leading Principles," pp. 324-341; and *supra*, Book III, Chap. II, § 4.

367.

The fact (sufficiently established by Mr. Brassey) is not considered also that England gives higher wages to operatives than the Continent, and yet England is able to undersell France and Germany in neutral markets. It is evident, however, that England can undersell only in occupations in which she has advantages.

368.
> Cairnes, "Leading Principles," pp. 382-388.

369.
> "Compendium," 1880, pp. 1343-1377.

370.
> "Princeton Review," 1883, p. 222.

371.
> The United States have at the present time but five persons engaged in agriculture for each square mile of settled area.

372.
> Book IV, Chap. I, § 2.

373.
> "Fifteenth Annual Report of the Massachusetts Bureau of Statistics, 1884," by Carroll D. Wright.

374.
> See Milnes's "Problems in Political Economy."